Environmental Protection
Text and Materials

Law in Context

Editors: William Twining (University College, London) and Christopher Mc Crudden (Lincoln College, Oxford)

Ashworth: *Sentencing and Criminal Justice*
Barton & Douglas: *Law and Parenthood*
Bercusson: *European Labour Law*
Birkinshaw: *Freedom of Information: The Law, the Practice and the Ideal*
Cane: *Atiyah's Accidents, Compensation and the Law*
Collins: *The Law of Contract*
Cranston: *Legal Foundations of the Welfare State*
Davies and Freedland: *Labour Law: Text and Materials*
Detmold: *Courts and Administrators: A Study of Jurisprudence*
Doggett: *Marriage, Wife-Beating and the Law in Victorian England*
Dummett and Nicol: *Subjects, Citizens, Aliens and Others: Nationality and Immigration Law*
Goodrich: *Languages of Law*
Hadden: *Company Law and Capitalism*
Harlow and Rawlings: *Law and Administration: Text and Materials*
Harris: *An Introduction to Law*
Lacey, Wells and Meure: *Reconstructing Criminal Law: Text and Materials*
Lewis: *Choice and the Legal Order: Rising above Politics*
Moffat: *Trusts Law: Text and Materials*
Norrie: *Crime, Reason and History*
Page and Fergusson: *Investor Protection*
Picciotto: *International Business Transaction*
Ramsay: *Consumer Protection: Text and Materials*
Richardson: *Law, Process and Custody*
Snyder: *New Directions in European Community Law*
Stapleton: *Product Liability*
Turpin: *British Government and the Constitution: Text, Cases and Materials*
Twining and Anderson: *Analysis of Evidence*
Twining and Miers: *How to do Things with Rules*
Ward: *A Critical Introduction to European Law*
Zander: *Cases and Materials on the English Legal System*
Zander: *The Law-Making Process*

Environmental Protection
Text and Materials

Sue Elworthy LLB, LLM
Research Associate
The Robert Gordon University, School of Public Administration and Law

Jane Holder LLB, PhD
Lecturer
University College, London

CAMBRIDGE UNIVERSITY PRESS
Cambridge, New York, Melbourne, Madrid, Cape Town,
Singapore, São Paulo, Delhi

Cambridge University Press
The Edinburgh Building, Cambridge CB2 8RU, UK

Published in the United States of America by Cambridge University Press, New York

www.cambridge.org
Information on this title: www.cambridge.org/9780521613538

First published by Butterworths 2001
Digitally reprinted (with corrections) by Cambridge University Press 2008

A catalogue record for this publication is available from the British Library

ISBN 978-0-521-61353-8 Paperback

What would the world be, once bereft
Of wet and of wilderness? Let them be left,
O let them be left, wildness and wet;
Long live the weeds and the wilderness yet.

(from 'Inversnaid', Gerard Manley Hopkins)

For Geoffrey Wilson

Preface

A book on environmental protection belongs in the Law in Context series. As graduates of Warwick University Law School, the original academic home of Law in Context, we have a long-standing commitment to the series' philosophy of openness and critical enquiry. We hope our readership includes our colleagues (many of whom belong to the Interdisciplinary Research Network on Environment and Society) – the engineers, philosophers, geographers, ecologists and social scientists with whom we have walked, worked and talked over the last few years, as well as fellow lawyers.

Sue Elworthy
Jane Holder
January 1997

Acknowledgements

William Twining, the series editor, gave us the freedom and encouragement to develop our interests in this field.

Special thanks go to Liz Anker and Jolyon Hall at Warwick University library for their close involvement in our research over the years. We thank our colleagues at University College, London, particularly David O'Keeffe and Margot Horspool for giving Jane the time to write; at The Robert Gordon University, Aberdeen; and at the University of Warwick, particularly Ken Foster for his interest and encouragement and Graham Moffat who generously shared his experience as a Law in Context author. Our special thanks go to John McEldowney for his valuable comments on our work and his clear perspective on the subject

Thanks also to John Love and all the others in the Scottish Natural Heritage office in Stilligarry who helped unstintingly with chapter 11.

Contents

Dedication v
Preface vii
Acknowledgements ix
Table of statutes xvii
Table of cases xxiii

PART I USING THE LAW FOR ENVIRONMENTAL PROTECTION

Chapter 1 Environmental law in context
1. Science and environmental law 7
   (a) Precaution: soft science/hard values 15
2. Nature and the environment 25
3. Spacial scales 34
4. The political environment 37
5. How we live 40

PART II HISTORICAL CONTEXT OF ENVIRONMENTAL LAW IN BRITAIN

Chapter 2 Building Babylon: industrial activities and early pollution controls
1. Introduction 47
2. Industrial activities, pubiic health and pollution 48
3. Scope and limitations of the common law 54
   (a) Riparian rights 54
   (b) Trespass 55
   (c) The rule in *Rylands v Fletcher* 56
   (d) The role of the common law of nuisance 56
   (e) Private property rights 59
4. Legislation and control of industrial activities 61
   (a) Air pollution 61
   (b) Water pollution 63
   (c) Interaction of statutory regimes and private law 64
5. Conclusions 65
6. A modern postscript: *Cambridge Water Company v Eastern Counties Leather* 67

Chapter 3 Containing Arcadia: early land use and development controls

1. Introduction 82
2. Origins and evolution of land use controls 82
   (a) Public health 82
   (b) Utopianism and the garden city movement 84
   (c) Miming nature 89
   (d) Early planning law 92
   (e) The post-war planning project: 1944 and onwards 97
3. Countryside protection 100
   (a) Separation of legal controls – the town and the country 103
   (b) Pressure for change 107
   (c) Access to the countryside 111
4. Conclusions 113
5. Millennium plotlands? 114

PART III DEVELOPMENT OF ENVIRONMENTAL LAW

Chapter 4 International initiatives

1. Introduction 123
2. Sources of international law 124
   (a) Treaties 125
   (b) International custom 130
   (c) Soft international law 131
3. Evolution of the concept of 'sustainable development' 132
   (a) Stockholm 1972 133
   (b) Principle 21 134
   (c) The United Nations Environment Programme 135
   (d) The Nairobi Declaration (1982) 135
   (e) The World Conservation Union (IUCN) 138
   (f) The World Commission on Environment and Development (the Brundtland Commission) 139
   (g) Caring for the Earth: A Strategy for Sustainable Living 140
4. The contradictions of sustainable development 142
5. Agenda 21 144
6. Linkage between sustainable development and the precautionary principle: *New Zealand v France* 154

Chapter 5 The development of environmental law in the European Community

1. Introduction 165
   (a) The EEC to the European Union: A market in polluting substances 166
2. Origins and development of EC environmental law and policy 168
3. Policy making 173
4. Legal and policy framework 179
5. Approaches and techniques of Community environmental law 183

(a) Sectoral controls ... 184
(b) Preventive and integrated law ... 184
(c) Regulation of land use ... 185
(d) Moving towards integration ... 185
(e) The imperative of subsidiarity ... 186
6. A case of selective implementation ... 189
7. Enforcement ... 191
(a) Procedure ... 191
(b) Individual protection ... 200
(c) *Francovich* liability ... 203
8. Losing the economic base: *Lappel Bank* ... 204

PART IV TECHNIQUES FOR ENVIRONMENTAL PROTECTION

Chapter 6 Beyond Babylon: the development of pollution controls
1. Introduction ... 215
2. Best Practicable Means ... 217
3. Control of smoke ... 221
4. Integrated Pollution Control: the expansion of BPM ... 223
(a) Best Practicable Environmental Option ... 225
(b) BATNEEC ... 228
5. Public participation ... 234
6. Environmental assessment ... 238
7. Monitoring air quality ... 238
8. Conclusion ... 240

Chapter 7 Land use control: town planning and countryside designation
1. Introduction ... 243
2. Town planning ... 243
(a) Elements of the town planning system ... 249
(b) Policy change: the fall and rise of the development plan ... 252
(c) Planning tools: conditions and obligations ... 261
3. Planning for environmental protection ... 266
(a) The 'greening' of planning ... 271
(b) Interrelation of planning and pollution controls ... 273
(c) Precautionary planning? ... 281
(d) Scope of planning controls ... 282
4. Control of land use in the countryside ... 285
(a) Countryside designation ... 286
(b) European designations ... 293
(c) Planning for conservation ... 295
5. Conclusion ... 296

Chapter 8 Alternative environmental protection
1. Introduction ... 299
2. Economic instruments ... 306

3. Oblique regulation 322
4. Self regulation: environmental management and auditing systems 324
5. Buying the green lifestyle 338
6. Voluntary simplicity and alternative lifestyles: post-materialism 346
7. Direct action and destabilisation: the new *Total Kritik* 349
8. Legal radicalism 353

PART V APPLICATIONS OF MODERN ENVIRONMENTAL LAW

Chapter 9 The case of nitrate: farming for environmental protection
1. Introduction 361
2. Nitrate pollution 361
3. The legal problem 365
4. European Community law 366
   (a) Emission standards or water quality objectives? 366
   (b) Directive 778/80/EEC on the quality of drinking water 367
   (c) Directive 91/676/EEC on the protection of water against pollution caused by nitrate from agricultural sources 372
5. The British response: proactive law 373
   (a) Information 374
   (b) Storage 374
   (c) Water Protection Zones 376
   (d) Nitrate Sensitive Areas 377
   (e) Code of Good Agricultural Practice for the Protection of Water 380
6. Conclusion 384

Chapter 10 The road ahead: environmental assessment
1. Introduction 388
2. The concept of environmental assessment – the accepted version 389
   (a) Characteristics of environmental assessment 390
   (b) Implementing sustainable development via environmental assessment 391
3. Environmental assessment in law and practice 394
   (a) Development of environmental assessment by the EC 394
   (b) Refining environmental assessment 398
4. Environmental assessment in the UK 400
   (a) Informal environmental assessment 400
   (b) Implementation of Directive 85/337/EEC 401
5. The Thanet Way bypass project 402
   (a) Alternative routes and the 'need' for the project 407
   (b) Mitigating measures and environmental gains 410
   (c) Cumulative effects of development 412
   (d) Role of the developer's environmental statement 413
   (e) Environmental assessment and the planning inquiry 414
   (f) Perceptions of the environment in environmental assessment 417
6. So what is going on here? 418
7. Is strategic environmental assessment the way forward? 419

Chapter 11 Room for the geese: conservation and designation

1. Introduction 422
2. The case study: Loch Druidibeg 425
3. Nature conservation 427
4. Designation 430
5. The post war conservation project 431
6. National Nature Reserves in Scotland 434
7. The National Parks and Access to the Countryside Act 1949 436
8. Establishment of the reserve 438
9. International law 439
   (a) Designation as a Ramsar Site 439
   (b) Designation as a Biosphere Reserve 449
   (c) Designation as a Geological Conservation Review Site 450
10. European Community Law 451
   (a) Designation as a Special Protection Area 451
   (b) Designation as a Special Area of Conservation 454
11. Agricultural designations 457
12. Crofting and rare species 461
13. Conclusion 461

Epilogue Environmental justice 465

Bibliography 467
Index 477

Table of statutes

References in this Table to *Statutes* are to Halsbury's Statutes of England (Fourth Edition) showing the volume and page at which the annotated text of the Act may be found. Page references in **bold** type indicate where sections of an Act are set out in part or in full.

PAGE

Acquistion of Land Act 1981 (9 *Statutes* 366) ... 402
Agricultural Holdings Act 1986 (1 *Statutes* 732) ... 378
Agriculture Act 1947 (1 *Statutes* 170) ... 107, 363
s 1 ... **106**
Agriculture Act 1986 (1 *Statutes* 546)
s 17(1) ... **459**
Alkali Act 1863 ... 47, 61, 65, 66, 217, 222, 223, 366, 391
Alkali Act 1874 ... 62, 63, 65, 66, 222, 366, 391
s 5 ... 217, 218
Alkali, etc, Works Regulation Act 1906 (35 *Statutes* 64) ... 66, 218, 219, 220, 221, 222, 391
s 7 ... 218
27 ... 62, **218**
Artizans and Labourers Dwellings Act 1868 94
Artizan's and Labourers' Dwellings Improvement Act 1875 ... 94
Clean Air Act 1956 ... 132, 222, 223
Clean Air Act 1968 ... 132, 222, 223
Control of Pollution Act 1974 (35 *Statutes* 349) ... 377, 381, 382
s 31(2)(c) ... 382
Countryside Act 1968 (32 *Statutes* 142) ... 286
Cross's Act *See* Artizan's and Labourers' Dwellings Improvement Act 1875
Electricity Act 1989 (15 *Statutes* 1555)
s 3 ... 18, 19
29 ... 18, 19, 20, 21, 22
Environment Act 1995 (32 *Statutes* 366) ... 227, 241, 243
s 4 ... 230, 231
(1), (2) ... **229**
(3)–(5) ... **229**
39 ... 229
(1) ... **230**
(2) ... **230**, 231
Pt III (ss 61–79) ... 286
Pt IV (ss 80–91) ... 238
s 82 ... 239
Sch 22 ... 375

PAGE

Environmental Protection Act 1990 (35 *Statutes* 791) ... 227, 234, 238, 243, 276, 280, 281, 325
Pt I (ss 1—28) ... 186, 227, 231, 276, 281, 391
s 2(1) ... **277**
6(1) ... **277**
(2)–(4) ... 278
7(1)(a) ... **228, 278**
(b)–(c) ... **228**
(2) ... 280
(a) ... **228**
(b) ... **228**, 229
(c) ... **228**
(4) ... **278**, 280
(a) ... **228**
(b) ... **229**
(5)–(7) ... **229**
Sch 1 ... 276
European Communities Act 1972 (17 *Statutes* 34)
s 2(2) ... 402
Green Belt (London and Home Counties) Act 1938 (32 *Statutes* 40) ... 111
Highways Act 1959
Sch 1
para 7 ... 400
Highways Act 1980 (20 *Statutes* 124) ... 402
Housing, Town Planning, etc, Act 1909 ... 92, 94, 95, 96, 99
s 49 ... 96
54(1) ... **92**
57 ... 96
(1), (2) ... **93**
58 ... 96
(1) ... **93**, 95
(2) ... **93**
59 ... 96
(1) ... **93**
(2) ... **93**, 96
60–66 ... 96
Housing, Town Planning, etc Act 1919 ... 96

PAGE

Land Drainage Act 1991 (22 *Statutes* 698)
s 12(1) ... 430
London Building Act 1894 ... 94
Metropolis Management Act 1855 (26 *Statutes* 16) ... 84
s 76 ... 59, 84
National Parks and Access to the Countryside Act 1949 (32 *Statutes* 63) ... 109, 111, 112, 114, 286, 430, 436
s 5(1) ... **112, 286**
(2), (3) ... **112**
15 ... **437**
16(1)–(3) ... **437**
17(1) ... **437**, 439
(2) ... **437**, 439
18 ... 438
19 ... 438, 439
20(1), (2) ... **438**
23 ... 436, **438**
59(1) ... **112**
(2) ... **112, 113**
61(1) ... **113**
Planning and Compensation Act 1991 ... 249, 256, 261
s 12 ... 275
26 ... 254, 257
Planning (Listed Buildings and Conservation Areas) Act 1990 (45 *Statutes* 995)
s 74 ... 256
Public Health Act 1848 ... 52, 59, 83
Public Health Act 1875 (35 *Statutes* 29) ... 94, 245
Reform Act 1832. See Representation of the People Act 1932
Removal of Nuisances Act 1846 ... 59
Representation of the People Act 1932 ... 53
Restriction of Ribbon Development Act 1935 ... 111
Rivers (Prevention of Pollution) Act 1951 (49 *Statutes* 151) ... 391
Rivers Pollution Prevention Act 1876 ... 47, 63, 64, 65, 66, 391
s 12 ... **217**
Pt II, III ... 63
Smoke Abatement, London Act 1853 ... 54, 217
Torrens' Act. See Artizans and Labourers Dwellings Act 1868
Town and Country Planning Act 1932 ... 96, 111
Town and Country Planning Act 1947 ... 98, 100, 106, 107, 114, 252, 255, 256, 270, 286, 436
s 5(1), (2) ... **99**
12(1), (2) ... **99**
14(1) ... **99**
Town and Country Planning Act 1968 ... 98, 252
Town and Country Planning Act 1971 ... 98, 253
s 25 ... 400
31A ... 292

PAGE

Town and Country Planning Act 1990 (45 *Statutes* 514) ... 98, 249, 252, 274, 278, 280, 286
s 12(3A) ... 255
31(3) ... **255**
35(1) ... 282
36(3) ... 255
54A ... 251, **254**, 255, **256**, 257, 258, 259, 260, 261, 272, 277, 402
55(1), (1A) ... **250**
(2)(a)–(d) ... **250**
(e) ... 106, **250**, 251
(f), (g) ... **250**
70 ... 255
(1) ... 251, **254, 256**
(2) ... 251, **254, 256**, 257, 258, 261
72(2) ... 277
79(4) ... 277
91, 92 ... 254
106 ... 251, 263, 273, 275
(5), (6) ... 262
288 ... 256, 260, 277
Town Development Act 1952 ... 98
Towns Improvement Clauses Act 1847 (35 *Statutes* 17) ... 54
Water Act 1973 (49 *Statutes* 201)
s 11 ... 368
Water Act 1989 (49 *Statutes* 298) ... 374, 375, 377, 378, 379, 383
s 52 ... 365
104, 105 ... 373
112 ... 377
116 ... 383
Sch 11 ... 383
Water Industry Act 1991 (49 *Statutes* 405)
s 3(2) ... 430
18 ... 193, 194
19 ... 193, 194, 197
22 ... 198
68(1)(a) ... 193, 197, 198
Water Resources Act 1991 (49 *Statutes* 704) ... 365, 383
s 5(2)(a), (b) ... **379**
16(1) ... 430
82(1), (2) ... **373**
83(1) ... **373, 374**
(2) ... **374**
84 ... 374
85(1) ... **365**
86 ... 374
92 ... 375
93 ... 376
94 ... 377
(3) ... **378**
(4)(d) ... **378**
(5) ... **379**
95 ... 103, 377

PAGE

Water Resources Act 1991–*contd*
s 97 .... 380, 383
161 375
161D 375
202 374
Sch 12 379
Wildlife and Countryside Act 1981 (32 *Statutes* 193) 286, 291, 293, 424
Pt I (ss 1–27) 291

PAGE

Wildlife and Countryside Act 1981–*contd*
s 15 287
Pt II (ss 28–52) 286
s 28 .... 103, 287, 288, 290, 439
(7) 288
29 103
Wildlife and Countryside (Amendment) Act 1985 (32 *Statutes* 306) 290

Table of statutory instruments

PAGE

Conservation (Natural Habitats, &c) Regulations 1994, SI 1994/2716 .... 294, 454
 reg 22 295
 33 449
 54 295

Control of Substances Hazardous to Health Regulations 1988, SI 1988/1657 323

Control of Substances Hazardous to Health Regulations 1994, SI 1994/3246 323

Environmental Protection (Prescribed Processes and Substances) Regulations 1991, SI 1991/472
 reg 2 276

Nitrate Sensitive Areas Designation Order 1990, SI 1990/1013 .... 377, 378

Town and Country Planning (Assessment of Environmental Effects) Regulations 1988, SI 1988/1199 ..... 401, 402, 404, 414
 Sch 3 .... 407, 410

Town and Country Planning General Regulations 1976, SI 1976/1419
 reg 4 404

Town and Country Planning General Development Order 1977, SI 1977/289 400

Town and Country Planning (General Permitted Development) Order 1995, SI 1995/1418 251

Town and Country Planning (Use Classes) Order 1987, SI 1987/764 251

Water Supply (Water Quality) Regulations 1989, SI 1989/1147 .... 193, 194, 365

Table of Community law

PAGE

EC TREATIES

Single European Act 1986 .... 80, 167, 176, 181, 191
  Art 18 168
    25 171
Treaty on European Union 1992 (Maastricht Treaty) 19, 168, 171, 281
  Art 2 172
    3b **187**
    5 202
Title XVI 181
  Art 100 395
    130r **181, 182**
      (1) 183
      (2) 160, 186, 281
    130s **182, 183**
      (2) 281
    130t 183
    169 .... 191, 370
    170 191
    171(2) 192
    177 199
    189 189
      (3) 200
Treaty of Paris 1951 .... 158, 166
Treaty of Rome 1957 (EC Treaty) 165, 166
Title VII 181
  Art 2 169
    3b 19
    3h 167
    8a 168
      (1) 167
    100 176
    100a 168
    102a-109m 168
    130r 19, 80, 172
      (2) 18, 186
      (4) 186
    130s 171
      (3) 179
    189c 171
    235 176

DIRECTIVES

Directive 75/268/EEC (OJ [1975] L 128/1) 458

PAGE

Directive 75/439/EEC (OJ [1975] L 194/23) 80
  Art 2–4 .... 170, 171
    5, 6 170
Directive 75/440/EEC (OJ [1975] L 194/26) 201, 367
Directive 75/442/EEC (OJ [1975] L 194/39) 80
Directive 76/207/EEC (OJ [1976] L 39/40) 200
Directive 76/464/EEC (OJ [1976] L 129/23) 367, 373
Directive 78/319/EEC (OJ [1978] L 84/43) 80
Directive 79/409/EEC (OJ [1979] L 103/1) 185, 204, 207, 210, 293, 294, 399, 452, 454, 455, 462
  Preamble **452**
  Recital (9) **207–208**
  Art 1(1), (2) **452**
    2 .... 204, 205, 207, 208, 209
    3 .... 205, 208
    4 .... 204, 208, 209, 291
      (1) 205, 206, 207, 208, 209, 210, **452**
      (2) 205, 207, 208, 209, 210, **452, 453**
      (3) **453**
      (4) **205**, 209, 210, 293, **453**, 454
  Annex I 205, 206, 208, 452
Directive 80/778/EEC (OJ [1980] L 229/11) 67, 69, 78, 184, 187, 189, 190, 192, 194, 195, 198, 199, 201, 203, 204, 365, 367, 372, 379, 388
  Art 7(6) 371
    9 .... 369, 371, 372
      (1) 368, 369, 370
        (a) 368
    10, 18 371
    19, 20 .... 371, 372
  Annex I 369, 371
Directive 82/501/EEC (OJ [1982] L 230/1) 324
Directive 84/631/EEC (OJ [1984] L 326/31) 80
  Recital (19) 80
  Art 11(3) 80

PAGE
Directive 85/337/EEC (OJ [1985] L 175/40): 184, 191, 192, 202, 388, 389, 394, 400, 401, 402, 404, 417, 418, 420
Preamble **395**, **396**
Art 1(1)–(3) **396**
2 .... 394, 395
(1), (2) **396**
3 .... 395, **397**
4(1) 394, **397**
(2) 395, **397**
5(1), (2) **397**
(3) **398**
6 201
(1), (2) **398**
7 398
8 .... 397, **398**
9–11 397
Annex I 394
Annex II 394, 395, 399
Annex IIa 399
Annex III 399
Directive 85/374/EEC (OJ [1985] L 210/29) 79
Directive 87/216/EEC (OJ [1985] L 85/36) 324
Directive 90/313/EEC (OJ [1990] L 158/56) .. 184
Directive 91/244/EEC (OJ [1991] L 115/41) .. 455
Directive 91/676/EEC (OJ [1976] L 375/1) ... 372, 373, 377, 387
Preamble **372**
Directive 92/43/EC (OJ [1992] L 206/7) 185, 202, 206, 209, 210, 293, 294, 295, 395, 399, 444, 445, 454, 462
Preamble **455**
Art 3 .... 453, **455**, **456**
4(1) **456**

PAGE
Directive 92/43/EC–*contd*
Art 6 .... 185, 294, 295, 453
(1) **456**
(2) **205**, **456**
(3) **205**, **206**, 210, **294**, **456**
(4) **206**, 207, 209, 210, 453, **456**
7 .... 205, 210
11, 21 456
Annex I 294, 296, 455, 456
Annex II 294, 455
Annex III
Stage I 294, 455, 456
Directive 92/81/EEC (OJ [1992] L 316/12) 321
Directive 94/74/EC (OJ [1994] L 365) 321
Directive 96/61/EEC (OJ [1996] L 257) 186

REGULATIONS

Regulation 85/797/EEC (OJ L93, p 1, 30.3. 1985)
Art 19 (1), (2) 458
Regulation 92/880/EEC (OJ L99, 11.4.92) 184, 339
Regulation 93/1836/EEC (OJ L168, 10.7.93): 184, **327**, 332, 339
Art 1 .... **328**
2 .... **329**
3 .... **329**, 333
4 .... **330**
5 334
9 .... **330**
11, 12 334
Annex I **331**, **332**

RECOMMENDATIONS

Recommendation 79/3/EEC (OJ L5, 9.1.79, p 29) 80

Table of international treaties and conventions

PAGE

Agenda 21 (Rio, June 1992) 37, 38, 39, 40, 123, 124, 138, 144, 145, 146, 147, 148, 150, 151, 152, 153, 154, 158, 161, 234
  Ch 4 .... **145–150**
  Ch 22
    para 22.5(c) **161**
      28 38
  Ch 28 38
ASEAN Agreement 1985 158
Bergen ECE Ministerial Declaration on Sustainable Development 1990
  Art 7 159
Berne Convention 291
Charter of the United Nations 1946 124
Convention for the Preservation of Wild Animals, Birds and Fish in Africa 1900 168
Convention for the Protection of Birds Useful to Agriculture 1902 168
Convention for the Protection of the Marine Environment of the North-East Atlantic (OSPAR Convention) 1992 160
Convention on Biological Diversity (Rio de Janeiro, 31 ILM 818, 1992) 125, 158, 449, 453
Preamble **126**
  Art 1 .... **127**
    2-7 .... **128**
    8 .... **129**
    12, 15 129
    16, 20 129
Convention on Wetlands of International Importance especially as Waterfowl Habitat (Ramsar, 2.2.1971) 440, 443, 444, 445, 453
  Art 1, 2 .... **441**
    3 .... **441**
    3.2 .... 446, 447
    4 .... **442**
  6 .... **4**

PAGE

Convention on Wetlands of Internationl Importance–*contd*
  Art 6.1 (d) 442
    7 .... **442**
  Protocol (3.12.1982) 440
Declaration of the United Nations Conference on the Human Environment (Stockholm 1972) 135, 136, 168, 169
  Principle 1 .... **133**, 159
    8, 21 .... **134**
    23 134
ESPOO Convention 1991 .... 158, 400
Nairobi Declaration on the State of Worldwide Environment (Nairobi 1982) 135, 139, 465
  Principle 1-4 .... **136**
    5-10 .... **137**
Noumea Convention 1986
  Art 10 158
    12 .... **157**
    16 157
Protocol on Environmental Protection to the Antarctic Treaty 1991 158
Rio Declaration on Environment and Development of 13 June 1992, UNCED, A/Conf 151/4
  Principle 17 .... **391**
Statute of the International Court of Justice
  Art 38 130
United Nations Environment Programme Guidelines 1987
  Principle 1 .... **160**
    4 .... 160, **161**
United Nations Law of the Sea Convention 1982
  Art 205, 206 158
Vienna Convention on the Law of Treaties 1969 125
World Bank Operational Directive 1989 158
World Charter for Nature (1982)
  Principle 21 .... **138**
    22-24 .... 138, **139**

Table of national legislation

PAGE

BELGIUM

Belgian Civil Code
  Art 714 335

FRANCE

French Civil Code
  Art 714 335

PAGE

UNITED STATES

National Environmental Policy Act (NEPA) 1969 (42 USC 4321-4361)
  s 102(2)(c) 389

List of cases

PAGE

A

Algemene Transport-en Expeditie Onderneming van Gend & Loos NV v Nederlandse Belastingadministratie: 26/62 (1963), ECJ 165
Association pour la Protection des Animaux Sauvages v Préfet de Maine-et-Loire and Préfet de la Loire-Atlantique: C-435/92 (1994), ECJ 208
A-G v Birmingham Borough Council (1858) 64
A-G v Birmingham Council (1880), CA 65

B

Ballard v Tomlinson (1885), CA 68, 69, 70
Bamford v Turnley (1860); on appeal (1862), Ex Ch 72
Becker v Finanzamt Münster-Innenstadt: 8/81 (1982), ECJ 200
Board of Education v Rice (1911), HL 247
Brasserie du Pêcheur SA v Germany: C-46/93 (1996), ECJ 203
Bushell v Secretary of State for Transport and the Environment (1980) 416
Buxton v Minister of Housing and Local Government (1960) **100**

C

Cambridge Water Co Ltd v Eastern Counties Leather plc (1994), CA; revsd (1994), HL 47, **67**, **69**, 77, 273
Chasemore v Richards (1859) 70
Collins v Secretary of State for the Environment and Langbaurgh on Tees Borough Council (1996) 283
Comitato di Coordinamento per la Difesa della Cava v Regione Lombardia: C-236/92 (1994), ECJ 201
Cooper v Wandsworth Board of Works (1863) 59, 83, **84**, 245

D

de Merode v World Bank (1981) 165
Detergents Directive, Re: EC Commission v Italy: 91/79 (1980), ECJ 169
Duke v GEC Reliance Ltd (formerly Reliance Systems Ltd) (1988), HL 202

E

EC Commission v Belgium: C-42/9 (1990), ECJ 372
EC Commission v France: C-13/90 (1991), ECJ 190
EC Commission v Germany: C-361/88 (1991), ECJ 190, 356, 357, 373
EC Commission v Germany: C-57/89 (1991), ECJ 207, 209, 293, 453
EC Commission v Germany: C-59/89 (1991), ECJ 201, 356, 357
EC Commission v Spain: C-355/90 (1993), ECJ 203, 293, 453
EC Commission v United Kingdom: C-337/89 (1992), ECJ 190, 192, 203, **370**
Ellis and Ruislip-Northwood UDC, Re (1920), CA **95**

F

Faccini Dori v Recreb Srl: C-91/92 (1994), ECJ 202
Francovich and Bonifaci v Italy: C-6, 9/90 (1991), ECJ 203, 356

PAGE

G

Gateshead Metropolitan Borough Council v Secretary of State for the Environment (1994); affd sub nom Gateshead Metropolitan Borough Council v Secretary of State for the Environment and Northumbrian Water Group (1995), CA 275, **276**, 297
Gourmetterie van den Burg, Criminal Proceedings against: C-169/89 (1990), ECJ 208
Griffin v South West Water Services Ltd (1995) 202

H

Humphries (or Humphreys) v Cousins (1877) 74

L

Leatch v National Parks & Wildlife Service and Shoalhaven City Council 19
Local Government Board v Arlidge (1915), HL 247

M

McAlpine (Alfred) Homes (North) Ltd v Secretary of State for the Environment (1994), CA 281
Marleasing SA v La Comercial Internacional de Alimentación SA: C-106/89 (1990), ECJ ... 202
Marshall v Southampton and South West Hampshire Area Health Authority (No 1): 152/84 (1986), ECJ 200, 202

N

Nawar v Secretary of State for the Environment (1994); affd (1995), CA 272
New Zealand v France (1995) 154
Newbury District Council v Secretary of State for the Environment (1981), HL 262, 282
Nicaragua v United States (Merits) (1986) **131**
Nuclear Tests Case (Judgment) (1974) **155**

O

Overseas Tankship (UK) Ltd v Miller SS Co Pty, The Wagon Mound (No 2) (1967), PC 73

P

Pehrsson v Secretary of State for the Environment (1990), CA 257
Peralta, Re: C-379/92 (1994), ECJ 154
Pretura Unifacata di Torino v Persons Unknown: 228/87 (1988), ECJ 371
Procureur de la République v Association de défense des brûleurs d'huiles usagées: 240/83 (1985), ECJ 169, **170**, 204
Pubblico Ministero v Ratti: 148/78 (1979), ECJ 200

R

R v Canterbury City Council and Robert Brett & Sons Ltd, ex p Springimage Ltd (1994): 259
R v London Borough Transport Committee v Freight Transport Association Ltd (1992) ... 187
R v Plymouth City Council, ex p Plymouth & South Devon Co-operative Society Ltd (1993), CA 264
R v Poole Borough Council, ex p Beebee (1991) 288, **289**
R v Secretary of State for Trade and Industry, ex p Duddridge (1995); affd (1996), CA 18, 154, 187
R v Secretary of State for Transport, ex p Factortame Ltd: C-48/93 (1996), ECJ 203
R v Secretary of State for the Environment (1995) 201
R v Secretary of State for the Environment, ex p Friends of the Earth Ltd (1994); affd (1995), CA **192**
R v Secretary of State for the Environment, ex p Royal Society for the Protection of Birds (Lappel Bank): C-44/95 (1996), ECJ **204**, 293, 453
R v Swale Borough Council and Medway Ports, ex p Royal Society for the Protection of Birds (1991) 203, 402
Rainham Chemical Works Ltd v Belvedere Fish Guano Co Ltd (1921), HL 74, 76
Read v J Lyons & Co Ltd (1947), HL 56, 71, 75

PAGE

Rickards v Lothian (1913) 72
Ross v Fedden (1872) 71
Ruiz Bernáldez, Criminal proceedings against: C-129/94 (1996), ECJ 210
Rylands v Fletcher (1866); affd (1868) 54, 56, 73

S

Sainsbury plc v Secretary of State for the Environment (1993) **259**
St Albans District Council v Secretary of State for the Environment and Allied Breweries Ltd (1993) 255, **256**
St Helen's Smelting Co v Tipping (1865) 56, **57**, 61, 65, 354
Simpson v Edinburgh Corpn (1960) 257
Southern Water Authority v Nature Conservancy Council (1992), HL 288
Staffordshire County Council v Seisdon RDC (1907) 63, **64**
Sturges v Bridgman (1879), CA 245
Sweet v Secretary of State for the Environment and Nature Conservancy Council (1989) .. 287, 430

T

Tenant v Goldwin (or Golding) (1704) 56
Tesco Stores Ltd v Secretary of State for the Environment (1995), HL 263, **264**, 285
Trail Smelter Case, Re (1939) 131
Tulk v Moxhay (1848) 54
Twyford Parish Council v Secretary of State for the Environment (1992) 202

V

Van Duyn v Home Office (No 2): 41/74 (1974), ECJ 200
Von Colson and Kamann v Land Nordrhein-Westfalen: 14/83 (1984), ECJ 202

W

Wagon Mound (No 2), The. See Overseas Tankship (UK) Ltd v Miller SS Co Pty, The Wagon Mound (No 2)
Webb v EMO Air Cargo (UK) Ltd: C-32/93 (1994), ECJ; revsd sub nom Webb v Emo Air Cargo (UK) Ltd (No 2) (1995), HL 202
West v Bristol Tramways Co (1908), CA 74, 76
Western Fish Products Ltd v Penwith District Council (1981), CA 283
Wimpey Homes Holdings Ltd v Secretary of State for the Environment (1993) 283
Wychavon District Council v Secretary of State for the Environment, ex p Velcourt (1994); on appeal (1994), CA 201, 203

Y

Young (John) & Co v Bankier Distillery Co (1893), HL **55**, 78

Decisions of the European Court of Justice are listed below numerically. These decisions are also included in the preceding alphabetical list.

26/62: Algemene Transport-en Expeditie Onderneming van Gend & Loos NV v Nederlandse Belastingadministratie (1963), ECJ 165
41/74: Van Duyn v Home Office (No 2) (1974), ECJ 200
148/78: Pubblico Ministero v Ratti (1979), ECJ 200
91/79: Re Detergents Directive: EC Commission v Italy (1980), ECJ 169
8/81: Becker v Finanzamt Münster-Innenstadt (1982), ECJ 200
14/83: Von Colson and Kamann v Land Nordrhein-Westfalen (1984), ECJ 202
240/83: Procureur de la République v Association de défense des brûleurs d'huiles usagées (1985), ECJ 169, **170**, 204
152/84: Marshall v Southampton and South West Hampshire Area Health Authority (No 1) (1986), ECJ 200, 202
228/87: Pretura Unifacata di Torino v Persons Unknown (1988), ECJ 371

PAGE
C-361/88: EC Commission v Germany (1991), ECJ 190, 356, 357, 373
C-42/89: EC Commission v Belgium (1990), ECJ 372
C-57/89: EC Commission v Germany (1991), ECJ 207, 209, 293, 453
C-59/89: EC Commission v Germany (1991), ECJ 201, 356, 357
C-106/89: Marleasing SA v La Comercial Internacional de Alimentación SA (1990), ECJ ... 202
C-169/89: Criminal Proceedings against Gourmetterie van den Burg (1990), ECJ 208
C-337/89: EC Commission v United Kingdom (1992), ECJ 190, 192, 203, **370**
C-6, 9/90: Francovich and Bonifaci v Italy (1991), ECJ 203, 356
C-13/90: EC Commission v France (1991), ECJ 190
C-355/90: EC Commission v Spain (1993), ECJ 203, 293, 453
C-91/92: Faccini Dori v Recreb Srl (1994), ECJ 202
C-236/92: Comitato di Coordinamento per la Difesa della Cava v Regione Lombardia (1994), ECJ 201
C-379/92: Peralta, Re (1994), ECJ 154
C-435/92: Association pour la Protection des Animaux Sauvages v Préfet de Maine-et-Loire and Préfet de la Loire-Atlantique (1994), ECJ 208
C-32/93: Webb v EMO Air Cargo (UK) Ltd (1994), ECJ 202
C-46/93: Brasserie du Pêcheur SA v Germany (1996), ECJ 203
C-48/93: R v Secretary of State for Transport, ex p Factortame Ltd (1996), ECJ 203
C-129/94: Criminal proceedings against Ruiz Bernáldez (1996), ECJ 210
C-44/95: R v Secretary of State for the Environment, ex p Royal Society for the Protection of Birds (Lappel Bank) (1996), ECJ **204**, 293, 453

PART I

Using the law for environmental protection

CHAPTER 1

Environmental law in context

Much of the law to protect the environment has roots that are deep in history, but the conceptual basis of environmental law is still developing. It is guided by distinctive principles, but there is as yet no 'Grand Theory' and it remains characterised by 'ad hoc-ery', without even agreement as to its boundaries. Legal evolution, like social and biological evolution, proceeds by fits and starts and in a fragmentary manner, with law being laid down in response to immediately pressing problems. This relatively undeveloped quality of environmental law means it is still possible to shape it.

An optimistic view is often taken of environmental law; that a new law will cure our environmental ills, whatever these are perceived to be. However, a theme of the book is that this optimism is frequently absorbed into the shadow between aspirations for a better life and reality:

> Between the idea
> And the reality
> Between the motion
> And the act
> Falls the Shadow[1]

It is therefore important that environmental law is read critically and that the inherent limitations of relying on law alone are acknowledged. Still, as environmental protection will for the most part have to be effected through the medium of environmental law, we hope to encourage creative use of it.

To focus on environmental law, exclusively, is to tell an incomplete story of environmental protection. So we include, for example, consumption patterns or, more colloquially, 'lifestyle choices' and management systems. We are also uneasy with the way law has so far conceptualised the environment, and with the introspective way environmental law has developed. It still reflects old thinking that juxtaposes people and nature. Relationships between people and nature are being explored more thoroughly in other disciplines, particularly from an ethical perspective. But, law has to deal on a daily basis with practical environmental problems and has, so far, failed to take much account of philosophical and political developments. Law deals with environmental problems in the same way as it has traditionally dealt with other problems: in an individualist manner and favouring property. At the same time, it is attempting to deal with the complexities of a time of great social and ecological change and does in parts reflect the developments in thinking which arise

1 TS Eliot, 'The Hollow Men', *Selected Poems* (London: Faber and Faber, 1961), p 80.

from these changes. For example, legal principles and techniques have been developed in response to the challenges posed by 'sustainable development' and 'biodiversity'. In recognising the restricted nature of environmental law to date, we expand the definition of 'legal' so as to include styles of administration, the policy underlying the law, as well as different types of legal instruments. To approach the law in a critical, but constructive, way we draw upon a wide range of disciplines, periods and media. Understanding environmental problems requires making forays into other disciplines because the sources of environmental harm are diverse, multi-causal and themselves cross disciplinary boundaries; 'environmental studies' being perceived by academic purists as messy. We hope the cases, reports and literature will illuminate the law, and also stimulate debate beyond the law. We do not adopt what has, already, become the conventional approach of looking at laws relating to air, water and land; rather we contextualise environmental law in history, space and culture.

In Part V, we use case studies to ground the law in practical projects and bring it to life. This allows explanation of the practical nature of procedures and processes so that the complexities of decision making are not glossed over. It also allows us to include differing perceptions of the significance of laws by those involved in administration and those affected by environmental law. Our case studies grapple with contemporary, contentious social issues: adjusting agriculture, road building, and conservation. These illustrate important legal themes; in particular, that different layers of law – international, European Community and domestic – interact and are superimposed onto existing structures of law and administration. All three case studies are examples of the practical application of the precautionary principle. Related to this is the development of integrated procedures which attempt to achieve that holy grail of environmentalists – holism. We also identify in the case studies some parameters of environmental law – science, space and property – which have determined its scope and content.

Understanding ecological change is fundamental to environmental protection. We therefore begin with an extract which approaches this core issue by relating ideas of resilience to sustainable development. Of importance is the human and social element in ecological change.

D Pearce *Blueprint for a Green Economy* (London: Earthscan, 1989), pp 40-43

Sustainability as resilience

To understand the process by which ecosystems respond to environmental change, ecologists have developed the concept of *resilience* – the ability of the system to maintain its structure and patterns of behaviour in the face of external disturbance, i.e., its ability to adapt to change. This is usually distinguished from ecological *stability* – the ability of the system to maintain a relatively constant condition (its "equilibrium") in terms of its species composition, biomass and productivity, in response to normal fluctuations and cycles in the surrounding environment. The basic system properties for natural populations, communities and ecosystems are therefore *productivity* (in terms of numbers/ biomass of individual species), *stability* (constancy) and *resilience* (sustainability).

Understanding ecological resilience in the face of external disturbances is also of importance in managed ecosystems, particularly agriculture where the purpose of human activity is to transform an ecosystem deliberately. The key question is whether or not the human modification and transformation of ecosystems affect their stability and resilience (sustainability). If the natural mechanisms of control and stabilization are replaced by increased human management and control, the application of human knowledge, and the use of both human and natural resources – all with minimum ecological disturbance – the result may be little change in ecological stability or sustainability.

For both managed and natural ecosystems, the resilience of the system may differ depending on whether the external disturbance is a sudden shock or a cumulative, continuous stress. Especially for agricultural systems – or more appropriately "agro-ecosystems" – it may be more useful to define *sustainability* as the ability of an agro-ecosystem to maintain productivity when subject to stress or shock. *Productivity* can be re-defined as the output of valued product per unit of resource input, with common measures of productivity being yield or income per hectare, or total production of goods and services per household or nation. Stress in this context would be a regular, sometimes continuous, relatively small and predictable disturbance on agricultural productivity over time, for example the effect of salinity, toxicity, erosion, declining market demand or indebtedness. *Shock* on the other hand would be an irregular, infrequent, relatively large and unpredictable disturbance to the agricultural system, such as a rare drought or flood, a new pest or a sudden rise in input prices, like oil in the mid-1970s.

The unchecked abuse of resources within an *agro-ecosystem*, whether as a result of the inappropriate use of agro-chemicals and fertilizers, the overcropping of erodible soils, poor drainage, etc, not only directly affects the sustainability of the agro-ecosystem but may also increase its susceptibility to other external stresses and shocks, such as changes in market conditions, prolonged dry seasons, changes in land tenure, and so on.

As a consequence, a crucial component of sustainability, as defined in terms of the resilience of an agricultural system to external stresses and shocks, is maintaining the environmental resources and ecological functions upon which the system depends.

In the same way, we can consider the sustainability of an *economic* system in terms of its ability to maintain productivity when subject to stress in an economic system that may make it less "resilient" over time. In this context, "conservation of natural capital" essentially means exploiting the various functions of the environment – the production of material and energy inputs, the assimilation of waste and the maintenance of essential ecological functions and cycles – so as to minimize the stress imposed by environmental degradation on the economic system. Thus if the environment is likened to a stock of "natural" capital yielding a flow of services to the economic system (i.e. its essential economic functions), then sustainable development of that system involves maximizing the net benefits of economic development, subject to maintaining the services and quality of the stock of natural resources over time.

This rationale for natural capital conservation is often considered strongest for the developing world, where direct dependence on natural resource exploitation to sustain economic livelihoods, and in many cases to ensure economic growth and development, is so evident. But the rationale seems less applicable to advanced industrialized economies, with perhaps the exception of their agricultural and resource-based sector. The considerable accumulation and innovations in man-made capital and technology in these economies contribute to their resilience with respect to external acute or chronic shocks and stresses. Margins of flexibility are also greater than in poorer countries where population growth and poor economic performance in general often produce very narrow risk margins in the face of external disturbances, such as drought and changes in resource prices.

But the comparative resilience of advanced industrialized economies to environmental stresses and shocks might actually be illusory. First, although both man-made and natural capital contribute to the resilience of these economies, it does not imply that the two forms of capital are perfectly substitutable. As noted earlier, essential functions of the environment, such as complex life-support systems, biological diversity, aesthetic functions, micro-climatic conditions and so forth, have yet to be replicated by man-made capital, or can only be substituted at an unacceptably high cost. The risks of irreversible transformations of natural capital may therefore be high.

In addition, degradation of one or more parts of an ecosystem beyond some threshold level may lead to a breakdown in the integrity of the whole system, dramatically affecting recovery rates and resilience of the system. The total costs of the system breakdown may exceed the value of the activity causing the initial degradation.

Man-made capital often lacks an important feature of natural capital – *diversity*. The resilience justification for conserving the natural capital stock is thus based on the idea that diverse ecological and economic systems are more resilient to shocks and stress.

In turn, to maintain diversity it is essential to avoid irreversible choices. Since knowledge is rarely lost for ever, irreversibility involving man-made capital is rare – discontinued machines can be re-constructed, structures rebuilt, technology recreated, and so on. But ecological irreversibility is not unusual – natural species are lost every year, unique ecosystems are destroyed and environmental functions are irreparably damaged. This again reinforces the notion that we should only degrade or deplete our natural capital stock – particularly resources that may be irreversibly lost – if the benefits of doing so are very large.

In summary, then, conserving natural capital – ensuring that the natural environment is at least not degraded further – is consistent with:

* intergenerational equity
* intragenerational equity at least as far as poorer countries are concerned, and maybe also for richer countries
* resilience to stress and shock
* risk aversion.

Describing environmental harm in this way is particularly helpful when considering the role of law in environmental protection. To take the example of nitrate pollution from farming,[2] a 'shock' is when, for instance, a slurry tank bursts and pollutes a river, compared with the 'stress' of continuous run-off to the river of fertiliser from agricultural land. Law is quite good at dealing with one-off shocks but less so with stresses: neither, unfortunately, are ecosystems. Law is, however, being developed in response to this limitation.

1 SCIENCE AND ENVIRONMENTAL LAW

Much environmental law is developed and sustained by the scientific community. Scientists engage with law when they sit on Royal Commissions, give evidence to parliamentary committees, inquiries and to courts, collect data on the state of the environment, manage nature reserves, develop sampling techniques and make predictions for the purpose of environmental assessments. This crucial contribution from scientists gives environmental law its distinctive flavour: unlike other areas it does not develop primarily by the accidents of litigation.

The relationship between scientific knowledge, policy and law is complex and changing. Law relies on science for much of its legitimacy. Even the precautionary principle, which suggests that it may not be necessary to wait for scientific certainty before taking action, does not operate in a scientific vacuum. And, even if the relationship between a harm and a presumed cause is imperfectly understood, there may be an underlying statistical association which is itself the product of sophisticated mathematics. In practice, much environmental law operates in conditions of scientific uncertainty and hence may struggle for legitimacy. The following readings discuss the complexity of this relationship between science, policy, and law, and highlight the multi-faceted nature of scientific knowledge itself.

S Crook, J Pakulski & M Waters, *Postmodernization: Change in Advanced Society* (London: Sage, 1992) pp 210-211

Paradoxes of a Rationality of 'Control'

The radical Weberian critique of science and technology is based on assumptions about a 'logic' of control... The critique claims, in effect, that the Grand Design for the control of nature has been realized, but that its realization has brought unforeseen and terrible social costs. The rather different case that 'control' has always been problematic, and that a visible *failure* to deliver control is a disorganizing force in contemporary science, can be sketched here in relation to increasingly prominent concerns about the environment.

One impact of environmental concerns has been to alter the meaning of 'control' in claims about the 'control of nature'. Perhaps the most influential

2 See ch 9.

modern image of control has been that of 'harnessing' natural forces. Science discerns order in the protean unruliness of natural forces so that these forces can be tamed by technology and put to productive use. The paradigm here, and perhaps for all modern technology, is the development of energy sources: the forces which produce fire, lightning, flood, or even the forces which hold together matter itself, become the servants of human industry. A related image is that of 'transformation'. Not only are natural materials processed and shaped into objects of use, but modern science conjures up new materials from base elements, and turns them to new purposes.

The environmentalist critique of science and technology insists that pay-back time has arrived for the project of harnessing and transforming nature and for the industrial economy which is premised upon it. Of course, the argument that scientific-industrial civilization rests on an alienating human relationship with nature is familiar from the radical-Weberian critique and stretches back to Romanticism...Two peculiarities, at least, mark out contemporary concerns from the established tradition. The first can be indicated by way of contrast. Campaigns such as those to prevent damming, logging and mining in the temperate rainforests of south-west Tasmania have a relatively traditional relationship with the 'lifeworlds' of campaigners. They invoke images of a 'special' region that embodies the virtues of a wilderness which can be experienced by visiting the region or intimated by way of films and photographs. Concerns about global warming and ozone depletion, on the other hand, are not related to the lifeworld in the same way: they exist as concerns only by virtue of scientific measurement and hypothesis. No particular value attaches to the ozone layer other than its role as a global sunscreen, and ozone depletion cannot be seen in the way that the desolate results of clear-felling in native Australian forests can be seen.

The second peculiarity of contemporary global concerns is that they are unsettling because they suggest the failure of the project for 'control' of nature understood as harnessing and transformation. As Newby...notes in relation to the shifting focus of British environmental concerns, 'there is now a greater emphasis on the finite nature of the earth's resources and a growing suspicion that we may, in ways which remain not yet fully understood, be irreversibly tampering with the habitability of our planet'. Two dimensions of failure can be distinguished. The theme of 'scarcity' surfaced in the 1970s. It challenges the idea that nature will furnish raw materials for an indefinite prolongation of harnessing and transformation. A twist in the more recent versions of the theme points to the second dimension. Scarcity is due not simply to the exhaustion of natural resources, but to their despoliation by the practices through which they are exploited. So, modern agriculture threatens long-term productivity by reducing biological diversity, promoting soil erosion and increasing salinity...The twist, and the second dimension of failure, is that the project for control of nature is self-defeating in the long term; attempts at control set in train unforeseen consequences (soil degradation, ozone depletion, warming) which subvert the original attempt.

Increasingly, science and technology are required to turn their attention to another kind of control: the 'damage control' of the unforeseen consequences of the project for the control of nature. This kind of control is not new. Medicine has always aimed at a control of nature which, while informed by theoretical knowledge, establishes pragmatic criteria of success in terms of a capacity to halt or reverse pathological processes. Science and technology, one might say, are required to become more like medicine, to diagnose and (more problematically) to cure the diseases that scientific-industrial civilization has induced in the planet.

This shift in emphasis carries a disorganizing, postmodernizing, potential. Most generally, the question mark it places over the 'Grand Design' challenges the most potent of meta-narratives of modern science. If they are no longer in the vanguard of a 'progress' understood as unalloyed benefit, science and technology can be subject to more pragmatic and piecemeal judgements of worth. Perhaps more fundamentally, the clear lines between 'natural', 'technical' and 'social' processes are eroded. When Brown et al....try to depict a sustainable society, for example, the issues they raise illustrate the complex and fine-grained interdependence of choices made at each of these levels. So to shift the advanced societies from their reliance on private petrol-driven automobiles requires the development of new transport and energy techniques, as well as the revival of old ones (bicycles), the transformation of the social geography of cities, and shifts in the relations between home and work. The traditional model, in which science and technology connect with social processes only at the points of 'application' or 'use' is not adequate to these complexities.

A great deal of work is being done to predict ecological change. 'Model makers' are developing techniques to aid decision making by 'policy makers'. The following seeks to get behind the modelling process using the example of climate change.

S Shackley, 'Mission to Model Earth', in S Elworthy et al (eds) *Perspectives on the Environment 2* (Aldershot: Avebury, 1995) pp 11-23

...

Scientism

According to many, science is the most authoritative source of knowledge of the environment and good policy must, therefore, be based on good science. This linear extension from science to policy is a form of scientism, the extrapolation of scientific idioms and methods to conventionally or currently nonscientific realms in the belief that the conditions which make science authoritative and effective in producing knowledge of the natural world are applicable in those other fields and should be applied. An example is provided by the evidence of the former head of the UK Meteorological Office, Sir John Mason, before a Select Committee of the House of Lords. He commented that:

> It is very important in my view that any major policy that you make, which is likely to have either major economic or social consequences, should as far as possible be based on good science. If it does not make good scientific sense, it almost certainly will not make good economic sense and in the long run will not make good political

> sense. If it is basically a scientific and technical problem not based on good science and good technology and real understanding of that, then I think you are in a dangerous situation.

According to this view, science, as a unique source of knowledge of the 'real world', circumscribes what is real and hence feasible and desirable in economic and political terms. The natural and social worlds are therefore seen as continuous realities, in which failure to recognize actual limitations (which are naturally given, whether by physical or socio-economic laws) has serious consequences for policy success.

...

Criticisms of scientism

The criticisms of scientism are wide ranging and well known. One common argument has been that the social realm has quite different dynamics and epistemology from the natural. For example, if social reality is socially constructed then culture, institutions, political systems and understandings will influence, or, some would say, wholly determine, how the environment is viewed and treated by individuals and organizations. However natural scientists define 'dangerous climate intervention', therefore, this may or may not bear comparison to 'lay' understandings. Seen from the social end, the scientific definition may be readily rejected if it does not correspond to the definition which is achieved through political negotiation; there is no reason why science, even if it is 'right', should prevail.

...

The conflation of science and technology has been a particularly powerful expression of scientism, at least in policy cultures in the UK. If technological change, say to limit greenhouse gas emissions or develop alternative energy production systems, is beholden to precise scientific knowledge inputs, such as risk assessment and corresponding amelioration and mitigation strategies, some evidence suggests that the independent process of technological innovation can be inhibited. If so, this not only limits the availability of technological options but also curtails economic performance irrespective of the success of the scientific programme.

...

It is also clear that science cannot provide the synoptic overview of an environmental issue which is sometimes assumed from the perception of a few areas of apparent certainty let alone prescribe and institute credible and effective policy responses and social actions. So, for example, a record of half a degree celsius warming in the past century cannot be attributed unambiguously to anthropogenic emissions of greenhouse gases since it may be natural variability. The scientific basis for concern about global warming is more rooted in the findings of general circulation models (GCMs) of the climate system. Yet, there is a basic indeterminacy in the scenarios of climate change from such models since there is no way of confirming their predictive success in advance of the events being predicted.

...

The rhetorical force of scientism

The above comments are critical of scientism on two counts. There is the point that the advocates of scepticism rarely make explicit or justify their assumptions, for example that the natural and social worlds are continuous. They are being selective in which strands of their arguments they wish to raise and argue for, as if beyond that we should simply trust in their judgements. The second point relates to the implicit values behind scientism, such as the a priori value ascribed to scientific and technical information. These criticisms do not, however, deny the rhetorical force of scientific arguments.

...

Science as politics by other means

A very different approach from scientism is to regard science as irredeemably imbued with political, institutional or structural interests...The scientific community, or sections of it, can itself be regarded as a political agent, attempting to secure resources for its own survival and expansion. Boehmer-Christiansen claims, for example, that a scientific policy elite at the IPCC WGI manicured the representation of the scientific uncertainties in its reports, and through other avenues, such as meeting with high ranking policy officials, so as to put the issue of climate change on the political agenda as well as making itself indispensable as a source of expertise. Implicit in this account is the notion of elites as essentially self serving and interested in securing autonomy, resources and prestige. Scientific elites have generally been excused the attribution of less than respectable motives because the objectivity of 'the scientific method' and the knowledge so generated, was thought to maintain its integrity beyond reproach.

A problem with such political accounts, however, is their reliance on an a priori and stable definition of interests since on what basis can we attribute interests to actors? The problem is clear when the actors are large, multifaceted institutions or heterogenous collections of individuals and networks, since multiple, perhaps contradictory, articulations of 'interest' are routine, but qualitative research has also indicated widespread ambivalence at the level of the individual actor. A 'single story' is therefore unlikely to account for different understandings of what autonomy, resources, prestige or the furtherance of scientific knowledge mean, in practice, to different people and organizations.

Complexity argues, therefore, against a simple or single resolution of the relation of science and politics.

...

Scepticism

A programmatic, and sometimes radical, scepticism towards scientific knowledge is one approach within the sociology of science. The claim that scientific knowledge is in some senses superior knowledge, hence uniquely rational, objective or universal, comes under critical scrutiny, by inter alia detailed, micro level studies of scientific reasoning and practice in the work place. How then should closure around particular knowledge be understood? There are different responses in sociology of science, from exploring social processes, institutions and commitments, to analyzing how networks of scientists, institutions and nonhuman actors, such as greenhouse gases or the algae which respond to them, become stable and durable. One of the key theoretical issues of disagreement is the degree to which closure can be reduced to social processes, especially if the latter are themselves undergoing change. These sorts of approaches are especially attuned to the ways in which changing knowledge claims and new social processes, forms of organization and alliance become mutually producing and justifying.

...

Criticisms of scepticism

One possible problem with programmatic scepticism is that it undermines the authority of science and hence the seriousness and legitimacy of global environmental phenomena. This sentiment is expressed well by Geoff Mulgan:

> ...the green movement has itself contributed to [the] decay of deference and authority. It was nurtured in a libertarian, anti-statist culture that doubted government scientists and ministers, and was prepared to show why their authority was fatuous. Militant scepticism was a good tool for blocking grandiose developments. But now that the greens need a legitimate authority to take tough decisions in the name of the future, they find it is no longer there.

It is critical, however, to reject this argument in so far as it refers to the rhetorical force of scientific argumentation: unless, that is, one accepts this form of rhetoric as positive. My reasons for not doing so are that such forms of persuasion seem to generate a 'politics of fear', in which the rationale and motivation for change is some dreadful consequence or global catastrophe, knowledge about which has to be taken almost entirely on trust. I find it difficult to believe that the politics of fear is the right or desirable way to create the conditions for change.

...

New forms of science

My last category, new forms of science, adopts a posture of constrained scepticism. In this approach it is argued that the present scientific endeavour is in some senses flawed, for example through adoption of reductionist methodologies, overly mechanistic modes of analysis, overspecialization and segmentation of research activity, overbureaucratization of research organization, and so on. The implication is that if scientific thought and practice were to change appropriately, the credibility, and hence authority, of scientific knowledge would be enhanced.

...

Discussion: multiple stories, reduced realities

A major argument here is that there is no single way of describing the relation between environmental science and policy making. The four different approaches discussed differ in the extent to which they accept that point: scientism deals in an unproblematic but highly reduced reality, whereas sociology of science tends to problematize and unpick multiple constructions of reality and to aim for holistic understandings. The other two approaches are agnostic, and sometimes schizophrenic, on these issues. Many policy actors use more than a single type of argument in different contexts. For example, one research manager expressed the following views: GCMs should be the key input to climate impacts research (scientism); the satellite lobby had used scientific arguments opportunistically to appropriate resources (science as politics); and the arguments concerning climate change of the 'contrarians', as well as many environmentalists, should be treated with much incredulity (scepticism).

What, however, are the implications of these arguments for climate change research and policy? Perhaps the most important consequence will be the increasing tensions in an account of global environmental problems founded on scientific certainties. The universal claims of science are especially attractive in the context of the globalization of economic, political and cultural systems. The pressures towards standardization of science, and its relation to policy, will be undermined, however, by the multiple ways in which the science policy relationship is interpreted and used by policy actors as well as academics.

On a more prescriptive level, it seems to me that claims about 'good', or 'superior', science, or 'privileged knowledge', should be subject to critical scrutiny and, where appropriate, challenged. In practice, this means examining the arguments and values constituting scientism, given the latter's unstated dominance in many science and policy circles. To be consistent the claims made by those developing new forms of science to produce a richer understanding should also be studied, though sympathetically. This approach should hopefully have the effect of strengthening new forms of understanding, and encourage exploration of the way in which knowledge is, and can be, used in policy making. In time, we might even want to use that experience to fashion our knowledge 'through' supporting those institutions, local cultures, values and commitments which favour particular knowledge styles.

The following article is a similarly critical account of the potential use or abuse of science in environmental law. Law deals in dichotomies such as 'guilty/innocent'; a danger is that law similarly divides scientific knowledge into categories of 'good' and 'bad'.

AD Tarlock, 'The Futile Search for Environment Laws Based on "Good Science"', (1996) *International Journal of Biosciences and the Law* Vol 1, No 1, 9-11

Environmentalism derives its legitimacy from ethics, economics, politics and science, but science provides the most powerful explanation and justification for stringent laws to protect the public from toxic risks and to preserve biodiversity. Toxicology and ecology have identified a wide range of harms potentially caused by human activities such as the production and use of synthetic organic chemicals, waste discharges, and energy production. Science has also provided the basis for regulatory strategies to remedy these harms. Without science, environmentalism would be a minor nature preservation 'cult'. Science's success in influencing the content of environmental policy has come despite a profound tension between the ethics of modern research science and the demands of the regulatory state for immediate science-based causal justifications for its laws and regulations. Environmental regulation constantly pushes the limits of current scientific understanding and thus most important decisions must be made under extreme conditions of scientific uncertainty. This constraint is taken as a given in modern, probabilistic science, but uncertainty presents major problems when science is used either to assign liability for a 'toxic tort' or to justify a government risk reduction regulation. Judges have been trained to expect more certainty and rationality because the law has long rejected 'speculative' injuries; specifically, they demand 'traceable causal chains leading from actor to harm'. In the United States, the tension manifests itself in the intense debate over the legal standards for the admission of expert scientific evidence and for the judicial review of the science underlying environmental regulations. In both cases, courts have oscillated between almost total deference to 'science' and attempts to make an independent judgment about the validity of the science. This oscillation reflects a deeper debate about how to hold science socially accountable and how the law should adjust to the contingent nature of modern knowledge.

The tension between science and environmental regulation is fuelled by sharply differing views about the need for environmental regulation, about the nature of the science necessary to support this regulation, and exasperation with the inability of science to tell us unambiguously what regulation is necessary to protect public health and the integrity of natural systems. Science is the best neutral standard to resolve these debates, as it is widely accepted as a source of legitimacy. But, it cannot meet society's expectations. Instead, in the spirit of Milton, the debate about the scientific basis of environmental regulation has been cast as a choice between 'good science' and 'bad science' or 'junk' versus 'acceptable scientific reasoning'. The legal debate has focused on the level of science necessary to support a causal link between an activity and suspected harm. Like most dichotomies, the good versus bad science one is false, but it is deeply entrenched in all societies and influences the substance of science-based rules.

The United States Supreme Court recently decided a case... that assumes that the dichotomy is valid and that judges can effectively police the scientific validity of the methodology experts use to justify the imposition of civil liability. This decision technically applies only to civil and criminal suits rather than to the review of environmental regulations, but the case will be used to urge courts to invalidate regulations aimed at protecting public health and biodiversity. Their scientific basis will be attacked as too speculative. Although the precedent comes out of the United States legal system, which sends all manner of controversies to court, the issues arise in all political and legal systems. For example, under the rules of the World Trade Organization, a nation which adopts a high environment standard which potentially discriminates against international trade must bear the burden of justifying the standard's scientific necessity...

...My basic argument is that the good versus bad science debate will not provide meaningful legal controls on the use of science in environmental regulation and may make it more difficult to protect legitimate public health and biodiversity objectives.

(a) Precaution: soft science/hard values

The law's 'demand for traceable causal chains leading from actor to harm', discussed by Tarlock, is a fundamental hurdle that environmental law must either overcome or circumvent. Lawyers are trained to think in terms of causal chains. These are usually understood as linking an actor with a harm, in that direction. But these chains are legal constructs. In the real world a harm becomes apparent, next, if lawyers are involved at all, then they operate a legal 'blame beam', retrospectively, to find an activity to which the harm can be attributed. And then, in that frame, will look for an actor to whom liability can be attached. At each of these three stages, legal presumptions and expectations will filter reality into legally relevant and legally irrelevant facts.

For environmental harms, the extent of scientific uncertainty often makes this legal construction of causal chains very difficult. Consequently, an emerging feature of law is an attempt to prevent harms before they occur by adopting a precautionary approach.

Royal Commission on Environmental Pollution, Twelfth Report, *Best Practicable Environmental Option,* Cmnd 310 (London: HMSO, 1988)

The *Vorsorgeprinzip* in West German Environmental Policy

A report prepared in 1987 by Dr Konrad von Moltke for the Institute for European Environmental Policy at the request of the Royal Commission on Environmental Pollution. The views expressed are those of the author and do not necessarily reflect the views of the Royal Commission.

1. Introduction

One of the fables told by La Fontaine, in fact the very first in Book I, concerns an improvident cicada:

La cigale ayant chanté
Tout l'été
Se trouva fort dépourvue
Quand la bise fut venue:
Pas un seul petit morceau
De mouche ou de vermisseau.[3]

3 Fables de La Fontaine, 1.1. In the translation of Marianne Moore this is rendered as: Until fall, a grasshopper/Chose to chirr;/With starvation as a foe/When the northeasters would blow,/And not even a gnat's residue/Or a caterpillar's to chew. *The Fables of La Fontaine,* New York: Viking Press, 1954 p 13.

That, most Germans would say, is what comes from a lack of *Vorsorge*. While the cicada thought there was a solution to its troubles, it turns out that its circumstances were more adverse than anticipated. The literal translation of the German word *Vorsorge* is "precaution" or "foresight", but whereas the English words frequently connote something which goes beyond normal caution, in German usage it includes a notion of good husbandry which represents what one might also call best practice. The word *Vorsorge* is the key term in a principle of West German environmental policy, the *Vorsorgeprinzip*, enunciated some time ago by the German government and now the focus of increasing attention in that country.

...

2. Emergence of the *Vorsorgeprinzip*

The *Vorsorgeprinzip* was enunciated in 1976 by the federal government: "Environmental policy is not fully accomplished by warding off imminent hazards and the elimination of damage which has occurred. Precautionary environmental policy requires furthermore that natural resources are protected and the demands on them are made with care."[4] This formulation was based on earlier declarations of policy such as the 1971 environmental policy programme[5] which outlined the principle without giving it a name. In West German policy documents, the *Vorsorgeprinzip* generally figures with other principles of environmental policy, such as the polluter pays principle, all of which tend to be widely accepted without giving rise to specific prescriptive conclusions for policy.

Until recently, the polluter pays principle was much the most widely discussed of these principles in the Federal Republic of Germany, not least because of the felt need to justify a number of exceptions and thus the practice of providing assistance for pollution control measures from public funds.[6]

The *Vorsorgeprinzip* was first discussed in 1980, in relation to air pollution control[7] and in a special report on the North Sea by the West German Council of Experts for the Environment.[8]

Initial debate concerned the degree to which existing law fulfilled the demands of *Vorsorge* and the possibility of using the principle to justify furthergoing measures. There is a certain consensus that current West German air quality legislation is appropriately based upon the *Vorsorgeprinzip*.

4 *Umweltbericht 76 – Fortschrebung des Umweltprogramms der Bundesregierung vom 14.7.1976 (BT-Drs. 83713), Rdnr 4-Umweltpolitik erschöpft sich nicht in der Abwehr drohender Gefahren und der Beseitigung eingetretener Schäden. Vorsorgende Umweltpolitik verlangt darüber hinaus, daf die Naturgrundlagen geschützt und schonend in Anspruch genommen werden.*

5 *Umwelt programm der Bundesregierung vom 29.9.1971* (BT-Drs VI-Drs VI/2710).

6 Günter Hartkopf, Eberhard Bohne, *Umweltpolitik. Band 1. Grundlagen, Analysen, und Perspektiven*, Opladen: Westdeutscher Verlag, 1983, pp 112-113.

7 Gerhard Feldhaus, 'Der Vorsorgegrundsatz des Bundes-Immissionsschutzgesetzes', in *Deutsches Verwaltungsblatt* 1980, pp 133-139.

8 Rat von Sachverständigen für Umwelfragen, *Umweltprobleme der Nordsee*, Stuttgart: Kiepeneuer & Witsch, 1980, pp 444-446.

This theme of precaution is central to environmental protection but it is not without its critics, because too often precaution is conflated with safety.

F Füredi, 'The Dangers of Safety', (1996) *Living Marxism*, 16-22

Safety has become the fundamental value of the nineties. Passions that were once devoted to a struggle to change the world (or to keep it the same) are now invested in trying to ensure that we are safe. The label "safe" gives new meaning to a wide range of human activities, endowing them with unspoken qualities that are meant to merit our automatic approval. "Safe sex" is not just sex practised "healthily" – it implies an entire attitude towards life. And safe sex is only the most high profile of the safety issues today.

...

The Worship of Safety

So how to account for the worship of safety? It is generally acknowledged that we are living through insecure times and that as a result people are more anxious and predisposed towards fearing risks. In an interesting contribution, Mary Douglas and Aaron Wildavsky have argued that modern societies are confronted with an increased awareness of risks because more decisions are now taken in an atmosphere of uncertainty. This approach has the merit of interpreting the sense of risk as a social construct, related to the prevailing subjective consciousness of society, rather than a reflection of increased real dangers. But what is the connection between insecurity and risk-consciousness?

Insecurity is useful as a descriptive but not as an analytical category. Insecurity as such does not necessarily lead to risk-aversion or a fear of science and technology. In some cases, societies that feel insecure may well look to science and technology to provide security. Today, by contrast, insecurity is bound up with a strong, conservative sense of caution.

The importance of the so-called Precautionary Principle suggests that we are not merely concerned about risks, but are also suspicious of finding solutions to our predicament. According to the Precautionary Principle, it is best not to take a new risk unless its outcome can be understood in advance. Under this principle, which is now widely accepted as sound practice in the sphere of environmental management, the onus of proof rests with those who propose change. Since the full consequences of change are never known in advance, the full implementation of this principle would prevent any form of scientific or social experimentation. By institutionalising caution, the Precautionary Principle imposes a doctrine of limits. It offers security, but in exchange for lowering expectations, limiting growth and preventing experimentation and change.

Although the Precautionary Principle is usually discussed in relation to environmental management, it now provides a guide to life in many other spheres – health, sexuality, personal safety or reproductive technology. What seems particularly striking about the contemporary period is not its insecurity, but the profoundly conservative manner in which this condition is experienced. Yet most commentators on risk do not make a connection between the preoccupation with safety and the impulse of conservatism. Indeed many of the supporters of the Precautionary Principle, or advocates of the different safety campaigns, would see themselves as critics of the system rather than as conservatives. Consequently safety and the attitude of caution are now treated as inherently positive values across the entire political spectrum.

...

From this perspective, where every new technological process is suspected of causing unseen damage to the environment, the experts and academics insist that a heightened consciousness of risk is a rational response to the dangers of modern living. Even many sociological accounts of risk believe that an awareness of the destructive consequences of technology and science provides the basis for the wide-ranging concern with safety today. Disasters such as the nuclear accident at Chernobyl or the oil tanker spillages of recent years are said to have helped to alert the public to the dangers around us. Many theorists of risk regard the heightened public concern with safety as a sign of responsible citizenry, newly and personally aware of the problems of pollution and environmental damage...

...

The end result of the obsession with risk is to endorse a diminished sense of humanity and of the human potential for improvement.

Assessments of risk are central to the precautionary principle, as illustrated by the following case. The applicants' fears about the effect on their health of high voltage electromagnetic fields are fitted into existing legal categories of harm and causes of action. However, notwithstanding the radical nature of the applicants' arguments – that the precautionary principle should apply so as to *require* action to be taken – their case was broadly accepted. The case has a European dimension: Article 130r(2) of the Treaty Establishing the European Community gives precaution as a principle of policy making. The case therefore suggests the future possibility of a fusion of the precautionary principle with the obligations of Community law.

R v Secretary of State for Trade and Industry, ex p Duddridge **[1995] 3 CMLR 231, QBD**

Section 29 Electricity Act 1989 provides (*inter alia*) for regulations to be made by the Secretary of State for Trade and Industry for the purpose of protecting the public from dangers arising from the transmission or supply of electricity and for eliminating or reducing the risks of personal injury arising from transmission or supply.

Section 3 of the 1989 Act also imposes a duty upon the Secretary of State to exercise any of the functions assigned to him by the Act in a manner which is considered best calculated to protect the public from dangers arising from the generation, transmission or supply of electricity.

The applicants were three children living in an area of North East London where The National Grid Company was laying a new high voltage underground cable. The applicants alleged that the non-ionising radiation which would allegedly be emitted from the new cables when commissioned would enter their homes and schools and would be of such a level as would or might expose them to a risk of developing leukaemia.

Solicitors for the applicants wrote to the Secretary of State asking him to exercise his powers under section 29 and issue regulations to safeguard the health of the applicants and to take "a precautionary view" of the risk of damage to health.

The Secretary of State replied saying that he had never regarded it as necessary or appropriate to take specific measures to limit electric and magnetic fields to protect the public from the possibility of the very small risk of cancer.

The applicants sought a judicial review of this decision. They sought an order to compel the Secretary of State to issue regulations, guidelines or some other directive to licence holders (under the 1989 Act) so as to ensure that the electric and magnetic fields associated with electric cables to be laid as part of the National Grid did not exceed 0.2 micro-teslas to the nearest point of houses adjoining the cables; or some other level at which on current research, there was no evidence to suggest or otherwise hypothesise any possible risk to health. In the alternative they sought an order of mandamus to require the Secretary of State to advise the Crown to issue such regulations, guidelines or other form of directive. In the further alternative, they sought a declaration that, in refusing to issue such regulations, guidelines or directives, the Secretary of State had failed to comply with his duty under section 3 of the Electricity Act 1989.

The applicants argued that the Secretary of State was obliged to apply the precautionary principle as a result of either an obligation of European Community Law, under the policy of the present Government, or as a matter of common sense:

1. *EC Law*
The applicant argued that Article 130r of the EC Treaty as amended by the Treaty on European Union signed at Maastricht was binding on Member States and that the Secretary of State was under a duty to consider his powers and duties under the 1989 Act in the light of the article.

2. *Government policy*
The applicants argued that the Government White Paper "This Common Inheritance" Cm 1200 laid down the Government's support for the precautionary principle and in failing to issue guidelines in respect of electric and magnetic fields he was in breach of his own policy.

3. *Common sense*
The applicants referred to the judgment of Stein J. in the Land and Environment Court of New South Wales in *Leatch v National Parks & Wildlife Service and Shoalhaven City Council* 81 LGERA 270 and argued that the precautionary principle should be applied as a matter of common sense and reasonableness.

The respondent argued that the resolution of the European Parliament on combatting the harmful effects of non-ionising radiation took into account the precautionary principle. This resolution strongly suggested that Article 130r was nothing more than a general principle and no policy had been formulated nor had any binding legislation been passed.

Appearing as an interested party, the National Grid Company relied upon Article 3b of the Treaty in arguing that Article 130r does not impose an obligation on member states to legislate in light of the precautionary principle or any other principle set out in the article.

SMITH J

...

Behind this application lies the concern of residents of South Woodford, particularly those who are the parents of young children, who saw a BBC Panorama television programme transmitted on January 31, 1994. The programme discussed a number of epidemiological studies which examine the possible connection between exposure to high levels of non-ionising radiation in the electromagnetic fields (EMFs) created by high voltage cables and the incidence of childhood leukaemia. To the non-expert, some of these studies might appear to suggest that children who have substantial exposure to EMFs from high voltage cables passing near their homes face a three to fourfold (or even possibly sixfold) increased risk of developing leukaemia. However, as has been readily accepted by counsel appearing for the applicants, the study of the effects of EMFs by epidemiology is fraught with difficulty and the results of these studies, when expertly evaluated, do not allow, let alone require, any such positive or alarming conclusions to be drawn.

...

...However, it is important to make clear at the outset that it is not the function of this court to decide whether there is in fact an increased risk of leukaemia from exposure to high levels of EMFs. Still less is it for the Court to decide whether these applicants will be at any such increased risk. This court appreciates that the parents of these children are deeply concerned about these issues and it is not through any lack of sympathy with that concern that the court must decline to decide them. The only issue before the court is whether the Secretary of State, in declining to take specific measures to limit the level of EMFs, has acted unlawfully.

...

It is clear that the statutory scheme requires the Secretary of State to judge whether there exist any 'dangers' or risks of personal injury and whether he ought to exercise his power to make regulations under section 29. The provisions confer a wide discretion upon him. In order to make that judgment, he must of necessity rely upon advice given to him by experts.

The applicants argue that, in considering the issue whether there exist any dangers or risks of personal injury from EMFs, the Secretary of State has approached the matter in the wrong way. They submit that he has asked himself whether there is evidence that exposure to EMFs does in fact give rise to a risk of childhood leukaemia. Because, as we shall see, the scientific evidence does not establish that there is such a risk, he has concluded that he need not use his power under section 29 of the 1989 Act to regulate exposure to EMFs. They say the proper approach would be to ask himself whether there is any evidence of a possible risk even though the scientific evidence is presently unclear and does not prove the causal connection. They submit that if he had asked the question in that way, pitching the threshold for action at a lower level of scientific proof, that answer would have been 'yes' and he would then have been obliged to make regulations...

The basis of the applicants' argument in favour of the lower threshold of scientific proof, is that, either under Community law or under the policy of the White Paper or as a matter of common sense, the Secretary of State is obliged to apply what is known as 'the precautionary principle', when considering whether he is to take action under section 29 for the protection of human health.

There is, at present, no comprehensive and authoritative definition of the precautionary principle. It is an expression which has in recent years been used in a number of international declarations, conventions and treaties, to some of which the United Kingdom is a party. These include the Treaty of European Union, the Maastricht Treaty. In none of these documents is the principle comprehensively defined, although often the document describes what the principle is intended to mean in the context of the subject matter concerned.

...

It appears to me, from both these formulations [Australia's 1992 Inter-Governmental Agreement on the Environment, and Stein J.'s formulation in *Leatch*] that the principle is primarily intended to avoid long term harm to the environment itself rather than damage to human health from transitory environmental conditions. However, as we shall see, in some circumstances, the principle has been declared to be applicable for the purpose of safeguarding human health. Although it does not appear to me that either formulation of the principle supports their contention, the applicants submit that the principle requires that precautionary action be taken where the mere possibility exists of a risk of serious harm to the environment or to human health. Where this possible risk exists, a cost-benefit analysis must be undertaken so as to determine what action would be appropriate. Thus, application of the principle in this case would require the Secretary of State to conduct a cost-benefit analysis to ascertain what action could be taken and at what cost so as to reduce any possible risk, even though the scientific evidence does not show that the risk to health actually exists. The Secretary of State has not done this and, say the applicants, this failure vititiates the exercise of his discretion and renders his decision open to challenge.

In response, the Secretary of State argues that he has given careful consideration to his duties under the Electricity Act. He has considered the scientific evidence available and has taken advice from a special Advisory Group of the National Radiological Protection Board (NRPB) under the chairmanship of the very eminent epidemiologist Sir Richard Doll. This Group comprises highly qualified scientists who have exhaustively considered whether there is any evidence of adverse health effects from exposure to EMFs. In reliance upon their advice, which he has accepted, the Secretary of State has concluded that it is neither necessary nor appropriate to take the specific measures contended for by the applicants.

...

The applicants submit however, that if the Secretary of State is under a duty to take account of the precautionary principle when considering his duties under the 1989 Act, the basis for its application is laid, even on the advice given by the NRPB. That is so because the NRPB has advised that there is a possibility that there exists an increased risk of leukaemia from exposure to

EMFs. That submission appears to me to be correct, especially now that the Secretary of State is aware of the levels of EMFs to which these applicants will be exposed when the Tottenham to Redbridge cable is energised. No challenge was offered to the applicants' calculation, based on National Grid Company data, that some residents could be exposed to as much as 374 microtesla or 3,740 nanotesla. The effects of this level of exposure are not known but the exposure is significantly greater than the ordinary domestic levels of exposure, of up to 150 nanotesla. I am prepared to accept that, if the Secretary of State is shown to be under a legal obligation to apply the precautionary principle to legislation concerned with health and the environment, the possibility of harm raised by the existing state of scientific knowledge is such as would oblige him to apply it in considering whether to issue regulations to restrict exposure to EMFs. He would at least in my view be obliged to conduct the cost-benefit analysis necessary for the proper application of the principle. The Secretary of State accepts that he has not considered the precautionary principle, except to the limited extent required by the policy set out in the 1990 White Paper. If he were to be under an obligation to apply the principle, I would be in favour of granting relief limited to requiring the Secretary of State to reconsider the need for the regulation of EMFs in the light of that principle.

Smith J did not, however, consider that EC law, UK policy nor common sense obliged the Secretary of State to apply the precautionary principle by making regulations under his power to do so in section 29 of the Electricity Act 1989.

Risk assessment is not the prerogative of scientists. Risk is culturally constructed too. For the applicants in Duddridge, the *fear* of harm is significant, even if the scientific accounts of 'reality' do not support their views.

J Adams, *Risk* (London: UCL Press, 1995) pp 38-45

Divergent perspectives on environmental threats: an example of the cultural construction of risk

Capital Killer II: still fuming over London's traffic pollution (Bell 1993) is a report by the London Boroughs Association on the health effects of traffic pollution. It is an example of a common problem – the never-ending environmental dispute that appears to be unresolvable by science. The London Boroughs Association (LBA) has a membership of 19, mainly Conservative controlled London boroughs plus the City of London. As the subtitle of this report indicates, the association is unhappy – indeed fuming – over the lack of action by the Conservative central government to reduce traffic pollution in London. The report complains about the lack of resources provided by central government to deal with 'this most serious of issues', and reproaches the government for its failure to follow its own policy advice as propounded in its White Paper on the Environment: 'Where there are significant risks of damage to the environment, the government will be prepared to take precautionary action...even where scientific knowledge is not conclusive'. The particular precautionary action that the LBA seeks is 'action...now to reduce levels of traffic and pollution in London'.

Why should political allies (or at least politicians belonging to the same party) fall out over this issue? Why should the local government counterparts plead that there is insufficient evidence to justify such action? Let us look at the evidence on the health effects of traffic pollution summarized in the LBA report. The summary begins by citing the conclusions of its 1990 report *Capital Killer*: 'exhaust emissions from road vehicles *may* cause major health problems. Since publication of the report research has continued to *suggest* links between air pollution and health'. It accepts that it will be *difficult to get hard information on the long-term effects of air pollution on health.* It says that '*the link between air pollution and health is not proven* but research is increasingly *suggesting* that there is such a link'.

The report notes an alarming fivefold increase in the number of hospital admissions nationally for childhood asthma between 1979 and 1989 and says '*it may well be*' that air pollution is one of the factors contributing to the increased incidence and severity of asthma and that 'traffic exhausts *may* exacerbate' asthma and allergic disease. Unfortunately for this hypothesis, the magnitude of the changes in traffic and emissions between 1979 and 1989 are small relative to the health effects they are invoked to account for. Although childhood asthma is reported to have increased by 400 per cent, traffic nationally increased by only 57 per cent, and in urban areas, where the concentrations of pollutants are greatest, by only 27 per cent; further, during this period, reported emissions of nitrogen oxides, sulphur dioxide and lead increased by only 8 per cent and volatile organic compounds by only 3 per cent (DOT 1990). For such large change in the incidence of asthma requires a sensitivity of response for which the report presents no evidence.

...

The report presents more evidence in similar, heavily qualified, vein, and then quotes, in tones of disappointment and incredulity, the government's response to the evidence: 'there is [the Government says] *perceived to be* a growth in the incidence of respiratory illnesses, and many respiratory physicians do *believe* that there is an increase in the prevalence of asthma; but suggestions that the change in asthma levels is as a result of air pollution remain unproven'. In the previous ...paragraphs all the italics have been added by me to stress the LBA's acknowledgment of the tenuous nature of the evidence linking air pollution and ill health. In this paragraph the italics are added by the author of the LBA report. The LBA's italics appear to be intended to encourage a sense of anger and incredulity in the reader. How, the report seems to ask, could the Government respond to such compelling evidence by suggesting that it was mere perception and belief? How could the Government not be moved to action?

Adams continues:

These contrasting responses to the same evidence, or lack of it, provide an excellent example of the *cultural construction of risk*. This phenomenon can be found at work wherever disputes about health and safety are unresolved, or unresolvable, by science. For years the nuclear industry and environmentalists have argued inconclusively, producing mountains of 'scientific' evidence in the process. Food safety regulations, AIDS, the greenhouse effect, seat belts and bicycle helmets are but a few other examples, from many that could be chosen, of health and safety controversies that have generated a substantial 'scientific' literature without generating a consensus about what should be done. In all these cases, and a multitude of others, the participants commonly base aspersions on the rationality of those who disagree with them. The approach of cultural theory suggests not that some are rational and others irrational, but that the participants are arguing rationally from different premises. This can be illustrated by the disagreement between the LBA and the Government about traffic pollution in London.

...

The cultural construction of pollution

The debate about the health effects of traffic pollution is unlikely to be settled conclusively for some time, if ever. Describing the risks of traffic pollution as culturally constructed is not to say that they are mere figments of fevered imaginations. There is an obvious cause for concern; the exhaust emitted by cars contains many toxins, plus carbon dioxide, which is implicated in the greenhouse effect – a scientific controversy in its own right. The toxins are dispersed unevenly, in highly diluted form, over long periods of time. Some may be concentrated in the food chain, others may be transported great distances and/or combined with other pollutants to be rendered harmless, or more damaging. The environment into which they are dispersed contains plants, animals and people with varying susceptibilities to different toxins. Some toxins will be persistent and their effects cumulative. Some might have direct effects, others might weaken immune systems with results being manifest in the symptoms of a wide variety of opportunistic diseases. There are often long time-lags between exposure to pollutants and consequent damage to health, and most of the symptoms of illness caused by the ingredients of exhaust emissions could have other causes. Some emissions might even be beneficial; in certain circumstances, for example, acid rain and carbon dioxide increase plant yields.

With few exceptions the toxic nature of the emissions is not in dispute. The unresolved question is whether they are emitted in quantities that cause significant damage, and if so whether this damage outweighs the benefits of the activity, motoring, that produces them. The LBA report reviewed here ostensibly addresses the health effects of traffic emissions, but it does so in the context of a wider debate about the benefits of a Government transport policy that is fostering an increase in traffic. Both the Government and the LBA are agreed that the evidence linking pollution to ill health is somewhat tenuous. They disagree about the appropriate policy response. This suggests that the real difference between them lies not in their view of the damage done by traffic emissions, but in their view of the benefits of traffic. If the benefits are considered great, then the evidence required to justify a sacrifice of some of the benefits to reduce emissions should be compelling. The smaller the benefits, the stronger becomes the case for invoking the precautionary principle. And if the benefits are considered *negative* then even a suspicion that damage might result from emissions becomes an *additional* justification for curbing traffic.

...

Groping in the dark

The above speculations are relevant to *all* disputes that are unresolved or unresolvable by science. Wherever the evidence is inconclusive, the scientific vacuum is filled by the assertion of contradictory certitudes. For the foreseeable future scientific certainty is likely to be a rare commodity, and issues of health and safety – matters of life and death – will continue to be decided on the basis of scientific knowledge that is not conclusive. The conventional response to this unsatisfactory state of affairs is to assert the need for more science.

More trustworthy scientific information will do no harm, but the prospect is remote of settling most current controversies within the time available to make decisions; where adherents to the precautionary principle perceive the possibility of serious harm, they press for action as a matter of urgency.

...

2 NATURE AND THE ENVIRONMENT

So far, we have been talking about 'the environment' as though it were axiomatic. However, the environment is not a given. People's perceptions of nature, the environment and harms are often very different, informed as they are by upbringing, art, and literature, as well as by their professional perspectives.

AS Byatt, *Possession* (London: Vintage, 1991), pp 68-69

The wolds of Lincolnshire are a small surprise. Tennyson grew up in one of their tight twisting valleys. From them he made the cornfields of immortal Camelot.

> On either side the river lie
> Long fields of barley and of rye
> That clothe the wold and meet the sky.

Roland saw immediately that the word "meet" was precise and surprising, not vague. They drove over the plain, up the rolling road, out of the valley. The valleys are deep and narrow, some wooded, some grassy, some ploughed. The ridges run sharply across the sky, always bare. The rest of the large, sleepy county is marsh or fen or flat farmed plain. These slightly rolling hills appear to be folded out of the surface of the earth, but that is not the case; they are part of a dissected tableland. The villages are buried in the valleys, at the end of blind funnels. The green car went busily along the ridgeway, which was patterned with roads and paths like the branches of spines. Roland, who was urban, noted colours: dark, ploughed earth, with white chalk in the furrows; a pewter sky, with chalk-white clouds. Maud noticed good rides and unmended gates, and badly crunched hedgerows, gnashed by machine teeth.

...

N Evernden, *The Social Creation of Nature* (Baltimore: John Hopkins, 1993) pp 4-9

...

In his survey of the opinions of different sectors of British society, sociologist Stephen Cotgrove detected some interesting differences in the apprehension of environmental risk. Two of his categories showed wide divergence: the 'environmentalists' (composed of a sample drawn from membership lists of the Conservation Society and the Friends of the Earth), and the 'industrialists' (selected from *Business Who's Who* and *Who's Who of British Engineers*). As one would expect, the environmentalists perceived considerably more environmental danger than did the industrialists. But what is interesting is that the latter group does not seem to be deliberately acting in an irresponsible way, but rather seems not to perceive significant risk at all.

If pollution is regarded as a matter of empirical fact, it may seem odd that such disagreements can persist. But since pollution involves questions not only of concentrations but also of consequences, even 'hard' evidence is inevitably open to interpretation – hence the frequent spectacle of contradicting experts. Equally significant, however, is our tendency to treat pollution as a purely material phenomenon, a bias that tends to establish arbitrary boundaries to environmental debate.

We must bear in mind that the current understanding of pollution is just that: the current understanding. Yet there is no reason to limit the definition to physical abuse alone. The dictionary definition is much broader and entails 'uncleanness or impurity caused by contamination (physical or moral)'. Our attention to physical pollution may distract us from the fact that much of the debate is over the perception of moral pollution. For example, while voicing their opinions about how many parts per billion of a toxin are 'acceptable', both environmentalists and industrialists may be responding to a perceived instance of moral contamination. This emerges occasionally when one or other makes predictions about future consequences, or about what 'standard of living' ought to be protected. Environmentalists will assert that if the current action continues, our future well-being will be imperiled and our children will inherit a blighted planet. Cease, they say, and learn to live in a small-scale, cooperative society without the constant pressure for growth and transformation. Industrialists may reply that it is all very well for the impratical environmentalist to advocate such irresponsible action, but if their policies were ever to be put in place, our life-style would be in jeopardy, jobs would be lost, and food shortages would loom. To the environmentalists, what is at risk is the very possibility of leading a good life. To the industrialists, what is at risk is the very possibility of leading a good life. The debate, it appears, is actually about *what constitutes a good life*. The instance of physical pollution serves only as the means of persuasion, a staging ground for the underlying debate.

This is by no means a phenomenon unique to our times or our society. In *Purity and Danger*, the eminent anthropologist Mary Douglas makes it clear that the concept of pollution is a universal feature of human societies, and that our use of it is not fundamentally dissimilar to that of 'primitives'. All identify a contaminant, something that is out of place and hostile to the environment, as a danger to the well-being of individuals or society. On a personal basis, we respond to threats of pollution each time we wash our hands or clean the house: we attempt to get rid of dirt. But what is dirt? Not soil, but a contaminant, 'matter out of place'. Moreover, it is dangerous matter, at least when out of place. *But significantly, something can only be out of place if there is a system* of places to begin with.

That system in question here is, of course, the environment. In order for there to be perceptible pollution, there must first be an understanding of systemic order, an environmental norm. Only then is it possible to detect something that is 'out of place'. But when we see differing ideals in confrontation, we observe different perceptions of pollution and risk. In a homogeneous society with a single environmental ideal, this misunderstanding is unlikely to occur. But in any society, we find ideas about pollution being used as a means of social control. 'These danger-beliefs are as much threats which one man uses to coerce another as dangers which he himself fears to incur by his own lapses from righteousness. They are a strong language of mutual exhortation. At this level the laws of nature are dragged in to sanction the moral code'.

We witness just this use of pollution in the environmental debate. Ecology – the contemporary authority on nature's laws – is said to have revealed that such-and-such an action is dangerous to the environment, and that if it is continued both we and the environment will be imperiled. Hence, the polluter must be ordered to cease, lest he or she destroy us all. But notice that it is not just the environment that is at risk, but the very *idea* of environment, the social ideal of proper order.

...

...Being able to determine the 'parts per billion' of a contaminant enables the environmentalist to argue that pollution has indeed occurred, and thus to infer that the entire *position* of the polluter is untenable – the polluter has clearly done something 'unnatural' and in so doing has placed nature, and ourselves, at risk. The polluter is condemned not only for a physical pollution but also, implicitly, for a moral pollution that is revealed by the physical pollution. Hence the highly charged emotional tone of much environmental debate: far more is at stake than the chemical composition of a river.

...

In public discussions of environmental affairs, ecology is frequently a rather loosely defined entity, often treated as the environmentalists' chief ally and occasionally even as a synonym for the natural environment. Indeed, the very plasticity of our concept of nature may be illustrated by the contrasting uses to which ecology is put. It is pressed into the service of a variety of social alternatives, ranging from various forms of Aldo Leopold's land ethic to the bio-egalitarianism of Arne Naess and the eco-humanism of Murray Bookchin. But exactly what is advocated is of less interest here than that ecology functions as the exemplar of the natural and the healthy, and in so doing seems to indicate to us how we might re-orient our lives. Indeed, ecology will inevitably be so used if our understanding of ecology includes the establishment of norms as part of its function.

...

So far I have spoken of the use of ecology only by those in support of social reform. There is, however, a much heavier reliance on ecology by those who defend the status quo. I speak of the use of ecology in such officially sanctioned activities as environmental impact assessment, wildlife management, and land reclamation. While these may be useful in the immediate support of environmental integrity, they constitute a use of ecology in the service of technological and bureaucratic intervention. There is a tacit expectation that some form of environmental engineering must emerge that will facilitate continued growth with a minimum of environmental backlash. Ecology is to help us anticipate difficulties, so that alternative technologies can be forged to circumvent them.

...

These are two contrasting interpretations of the function of ecology. Undoubtedly they are caricatures of actual attitudes and assumptions, but they serve to illustrate the possibility of alternative uses of ecology, the contemporary nature-explainer that we expect to be 'objective' and, of course, 'value neutral'. Persons with contrasting viewpoints can draw upon this discipline, one group regarding it as a revealer of the natural and proper, the other as a source of power and control (which it is natural to use). Each group believes its stance to be correct, and each expects endorsements from ecology.

...

Yet perhaps no society other than our contemporary one has had so urgent a need to reconsider its motives in how it defines and uses nature. To untangle the knot of reasons and platitudes that binds us to our present understanding, we must consider not only the claims of the present-day interpreters but also those earlier transformations that have set the stage for the contemporary confrontation with the natural world. We must ask, in short, where 'nature' came from.

The many different perspectives on nature have everyday practical relevance for law and policy. For example, pollution control took more than a century to come to terms with the fact that air, water and earth are all parts of an integrated system. Agricultural designations, environmental assessments, and conservation of habitats, fauna and flora, to take the subjects of our case studies in Part V, all depend on assumptions about what is to be protected and for what reasons and, fundamentally, the proper place of people in ecosystems. We also see these differing assumptions in cases such as *Duddridge*, in which Smith J drew a distinction between protecting human health and protecting 'the environment' by adopting the precautionary principle.

The relationship between people and nature is not dichotomous, but is rather complicated and embedded. Presently, though, this is better understood in philosophy than law, which has still to work out the practical implications of a changing relationship with nature.

When reading the following, it might be questioned how far 'man' and 'mankind' includes all people?

J Passmore, *Man's Responsibility for Nature* (Duckworth, 1974) pp 28-46

Stewardship and co-operation with nature

Western civilisation...is anything but monolithic. I shall have a little to say later about the Western mystical tradition. For although nature-mysticism, with its veneration of nature as sacred or divine, is incompatible with the central, Christian or scientific, Western tradition, it has nevertheless had a continuing importance, with such influential representatives as, in their different ways, Wordsworth and Emerson – to say nothing of the more quirky Thoreau. It has helped to establish the value of the contemplative enjoyment of nature; it has insisted on the unifying links between human life, on the one hand, and the life of nature on the other. On that last point, if on scarcely any other, the Darwinians and the nature-mystics could find themselves at one. They both rejected that view of man, Platonic in origin, which saw him, in respect to his soul at least, as an alien in a world of change and decay.

Two other traditions are also of considerable importance, in so far as they both deny that man, in relation to nature, is essentially a despot: the tradition that sees him as a 'steward', a farm-manager, actively responsible as God's deputy for the care of the world, and the tradition that sees him as co-operating with nature in an attempt to perfect it. The tradition of 'stewardship' – never strong but persistent – dates back to the post-Platonic philosophers of the Roman Empire and especially to the teachings of Iamblichus, in the third century AD.

...

At this point in our discussion, it is time to revert to the *Republic*, with its debate between Socrates and the sophist Thrasymachus which...turns around the responsibility of governors. Thrasymachus thought it self-evident that the ruler acts entirely in his own interests; Socrates denied this. As ruler, his responsibility, according to Socrates, is the welfare of those he governs. That is the sort of government over nature Iamblichus had in mind when he said that man is sent to administer earthly things. It is now sometimes argued that this, too, is what Yahweh intended when he told the Hebrews to subdue the world. Or at the very least – for the Hebrew word translated as 'subdue' is a very strong one, with military connotations – that this is how Christianity interprets man's governorship. 'Men hold their dominium over all nature', so the Anglican Bishop Hugh Montefiore tells us, 'as stewards and trustees for God.' And he goes on to deduce a crucially important consequence. 'They are confronted,' he writes, 'by an inalienable duty towards and concern for their total environment, present and future; and this duty towards environment does not merely include their fellow man, but all nature and all life.'

Genesis, the environmentalist John Black maintains in the same spirit, makes this duty clear when it tells us that God put Adam into the Garden of Eden 'to dress it and to keep it', i.e. to manage and protect it. Man, Black goes on to argue, is made in God's image; this implies that he should act 'in a responsible way as God acts upon man'. Man is to nature, that is, as God is to man. On this interpretation, then, it is a gross error to suppose that Christianity passes no moral judgment on man's relationship to nature, to suppose that it not only permits but actually enjoins him to deal with it as he pleases, in the manner of an absolute despot. His responsibilities rather are those of the shepherd ruler, as Socrates described them.

What evidence is there in support of such an interpretation of Christian teaching? Very little, I should say. Admittedly, there is a recurrent New Testament image, as Black points out, in which man figures as a steward and as, in his stewardship, representing God. Man's stewardship, however, relates to the Church, not to nature; the vineyard functions, in Christian teaching, only as a down-to-earth analogue of man's relationship to God.

...

For an explicit presentation of the idea of stewardship over nature Black refers us only to a passage from the seventeenth century Chief Justice, Sir Matthew Hale – a passage so often quoted in this connection that one has good reason for suspecting that it would be embarrassing to ask for another example. 'The end of man's creation,' Hale tells us in his characteristically legal terminology, 'was, that he should be the viceroy of the great God of heaven and earth in this inferior world; his steward, *villicus* [farm manager], bailiff or farmer of this goodly farm of the lower world.' Only for this reason was man 'invested with power, authority, right, dominium, trust and care, to correct and abridge the excesses and cruelties of the fiercer animals, to give protection and defence to the mansuete [tame] and useful, to preserve the species of divers vegetables [growing things], to improve them and others, to correct the redundance of unprofitable vegetables, to preserve the face of the earth in beauty, usefulness and fruitfulness'.

Man is still to think of himself, on Hale's view, as master over the world, not as simply contemplating it or simply preserving it in its original condition. But his high estate does not entitle him to use nature as he wills, to exploit its resources without regard to the effects of his action. The fiercer animals he is at liberty to restrain, but the tame and useful he must protect. He can weed his farms 'to correct the redundance of unprofitable vegetables' and cut down trees to make new farms only if, in so doing, he does not destroy the beauty, the usefulness and the fecundity of the earth. Like a farm-manager, he can be called to account if he wilfully or carelessly degrades the earth's resources.

With Hale's eloquent description of man's responsibilities, modern conservationists – although not preservationists – would be in complete sympathy, whether or not they suppose these responsibilities to derive from man's being God's deputy. But this interpretation of man's relationship to nature stems from seventeenth-century humanism, with its Pelagian emphasis on what can be accomplished by the human will and its playing-down of original sin, rather than from the standard Augustinian tradition. Hale still grants, no doubt, that in some measure Adam's sin deformed the face of nature. But, like Black after him, he admonishes us to take as our guiding principle the prelapsarian injunction to 'dress and keep the garden', quite as if Adam had never been driven out of the garden to till a soil cursed for his sake.

...

To a certain degree, the tradition of stewardship coalesces with the...tradition that man's responsibility is to perfect nature by co-operating with it... Just as for Aquinas God's grace perfects human nature so, on this view, man's grace...perfects nature. The perfecting of nature, it is admitted, requires skill and, in this sense, mastery. But a mastery which perfects, not a mastery which destroys or enslaves. Man's duty in respect to nature, then, is to seek to perfect it by working with its potentialities.

How is perfection to be judged? The presumption is still, in Aristotle's manner, that nature is at its best when it fulfils men's needs – that this, indeed, is its reason for existing, what its potentialities are for. So to perfect nature is to humanise it, to make it more useful for men's purposes, most intelligible to their reason, more beautiful to their eyes. But like good artists, men should, it is urged, respect their material; they should not try to shape it in ways which cut across its own tendencies, any more than a good sculptor treats bronze as if it were marble or marble as if it were wood.

...

On the face of it, Genesis rules out any such supposition for the Jew or the Christian. The world, for Genesis, was created complete, by a series of divine acts; it was perfect until Adam sinned. Bacon might suggest that men had the task of recreating by their own efforts the Garden from which Adam had been driven, but Augustinian Christianity neither laid that task on man's shoulders nor promised him God's help if he should undertake it. It was left to Fichte, and the German metaphysicians who followed him, to reinstate the idea of a universe-in-the-making which man helps to form, in co-operation with a Spirit intent on civilising it. No doubt in Fichte the element originally supplied by nature, as distinct from Spirit, is reduced to a minimum...

The German metaphysicians emphasise the fact that what we commonly call 'nature' has already been largely modified by man – this, of course, is most obviously true in Europe with its tamed landscapes. So co-operation with Spirit means co-operation with a spiritualised nature, co-operation, indeed, with one's human predecessors. And men, at first forced to dominate, are now able to deal with nature in a gentle way; it no longer resists but welcomes their attentions – somewhat like a horse that has been broken in. They can rule over it as its natural lord, not as tyrants...'Nature [shall] ever become more and more intelligible and transparent even in her most secret depths; human power, enlightened and armed by human invention, shall rule over her without difficulty'. There could scarcely be a better expression of the optimistic spirit of civilisation – a civilisation restoring in a higher form the Garden of Eden, converting man the tyrant into man the lord – which prevailed during the nineteenth century and well into our own century; we read Fichte now with a sigh or an ironic smile.

In our own time, Teilhard de Chardin set out to formulate an evolutionary metaphysics in which the idea of co-operating with nature...is central. Traditional Christianity, according to Teilhard, has made two fundamental mistakes. In the first place it has supposed nature to be static, created once and for all by God at the creation...The second Christian mistake was to suppose that in order to save themselves men must free themselves from, must rise above, the world.

Rather, according to Teilhard, they must work *with* the world. They are the first beings sufficiently rational to see what nature, through gradual evolution, is doing, and sufficiently powerful to help it on its path towards that final consummation for which 'the whole creation groaneth and travaileth until now.'

The importance of such metaphysical systems, from our present point of view, is that they testify to the operation in Western civilisation of an attitude to nature not reducible either to despotism or to stewardship. As opposed to both of these it rejects the conception of nature which is complete in itself, simply *there*, to be struggled against or conserved. Nature, for it, is still in the making.

...

Herbert Marcuse, an inheritor of the German Idealist tradition, distinguishes, like Fichte, 'two kinds of mastery: a repressive and a liberating one'. Man's relationship to nature, Marcuse is prepared to admit, must at first be repressive, but as he civilises nature, he at the same time liberates it, frees it, as Hegel also suggests, from its 'negativity', its hostility to spirit. Civilisation, Marcuse argues, has most noticeably achieved that liberating, transformation of nature in parks and gardens and reservations. 'But outside these small, protected areas', he adds, 'it has treated Nature as is has treated man -as an instrument of destructive productivity'. So what is wrong with our treatment of nature is not that we have failed sufficiently to contemplate it but that we have used it destructively, as distinct from seeking to humanise it, spiritualise it.

...

There are, then, two important minority traditions in Western civilisation both of which think of men as having responsibilities towards nature. The first is, in feeling, conservationist. It emphasises the need to conserve the earth's fertility, by culling and pruning and good management. The second is rather bolder: it looks to the perfection of nature by man, but a perfection which always takes account of nature's own resources and of what man has already achieved in his civilising of the world. It has often been formulated, and still is often formulated, in a metaphorical way, as if nature were a friendly power or, in the Hegelian version, a prisoner to be liberated from her fetters. We ought not to think of it as for this reason useless in our present situation. It suggests an attitude to nature which would warn us against setting up sea-walls as a substitute for yielding dunes, building freeways as gashes on the hillside, designing towns and buildings out of relationship to their sites.

How far it will carry us is quite another matter. Mill warns us against loose and sentimental talk about 'harmony with nature'. 'There still exists a vague notion', he writes, 'that...the general scheme of nature is a model for us to imitate: that with more or less liberty in details, we should on the whole be guided by the spirit and general conception of Nature's own ways: ... and that, if not the whole, yet some particular parts of the spontaneous order of nature, selected according to the speaker's predilections, are in a peculiar sense, manifestations of the Creator's will; a sort of fingerpost pointing out the direction which things in general, and therefore our voluntary actions, are intended to take.' The geometrical garden has a beauty of its own – remember *Last Year at Marienbad* – and so has the city of great boulevards, however 'unnatural' the square and the straight line. A road cannot imitate a riverbed, and it may be dangerous for it to follow closely at all points the contours of the countryside.

But without sentimentality, without recourse to metaphysics, we can still recognise that it is better to look first at the way things happen in nature and help them to work more effectively than to try to ride rough-shod over them merely in order to demonstrate the superiority of a rationality defined in wholly mathematical, or wholly economic, terms.

...

...The fact that the West has never been wholly committed to the view that man has no responsibility whatsoever for the maintenance and preservation of the world around him is important just because it means that there are 'seeds' in the Western tradition which the reformer can hope to bring to full flower. Were something like this not the case, the momentary agitation to which [the reformer's] strictures give rise is unlikely to issue in firm and consistent action over a long period of time; the familiar traditions are almost certain to reassert themselves...

The following critiques the contemplative consciousness-raising relationship between man and nature.

J Barry, 'Deep Ecology and the Undermining of Green Politics' in J Holder et al (eds) *Perspectives on the Environment* (Aldershot: Avebury, 1993), pp 49-50

Nature as wilderness and garden

The 'wilderness experiences' advocated by many deep ecologists like Devall and Sessions (1985), and eco-feminists like Warren (1990) are arguably an aesthetic form of 'green consumerism' (to which deep ecologists and most greens are formally opposed) as the way to create a new eco-friendly consciousness. Both are individualistic, they appeal to the person as consumer or experiencing subject, not as a citizen, thus both are apolitical, and largely a function of income distribution. This is especially true in the case of 'wilderness experiences'. It also gives another elitist dimension to deep ecology...The elitism here comes from the fact that deep ecologists do not think that the experience of nature one gets from working on an allotment, for example, is of the same consciousness raising quality as, say, Warren's personal experience of climbing a rockface...The obvious bias here is that only those who can afford these experiences will truly have their consciousness raised, leaving the rest of us perhaps to have a 'mediated' eco-consciousness authoritatively inculcated as indicated above. On the other hand perhaps Elkins is nearer the mark, and offers a less 'draconian' interpretation, when he asserts that for deep ecologists: 'Since social and ecological problems are ultimately seen to be the consequences of misconceived values and ideas, social change is contingent on the ability to communicate the insights of the new paradigm.'... But it seems that this more benign interpretation is purchased at the cost of rendering deep ecology politically impotent, leaving it as a sort of whispering campaign against the modern worldview.

A more obvious practical problem concerning 'wilderness experience' as a strategy even for consciousness-raising purposes, relates to people's actual access to wilderness. Access to wild nature is increasingly what Hirsch (1976) has called a 'positional good', where the zero-sum nature of the good means that only those with progressively increasing amounts of income can enjoy them. The whole point about positionality is that the more people who have access to a positional good the more that good loses its value. Thus encouraging modern urban populations en masse to 'contemplate a mountain' will lead to the diminution of the 'consciousness-raising' potential of the experience. Thus even when deep ecologists do talk about 'strategy', (although there is nothing political about isolated 'wilderness experiences') it is so fraught with inconsistencies and naivete, that it is better abandoned as an integral part of green political theory and practice.

This access to wilderness also has to do with its distribution across the globe. For example, it is clear that in the western European context there is little 'wilderness' in the requisite sense required by deep ecologists. In Europe a conception of nature as 'garden' seems more appropriate, given the fact that humans have largely made the modern European landscape, from the Dutch reclaiming land from the sea, to the hedgerows of the English and Irish countryside. In a very real sense then there is not much 'wilderness' left in Europe. Therefore to talk of 'wilderness experience' is to talk in a foreign language when addressing the populations of Europe. There can be no going back to a pre-humanized environment, and to suggest attempting to do so resonates with nostalgia and utopianism.

3 SPACIAL SCALES

Asking what the environment is leads to many further questions. Can one relate to a global environment, as well as a locality? Where does 'the environment' stop?

Law is preoccupied with jurisdiction. It talks in terms of international law, Community law, domestic law and local law. Such boundaries lead to practical difficulties in putting 'ecologically correct' thinking into action.

D Harvey, *Justice, Nature and the Geography of Difference* (Oxford: Blackwell, 1996) pp 203–204

The Question of Temporal and Spatial Scales

At first sight, the question of scale appears as a purely technical matter. Where, for example, do ecosystems (or socio-ecological projects) begin and where do they end, how does a pond differ from the globe, how is it that processes which operate with profound effect at one scale become irrelevant at another. 'Issues of appropriate scaling', Haila and Levins argue, 'are among the fundamental theoretical challenges in the understanding of society-nature interactions'. There is, they say, 'no single correct way' to define temporal and spatial scales: these are constituted by the organisms considered so that different scales are simultaneously present at any particular site in nature ... If, as in the dialectical view ... there are no basic units to which everything can be reduced, then the choice of scale at which to examine processes becomes both crucial and problematic. The difficulty is compounded by the fact that the temporal and spatial scales at which human beings operate as ecological agents have also been changing. Cronon notes, for example, how even before colonial settlement began in New England, long-distance trade from Europe was bringing two hitherto largely isolated ecosystems into contact with one another in such a way as to commercialise the Indians' material culture and dissolve their earlier ecological practices. If we think these days of the scale defined by the commodity and money flows that put our breakfasts upon the table, and how that scale has changed over the last hundred years, then immediately it becomes apparent that there is an instability in the definition of scale which arises out of practices of capital accumulation, commodity exchange, and the like.

Yet, as Smith remarks, 'the theory of the production of geographical scale' (to which I would add also the production of temporalities) – 'is grossly underdeveloped'. It seems to imply the production of a nested hierarchy of scales (from global to local) leaving us always with the political-ecological question of how to 'arbitrate and translate between them'. The ecological argument is incredibly confused on exactly this point. On the one hand the Gaian planetary health care specialists think globally and seek to act globally, while the bioregionalist and social anarchists want to think and act locally, presuming, quite erroneously, that whatever is good for the locality is good for the continent or the planet. But at this point the issue becomes profoundly political as well as ecological, for the political power to act, decide upon socio-ecological projects and to regulate their unintended consequences has also to be defined at a certain scale (and in the contemporary world the nation states mostly carved out over the last hundred years maintain a privileged position even though they make no necessary politico-ecological sense). But this also says something very concrete about what any ecosocialist project must confront. On the one hand there will presumably be continuing transformations in human practices that redefine temporal and spatial scales, while on the other hand political power structures must be created that have the capacity to 'arbitrate and translate between' the different scales given by different kinds of projects. Here, too, it seems that an ecosocialist perspective has an enormous import for socialist thinking, on how human potentialities are to be explored and what kinds of political institutions and power structures can be created that are sensitive to the ecological dimensions of any socialist project.

E Shove, 'Threats and Defences in the Built Environment', in S Elworthy et al (eds) *Perspectives on the Environment 2* (Aldershot: Avebury, 1995), pp 45-57

In popular imagination, the environment is 'everything out there': it is the outdoor world of fields and trees, birds and bees. Actions and policies for environmental protection implicitly relate to this domain, some focusing upon the intrinsic qualities of nature, others viewing the environment as a finite stock of natural resources, or as an endangered and fragile system. This, it seems, is the world which is to be saved and valued. It is important, however, to acknowledge that this is not the place in which we routinely live. Although whales and the ozone layer are critical elements in the environmental iconography, this outside world is not the one which most people inhabit most of the time. The environment of everyday life, is, of course, the indoor environment. Current definitions of the environment as 'everything out there' place people in a specific relationship to nature, setting them apart from the real environmental action. This has not always been the case for meanings of 'out there' and 'in here' have changed over time.

...

...heating and ventilation industries, together with building scientists and engineers have specified and created a global indoor climate. At the same time, increasingly standardized buildings accommodate increasingly convergent patterns of social activity. In these circumstances the outside environment must be excluded as efficiently as possible if there is to be any chance of maintaining the desired conditions inside. There is no place here for local variation, for site specific complexities or for the subtle interaction of indoor and outdoor climate.

Standing between the inside and the outside environment, buildings provide a tangible illustration of changing beliefs about the relationship between the two worlds. Taking concern about environmental change to heart means acknowledging complex interrelations between the different environmental spaces we inhabit. Now viewed as a vulnerable as well as a potentially inhospitable domain, the outside world is managed cautiously. Because of a growing recognition of the fragility of the global environment, buildings are redesigned to use less energy and to make fewer demands on limited natural resources. Perceptions of the indoor environment have changed as well. Technologies of indoor environmental control have begun to frighten the very people they were designed to protect and alternative, more 'natural' methods of environmental management are sought in response. However, these more variable strategies of climate control run counter to the interests of the international construction industry, to the interests of those involved in heating and ventilating, and even to the interests of building occupants who have come to expect an utterly predictable indoor environment. Indoor climatic conditions, initially established with the aid of energy intensive technologies, have taken root in the international culture. Indeed this global climatic revolution has been so wide ranging and so effective, that many taken for granted features of everyday life now depend upon the maintenance and management of a uniformly acceptable indoor environment. There is no way back to nature.

Accordingly, discussion concentrates on the technologies of energy efficiency, on future energy demand, and on the environmental consequences of CO_2 emissions. The challenge, it seems, is one of identifying commercially viable, environmentally friendly ways of sustaining the artificially uniform conditions to which we have become accustomed.

What is missing is more serious questioning of the indoor environment itself. While there is no way back to nature the process of indoor climatic convergence is neither inherently necessary nor totally irreversible. As suggested here, developments within the indoor environment form part of a complex sociotechnical process in which machinery is sold, definitions of comfort shift, social practices change, lifestyles evolve, and designers make decisions. We clearly need a much better understanding of these critical developments if we are to explore ways of minimizing outdoor environmental damage. Yet the indoor climate is not even on the outdoor environmental agenda.

By defining the environment as 'everything out there', environmentalists have overlooked important changes in the indoor environment. They have, in effect, failed to notice the world wide manufacture of a standard indoor climate despite the fact that this is a development of considerable global cultural, technological, economic, and wider environmental significance. So it is time to refocus the environmental debate. It is time to come inside and to recognize the degree to which events in the outside world relate to what goes on indoors.

4 THE POLITICAL ENVIRONMENT

Throughout this book we characterise environmental law as dynamic and pervasive, with the potential to destabilise established legal doctrine. This may have effects beyond law and lead to changes in institutions and political culture. As the following shows, the international legal instrument, Agenda 21,[9] is having marked effects at the level of local government: its emphasis on citizen participation is creating tensions in a political culture based on representation. It is an attempt to mediate between spatial scales.

P Selman and J Parker, 'Democracy, Scientific Expertise and Participation in Local Sustainability Programmes', paper presented to Interdisciplinary Research Network on Environment and Society Annual Conference, Lancaster University, (1996) pp 1-6

...

In this paper, we are concentrating on three aspects which may be associated with active environmental citizenship. First, the processes of *democracy* in Local Agenda 21 are not straightforward and, whilst it is often fashionable to talk of grass-roots involvement of community champions, this can create tensions with the traditional, representative, ward-based councillor system. Second, responsible action must be based on comprehensible, accessible and trusted information and behaviour change, the ways in which information can most readily be disseminated, and the nature of official indicators of local environmental quality. Third, we look at the changing nature of public *participation* in the context of local sustainability, and the various barriers to and opportunities for effective involvement.

'Local Government and the Environment' or 'Local Governance and Sustainability'?

Many issues arise because of the broad scope of LA21. In the early stages, beyond which many local authorities have yet to progress, the expectation was that LA21 would merely involve another 'green plan', and could often be met by Council-led strategy of re-badging existing environmental projects. The

9 See ch 4, p 144 et seq.

reasons for this are not always 'minimalist' – often they arise from a positive concern to make an early impact in terms of achievement and the delivery of observable products, which in turn might help convince citizens and councillors of the seriousness of their intent to pursue sustainable development. However, local authorities are widely beginning to recognise that, if a serious response is to be made to the sustainability issues of the 21st century, then the general population will not accept claims of environmental performance, or edicts to change their behaviour, which are delivered in a top-down manner. Equally, if 'sustainability' is to be seen as an equitable and relevant pursuit, then it cannot be construed either as a means of dampening the expectations of the disadvantaged, nor a *carte blanche* for NIMBYs to obstruct proposed development. It must relate to a popular agenda, which has been widely debated. Hence, whilst some participants initially expected LA21 to be a fairly limited exercise focusing on familiar 'green' issues, it has often become one involving radical new approaches to local democracy, and embracing a wide spectrum of quality of life issues (e.g. health, crime, employment). As this equates to, or even exceeds, the local authority's overall purview, it is not so much an add-on as an alternative channel of democracy and community action.

LA21 programmes tend to be of two types: those which are very much council-led, with an executive agenda produced mainly by some kind of officer-member working group; and those whose contents are more locally defined, with the community taking a prominent role in the identification and prioritisation of issues and the production of documents. The former has the advantage that it may achieve a high initial impact, but do little to capture citizens' imagination, whereas the latter may be associated with apparent non-activity in the earlier stages, yet acquire a stronger internal dynamic in the long-term. There are, of course, intermediate balances between the two poles. Whilst 'transparent, open and participatory' approaches have been most fashionable, this may simply be because they lend themselves most readily to current rhetoric. Increasingly, we are tempted to explore, in the context of 'sustainability', the tensions between local government and local governance, and between representative and participatory democracy.

Fundamentally, one might question whether the LA21 process should be instigated by local government at all, or whether it is merely habit that leads us to view local authorities in this role. Whilst the choice is by no means self-evident, it has been noted that local authorities are important precisely because they are local and have authority. They have a long heritage of representing citizens within their area of statutory and geographical jurisdiction, have a direct responsibility for many of the services which naturally form the core of an LA21. Chapter 28 of Agenda 21 certainly assumes that local government will have a pivotal role, and many commentators argue that a local sustainability programme which was too divorced from the local authority would be fundamentally against the spirit of Agenda 21. The Model Communities Program of the International Council for Local Environmental Initiatives, whilst seeking a radically new approach to the local delivery of services, still sees local government as playing the central role. Whilst most of our respondents agreed that local authorities should, if they had not already done so, withdraw from a controlling position in LA21s, no-one felt that they should adopt complete exit strategies. There was a stronger feeling that local authorities were a key stakeholder, who had a duty to ensure that sustainability maintained a position of importance.

Democracy

In Europe generally, there has been a trend towards a greater decentralisation of government structures. However, whilst there has been a fairly comparable degree of attention given throughout European countries to common local government issues such as deregulation, popular choice, efficiency and responsiveness, the emphasis given to local democracy has varied widely. Whereas in continental Europe there has been a concern to improve the functioning of local democracy, in Britain the trend has been to restrict the scope and powers of local government. Yet, whilst in Britain local democracy apparently has been eroded, there has (at least on paper) been a resurgence of interest in empowering local communities.

This concern for more active citizenship has assumed an unforeseen centrality in LA21. 'Civicness' is now widely perceived to underpin the pursuit of sustainable development, and the reinvigoration of social concern and caring is seen to be at the forefront of LA21. Researchers at the University of British Columbia have coined the terms Appropriated Carrying Capacity (ACC) and Social Caring Capacity (SCC) as the twin facets of local sustainability. ACC refers to the scale and intensity of an area's 'ecological footprint', which generally needs substantially to be reduced, while SCC reflects the supportive community networks, ideally to be extended and reinforced, which sustain 'social capital'. They argue that the latter can substitute for the former and that, in practice, a more 'civic' community should be able significantly to reduce its environmental impact. In practice, however, this is creating a paradox for local governance, deriving from a tension between the traditional *representative* role of elected members, whose powers have been steadily eroded, and an alternative *participatory* role for active citizens. This dilemma creates scope for both friction and synergy.

The 'representative' model suggests a council-led approach, with an agenda driven by normal committee and consultative processes. By contrast, the 'participatory' approach proposes an agenda which is defined, formalised and substantially implemented at the neighbourhood level. Some current evidence points towards a strong mistrust of politicians, officialdom, and government exhortations to change our lifestyles. This indicates the need for an agenda which is distilled and 'owned' at a level much closer to the community. Yet the practice of achieving this is far from straightforward. Whilst many LA21 activists claim high levels of participation, closer examination suggests that most actions are progressed by a small (and often unelected) motivated minority; whilst this is not necessarily undesirable, it clearly poses some problems of the representativeness of 'local' agendas. Some councillors seem to be concerned at, and even feel threatened by, this phenomenon. The traditional role of elected members is clearly one founded on representative democracy. This provides a ward-based focus, which can give a very positive feeling of 'ownership' and association, yet, equally, can be slow and obstructive or indifferent to radical sustainability issues.

...

Some general observations that we infer from our interviews regarding the 'populist' approach to LA21 is that the impressive levels of participation mean that momentum may be unstoppable, even if the Council 'pulls the plug'. It also creates a greater likelihood of breaking the mould of traditional policy, going beyond formal policy-making to create a wider debate. This view is fuelled by the feeling that local government has a structure which militates against radical change, albeit officers and members are credited with having learned the lesson that they cannot 'go it alone', and several have been described as unexpectedly open and receptive to the sustainability agenda. The active role of local government continues to be important, however, in view of its valued financial support and its ability to achieve significant results.

A further issue which arises in relation to LA21 is the scale at which the sustainability agenda is most appropriately addressed. In general, we encountered the view that, the larger the scale of the exercise, the easier it was to secure agreement; at a smaller scale, issues tend to be more controversial, with more sticking points. However, the more local the scale of debate, the more likelihood there was of action, as opposed to pious and eloquent statements.

...

5 HOW WE LIVE

We now turn from scientific, spiritual, spacial and political perspectives on the environment, to the mundane – of how we get from 'A' to 'B'. Poor air quality is caused by our day to day activities, which are, in turn, determined by these contexts.

Royal Commission on Environmental Pollution, Eighteenth Report *Transport and the Environment*, Cmnd 2674 (London: HMSO, 1994), pp 16-18

Changes in lifestyles

2.17 The growth in personal travel has been closely linked with social changes. Some of the key features can be briefly identified. There have been demographic changes. Although the population of the UK increased by only 14.5% between 1951 and 1991, there was a more rapid increase in the number of people over 16 and an increase of 44% in the number aged 65-79. People are remaining active longer and making more use of post-retirement leisure. In doing so they are even more likely than younger people to welcome the comfort and convenience of a car.

2.18 Women use buses more frequently than men. In 1989/91 women aged 16-29 made 133 trips by bus a year on average compared to only 84 by men, and women aged 30-59 made 83 trips by bus a year on average compared to only 38 by men. However, women now increasingly have a car or access to a car, and the gap between women's and men's travel patterns is narrowing. The proportion of car mileage driven by women rose from 16% in 1975/76 to 25%

in 1989/91. Over the same period the ratio of average annual distance travelled in a car by women to the average for men rose from 0.53 to 0.67 in the 17-29 age group and from 0.43 to 0.56 in the 30-59 age group.

2.19 The organisation of work is becoming more flexible and decentralised. For a number of reasons, including the shift from manufacturing services and improvements in labour productivity, employment is now spread more thinly over a larger number of establishments. There have been increases in the numbers of self-employed, part-time workers, women workers and workers with more than one job. An increase in the number of workers without a fixed place of employment may help to account for the increase by a third in the late 1980s in the average number of journeys made on business, which now represent over a tenth of distance travelled. ...

2.20 The travel patterns of parents and children have also changed. Partly because of the increase in female employment, the number of places in day nurseries and playgroups and with registered child-minders has grown by 400,000 in the last 15 years. Many more children now start school before the age of 5. There has been a marked change in the way older children travel to school. The proportion of children aged 7-11 taken to school by car increased to 30% in a 1990 sample from 1% a generation earlier; the proportion walking dropped from 87% to 67%. One factor has been the closure of many smaller schools. Despite that, 80% of the 1990 sample lived within a kilometre of their school; but parents now have a heightened perception of the risks to children, their main concerns being danger from traffic (43%), unreliability of the child (21%) and fear of molestation (21%). The trend towards use of cars has been partly offset as a cause of traffic growth by a reduction of 13% in the late 1980s in the average number of journeys made primarily for education, as a result of a fall in the school age population.

2.21 There have been major changes in the way people shop. Between 1982 and 1992 more than half of new retail floorspace opened was at out-of-town sites, compared with only one-seventh between 1960 and 1981. Between 1988 and 1992, the number of superstores (defined as having an area of more than 25,000 square feet, and mostly on out-of-town sites) increased by more than half. There are also estimated to be over 2,000 retail warehouses. Half of do-it-yourself sales are now at out-of-town locations, which are also becoming increasingly important for electrical goods, clothing, sports equipment, footwear and office supplies. The last decade has seen the creation of a small number of massive out-of-town shopping centres, each containing hundreds of shops: the Gateshead Metro Centre, Lakeside at Thurrock (Essex), Meadowhall at Sheffield and Merry Hill at Dudley. In all, 37% of retail sales in 1992 were in out-of-town locations, compared to only 5% in 1980.

2.22 The growth of out-of-town stores and centres has increased dependence on cars. Customers travelling by car account for 97% of the sales from Marks and Spencer edge-of-town stores compared with about 70% from high street stores. An early survey of people shopping at the Gateshead Metro Centre found 80% had travelled by car, compared with 27% of those shopping in Newcastle city centre. At a site adjacent to the M40, 98% of customers at an Asda food store came by car. These customers tend to come from a wide area. About a quarter of customers at the Asda store had a journey time of 20 minutes or more and most used the motorway. Marks and Spencer define the catchment area of an edge-of-town store as 40 minutes driving time (which can be equivalent to a distance of more than 40 miles), compared with 20 minutes for minor high street stores. Lakeside in Essex attracts visitors along the A12 and M25 from as far away as Ipswich and Norwich.

2.23 The government has recently made important changes in planning policies on out-of-town stores ... The success of out-of-town stores and centres reflects a fundamental modification in the way people view shopping, the result ultimately of increasing affluence. It is now for many people a form of leisure, and stores and centres are designed and operated on that basis. In other spheres of life as well, the increased opportunities for mobility have highlighted the scope for choice and variety. People are now less likely to use a particular shop or school or other facility simply because it is the nearest. Many of them choose to travel further in order to obtain a quality or kind of service which they see as more desirable. Between 1985/86 and 1989/91 the number of journeys made for leisure increased by 10% on average, but the average distance travelled for leisure increased by 23%. The corresponding figures for shopping journeys were 16% and 24%. Another strong trend has been towards the 'chaining' of journeys to serve a number of purposes in succession. For example the journey to work may be combined with delivering one or more children to school or playgroup; the journey home from work may be combined with collecting children and with shopping. In order to make such chains of journeys a car is almost essential.

2.24 These new lifestyles are not shared by everyone. Two-thirds of people do not shop out of town. Some of them dislike the wide ranges of often unfamiliar products stocked by out-of-town stores and the time taken up by a visit to one. Others are among the third of households which do not have access to a car. For those households opportunities have often been reduced: the growth of superstores and out-of-town centres has reduced the profitability of many shops which could be easily reached on foot or by public transport, and in some cases brought about their closure. Many households, especially in rural areas, have difficulty in affording a car but find they now need one in order to buy food and obtain employment.

2.25 Although only limited statistics are available, it is clear that increased use of cars, especially for short journeys, has greatly reduced the distances many people walk or cycle. This is of considerable concern in a health context. Physical activity contributes to the prevention and management of weight problems and obesity and protects against coronary heart disease. Present levels of fitness are very low. About one-third of men aged 55-64, almost two-fifths of women aged 45-54 and over half of women aged 55-64 are not fit enough to walk on level ground at 3 mph. In the light of findings like this the government is developing strategies for promoting physical exercise.

2.26 The changes that have taken place in lifestyles can be regarded as a response to the greater opportunities for mobility. Their general effect, however, is to provide a powerful further stimulus to the use of cars and, as a result of changes in the location of population and the pattern of land use ..., they have now developed a dynamism of their own. The car has also developed deep and powerful symbolic meanings, which add to its attractiveness. If our lifestyles are not sustainable, however, they will have to be modified sooner or later.

2.27 Travel by car has shown a rapid growth in all developed countries, but there is no simple relationship between car use and ownership and GDP per head. Britain has the lowest GDP per head of the ten developed countries shown in figure 2-VI, and comes seventh in terms of car ownership per thousand people, but third in the average distance travelled by car annually. The USA has the most car-intensive lifestyle; but people in the other countries listed have a less car-intensive lifestyle at present than the British either in absolute terms (Belgium, France, Germany, Italy, Japan, Netherlands) or in relation to their wealth (Denmark, Sweden). We do not believe that the extrapolation of past trends in the UK represents the only possible future.

...

The need to improve air quality

3.41 The monitoring data show that many people in the UK are exposed from time to time to concentrations of pollutants which exceed WHO guidelines. This is mainly the result of emissions from road vehicles. In particular:

The health-based guidelines for **ozone** are exceeded on occasions in both urban and rural areas, particularly in southern Britain. In 1992 the lower bound of the guidelines was exceeded for a total of 41 hours at 7 urban monitoring sites, for 35 hours at the sole suburban site and for 551 hours at 15 rural sites; the upper bound was exceeded for 38 hours in the rural network. ...

The guidelines for **nitrogen dioxide** are exceeded on occasions at urban sites. The highest urban background levels ever recorded in the UK were measured in 1991 and 1992. ... In 1992 the daily guideline was exceeded for 8 days at the sole kerbside site and for 15 days in total at the 13 urban sites; the hourly guideline was exceeded for 10 hours in total at the urban sites.

The results of the first year's monitoring show that, although the daily guideline for thoracic particles has not been exceeded, there have been shorter periods when levels of **PM10** exceeded the concentration specified in that guideline.

3.42 Although the monitoring data are from a small number of sites, there is no reason to suppose they are not representative of conditions in many areas of the UK. Modelling studies submitted in evidence by the Meteorological Office indicate that the hourly mean concentration of nitrogen dioxide would frequently exceed the EC standard of 200 mg/m^3 (expressed in the Directive as the 98th percentile of hourly means over a year) near any road carrying more than 10,000 fast-moving vehicles an hour if these are not in most cases fitted with three-way catalytic converters.

3.43 We are concerned that the present use of road vehicles may be causing serious damage to human health by triggering or exacerbating respiratory symptoms and by exposing people to carcinogens from vehicle emissions. The situation should therefore be regarded as unsustainable... Despite the many uncertainties about the effects of transport pollutants on human health and the environment, there is a clear case, on the basis of what is already known, for increasing the precautionary action taken to improve air quality. It is especially important to reduce concentrations of particulates and nitrogen oxides. The overall policy objective should be:

TO ACHIEVE STANDARDS OF AIR QUALITY THAT WILL PREVENT DAMAGE TO HUMAN HEALTH AND THE ENVIRONMENT

PART II

Historical context of environmental law in Britain

CHAPTER 2

Building Babylon: Industrial activities and early pollution controls

And dream of London, small and white and clean
The clear Thames bordered by its gardens green

W Morris, *The Earthly Paradise* (1898) Prologue

1 INTRODUCTION

Pollution has been a concern of government, property owners and citizens for a long time and law has been laid down in response. Acts from the fourteenth century have been passed to forbid citizens to 'annoy' the River Thames or to desist from throwing carcasses into rivers within city walls. The effects of pollution were limited until the nineteenth century by the scale of polluting activities and the size of cities. Many cities could, until then, still be described as 'islands', with water or green fields flowing up their shores, or they were contained behind city walls.[1] This altered in the nineteenth century when cities began to swell. London became 'the murky, modern Babylon', Manchester 'a Babel built of brick', its warehouses 'Babylonian monuments'.[2] In this chapter we pay particular attention to the types of pollution and public health problems which led to these descriptions in the nineteenth century. We chart the development of statutory controls in response to the limitations of the common law to control polluting activities using the example of two major enactments concerned with air and water pollution: the Alkali Act 1863 and the Rivers (Pollution Prevention) Act 1876. A decidedly modern postscript is added: *Cambridge Water Co Ltd v Eastern Counties Leather plc.*[3] This case suggests a continuing restricted role for civil liability in environmental protection and might be used to question the strength of a number of key principles of modern environmental law.

1 M Girouard, *Cities and People: A Social and Architectural History* (New Haven and London: Yale University Press: 1985), p 343.
2 Ibid.
3 [1994] 2 AC 264, [1994] 1 All ER 53, HL.

2 INDUSTRIAL ACTIVITIES, PUBLIC HEALTH AND POLLUTION

Britain was the first country to industrialise. Throughout the nineteenth century the economy grew rapidly and diversified but was frequently unstable. A number of factors contributed to the rapid expansion of industry and trade. The end of the Napoleonic War in 1815 brought increased prosperity as traders exported cotton, hardware and iron to markets that had been starved of such goods.[4] Manufacturing received an immense impetus from technical progress: the invention of steam-generated mechanical power to supplement water power leading to the development of advanced machine tools and the Leblanc process in chemical production. During the 1820s and 1830s large scale investment was funnelled into docks, railways, gasworks, water companies and shipbuilding. A great expansion of trade in cotton and natural resources also occurred with North and South America, Africa and Asia.

In the late 1830s to early 1840s depression caused by a series of bad harvests and the need for substantial grain imports damaged the cotton industry. Mill owners responded by installing power looms in an attempt to increase capacity. Better profits were achieved in the mid-1840s and new capital poured into the cotton industry. Similar investment occurred in the woollen industry and in the coal fields. The rate of investment ensured that the economic system adapted to increased industrial growth; and indeed was from then heavily dependent upon its continuance. The remainder of the century saw periods of economic difficulty alongside growth by leaps and bounds. One period of growth was in the 1870s, resulting from the expansion of British exports and a continued fall in the real cost of production due to technical progress. Confidence in worldwide industrial acceleration and new gold discoveries in California and Australia made it possible for European and American bankers to invest further in British industry.

As early as the first quarter of the century the environmental effects of intense economic activity became apparent in the form of polluted air, blackened and effluvial rivers. The concomitant growth of cities led to outbreaks of epidemic diseases, such as cholera. While air and watercourses had been polluted in the pre-industrial era, the rise of industrial society saw abuse of the environment on a different scale and of a significantly different type: smoke emissions were combined with noxious acid gas compounds, commonly hydrochloric acid gas. Rivers had frequently been obstructed by waste but, following industrialisation, pollution by sulphuric acid and other deleterious matter and sewage led to acute degradation of water.

A whole range of industrial activity generated both national income and pollution – chemical production, manufacturing, metal industries, building, and engineering, as well as secondary sectors such as the manufacture of domestic goods and distilling. Particularly severe environmental harm was caused by the chemical industry which came to dominate Lancashire, first in

4 SG Checkland, *The Rise of Industrial Society in England 1815-1855* (London: Longman, 1969), p 8.

St Helens and, following litigation, in Widnes and Runcorn. Minor centres of chemical works were located in South West Wales, the West Riding of Yorkshire and in Scotland. The manufacture of chemicals involved the bringing together of vast quantities of bulky materials – salt, kelp, and limestone – and processing them to produce chemicals such as the acid and alkali used in the manufacture of glass, soap and textiles. The processing of such bulk, often only into a single product, produced much waste and pollution. For example one stage of the process, the decomposition of common salt by sulphuric acid in furnaces, resulted in a vigorous reaction which produced large quantities of hydrochloric acid gas (muriatic acid). A contemporary noted that this process 'is attended by an inevitable creation of nuisances which desolate its surroundings'.[5] The location of the chemical industry altered as manufacturers chose sites convenient for transport by sea, canal and rail and where wastes, fumes and effluvia could be dispersed with minimum complaint.

Early attempts to reduce air pollution from the release of hydrochloric acid gas from chemical works by wide dispersal of the noxious fumes from remarkably high chimney 'stalks' were unsuccessful: the cold, wet fumes rapidly descended to the ground where they inflicted greater harm over a wider area. Metal objects such as gutters were eroded and crops and fruit trees were blighted. Refuse from the manufacture of chemicals, containing a large proportion of sulphur, accumulated in huge mounds at the works. This was liable to combustion and gave out offensive vapours. When exposed to heavy rains it would pollute neighbouring streams and meadows and destroy vegetation with which it came into contact.

Public complaint was such that in 1862 a Select Committee of the House of Lords was set up under the chairmanship of the Earl of Derby to 'inquire into the injury resulting from noxious vapours evolved in certain manufacturing processes and into the state of the law relating thereof'. The Derby Committee was not concerned with the effects of noxious vapours on human health, but was preoccupied with the considerable depreciation of the value of agricultural land affected by the vapours. Most of the available evidence on the impact of the chemical industry upon air quality is taken from the St Helens area, a scene of desolation. The following extract is taken from the Derby Committee report.

Report of the Select Committee of the House of Lords, *Injury from Noxious Vapours* BPP 14 (London: HMSO, 1862) pp v-viii

...

It is difficult to exaggerate the amount of injury to the adjoining district, which in some instances is caused by the neighbourhood of these works. The pungent vapour is perceptible, in certain states of the atmosphere, at the distance of five or six miles: and its effects, within a radius of one or two miles, are fearful. Trees appear to suffer the most: "they lose their leaves; the top branches begin to decay; afterwards the bark becomes discoloured and hardened; when very much affected it adheres to the tree and the tree is ultimately killed." The same witness, describing the neighbourhood of St Helens, where there are numerous

5 F Wyatt, *The Progress of the Chemical Industry in Rothwell* (1893), p 58.

works of this description says: "It is one scene of desolation. You might look around for a mile, and not see a tree with any foliage on whatever. I do not mean to say there are not individual trees within a mile of St Helens that have any foliage on; but I do not think there is a tree within a mile of St Helens that possesses half its natural vigour; and I should think that three-fourths of the trees are totally dead.

...

Other witnesses speak to the destruction of trees, by hundreds, in successive years, from the effects of the vapours. Farms recently well wooded, and with hedges in good condition, have neither tree nor hedge left alive; whole fields of corn are destroyed in a single night, especially when the vapour falls upon them while in bloom; orchards and gardens, of which there were great numbers in the neighbourhood of St Helens, have not a fruit tree alive; pastures are so deteriorated that graziers refuse to place stock upon them; and some of the witnesses have attributed to the poisonous nature of the grass the fact that their sheep and cattle have cast their young in considerable numbers.

It is right to add that in the immediate neighbourhood of St Helens, there are, in addition to the seven or eight alkali works existing in that locality, six or eight large copper smelting works, beside a large number of collieries, glass works, and other manufactories.

The coal industry also had injurious effects. The industry began to operate powerfully on the British economy and society in the 1820s and 1830s when enormous reserves to the south and south east of Durham were opened up.[6] Increased industrial and domestic demand provided the basis for steady expansion in most coalfields, particularly Lancashire and Yorkshire. Simultaneously, the ironstones of North Stafford were worked following the discovery of new ores providing brass, tin and steel for household goods, plating and railway rolling stock. Coal and lesser metal production had a cumulatively destructive effect upon the landscape and river quality. In particular, pollution of water from the mining industry arose from the discharge of solid matter during coal washing, from tin and zinc mines which clogged flowing streams and from the emission of other poisonous, noxious solid or liquid waste from the mines. This was acknowledged formally in a Royal Commission Report on Salmon Fisheries in 1861. The following extract from the Report describes how the blocking of rivers and breeding grounds by solid matter from mines, and poisoned water by mine efflux, diminished the supply of salmon from rivers and fisheries in England and Wales. The report attempts to balance such losses with the economic advantages of a healthy mining industry.

Royal Commission on Salmon Fisheries, *Report on Fisheries in England and Wales* BPP 2768 (London: HMSO, 1861)

We regret to state that it has been fully substantiated by the evidence. In some rivers the fact is patent and notorious. Salmon formerly abounded, but have

6 SG Checkland, *The Rise of Industrial Society in England 1815-1855* (London: Longman, 1969), p 154.

now almost or altogether ceased to exist. Such are the cases in which mines or manufactures have poisoned the waters or obstructions have been erected by which the fish have been blocked out from the breeding grounds...The decrease of fish in most cases is stated to have been very great.

...

Poisoning by mine efflux

The most striking case of contamination of waters is by the efflux from mines. For example rivers form a junction as they fall into the sea at Aberystwyth and since machinery is employed at Goginan lead mines to make the crushing process more effectual a total extinction of animal life has taken place in the waters of the surrounding rivers. Furthermore, it has been proved beyond doubt that not only the fish in these rivers, but animals grazing on their banks, cows, pigs, horses and poultry, had been poisoned, not so much by drinking the water as by eating the grass which in times of floods had been covered by the infected waters....In Cornwall which is peculiarly mineral country, the salmon fisheries may be said to have been virtually destroyed by the mines.

The first question is thus whether it is possible to reconcile the interests of mines and fisheries, either by diverting mine water or by rendering it by mechanical or chemical means innoxious to the fish. Secondly, if this cannot be done at least not without an expense which would be unreasonable or prohibitory and if, consequently it becomes necessary to elect between conflicting interests. The comparative extent of industry and capital invested in the respective undertakings form an important ingredient in the consideration of this question.

On grounds of superior public importance it may be considered that established mineral undertakings of great value ought not to be interfered with, although the consequences of their working may be to destroy the fish in those rivers into which they drain.

The manufacture of cotton, wool, worsted, silk and jute goods reached its height in the middle decades of the nineteenth century. The cotton industry was centred upon Manchester, described by a Board of Trade Committee in 1843 as 'one vast workshop'.[7] A Royal Commission report on pollution of the Rivers Aire and Calder (1867) stated that in the West Riding of Yorkshire, the principal seat of the woollen and cotton trades, 'the water became fouler and more foul after leaving each successive mill'.[8] A later Royal Commission report on Pollution Arising from Woollen Manufactures (1871) noted, however, that in areas of great industrial activity with polluted rivers the preponderance of cotton or woollen manufacturers did little to impress a specific character on the condition of the already polluted river water.

7 Board of Trade Committee Report (1845), quoted in K Warrens, *Chemical Foundations: The Alkali Industry in Britain Until 1926* (Oxford: Clarendon, 1980), p 92.

8 Royal Commission on the Pollution of Rivers (of 1865), Third Report, *The Rivers Aire and Calder* BPP 3850 (London: HMSO, 1867) p (xxi).

Sewage was a major and related source of pollution alongside that of industrial activity. Concern about public health problems caused, in the main, by sewage pollution was reflected in a report by Edwin Chadwick on the Sanitary Condition of the Working Classes in 1842 and two reports of the Royal Commission on the State of Large Towns and Populous Districts in 1842 and 1843. As a result of these reports the Public Health Act 1848 was passed, requiring the building of sewage systems and the provision of water supplies. The 1848 Act was an early legal response to the problem of sanitation. However, it came to cause a different environmental problem: the Act authorised local Boards of Health to empty their new sewage systems 'into such places as may be fit and necessary', which was generally the nearest river. In 1869 the Royal Sanitary Commission reported on the consequences of the Act:

> Encouraged by the facilities which the Public Health Act 1848 offered, the towns began to carry out large works for their own sewerage and drainage, taking the rivers, on which most of them had been situated for water supply, as the means of discharging what they simply looked upon as refuse, regardless of the loss to themselves of pure water, of the waste of sewage and of the injury to the inhabitants of the valleys through which these poisoned waters were afterwards to flow.

Pollution from sewage increased with the growth of urban areas, causing streams to be converted into common sewers. The Royal Commission Report on the Process of Treating Sewage (1870) noted: 'of all forms of pollution to which rivers are subject, that from sewers is the most objectionable...often masked and overborne by the foul contribution of manufactories'.[9] A clear link between the growth of industry and pollution by domestic sewage was identified in a Royal Commission Report on Rivers in Scotland (1872): 'in the case of the Clyde basin the liquid refuse of all kinds of manufactures is so mixed with the personal waste of the immense population engaged in them that the river becomes in every way offensive'.[10]

The various Royal Commission reports and contemporary accounts mentioned above provide vivid pictures of the state of the environment. Rivers were poisoned, clogged and corrupted by refuse from various manufacturing processes, mining operations and sewage. The population of towns such as St Helens lived under a low hanging roof of smeary smoke. But, national income and employment were important consequences of expansive, albeit environmentally harmful, industrial activities. In its Report on Pollution of the Rivers Aire and Calder (1867) the Royal Commission on the Pollution of Rivers (of 1865) shows an express interest in the economic importance of industrialisation:

> It would be impossible to calculate the extent of the profit which the national products of the West Riding, stone, iron, coal and other mines have been worked, while the profits of the textile manufacture of worsteds and woollens might perhaps exceed the amount of our national debt.[11]

9 Royal Commission on Pollution of Rivers, *Report on the Process of Treating Sewage*, (1870), C 181, p 23.

10 Royal Commission on the Pollution of Rivers, *Fourth Report on the Pollution of Rivers in Scotland* (1872), Cmnd 603, p 100.

11 Royal Commission on the Pollution of Rivers (of 1865), Third Report, *The Rivers Aire and Calder* (1867), p (xi).

Parliament and the courts were faced with the dilemma of balancing industrial interests with those of public health and the protection of property from pollution. The Reform Act 1832 further complicated this task by granting, in effect, an electoral mandate for industrial interests. The following passage describes the problem facing the legislature and judiciary in the nineteenth century.

G Wilson, 'The Development of Environmental Law in Nineteenth Century Britain', in G Weick (ed), *National and European Law on the Threshold to the Single Market* (Frankfurt am Main: Peter Lang, 1993), pp 13-14

A radical transformation

The development of law relating to the environment in nineteenth century England takes us straight away into the heart of the Victorian predicament; how to deal with the cost of material development, with no precedents to guide, with advances in production outstripping the scientific and technical knowledge needed to cope with the problems to which they gave rise, with no tradition of collective action, no state apparatus at central or local government level, with siren voices urging that untrammelled enterprise was the best way of releasing the productive energies of the nation and obtaining the material benefits of becoming the world's first industrial nation. The slow acceptance that something more had to be done, that government had to take responsibility, that legislation was needed to supplement the judge-made law, that administrative action was needed to supplement judicial administration, that bureaucrats were needed to work alongside judges and legislators, all this was not simply part of the context of the development of the law relating to the environment, it was an essential part of that development itself. The lack of organisation, the absence of a tradition of state intervention, the heavy reliance on private law administration by the ordinary courts, were as much obstacles that had to be overcome, if the problems were first to be understood and then dealt with, as the scientific and technical ignorance.

And a slow response

The response was slow and piecemeal, an evolutionary response to a revolutionary situation. It was also fragmented. In the same way as judge-made law was developed in the context of particular fact situations so here too the new principles and the new legal instruments and institutions which were introduced to meet the problems, were developed in the context of what were seen as separate problems, problems of the administration of the poor law, problems of public order, problems of the conditions in factories, problems of public health, problems of the pollution of rivers, problems of the emission of noxious gases. There was not even at first an overall picture of the role and techniques of government let alone an overall view of the environment. And much of the debate was fragmented as well and conducted in the context of particular problems. Questions about state intervention, the reliance on legislation to supplement actions and prosecutions at law, the balance between central and local government, the justifications for interference with private property and the freedom to trade, were all discussed not only in Parliament, the natural constitutional forum of debate, and in the writings of economists and political theorists, but in evidence to, and in the reports of, Select Committees and Royal Commissions, arguments to and judgments in the courts, in pamphlets and periodicals, even in novels. All contributed to the slow, and what often seems reluctant, transition from the barebones State of the beginning of the nineteenth century to the fully fledged State with its organised central government assisted by a central bureaucracy and a uniform system of local government, armed with statutory powers which gave them wide discretion to initiate, decide and act, which existed at the beginning of the twentieth.

Legislation in the early nineteenth century offered only piecemeal protection of the environment and gave little opportunity for *preventing* industrial pollution. For example, the Towns Improvement Clauses Act 1847, enacted to control smoke emissions from furnaces, specifically contained an exemption for industry and excluded noxious vapours or gas from its ambit. Public health legislation was not uniform across the country: for instance the Smoke Nuisance Abatement Act 1850 applied only to London. Until at least the middle of the century the common law, as distinct from statute law, provided the primary means of environmental protection.

3 SCOPE AND LIMITATIONS OF THE COMMON LAW

We now turn to the scope and limitations of the common law. The system of common law developed from the time of the Norman Conquest in an attempt to cope with new disputes over the use and abuse of land. As it developed it incidentally became a mechanism for environmental protection through controlling the use of land rather than by regulating the use of natural resources per se.[12] In the nineteenth century, as now, people seeking a remedy in the civil law were entitled to redress for injury caused by environmental harm and a legal remedy only if they possessed certain riparian rights, or if the case fell within the boundaries of one of three tortious actions: trespass; the rule in *Rylands v Fletcher* (1866); and private nuisance. The law of tenure, particularly the use of restrictive covenants[13] offered a further means by which landowners might exercise control over the use of land in private law.

(a) Riparian rights

Riparian rights are common law rights relating to the use of water associated with the ownership of a bank of a watercourse. Riparian owners do not own

12 S Ball and S Bell, *Environmental Law* 2nd edn (London: Blackstone Press, 1994), p 142.

13 See *Tulk v Moxhay* (1848) 2 Ph 774, 41 ER 1143 which marks a restrictive covenant as an equitable proprietary interest in land; see further M Grant, *Urban Planning Law* (London: Sweet and Maxwell, 1982), pp 2-3.

the water which flows in streams and watercourses but the landowner does have certain rights over it.[14] These are regarded as akin to a proprietary right and invasion of them is treated as damage to land. The nature of a riparian owner's right to clean water is stated clearly by Lord MacNaughten in *John Young & Co v Bankier Distillery Co.*[15] In this case the appellant company owned a distillery situated on the banks of a stream and used water from the stream in its operations. The respondents owned a mine higher up the stream and used the water in the working of the mine. The water that the mine owners discharged back into the stream was pure, but its chemical properties were altered by its use, making it hard and unsuitable for distilling. The House of Lords found that the lower riparian owner, the distillery company, had the right to receive water without alteration of its 'natural' character.

John Young & Co v Bankier Distillery Co [1893] AC 691 at 698, [1891-4] All ER 439 at 441, HL

Lord MacNaughten: A riparian proprietor is entitled to have the water of the stream on the banks of which his property lies, flow down as it has been accustomed to flow down to his property, subject to the ordinary use of the flowing water by upper proprietors, and to such further use, if any, on their part in connection with their property as may be reasonable under the circumstances. Every riparian owner is thus entitled to the water of his stream in its natural flow, without sensible diminution or increase, and without sensible alteration in its character or quality. Any invasion of this right causing actual damage, or calculated to found a claim which may ripen into an adverse right, entitles the party injured to the intervention of the court.

In practice, opportunities for relying on riparian rights were limited. They depend on ownership and not possession. Consequently, in the nineteenth century, manufacturers and mine owners often bought up stretches of land adjoining a watercourse downstream which were then leased out. Industrialists would also pipe pollutants downstream beyond a riparian owner's land. A further difficulty was proving that the pollution suffered was caused wholly by a riparian owner upstream; this was nearly impossible where a river or stream was subject to pollution discharged from a number of sites.

(b) Trespass

The action in trespass protects against interference with land whether or not damage is caused. In terms of water pollution the tort of trespass arises where an unauthorised person brings about the direct entry of polluting matter into the water of another person without justification. An advantage is that trespass to land or goods is a wrong to possession rather than to ownership. However its major disadvantage in terms of environmental protection is that the

14 See W Howarth *Wisdom's Law of Watercourses* 5th edn (London: Shaw and Sons, 1992), pp 90-91.

15 [1893] AC 691 at 698, [1891-4] All ER 439 at 441, HL.

interference must be *direct*. Most pollution of water occurs indirectly by diffuse and commonly natural processes and therefore falls outside its scope.

(c) The rule in *Rylands v Fletcher*

The rule in *Rylands v Fletcher* (1866), the tort of 'escaping nuisances', imposes strict liability for the 'escape' of dangerous substances which have been brought onto land where the accumulation of the substance could not be regarded as a 'natural user of land'. In *Rylands v Fletcher*,[16] in the Exchequer Chamber, the defendant employed independent contractors to construct a reservoir on his land. The contractors failed to shut off connected mine shafts so that when the reservoir filled with water the mine was flooded. Although the defendant had not been negligent and could not be held liable for the negligence of the contractors, the House of Lords[17] held that the plaintiffs should succeed.

Notwithstanding the apparent breadth of this rule, that a plaintiff must prove the activity complained of constituted a non-natural use of land, it has proved to be a major stumbling block for plaintiffs seeking to apply the rule. Many uses of land which cause pollution, such as the working of mines and munitions works, have been regarded by the courts as constituting a natural use of land,[18] thus providing an opportunity to balance competing interests, often in favour of industrial and polluting activities. The rule in *Rylands v Fletcher* has therefore proved virtually useless in cases involving escapes from industrial premises (see, however, 'A Modern Postscript: *Cambridge Water*', below).

(d) The role of the common law of nuisance

In the nineteenth century, private nuisance was the most common basis for tortious action for industrial pollution. This arises where there has been an intentional or negligent act which causes unreasonable and indirect injury to land, buildings or vegetation, or substantial interference with a landholder's interest in the use or enjoyment of the land by excessive noise, dust, fumes, smells and so on. The reason for the rule of nuisance was explained by Lord Holt in 1705 that 'every man must so use his own as not to indamnify another' (*sic intere tuo ut alienum non laedus*).[19] The main remedies are an award of damages to compensate for injury suffered as a result of the nuisance and an injunction to restrain the defendant from beginning or continuing the nuisance.

The centrality of private ownership of property to the tort is clear: an action will lie in the case of unreasonable interference with the reasonable use and enjoyment of *land*;[20] an individual's ability to obtain redress is therefore tied to a property interest in a specific parcel of land. On the other hand, the limitations which operate in private nuisance actions, for example that nuisance

16 (1866) LR 1 Exch 265.
17 (1868) LR 3 HL 330.
18 *Read v J Lyons & Co Ltd* [1947] AC 156, [1946] 2 All ER 471, HL.
19 *Tenant v Goldwin* (1704) 92 ER 222.
20 See *St Helen's Smelting Co v Tipping* (1865) 11 HL Cas 642, 11 ER 1483.

applies only to certain types of environmental harm such as those from easily identified sources, mean that *property owners'* freedom of action with respect to their own land, including its degradation and pollution, is also preserved. By conferring rights of exploitation of natural resources, possession or land ownership also provides a *defence* to causing environmental harm.

The scope of the doctrine of nuisance is illustrated by *St Helen's Smelting Co v Tipping* (1865). Mr Tipping purchased a valuable estate in St Helens, which lay within a mile and a half of large smelting works from which noxious vapours were emitted. In 1863 Tipping brought an action to recover damages for injury to trees, hedges, fruit and cattle, and for substantial personal discomfort. At trial, Mellor J stated that for the injury to be actionable it must visibly diminish the value, comfort and enjoyment of the property. The jury returned a verdict with damages for Tipping. The House of Lords upheld the Exchequer Chamber's ruling that the company was liable for any physical damage it caused, but that it was not liable for deterioration of the plaintiff's comfort. In the following extract Lord Westbury differentiates between the two types of injury and invokes the locality doctrine.

St Helen's Smelting Co v Tipping (1865) 11 ER 1483 at 1486-7

Lord Westbury: My Lords, in matters of this description it appears to me that it is a very desirable thing to mark the difference between an action brought for a nuisance upon the ground that the alleged nuisance produces material injury to the property, and an action brought for a nuisance on the ground that the thing alleged to be a nuisance is productive of sensible personal discomfort. With regard to the latter, namely the personal inconvenience and interference with one's enjoyment, one's quiet, one's personal freedom, anything that discomposes or injuriously affects the senses or the nerves, whether that may or may not be denominated a nuisance, must undoubtedly depend greatly on the circumstances of the place where the thing complained of actually occurs. If a man lives in a town, it is necessary that he should subject himself to the consequences of those operations of trade which may be carried on in his immediate locality, which are actually necessary for trade and commerce, and also for the enjoyment of property, and for the benefit of the inhabitants of the town and the public at large. If a man lives in a street where there are numerous shops, and a shop is opened next door to him, which is carried on in a fair and reasonable way, he has no ground for complaint, because to himself individually there may arise much discomfort from the trade carried on in that shop. But when an occupation is carried on by one person in the neighbourhood of another, and the result of that trade, or occupation, or business, is a material injury to property, then, there unquestionably arises a very different consideration. I think, my Lords, that in a case of that description, the submission which is required from persons living in society to that amount of discomfort which may be necessary for the legitimate and free exercise of the trade of their neighbours, would not apply to circumstances the immediate result of which is sensible injury to the value of the property.

Lord Wensleydale (concurring):....In these few sentences I think everything is included: The Defendants say, "If you do not mind you will stop the progress of works of this description." I agree that is so, because, no doubt, in the county of Lancaster above all other counties, where great works have been created and carried on, and are the means of developing the national wealth, you must not stand on extreme rights and allow a person to say, "I will bring an action against you for this and that, and so on." Business could not go on if it were so. Everything must be looked at from a reasonable point of view; therefore the law does not regard trifling and small inconveniences, but only regards sensible inconveniences, which sensibly diminish the comfort, enjoyment or value of the property which is affected.

On the facts of the case, the appeal was dismissed with costs against the defendant, the smelting manufacturer. The House of Lords' decision was a compromise, but one which constituted a new balance in favour of industrial activity. The decision confirmed the judicial concern to protect private property rights which had long directed the development of nuisance law. The case shows the powerful combination of protection of property and space (in the working of the locality doctrine) in law.

Given the nature of strict liability in actions for nuisance the doctrine may be described as a mechanism for the private control of environmental pollution. However, in the nineteenth century at least, nuisance law did not provide the level of protection against environmental damage that might have been expected and industrial development continued apace. There was a dearth of case law involving industrial pollution in the courts of the common law in the period 1770-1870, with on average only one or two actions for air pollution every ten years.[21] The record in noise pollution is even sparser. The working of the locality doctrine, as seen in *St Helen's Smelting Co v Tipping*, was one reason why nuisance law was not more successful in arresting pollution. Others include the expense for plaintiffs of going to law and the difficulties they faced pinpointing the exact source of the nuisance. The limitations of the tort in offering protection against polluting activities are summarised in the following passage.

G Wilson, 'The Development of Environmental Law in Nineteenth Century Britain', in G Weick (ed) *National and European Law on the Threshold to the Single Market* (Frankfurt am Main: Peter Lang, 1993) pp 14-15

The law of nuisance was, it is true, a law about activities which were regarded as offensive because they interfered with the quality of life and caused damage to property, but it was not the community at large that was the concern, let alone the environment as such. The law was there to regulate the relations between neighbours. It was not designed to protect the community but to protect individual owners' enjoyment of their property. And it was not about the kinds

21 JPS MacLaren, 'Nuisance law and the Industrial Revolution – Some Lessons from History' (1983) *Oxford Journal of Legal Studies* Vol 3, No 2, 155-221, at 161; see also JF Brenner, 'Nuisance Law and the Industrial Revolution' (1974), 3 *Journal of Legal Studies* 403-431, and PS Atiyah, 'Railway Nuisances in the English Common Law: A Historical Footnote', (1980) 23 *Journal of Law and Economics*, 191 et seq; see also A Ogus and G Richardson, 'Economics and the Environment: A Study of Private Nuisance (1977) *Cambridge Law Review* Vol 36, 284.

of large scale industrial activities and urban concentrations which became characteristic of the nineteenth century. It was about pigsties, privies, private breweries, the burning of bricks, and complaints by owners of land on river banks that defendants higher up the river were obstructing, diverting or diminishing the flow of water to their premises. And although the cases might involve the conduct of offensive trades such as soap or candle-making or the operation of slaughterhouses or the working of a water mill these were small scale affairs compared to what was to come.

(e) Private property rights

The most significant limitation of the role of the common law in controlling nuisances and securing public health was, and continues to be, that the protection of private property is the rationale of private law and its motivation. Private property rights give the property owner (whether freeholder or lessee) a right to exclude anyone else from the use or benefit of the land unless they have a better title to it, and mean also that an individual's ability to obtain redress for environmental damage is tied to a property interest in a specific parcel of land. Environmental protection may be effected through the protection of property rights. But, private law will act only to protect the individualised, self-interested claim, which considerably constrains legal action. The main doubt about the ability of private law to provide an appropriate means of protecting the environment is that environmental problems demand collective action; there is therefore some resistance to the idea that individual rights might contribute to collective progress towards environmental protection.[22]

In the nineteenth century, further difficulties in engaging the common law in protecting the environment and freeing individuals from nuisances existed, not least that the general legal culture and day to day running of the courts was biased towards the protection of private property interests.[23] The protection of private property by law was challenged by legislation directed to improve the living conditions of the urban working class. For example the Removal of Nuisances Act 1846 and the Public Health Act 1848, concerned with nuisances in individual houses, empowered Local Boards of Health to install drains and register and inspect lodging houses, even to demolish unauthorised houses.[24] Presented with such government action, the courts, unused as they were to making an assessment of the inroads which were to be made on the prevailing ethos of proprietary freedom, developed principles, precedents and rules of statutory interpretation which worked so as to continue to protect property owners.[25] 'Final straws' were that the common law was also complex and expensive.

22 See discussion in J Steele, 'Private Law and the Environment: Nuisance in Context', (1995) *Legal Studies* Vol 15, No 2, 236 at 237.

23 Ibid.

24 P McAuslan, *Land, Law and Planning* (London: Weidenfeld and Nicholson, 1975), pp 38-39.

25 Ibid, p 3; for example, in *Cooper v Wandsworth Board of Works* (1863) 143 ER 414, concerning the demolition of the plaintiff's house for failure to give notice to the district board of his intention to build the house, as required by section 76 of the Metropolis Local Management Act 1855, the House of Lords held that before a person's property is interfered with by public authorities the person must be given an opportunity to be heard.

Even in the nineteenth century, there was some awareness that the law was constrained by reason that only 'men of property' could bring actions against nuisances and river abuses. The following extract is taken from a report by the Royal Commission on the Pollution of Rivers in 1867. The Report is concerned with the basic fact that river abuses affect only *private* rights and that the expense of litigation generally far exceeded the value of the personal interest of any individual in arresting the nuisance, thereby rendering legal action unattractive.

Royal Commission on the Pollution of Rivers (of 1865), Third Report, *The Rivers Aire and Calder* (1867) Cmnd 3850, pp li-liii

Defects of Existing Law Relating to River Pollution

So far as river abuses affect only private rights, each individual is left to protect himself by putting the law in motion. An aggrieved proprietor has the option of bringing an action for damages in the Common Law Courts or of filing a bill in Chancery for an injunction. Either course is necessarily invidious, expensive and doubtful in its result. It is invidious because neighbour is set against neighbour and because it must seem unjust that one manufacturer should be proceeded against and mulcted for doing that which hundreds of others, who do not happen to offend a powerful neighbour, are doing with impunity. It is an expensive remedy. For the same money which is spent over a hardly fought litigation against a single manufacturer, a Conservancy Board, armed with proper powers, might for years keep safe from all abuse, a long extent of river with hundreds of manufactories situated on its banks....Legal proceedings are also a very doubtful remedy. The plaintiff has also to prove that he has suffered injury from the pollution of the river and that the defendant has polluted the river above him; but this is not enough. The plaintiff has also to prove that what he has suffered has been caused wholly or in part by the special act of the defendant, which is always difficult – often impossible. For besides the defendant there is probably a multitude of manufacturers who, at various points higher up the stream, cast in liquid refuse from their works; these impurities are carried down by the current, and are all mingled confusedly together, and the offence of the defendant has proved to be indistinguishable. The plaintiff accordingly fails to establish his case.

Even where successful these private attempts to protect the river are but little gain to the public. Several instances have come before us where a manufacturer, sued for polluting running water, has brought the litigation to a close, not by ceasing to foul the water, but by simply removing the discharge into the river to a point below the works of the complainant.

....

The expense of such litigation generally far exceeds the value of the personal interest of any individual in the stoppage of the nuisance. Accordingly, whatever the inconvenience to the public, the nuisance continues unabated. Rich and poor alike submit to it as a sort of destiny.

4 LEGISLATION AND THE CONTROL OF INDUSTRIAL ACTIVITIES

By the middle of the nineteenth century, the limitations of the common law as a means to prevent pollution were clear. Reports such as the Royal Commission's Report on the Rivers Aire and Calder, extracted above, provided the stimulus for the development of a second tier of control of legislation and enforcement regimes to supplement the common law of nuisance and other private law actions in the control of primarily industrial activities which caused pollution and associated public health problems. Legislation dealing specifically with problems of environmental pollution was enacted, although the absence of a tradition of state intervention and the fact that there was little state apparatus at central or local levels of government meant that this proved difficult. And, as the courts engaged in balancing industrial interests with public health and conservation in the nineteenth century, so the legislature conducted a similar exercise.

The hallmark of environmental legislation in this period was that it was problem specific – air, water and land pollution were examined as distinct subjects. The following offers an outline of statutory responses to air and water pollution and the different techniques which were employed in this period.

(a) Air pollution

In 1862 the House of Lords Select Committee (the 'Derby Committee') recommended in their Report on Injury from Noxious Vapours[26] that the law of nuisance should be consolidated and made uniform throughout the country. By the middle of the century parliamentary bodies had directed their attention to the more specific and direct consequences of air pollution and, prompted by the hearing in *St Helen's Smelting Co v Tipping* (1865),[27] the recommendations of the Derby Committee and the later Royal Commission Report on Noxious Vapours (1878) were enacted in a series of Alkali Acts which significantly changed the law relating to air pollution.

The Alkali Act 1863 required the condensation of 95 per cent of muriatic acid produced in the alkali-making process. It also mandated the registration of all alkali works and the establishment of the first national public pollution agency, the Alkali Inspectorate. No provision was made to prohibit the release of fumes from copper smelting, for which no abatement technique yet existed. The Ninth Annual Report of the Chief Inspector of the Inspectorate (1873)[28] detailed two serious problems with the effective control of air pollution under the 1863 Act. The first was that an increasing number of processes lay outside the ambit of the Act with the consequence that sulphurous acids were emitted

26 House of Lords Select Committee on Noxious Vapours, *Report on Injury from Noxious Vapours*, BPP 14 (London: HMSO, 1862).

27 (1865) 11 HL Cas 642, 11 ER 1483.

28 Chief Inspector of the Alkali Inspectorate, Ninth Annual Report (1873), quoted in M Frankel, *The Alkali Inspectorate: The Control of Industrial Air Pollution* (London: Social Audit, 1974).

freely from copper smelting works. The second difficulty lay in the fact that the uniform emission standard of condensing 95% of muriatic acid did not ensure clean air since more alkali works were opening in areas such as Merseyside.

An amendment Alkali Act was passed in 1874 in response to the Chief Inspector's report.[29] This extended the definition of noxious gases to include sulphurous acid from copper works. In response to the second problem identified by the Chief Inspector, the 1874 Act provided that, in addition to the condensation of sulphurous acid, the owner of every alkali works should use the 'best practicable means' to prevent the escape of all other noxious or offensive gases from the works. 'Best practicable means' was first applied in 1842 as an attempt to curb smoke nuisance in Leeds, but it was not until 1906 that it received a statutory formulation in section 27 of the Alkali Etc Works Regulation Act of that year:

> The expression 'best practicable means' when used with respect to the prevention of the escape of noxious and offensive gases, has reference not only to the provision and efficient maintenance of appliances adequately for preventing such escape, but also to the manner in which such appliances are used and to the proper supervision by the owner of any operation in which such gases are evolved.

The 'best practicable means' did not include any clearly defined, formal, environmental quality standards. However, consideration was given to it to guide standard setting and enforcement in relation to air and, implicitly, to other environmental media. The concept had a number of practical effects. It encouraged the Alkali Inspectorate to adopt a conciliatory and cooperational approach to achieve compliance because it could be applied flexibly and on an individualised basis to ensure that, in each particular case, the emission controls were 'practicable'. The 'standards' contained within the concept represented a tacit agreement between pollution inspectors and industry about the acceptable level of costs of pollution control. The use of 'best practicable means' suggests that pollution standards reflected judgments of economic as well as technical feasibility. Such judgments are described by a former Alkali Inspector in his Annual Report (1873):

> There must be a compromise between (i) the natural desire of the public to enjoy pure air, (ii) the legitimate desire of the manufacturer to meet competition, (iii) overriding national interests. The answer to those opposing interests lies in the honest use by the manufacturer of the best practicable means.[30]

That the legislature tackled the problem of pollution abatement according to individual sectors of industry and with little appreciation of the *integrated* nature of environmental problems, is apparent in a study of the Alkali Acts of 1863 and 1874: more effective air pollution controls, required under the Acts, led to a substantial increase in water pollution as the liquid products from the condensation of noxious gas were released into rivers and streams.

29 See further ch 6.
30 Quoted in Frankel, op cit, p 8.

(b) Water pollution

Royal Commissions on River Pollution were established in 1865 and 1868 to inquire into the pollution of rivers and the means of preventing such pollution.[31] The primary recommendation of the Commissions was that it was necessary strictly to prohibit the casting of solid matter into river channels, to enact standards of purity and to give manufacturers the power to discharge drainage waters into town sewers. In the event, the first major piece of legislation, the Rivers (Pollution Prevention) Act 1876, embodied a more cautious approach. This Act placed a prohibition on pollution by solid matter, sewage pollution and pollution by manufacturing and mining. Under Part II of the 1876 Act an offence was created where any person caused any solid or liquid sewage matter to fall or flow or be carried into any stream. However, a defence was available if the person was able to show that the 'best practicable and available means' to render the sewage harmless had been taken. The requirement to employ the best practicable means or techniques, promulgated in the Alkali Act 1874, was thereby translated into a defence in the 1876 Act. Part III of the 1876 Act was concerned with pollution caused by manufacturing and mining. The basic offence of causing or knowingly permitting poisonous, noxious or polluting matter to be carried into a stream, was similarly subject to a proviso that it was not committed where the defendant could show that the 'best practicable and reasonably available means' had been used.

Part III of the 1876 Act also laid down that enforcement proceedings with regard to manufacturing and mining pollution were to be taken solely by a sanitary authority and only with the consent of the Local Government Board,[32] forming a double filter. The Board was not to give consent to such proceedings in any district that was the 'seat of any manufacturing industry' unless it was fully satisfied 'that no material injury will be inflicted by such proceedings on the interests of such industry'. The rationale for this test was given in a later Royal Commission report:

> In such centres the interests of the community are largely bound up with the interests of the manufacturer and that to demand from manufacturers costly schemes of purification might injure the community without any corresponding improvement in the character of the river which is already materially, if not hopelessly impaired.[33]

Under the Rivers (Pollution Prevention) Act 1876, the combination of the best practicable means defence and the obstructive limitation in the Act's enforcement in areas regarded as a 'seat of any manufacturing industry', ensured that a compromise was reached between industrial and conservatory interests. Nevertheless, in cases such as *Staffordshire County Council v Seisdon RDC* (1907),[34] concerning the cumulative effects of pollution, the courts offered a

31 Reports included: Royal Commission on Pollution of Rivers (of 1865) Third Report, *The Rivers Aire and Calder* (1867) Cmnd 3850 and Royal Commission on Pollution of Rivers (of 1868) Fifth Report, *Pollution Arising from Mining Operations and Metal Manufacturing* (1874) Cmnd 951.

32 The forerunner of local government as elected local authorities.

33 Royal Commission on Sewage Disposal, Ninth Report, *Disposal of Liquid Wastes from Manufacturing Processes* (1914-16) Cmnd 7819, p 3.

34 (1907) 71 JP 185.

strict interpretation of the provisions of the 1876 Act. The case concerned an application before the county court by Staffordshire County Council for an order under the Rivers (Pollution Prevention) Act 1876 requiring Seisdon Rural District Council to stop polluting the River Stour with sewage as it flowed through a town. The county court judge refused to make an order on the ground that the pollution was not appreciable; it could not be said that the sewage substantially harmed the quality of the River Stour because its waters were already polluted. On appeal, in the King's Bench Division, it was held that the county court judge was wrong in law to decide that an order may not be made on the ground that the stream was not rendered more foul by the entry of the sewage. The test was whether the river in its *pristine* state would be polluted.

Staffordshire County Council v Seisdon RDC (1907) 71 JP & LGR 185 at 187

Darling J: ...It must not be said: 'See what a lot of filth other people put into it, and therefore you must excuse us', because that leads to this logical conclusion: You must proceed at once against all the offenders or else against none, because everyone could make that answer and the river would not be purified at all.

...

In considering what is an appreciable pollution, what is the evidence? That practically all the liquid from the sewage which was put into the river (and we have heard what an offensive kind of stuff it was) had some effect on the stream, no one could dispute. My conclusion is that the learned judge would have decided in accordance with the facts if he had said 'I must view the stream as hypothetically pure; but into it goes the stuff of Kinver. Does it pollute it? Looking at what it is, does it pollute the stream?' What does the statute require? The statute does not mean that rivers must not be what you call appreciably polluted by one person, in addition to others who have already polluted them. The statute aims at the bringing back of rivers to a pristine state.

(c) Interaction of statutory regimes and private law

The new body of public law relating to air and water pollution interacted with private law which had previously controlled environmental harm affecting the use or enjoyment of land. For example, statutes concerned with the sanitation of towns specified that common law rights would continue: actions could therefore be brought by the Attorney General on behalf of private persons who suffered nuisance from the building, or use of sewers. In *A-G v Birmingham Borough Council*,[35] a wealthy landowner sought an injunction against the defendant corporation to restrain it from dumping sewage in the river which ran through his property. Page-Wood VC found for the plaintiff, saying 'he is entitled to the full use and benefit of the river, just as he enjoyed them before the passing of the Municipal Act 1850'.[36] As rights, such as those enjoyed by

35 (1858) 70 ER 220.
36 (1858) 70 ER 220 at 225.

the plaintiff, could not be tampered with, equitable remedies were used in a flexible way. In a case concerning the same council, *A-G v Council of Birmingham*,[37] the operation of an injunction on the defendant council was suspended for five years in order to give the defendants time to carry out works to prevent river pollution by sewage. The abatement of nuisance caused by pubic works undertaken to improve general public health also provided a spur to councils to build proper sewage works which did not rely on disposal into the nearest river.

5 CONCLUSIONS

During the nineteenth century two tiers of control developed in response to the considerable problems of pollution from industrial and associated activities: the common law of private nuisance and statutory regimes. As seen above, there was some interaction between these two tiers of control. There was a tendency on the part of the judiciary to link the development of industry with the public benefit to be gained from a strong local and national economy. In emphasising this link the common law courts provided a forum in which the costs and benefits of industrial activity could be weighed. They therefore played an important part in legitimating and sanctioning polluting industrial activity which caused discomfort and injury, but also contributed to the nation's economic welfare, with one qualification: the courts continued to be sensitive to the protection of private property as seen in *St Helen's Smelting Co v Tipping* (1865). Furthermore, the principle of private property was elaborated by the courts to provide some protection for landowners against government action designed to improve public health, as seen in the public works cases brought against Birmingham Council by the Attorney General in 1855 and 1880.

On the whole, statutory controls were not premised upon the protection of property. A number of different legislative approaches and techniques was deployed to control air and water pollution. The formation of a national inspectorate under the Alkali Act 1863 was an innovative response to pollution problems. The use of obstructive limitations in statutory enforcement proceedings, for example in areas regarded as 'seats of the manufacturing industry' under the Rivers (Pollution Prevention) Act 1876 was a further technique. The central technique, though, was the use of the 'best practicable means' concept, either in the form of a requirement, as in the Alkali Act 1874, or as a defence to a statutory offence in the Rivers (Pollution Prevention) Act 1876. The concept was premised upon a system of cooperation and conciliation between industrial interests and the regulatory body. The legislature favoured this presumptive, but ultimately abstract concept, in contrast to more clearly defined, substantive, environmental quality standards, such as those later drawn up by the Royal Commission on Sewage Disposal in a Report of 1912-13.[38]

37 (1880) 43 LT 77.

38 Royal Commission on Sewage Disposal, Eighth Report, *Standards and Tests for Sewage and Sewage Effluents Discharging into Rivers and Streams*, (1912-13) Cmnd 6464, stated that inland waters should not have a biological oxygen demand of more than two parts per 100,000.

The common law is inherently reactive to problems of pollution. In the nineteenth century, the legislature similarly reacted to environmental problems rather than pre-empting them. Significantly, the legislature did not countenance the idea of *preventive* legal controls. In a report on the disposal of liquid wastes from manufacturing processes (1914-16), the Royal Commission on Sewage Disposal considered representations that the law should be altered so that every person who proposes to set up works might be required to give notice to the sanitary authority or Rivers Board specifying the steps to be taken to prevent liquid refuse from becoming polluting and that any person failing to give notice or commencing to discharge liquid refuse after his proposals have been disapproved, should incur a penalty. The Commission rejected the representations, believing that 'the suggested procedures might involve needless interference with manufactures'.[39] For this and similar reasons, in the case of air pollution, it was not until the Alkali Etc Works Regulation Act 1906 that legislation introduced a system of prior authorisation for 'scheduled processes'.

In the nineteenth century, environmental protection was viewed as a matter of pollution control over specific areas or activities. The legislature dealt with environmental problems sector by sector, according to either industrial activities such as the Alkali Acts 1863 and 1874, or by environmental media as in the Rivers (Pollution Prevention) Act 1876. As judge-made law was developed in the context of particular fact situations, so too was legislation relating to the environment developed in the context of what were seen as *separate* problems. Little consideration was therefore given to the possible consequences of imposing control on one sector in relation to the others. Such a sectoral and fragmented approach failed spectacularly to appreciate the integrated nature of environmental problems, typically the transfer of pollutants between environmental media, as seen by the pollution of freshwaters by sulphuric acid following compulsory condensation of noxious gases under the Alkali Act 1863 and the building of sewage works which, typically, discharged effluent into the nearest river. Despite the recommendation made by the Derby Committee in 1862 that the laws respecting nuisance should be consolidated and made uniform, 'environmental law' continued to be split between a number of statutes and administered by a number of bodies. The legacy of nineteenth century environmental law is that of a reactive, sectoral, and fragmentary approach to the control of pollution.[40] The roots of the British ad hoc and pragmatic approach to environmental problems are located firmly in this period.

39 Royal Commission on Sewage Disposal, Final Report, *General Summary of Conclusions and Recommendations* (1914-16) Cmnd 7821, at p 17.

40 On the general characteristics of environmental law, see R Macrory 'British Environmental Law: Major Strands and Characteristics' (1989) *Connecticut Journal of International Law* Vol 4, No 2, 287-304.

6 A MODERN POSTSCRIPT: *CAMBRIDGE WATER CO LTD V EASTERN COUNTIES LEATHER PLC*[41]

Cambridge Water Co Ltd v Eastern Counties Leather plc led to a resurgence of interest in the potential contribution of civil liability to protect the environment. In the event, the case brought the limitations of tortious liability sharply into focus again. Cambridge Water Company sought injunctive relief and damages from the defendant manufacturing company, Eastern Counties Leather, in nuisance, negligence, and the rule in *Rylands v Fletcher* for the cost of sinking a borehole into an aquifer on land which it had purchased in 1976. The leather company had polluted water abstracted from the bore-hole with an organic solvent, perchloroethene, so that the water failed to comply with limit standards for the substance which had been set to fulfil European Community obligations under Directive 778/80/EEC on the quality of water intended for human consumption.[42] The tanning process which led to the seepage of the solvent into the water supply had stopped *before* the relevant standards for perchloroethene had been set in the Directive. This is an example *par excellence* of 'historic pollution'.

At first instance, Kennedy J rejected the plaintiff's case in nuisance and negligence on the grounds that the plaintiff must establish that the defendant foresaw the damage occurring and that, in this case, this was not possible: the defendant's employees could not have reasonably foreseen in 1976 or before that solvents were capable of seeping through a concrete floor to the water supply and would therefore result in detectable quantities of perchloroethene being found in the aquifer. He considered that the plaintiff must also fail on the ground of the rule in *Rylands v Fletcher*. The setting of Eastern Counties Leather's works in the 'industrial village' of Sawston, Cambridgeshire, and the benefit of the activity to the local community in terms of employment, meant that the process of tanning leather by applying solvents was not a 'non-natural use' of the land, and thus fell into the broadening category of exceptions under this rule.

Cambridge Water Co Ltd v Eastern Counties Leather plc (1992) JEL Vol 4, No 2, 81 at 97, per Kennedy J

In my judgment, in considering whether the storage of organochlorines as adjunct to a manufacturing process is a non-natural use of land, I must consider whether that storage created special risks for adjacent occupiers and whether the activity was for the general benefit of the community. It seems to me inevitable that I must consider the magnitude of the storage and the geographical area in which it takes place in answering the question. Sawston is properly

41 [1994] 2 AC 264, [1994] 1 All ER 53, HL, and commentary by A Ogus, 'Water Rights Diluted: *Cambridge Water Co Ltd v Eastern Counties Leather plc*' (1994) JEL Vol 6, No 1, 151; see also *Cambridge Water Co Ltd v Eastern Counties Leather plc* [1994] 2 AC 264, [1994] 1 All ER 53, CA.

42 OJ L 229 30.8.80.

described as an industrial village, and the creation of employment is clearly for the benefit of the community. I do not believe that I can enter upon an assessment of the point on a scale of the desirability that the manufacture of wash leathers comes, and I content myself with holding that this storage in this place is a natural use of land. The Plaintiffs have not sought to make any particular point on the proximity of either works to residential areas...I hold that the storage of these chemicals did not amount to a non-natural user of land.

In the Court of Appeal, Mann LJ, giving judgment, found for the appellant water company. He revised the assumption that the appellant's claim in nuisance failed for a reason which assumes that the respondent could be liable for the consequences of the accidental spillage of the solvent only if the respondent had broken a duty to avoid foreseeable damage of a particular kind. Mann LJ was of the view that the courts have identified as an incident of *ownership* of land 'natural rights', such as the right of an owner in regard to naturally occurring water which comes beneath his land by percolation through undefined channels. He considered that the owner's right is to have such of the water as he appropriates by abstraction come to him in an *uncontaminated* condition. The authority for such a proposition is *Ballard v Tomlinson* (1885),[43] another nineteenth century case the facts of which were thought by Mann LJ to be so similar as to be indistinguishable to those in *Cambridge Water*. In *Ballard v Tomlinson*, the plaintiff and defendant were adjacent landowners who each owned a well sunk into a chalk aquifer. The plaintiff pumped water from his well for the purposes of his brewery but the defendant came to use his well as a receptacle for sewage and refuse from his printing house. The sewage and refuse contaminated the water in the chalk to such an extent that the water which the plaintiff pumped became unusable for the brewing process. In the Court of Appeal in *Ballard*, Brett MR described an aquifer as a 'common source', and said: 'it seems to me that although nobody has any property in the common source, yet everybody has a right to appropriate it and appropriate it in its natural state, and no one of those who have a right to appropriate it has a right to contaminate that source so as to prevent his neighbour from having the full value of his right of appropriation'.[44] Applying this judgment in *Cambridge Water*, Mann LJ concluded that *Ballard v Tomlinson* decided that where the nuisance is an interference with a natural right incident to *ownership*, then the liability is strict and negligence plays no part. *Ballard v Tomlinson* was taken to extend the principles applying to riparian rights to abstracters of percolating underground waters and was therefore in favour of the appellant.

The Court of Appeal judgment in *Cambridge Water* is a simplistic form of rights-based liability, so that liability attaches should infringement of a right take place, in this case the 'natural' right to percolating water which is an incident of ownership. The judgment therefore prioritises property rights.[45] The Court of Appeal's decision also appears to have been influenced by aspects

43 (1885) 29 Ch D 115.
44 (1885) 29 Ch D 115 at 121 and 122.
45 Steele, *supra*, at 252.

of contemporary environmental policy. For example it draws upon, and extends, the polluter pays principle to cases of 'historic pollution': the polluting activities took place when the solvent would not have counted as harm for the purposes of tort law; the harm having occurred after the coming into force of Directive 80/778/EEC on the quality of drinking water.

The House of Lords took a very different view. The key part of the judgment is to be found in Goff LJ's distinguishing *Ballard v Tomlinson* on the grounds that the water pollution in that case had been intentional (the discharge of sewage into a sewer) and the water was contained in a definite channel; in *Cambridge Water*, the discharge of solvent was not intentional and the pollution occurred after the solvent had seeped through a floor and percolated through layers of soil and gravel. Goff LJ interprets *Ballard v Tomlinson* as meaning no more than that the owner of land can, without a grant, lawfully *abstract* water which percolates beneath his land – in whatever condition it happens to be in.[46] The plaintiff, therefore, has no right to abstract *uncontaminated* water. Importantly, *Ballard v Tomlinson* is not disapproved, but is described as providing no stricter liability than nuisance.

The House of Lords confirmed the test of foreseeability in actions in nuisance applied by the first instance judge. More surprisingly, the test was also affirmed in the rule of *Rylands v Fletcher* (previously categorised as a classic example of a strict liability offence in tort) for reason that *Rylands v Fletcher* was considered by Goff LJ to be an offshoot of nuisance and therefore not creating a novel form of liability. *Obiter dicta*, Goff LJ considered that Eastern Counties Leather could not possibly have foreseen the damage that would result from their manufacturing process and storage arrangements because of the nature of the pollution and the fact that a test had not been developed for measuring quantities of the solvent in water at the time that the tanning process was carried out.

Cambridge Water Co Ltd v Eastern Counties Leather plc [1994] 2 AC 264, [1994] 1 All ER 53, HL

LORD GOFF OF CHIEVELEY

...

The Decision of the Court of Appeal: *Ballard v Tomlinson*

...

In his judgment in *Ballard v Tomlinson* (1885) 29 Ch D 115, 124 Cotton LJ spoke of the plaintiff's right to abstract percolating water beneath his land as '...a natural right incident to the ownership of his own land...'. In the present context, however, this means no more than the owner of land can, without a grant, lawfully abstract water which percolates beneath his land, his right to do so being protected by the law of tort, by means of an action for an injunction or for damages for nuisance...There is no natural right to percolating water, as

46 See SC Smith, 'How Law Hides Risk', in G Teubner et al (eds) *Environmental Law and Ecological Responsibility* (Chichester: Wiley, 1994) p 132.

there may be to water running in a defined channel; see *Chasemore v Richards* (1859) 7 HL Cas 349, 379, *per* Lord Cranworth, and *Halsbury's Laws of England* 4th ed, vol. 49, para 392. In the present case Mann LJ stated (at p 15B) that *Ballard v Tomlinson* (1885) 29 Ch D 115 decided that 'where the nuisance is an interference with a natural right incident to ownership then the liability is a strict one'. In my opinion, however, if in this passage Mann LJ intended to say that the defendant was liable which he could not reasonably have foreseen, that conclusion cannot be drawn from the judgments in the case, in which the point did not arise. As I read the judgments, they disclose no more than that, in the circumstance of the case, the defendant was liable to the plaintiff in tort for the contamination of the source of water supplying the plaintiff's well, either on the basis of the rule in *Rylands v Fletcher* or under the law of nuisance, by reason of interference with the plaintiff's use and enjoyment of his land, including his right to extract water percolating beneath his land. It follows that the question whether such a liability may be attached in any particular case must depend upon the principles governing liability under one or other of those two heads of the law. To those principles, therefore, I now turn.

Nuisance and the rule in Rylands v Fletcher

As I have already recorded, there was no appeal by CWC to the Court of Appeal against the judge's conclusion in nuisance. The question of ECL's liability in nuisance on the principle was laid down, as they saw it, in *Ballard v Tomlinson.* Since, for the reasons I have given, that case does not give rise to any principle of law independent of the ordinary law of nuisance or the rule in *Rylands v Fletcher,* the strict position now is that CWC, having abandoned its claim in nuisance, can only uphold the decision of the Court of Appeal on the basis of the rule in *Rylands v Fletcher.* However, one important submission advanced by ECL before the Appellate Committee was that strict liability for an escape only arises under that rule where the defendant knows or reasonably ought to have foreseen, when collecting the relevant things on his land, that those things might, if they escaped, cause damage of the relevant kind. Since there is a close relationship between the nuisance and the rule in *Rylands v Fletcher,* I myself find it very difficult to form an opinion as to the validity of that submission without first considering whether foreseeability of such damage is an essential element in the law of nuisance. For that reason, therefore, I do not feel able altogether to ignore the latter question simply because it was no longer pursued by CWC before the Court of Appeal.

In order to consider the question in the present case in its proper legal context, it is desirable to look at the nature of liability in a case such as the present in relation both to the law of nuisance and the rule in *Rylands v Fletcher,* and for that purpose to consider the relationship between the two heads of liability.

I begin with the law of nuisance. Our modern understanding of the nature and scope of nuisance was much enhanced by Professor Newark's seminal Article on 'The Boundaries of Nuisance' (1949) 65 LQR, 480. The Article is avowedly a historical analysis, in that it traces the nature of the tort of nuisance to its origins, and demonstrates how the original view of nuisance as a tort of land (or more accurately, to accommodate interference with servitudes, a tort directed against the plaintiff's enjoyment of rights over land) became distorted as the tort was extended to embrace claims for personal injuries even where the plaintiff's injury did not occur while using land in his occupation. In Professor Newark's opinion (p. 487), this development produced adverse effects, viz that liability which should have arisen only under the law of negligence was allowed under the law of nuisance which historically was a tort of strict liability; and that there was a tendency for 'cross-infection to take place, and notions of negligence began to make an appearance in the realm of nuisance proper'. But in addition, Professor Newark considered (pp. 487-488), it contributed to a misapprehension of the decision in *Rylands v Fletcher.*

'This case is generally regarded as an important landmark, indeed a turning point – in the law of tort; but an examination of the judgments shows that those who decided it were quite unconscious of any revolutionary or reactionary principles implicit in the decision. They thought of it as calling for no more than a restatement of settled principles, and Lord Cairns went so far as to describe those principles as "extremely simple". And in fact the main principle involved was extremely simple, being no more than the principle that negligence is not an element in the tort of nuisance. It is true that Blackburn J in his great judgment in the Exchequer Chamber never once used the word "nuisance", but three times he cited the case of fumes escaping from an alkali works – a clear case of nuisance – as an instance of liability, under the rule which he was laying down. Equally it is true that in 1866 there were a number of cases in the reports suggesting that persons who controlled dangerous things were under a duty to take care, but as none of these cases had anything to do with nuisance Blackburn J did not refer to them.

'But the profession as a whole, whose conceptions of the boundaries of nuisance were now becoming fogged, failed to see in *Rylands v Fletcher* a simple case of nuisance. They regarded it as an exceptional case – and the rule in *Rylands v Fletcher* as a generalisation of exceptional cases, where liability was to be strict on account of the "magnitude of danger, coupled with the difficulty of proving negligence" [*Pollock, Torts,* 14th ed, p. 386] rather than on account of the nature of the plaintiff's interest which was invaded. They therefore jumped rashly to two conclusions: firstly, that the rule in *Rylands v Fletcher* could be extended beyond the case of neighbouring occupiers; and secondly, that the Rule could be used to afford a remedy in cases of personal injury. Both these conclusions were stoutly denied by Lord Macmillan in *Read v J Lyons & Co Ltd* [1947] AC 156, [1946] 2 All ER 471, but it remains to be seen whether the House of Lords will support his opinion when the precise point comes up for decision.'

We are not concerned in the present case with the problem of personal injuries, but we are concerned with the scope of liability in nuisance and in *Rylands v Fletcher.* In my opinion it is right to take as our starting point the fact that, as Professor Newark considered, *Rylands v Fletcher* was indeed not regarded by Blackburn J as a revolutionary decision: see, e.g., his observations in *Ross v Fedden* (1872) 26 LT 966, 968. He believed himself not to be creating new law, but to be stating existing law, on the basis of existing authority; and, as is apparent from his judgment, he was concerned in particular with the situation where the defendant collects things upon his land which are likely to do mischief if they escape, in which event the defendant will be strictly liable for damage resulting from any such escape. It follows that the essential basis of liability was the collection by the defendant of such things upon his land; and the consequence was strict liability in the event of damage caused by their escape, even if the escape was an isolated event. Seen in its context, there is no reason to suppose that Blackburn J intended to create a liability any more strict than that created by the law of nuisance; but even so he must have intended that, in the circumstances specified by him there should be liability for damage resulting from an isolated escape.

Of course, although liability for nuisance has generally been regarded as strict, at least in the case of a defendant who has been responsible for the creation of a nuisance, even so that liability has been kept under control by the principle of reasonable user – the principle of give and take as between neighbouring occupiers of land, under which '...those acts necessary for the common and ordinary use and occupation of land and houses may be done, if conveniently done, without subjecting those who do them to an action': see *Bamford v Turnley* (1860) 3 B & S 62, 83, *per* Bramwell B. The effect is that, if the user is reasonable, the defendant will not be liable for consequent harm to his neighbour's enjoyment of his land; but if the user is not reasonable, the defendant will be liable, even though he may have exercised reasonable care and skill to avoid it. Strikingly, a comparable principle has developed which limits liability under the rule in *Rylands v Fletcher*. This is the principle of natural use of the land. I shall have to consider the principle at a later stage in this judgment. The most authoritative statement of the principle is now to be found in the advice of the Privy Council delivered by Lord Moulton in *Rickards v Lothian* [1913] AC 263, 280 when he said of the rule in *Rylands v Fletcher*:

> 'It is not every use to which land is put that brings into play that principle. It must be some special use bringing with it increased dangers to others, and must not merely be the ordinary use of the land or such a use as is proper for the general benefit of the community.'

It is not necessary for me to identify precise differences which may be drawn between this principle, and the principle of reasonable user as applied in the law of nuisance. It is enough for the present purposes that I should draw attention to a similarity of function. The effect of this principle is that, where it applies, there will be no liability under the rule in *Rylands v Fletcher*, but that where it does not apply, ie where there is a non-natural use, the defendant will be liable for harm caused by the plaintiff by the escape, notwithstanding that he has exercised all reasonable care and skill to prevent the escape from occurring.

Foreseeability of damage in nuisance

It is against this background that it is necessary to consider the question whether foreseeability of harm of the relevant type is an essential element of liability either in nuisance or under the rule in *Rylands v Fletcher*. I shall take first the case of nuisance. In the present case, as I have said, this is not strictly speaking a live issue. Even so, I propose briefly to address it, as part of the analysis of the background to the present case.

...We are concerned with the liability of a person where a nuisance has been created by one for whose action he is responsible. Here, as I have said, it is still the law that the fact that the defendant has taken all reasonable care will not of itself exonerate him from liability, the relevant control mechanism being found within the principle of reasonable user. But it by no means follows that the defendant should be held liable for damage of a type which he could not reasonably foresee; and the development of the law of negligence in the past sixty years points strongly toward a requirement that such foreseeability should be a prerequisite of liability in damages for nuisance, as it is of liability in negligence. For if a plaintiff is in ordinary circumstances only able to claim damages in respect of personal injuries where he can prove such foreseeability on the part of the defendant, it is difficult to see why, in common justice, he should be in a stronger position to claim damages for interference with the enjoyment of his land where the defendant was unable to foresee such damage. Moreover, this appears to have been the conclusion of the Privy Council in *Overseas Tankship (UK) Ltd v Miller Co Pty, The Wagon Mound (No 2)* [1967] 1 AC 617. The facts of the case are too well known to require repetition, but they gave rise to a claim for damages arising from a public nuisance caused by a spillage of oil in Sydney Harbour. Lord Reid, who delivered the advice of the Privy Council, considered that, in the class of nuisance which included the case before the Board, foreseeability is an essential element in determining liability. He then continued, at p. 640:

> 'It could not be right to discriminate between different cases of nuisance so as to make foreseeability a necessary element in determining damages in those cases where it is a necessary element in determining liability, but not in others. So the choice is between it being a necessary element in all cases of nuisance or in none. In their Lordships' judgment the similarities between nuisance and other forms of tort to which the *Wagon Mound (No 1)* applies far outweigh any differences and they must therefore hold that the judgment appealed from is wrong on this branch of the case. It is not sufficient that the injury suffered by the respondents' vessel was the direct result of the nuisance if that injury was in the relevant sense unforeseeable.'

It is widely accepted that this conclusion, although not essential to the decision of the particular case, has nevertheless settled the law to the effect that foreseeability of harm is indeed a prerequisite of the recovery of damages in private nuisance, as in the case of public nuisance.

...

Foreseeability of damage under the rule in Rylands v Fletcher

It is against this background that I turn to the submission advanced by ECL before your Lordships that there is a similar prerequisite of recovery of damages under the rule in *Rylands v Fletcher*.

I start with the judgment of Blackburn J in *Rylands v Fletcher* itself (1866) LR 1 Exch 265. His celebrated statement of the law is to be found at pp. 279-280, where he said:

> 'We think that the true rule of law is, that the person who for his own purposes brings on his lands and collects and keeps there anything likely to do mischief if it escapes, must keep it in at his peril, and, if he does not do so is prima facie answerable for all the damage which is the natural consequence of its escape. He can excuse himself by showing that the escape was owing to the plaintiff's default: or perhaps that the escape was the consequence of vis major, or the act of God; but as nothing of this sort exists here, it is unnecessary to inquire what excuse would be sufficient. The general rule, as above stated, seems on principle just. The person whose grass or corn is eaten down by the escaping cattle of his neighbour, or whose mine is flooded by the water from his neighbour's privy, or whose habitation is made unhealthy by the fumes and noisome vapours of his neighbour's alkali works, is damnified without any fault of his own; and it seems but reasonable and just that the neighbour, who has brought something on his property which was not naturally there, harmless to others so long as it is confined to his own property but which he knows to be mischievous if it gets on his neighbour's, should be obliged to make good the damage which ensues if he does not succeed in confining it to his own property. But for his act in bringing it there no mischief could have accrued, and it seems but just that he should at his peril keep it there so that no mischief may accrue, or answer for the natural and anticipated consequences. And upon authority, this we think is established to be the law whether the things brought be beasts, or water, or filth, or stenches.'

In that passage, Blackburn J spoke of 'anything *likely* to do mischief if it escapes'; and later he spoke of something 'which he *knows* to be mischievous if it gets on to his neighbour's [property]', and the liability to 'answer to the natural *and anticipated* consequences'. Furthermore, time and again he spoke of the strict liability imposed upon the defendant as being that he must keep the thing in at his peril; and, when referring to liability in actions for damage occasioned by animals, he referred (p. 282) to the established principle 'that it is quite immaterial whether the escape is by negligence or not'. The general tenor of his statement of principle is therefore that knowledge, or at least foreseeability, of the risk is a prerequisite of the recovery of damages under the principle; but that the principle is one of strict liability in the sense that the defendant may be held liable notwithstanding that he has exercised all due care to prevent the escape from occurring.

There are, however, early authorities in which foreseeability of damage does not appear to have been regarded as necessary (see, eg, *Humphries v Cousins* (1877) 2 CPD 239). Moreover, it was submitted by Mr Ashworth for CWC that the requirement of foreseeability of damage was negatived in two particular cases, the decision of the Court of Appeal in *West v Bristol Tramways Co* [1908] 2 KB 14, and the decision of this House in *Rainham Chemical Works Ltd v Belvedere Fish Guano Co Ltd* [1921] 2 AC 465.

[Lord Goff discusses the latter two cases and continues]

...

Even so, the question cannot be considered solely as a matter of history. It can be argued that the rule in *Rylands v Fletcher* should not be regarded simply as an extension of the law of nuisance, but should rather be treated as a developing principle of strict liability from which can be derived a general rule of strict liability for damage caused by ultra-hazardous operations, on the basis of which persons conducting such operations may properly be held strictly liable for the extraordinary risk to others involved in such operations. As is pointed out in *Fleming on Torts*, 8th ed., pp. 327-328, this would lead to the practical result that the cost of damage resulting from such operations would have to be absorbed as part of the overheads of the relevant business rather than be borne (where there is no negligence) by the injured person or his insurers, or even by the community at large. Such a development appears to have been taking place in the United States, as can be seen from paragraph 519 of the *Restatement of Torts* (2d), vol. 3 (1977). The extent to which it has done so is not altogether clear; and I infer from paragraph 519, and the comments on that paragraph, that the abnormally dangerous activities there referred to are such that their ability to cause harm would be obvious to any reasonable person who carried them on.

I have to say, however, that there are serious obstacles in the way of the development of the rule in *Rylands v Fletcher* in this way. First of all, if it was so to develop, it should logically apply to liability to all persons suffering injury by reason of the ultra-hazardous operations; but the decision of this House in *Read v J Lyons & Co Ltd* [1947] AC 156, which establishes that there can be no liability under the rule except in circumstances where the injury has been caused by an escape from land under the control of the defendant, has effectively precluded any such development. Professor Fleming has observed that 'the most damaging effect of the decision in *Read* v *Lyons* is that it prematurely stunted the development of a general theory of strict liability for ultra-hazardous activities' (see *Fleming on Torts*, 8th ed, p. 341). Even so, there is much to be said for the view that the courts should not be proceeding down the path of developing such a general theory. In this connection, I refer in particular to the Report of the Law Commission on Civil Liability for Dangerous Things and Activities (Law Comm. No. 32), 170. In paragraphs 14-16 of the Report, the Law Commission expressed serious misgivings about the adoption of any test for the application of strict liability involving a general concept of 'especially dangerous' or 'ultra hazardous' activity, having regard to the uncertainties and practical difficulties of its application. If the Law Commission is unwilling to consider statutory reform on this basis, it must follow that judges should if anything be even more reluctant to proceed down that path.

...I incline to the opinion that, as a general rule, it is more appropriate for strict liability in respect of operations of high risk to be imposed by Parliament, than by the courts. If such liability is imposed by statute, the relevant activities can be identified, and those concerned can know where they stand. Furthermore, statute can where appropriate lay down precise criteria establishing the incidence and scope of such liability. It is of particular relevance that the present case is concerned with environmental pollution. The protection and preservation of the environment is now perceived as being of crucial importance to the future of mankind; and public bodies, both national and international, are taking significant steps towards the establishment of legislation which will promote the protection of the environment, and make the polluter pay for damage to the environment for which he is responsible – as can be seen from the WHO, EEC, and national regulations to which I have previously referred. But it does not follow from these developments that a common law principle, such as the rule in *Rylands v Fletcher*, should be developed or rendered more strict to provide for liability in respect of such pollution. On the contrary, given that so much well-informed and carefully structured legislation is now being put in place for this purpose, there is less need for the courts to develop a common law principle to achieve the same end, and indeed it may well be undesirable that they should do so.

Having regard to these considerations, and in particular to the step which this House has already taken in *Read v Lyons* to contain the scope of liability under the rule in *Rylands v Fletcher*, it appears to me to be appropriate now to take the view that foreseeability of damage of the relevant type should be regarded as a prerequisite of liability in damages under the rule. Such a conclusion can, as I have already stated, be derived from Blackburn J's original statement of the law; and I can see no good reason why this prerequisite should not be recognised under the rule as it has been in the case of private nuisance. In particular, I do not regard the two authorities cited to your Lordships, *West v Bristol Tramways Co* [1908] 2 KB 14 and *Rainham Chemical Works Ltd v Belvedere Fish Guano Co* [1921] 2 AC 465, as providing any strong pointer towards a contrary conclusion. It would, moreover, lead to a more coherent body of common law principles if the rule were to be regarded essentially as an extension of the law of nuisance to cases of isolated escapes from land, even though the rule as established is not limited to escapes which are in fact isolated. I wish to point out, however, that in truth the escape of the PCE from ECL's land, in the form of the trace elements carried in percolating water has not been an isolated escape, but a continuing escape resulting from a state of affairs which has come into existence at the base of the chalk aquifer underneath ECL's premises. Classically, this would have been regarded as a case of nuisance; and it would seem strange if by characterising the case as one falling under the rule in *Rylands v Fletcher*, the liability should thereby be rendered more strict in the circumstances of the present case.

The facts of the present case

Turning to the facts of the present case, it is plain to see that, at the time when the PCE was brought onto ECL's land, and indeed when it was used in the tanning process there, nobody at ECL could reasonably have foreseen the resultant damage which occurred at CWC's borehole at Sawston.

...

Cambridge Water is evocative of the nineteenth century cases and legal preoccupations we have discussed above – the protection of the environment within a legal framework of protection of private property, a concern not to damage 'any seat of manufacturing industry', and concepts of 'natural rights' in natural resources. The importance of the case lies in its implications for a future restricted role of civil liability in environmental protection, due largely to the requirement that a plaintiff must establish a defendant had foreseen that environmental harm would be the consequence of his or her actions and activities. It is possible that, by softening traditional notions of strict liability, *Cambridge Water* may create further obstacles to the protection of the environment through enforcement of private property rights in circumstances in which rights are more certain than those asserted in the case.[47] The restricted nature of the role of the common law in environmental protection is recognised by Lord Goff in his examination of the interaction between common law principles and environmental protection legislation: '...given that so much well-informed and carefully structured legislation is now being put in place for this purpose, there is less need for the courts to develop a common law principle to achieve the same end, and indeed it may well be undesirable that they should do so.'[48] Contrasting the regimes in such a way highlights that common law is, by its very nature, reactive, with its primary concern to compensate for past damage, notwithstanding the role of the injunction; and is thus limited in terms of *preventing* environmental harm.

In *Cambridge Water* one can see the development of legal responses to pollution coming full circle. In the nineteenth century, the limitations of private common law in controlling industrial activities provided the stimulus for the development of statutory regimes. In the current political climate of deregulation in the environmental field, *Cambridge Water* performed the part of a test case for determining what role private common law should play, should extensive deregulation materialise. In other words, to what extent can systems of compensation (with insurance at centre stage) take the place of 'command and control' systems of environmental protection? The message sent by Lord Goff is that regulatory responses are fully worked out and currently satisfy the needs for protection in a manner which cannot yet be replaced by private common law actions. In *Cambridge Water*, emphasis was placed upon the fact that future legislation on civil liability for pollution was unlikely to extend to cases of 'historic pollution'.[49] The imposition of liability for such pollution at common law in *Cambridge Water* would therefore have been an unusual step. In the event, the House of Lords' decision not to extend liability to such cases reveals an unwillingness to contemplate a separate role for the common law where the legislature is already showing signs of activity, or a role beyond that offered by existing statutory regimes.[50]

Remarkable though it might seem, it has been said that environmentalists might draw some comfort from the House of Lords' decision in *Cambridge Water*. First, although admittedly *obiter*, Lord Goff's judgment suggests that in cases where harm can be said to be reasonably foreseeable, such as *continuing* to allow perchloroethene to seep through ground post-*Cambridge Water*, there is support for plaintiffs to sue in nuisance or under the rule in *Rylands v Fletcher*. The second, possibly cold comfort, is Lord Goff's tightening up of the 'non-natural user of land' exception to the rule in *Rylands v Fletcher*. Having established that the storage of chemicals in substantial quantities and their use in the manner employed by Eastern Counties Leather cannot fall within the exception, he exposes the artificial use of the term 'non-natural user of land':

47 A Ogus, 'Water Rights Diluted', (1994) JEL Vol 6, No 1, 151 at 156.

48 *Cambridge Water Co v Eastern Counties Leather* [1994] 2 AC 264, [1994] 1 All ER 53.

49 See, for example, European Commission, *Green Paper on Remedying Environmental Damage* COM (93) 47 final.

50 Steele, *supra*, at 250.

> 'It may well be that now that it is recognised that foreseeability of harm of the relevant type is a prerequisite of liability in damages under the rule, the courts may feel less pressure to extend the concept of natural use to circumstances such as those in the present case; and in due course it may become easier to control this exception, and to ensure that it has a more recognisable basis of principle.'[51]

These lighter points apart, *Cambridge Water* still serves as a reminder of the continuing reliance of environmental law on the state of scientific knowledge and methods. In this case, the test for the solvent was developed some years after the spillages of the substance had occurred. This gap in knowledge, critically, made the House of Lords unwilling to impose what would amount to retrospective liability on the defendant company. The infusion of foreseeability in nuisance and *Rylands v Fletcher* might also be seen to mitigate further against the acceptance of the precautionary principle. The judgment states that a polluter should not be liable for environmental or other harm should that harm not be foreseeable. This contradicts the fundamental premise of the precautionary principle: that action should be taken, and, potentially, liability should bite in a prima facie case. A strong version of the principle would require action even in the absence of proof of harm. *Cambridge Water* represents a significant 'anti-precautionary' trend which may prove difficult to disengage in future. The result of the case also leaves the polluter pays principle redundant. If Eastern Counties Leather does not pay for the pollution it caused, who should?

Notwithstanding the distinctly Victorian flavour of the case, the further significance of *Cambridge Water* is its highlighting that European Community law plays a central role in attributing environmental responsibilities and conferring environmental rights in law in the United Kingdom, a central theme of this book. The *Cambridge Water* saga was triggered by the implementation of Directive 80/778/EEC on the quality of drinking water which potentially rendered illegal the seepage of the solvent to groundwater to be used for drinking and for use in food. Notably, the 'absolute' limit for substances such as solvents set by the Directive differs considerably from the more abstract and relative concepts and principles which characterise tort law such as the 'natural' state of water, in *John Young & Co v Bankier Distillery Co*,[52] and the 'non-natural user of land' exception in *Rylands v Fletcher*. There is also an uncommunautaire reluctance on the part of some of the judges in this case to impose liability for exceeding an environmental quality standard for perchloroethene set by the European Community, which was considered to be a stricter standard for the substance than that recommended by the World Health Organisation.[53] Such a reluctance may also be seen with regard to other Community environmental legislation, as discussed in chapters 9, 10 and 11.

To continue the European theme, the European Commission has proposed a Community-wide system of civil liability for environmental damage. Although it is by no means clear that cases of historic pollution, such as in *Cambridge Water* will be caught by a European measure, the Comission's paper sees that

51 (1994) JEL, Vol 6, No 1, 137 at 151.
52 [1893] AC 691, [1891-4] All ER Rep 439, HL.
53 See ch 9.

civil liability for the cost of cleaning up environmental contamination would be in line with the imperatives of the polluter pays principle and principle of prevention. The following extract from the proposal begs the question whether civil liability systems in the area of product safety and consumer protection can be successfully transferred to the environmental field in cases such as *Cambridge Water*.

Commission of the European Communities, *Green Paper on Remedying Environmental Damage* COM(93) 47, Brussels

A Community-wide system of civil liability for environmental damage would draw on a basic and universal principle of civil law, the concept that a person should rectify damage that he causes. This legal principle is strongly related to two principles forming the basis of Community environmental policy since the adoption of the Single Act, the principle of prevention and the "polluter pays" principle.

The "polluter pays" principle is evoked because civil liability is a means for making parties causing pollution to pay for damage that results. The prevention principle is involved in that potential polluters who know they will be liable for the costs of remedying the damage they cause have a strong incentive to avoid causing such damage.

If civil liability for environmental damage operates differently in Member States, industries in some Member States will be required to pay the costs of the damage they cause, while industries in other Member States will be able to avoid those costs, because restoration is not required or the cost is passed on to the taxpayers. Industries not required to pay restoration costs receive, in effect, a competitive advantage.

...

2.2.3 The position taken at Community level

Community-wide action involving the doctrine of civil liability has been taken primarily in the area of product safety and consumer protection. In 1985, the Council adopted Directive 85/374/EEC instituting strict liability for the producer of defective products.[54] The Directive is based on the concept of the "defective product", i.e. a product which does not provide the safety which a person is entitled to expect. It provides that the *manufacturer of the defective product* is liable for the damage, even where not at fault, unless he can prove that the product's defect is due to compliance with mandatory regulations issued by public authorities. The Directive covers only losses suffered by a private consumer. It does not cover *damage to the environment*, if that damage is not damage to property owned by a private person. The question of *insurability* is not addressed in the framework of this Directive.

54 Council Directive 85/374/EEC of 25 July 1985 on the approximation of the laws, regulations and admininstrative provisions of the Member States concerning liability for defective products (OJ No L 210, 7.8.85, p 29).

Applications of civil liability for environmental protection purposes have been discussed for some time. In 1984, for instance, the Council adopted Directive 84/631/EEC on the supervision and control within the European Community of the transfrontier shipment of hazardous waste.[55] The 19th recital called for defining of the liability of the producer and any other person accountable for damage "in order to guarantee effective and fair compensation for damage which may be caused during the shipment of dangerous waste". Article 11(3) expressly provided for the Council to determine the conditions for implementing civil liability for the producer.

In 1986, following the Sandoz fire which resulted in the poisoning of the Rhine River, the Council declared that the key to more effective protection of Community waterways lay in, inter alia, prompt cleanup and restoration, coupled with equitable arrangements for liability and compensation by the polluters for any damage caused.[56] It called on the Commission to review the Community's existing measures for preventing pollution and for remedying damage caused by pollution and, if necessary, to submit appropriate proposals. Two weeks later the European Parliament adopted a complementary resolution calling expressly on the Commission to "put forward proposals for a Community system governing fault [sic] liability for accidents connected with all chemical and high risk activities".[57]

The adoption of the Single Act in 1986 and the insertion of Art. 130r into the EEC Treaty provided impetus for further discussion of civil liability for environmental damage. This Article provides that action by the Community relating to the environment shall be based, *inter alia*, on the principle that the polluter should pay. The *"polluter pays" principle* seeks to properly attribute external costs of pollution. Community applications to date have aimed at making operators bear the costs of environmental protection measures imposed on the public authorities.[58] In addition, the Directives on waste, waste oil, and toxic and dangerous waste[59] make express reference to the "polluter pays" principle as the basis for a system making the holder and/or the producer of waste responsible for the costs of safe disposal. Civil liability for the cost of cleaning up environmental contamination would be a concrete application of this principle.

In response to these developments, the Fourth Environmental Action Programme,[60] released in 1987, declared that the Commission would consider the scope for arriving at a better definition of responsibility in the field of the

55 OJ No L 326, 13.12.84, p 31.

56 Bull EC 11-1986, point 2.1.146.

57 Doc B2 – 1259/86, OJ No C 7, 12.01.87, p. 116. The French text calls for 'responsabilité civile sans faute'.

58 An elaboration of the 'polluter pays principle' can be found in Council Recommendation 79/3/EEC, OJ No L 5, 9.1.79, p 29.

59 Council Directive 75/442/EEC, OJ No L 194, 25.7.75, p 39; Council Directive 75/439/EEC, OJ No L 194, 25.7.75, p 23; Council Directive 78/319/EEC, OJ No L 326, 13.12.84, p 31.

60 Resolution of the Council and of the representatives of the Governments of the Member States, meeting within the Council of 19 October 1987, on the continuation and implementation of a European Community policy and action programme on the environment (1987-1992), OJ No C 328, 7.12.87, p 15, paragraph 2.5.5.

environment, and envisaged the possibility that the polluter should assume greater liability for damage caused by products or processes. In addition, after requests in 1989 and 1990 from the European Parliament for an absolute liability regime for damage resulting from the release into the environment of genetically modified organisms, the Commission pledged to consider the issue of civil liability for damage to the environment horizontally.[61]

In October 1989, the Commission presented a proposal for a Council Directive on civil liability for damage caused by waste.[62] This proposes a no-fault liability regime. As regards the *channelling of liability* the Directive states that the producer of waste shall be strictly liable for damage and impairment of the environment caused by waste. The party bringing the action must demonstrate the causal link between the waste and the damage. The draft Directive extends the notion of *damage* to "impairment of the environment" ... This definition of impairment is capable of including cases where the environment is affected in a continuing manner. Regarding the question of *insurance* the draft Directive requires the producer and eliminator of waste to be covered by insurance or other financial security. Article 3(2) of the proposed Directive states that the producer must include in his annual report the name of his insurers for civil liability purposes. The draft Directive also authorizes the Commission to study the feasibility of setting up a compensation fund for damage and impairment to the environment caused by waste in cases where the person liable cannot be identified or is insolvent. The initial proposal for a Directive has been amended to incorporate proposals made by the Parliament,[63] and is under consideration by the Council.

In the Commission proposal for a Council Directive on the Landfill of Waste Article 14 provides that "the operator shall be liable under civil law for the damage and impairment of the environment caused by the landfilled waste, irrespective of fault on his part".[64]

61 SEC (89) 2091 final – SYN 131, 6.12.89.
62 OJ No C 251, 4.10.89, p 3.
63 OJ No C 192, 23.07.91, p 6.
64 OJ No C 190 22.07.91, p 1.

CHAPTER 3

Containing Arcadia: early land use and development controls

1 INTRODUCTION

In this chapter we critically analyse the development of controls over land use and development which, with those over industrial activities described in the previous chapter, constituted early environmental regulation. We take land use controls to include not just town planning but also controls over makeshift development in rural areas, and the fashioning of the 'made' environment – gardens and parks – in country estates. The development of controls over the use and development of land is usually presented in an uncritical manner. There is another point of view: that controls arose to contain, or incorporate into legal form, radical socialist movements, social welfare experiments and utopian or arcadian visions. More prosaically, but no less idealistically, some social movements and groups formed primarily to protect wildlife or to campaign for access to the countryside contributed to legal development in this area. The inclusion of radical and utopian ideals within legal regimes is instructive, particularly when viewed in the light of contemporary attempts to engender social change, both by using law and outwith the legal system. A modern example of an attempt to build a better world (outside the constraints imposed by planning law) – 'millennium plotlands' – is therefore included as a new twist on the idealism of the garden city movement which informed town planning and the utopian heritage of the environmental movement. The vocabulary, ideology, and frustrations of those advocating the use of rural areas for self-sufficient, sustainable farming are familiar, as is the legal response.

2 ORIGINS AND EVOLUTION OF LAND USE CONTROLS

(a) Public health

The roots of land use and development controls lie predominantly in the public health movement of the second half of the nineteenth century with its concerns for the, usually urban, community's health, the removal of nuisances and sanitation. To achieve these objectives, there were powers to make and enforce by-laws for controlling street widths, and the height, structure and layout of buildings. Edwin Chadwick's Public Health Act 1848 made provision for the registration of lodging houses and requirements for water supply, drains and the provision of water closets. The legal provisions were strong and prescriptive.

1848 Public Health Act

XLLX. And be it enacted, That it shall not be lawful newly to erect any House, or to rebuild any House which may have been pulled down to or below the Floor commonly called the Ground Floor, or to occupy any House so newly erected or rebuilt, unless or until a covered Drain or Drains be constructed, of such Size and Materials, and at such Level and with such Fall as upon the Report of the Surveyor shall appear to be necessary and sufficient for the proper and effectual Drainage of the same and its Appurtenances; and if the Sewer of the Local Board of Health, or a Sewer which they are entitled to use, be within One hundred Feet of any Part of the Site of the House to be built or rebuilt, the Drain or Drains so to be constructed shall lead from and communicate with such one of those Means of Drainage be within One hundred Feet of any Part of the Site of the House to be built or rebuilt, the Drain or Drains shall lead from and communicate with such one of those Means of Drainage as the said Local Board shall direct, or if no such Means of Drainage be within that Distance then the last-mentioned Drain or Drains shall communicate with and be emptied into such covered Cesspool or other Place, not being under any House, as the said Local Board shall direct; and whosoever erects or rebuilds any House or constructs any Drain contrary to this Enactment shall be liable for every such Offence to a Penalty not exceeding Fifty Pounds, which may be recovered by any Person, with full Costs of Suit, by Action of Debt; and if at any Time, upon the Report of the Surveyor, it appear to the said Local Board that any House, whether built before or after the Time when this Act is applied to the District in which it is situate, is without any Drain, or without such a Drain or Drains communicating with the Sea...they shall cause Notice in Writing to be given to the Owner or Occupier of such House, requiring him forthwith, or within such reasonable Time as shall be specified therein, to construct and lay down, in connexion with such House and One of those Means of Drainage...and if such Notice be not complied with the said Local Board may, if they shall think fit, do the Works mentioned or referred to therein and the Expenses incurred by them in so doing shall be recoverable by them from the Owner in a summary Manner...

Pragmatic though his health reforms were, Chadwick was as much an idealist as the utopian thinkers who were his contemporaries. His general concern was with the dignity of humans – particularly when they were diseased and dying. The public health movement, headed by Chadwick, challenged the prevailing ethos of the sanctity of the landlords' rights to develop and use property as and how they desired. The conflict which arose between proprietorial rights and local government powers to regulate the use and development of land is seen clearly in *Cooper v Wandsworth Board of Works*[1] in which the plaintiff had failed to give notice to Wandsworth Board of Works of building works as required

1 (1863) 143 ER 414.

under the Local Management Act 1855, thus denying the Board the opportunity of directing the plaintiff developer how to build sewerage and drainage systems. In this case the 'public interest' is aligned with the plaintiff's proprietorial rights.

This judicial approach to the task of mediating between the interests of the general public and the individual landowner has informed modern planning law.

Cooper v Wandsworth Board of Works (1863) 143 ER 414

Erle, C.J.: I am of the opinion that this rule ought to be discharged. This was an action of trespass by the plaintiff against the Wandsworth district board, for pulling down and demolishing his house; and the ground of defence that has been put forward by the defendants has been under the 76th section of the Metropolis Local Management Act, 18 & 19 Vict. c. 120. By the part of the section which applies to this case, it is enacted that, before any person shall begin to build a new house, he shall give seven days' notice to the district board of his intention to build; and it provides at the end that, in default of such notice it shall be lawful for the district board to demolish the house. The district board here say that no notice was given by the plaintiff of his intention to build the house in question, wherefore they demolished it. The contention on the part of the plaintiff has been that, although the words of the statute, taken in their literal sense, without any qualification at all, would create a justification for the act which the district board has done, the powers granted by the statute are subject to a qualification which has been repeatedly recognised, that no man is to be deprived of his property without his having an opportunity of being heard. The evidence here shews that the plaintiff and the district board have not been quite on amicable terms. Be that as it may, the district board say that no notice was given and that consequently they had a right to proceed to demolish the house without delay, and without notice to the party whose house was to be pulled down, and without giving him the opportunity of shewing any reason why the board should delay. I think that the power which is granted by the 76th section is subject to the qualification suggested. It is a power carrying with it enormous consequences. The house in question was built only to a certain extent. But the power claimed would apply to a complete house. It would apply to a house of any value and completed to any extent; and it seems to me to be a power which may be exercised most perniciously, and that the limitation which we are going to put upon it is one which is required by a due consideration for the public interest.

(b) Utopianism and the garden city movement

The roots of land use controls might lie primarily in the public health movement, but utopian and socialist thinkers were also influential in planning experiments such as the creation of the 'industrial paradise' at Bourneville and the building of garden cities, both of which had an impact on the course of planning. Such experiments advocated not just interference with property rights, as was the case with much public health legislation, but a radical rethinking of property ownership and organisation of space, sometimes along utopian lines. Ideas of 'the environment' have a rich heritage in utopian writing. A common strand is that the control of land use and the appurtenances of the land – fruits, animals, soil – is to be achieved by wide-scale social reform rather than by individual legal mechanisms. These social reforms centre upon the common ownership and equal distribution of land, and the relationship of man to the natural world. The ties between society and the environment were perceived by utopian thinkers to be very strong; a deeply *social* notion of the environment prevailed.

An idea of the environment as utopia can be traced to the ideas of Thomas Spence in the eighteenth century. For Spence, land and liberty were fundamental rights, neither of which could exist without the other. In his *Rights of Man*, he wrote 'the country of any people in a native state is properly their common, in which each of them has an equal property, with free liberty to sustain himself and connexions with the animals, fruits and other products thereof'. Spence describes how land, with all its appurtenances, was claimed by landlords, usurpers and tyrants and divided among themselves. In contrast, in Spence's utopia, 'Spensonia', an imaginary island off the coast of America, the inhabitants reassert their natural rights to common land and its products.

T Spence, *The Rights of Man* (London: Philosophical Society, 4th edn, 1793) pp 11-12

Therefore, a day is appointed on which the inhabitants of each parish meet, in their respective parishes, to take up their long lost rights into possession, and to form themselves into corporations. So then each parish becomes a corporation, and all the men who are inhabitants become members or burghers. The land with all that appertains to it, is in every parish made the property of the corporation or parish with as ample power to let, repair or alter all, or any part thereof as a Lord of the manor enjoys over his lands, houses, etc., but the power of alienating the least morsel in any manner, from the parish, either at this or any time thereafter, is denied...Thus there are no more or other landlords, in the whole country than the parishes; and each of them is sovereign landlord in its own territories.

Rents which had hitherto been paid to the landlords would accordingly fall to the parishes which, as sovereign bodies, would employ them in 'building, repairing and adorning its houses, bridges, and other structures; in making and maintaining convenient and delightful streets, highways and passages for foot and carriages and in making and maintaining canals...and in planting and taking in waste grounds'. Spence described autonomous, self-governing communities, and communal ownership of land, all contributing to, in his words, a 'delightful' environment.

A similar strand of thought exists in the works of William Morris, a socialist poet, craftsman and artist. In a series of lectures on art and architecture for the Society for the Protection of Ancient Buildings in 1877, Morris explored the relationship between art and society. He concluded that the degraded state of design and art was associated with the degraded condition of the workman: he felt that change in either could only come about through radical social reform. Morris committed himself to socialism in 1883 by joining the Democratic Federation. He also became editor of *The Commonweal*, the journal of the Socialist League. In this he published his utopian novel, 'News From Nowhere' in which he explores humanity's relationship with the natural world. Morris, as the narrator, wakes up from sleep to find that a socialist revolution has taken place. He finds an ideal society in which there is equality between the sexes, private property has been abolished, and people live in small communities, working on the land and at hand-crafts in harmony with nature. The big murky places which were once the centres of manufacture disappear in his utopia, and ecological change in the human environment occurs as a result of a change in the purpose of work.

Morris anticipated the tenets of the garden city movement. This arose out of his concern that art and architecture should never ignore the relationship of humanity with nature, as he declares in an 1877 lecture.[2]

Lecture to the Trades Guild of Learning, *Hopes and Fears for Art as the Lesser Arts of Life* (1877) Collected Works Vol XXII (London: Longman, 1914), p 3

I do not want art for a few, any more than education for a few, or freedom for a few...art will make our streets as beautiful as the wood, as elevating as mountain-sides: it will be a pleasure and a rest to come from the open country into a town; every man's house will be fair and decent, soothing to his mind and helpful to his work, all the works of man that we live amongst and handle will be in harmony with nature, will be reasonable and beautiful...in no private dwelling will there be any signs of waste, pomp, or insolence, and every man will have his share of the best.

A contemporary of William Morris, Prince Peter Kropotkin, a Polish geographer and anarchist, was also concerned by the nature of productive work and the urban environment of human towns. In his *Fields, Factories and Workshops* (1899), he argued in favour of mixing factory work with farm work, brain work with manual work, and town jobs with country jobs. Looking at the enormous productivity of small workshops and horticulture as opposed to large-scale industry and farming, Kropotkin claimed that the future lies with the dispersal of both. He makes a plea for: 'a new economy in the energies used in supplying the needs of human life, since these needs are increasing and the energies are not inexhaustible.'[3]

A deist prescription for an industrial utopia or paradise was developed by Robert Owen, an idealistic owner of industrial works. He believed that the millennium did not have to be waited for, but could be created on earth:

> 'What idea individuals may attach to the term Millennium I know not; but I know that society may be formed so as to exist without crime, without poverty, with health greatly improved, with little, if any, misery, and with intelligence and happiness increased an hundredfold; and no obstacle whatsoever intervenes at this moment, except ignorance, to prevent such a state of society becoming universal'.[4]

2 See also *Art and the Beauty of the Earth*, Collected Works, Vol XXII (London: Longman, 1914), p 155.
3 See P Kropotkin *Address to the Young* (London: Lighthouse Publications, 1855).
4 Quoted in WHG Armytage (1961), *Heavens Below*, p 77.

Changing the physical form of the land was an important part of Owen's plans. The towns of New Lanark, Bourneville, and Port Sunlight were suburban in character, and allowed for light, openness, and greenery.

Many strands of utopian thought – the rights of man, the earthly and industrial paradise, the sovereign, self-sufficient community, harmony between people and the natural world, and between rural and city interests – came together and were given practical expression in the garden city movement, headed by Ebenezer Howard, in the 1890s.[5] Living in the United States for five years as a young man, Howard saw social experiments organised on cooperative principles in the 'planned' cities in Massachussetts and Connecticut. His insights into the condition of 'healthy' American cities with their low population density, good housing, wide thoroughfares, and plenty of open space, fed into his philosophy of encouraging a sense of community and good quality of life for the individual through planning:

> 'I realised, as never before, the splendid possibilities of a new civilisation based in service to the Community and not on self interest: at present the dominant motive...I was led to put forward proposals...to build by private enterprise pervaded by a public spirit an entirely new town, industrial, residential and agricultural.'[6]

Howard saw this form of social organisation as creating a new industrial system in which the productive forces and wealth were to be used and *distributed* with far greater effectiveness and fairness. His grand principle was that all men are equally entitled to the use of the earth. Howard wrote a book of his vision, *Garden Cities of Tomorrow* (1889), and formed the Garden City Association in 1899. He adopted a utopian approach, testing out his ideas on a small scale by using a single city. The name given to this utopia, the garden city, has since been attributed to the description of Chicago as a garden city because of its plentiful public parks. Chicago itself was called the City Beautiful.

In *Garden Cities of Tomorrow*, Howard describes a marriage of town and country in a single community and the *common* ownership of the land by that community. The city was to be planned, built, and generally governed by the community. He envisaged a garden city built in concentric circles. At the centre there is a group of civic buildings, midway there is a circular Grand Avenue with trees and green verges. The outermost circle is an agricultural belt for growing fruit and vegetables for the city and supplying it with eggs and milk, and acting as a buffer to keep the garden cities a wholesome distance apart. Six boulevards radiate from the centre, creating a manufacturing area, several residential areas, a shopping centre and playing fields. The central premise – the combining of the town and the country – and further practicalities of this plan are summarised by Howard below.

E Howard, *Garden Cities of Tomorrow* (London: Faber & Faber, 1946)

There are in reality not only...two alternatives; town life and country life, but a third alternative, in which all the advantages of the most energetic and active

5 The idea of the garden city can be traced back to John Evelyn writing *Fumifugium* in 1661. His ideas led to great tree planting on estates and in London (see ch 6).

6 Quoted in D MacFadyen, *Sir Ebenezer Howard and the Town Planning Movement* (Manchester: Manchester University Press, 1970), p 21.

town life, with all the beauty of and delight of the country may be secured in perfect combination. And the certainty of being able to live this life will be the magnet which will produce the effects for which we are all striving: the spontaneous movement of the people from the crowded and unhealthy cities to the bosom of our kindly mother earth.

...

An estate of 6,000 acres was to be bought at a cost of £40 an acre, or £240,000. The estate was to be held in trust, 'first, as a security for the debenture-holders, and secondly, in trust for the people of Garden City'. A town was to be built near the centre of the estate to occupy about 1,000 acres. In the centre was to be a park in which were placed the public buildings, and around the park a great arcade containing shops etc. The population of the town was to be 30,000. The building plots were to be of an average size of 20 by 130 feet. There were to be common gardens and cooperative kitchens. On the outer ring of the town were to be factories, warehouses, etc. fronting on a circular railway. The agricultural estate of 5,000 acres was to be properly developed for agricultural purposes as part of the scheme, and the population of this belt was taken at 2,000.

The entire revenue of the town was to be derived from ground rents, which were considered to be amply sufficient (a) to pay the interest on the money with which the estate is purchased, (b) to provide a sinking fund for the purpose of paying off the principal, (c) to construct and maintain all such works as are usually constructed and maintained by municipal and other local authorities out of rates compulsorily levied, and (d) after redemption of debentures to provide a large surplus for other purposes, such as old-age pensions or insurance against accident and sickness.

...

Some of my friends have suggested that such a scheme of town clusters is well enough adapted to a new country, but that in an old-settled country, with its towns built and its railway system for the most part constructed, it is quite a different matter. But surely to raise such a point is to contend, in other words, that the existing wealth forms of the country are permanent, and are for ever to serve as hindrances to the introduction of better forms; that crowded, ill-ventilated, unplanned, unwieldy, unhealthy cities - ulcers on the very face of our beautiful island – are to stand as barriers to the introduction of towns in which modern scientific methods and the aims of social reformers may have the fullest scope in which to express themselves. No, it cannot be; at least, it cannot be for long. What Is may hinder What Might Be for a while, but cannot stay the tide of progress. These crowded cities have done their work; they were the best which a society largely based on selfishness, acquisitiveness and fear could construct, but they are in the nature of things entirely unadapted for a society in which the social side of our nature is demanding a larger share of recognition – a society where even the very love of self leads us to insist upon a greater regard for the well-being of our fellows. The large cities of to-day are scarcely better adapted for the expression of the fraternal spirit than would a work on astronomy which taught that the earth was the centre of the universe be capable of adaptation for use in our schools.

Howard's idealistic principles and theories on the garden city were put into practice first in Letchworth, an estate near Hitchin in Hertfordshire which was purchased from fifteen different owners in 1903 by the First Garden City Company. The planning of the town was carried out by the First Garden City Company by means of its powers as sole owner of the Estate, and not by the Local Authority under the powers of the Town Planning Acts. However, the Urban District Council had a voice in the Town Plan, deposited with the Council by the Company. This Plan laid out the defining use, character and density of buildings; the Company agreed not to depart from the provisions of the plan without first consulting the Council. The establishment of Letchworth Garden City was followed by the purchase of a second estate at Welwyn, also in Hertfordshire and the foundation of Welwyn Garden City. These garden cities, which still exist, were part of Howard's plan to create a cluster of such cities and the eventual rebuilding of London itself. There was some disappointment with the realisation of Howard's plans; the planned nature of the towns meant that they lacked a certain energy and character. And their building stopped far short of redirecting the geography and development of London.

Howard's utopian vision of combining town and country, thus alleviating the 'crowded, ill-ventilated, unplanned, unwieldy, unhealthy cities', and establishing conditions for the creation and distribution of new forms of wealth, followed Thomas Spence's utopian writings of the eighteenth century. However, his vision of the garden city had a distinctly contemporary feel: it reflected Ruskin's ideal of ethical principles in industry, Herbert Spencer's doctrine of social evolution, and the foundation of the Labour Party. Howard was also influenced by aspects of Peter Kropotkin's anarchism – local economic initiative, self-government, and self-sufficiency. He cited Kropotkin's *Fields, Factories and Workshops* in his own *Garden Cities of Tomorrow* and considered that it was 'as by a hair's breadth' that Kropotkin, Morris and Ruskin had failed to give expression to the garden city idea themselves'.[7] As his biographer describes, in Howard's plans there was something for every kind of idealist: self-realisation to please the individualist, and a communal venture which pleased the socialist.[8]

(c) Miming nature

A very different type of experiment on land can be seen in the gardens and parks of country estates in the eighteenth and nineteenth centuries – the miming of natural form and features. This was a departure from the more autocratic, formal gardens of the seventeenth century and earlier which demonstrated dominance over nature. Passmore locates this shift in man's changing relationship with nature.

7 See R Beevers, *The Garden City Utopia* (Hampshire: Macmillan, 1988) p 17.
8 Macfadyen, op cit, p 38.

J Passmore, *Man's Responsibility for Nature: Ecological Problems and Western Tradition* (London: Duckworth, 1974), pp 36-38

Stewardship and Co-operation with Nature

...

The temptation to think of nature, in the Stoic manner, as a semi-divine or divinely activated being with whom men can choose to co-operate or not to co-operate is indeed a powerful one. But it would be wrong to suggest that the metaphysicians and the looser rhetoricians are nothing more than victims of hypostatisation. They have something to say about man's relationship with nature, even when they wrongly suppose that it is a relationship between two entities - 'Man' and 'Nature'. To find out what that 'something' is, I shall take a hint from Marcuse's remark that parks and gardens and reservations represent a liberating as opposed to a tyrannical mastery over nature. It is the more enlightening to do so in that Western thought has been obsessed with the ideal of a garden, that Paradisiacal garden from which Adam and Eve were driven.

In the seventeenth-century formal garden the idea of mastering or conquering nature is pre-eminent. 'Perfecting nature' is understood as imposing form on it. Man shows his unique rationality – identified with l'ésprit géométrique – by constructing gardens on a geometrical plan. The severe simplicity of the design contrasts with the waywardness of nature. Shrubs are pruned into triangles, spheres or cones, or into the likeness of men or animals – into shapes, in either case, which could not possibly occur without human intervention. Nothing could be more attractive, better calculated to display man's power over nature. 'Our British gardeners', wrote Addison in 1712, '...instead of humouring Nature, love to deviate from it as much as possible. Our trees rise in cones, globes and pyramids. We see the marks of the scissors upon every plant and bush.' Interestingly enough, the seventeenth century sometimes thought of the Garden of Eden in exactly these same terms, with 'clipt hedges, square parterres, strait walls, trees uniformly lopt, regular knots and carpets of flowers, groves nodding at groves, marble foundations, and water works'.

In contrast, the late eighteenth century gardener sought to construct gardens which would have the same sort of relation to wild nature as does a landscape painting to the landscape it portrays. The gardener was to take his materials from nature, to treat them reverently, but to arrange them in a better composition. To 'perfect' was not to *impose* form, but to *improve* form. We are told of the most famous of landscape gardeners, Lancelot Brown that it was his object to 'bring to life an improvement on rough Nature,...a raw goddess who was always struggling for improvement, but never achieved it without the Aristotelian dressing of man's divinely natural faculties'. His nickname 'Capability' arose out of his habit of describing a site as 'having capabilities'; his task, he thought, was to convert those capabilities into actualities. Nature supplied the matter but only suggested the form. As a poetic contemporary put it, 'Brown was to grace Nature and her works complete'. There could scarcely be a nicer example of the ideal of cooperative perfection – to grace nature, to complete her works, by realising their capabilities.

The civilising of nature, as its eighteenth and nineteenth century advocates saw the situation, has two advantages over leaving it as it is. It converts nature into something at once more agreeable and more intelligible than a wilderness; man understands domesticated nature, because he has helped to make it. He arranges nature in such a way that he 'can enter her world and enjoy our origins'. From the wilderness he is always in some measure alienated; it stands in a relationship to him of pure externality. Yet at the same time the civilised garden does not involve the mutilation of nature, at least in the topiarist's manner. Its trees are still recognisably elms and limes and oaks, but by skilful placing and pruning thay have been brought to a perfection of shape they rarely achieve in the forest.

The geometrical gardeners were, in a general sense, Platonists, convinced that to perfect nature it had first to be reshaped. The Cartesian-Platonist Malebranche once wrote: 'The visible world would be more perfect if the seas and lands made more regular figures' – in contrast to the followers of Rousseau, for whom everything is good as it comes from the hands of the Creator and man's task is to remove hindrances to its free development. In removing dead limbs, in cutting off branches the tree is not strong enough to bear or which would prevent the free growth of other branches, the pruner, on the Rousseau view, helps the tree to assume its perfect form. To the Platonic topiarist, in contrast, no natural shape, but only a humanly-imposed and geometrical form, can be perfect.* The first view encourages man in his relationship with nature to think of himself as a ruthless despot, imposing order on what would otherwise be a meaningless chaos; on the second view he shows his skill, rather, by bringing to light the potentialities of the nature on which he operates.

* The more practically minded, of course, lop trees into any shape which will ensure that they 'keep their place', so that they will not interfere with such civilised projects as overhead transmission wires. One sometimes feels, indeed, that trees are planted only in order to be thus lopped; their mutilated branches are the modern equivalent of the mutilated men with which some tyrants have liked to decorate their cities – a reminder of power.

...

Passmore uses town planning as another example of how people relate to nature and shape their environment:

Town planning will serve as a second example of this conflict of ideals. Nothing could better display the despotic concept of perfection than the American-style grid town, with its echoes of Rome and, more remotely, of Pythagoras. Whatever the character of the landscape, the roads run straight. The blocks are evenly square, whether on a hillside or on a flatplain, just as Roman centuriation was superimposed as much on the valley of the Po as on the near-deserts of Tunisia.

In contrast, the town planner now often seeks to 'design *with* Nature', to take over the title of a book written by a leading exponent of this type of town planning, Ian McHarg. It is interesting to observe the assumptions on which McHarg works: 'Canvas and pigments lie in wait, stone, wood and metal are ready for sculpture, random noise is latent for symphonies, sites are gravid for cities'. Notice the language: it is not just that stone, metal, wood, noise, sites are 'at hand', as Heidegger would say, ready for man to use; they 'lie in wait', they are 'ready', 'gravid', for man the deliverer. Lewis Mumford sums up McHarg's purpose in a way which still more closely links it with the German tradition I have already described: 'He seeks, not arbitrarily to impose design, but to use to the fullest the potentialities – and with them, necessarily, the restrictive conditions – that nature offers. So, too, in embracing nature, he knows that man's own mind, which is part of nature, has something precious to add that is not to be found at such a high point of development in raw nature, untouched by man'.

The designers with nature, it will be observed, are by no means primitivists; they do not think of man as being wholly a despoiler. Nor do they imagine that they can 'perfect' nature without effort, as if what they try to do will always be aided by an invisible, guiding hand. But they seek to break down the attitude enshrined in Mill's essay on 'Nature': 'All praise of civilisation, or art, or contrivance is so much dispraise of Nature'. If we praise the architects of the *tholos* at Delphi, this is not a way of depreciating the beauty of the site the architects chose for it. Men can – and this is what the 'designers with nature' are talking about – use their ingenuity to enhance rather than to destroy the qualities of a site. The road or city builder too often adopts as his principle of action Isaiah's (and Luke's): 'Every valley shall be filled, and every mountain and hill shall be brought low; and the crooked shall be made straight, and the rough ways shall be made smooth.' But alternatively, he can try so to construct his city or his road that mountains and valley are, as with some Alpine roads or the Tuscan hill cities, more strikingly related than before. He will not always choose to make a road smooth or straight, if this involves too extensive a destruction.

(d) Early planning law

Planning is all encompassing – from drains to 'designing' nature. Early planning legislation had as at least one of its goals the provision of a healthier environment in the sense of a concern with amenity rather than environmental protection per se. Even 'amenity' was at this date combined with predominant concerns of nuisances and sanitation. The Housing, Town Planning, Etc Act 1909 is generally referred to as the first Planning Act. Howard's physical planning ideals, such as low density housing, were applied to new urban development by this Act.

PART II. TOWN PLANNING

Preparation and approval of town planning scheme

54.-(1) A town planning scheme may be made in accordance with the provision of this Part of this Act as respects any land which is in the course of development or appears likely to be used for building purposes, with the general objective of securing proper sanitary conditions, amenity, and convenience in connexion with the laying out and use of the land, and of any neighbouring lands.

...

Power to enforce scheme.

57.-(1) The responsible authority may at any time, after giving such notice as may be provided by a town planning scheme and in accordance with the provisions of the scheme -

(a) remove, pull down, or alter any building or other work in the area included in the scheme which is such as to contravene the scheme, or in the erection or carrying out of which any provision of the scheme has not been complied with; or

(b) execute any work which it is the duty of any person to execute under the scheme in any case where it appears to the authority that delay in the execution of the work would prejudice the efficient operation of the scheme.

(2) Any expenses incurred by a responsible authority under this section may be recovered from the persons in default in such manner and subject to such conditions as may be provided by the scheme.

...

Compensation in respect of property injuriously affected by scheme, &c.

58.-(1) Any person whose property is injuriously affected by the making of a town planning scheme shall, if he makes a claim for the purpose within the time (if any) limited by the scheme, not being less than three months after the date when notice of the approval of the scheme is published in the manner prescribed by regulations made by the Local Government Board, be entitled to obtain compensation in respect thereof from the responsible authority.

(2) A person shall not be entitled to compensation under this section on account of any building erected on, or contract made or other thing done with respect to, land included in a scheme, after the time at which the application for authority to prepare the scheme was made, or after such other time as the Local Government Board may fix for the purpose:

...

Exclusion or limitation of compensation in certain cases.

59.-(1) Where property is alleged to be injuriously affected by reason of any provisions contained in a town planning scheme, no compensation shall be paid in respect thereof if or so far as the provisions are such as would have been enforceable if they had been contained in byelaws made by the local authority.

(2) Property shall not be deemed to be injuriously affected by reason of the making of any provisions inserted in a town planning scheme, which, with a view to securing the amenity of the area included in the scheme or any part thereof, prescribe the space about buildings or limit the number of buildings to be erected, or prescribe the height or character of buildings, and which the Local Government Board, having regard to the nature and situation of the land affected by the provisions, consider reasonable for the purpose.

...

The rationale and main provisions of the Act are critically analysed in the following piece.

JB Cullingworth and V Nadin, *Town and Country Planning in Britain* (London: Routledge, 11th edn, 1994), p 2

THE FIRST PLANNING ACT

The movement for the extension of sanitary policy into town planning was uniting diverse interests. These were nicely summarised by John Burns, President of the Local Government Board when he introduced the first legislation bearing the term 'town planning' – the Housing, Town Planning, Etc Act 1909:

> The object of the bill is to provide a domestic condition for the people in which their physical health, their morals, their character and their whole social condition can be improved by what we hope to secure in this bill. The bill aims in broad outline at, and hopes to secure, the home healthy, the house beautiful, the town pleasant, the city dignified and the suburb salubrious.

The new powers provided by the Act were for the preparation of 'schemes' by local authorities for controlling the development of new housing areas. Though novel, these powers were logically a simple extension of the existing ones. It is significant that this first legislative acceptance of town planning came in an Act dealing with health and housing. And, as Ashworth has pointed out, the gradual development and the accumulated experience of public health and housing facilitated a general acceptance of the principles of town planning.

> Housing reform had gradually been conceived in terms of larger and larger units. Torrens' Act (Artizans and Labourers Dwellings Act 1868) had made a beginning with individual houses; Cross's Act (Artizans and Labourers Dwellings Improvement Act 1875) had introduced an element of town planning by concerning itself with the reconstruction of insanitary areas; the framing of bylaws in accordance with the Public Health Act 1875 had accustomed local authorities to the imposition of at least a minimum of regulation on new building, and such a measure as the London Building Act 1894 brought into the scope of public control the formation and widening of streets, the lines of buildings frontage, the extent of open space around buildings, and the height of buildings. Town planning was therefore not altogether a leap in the dark, but could be represented as a logical extension, in accordance with changing aims and conditions, of earlier legislation concerned with housing and public health.

The centrality of amenity to planning is emphasised in the following extract. This also makes clear the continuity of ideas in the planning system: in this case as between amenity and sustainable development.

D Millichap, 'Law, Myth and Community: A Reinterpretation of Planning's Justification and Rationale', (1995) *Planning Perspectives*, Vol 10, 279-293, at 279-280

'Amenity' and *The Housing, Town Planning &c Act 1909*

The first planning Act, The Housing, Town Planning &c Act 1909 ('the 1909 Act'), was a landmark in the development of the UK planning system. This was the first time that the word 'planning' had been used in legislation. The term 'amenity' was another key element. The legislation offered public authorities the powers to regulate certain types of development for 'planning' and 'amenity' reasons. Earlier legislation on land-use and development had not attempted to regulate land-use on the basis of amenity. This incorporation of the term 'amenity' into the first modern piece of planning legislation reflected the pioneering work of those advocating a broader approach to land-use control. So the concept reflected the efforts of planning pioneers of the era to move on from the 'sanitation'-based approach of the public health version of regulation, to an approach that also encompassed amenity. Such a concern for wider aspects of land-use control still informs much of current planning practice. 'Amenity' is still a term found in the planning legislation. It is arguably a concept that links the most recent concerns for sustainable development with that first planning legislation...What is more relevant in terms of the concepts, ideology and cultural trappings of planning in its infancy is that the key role to be played by the term 'amenity' was not lost on those supporting the passage of the legislation through Parliament...

'Amenity' is thus not only a core statutory term, it is also a rallying cry to those in the vanguard of planning. It was meant to go beyond the rather drab and sterile urban environment which the focus on 'public health' had produced. Regulatory control was also to take as a central aim a new dimension of urban life - beauty: 'amenity' encapsulated that approach.

Although 'amenity' was a central term in the 1909 Act, it was left undefined. One understanding of this is that since the Act sought to regulate the development of land, and had such a bearing on landowners, the legislature thought it best not to prescribe a restrictive, legal meaning which might jeopardise cooperation between landowners and the local authorities charged with creating 'schemes' for residential development.[9] It was left to the courts to give meaning to 'amenity' in the planning legislation, as in *Re Ellis and Ruislip-Northwood UDC*. This case goes to the heart of the rationale for planning legislation – to alter the position and duties of the landowner – and signals the significant inroads of planning powers on the economic interests of landowners.[10] Note particularly the references to the community rights and duties of the landowner.

Re Ellis and Ruislip-Northwood UDC [1920] 1 KB 343

Scrutton L.J.: Mr Ellis, the appellant, owned some land at Ruislip, bordering on the main street, and complained that it was injuriously affected by the provisions of a scheme made under the Housing, Town Planning, &c., Act 1909.

...

It is clear that a strip of Mr. Ellis's land 7 feet in depth adjoining the street is injuriously affected, and under s. 58, sub-s.1, of the Housing, Town Planning, &c., Act 1909, he is, subject to other provisions of the Act, entitled to compensation. But it is said and the arbitrator and judge have found that certain

9 D Millichap, 'Law, Myth and Community: A Reinterpretation of Planning's Justification and Rationale', (1995) *Planning Perspectives*, Vol 10, 279-293, at 280-281.

10 Ibid, at 282; see also BJ Pearce, 'Property Rights v Development Control', (1981) *Town Planning Review*, Vol 52, 45.

other provisions of the Act deprive him of the compensation he is prima facie entitled to, and while the Courts will be slow to deprive anyone of his property without compensation, if Parliament has clearly intended that consequence to follow, the Courts can only give effect to the expressed intention of Parliament, though in cases of doubt the presumption would be against taking away private property without compensation. I agree with my brethren on this point; the question is whether this Act of Parliament, and this scheme, which has the force of an Act of Parliament, have this effect.

...

Sect. 59, sub-s. 2, uses the language: "Prescribe the space about buildings with a view to securing the amenity of the area." The scheme has clauses 36-48: `Space about buildings, including building lines"; 49, "Limitation of number of buildings to the acre"; 57-66, "Sanitary conditions and amenity." The word "amenity" is obviously used very loosely; it is, I think, novel in an Act of Parliament, and appears to mean "pleasant circumstances or features, advantages". Wide streets and plenty of air and room between houses seem clearly to be amenities, and a provision securing them by setting back houses to a given line seems to me to be a provision with a view to securing amenity. It follows that damage done to Mr. Ellis's land by the operation of clause 36 of the scheme is damage for which, by the operation of s. 59, sub-s. 2, of the Act he is not entitled to compensation. Parliament appears to have sacrificed the individual to the welfare of the area possibly thinking that the increased value of the rest of the land would compensate him for the fetter imposed on part of the land. However, its motives are not for me; it is only my duty to interpret and apply its enactments.

...

Mr. Ellis addressed to us a very sincere and earnest appeal that the Courts do him justice which the local authority and Government department denied him. I think the result of the legislation we have been considering is to inflict a hardship on him in depriving him of the use of his property without compensation, but it is the result of the action of Parliament, and the Courts are established to administer the laws, not to strain them in order to redress individual cases which appear to them hard. Hard cases make bad law. In my view the express provisions of the Act of Parliament, when fairly construed, require me to give them a meaning which excludes Mr. Ellis's claim to compensation because he is not allowed to build right up to the edge of his land in a narrow street. I can quite understand that Parliament may have taken a view that a landowner in a community has duties as well as rights, and cannot claim compensation for refraining from using his land where they think that it is his duty so to refrain.

It follows that in my view Mr. Ellis's appeal, which appears to me to raise questions far more important than the individual interests of Mr. Ellis, fails.

The 1909 Act was followed by the Housing, Town Planning Act 1919 and the Town and Country Planning Act 1932, both of which required that all borough and urban districts prepare schemes to regulate *general* land use. In theory the schemes led to the zoning of land for particular uses such as residential or industrial. Developers did not have to apply for planning permission but, should the development fail to conform to the scheme, the planning authority could require that the owner remove or alter the development (without compensation). In practice, a number of difficulties arose with the administration of the planning schemes. By 1942, only 5% of England and 1% of Wales was subject to development schemes; large country districts, towns and cities were not covered by a scheme at all. Of those which were made, most merely ratified existing trends of development because a more radical reappraisal of sites for development would have involved the planning authority in paying out compensation to landowners for restrictions or prohibitions on development which most authorities could ill afford. The schemes therefore placed few restrictions on developers. The system of paying compensation for loss of development rights was changed radically in the post-war reassessment of the planning system, representing a fundamental shift away from protecting property ownership and the associated right to develop land. The context in which this change takes place is described below.

D Hardy and C Ward, *Arcadia for All: The Legacy of a Makeshift Landscape* (London: Mansell, 1984), p 49

...to remedy the situation there was no shortage of ideas. For all their variety, more rather than less public intervention was generally accepted as a prerequisite. Increasedly, a notion of the 'common good' was equated with the State, in opposition to selfish acts of individualism. In political terms this formula proved to be unworkable until after 1945, but the seeds were carefully sown for what was later to become a new consensus.

In the late-1930s there was widespread support for something akin to a 'Ministry of Amenities' – 'a new Government department charged with the duty not only of restraining and advising the other Departments of State...'. Centralized ministerial control was generally considered to be preferable to the divided planning responsibilities that prevailed, in which the Ministry of Health held the main brief for amenity.

There was also a growing call for land nationalization as the only way to secure development in the common good. In turn, though, this was sometimes tempered by doubts as to whether administration by public officials would necessarily be any better than that of private landowners. At the very least, it was suggested that everyone would benefit from a good dose of environmental education. One writer even went so far as to say that the public at large should not be allowed into the countryside until they were properly educated in its ways. But if there were doubts as to unbridled nationalization, there was almost total support for a network of national parks, where large areas of valuable landscape (including the Sussex Downs in southern England) could be protected for all time.

(e) The post-war planning project

Radical developments in the control of land use followed the end of the Second World War. There was at this time a newly acquired confidence to tackle long-standing social and economic problems: town planning formed part of this idea of regeneration. The 1944 White Paper, *The Control of Land Use*, sets the changes in a climate of social idealism. The utilitarian, but also utopian, heritage of planning is apparent in the following extract from the White Paper.

White Paper, *The Control of Land Use* Cmnd 6537 (London: HMSO, 1944)

Provision for the right use of land, in accordance with a considered policy, is an essential requirement of the government's programme of postwar reconstruction. New houses, whether of permanent or emergency construction; the new layout of areas devastated by reason of age or bad living conditions; the new schools which will be required under the Education Bill now before Parliament; the balanced distribution of industry which the government's recently published proposals for maintaining employment envisage; the requirements of sound nutrition and of a healthy and well-balanced agriculture; the preservation of land for national parks and forests, and the assurance to the people of enjoyment of the sea and countryside in times of leisure; a new and safer highway system better adapted to modern industrial and other needs; the proper provision of airfields – all these related parts of a single reconstruction programme involve the use of land, and it is essential that their various claims on land should be so harmonised as to ensure for the people of this country the greatest possible measure of individual well-being and national prosperity.

The Town and Country Planning Act 1947 was essential to the post-war nationalisation programmes and attempts to rebuild devastated areas. The 1947 Act considerably strengthened the state's control over the use and development of privately owned land by making all development subject to prior authorisation. Development plans were to be prepared in every area in the country. These were to outline the way in which each area was to be developed or preserved and thereby guide the authority in its decision-making. The authority was also to have regard to 'any other material considerations' in making decisions about planning permission. All development values in land were nationalised. This meant that compensation for loss of development rights was to be paid once and for all, after which the grant of development consent was to be decided on the basis of 'good planning principles'. The refusal of planning permission for development was therefore no longer compensatable. In addition, a development charge was imposed upon development value accruing to land by virtue of a grant of planning permission; although significant, this was short lived.[11] The main provisions of the 1947 Act have been re-enacted in the Town and Country Planning Acts of 1968, 1971 and 1990.[12] The following is from the 1947 Act.

11 The system of charging for development was repealed by the Town and Country Planning Act 1952; see further M Grant, *Urban Planning Law* (London: Sweet and Maxwell, 1982) pp 18-27 on compensation, betterment and charges for development.

12 See further Grant, op cit, pp 14-16 and JB Cullingworth and V Nadin, *Town and Country Planning in Britain* (London: Routledge, 11th edn, 1994) pp 10-20.

PART II. DEVELOPMENT PLANS

Surveys of planning areas and preparation of development plans.

5.-(I) As soon as may be after the appointed day, every local planning authority shall carry out a survey of their area, and shall, not later than three years after the appointed day, or within such extended period as the Minister may in any particular case allow, submit to the Minister a report of the survey together with a plan (hereinafter called a "development plan") indicating the manner in which they propose that land in that area should be used (whether by the carrying out thereon of development or otherwise) and the stages by which any such development should be carried out.

(2) Subject to the provisions of any regulations made under this Act for regulating the form and content of development plans, any such plan shall include such maps and such descriptive matter as may be necessary to illustrate the proposals aforesaid with such degree of particularity as may be appropriate to different parts of the area; and any such plan may in particular-

(a) define the sites of proposed roads, public and other buildings and works, airfields, parks, pleasure grounds, nature reserves and other open spaces, or allocate areas of land for use for agricultural, residential, industrial or other purposes of any class specified in the plan;
(b) designate, as land subject to compulsory acquisition by any Minister, local authority or statutory undertakers any land allocated by the plan for the purposes of any of their functions...

...

PART III. CONTROL OF DEVELOPMENT, ETC.

Permission to develop land.

12.-(I) Subject to the provisions of this section and to the following provisions of this Act, permission shall be required under this Part of this Act in respect of any development of land which is carried out after the appointed day.

(2) In this Act, except where the context otherwise requires, the expression "development" means the carrying out of building, engineering, mining or other operations in, on, over or under land, or the making of any material change in the use of any buildings or other land.

...

14.-(I) Subject to the provisions of this and the next following section, where application is made to the local planning authority for permission to develop land, that authority may grant permission either unconditionally or subject to such conditions as they think fit, or may refuse permission; and in dealing with any such application the local planning authority shall have regard to the provisions of the development plan, so far as material thereto, and to any other material considerations.

The main theme of the 1947 Act was economic regeneration. However, a link with the 1909 Act existed in the retention of the 'amenity' term and more broadly in the notion that public bodies had wide powers over land use and development. Landowners' economic interests were seriously affected by the

1947 Act, leading to litigation which examined the rights of landowners in the post-war planning system.[13]

***Buxton v Minister of Housing and Local Government* [1960] 3 All ER 408 at 411**

July 28. **SALMON, J.,** ...Before the town and country planning legislation any landowner was free to develop his land as he liked, provided he did not infringe the common law. No adjoining owner had any right which he could enforce in the courts in respect of such development unless he could show that it constituted a nuisance or trespass or the like. The scheme of the town and country planning legislation, in my judgment, is to restrict development for the benefit of the public at large and not to confer new rights on any individual members of the public, whether they live close to or far from the proposed development. The legislature made the local planning authority, under the general supervision of the Minister, custodians of the public's rights.

In the development of planning controls we see a powerful combination of social forces, economic plans and welfarist ideals. The legal apparatus for bringing about a pleasant city, salubrious suburbs and healthy environs, primarily the development scheme, was built on the bedrock of powers granted to local authorities for basic public health requirements.

Even in this early period of land use controls, we already see the ability of the planning system to reflect the concerns of the time and to 'deliver the goods' in terms of public health, and economic regeneration. Environmental protection had yet to be developed fully as one such concern, although the emphasis on amenity foreshadows this. Further common concerns include notions of the 'public interest' and 'community rights and duties'.

3 COUNTRYSIDE PROTECTION

We have looked at public health and early planning legislation from the point of view of interfering with landowners' rights in the 'public interest'. We now turn to the use of planning in the pre-war period as a legal mechanism to contain or order popular trends and movements such as those discussed below. The main trend identified by the authors in the following – the makeshift landscape – contrasts sharply with that of the 'made' landscape of naturalist gardens and parks in country estates of the nineteenth century.

D Hardy and C Ward, *Arcadia for All: The Legacy of a Makeshift Landscape* (London: Mansell, 1984), pp 1-15

For holidays as well as homes, towns reached ever further into the countryside – a fragile countryside already in the throes of change. Demands for green field

13 See analysis of this case law by Millichap, supra, at 284-285.

sites, fresh air and a sight of the sea seemed insatiable. Even the new suburbanites, themselves refugees from the city, joined the seasonal exodus for weekend breaks and holidays. Sylvan retreats, romantic river valleys, gentle hills and vantage points but, most of all, the evocative features of a varied coastline lured more and more away from the towns to a lost Arcadia.

England was suddenly a smaller place. Beyond the suburbs, themselves a product of people moving out, the new ways were soon to make their mark. Roadhouses along the arterials, teahouses perched on clifftops, riverside hotels, petrol pumps in picturesque villages, advertisements painted on cottage roofs and walls, charabancs and caravans all bore witness to a process of dispersal.

It was as part and parcel of this new landscape, alongside more conventional developments, that a curious makeshift world emerged. Defying even the minimal building codes of the day, a motley of makeshift structures, often on the most unlikely sites, carried dispersal to its very limits.

...

Invariably it was a landscape put together on the cheap, a manifestation by poor people of the fashionable trend for a place in the country. Plots of land were bought cheaply and sometimes, through squatting, acquired at no cost at all. And the varied structures they accommodated were more a product of necessity than of a conscious sense of Arcadian design.

...

No less distinctive in the early plotlands was the lack of any overall planning and provision of services. Land was subdivided to enable the quickest and cheapest means of disposal, and the results showed little regard for amenity or for convenient access. Indeed, it was not uncommon to have to cross another plot to reach one's own. Roads were little more than lines on a map, and remained unmade for many years – rutted in the summer months, and waterlogged in winter. A mains water supply, sewerage system, electricity and other services passed the plotlands by. Likewise, shops, schools and other facilities which one would expect in a small community were few and far between. With their unfinished appearance and lack of amenities the plotlands were in some ways akin to frontier settlements in the New World.

...

The makeshift landscape of the early twentieth century was very much a product of its age – with new social opportunities to weigh against new demands on the environment. And yet, at the same time, there are elements in the new scene with roots running deep into a history of popular movements. Two traditions in particular, can be discerned – the one, "pastoralism" with its call back to an image of lost rural bliss and to an affinity with Nature; the other "agrarianism", with its ideal of peasant proprietorship and of reclaiming land which had been wrongly appropriated in times past. Though diverse in origin, the two traditions can be seen to coalesce in twentieth-century plotlands.

"Sweet Arcady"

In pastoralism is an image of a purer way of life rooted in a past, more natural setting. It is a fantasy of gentle scenery, of mellow farms and villages and of beautiful people filled with love; it is a world of perfection and harmony, of the

Garden of Eden before the Fall. Poets, painters, musicians and writers enriched and varied the image over centuries.

...

Earlier in the nineteenth century, Shelley, Coleridge, Southey and Wordsworth were amongst those who idealized Nature against a growing backcloth of towns and factories. And some years later the pre-Raphaelites in their various ways sought to depict the essence and truth of Nature.

Romanticism opened up two routes. The one was of sentimentality and nostalgia; Victorian profiles of rose-covered country cottages and ruddy-faced yeomanry. The other was a synthesis of intellect and emotion, or rationality and imagination; Thoreau's contemplation of his experience in a log cabin by a lake, or the writings of William Morris. Each had its own following, and each contributed to a consensus of powerful emotions that country life was better than town life, a feeling that grew stronger as the century progressed.

This idealization of the country was strengthened by political writers, like Morris, Kropotkin and Tolstoy, portraying a new form of society without cities. And an interest, if not a total commitment in "Back to Nature", showed itself in natural history societies, in organized rambles and cycling excursions from the towns, and in a variety of practical schemes for decentralized settlements (amongst which Ebenezer Howard's for garden cities attracted most attention).

...

By the turn of the century those ordinary folk who sought to leave the city, if only for the weekend, were already bound up in a long and powerful tradition of "anti-urbanism". Love of the countryside and scorn for the towns had become a cultural trait, touching the very heart of unspoken consciousness and desires. For those who acted on impulse, it mattered not whether this idealization of the countryside was born of dreams or reality. What mattered was the attraction of an image, powerful enough to lure townsfolk to their tiny plots in woodland and marsh, on gentle southern hills or quiet river valleys. In all innocence thousands followed a path charted by poets and others for centuries past.

"Land for the people"

No less deep-rooted than pastoralism is a parallel tradition of agrarianism. Unique in Europe, the English peasant was not, as a rule, a landowner. That this was so contributed to a long-standing sense of grievance, surfacing from time to time in outright attempts to reclaim the few acres which individual farm labourers believed were rightly theirs. The injustice of the massive land reallocation following the Norman Conquest was never forgotten, though it was the tangible evidence of a long process of "enclosures" which served periodically to fuel the fires of discontent. Even into the nineteenth century common rights were usurped, and historic smallholdings and cottagers' farms disappeared.

"Agrarianism" amounted to repeated attempts to retrieve the situation and to "resettle" a dispossessed peasantry. Medieval peasant revolts, the Diggers and others in the seventeenth century, the Chartist land campaign in the 1840s, and various land movements in the late nineteenth century all reflected the endurance of this basic impulse. The goal of a peasant proprietorship was seldom far down on a radical political agenda; a few acres of land retained a powerful lure.

What was it that drove people, time and again, to claim a few acres of land as their right? Undoubtedly, as those who achieved their goal found, wealth and an easy life were never amongst the rewards. Instead, what stands out is a sense of seeing justice done - of getting back that to which everyone has a right; and a belief that owning one's plot of land would secure independence and freedom. Added to these objectives, later in the nineteenth century, Robert Blatchford and others stressed the healthy life, in contrast to the debilitating conditions in towns.

Irrationally, perhaps, but understandably, the modern plotlanders themselves drew on these historic reasons for settlement. Far removed though they were from the situation which gave rise to early agrarianism, there were still grounds for echoing the original claims. Their little plots – rarely of a size that could enable economic subsistence – were still to many a living symbol of freedom and independence.

Moreover the process of acquiring modern plots bears more than a passing resemblance to "rural squatting", the means by which many staked a claim to land in times past. Squatting dates back as long as the process of land settlement itself, and most cultures have a traditional belief in "squatters' rights" whether these are recognized by statute or not.

...

Squatting becomes, as it did at various times in the past a product of the "marginality" of the process. People attracted by the idea of a place out of town, yet denied the economic means to follow the conventional route of paying market prices and dealing with professional traders in land, will look for cheaper alternatives. And these will inevitably be found not on high value land but in areas neglected because they flood, or yield a poor crop, or have long been in disputed ownership. It is to such areas of opportunity that common people, of necessity, have turned in the past - the twentieth century plotlands simply adding a new chapter to a long history of popular possession of land.

(a) Separation of legal controls – the town and the country

To order the 'makeshift landscape', legal controls over the use and development of land were needed. These controls evolved separately from those in urban areas. This state of affairs originates in the Report of the Committee on Land Utilisation in Rural Areas (the Scott Report) (1943). The Committee had a wide brief to review physical, social and economic development in the countryside. The Report came out strongly with the view that prosperous farming was essential for the whole country. This was for aesthetic and social reasons as well as for food production. Interestingly, the Scott Report includes a dissenting opinion given by Professor SR Dennison in which he advocates that farmers be paid for *conservation* rather than for working the land. His minority report is usually overlooked but shows much foresight in predicting the social and environmental problems that have been caused by the favoured position of farming (encouraged by the majority's opinion) and the main legal technique developed to resolve such problems, the voluntary management schemes provided for in sections 28 and 29 of the Wildlife and Countryside Act 1981 and section 95 of the Water Resources Act 1991. These schemes compensate farmers for loss of exploitation rights and profit foregone. Professor Dennison also recommended that planning controls be extended to the use and development of land in countryside areas. An extract from the main body of the Scott Report, as well as Professor Dennison's dissenting opinion, follows.

Scott Report *Report of the Committee on Land Utilisation in Rural Areas, 1941-42, Cmnd 6378 (London: HMSO, 1943)*

160. *The Preservation of Amenities.*- We regard the countryside as the heritage of the whole nation and, furthermore, we consider that the citizens of this country are the custodians of a heritage they share with all those of British descent and that it is a duty incumbent upon the nation to take proper care of that which it thus holds in trust.

In large part the beauties of Britain are man-made. Left to themselves the fields would quickly revert to thickets of shrub and brambles interrupted by bogs choked with reeds and rushes. The British countryside to-day owes its characteristic features to the fact that it has been used – in other words it has been farmed. The countryside cannot be "preserved" (though its peculiar value to the nation can be); it must be farmed if it is to retain those features which give it distinctive charm and character. For this reason neither the farmer nor the forester can be regarded as simply members of an industry or on the same footing with those in other great industries. In addition to their function of producing food and timber from the land, farmers and foresters are unconsciously the nation's landscape gardeners, a privilege which they share with landowners.

We regard this principle as of fundamental importance; even where there are no economic, social or strategic reasons for the maintenance of agriculture, the cheapest way, indeed the only way, of preserving the countryside in anything like its traditional aspect would still be to farm it. This principle is recognised in the management of their properties by the National Trust.

The complex pattern of the English and Welsh countryside, with its mosaic of hedged fields of varied shapes and sizes, is of comparatively recent origin - since the time when enclosure began and mainly within the last two hundred years. The pattern evolved was a utilitarian one: the resulting beauty was incidental. Only in the case of the laying out of great parks has there been a deliberate attempt to mould the landscape. Each type of English or Welsh scenery has its devotees - there are those who find their greatest satisfaction in the waving cornfields of East Anglia or the rich dark earth and shining dykes of the Fens: others who would choose a remote Welsh valley or the fringe of Exmoor. Because of this catholicity of taste we do not fear the effect of changes on the character and type of farming and we agree with the Councils for the Preservation of Rural England and Wales and kindred bodies that efforts to preserve the countryside should be directed towards the conservation on the one hand of intrinsically interesting, old and beautiful structures which may be in danger of being swept away and towards directing on the other hand, the design of new construction so that the new will not offend by reason of bad taste or incongruity with the old.

We consider that the land of Britain should be both useful and beautiful and that the two aims are in no sense incompatible.

...

Minority Report by Professor SR Dennison

III THE PRESERVATION OF AMENITIES

41. The view of the Majority is that the beauties of the countryside depend essentially on agriculture, and the extension of this view is that anything which is hurtful to agriculture helps to destroy those beauties: thus (paragraph 160) "the countryside cannot be 'preserved' (though its peculiar value to the nation can be); it must be farmed if it is to retain those features which give it distinctive charm and character."...

42. Now if it were indeed true that amenities depended thus closely on agriculture, there might be a case for the extension and protection of agriculture and the limitation of any construction which would be harmful to it. This would not rest on economic grounds, for it would involve a considerable cost to the whole community. It would rest on the deliberate choice of the community to retain amenities at the expense of lower material standards of life; in this event, the cost should not fall on the agricultural worker more than on other members of the community - he should be paid in respect of his function as a landscape gardener and not as an agriculturalist. The cost would certainly be very great, and it is doubtful whether such beauty would be a luxury which we could afford; our standards of living are not so high that there would be a margin sufficient to allow it.

43. The question is, however, in fact one of degree. This is for two reasons. First, the area likely to be covered by new construction, even though there were widespread dispersal of congested cities, is but a small part of the total of agricultural land. Thus (taking the figures quoted in paragraphs 8 and 88 of the Majority Report) in the twelve years up to 1939, the average annual use of land for building and general construction amounted to 0.15 per cent of the agricultural acreage. Even if this were doubled, the rate of destruction of beauty would not be very formidable.

44. It is, however, one purpose of planning to prevent new construction from destroying beauty, so that even this relatively small amount of encroachment on the countryside need not involve a comparable loss of amenity. There are areas in the country where it would be generally agreed that construction should be severely restricted, if not completely prevented, and intelligent and comprehensive control would ensure that such areas would be left unspoilt. While construction might thereby be kept entirely away from certain areas, there would still be left the major part of the countryside, and here planning control should make it possible to reduce to a minimum any sacrifice of amenity.

...

50. The solution must lie in more comprehensive planning control. Not only is it necessary to prevent the spoilation of a particular piece of beauty (such as may occur through bad design or siting, or, indeed, in some cases by the intrusion

of any construction), but it is also necessary that new construction should be so ordered as to give the best possible conditions for those who are to live in the new communities. It is in this way that a new beauty can be created - not, it is true, the beauty of a purely rural countryside (though much of that will remain), but a beauty with a greater social significance, enjoyed by many more than now have that privilege.

...

75. *Recommendations*

(1) All land in the countryside should be included in planning schemes, and no interests of national importance should be excluded from the aims of planning.

(2) While particular planning schemes will certainly involve preservation of much land in agricultural use, it should not be accepted as a *necessary principle* that construction in the countryside must be prevented in order to maintain agriculture, to preserve rural communities, or to preserve amenities.

(3) The introduction of industry into the countryside, under effective planning control, could be of considerable benefit to rural communities; rather than preventing such development, some measure of it should be encouraged as part of the dispersal of existing concentrations.

(4) The needs of agriculture (including the protection of good quality land) should be met through the normal machinery of planning schemes, and not given any prior rights. They would be met, without undue hindrance to development, if the agricultural user were given opportunity to show why change of use of a particular piece of land should not be allowed...

Professor Dennison's recommendation for 'more comprehensive planning control' was not heeded: the Town and Country Planning Act 1947 excluded farming and forestry activities from the definition of 'development',[14] thus granting farming and forestry a preemptive claim over uses of rural land and making clear that the modern system of town and country planning would not place restrictions on farmers. The split between the 'countryside' activities of agriculture and forestry and all other types of development, fostered by the majority opinion of the Scott Report, therefore became settled in planning law and led to the evolution of different legal techniques for environmental protection in urban and countryside areas. The esteem with which farming was held by the majority of the Committee and their general approach towards farming is implicit also in the Agriculture Act 1947 which set up the conditions for considerable post-war expansion of farming. The general objectives of agriculture were given in section 1 of the Agriculture Act 1947:

> ... promoting and maintaining...a stable and efficient agricultural industry capable of producing such part of the nation's food and other agricultural produce as in the national interest it is desirable to produce in the United Kingdom, and of producing it at minimum prices consistently with proper remuneration and living conditions

14 See definition of 'development' in s 55 of the Town and Country Planning Act 1990 and, particularly, exclusion of agricultural and forestry activities from this definition in s 55(e).

for farmers and workers in agriculture and an adequate return on capital invested in the industry.

The two 1947 Acts were complementary: the Town and Country Planning Act 1947 ensured security of land use for agriculture and unhampered agricultural development; the Agriculture Act 1947 achieved security of investment in farming.

(b) Pressure for change

The late nineteenth century to early twentieth century saw varied forms of environmental and land use concern in Britain develop into social movements and early pressure groups. These arose in response to the decline of traditional agriculture, rural communities and populations, and the corresponding expansion of urban areas. Different groups formed with their own sets of interests, methods and activities, but with a common desire to prevent rural decline. These spanned the political spectrum. As some socialist writers looked towards an environmental utopia in the radical tradition of William Morris and Peter Kropotkin, so there is also a history of groups on the right and far-right portraying themselves as the guardians of a rural tradition. Particularly in the inter-war period, environmental concerns were also caught up with ideas of nationalism. Images of England's green and pleasant land were employed to legitimise hierarchical social relations and foster patriotic appeals to a British national identity.

The following is Coates' account of the formation, membership and activities of three groups which reveal their common concern for the environment and their varying methods: the Soil Association; the Ramblers' Federations; and the Council for the Preservation of Rural England. These demonstrate also the political balancing and involvement in such groups: whilst many of the Ramblers' groups were associated with socialist ideals, the Soil Association had a reputation as a right-wing organisation. In the case of the first group, 'experiential holism' is used to describe the pursuit of alternative lifestyles involving a return to the land to live a simple life through gardening or smallholding, arts and crafts, and health food diets.[15]

I Coates, 'Environmental Concern in Britain 1919-1949: Diversity and Continuity', in S Elworthy et al (eds) *Perspectives on the Environment* 2 (Aldershot: Avebury, 1995) pp 65-72

Experiential holism: the Soil Association

The Soil Association had its origins in the experimental programme undertaken by Eve Balfour. She established a research trust to compare organic and non-organic farming methods in terms of their effects on the soil and the quality of the food produced. The experiment was described in her book *The Living Soil*, which also presented a summary of recent research on the link between soil

15 See further ch 8.

fertility, food quality, and human health.[16] Balfour, a critic of modern farming methods, sought scientific validation to support alternative approaches. Though her quest for wholeness undoubtedly drew on spiritual and vitalist currents, she also looked to the new science of ecology to outline the wider consequences of attempting the conquest of nature through industrial and chemical farming. Her discussion of these issues was also set in the context of contemporary debates concerning postwar reconstruction and the need to plan and build a better society. Though not taking a specific political stance, Balfour favoured a democratic and decentralised approach, arguing that private ownership of land led to over-exploitation and that some form of public ownership might be a better option.

Following the positive response to her book, the initial meeting of the Soil Association in 1945 was attended by over one hundred people and by 1947 it had membership of more than one thousand. The aims of the Soil Association can be summarised as being: to bring together all those working towards a fuller understanding of the vital relationship between soil, plants, animals and humans; to initiate, coordinate and assist research in this field; and to collect and distribute information to create a body of informed public opinion. Though successful in its role as an advisory and coordinating body for the organic farming movement, the Soil Association's experimental programme was always short of the kinds of funds necessary to run a long term comparative trial. This proved a drain on the Soil Association's meagre resources and after a series of financial crises the research had to be abandoned. A related problem was that despite the involvement of a number of reputable scientists, the Soil Association's research programme was dismissed as the work of cranks by a scientific and policy community committed to a chemical and energy intensive agriculture.

...

Popular appreciation of the countryside: the Ramblers' Federations

Estimates of the numbers of people involved in outdoor activities in the 1930s have been placed as high as 500,000. Walking was one of the most popular outdoor pastimes, especially with young people, from both working class and middle class backgrounds. In the interwar period hiking became associated with ideas of health, fitness and social permissiveness. For those experiencing the enforced leisure of unemployment it also had the advantage of being a cheap means of escaping from the bleakness of urban life. Bus and railway companies often organised special excursions and granted concessionary fares to ramblers.

The first rambling clubs had been established in the 1880s and 1890s, a number of which were associated with the *Clarion*, a socialist newspaper. The Clarion Field Clubs were sociable and family oriented, aiming to cultivate an appreciation of the countryside by bringing 'the town dweller more frequently into contact with the beauty of nature, to help forward the idea of the simple life, plain living and high thinking', the idea being that creating better people

16 Lady Eve Balfour, *The Living Earth* (London, Faber, 1941).

would help build a better society.[17] The same ethos informed groups like the Sheffield Clarion Ramblers, founded in 1900, who were to significantly influence the direction of the rambling movement.

...

The lack of free access to private land remained the key issue for ramblers. This was less of a problem in the South where public footpaths were well established and walkers on downland and pasture were not seen as a threat. In the North of England where rambling was much more a mass working class movement, the upland areas near the major cities were predominantly used for grouse shooting. Claiming that free access would cause damage and loss of income, large landowners employed keepers, generally armed with clubs or guns and accompanied by dogs, to keep walkers out. Even some council owned land was subject to a no access policy, either on the grounds of possible contamination of water catchment areas, or because the councils themselves were letting the land for private shooting.

The Ramblers' Federations responded with a series of rallies and demonstrations, with the Manchester and Sheffield Federations being amongst the most militant. Their annual demonstration at Winnats Pass in Derbyshire attracted 10,000 protesters in 1932. Also in 1932, the British Workers' Scouts Federation organised a mass trespass near Kinder Scout, a peak between Manchester and Sheffield, where only 764 out of 84,000 acres of moorland were open to the public. About 500 protesters were met by 60 keepers, one of whom was knocked unconscious. Arrests followed and five protesters received prison sentences. The Ramblers' Federations were not actively involved, preferring to stay within the law and work through negotiation, though some did organise mass trespass themselves. Such events were certainly a symptom of the resentment felt by ramblers on this issue. An Access Bill eventually became law in 1939, but ramblers regarded this as a landowners' charter. It was only in 1949 with the Access to the Countryside Act, in which the Ramblers' Association had taken an influential consultative role, that wider rights of access were granted.

Whereas on one level this was a conflict about access for recreation, it also raised wider issues of property rights, land use and environmental impacts. The owners were arguing that free access would lead to environmental damage and loss of income, but the use of moorland areas for private shooting meant that other forms of land use were not considered. As these moors were exclusively managed to protect game this led to the systematic eradication of all predators, including rare species, with all the undesirable ecological consequences resulting from such a policy. People were also seen as a threat to commercial interests, even though it was shown that grouse were not affected by public access. The ramblers' attack on property rights could be seen not merely to guarantee legal access, but also to preserve the character of the landscape, its flora and fauna, to be enjoyed for their own sake.

17 D Prynn, 'The Clarion Clubs, Rambling and the Holiday Associations in Britain Since the 1890s', (1976) *Journal of Contemporary History* No 11, 65-77.

Corporate conservationism: Council for the Preservation of Rural England

The question of access to the countryside had also involved the Council for the Preservation of Rural England. In 1928, along with the representatives of other interested groups, they had organised a Countryside Conference where the Federation of Rambling Clubs had demanded an Access to Mountains Bill. Though the CPRE was in favour of increased access it wanted this to be controlled, and was certainly opposed to it being 'without let or hindrance'. This could be explained by the fact that large landowners were one of the interest groups represented by the CPRE, which drew its support from institutions which were very much part of the establishment.

There were already a number of amenity and conservation groups in Britain, dating back to 1865 with the founding of the Commons Preservation Society. This was followed by, amongst others, the Society for the Protection of Ancient Buildings, the Society for the Protection of Birds, the Society for Checking Abuses in Public Advertising, the National Trust and the Society for the Promotion of Nature Reserves.[18] Though campaigning on behalf of the public interest, these groups tended to stick to their specialist area and worked to bring about the changes they desired through appeals to property interests and political elites. The National Trust epitomised this approach, itself becoming a large landowner and forming a close relationship with government, which almost regarded it as a public agency. However, this also limited the scope of its activities.

The CPRE was brought into being in order to undertake a role not being met by existing amenity groups. The initiative to found the CPRE had come from Patrick Abercrombie, a Professor of Town Planning who wished to find a balance between the needs of modern life and aesthetic considerations. Abercrombie thought that through planning it would be possible to exploit the countryside without destroying its essential qualities.[19] The inaugural meeting of the CPRE in 1926 was attended by the representatives of twenty organisations including established amenity groups like the National Trust, along with other interested parties such as the Royal Institute of British Architects, the Town Planning Institute, the Urban, County and Rural Councils Associations, the Central Landowners Association, and even the AA and the RAC.[20] Within ten years the CPRE represented 42 constituent bodies, 140 affiliated bodies, 28 local county branches and a large associate membership, all contributing towards administration costs of £5,000 per year for a headquarters and permanent staff.

The CPRE stated its aims as being to protect rural scenery and amenities, to provide advice and inform policy on these issues, and to educate public opinion. Other activities undertaken by the CPRE included the coordination of the work of different amenity groups, with whom they often formed special joint committees on particular issues, commissioning surveys and reports, and the

18 P Lowe, 'The Rural Idyll Defended: From Preservation to Conservation', in GE Mingay (ed) *The Rural Idyll* (London: Routledge, 1989), pp 113-139.

19 P Abercrombie, 'Country Planning', in CW Ellis (ed) *Britain and the Beast* (London: Dent, 1937), pp 133-140.

20 *The Times*, 8 December 1926, p 13.

organising of exhibitions and lectures around the country. The CPRE had considerable influence, overseeing planning schemes at national and local levels, as well as formulating and promoting legislation. In these roles it was regularly consulted by central and local government and various public bodies. Though the CPRE sought to work with the government they were highly critical of a lack of policy and the absence of coordination between government departments.

An early aim was to limit urban sprawl and ribbon development, which the CPRE did to some extent through its input into the 1932 Town Planning Act, the 1935 Ribbon Development Act and the 1938 London Green Belt Act. Another initiative began in 1929 when the CPRE submitted a memorandum to the Prime Minister on the need to create National Parks in Britain. A commission was established and a report published, but when the government failed to implement it, the CPRE formed the Standing Committee on National Parks to campaign for their establishment and to generally provide more public access to the countryside. This objective was finally achieved with the creation of the National Parks in 1949. However, the CPRE was also concerned to minimise the impact of public access, which they sought to do through an education programme promoting a country courtesy code and by the provision of Countryside Wardens wearing the CPRE badge.

Though the CPRE was undoubtedly made up of elite and established groups, including landed interests, it did take on an active campaigning role on a number of issues and took a critical stance to many government bodies. It cannot be seen as a backward looking movement concerned simply with preserving the past. The CPRE was arguing for a planned approach that would achieve a balance between the needs of modern life and conserving the aesthetic appearance of the landscape. Often the conception of what constituted an aesthetically pleasing landscape was surprisingly modernist in outlook. For example Abercrombie was not against motorways as long as they were sited with care.[21] They saw their role as being 'to promote suitable and harmonious development and to encourage rational enjoyment of rural areas by urban dwellers', allowing the physical and mental improvement of the citizen.[22]

(c) Access to the countryside

The success of these movements may be accounted for by the great political and social changes during and following the Second World War. Wartime experience generated two things in particular: the acceptance of a massive increase in the role of the government and, related to that, a commitment to greater equality through the welfare state. Access to land was affected by these changes. Despite the pressures of war, two government committees considered long distance paths and national parks in 1942 (the Scott Committee) and 1943 (the Dower Committee). A further Committee on Footpaths and Access

21 P Abercrombie, *The Preservation of Rural England* (London, University Press of Liverpool and Hodder and Stoughton, 1926), p 25.

22 J Sheail, *Rural Conservation in Inter-War Britain* (Oxford: Clarendon Press, 1981), p 64.

to the Countryside in 1947 strongly supported the creation of national footpaths which would allow greater access to the countryside.

The National Parks and Access to the Countryside Act 1949[23] was landmark legislation for creating long distance paths. Reports at the time spoke of the spirit of optimism in the 1949 legislation, that, unthinkable just a few years previously, land might be obtained by law for paths and national parks.

National Parks and Access to the Countryside Act 1949

An Act to make provision for National Parks and the establishment of a National Parks Commission; to confer on the Nature Conservancy and local authorities powers for the establishment and maintenance of nature reserves; to make further provision for the recording, creation, maintenance and improvement of public paths and for securing access to open country, and to amend the law relating to rights of way; to confer further powers for preserving and enhancing natural beauty; and for matters connected with the purposes aforesaid.

...

PART II NATIONAL PARKS

5. (1) The provisions of this Part of this Act shall have effect for the purpose of preserving and enhancing the natural beauty of the areas specified in the next following subsection, and for the purpose of promoting their enjoyment by the public.

(2) The said areas are those extensive tracts of country in England and Wales as to which it appears to the Commission that by reason of -

(a) their natural beauty, and

(b) the opportunities they afford for open-air recreation, having regard both to their character and to their position in relation to centres of population,

it is especially desirable that the necessary measures shall be taken for the purposes mentioned in the last foregoing subsection.

(3) The said areas, as for the time being designated by order made by the Commission and submitted to and confirmed by the Minister, shall be known as, and are hereinafter referred to as, National Parks.

...

PART V ACCESS TO OPEN COUNTRY

59. (1) The provisions of this Part of this Act shall have effect for enabling the public to have access for open-air recreation to open country -

(a) to which the provisions of the next following section are applied by an agreement under this Part of this Act (hereinafter referred to as an "access agreement") or by an order under this Part of this Act (hereinafter referred to as an "access order"),

(b) acquired under this Part of this Act for the purpose of giving to the public access thereto.

(2) In this Part of this Act the expression "open country" means any area appearing to the authority with whom an access agreement is made or to the authority by whom an access order is made or by whom the area is acquired,

23 See further ch 11.

as the case may be, to consist wholly or predominantly of mountain, moor, heath, down, cliff or foreshore (including any bank, barrier, dune, beach, flat or other land adjacent to the foreshore).

...

61. (1) Every local planning authority, except as hereinafter provided, shall within two years from the commencement of this Act review their area for the purpose of ascertaining what land there is in their area of the descriptions specified in subsection (2) of section fifty-nine of this Act, and of considering what action should be taken as respects their area, whether by the making of access agreements or orders or by the acquisition of land, for securing access by the public for open-air recreation.

4 CONCLUSIONS

Land use controls in Britain, including the modern system of town planning, are the product of an intriguing and peculiar mix of social forces, which had in common a desire to fashion or impose order on nature and chaotic urban areas in the cause of creating the conditions for a better, healthier, society. In this mix we can identify utopian and socialist thought, and the pragmatism and idealism of zealous public health reformers and popular social movements and groups. These influences were then combined with the opportunities and conditions for regeneration which followed the Second World War. The effects of the developing land use controls were not always benign. Planning offered a powerful means by which law defined what is meant by 'amenity', and the 'public benefit'. The planning system, by containing the radicalism of popular social movements, ordered living and working patterns and conditions, and relations between individuals and communities. The strength and prescriptiveness of planning controls was softened by references to planning serving the public interest or common good.

Nevertheless the utopian influence on planning controls is seen clearly in the building of garden cities. The emphasis of the garden city movement on land as the source of wealth, on cooperation, and community, has had an impact on the principles and practice of town planning beyond the confines of Letchworth and Welwyn. The idealism of the garden city movement can be seen in the modern town planning system in terms of the role that planning is expected to perform in protecting the environment and particularly now its contribution to achieving sustainable development.[24] This is not surprising since some of the ideas and principles which informed the building of garden cities and new towns also helped develop the town planning movement.[25] The nomenclature of the movement is significant: the Garden City Association

24 See ch 7; see D Millichap, 'Sustainability: A Long Established Concern of Planning, [1993] JPEL 1111-1119, for a discussion of the fundamental similarity between the concerns of sustainability and those of planning from the Victorian era onwards.

25 D Hardy, *From Garden Cities to New Towns: Campaigning for Town and Country Planning, 1889-1946* (London: Spon, 1991); D Hardy, *From New Towns to Green Politics: Campaigning for Town and Country Planning 1946-1990* (London: Spon, 1991).

became the Garden City and Town Planning Association in 1908 and the Town and Country Planning Association in 1932. There is also a sense of continuity of purpose and content of law; references in the early planning legislation to 'amenity' and the 'public interest' are made in the later Planning Acts. Recent environmental concerns have also led to proposals to revive the system of charging for development, as introduced by the 1947 Act. A form of this might implicitly be seen in the present use of planning obligations.[26]

During industrialisation, we see the social and physical 'construction' of the town and countryside – in relation to each other and also in opposition. The countryside can only exist as a peaceful haven (as nature) when contrasted with the industrial city's man-made landscape of chimneys, factories and streets. The garden city idealists attempted to break down this division so as to create a 'marriage' of the town and country. It is telling that the two important land use Acts in the post-war period, the Town and Country Planning Act 1947 and the National Parks and Access to the Countryside Act 1949, separated controls over urban and countryside areas. In broad terms, the separation of legal controls over land use and development in rural and urban areas, settled in the Town and Country Planning Act 1947, may still be seen in the modern town planning and countryside designations regimes. This continues to mitigate against an integrated approach to environmental protection.

5 MILLENNIUM PLOTLANDS?

Some of the ideas and principles of the garden city movement and the independent spirit of those who sought Arcadia in disused railway carriages, roadhouses, charabancs and caravans have been resurrected in pockets of the modern ecological movement by those who advocate self-sufficiency and a radical form of sustainablility. This modern variant of utopianism is anarchist, or at the very least distinctly alternative, and reflects deep, as opposed to shallow or social, ecological thought. The planning system, tending to prefer a tamer version of sustainable development and doggedly adhering to a particular view of the countryside and environmental and amenity problems, gives attempts to build eco-hamlets and settlements short shrift.

Department of the Environment, Planning Research Programme, *Planning Controls over Agricultural and Forestry Development and Rural Building Conversions*, A report by Land Use Consultants and Countryside Planning and Management (London: HMSO, 1995) pp 93-100

CHAPTER 10: CAR PARKS, MOBILE UNITS, AND TEMPORARY STRUCTURES ON FARMS

10.1 The particular issues which this research sought to address related to:

* very large purpose designed mobile structures which are now on the market

26 See ch 7, pp 261–266.

for farm enterprises;

* non-purpose designed temporary/moveable structures which appear on farms, from old railway carriages and portacabins to caravans and containers, supposedly used for storage purposes;
* farm car parks on pick-your-own enterprises and equivalent, especially those involving considerable areas of hardstanding.

...

Temporary/mobile structures not designed for the purposes of agriculture

10.14 Of far greater concern to local authorities and national conservation agencies, were moveable structures not designed for the purpose of agriculture, such as old railway coaches, containers, portacabins and caravans, used for storage, shelter and temporary accommodation of farm workers. Such structures are particularly prevalent in the urban fringe where they may serve sub-divided paddocks associated with hobby farming and horse-keeping. In situations where they are not serving an agricultural purpose, they are normally deemed to be permitted "development" under Part 4 of Schedule 2 to the GDO [General Development Order]... but where they are serving an agricultural purpose they may be deemed to be "a use of land for agriculture"...

10.15 Structures such as portacabins, containers, etc., are also found on agricultural units in the deeper countryside, particularly those of a part-time nature, including in designated landscapes and upland areas, where they sometimes replace the more traditional lambing marquees. They may be found either scattered around the farmstead or, occasionaly, in isolated and visually prominent locations.

10.16 Although not enormous in overall numbers, all our LPAs pointed to these structures as being a particular problem, because they are a major source of public complaint, and because LPAs are often helpless to take action, frequently bringing the planning system into disrepute. It was felt by LPAs that the problems caused by these structures are entirely disproportionate to their actual numbers. In addition, they can be larger than some legitimate agricultural developments constructed under the determination process. ...

10.17 It was also noted that there are currently no restrictions on the number of temporary structures allowed on a holding, regardless of its size, often leading to considerable areas of "shackery", particularly in the urban fringe. Some LPAs noted that temporary structures are used as a "threat" to planning officers by applicants seeking permission for an agricultural dwelling or equivalent. So, whereas in the past officers were sometimes threatened with an agricultural development constructed as permitted development, if planning permissions were not granted, since introduction of the determination process, the emphasis has shifted to temporary structures.

Current controls adopted by LPAs over temporary and mobile structures

Temporary/mobile structures deemed to be a use of land for agriculture

10.18 All our sample LPAs felt helpless to control temporary/mobile structures which are deemed to be "a use of land for agriculture". Although Discontinuance

Orders ... are technically available to cover this eventuality, they were considered generally inappropriate and unwieldy in that they can only be served on a site and not a structure and, in disputed cases, the structure could simply be moved to an alternative site. In addition, like Article 4 Directions:

* they require the approval of the Secretary of State;
* they attract compensation.

10.19 For these reasons none of our sample LPAs had or intend to use a Discontinuance Order for this purpose.

10.20 The only controls which LPAs have used is in the form of conditions or a legal agreement associated with a separate planning permission for say, an agricultural dwelling or a change of use. In one case history, permission for an agricultural dwelling was subject to a legal agreement which sought the removal of old car bodies and temporary structures scattered around the farmstead. In another, part of the legal agreement associated with a permission for building re-use, required that no lorry containers should be placed anywhere on the site. Obviously the scope of this form of control is limited, as it depends on planning permission being sought for other forms of development on the same holding.

...

RECOMMENDATIONS

10.33 Against this background it is recommended that:

R11 DOE should give serious consideration as to how to exercise control over temporary structures which are deemed to be a "use of land for agriculture" and therefore currently fall outside planning control (...) In particular, attention should focus on those structures which are not designed for the purpose of agriculture recognising the considerable landscape impact which they can have (...).

This is a complex subject since the definitions for temporary structures have been established by the Courts. A change in primary legislation may be required to bring what is deemed to be "an agricultural use of land" under some form of planning control. One approach might be to require that before a temporary structure can be considered as "an agricultural use of land" thereby falling outside planning control, it must pass two tests:

* it must be designed for the purposes of agriculture following the definition which applies to agricultural development under Part 6 of Schedule 2 to the GDO;
* it must be demonstrated to be temporary/moveable in terms of both design and use, in other words a time limit should be set specifying the maximum time that a moveable/temporary structure can stay in one location.

R 12 Consideration should be given to simplifying Article 4 Directions and removing the requirement for compensation payments (...)

This is required to allow LPAs to respond rapidly to situations where there is a need to control:

- ...
- the proliferation of temporary buildings associated with hobby farming and horse-keeping (para 10.14).

The Department of the Environment's view of an ideal countryside bears a resemblance to that of the Council for the Protection of Rural England: the CPRE has consistently argued for a planned approach to conserve the aesthetic appeal of the landscape (see the extract from Coates, above, p 110). As the following extract suggests, this 'preservation' of rural England cannot be squared with a vision of a countryside that is vital, productive and, above all, sustainable.

S Fairlie 'Planning's blot on the landscape', *The Guardian* 14.8.96, p 4

How can there be sustainable development in the countryside when the British planning system explicity *discourages* development in the countryside? The powerful environmental movement in England and Wales has so far failed to tackle this basic question. If it continues to ignore it, then an already perceptible rift between conservationists and advocates of sustainability will widen.

On one side, a wide range of groups and individuals – organic farmers, permaculturists, low-impact dwellers, builders of energy-efficient houses and advocates of eco-hamlets and settlements – are finding the main obstacle to sustainable rural development is the planning system.

On the other side, the countryside lobby, championed by the Council for the Protection of Rural England (CPRE) is pressing for stiffer planning restrictions on rural development, without making a firm distinction as to whether such development is sustainable or not. It is the countryside protection lobby which is informing Government policy.

The influence of the CPRE and similar organisations can be seen in a 1995 Department of the Environment research report, Planning Control over Agricultural and Forestry Developments and Rural Building Conversions. It examines what both the CPRE and the DoE have identified as the "fragmentation" of British farmland. As a result of changes in agricultural policy, uneconomic farms, instead of being amalgamated into larger units, are increasingly being broken up and sold off in lots. While the original farmhouse, and sometimes the outbuildings as well, are bought for prodigious sums by urban in-comers and commuters, the bare land tends to be sold off in small parcels, often to prospective smallholders and part-time farmers.

Fragmentation, say the DoE researchers, "may result in considerable pressure for new buildings, and can have a profound effect upon landscape character". The aspiring smallholders install makeshift barns, cowsheds, stables, pig arks, caravans, lorry containers and what have you – "shackery", as the report calls it – on their bare land plots, then often go on to apply for planning permission for a new house.

...

These proposals [see extract above this one] bear more than a passing resemblance to recommendations made in a 1990 report by the Council for the Protection of Rural England (CPRE), called Planning Controls over Farmland.

Ideally the CPRE would like to see planning controls enforced upon all farmers in a way that would make some distinction between, say, organic producers and intensive livestock units. But, with the present government unlikely to sanction the imposition of burdens upon its friends in the Country

Landowners Association, the CPRE is prepared (so the DoE researchers tell us) to settle for controls upon smallholders "as a step in the right direction".

The DoE thus claims the backing of the countryside protection lobby for a policy which is designed to hit small enterprises responding to changes in agricultural conditions, but which hardly touches the "big boys". And hit small farmers it will. If the policy is rigorously enforced, the operation of a holding with no existing buildings attached will be virtually impossible.

Plants For A Future is a co-operative employing four people who are converting 38 acres of land in Cornwall to organic horticulture and selling more than 1,500 species of plants by mail order. When the project started up in 1988, its founders wanted to live on their land in a mobile home, but, after an unsuccessful planning appeal, were forced to find rented accommodation from which they now commute in a car. Then, to make matters worse, an Article 4 Direction was placed on their property. And recently they were refused permission to erect a poly-tunnel and lay gravel on their visitors' car park, on visual impact grounds.

Phil Warsop, of the co-operative, says: "The planners don't take into account the fact that we have planted 12,000 trees on the land and some two miles of hedges. The Article 4 Direction makes it almost impossible to manage our land properly and we are thinking of relocating the centre of our operation to another district."

Most people would rather not see recycled shackery, mobile homes and new agricultural bungalows sprouting over the countryside, particularly when there are traditional farm buildings built to fulfil the same purposes. But neither the CPRE nor the DoE reports begin to consider whether small-scale farming might not be a constructive response to fragmentation. They do not take into account the view of the Rural Development Commission that small and part-time farms may benefit from Common Agricultural Policy reforms, because "relatively low indebtedness means that they can operate with very low returns".

Nor do they acknowledge that small, labour-intensive farms are consistently found by agro-economists to be more productive per acre and per unit of energy used than large ones. And they do not examine whether since the amalgamation of farmland has been so destructive, fragmentation might not lead to environmental improvements.

And neither report gives any inkling of what is supposed to happen to this land if small scale agriculture is to be discouraged. Are members of the CLA to be paid with taxpayers' money to keep it in a state of suspended animation?

For people who seek to live and work in the country, and for many in the environmental movement, the release of farmland represents not a threat but a way forward: an opportunity to revive more labour-intensive farming methods that work with nature, rather than against it; to regenerate woodland and coppice to provide better timber and more satisfying livelihoods; to develop permaculture as a new form of intensive land-use; and to evolve low-impact ways of accommodating people and animals which enhance the environment.

Instead of a moonscape of caravans, lorry containers and bungalows, many prospective smallholders and country dwellers want to contribute towards an environment with more trees, more hedges, more birds and butterflies, fine buildings that are part of the landscape – and more people to provide the necessary labour and craftsmanship.

There is a growing concern among many in the environmental movement that the CPRE national executive, rather than its membership, is more interested in turning the countryside into a drive-in museum than supporting sustainable rural development. There is an argument for extending planning controls over major agricultural activities, but controls should be introduced in a way that is not unduly prejudicial against small holders and aspiring farmers.

...

PART III

Development of environmental law

CHAPTER 4

International initiatives

1 INTRODUCTION

In this chapter we will trace the evolution and development in international law of the concept of sustainable development. We choose the topic because it illustrates both the problems that must be overcome when attempting to regulate use of the resources of the entire planet and also the remarkable developments in international environmental law over the twenty years between the international conferences devoted to global environmental protection held in Stockholm in 1972 and in Rio in 1992.

Classical international law regulates relations between sovereign states. The developing field of international environmental law faces challenges because it is concerned with natural systems. It follows the forms and procedures of international law and so is constrained by national frontiers but it also seeks to mediate the relationship between people and nature, safeguarding the integrity of ecosystems.

A distinct body of international law specifically concerned with environmental protection has developed since the early 1970s. This development has been rapid and is still proceeding with bursts of growth and change. One commentator describes international environmental law as 'beyond infancy but not yet adolescent'.[1]

N Robinson (ed) *Agenda 21: Earth's Action Plan* (New York/London/Rome: Oceana Pubs Inc, 1993) pp xiv-xv

International Environmental Law links individuals and their local governments into a world-wide network. This system is not often perceived locally, because each country's own legislation and institutions are assigned the job of applying the shared environmental rules. However, when one considers how the weather transports pollution, how species migrate, how trade of a food product like coffee can carry pesticide residues, how tourists, business staff, or visitors move daily around the world, it is evident that each country needs to undertake roughly equivalent environmental protection measures. Law is the mechanism for defining and applying those services.

Moreover, Environmental Law is unlike the model of classic International Law in which a few agreed norms guide how independent sovereign states act

1 N Robinson (ed) *Agenda 21: Earth's Action Plan* (New York/London/Rome: Oceana Pubs Inc, 1993) p xxxv.

to establish their own rules and keep their national territory safe by a balance of power. The new paradigm of Environmental Law provides for rules which are based on ecology and other sciences; the "laws of nature" exist quite apart from the will of sovereign states. These environmental rules cut across all artificial national borders, just as watersheds or wind patterns do. Environmental Law functions wherever nature's systems are found, and adapts human behaviour to work within the constraints of the environment.

If human conduct is not guided by the teachings of environmental sciences, the "tragedy of the commons" results; each person maximizes a narrow, immediate gain, while failing to see how a natural resource may be depleted or a pollutant may harm a distant person. If socio-economic development is to be sustained over time, it cannot unknowingly waste its capital or freely discard its unwanted by-products. The role of Environmental Law is to compensate for such dysfunctions in the economic and social sectors.

We focus on sustainable development because it is the theme of Agenda 21, arguably the most important outcome of the Rio conference in June 1992, and because it is an example of how environmental law is dynamic and pervasive, challenging established legal concepts and institutions in order to protect the environment. The existence of Agenda 21 represents a remarkable achievement in international diplomacy. It is having appreciable effects already and it promises to have further effects in the future. This is all the more interesting since, in strict legal terms, Agenda 21 was originally viewed as something of a failure as it did not achieve treaty status. Its status is that of 'soft law'. We discuss this in the next section which describes and illustrates the main sources of international law.

2 SOURCES OF INTERNATIONAL LAW

There is no supreme international body responsible for law making, so international law is derived from a number of sources and a diversity of institutions.

The International Court of Justice was established by the Charter of the United Nations in 1946 as a successor to the Permanent Court of International Justice set up by the League of Nations. There is a President of the Court, a Vice-President and a panel of a dozen judges. As international law exists by virtue of the consent of states, it follows that the assertion of a claim under international law by one state against another is contentious; so every diplomatic channel is exhausted before a case comes before the Court. There are consequently very few cases. More often states will agree to arbitration by a tribunal or by an agreed arbitrator. Occasionally the Secretary General of the United Nations will be asked for a ruling. The '*Rainbow Warrior* Affair' resulted in such a ruling.

In July 1986 the *Rainbow Warrior*, a ship owned by Greenpeace, was sunk in Auckland Harbour, New Zealand, as a result of damage caused by explosions. A Dutch crewman drowned when the ship went down. Greenpeace had been using the *Rainbow Warrior* for its campaign against French nuclear tests in the Pacific. Two agents of the French secret service were arrested in New Zealand and prosecuted for the crime. New Zealand and France were unable to reach agreement on reparations and referred the matter to the Secretary General of the United Nations, agreeing to abide by his ruling. New Zealand's claims were that France had violated its sovereignty and rights under international law and so France should give an unqualified apology and pay compensation. The Secretary General ruled that France should convey to the Prime Minister of New Zealand a formal and unqualified apology for the attack and pay NZ$7 million to the Government of New Zealand as compensation. New Zealand did not have standing to claim compensation on behalf of the family of the Dutch seaman but wanted to make sure that France compensated them. France did so. France agreed with Greenpeace to submit the matter of compensation for the ship to an arbitral tribunal which later awarded Greenpeace NZ$8,159,000.[2]

(a) Treaties

Treaties are agreements made between states with the intention that they should be binding under international law. They are generally the result of lengthy deliberations and negotiations and may be multi-lateral, applying to all states, or bi-lateral, in which case they are only binding on the signatory states. They may not always be titled treaties but may also be called conventions, protocols, covenants, pacts and so on. The 1969 Vienna Convention on the Law of Treaties (the treaty on treaties) lays down the rules which govern treaties on such matters as entry into force, interpretation, invalidity and termination. Unless the treaty specifically does not allow it, states may make reservations to treaties provided the reservation is not incompatible with the treaty's objectives.

Treaty making is a two stage process. First, a treaty is signed by states, with a later ratification date. This enables individual states to obtain approval of the treaty from whatever may be their internal law making institution: this may be a parliament, a president, or, alternatively, a dictator. During this interval between signing and ratification, states which have signed the treaty may not do anything that undermines its purposes. Only when the agreed ratification process is complete does the treaty become fully legally binding.

We have reproduced below parts of the Convention on Biological Diversity agreed at Rio in 1992 as an example of a treaty. We have chosen this because maintaining biodiversity and preserving and disseminating the knowledge of indigenous peoples is central to sustainable development. It illustrates the dynamism of international environmental law, and acknowledges the important role played by non-governmental organisations.

Note first that it is called a 'convention'. The purposes of the treaty are set out in the preamble. The intention that it should be legally binding can be discerned from the language of the Articles which use such mandatory words as 'Each Contracting Party shall', though this is frequently qualified by other

2 JM Sweeney, CT Oliver and NE Leech, *The International Legal System, Cases and Materials* 3rd edn (Westbury, New York: Foundation Press, 1988), pp 38-40.

phrases such as 'in accordance with [a state's] particular conditions and capabilities'.

CONVENTION ON BIOLOGICAL DIVERSITY

Done at Rio de Janeiro, June 5, 1992, Cite as 31 I.L.M. 818 (1992). Reproduced from the text provided by the United Nations Environment Programme. The Convention was adopted by the Conference for Adoption of the Agreed Text of the Convention on Biological Diversity, held at UNEP Headquarters, Nairobi, on May 22, 1992. It was opened for signature at the UNCED Conference in Rio de Janeiro by all states and regional economic integration organisations, and remained open for signature at U.N. Headquarters in New York until June 4, 1993.

Preamble

The Contracting Parties

Conscious of the intrinsic value of biological diversity and of the ecological, genetic, social, economic, scientific, educational, cultural, recreational and aesthetic values of biological diversity and its components,

Conscious also of the importance of biological diversity for evolution and for maintaining life sustaining systems of the biosphere,

Affirming that the conservation of biological diversity is a common concern of humankind,

Reaffirming that States have sovereign rights over their own biological resources,

Reaffirming also that States are responsible for conserving their biological diversity and for using their biological resources in a sustainable manner,

Concerned that biological diversity is being significantly reduced by certain human activities,

Aware of the general lack of information and knowledge regarding biological diversity and of the urgent need to develóp scientific, technical and institutional capacities to provide the basic understanding upon which to plan and implement appropriate measures,

Noting that it is vital to anticipate, prevent and attack the causes of significant reduction or loss of biological diversity at source,

Noting also that where there is a threat of significant reduction or loss of biological diversity, lack of full scientific certainty should not be used as a reason for postponing measures to avoid or minimize such a threat,

Noting further that the fundamental requirement for the conservation of biological diversity is the in-situ conservation of ecosystems and natural habitats and the maintenance and recovery of viable populations of species in their natural surroundings,

Noting further that ex-situ measures, preferably in the country of origin, also have an important role to play,

Recognizing the close and traditional dependence of many indigenous and local communities embodying traditional lifestyles on biological resources, and the desirability of sharing equitably benefits arising from the use of traditional knowledge, innovations and practices relevant to the conservation of biological diversity and the sustainable use of its components,

Recognizing also the vital role that women play in the conservation and sustainable use of biological diversity and affirming the need for the full participation of women at all levels of policy-making and implementation for biological diversity conservation,

Stressing the importance of, and the need to promote, international, regional and global cooperation among States and intergovernmental organizations and the non-governmental sector for the conservation of biological diversity and the sustainable use of its components,

Acknowledging that the provision of new and additional financial resources and appropriate access to relevant technologies can be expected to make a substantial difference in the world's ability to address the loss of biological diversity,

Acknowledging further that special provision is required to meet the needs of developing countries, including the provision of new and additional financial resources and appropriate access to relevant technologies,

Noting in this regard the special conditions of the least developed countries and small island States,

Acknowledging that substantial investments are required to conserve biological diversity and that there is the expectation of a broad range of environmental, economic and social benefits from those investments,

Recognizing that economic and social development and poverty eradication are the first and overriding priorities of developing countries,

Aware that, ultimately, the conservation and sustainable use of biological diversity will strengthen friendly relations among States and contribute to peace for humankind,

Desiring to enhance and complement existing international arrangements for the conservation of biological diversity and sustainable use of its components, and

Determined to conserve and sustainably use biological diversity for the benefit of present and future generations,

Have agreed as follows:

Article 1. Objectives
The objectives of this Convention, to be pursued in accordance with its relevant provisions, are the conservation of biological diversity, the sustainable use of

its components and the fair and equitable sharing of the benefits arising out of the utilization of genetic resources, including by appropriate access to genetic resources and by appropriate transfer of relevant technologies, taking into account all rights over those resources and to technologies, and by appropriate funding.

Article 2. [Use of terms]

Article 3. Principles
States have, in accordance with the Charter of the United Nations and the principles of international law, the sovereign right to exploit their own resources pursuant to their own environmental policies, and the responsibility to ensure that activities within their jurisdiction or control do not cause damage to the environment of other States or of areas beyond the limits of national jurisdiction.

Article 4. [Jurisdictional Scope]

Article 5. [Cooperation]

Article 6. General Measures for Conservation and Sustainable Use
Each Contracting Party shall, in accordance with its particular conditions and capabilities:

(a) Develop national strategies, plans or programmes for the conservation and sustainable use of biological diversity or adapt for this purpose existing strategies, plans or programmes which shall reflect, inter alia, the measures set out in this Convention relevant to the Contracting Party concerned; and
(b) Integrate, as far as possible and as appropriate, the conservation and sustainable use of biological diversity into relevant sectoral or cross-sectoral plans, programmes and policies.

Article 7. Identification and Monitoring
Each Contracting Party shall, as far as possible and as appropriate, in particular for the purposes of Articles 8 to 10:

(a) Identify components of biological diversity important for its conservation and sustainable use having regard to the indicative list of categories set down in Annex I;
(b) Monitor, through sampling and other techniques, the components of biological diversity identified pursuant to subparagraph (a) above, paying particular attention to those requiring urgent conservation measures and those which offer the greatest potential for sustainable use;
(c) Identify processes and categories of activities which have or are likely to have significant adverse impacts on the conservation and sustainable use of biological diversity, and monitor their effects through sampling and other techniques; and
(d) Maintain and organize, by any mechanism, data derived from identification and monitoring activities pursuant to subparagraphs (a), (b) and (c) above.

Article 8. In-situ Conservation

Each Contracting Party shall, as far as possible and as appropriate:

(a) Establish a system of protected areas or areas where special measures need to be taken to conserve biological diversity;
(b) Develop, where necessary, guidelines for the selection, establishment and management of protected areas or areas where special measures need to be taken to conserve biological diversity;
(c) Regulate or manage biological resources important for the conservation of biological diversity whether within or outside protected areas, with a view to ensuring their conservation and sustainable use;
(d) Promote the protection of ecosystems, natural habitats and the maintenance of viable populations of species in natural surroundings;
(e) Promote environmentally sound and sustainable development in areas adjacent to protected areas with a view to furthering protection of these areas;
(f) Rehabilitate and restore degraded ecosystems and promote the recovery of threatened species, inter alia, through the development and implementation of plans or other management strategies;
(g) Establish or maintain means to regulate, manage or control the risks associated with the use and release of living modified organisms resulting from biotechnology which are likely to have adverse environmental impacts that could affect the conservation and sustainable use of biological diversity, taking also into account the risks to human health;
(h) Prevent the introduction of, control or eradicate those alien species which threaten ecosystems, habitats or species;
(i) Endeavour to provide the conditions needed for compatibility between present uses and the conservation of biological diversity and the sustainable use of its components;
(j) Subject to its national legislation, respect, preserve and maintain knowledge, innovations and practices of indigenous and local communities embodying traditional lifestyles relevant for the conservation and sustainable use of biological diversity and promote their wider application with the approval and involvement of the holders of such knowledge, innovations and practices and encourage the equitable sharing of the benefits arising from the utilization of such knowledge, innovations and practices;
(k) Develop or maintain necessary legislation and/or other regulatory provisions for the protection of threatened species and populations;
(l) Where a significant adverse effect on biological diversity has been determined pursuant to Article 7, regulate or manage the relevant processes and categories of activities; and
(m) Cooperate in providing financial and other support for in-situ conservation outlined in paragraphs (a) to (l) above, particularly for developing countries.

Other articles cover matters such as Research and Training (Article 12), Access to Genetic Resources (Article 15) and Access to and Transfer of Technology (Article 16) as well, crucially, as Financial Resources (Article 20).

This Treaty specifically stated that no reservations are permitted. This being so, the United States declared at Rio that it would not sign and gave a declaration as to the reasons.

Environment Programme Conference for the Adoption of the Agreed Text of the Convention on Biological Diversity [May 22, 1992] Cite as 31 ILM 848 (1992). Reproduced from the text of the Declaration attached to the Nairobi Final Act provided by the United Nations Environment Programme.

Declaration of the United States of America

1. In signing the Final Act, the United States recognizes that this negotiation has drawn to a close.
2. The United States strongly supports the conservation of biodiversity and, as is known, was an original proponent of a convention on this important subject. We continue to view international cooperation in this area as extremely desirable.
3. It is deeply regrettable to us that – whether because of the haste with which we have completed our work or the result of substantive disagreement – a number of issues of serious concern in the United States have not been adequately addressed in the course of this negotiation. As a result, in our view, the text is seriously flawed in a number of important respects.
4. As a matter of substance, we find particularly unsatisfactory the text's treatment of intellectual property rights; finances, including, importantly, the role of the Global Environmental Facility (GEF); technology transfer and biotechnology.
5. In addition, we are disappointed with the development of issues related to environmental impact assessments, the legal relationship between this Convention and other international agreements, and the scope of obligations with respect to the marine environment.
6. Procedurally, we believe that the hasty and disjointed approach to the preparation of this Convention has deprived delegations of the ability to consider the text as a whole before adoption. Further, it has not resulted in a text that reflects well on the international treaty-making process in the environmental field.

(b) International custom

As a source of international law, custom is less easy to pinpoint. Article 38 of the Statute of the International Court of Justice stipulates that the Court should apply international customary law as 'evidence of a general practice accepted as law'. This evidence can be found in the actual behaviour of states coupled with the belief that the behaviour is required by law – *opinio juris*. It is not necessary that all practices by states should be entirely consistent with the rule provided they are aware that they are breaking it. In this sense there is an analogy with domestic laws: we do not all abide by all the laws all of the time but generally we know when we are acting unlawfully.

There is an important, and contested, question as to how long a time must elapse before a general practice of states can be said to have crystalised into a rule of customary international law. Given the extremely rapid development of international environmental law there is a body of opinion that maintains that new norms and principles can become instantaneous international customary law because of the lack of custom to be displaced.[3]

An example of customary international environmental law is the duty of a state to take adequate steps in order to prevent, reduce and control sources of pollution within its jurisdiction which cause harm in the territory of another state. In the *Trail Smelter* case[4] Canada was ordered to pay damages to the United States and to establish a regime for controlling future emissions from a smelter whose fumes had caused harm across the border.

The International Court of Justice was quite clear in the *Nicaragua* case that a treaty reservation could not displace customary international law.

Case Concerning Military and Paramilitary Activities In and Against Nicaragua (*Nicaragua v United States (Merits)*) [1986] ICJ 14

172. The Court has now to turn its attention to the question of the law applicable to the present dispute. In formulating its view on the significance of the United States multilateral treaty reservation, the Court has reached the conclusion that it must refrain from applying the multilateral treaties invoked by Nicaragua in support of its claims ...

...

179. It will therefore be clear that customary international law continues to exist and to apply, separately from international treaty law, even where the two categories of law have an identical content...

(c) 'Soft' international law

A further source of international law is what are known as 'soft law' instruments. In international law for environmental protection the use of soft law is extremely important. It takes the form of codes of practice, recommendations, guidelines, resolutions and declarations of principle to which states expect adherence.

P Birnie and A Boyle, *International Law and The Environment* (Oxford: Clarendon Press, 1993), p 27

Soft law is by its nature the articulation of a "norm" in written form, which can include both legal and non-legal instruments; the necessary abstract norms in issue which have been agreed by states or in international organisations are thus recorded in it, and this is its essential characteristic; another is that a considerable degree of discretion in interpretation and on how and when to

3 J Cameron and J Werksman, *The Precautionary Principle: A Policy for Action in the Face of Uncertainty*, CIEL Background Papers on International Environmental Law No 1/1991, p 6.
4 (1939) 33 American Journal of International Law 182.

conform to the requirements is left to the participants. Its great advantage over "hard law" is that, as occasion demands, it can either enable states to take on obligations that otherwise they would not, because these are expressed in vaguer terms, or conversely, a "soft law" form may enable them to formulate the obligations in a precise and restrictive form that would not be acceptable in a binding treaty. Despite the fact that states retain control over the degree of commitment, the very existence of such an instrument encourages the trend towards hardening the international legal order; not all "soft" instruments necessarily themselves become "hard" law nor is that an inherent aim of each one, but several have.

3 EVOLUTION OF THE CONCEPT OF 'SUSTAINABLE DEVELOPMENT'

A number of developments in the 1960s led to public concern that the rapid increase in industrialisation following the Second World War was degrading the natural world.

A Kiss and D Shelton, *International Environmental Law* (London: Transnational Publishers Inc and Graham & Trotman, 1991), pp 36-37

This movement of opinion was unprecedented in two ways. First it was entirely grass roots, not finding a power base until a few, then several more governments joined in. Second, the movement was grounded from the beginning at the international level. It also had a strong philosophical content corresponding to a changing concept of the world, incorporating new individual and social values as a reaction to the "consumer society". Rejecting ideologies to the degree that they were seen as materialistic, the ecological movement spanned all political factions and political parties, sustaining a great social consensus. As a result there exist few other subjects about which so many laws have been adopted unanimously by so many national parliaments. These factors explain the brevity of time it took for international organizations to recognize the emergence of a new problem...

Kiss and Shelton believe that three events, in particular, proved to be important. First was the publication in 1963 of Rachel Carson's book *The Silent Spring* which called into question the widespread use of pesticides in modern agriculture and mobilised a grass roots movement to force governments to take steps to protect the environment. Second was the death of forests in Sweden and the acidification of extensive fresh water lakes. The Swedes had become convinced that only action and cooperation at an international level could deal with the problem of acid rain. Sweden attributed the increase in acidity of rain by a factor of forty times the natural level to Britain's tall stack chimneys on power stations which had been built in response to the British Clean Air Acts of 1956 and 1968.[5] At the time the tall stacks were built it was thought,

5 See ch 6, pp 221-223.

optimistically, that the dispersal of emissions into the upper atmosphere would render them harmless. However, they were merely shifted by the prevailing westerly winds and were deposited further afield, pre-dominently over Scandinavian countries. The third event was the sinking of the oil tanker, *Torrey Canyon*, off the coast of Britain in 1967 which resulted in oil being washed ashore in England, France and Belgium.

It became clear that action to prevent the harms caused by pollution was needed at the international level. The United Nations General Assembly responded and passed a resolution which stated that there was 'an urgent need for intensified action at national and international level, to limit, and where possible, to eliminate the impairment of the human environment'.[6]

(a) Stockholm 1972

Following the General Assembly Resolution in 1968, in 1972 the United Nations convened a Conference on the Human Environment, hosted by Sweden in Stockholm. At the Stockholm Conference, for the first time, governments discussed the environment as a global policy issue. One hundred and thirteen states participated in the Conference, largely as a result of the report of a meeting of experts on environment and development in Switzerland in 1971 which reassured developing countries that their concerns would be taken into account at Stockholm.[7]

Consequently the Conference was of great importance because it was attended by representatives from both industrially developed and developing countries and it was recognised that environmental protection was linked with progress in economic development.[8] As well as official delegations from states there were representatives of intergovernmental organisations, 700 observers from 400 non-governmental organisations and 1,500 journalists.[9] A Declaration was produced at the end of the conference outlining principles. As well as the Declaration, an Action Plan made over a hundred recommendations and a resolution was made for financial and institutional implementation by the United Nations. The principle of sustainable development in international environmental law was first formulated in Principle 1 of the Stockholm Declaration.

Declaration of the United Nations Conference on the Human Environment (Stockholm), UN Doc, A/CONF/48/14/REV 1

Principle 1:
Man has the fundamental right to freedom, equality and adequate conditions of life, in an environment of quality that permits a life of dignity and well being, and he bears a solemn responsibility to protect and improve the environment for present and future generations...

6 G A Res 2398 (XXIII) of 3 December 1968.
7 Development and Environment: Report and Working Papers of a Panel of Experts Convened by the Secretary General of the UNCHE, Founex, 1971.
8 Report of the UN Conference on the Human Environment (Stockholm 1972) UN Doc. A/CONF/48/14/Rev 1).
9 A Kiss and D Shelton *International Environmental Law* (London: Transnational Publishers Inc & Graham & Trotman Ltd, 1991), p 38.

Stockholm was significant for recognising that environmental protection was linked to economic and social development:

Principle 8:
Economic and social development is essential for ensuring a favourable living and working environment for man and for creating conditions on earth that are necessary for the improvement of the quality of life.

(b) Principle 21

Principle 21 of the Stockholm Declaration reaffirms the sovereign right of states to exploit their own resources though this is subject to their responsibility not to cause harm to other states.

Principle 21:
States have, in accordance with the Charter of the United Nations and the principles of international law, the sovereign right to exploit their own resources pursuant to their own environmental policies, and the responsibility to ensure that activities within their jurisdiction or control do not cause damage to the environment of other states or of areas beyond the limits of national jurisdiction.

The United States submitted that Principle 21 did no more than restate an existing responsibility that states do not harm areas beyond their national jurisdiction.[10] The Principle has been applied in later international laws and requires states to do more than merely make reparation for damage, placing an obligation on them to take preventive measures to protect the environment – a precautionary approach.[11] What has emerged is an obligation on states to act with due diligence.[12] How this is to be fulfilled is not clear. It might be by the introduction of legislation and administration capable of protecting other states with special allowance made for developing countries' ability to do this under Principle 23 of the Stockholm Declaration, or it might be by the introduction of standards such as 'best available technology' or 'best practicable means'.[13]

If Principle 21 outlines the duty of states, and of international lending agencies such as the World Bank and the International Monetary Fund, to treat a precautionary approach as a higher, and therefore guiding, legal principle, as Cameron and Werksman assert,[14] the question still arises as to when it should come into play. If it is a policy for action in the face of uncertainty to take prior assessment of environmental impacts into account, the question remains as to what degree of risk should trigger precautionary action. Some states still insist that they are not bound to take action until clear scientific proof of actual harm has been provided.

Birnie and Boyle, however, adopt a stronger version of precaution.

10 See Canadian and US Comments in UN Doc A/CONF/48/14/Rev 1 at 64-66.
11 Discussed further below.
12 P Birnie and A Boyle *International Law and The Environment* (Oxford: Clarendon Press, 1993), pp 92-93.
13 See ch 6, pp 223-234.
14 J Cameron and J Werkman *The Precautionary Principle: A Policy for Action in the Face of Uncertainty*, CIEL Background Papers on International Environmental Law No 1/1991.

P Birnie and A Boyle, *International Law and the Environment* (Oxford: Clarendon, 1993) p 97

A more realistic approach, when the question is one of prevention of foreseeable harm, not responsibility for actual harm, is to lower the threshold of proof. Whilst still entailing some element of foreseeability, this would require measures of prevention at an earlier stage, when there is still some room for uncertainty. Expressions such as "reasonably foreseeable" or "significant risk" allow both the magnitude of harm and the probability of its occurrence to be taken into account.

(c) The United Nations Environment Programme (UNEP)

Perhaps the most significant outcome of the Stockholm Conference was the establishment of an infrastructure for intergovernmental cooperation in research, education and programme development taking environmental considerations into account.

Most importantly, in 1973 the United Nations Environment Programme (UNEP) was set up with the task of identifying research needs and stimulating environmental pro-grammes amongst other agencies of the United Nations and amongst regional groupings of states. Its role is essentially as a catalyst. UNEP is based in Nairobi, Kenya on the insistence of developing countries. Development of international law was not initially included in the UNEP priorities, which did include human settlements and habitats, the health of people and their environment, terrestial ecosystems, oceans, energy and natural disasters. However, in order to implement environmental programmes within the United Nations system, UNEP has progressively developed international law by producing guidelines, conventions and protocols to protect regional seas, regulate the movements of hazardous wastes and to protect the ozone layer.[15]

(d) The Nairobi Declaration (1982)

A tenth anniversary meeting of the Stockholm United Nations Conference on the Human Environment was held in Nairobi in 1982.The Nairobi Declaration on the state of the Worldwide Environment was adopted by the UNEP Governing Council.This document states that really radical changes had to be made if sustainable development, discussed at the 1972 Stockholm Conference, was ever to be achieved.

Nairobi Declaration on the State of Worldwide Environment (UNEP/GC.10/INF.5 of 19 May 1982)

Declaration adopted by the session of a special character

The world community of States, assembled in Nairobi from 10 to 18 May 1982 to commemorate the tenth anniversary of the United Nations Conference on the Human Environment, held in Stockholm, having reviewed the measures

15 A Kiss and D Shelton *International Environmental Law* (London: Graham and Trotman, 1991), p 38.

taken to implement the Declaration and Action Plan adopted at that Conference, solemnly requests Governments and peoples to build on the progress so far achieved, but expresses its serious concern about the present state of the environment world-wide, and recognizes the urgent necessity of intensifying the efforts at the global, regional and national levels to protect and improve it.

1. The Stockholm Conference was a powerful force in increasing public awareness and understanding of the fragility of the human environment. The years since then have witnessed significant progress in environmental sciences; education, information dissemination and training have expanded considerably; in nearly all countries, environmental legislation has been adopted, and a significant number of countries have incorporated within their constitutions provisions for the protection of the environment. Apart from the United Nations Environment Programme, additional governmental and non-governmental organizations have been established at all levels, and a number of important international agreements in respect of environmental co-operation have been concluded. The principles of the Stockholm Declaration are as valid today as they were in 1972. They provide a basic code of environmental conduct for the years to come.

2. However, the Action Plan has only been partially implemented, and the results cannot be considered as satisfactory, due mainly to inadequate foresight and understanding of the long-term benefits of environmental protection, to inadequate co-ordination of approaches and efforts, and to unavailability and inequitable distribution of resources. For these reasons, the Action Plan has not had sufficient impact on the international community as a whole. Some uncontrolled or unplanned activities of man have increasingly caused environmental deterioration. Deforestation, soil and water degradation and desertification are reaching alarming proportions, and seriously endanger the living conditions in large parts of the world. Diseases associated with adverse environmental conditions continue to cause human misery. Changes in the atmosphere – such as those in the ozone layer, the increasing concentration of carbon dioxide, and acid rain – pollution of the seas and inland waters, careless use and disposal of hazardous substances and the extinction of animal and plant species constitute further grave threats to the human environment.

3. During the last decade, new perceptions have emerged: the need for environmental management and assessment, the intimate and complex interrelationship between environment, development, population and resources and the strain on the environment generated, particularly in urban areas, by increasing population have become widely recognized. A comprehensive and regionally integrated approach that emphasizes this interrelationship can lead to environmentally sound and sustainable socio-economic development.

4. Threats to the environment are aggravated by poverty as well as by wasteful consumption patterns: both can lead people to over-exploit their environment. The International Development Strategy for the Third United Nations Development Decade and the establishment of a new international economic order are thus among the major instruments in the global effort to reverse environmental degradation. Combinations of market and planning mechanisms can also favour sound development and rational environmental and resource management.

5. The human environment would greatly benefit from an international atmosphere of peace and security, free from the threats of any war, especially nuclear war, and the waste of intellectual and natural resources on armaments, as well as from apartheid, racial segregation and all forms of discrimination, colonial and other forms of oppression and foreign domination.

6. Many environmental problems transcend national boundaries and should, when appropriate, be resolved for the benefit of all through consultations amongst States and concerted international action. Thus, States should promote the progressive development of environmental law, including conventions and agreements, and expand co-operation in scientific research and environmental management.

7. Environmental deficiencies generated by conditions of under-development, including external factors beyond the control of the countries concerned, pose grave problems which can be combated by a more equitable distribution of technical and economic resources within and among States. Developed countries, and other countries in a position to do so, should assist developing countries, affected by environmental disruption in their domestic efforts to deal with their most serious environmental problems. Utilization of appropriate technologies, particularly from other developing countries, could make economic and social progress compatible with conservation of natural resources.

8. Further efforts are needed to develop environmentally sound management and methods for the exploitation and utilization of natural resources and to modernize traditional pastoral systems. Particular attention should be paid to the role of technical innovation in promoting resource substitution, recycling and conservation. The rapid depletion of traditional and conventional energy sources poses new and demanding challenges for the effective management and conservation of energy and the environment. Rational energy planning among nations or groups of nations could be beneficial. Measures such as the development of new and renewable sources of energy will have a highly beneficial impact on the environment.

9. Prevention of damage to the environment is preferable to the burdensome and expensive repair of damage already done. Preventive action should include proper planning of all activities that have an impact on the environment. It is also important to increase public and political awareness of the importance of the environment through information, education and training. Responsible individual behaviour and involvement are essential in furthering the cause of the environment. Non-governmental organizations have a particularly important and often inspirational role to play in this sphere. All enterprises, including multinational corporations, should take account of their environmental responsibilities when adopting industrial production methods or technologies, or when exporting them to other countries. Timely and adequate legislative action is important in this regard.

10. The world community of States solemnly reaffirms its commitment to the Stockholm Declaration and Action Plan, as well as to the further strengthening and expansion of national efforts and international co-operation in the field of environmental protection. It also reaffirms its support for strengthening the United National Environment Programme as the major

catalytic instrument for global environmental co-operation, and calls for increased resources to be made available, in particular through the Environment Fund, to address the problems of the environment. It urges all Governments and peoples of the world to discharge their historical responsibility, collectively and individually, to ensure that our small planet is passed over to future generations in a condition which guarantees a life in human dignity for all.

(e) The World Conservation Union (IUCN)

Official agencies of the United Nations, such as UNEP, are not the only organisations which have an important role in the development of law for environmental protection. In this field, the World Conservation Union is a particularly important non-governmental organisation consisting of Member States as well as hundreds of environmental associations.[16] In 1980 the World Conservation Union, together with the United Nations Environment Programme and World Wide Fund for Nature published The World Conservation Strategy. This said that humanity, as part of nature, had no future unless nature and natural resources were conserved and conservation could not be achieved without development to alleviate poverty. The World Con-servation Strategy claims to have given the first currency to the term sustainable development.[17]

The World Conservation Union has also played a major role in the development of international environmental law by formulating the World Charter for Nature which was adopted by the General Assembly of the United Nations in 1982.[18] Whilst this Charter may also be soft law it was adopted in the United Nations with 111 states voting for its adoption, only 18 abstentions and just the United States voting against it.[19] Birnie and Boyle suggest that it has proved to have moral and political force since it has been restated in subsequent strategies for environmental protection and will have more force since it sets the ground rules for sustainable development.[20]

After an exhortatory preamble the Charter is divided into three sections: principles, functions, and implementation. Principles 21 to 24, in the section on implementation, together make up the foundation on which Agenda 21 was built.

World Charter for Nature UNGA Res. 37/7, 28 Oct. 1982, repr. in 23 ILM (1983), 455-60

21. States and, to the extent they are able, other public authorities, international organizations, individuals, groups and corporations shall:

16 A Kiss and D Shelton *International Environmental Law* (London: Graham & Trotman, 1991), p 45.

17 IUCN (The World Conservation Union), UNEP (United Nations Environment Programme), WWF (World Wide Fund for Nature) *Caring for the Earth: A Strategy for Sustainable Living* (Gland: IUCN–UNEP–WWF, 1991), p 1. See below pp 141 and 143.

18 UNGA Res 37/7, 28 October 1982, repr in 23 ILM (1983) 455-60.

19 P Birnie and A Boyle *International Law and the Environment* (Oxford: Clarendon, 1993), p 431, fn 32.

20 Ibid, p 432.

(a) Co-operate in the task of conserving nature through common activities and other relevant actions, including information exchange and consultations;
(b) Establish standards for products and manufacturing processes that may have adverse effects on nature, as well as agreed methodologies for assessing these effects;
(c) Implement the applicable international legal provisions for the conservation of nature and the protection of the environment;
(d) Ensure that activities within their jurisdiction or control do not cause damage to the natural systems located within other States or in the areas beyond the limits of national jurisdiction;
(e) Safeguard and conserve nature in areas beyond national jurisdiction.

22. Taking fully into account the sovereignty of States over their natural resources, each State shall give effect to the provisions of the present Charter through its competent organs and in co-operation with other States.

23. All persons, in accordance with their national legislation, shall have the opportunity to participate, individually or with others, in the formulation of decisions of direct concern to their environment, and shall have access to means of redress when their environment has suffered damage or degradation.

24. Each person has a duty to act in accordance with the provisions of the present Charter; acting individually, in association with others or through participation in the political process, each person shall strive to ensure that the objectives and requirements of the present Charter are met.

(f) The World Commission on Environment and Development (The Brundtland Commission)

The United Nations adopted the Nairobi Declaration, which, whilst emphasising the achievements since the Stockholm Conference, drew attention as well to the failures. It saw these as the result of the dynamics of development and underdevelopment. The United Nations General Assembly established the Brundtland Commission. The Commission's terms of reference were:[21]

> To propose long-term environmental strategies for achieving sustainable development by the year 2000 and beyond;
>
> To recommend ways concern for the environment may be translated into greater co-operation among developing countries and between countries at different stages of economic and social development and lead to the achievement of common and mutually supportive objectives that take account of the interrelationships between people, resources, environment, and development;
>
> To consider ways and means by which the international community can deal more effectively with environmental concerns; and
>
> To help define shared perceptions of long-term environmental issues and the appropriate efforts needed to deal successfully with the problems of protecting and

21 World Commission on Environment and Development *Our Common Future* (Oxford: OUP, 1987), p ix.

enhancing the environment, a long-term agenda for action during the coming decades, and aspirational goals for the world community.

The Commission held public hearings in five continents over four years, during which major disasters occurred: the African famines; the Bhopal leakage of chemicals and the Chernobyl nuclear reactor explosion. The Commissioners were, however, as much impressed by the chronic problems caused by the economic crisis in the developing world. In 1987 their report, *Our Common Future* (the Brundtland Report), was published. This discussed sustainable development.

World Commission on Environment and Development, *Our Common Future, Report of the Brundtland Commission* (Oxford: Oxford University Press, 1987), p 8

Humanity has the ability to make development sustainable – to ensure that it meets the needs of the present without compromising the ability of future generations to meet their own needs. The concept of sustainable development does imply limits – not absolute limits but limitations imposed by the present state of technology and social organization on environmental resources and by the ability of the biosphere to absorb the effects of human activities. But technology and social organization can be both managed and improved to make way for a new era of economic growth. The Commission believes that widespread poverty is no longer inevitable. Poverty is not only an evil in itself, but sustainable development requires meeting the basic needs of all and extending to all the opportunity to fulfill their aspirations for a better life. A world in which poverty is endemic will always be prone to ecological and other catastrophes.

Meeting essential needs requires not only a new era of economic growth for nations in which the majority are poor, but an assurance that those poor get their fair share of the resources required to sustain that growth. Such equity would be aided by political systems that secure effective citizen participation in decision making and by greater democracy in international decision making.

Sustainable global development requires that those who are more affluent adopt life-styles within the planet's ecological means – in their use of energy, for example. Further, rapidly growing populations can increase the pressure on resources and slow any rise in living standards; thus sustainable development can only be pursued if population size and growth are in harmony with the changing productive potential of the ecosystem.

Yet in the end, sustainable development is not a fixed state of harmony, but rather a process of change in which the exploitation of resources, the direction of investments, the orientation of technological development, and institutional change are made consistent with future as well as present needs. We do not pretend that the process is easy or straightforward. Painful choices have to be made. Thus, in the final analysis, sustainable development must rest on political will.

(g) Caring for the Earth: A Strategy for Sustainable Living

This report was published in 1991 by The World Conservation Union, UNEP and World Wide Fund for Nature. It was a response to the Brundtland Report

Our Common Future and a follow-up to the World Conservation Strategy of 1980. The report outlines the nine principles which must be adopted for sustainable living: to respect and care for the community of life; to improve the quality of human life; to conserve the earth's vitality and diversity; to minimise the depletion of non-renewable resources; to keep within the earth's carrying capacity; to change personal attitudes and practices; to enable communities to care for their own environments; to provide a national framework for integrating development and conservation; and to create a global alliance.

Part II outlines what needs to be done in different sectors. These are broken down as: energy; business, industry and commerce; human settlements; farm and range lands; forest lands; fresh waters; and oceans and coastal areas. Part III deals with implementation and follow-up of the Strategy.

Caring for the Earth is both visionary and practical. Significantly, it sets out the conflicts inherent in 'sustainable development' clearly. This is aided by clarifying some definitions.

IUCN, UNEP, WWF, *Caring for the Earth: A Strategy for Sustainable Living* (Gland: IUCN et al, 1991), p 10

Sustainability: a question of definition

Caring for the Earth uses the word "sustainable" in several combinations, such as "sustainable development", "sustainable economy", "sustainable society", and "sustainable use". It is important for an understanding of the Strategy to know what we mean by these terms.

If an activity is sustainable, for all practical purposes it can continue forever.

When people define an activity as sustainable, however, it is on the basis of what they know at the time. There can be no long-term guarantee of sustainability, because many factors remain unknown or unpredictable. The moral we draw from this is: be conservative in actions that could affect the environment, study the effects of such actions carefully, and learn from your mistakes quickly.

The World Commission on Environment and Development (WCED) defined "sustainable development" as "development that meets the needs of the present without compromising the ability of future generations to meet their own needs".

The term has been criticized as ambiguous and open to a wide range of interpretations, many of which are contradictory. The confusion has been caused because "sustainable development", "sustainable growth" and "sustainable use" have been used interchangeably, as if their meanings were the same. They are not. "Sustainable growth" is a contradiction in terms: nothing physical can grow indefinitely. "Sustainable use" is applicable only to renewable resources: it means using them at rates within their capacity for renewal.

"Sustainable development" is used in this Strategy to mean: improving the quality of human life while living within the carrying capacity of supporting ecosystems.

A "sustainable economy" is the product of sustainable development. It maintains its natural resource base. It can continue to develop by adapting, and through improvements in knowledge, organization, technical efficiency, and wisdom.

4 THE CONTRADICTIONS OF SUSTAINABLE DEVELOPMENT

This clarification of definitions is useful but 'sustainable development' had already become a fiercely contested concept in the international arena. Michael Redclift writes:

M Redclift *Sustainable Development: Exploring the Contradictions* (London: Routledge, 1991), pp 199-201

Sustainable development, if it is not to be devoid of analytical content, means more than seeking a compromise between the natural environment and the pursuit of economic growth. It means a definition of development which recognizes that the limits of sustainability have structural as well as natural origins.

It was suggested that the problem in achieving sustainable development was related to the overriding structures of the international economic system, which arose out of the exploitation of environmental resources, and which frequently operates as constraints on the achievement of long-term sustainable practices...Indeed the argument could be put that containing economic demands for material advance, in a highly unequal world, requires political measures that are so authoritarian they would immediately contradict the liberating, humane objectives that would make development sustainable in the first place.

The first contradiction that lies dormant within "sustainable development", then, is one which we ignore at our peril: if we cannot rely upon market forces to sustain our environment, we need to place very much greater reliance on international agreement and planning, without which individual, personal or national, interests will dictate the course of the development process...Most interventions in the development process on behalf of the environment are motivated by a desire to minimize the "externality" effects of development, rather than to provide lessons in how development should proceed. Where environmental considerations clash with strategic, political or national interests, they are unceremoniously forgotten...The debt crisis in Latin America and Africa today is a vivid illustration of a problem with serious environmental implications and causes which is routinely considered in exclusively economic, even financial terms.

A second contradiction concerns the relationship between the political struggles over the environment in developed and developing countries. In seeking sustainability in the North we are seeking to affirm a cluster of related values, concerning the way in which we want our environment to be preserved. We seek, with millions of other people in the developed world, to protect and conserve rural space, to recognize aesthetic values in the countryside, to provide better access to this space and to ensure the biological survival of threatened species. Environmental objectives in the South are rather different. The survival of species is equally important, although possibly for more crudely economic reasons. Otherwise the environment is contested for different reasons in developing countries. The environment, especially the rural environment, is a contested domain in the South because it is the sphere in which value is created through the application of human labour to nature. If people are to increase their share of material rewards in developing countries, it follows that they must extend their control over the environment, or over the way in which technology transforms the environment.

At this point it is important to remember the environment has an international character...the material standards of life in developed countries are intimately linked with the way resources and human labour are exploited in the South.

Caring for the Earth also draws attention to the role of the present international financial regime in preventing countries from living sustainably.

IUCN, UNEP, WWF, *Caring for the Earth: A Strategy for Sustainable Living* (Gland: IUCN et al, 1991), p 77

Thinking globally and acting locally is not enough. We must act globally as well. The environment links all nations. The atmosphere and oceans interact to provide the world's climate. Many great river systems are shared between several states. Pollution knows no frontiers, as it moves with the currents of air or water. Sustainability within a nation often depends on international agreements to manage shared resources. Nations must recognize their common interest in the world environment.

Climate change, ozone depletion, and pollution of the air, rivers and seas are worldwide threats. Neither wealth nor sovereignty can protect us from these pervasive influences. The affluent nations of the Western Pacific, Western Europe and North America – islands of wealth in an ocean of want – face a rising tide of migrants trying to escape from environmental degradation and economic stagnation. These and other factors – from long-range weapons to modern communications and international money markets – are continually eroding the significance of national frontiers.

At the same time the integrity of national frontiers – even though many are legacies of colonialism and make no ecological, ethnic or economic sense – is a principle that many governments passionately defend. A key issue for the future is whether frontiers will hold, be held by force or crumble before a tide of environmental refugees. The only chance of stabilizing the situation lies in international cooperation on an unprecedented scale to establish sustainability for all societies. Sovereign states must stop regarding themselves as self-sufficient units (which few, if any, are), and accept a future as components of a global system.

"Interdependence is one of the present day phenomena that has greatest impact on the fate of nations", declared the South Commission. "If the multiple bonds that characterize interdependence are convincingly present in any field, it is in that encompassing development and the environment. Human civilization is moving toward a global state. This is apparent in all dimensions: social, economic, cultural and political, as well as environmental. But the transition is not occurring smoothly and harmoniously: it is turbulent and beset with conflict."

International cooperation needs the backing of international law. To expand from nationalism to globalism, we need to reshape the law to reflect the need for the peoples of the world to live sustainably, and the obligations of nations towards the Earth they share. We need to build a global alliance, and to use international law (especially treaty law) to give it effect. The new alliance must have at its heart the understanding not only that all have a role to play in safeguarding the Earth, but also that those who have more economic and social resources must contribute more.

The Third World's cumulative debt is more than $l trillion, and interest payments alone have reached $60 billion a year. As a result, since 1984 there has been a net transfer of capital from lower-income to upper-income countries. The most indebted regions are sub-Saharan Africa, where debt now equals Gross National Product; and Latin America, where it is 60% of GNP. These massive debts can force countries simultaneously to curb living standards, accept growing poverty, and export greater amounts of scarce resources, thereby accelerating environmental destruction. Yet despite these constraints, many lower-income countries invest more money on conservation and environmental management, as a proportion of their Gross National Product, than do upper-income countries.

Most low-income countries obtain three-quarters or more of their export incomes from primary commodities. Prices of many of these, including copper, iron ore, sugar, rubber, cotton and timber, have fallen in recent years. These prices in any case do not include the environmental and user costs of producing the resources. So the natural wealth of the exporting countries is subsidizing the importers.

Political borders impede the flow of goods and services but not the much larger flow of money. Trade barriers by high-income countries cost lower-income countries two and a half times more than all the aid they get. Fluctuations and speculation in currency, commodity prices, and interest rates weaken vulnerable economies. Capital flight from Latin American nations, generally to United States and European banks, may have as big an impact as the Latin American debt. Transnational companies can move money freely, and while some have adopted an exemplary policy of maintaining the highest standards everywhere, others have played one country off against another to win cheap resources and weak environmental controls.

...To increase the capacity of low-income countries to support themselves – and in so doing to develop sustainably and protect their environments – their debts must be reduced and their terms of trade improved. Increased flows of finance are also essential, especially to Africa, Latin America, and low-income Asia. But it must be a different kind of assistance: a true partnership for sustainability.

...There is already a substantial body of international environmental law... It is important that existing measures are fully supported and implemented...There is also a need for a *global instrument* that gives expression to both the ethic of living sustainably and the obligations that stem from it.

5 AGENDA 21

Agenda 21: Earth's Action Plan, negotiated at the Rio Conference 1992, is the global instrument mentioned in 'Caring for the Earth'. It was painstakingly negotiated and was adopted by consensus at the largest conference the United Nations had ever held. It consists of integrated strategies and detailed programmes to reverse environmental degradation and to promote sustainable development throughout the world. What is fundamental, and innovative, is that it is to be monitored by the United Nations. The United Nations Commission on Sustainable Development is charged with reviewing progress in implementing the proposals contained in the document by 1997. The reports of all relevant organs of the United Nations system are to be analysed and evaluated. Governments are to provide information on what they have done to implement Agenda 21 and the problems they have faced, including the transfer of financial resources. Non-governmental sectors such as private business and the scientific community are also asked to submit reports for analysis to the Commission.

This massive document of nearly 700 pages consists of 39 chapters to make an 'agenda' for the 1990s and into the twenty first century to achieve 'sustainable development'. The chapters are divided into sections: social and economic dimensions; conservation and management of resources for development; strengthening the role of major groups; and, finally, means of implementation.

N A Robinson, IUCN Commission on Environmental Law on p iii in preface to N A Robinson (ed), *Agenda 21: Earth's Action Plan* (New York: Oceana Publications, Inc, 1993)

Agenda 21 is the blueprint, the consensus to guide our multi-faceted endeavors throughout the world. Change is afoot throughout the world – new scientific advances promise the better while failures to employ amply understood conservation knowledge promise the worse. Agenda 21 is the optimistic first step. A united world agreeing, amidst its common and differentiated circumstances, on the blueprint. Like an architect's vision, however, this hope is an aspiration, embellishing the pages of this volume. As its reader, your task is to participate in translating Agenda 21 from words to practice, from plan to reality.

In the introduction to this chapter, we have drawn attention to the fact that Agenda 21's legal status is that of soft law. While reading the extract from Agenda 21 below, contrast the language used with that of the Convention on Biodiversity: 'States *shall*' in the Treaty is here 'Governments *should*' and there is much use of the word 'encourage'. Nonetheless, the thrust of this part of the Agenda on consumption patterns reflects the contradictions in sustainable development, discussed above, and so bears testimony to the rigour of the negotiations that led to Agenda 21's adoption by consensus.

N A Robinson (ed), *Agenda 21: Earth's Action Plan* (New York: Oceana Publications, Inc, 1993), pp 32-40

Chapter 4

CHANGING CONSUMPTION PATTERNS

4.1. This chapter contains the following programme areas:

(a) Focusing on unsustainable patterns of production and consumption;

(b) Developing national policies and strategies to encourage changes in unsustainable consumption patterns.

4.2. Since the issue of changing consumption patterns is very broad, it is addressed in several parts of Agenda 21, notably those dealing with energy, transportation and wastes, and in the chapters on economic instruments and transfer of technology. The present chapter should also be read in conjunction with Chapter 5 (Demographic dynamics and sustainability).

PROGRAMME AREAS

A. Focusing on unsustainable patterns of production and consumption.

Basis for action

4.3. Poverty and environmental degradation are closely related. While poverty results in certain kinds of environmental stress, the major cause of continued deterioration of the global environment is the unsustainable pattern of consumption and production, particularly in industrialized countries, which is a matter of grave concern, aggravating poverty and imbalances.

4.4. Measures to be undertaken at the international level for the protection and enhancement of the environment must take fully into account the current imbalances in the global patterns of consumption and production.

4.5. Special attention should be paid to the demand for natural resources generated by unsustainable consumption and to the efficient use of those resources consistent with the goal of minimizing depletion and reducing pollution. Although consumption patterns are very high in certain parts of the world, the basic consumer needs of a large section of humanity are not being met. This results in excessive demands and unsustainable lifestyles among the richer segments, which place immense stress on the environment. The poorer segments, meanwhile, are unable to meet food, health care, shelter and educational needs. Changing consumption patterns will require a multipronged strategy focusing on demand, meeting the basic needs of the poor, and reducing wastage and the use of finite resources in the production process.

4.6. Growing recognition of the importance of addressing consumption has also not yet been matched by understanding of its implications. Some economists are questioning traditional concepts of economic growth and underlining the importance of pursuing economic objectives which take account of the full value of natural resource capital. More needs to be known about the role of consumption in relation to economic growth and population dynamics in order to formulate coherent international and national policies.

Objectives

4.7. Action is needed to meet the following broad objectives:

(a) To promote patterns of consumption and production that reduce environmental stress and will meet the basic needs of humanity;

(b) To develop better understanding of the role of consumption and how to bring about more sustainable consumption patterns.

Activities

(a) Management-related activities

Adopt an international approach to achieving sustainable consumption patterns

4.8. In principle, countries should be guided by the following basic objectives in their efforts to address consumption and lifestyles in the context of environment and development:

(a) All countries should strive to promote sustainable consumption patterns;
(b) Developed countries should take the lead in achieving sustainable consumption patterns;
(c) Developing countries should seek to achieve sustainable consumption patterns in their development process, guaranteeing the provision of basic needs for the poor, while avoiding those unsustainable patterns, particularly in industrialized countries, generally recognized as unduly hazardous to the environment, inefficient and wasteful, in their development processes. This requires enhanced technological and other assistance from industrialized countries.

4.9. In the follow-up of the implementation of Agenda 21 the review of progress made in achieving sustainable consumption patterns should be given high priority.

(b) Data and information

Undertaking research on consumption

4.10. In order to support this broad strategy, Governments, and/or private research and policy institutes, with the assistance of regional and international economic and environmental organizations, should make a concerted effort to:

(a) Expand or promote databases on production and consumption and develop methodologies for analyzing them;
(b) Assess the relationship between production and consumption, environment, technological adaptation and innovation, economic growth and development, and demographic factors;
(c) Examine the impact of ongoing changes in the structure of modern industrial economies away from materials intensive economic growth;
(d) Consider how economies can grow and prosper while reducing energy material use and production of harmful materials;
(e) Identify balanced patterns of consumption world wide which the Earth can support in the long term.

Developing new concepts of sustainable economic growth and prosperity

4.11. Consideration should also be given to the present concepts of economic growth, and the need for new concepts of wealth and prosperity, which allow higher standards of living through changed lifestyles and are less dependent on the Earth's finite resources and more in harmony with the Earth's carrying capacity. This should be reflected in the evolution of new systems of national accounts and other indicators of sustainable development.

(c) International cooperation and coordination

4.12. While international review processes exist for examining economic, development and demographic factors, more attention needs to be paid to issues related to consumption and production patterns and sustainable lifestyles and environment.

4.13. In the follow-up of the implementation of Agenda 21, reviewing the role and impact of unsustainable production and consumption patterns and lifestyles and their relation to sustainable development should be given high priority.

Financing and cost evaluation

4.14. The Conference secretariat has estimated that implementation of this programme is not likely to require significant new financial resources.

B. Developing national policies and strategies to encourage changes in unsustainable consumption patterns

Basis for action

4.15. Achieving the goals of environmental quality and sustainable development will require efficiency in production and changes in consumption patterns in order to emphasize optimization of resource use and minimization of waste. In many instances, this will require reorientation of existing production and consumption patterns which have developed in industrial societies and are in turn emulated in much of the world.

4.16. Progress can be made by strengthening positive trends and directions which are emerging, as part of a process aimed at achieving significant changes in consumption patterns of industries, Governments, households and individuals.

Objectives

4.17. In the years ahead, Governments, working with appropriate organizations, should strive to meet the following broad objectives:

(a) To promote efficiency in production processes and reduce wasteful consumption in the process of economic growth, taking into account the development needs of developing counties;
(b) To develop a domestic policy framework which will encourage a shift to more sustainable patterns of production and consumption;
(c) To reinforce both values which encourage sustainable production and consumption patterns and policies which encourage the transfer of environmentally sound technologies to developing countries.

Activities

(a) Encouraging greater efficiency in the use of energy and resources

4.18. Reducing the amount of energy and materials used per unit in the production of goods and services can contribute both to the alleviation of environmental stress and to greater economic and industrial productivity and competitiveness. Governments, in cooperation with industry, should therefore intensify efforts to use energy and resources in an economically efficient and environmetally sound manner by:

(a) Encouraging the dissemination of existing environmentally sound technologies;
(b) Promoting research and development in environmentally sound technologies;
(c) Assisting developing countries to use these technologies efficiently and to develop technologies suited to their particular circumstances;
(d) Encouraging the environmentally sound use of new and renewable sources of energy;
(e) Encouraging the environmentally sound and sustainable use of renewable natural resources.

(b) Minimizing the generation of wastes

4.19. At the same time, society needs to develop effective ways of dealing with the problem of disposing of mounting levels of waste products and materials. Governments, together with industry, households and the public, should make a concerted effort to reduce the generation of wastes and waste products by:
(a) Encouraging recycling in industrial processes and at the consumed level;
(b) Reducing wasteful packaging of products;
(c) Encouraging the introduction of more environmentally sound products.

(c) Assisting individuals and households to make environmentally sound purchasing decisions

4.20. The recent emergence in many countries of a more environmentally conscious consumer public, combined with increased interest on the part of some industries in providing environmentally sound consumer products, is a significant development that should be encouraged. Governments and international organizations, together with the private sector, should develop criteria and methodologies for the assessment of environmental impacts and resource requirements throughout the full life cycle of products and processes. Results of those assessments should be transformed into clear indicators in order to inform consumers and decision makers.

4.21. Governments, in cooperation with industry and other relevant groups, should encourage expansion of environmental labelling and other environmentally related product information programmes designed to assist consumers to make informed choices.

4.22. They should also encourage the emergence of an informed consumer public and assist individuals and households to make environmentally informed choices by:

(a) Providing information on the consequences of consumption choices and behaviour, so as to encourage demands for environmentally sound products and use of products;
(b) Making consumers aware of the health and environmental impact of products, through means such as consumer legislation and environmental labelling;

(c) Encouraging specific consumer-oriented programmes, such as recycling and deposit/refund systems.

(d) Exercising leadership through government purchasing

4.23. Governments themselves also play a role in consumption, particularly in countries where the public sector plays a large role in the economy and can have a considerable influence on both corporate decisions and public perceptions. They should therefore review the purchasing policies of their agencies and departments so that they may improve, where possible, the environmental content of government procurement policies, without prejudice to international trade principles.

(e) Moving towards environmentally sound pricing

4.24. Without the stimulus of prices and market signals that make clear to producers and consumers the environmental costs of the consumption of energy, materials and natural resources and the generation of wastes, significant changes in consumption and production patterns seem unlikely to occur in the near future.

4.25. Some progress has begun in the use of appropriate economic instruments to influence consumer behaviour. These instruments include environmental charges and taxes, deposit/refund systems, etc. This process should be encouraged in the light of country-specific conditions.

(f) Reinforcing values that support sustainable consumption

4.26. Governments and private-sector organizations should promote more positive attitudes towards sustainable consumption through education, public awareness programmes and other means such as positive advertising of products and services that utilize environmentally sound technologies or encourage sustainable production and consumption patterns. In the review of the implementation of Agenda 21, an assessment of the progress achieved in developing these national policies and strategies should be given due consideration.

Means of implementation

4.27. This programme is concerned primarily with changes in unsustainable patterns of consumption and production and values that encourage sustainable consumption patterns and lifestyles. It requires the combined efforts of Governments, consumers and producers. Particular attention should be paid to the significant role played by women and households as consumers and the potential impacts of their combined purchasing power on the economy.

Agenda 21 integrates environmental concerns with development. It is an example of the pervasiveness of environmental law in that it takes a macro view of the world economic system, with proposals for trade liberalisation and provision of adequate financial resources to developing countries, and stresses the need for public participation in decision making at a grass roots level with much emphasis placed on local communities. In particular, the need to include previously marginalised groups such as women and indigenous peoples is highlighted. Attention is also drawn to the importance of educating the world's children and involving young people in decision making.

Agenda 21 is also an example of the dynamic character of environmental law. Many of the proposals are for further research and the expectation is that increased knowledge will result in changed priorities and further actions. Integrating environmental and development issues into policy making will require breaking down departmental barriers within governments. If sustainable development is to be achieved it will need a style of management that is flexible enough to accommodate several goals and be able to change quickly in the light of new knowledge and experience. To this end, Agenda 21 suggests that the lowest level of public authority is the most appropriate and that indigenous methods of managing natural resources, for example using local building materials, are likely to be the most appropriate.

Agenda 21 may have started as soft law. It is arguable that it is already crystalising into customary international law because its effects have been profound and it is being taken seriously. It is too soon to say how widespread this process is but in Britain the government has drawn up a strategy document, some local authorities have departments for implementing Agenda 21 and many more have discussed how to put its proposals into practice. The monitoring requirement for states to report what action has been taken at the local level accounts for Agenda 21's widespread importance. The participatory requirements in Agenda 21, together with monitoring at the international level, have forced local government in Britain to try novel ways to find out citizens' views. As we saw in chapter 1 of this book one effect of this process has been a new political tension in local government. This extract from the community newspaper of the southern isles of the Outer Hebrides is a good example of the widespread consultation which has taken place.

Am Paipear, The News of the Southern Isles, October 1995, p 11

What is Agenda 21?

Agenda 21 is the blueprint for sustainable development into the 21st Century. Its basis was agreed during the "Earth Summit" at Rio in 1992, and signed by 179 Heads of State and Governments. At Rio an undertaking was given that local councils in the UK would produce their own plan – a Local Agenda 21. This would involve consulting with the community, because it is the people in the area who have the local knowledge needed to make sensible decisions for the future. This process has to be completed by 1996. As yet there is **no Local Agenda 21 plan for Uist or even the Western Isles!!**

Agenda 21 is a guide for individuals, businesses and governments in making choices for development that help society and the environment. If we do not tackle the issues and concerns, we all face higher and higher levels of human suffering and damage to the world we live in. It goes further than just looking at the environment – social factors are seen as very important as well.

Coming in November to Uist is Mr Barney Leith, member of Oxfordshire County Agenda 21 Steering Group and Member of United Nations Environment and Development Committee for the UK.

Mr Leith will hold public meetings throughout Uist with more information on Agenda 21 and will set up a Local Agenda 21 Committee for Uist with a view to preparing a Local Agenda 21 plan for Uist.

If you would like to attend a meeting/workshop and would like the chance to have your say about the local environment and social factors, and have the chance to serve on the Local Agenda 21 committee, or would just like more information please phone ...

The following piece, however, shows that meetings and workshops are only a beginning. Far more challenging, and potentially destabilising, is the process of changing established institutions to ensure real participation within a traditionally passive, representative political culture.

P Selman and J Parker, 'Democracy, Scientific Expertise and Participation in Local Sustainability Programmes', paper presented to Interdisciplinary Research Network on Environment and Society (IRNES) Annual Conference 1996, Lancaster University, pp 1-6.

Participation

If a cornerstone of local sustainable development is that of increased 'civicness', then it is axiomatic that LA21 processes need to be highly participatory. Consequently, ensuring that individuals and community groups help to design, endorse and implement LA21s is now taken as seriously as the more familiar task of greening the delivery of services and the manufacture of products. Especially in the 'first world', however, this must be set against an apparently declining appetite for active citizenship. The principal tension is likely to be the perennial one between an executive style of decision-making, which may be cost-effective and relatively rapid in achieving results, and a more open and transparent style which seeks wider consensus but may be time-consuming and demanding of human resources. Researchers at UBC [University of British Columbia] suggest that a duality exists between the maintenance of a certain level of centralised policy formulation and control, and the need to accommodate (and even prioritise) indigenous preferences. In the context of local sustainability programmes, we might usefully note their observation that community oriented approaches can sometimes 'produce perfunctory participation, overworked volunteers upholding the appearance of participation, and staff devoting so much time to the care and feeding of coalitions that they have little left for the programme implementation'. There are some potential solutions to this problem, but we should note its constant risk.

...

One means of extending the active network of supporters is through innovative mechanisms of community involvement. There seems to be a growing acceptance of the necessity for techniques such as 'planning for real', focus groups, participant observation, structured interviews, workshops, conferences and children's competitions; one 'third world' case study is conducting 10,000 interviews to help inform its sustainability programme. One concern which has been voiced is that the vast array of ideas which are produced by these exercises will inevitably result in some degree of prioritisation, and that the voice of minorities may be lost during this exercise. Also, especially in the 'third world', experience of corruption and political scandals may create a feeling of disempowerment, and hence apathy towards sustainability programmes.

Also crucial to the success of local sustainable development is the energy and determination of individual 'champions' or 'catalytic personalities'. These have come from all quarters – councillors, officials, volunteers – and they have a particular role in ensuring that a project is seen through from beginning to end. We have found problems when, for some reason (e.g. job move, maternity leave, competing workload), a champion must permanently or temporarily retreat from the front-line. Serious loss of momentum may occur where no structural provision has been made for the catalysis to continue. It has been suggested to us that it should be possible to include structural mechanisms which facilitate continuity and minimise the impact of loss or temporary absence of key personnel, and, equally importantly, ensure that people do not become over-committed.

Conclusion

There is little doubt that Agenda 21 has set in motion an encouraging and enthusiastic local response to the need for sustainable development. The importance of this has been enhanced by the changing nature of local government, and the growing interest in community involvement and elevated levels of 'civicness'. The quest for sustainability requires a comprehensive blend of statutory powers, improved planning and management, and changes in individual behaviour. Only a limited amount of this can be effected rapidly or by top-down centralised solutions. Agendas must be widely owned, and their implementation must be a shared responsibility.

Whilst local government must play an important role, often involving clear leadership and core funding, it must also proceed with humility. The way forward is neither one of bureaucractic imposition nor of outright community activism; it is one of blending the ward-based councillor system with local energies, and of seeking new mechanisms and alliances which maximise civicness yet protect community champions from excessive burdens. It must also involve the availability of high quality information and practical guidance, in a way which provides expertise without the imposition of 'expert' solutions. In many respects, therefore, LA21 has broadened the environmental agenda beyond expectations (and, indeed, beyond the level with which many 'greenies' feel comfortable). It is helping revise our understandings and expectations of local service delivery and governance, in ways which may help yield the improvements in levels of civicness which are necessary for sustainable development to occur.

As well as central government co-ordination and innovative attempts by local government to increase public participation, scientific research programmes are being designed around proposals in the Agenda. A wide diversity of groups have seized on parts of it to give a legitimacy to their claims to have their interests considered. This degree of attention to the document, if it continues, may amount to the *opinio juris* necesary for its status to be that of international customary law.

6 LINKAGE BETWEEN SUSTAINABLE DEVELOPMENT AND THE PRECAUTIONARY PRINCIPLE

Even if Agenda 21 is still soft law, as opposed to customary international law, this does not mean that it can be dismissed easily. Soft law should not be seen as 'mere rhetoric' but, following the original Greek meaning of rhetoric, as persuasion. As such it can be a more effective form of law than a treaty or convention because it leaves room for creativity.[22]

The creative nature of international environmental law is illustrated by the close linkage between sustainable development and the fundamental tenet of environmental law, the precautionary principle. This principle itself has been developing from its origin as a vague, common sense, policy approach to pollution control. Whether it has yet emerged as an important legal tool for environmental protection is open to question but it undoubtedly does exist in international law and now appears in many international documents. From German national law it has filtered to the European Community and Britain, although both the European Court of Justice and the English Court of Appeal have decided it is not justiciable law.[23]

In Principle 15 of the Rio Declaration the precautionary principle is expressed as:

> Where there are threats of serious or irreversible damage, lack of full scientific certainty shall not be used as a reason for postponing cost-effective measures to prevent environmental degradation.

There is an influential body of opinion that holds that the precautionary principle may now have become international customary law. It may be too soon to assert this with complete confidence, but it is now undoubtedly on the agenda and will have an effect in future international law, as seen in *New Zealand v France*, below. It is particularly significant that the Bergen Declaration[24] forged the first link in the chain specifically joining the precautionary principle with sustainable development: 'In order to achieve sustainable development, policies must be based on the precautionary principle'. This close connection between the precautionary principle and sustainable development in legal terms, probably as international customary law, has considerable practical importance because it obliges states to move beyond a rhetorical commitment to sustainable development.

To discover the meaning of the precautionary principle in law, as opposed to policy, we need to look at its practical effects. The kind of scenario in which we might expect it to play an important role came before the International Court of Justice in September 1995 when New Zealand requested the Court to examine the situation of France conducting a new series of nuclear tests in the South Pacific. Since there are so few environmental cases in the juris-

22 For example, see ch 11 on the development of the Ramsar Convention, pp 439-449.

23 See Case C-379/92: *Peralta* [1994] ECR I-3453; and *R v Secretary of State for Trade and Industry, ex p Duddridge* [1995] Env LR 151, CA.

24 Bergen Ministerial Declaration on Sustainable Development in the ECE Region, held in Bergen, Norway on 16 May 1990.

prudence of the International Court of Justice this is especially significant. Although the majority of the Court took a very conservative, procedural and legalistic approach to the Request, three judges delivered dissenting opinions which traced developments in international environmental law over the 20 years since 1974 when the *Nuclear Tests Case* was heard. These dissenting judgments will be extremely influential in future developments, the more so because the Court's majority decision precluded a full discussion of the case.

International Court of Justice Communiqué No 95/22 21 August 1995

New Zealand submits to the Court a Request for an Examination of the Situation in accordance with Paragraph 63 of the Court's 1974 Judgment in the *Nuclear Tests* Case (*New Zealand v France*)

Provisional Measures Requested

Today 21st August 1995, New Zealand submitted to the Court a Request for an Examination of the Situation "arising out of a proposed action announced by France which will, if carried out, affect the basis of the Judgment rendered by the Court on 20 December 1974 in the *Nuclear Tests Case (New Zealand v France)*". The request refers to a media statement of 13 June 1995 by President Chirac "which said that France would conduct a final series of eight nuclear weapons tests in the South Pacific starting in September 1995". New Zealand states that the request is made "under the right granted to New Zealand in paragraph 63 of the Judgment of 20 December 1974".

Paragraph 63 reads as follows:

"Once the Court has found that a State has entered into a commitment concerning its future conduct it is not the Court's function to contemplate that it will not comply with it. However, the Court observes that if the basis of this Judgment were to be affected, the Applicant could request an examination of the situation in accordance with the provisions of the Statute [the Statute laying down the procedures of the Court]; the denunciation by France, by letter dated 2 January 1974, of the General Act for the Pacific Settlement of International Disputes, which is relied on as a basis of jurisdiction in the present case, cannot constitute by itself an obstacle to the presentation of such a request."

New Zealand asserts that the rights for which it seeks protection all fall within the scope of the rights invoked by New Zealand in paragraph 28 of the 1973 "Application" in the above mentioned case, but that at the present time "New Zealand seeks recognition only of those rights that would be adversely affected by entry into the marine environment of radioactive material in consequence of the further tests to be carried out at Mururoa or Fangataufa Atolls, and of its entitlement to the protection and benefit of a properly conducted Environmental Impact Assessment". New Zealand asks the Court to adjudge and declare:

(i) that the conduct of the proposed nuclear tests will constitute a violation of the rights under international law of New Zealand, as well as of other States; further or in the alternative;

(ii) that it is unlawful for France to conduct such nuclear tests before it has undertaken an Environmental Impact Assessment according to accepted international standards. Unless such an assessment establishes that the tests will not give rise, directly or indirectly, to radioactive contamination of the marine environment the rights under international law of New Zealand, as well as the rights of other States, will be violated.

Also today New Zealand, referring to the Court's Order of 22 June 1973 indicating interim measures of protection and to the Court's Judgment of 20 December 1974 in the above mentioned case, requested the Court...to indicate the following further provisional measures:

(1) that France refrain from conducting any further nuclear tests at Mururoa and Fangataufa Atolls;
(2) that France undertake an environmental impact assessment of the proposed nuclear tests according to accepted international standards and that, unless the assessment establishes that the tests will not give rise to radioactive contamination of the marine environment, France refrain from conducting the tests;
(3) that France and New Zealand ensure that no action of any kind is taken which might aggravate or extend the dispute submitted to the Court or prejudice the rights of the other Party in respect of the carrying out of whatever decisions the Court may give in this case.

...

Communiqué No. 95/29 22 September 1995

Summary of the Order

...

The Court begins by citing paragraph 63 of the Judgment of 20 December 1974 [see above]...

It then indicates that the following question has to be answered *in limine*: "Do the Requests submitted to the Court by the Government of New Zealand on 21 August 1995 fall within the provisions of paragraph 63..., and that the proceedings have consequently been limited to that question?". The question has two elements; one concerns the courses of procedure envisaged by the Court in paragraph 63 of its 1974 Judgment, ...; the other concerns the question whether the "basis" of that Judgment has been "affected" within the meaning of paragraph 63 thereof.

...

... by inserting the above-mentioned words in paragraph 63 of its Judgment, the Court did not exclude a special procedure, in the event that the circumstances defined in that paragraph were to arise, in other words, circumstances which "affected" the "basis" of the Judgment. The Court goes on to point out that such a procedure appears to be indissociably linked, under that paragraph, to the existence of those circumstances; and that if the circumstances in question do not arise, that special procedure is not available.

...

Referring, among other things, to a statement made by the Prime Minister of New Zealand, the Court found that "for purposes of the Application, the

New Zealand claim is to be interpreted as applying only to atmospheric tests, not to any other form of testing, and as applying only to atmospheric tests so conducted as to give rise to radio-active fall-out in New Zealand territory" (ICJ 1974, p. 466, para. 29).

...The Court concludes that the basis of the 1974 Judgment was consequently France's undertaking not to conduct any further atmospheric nuclear tests; that it was only, therefore, in the event of a resumption of nuclear tests in the atmosphere that that basis of the Judgment would have been affected; and that that hypothesis has not materialised.

...

Finally, the Court indicates that it must likewise dismiss New Zealand's "Further Request for the Indication of Provisional Measures" as well as the applications for permission to intervene submitted by Australia, Samoa, Solomon Islands, the Marshal Islands and the Federated States of Micronesia and the declarations of intervention made by the last four States – all of which are proceedings incidental to New Zealand's main request. [By 12 votes to 3].

Three Judges (Judge Weeramantry, Judge Koroma and Judge ad hoc Sir Geoffrey Palmer, who was invited to hear the request because he had heard the 1974 case) delivered *dissenting* opinions. Note the connection made between the precautionary principle and environmental assessment.[25]

Dissenting opinion of Judge Koroma

... New Zealand also advanced the argument that as a result of the evolution of the law, there is now no basis for assuming that the law permits underground testing: that, on the contrary, international law in general and the Noumea Convention in particular impose on France an obligation not to contaminate the environment with radioactive material.

The Noumea Convention of 25 November 1986 (to which New Zealand and France together with other States are parties), New Zealand pointed out is concerned with the protection of the natural resources and environment of the South Pacific region, and that Article 12 of that treaty provides that:

> "The Parties shall take all appropriate measures to prevent, reduce and control pollution in the Convention Area which might result from the testing of nuclear devices."

New Zealand takes the position that France is under an obligation to carry out an Environmental Impact Assessment, in accordance with Article 16 of the Treaty, before embarking on nuclear testing, to determine whether such tests are environmentally acceptable to the location and that no radioactive material will be introduced into the environment as a result of those tests. New Zealand maintains that France has not carried out such an assessment, or that there is no available evidence to show that it has done so.

25 See further ch 10, pp 390-391.

New Zealand contends that apart from France's obligation under the Noumea Convention to carry out an Environmental Impact Assessment of the proposed underground nuclear tests, it is also obliged under customary international law to carry out such an assessment in relation to any activity which is likely to cause significant damage to the environment, particularly where such effects are likely to be transboundary in nature. In its view, nuclear tests, because of their significant deposits of radioactive material which could be released into the immediate marine environment, must be preceded by such an assessment. That obligation, according to New Zealand, is founded on concordant State practice, the 1987 UNEP Goals and Principles of Environmental Impact Assessment,

Articles 205 and 206 of the 1982 United Nations Law of the Sea Convention, the 1985 ASEAN Agreement, the European Community Environmental Impact Assessment Directive, the 1989 World Bank Operational Directive, the 1991 Espoo Convention, the 1991 Protocol on Environmental Protection to the Antarctic Treaty and the 1992 Convention on Biological Diversity, as well as the Euratom Treaty, all of which serve as a legal basis and as an illustration of the international standards accepted by France as applicable in this sphere of activity. New Zealand submits that France's refusal to carry out such a procedure for this class of activity is illegal.

...

It is also part of New Zealand's case that the introduction of radioactive material into the oceans is a matter of special concern to the international community, and calls for the most extensive, if not absolute prohibition. This principle, says New Zealand, is recognized by France both in terms of Agenda 21, paragraph 22.3(c), of the United Nations Conference on Environment and Development and in Article 10 of the Noumea Convention whereby: "The Parties agree to prohibit the dumping of radioactive wastes or other radioactive matter in the Convention area."

In sum, New Zealand maintains that France has accepted stringent requirements – which have now become law – which prohibit it from introducing radioactive material into the marine environment, and even prohibit the storage of radioactive wastes (including the produce of nuclear tests) unless there is compelling evidence to the effect that such storage will not lead to the introduction of radioactive material into the marine environment.

...

...New Zealand maintained that since 1974 the situation had changed so radically as to have materially affected the basis of the Judgment: that such changes had struck at the rationale on which the case was barred from proceeding in 1974 so as to warrant its resumption in 1995; that the Court's assumption that the cessation of atmospheric testing would protect New Zealand's right had been affected by further evidence in 1995 when France resumed underground testing in the South Pacific region of Mururoa and Fangataufa and that this would have had potentially adverse and detrimental effects on those atolls.

...

In my view the evidence, though not conclusive, is sufficient to show that a risk of radioactive contamination of the marine environment may be brought about as a result of the resumed tests. The Court should have taken cognizance of the legal trend prohibiting nuclear testing with radioactive effect, and it should have proceeded to an examination of the situation within the framework of the 1974 *Nuclear Tests* case. The Court should also have indicated the interim measures of protection as requested.

Dissenting opinion of Judge Weeramantry

... [The Stockholm Declaration] formulated nearly a quarter of a century ago the principle of "a solemn responsibility to protect and improve the environment for present and future generations" (Principle 1). This guideline sufficiently spells out the approach to this new principle which is relevant to the problem the Court faces of assessing the likely damage to the people of New Zealand. This Court has not thus far had occasion to make any pronouncement on this developing field. The present case presents it with a pre-eminent opportunity to do so, as it raises in pointed form the possibility of damage to generations yet unborn.

The Precautionary Principle

Where a party complains to the Court of possible environmental damage of an irreversible nature which another party is committing or threatening to commit, the proof or disproof of the matter alleged may present difficulty to the claimant as the necessary information may largely be in the hands of the party causing or threatening the damage.

The law cannot function in protection of the environment unless a legal principle is evolved to meet this evidentiary difficulty, and environmental law has responded with what has come to be described as the precautionary principle – a principle which is gaining increasing support as part of the international law of the environment (see Philippe Sands, *Principles of International Environmental Law*, Vol. 1, pp. 208-210).

In 1990, the Ministers from 34 countries in the Economic Commission for Europe and the Commissioner for the Environment of the European Community, meeting at Bergen, Norway, issued the Bergen ECE Ministerial Declaration on Sustainable Development. Article 7 of this Declaration formulated the precautionary principle in these terms:

> "In order to achieve sustainable development, policies must be based on the precautionary principle. Environmental measures must anticipate, prevent and attack the causes of environmental degradation. Where there are threats of serious or irreversible damage, lack of full scientific certainty should not be used as a reason for postponing measures to prevent environmental degradation." (Bergen ECE Ministerial Declaration on Sustainable Development, 15 May 1990 in Harald Hohmann (ed.) *Basic Documents of International Environmental Law*, Vol. 1. 1992 pp. 558-559).

...

The precautionary principle of course went further back in time than 1990. It is a principle of relevance to New Zealand in its application to this Court and one which inevitably calls for consideration in the context of this case.

New Zealand has placed materials before the Court to the best of its ability, but France is in possession of the actual information. The principle then springs into operation to give the Court the basic rationale for considering New Zealand's request and not postponing the application of such means as are available to the Court, to prevent on a provisional basis, the threatened environmental degradation, until such time as the full scientific evidence becomes available in refutation of the New Zealand contention.

Several environmental treaties have already accepted the precautionary principle (see Sands, *op cit.*, pp. 210 *et seq.*) Among these are the 1992 Baltic Sea Convention and the 1992 Maastricht Treaty (Treaty on European Union. Title XVI, Art. 130r (2)), which states the Community policy on the environment "*shall* be based on the precautionary principle" (emphasis added). It is noteworthy that under the 1992 Convention for the Protection of the Marine Environment of the North-East Atlantic (OSPAR Convention), the parties (France and the United Kingdom), wishing to retain the option of dumping low and intermediate level radioactive wastes at sea, would be required to report to the OSPAR Commission on:

> "the results of scientific studies which show that any potential dumping operations would not result in hazards to human health, harm to living resources or marine ecosystems, damage to amenities or interference with other legitimate uses of the sea" (Ann.II, Art.3(3)(c), cited from Sands, *op cit.*, p. 212).

This last application of the precautionary principle, to which France is a party, has particular relevance to the matter presently before the Court.

The provision in the Maastricht Treaty, incorporating the precautionary principle as the basis of European Community policy on the environment (Art. 130r(2)), would lead one to expect that the principle thus applicable to Europe would apply also to European activity in other global theatres.

Reference should be made finally to Principle 15 of the Rio Declaration on Environment and Development...[26]

Environmental Impact Assessment (EIA)

This principle is ancillary to the broader principle just discussed. As with the previous principle, this principle is gathering strength and international acceptance and has reached the level of general recognition at which this Court should take notice of it.

The United Nations Environment Programme (UNEP) Guidelines of 1987 on "Goals and Principles of Environmental Impact Assessment" states in Principle 1 that:

> "States (including their competent authorities) should not undertake or authorize activities without prior consideration, at any early stage, of their environmental effects. Where the extent, nature or location of a proposed activity is such that it is likely to significantly affect the environment, a comprehensive environmental impact assessment should be undertaken in accordance with the following principles." (Hohmann, *op. cit.*, p. 187)

A proper Environmental Impact Assessment should, according to Principle 4, include:

26 See above, p 154.

"(a) A description of the proposed activity;
(b) A description of the potentially affected environment, including specific information necessary for identifying and assessing the environmental effects of the proposed activity;
(c) A description of practical alternatives, as appropriate;
(d) An assessment of the likely or potential environmental impacts of the proposed activity and alternatives, including the direct, indirect, cumulative, short-term and long-term effects;
(e) An identification and description of measures available to mitigate adverse environmental impacts of the proposed activity and alternatives, and an assessment of those measures;
(f) An indication of gaps in knowledge and uncertainties which may be encountered in compiling the required information;
(g) An indication of whether the environment of any other State or areas beyond national jurisdiction is likely to be affected by the proposed activity or alternatives;
(h) A brief non-technical summary of the information provided under the above headings." (Hohmann, *op. cit.*, p. 188)

It is clear that on an issue of the magnitude of that which brings New Zealand before this Court the principle of Environmental Impact Assessment would prima facie be applicable in terms of the current state of international environmental law.

This Court, situated as it is at the apex of international tribunals, necessarily enjoys a position of special trust and responsibility in relation to the principles of environmental law, especially those relating to what is described in environmental law as the Global Commons. When a matter is brought before it which raises serious environmental issues of global importance, and a prima facie case is made out of the possibility of environmental damage, the Court is entitled to take into account the Environmental Impact Assessment principle in determining its preliminary approach.

Of course the situation may well be proved to be otherwise and fears currently expressed may prove to be groundless. But that stage is reached only after the Environmental Impact Assessment and not before.

...

The Report of the Rio Conference of 1992 deals in Chapter 22 of Agenda 21 with "Safe and Environmentally Sound Management of Radioactive Wastes". Paragraph 22.5 (c) deals specifically with this problem in terms that States should:

> "Not promote or allow the storage or disposal of high-level, intermediate-level and low-level radioactive wastes near the marine environment unless they determine that scientific evidence, consistent with the applicable internationally agreed principles and guidelines, that such storage or disposal poses no unacceptable risk to people and the marine environment or does not interfere with other legitimate uses of the sea, making, in the process of consideration, appropriate use of the concept of the precautionary approach." (*Report of the United Nations Conference on Environment and Development* (A/CONF, 151/26/Rev.1), Vol. I. Ann. II. pp. 371-372.)

France supported Agenda 21. Indeed, President Mitterrand gave it such strong support as to suggest that the Secretary-General of the United Nations should be entrusted with the task of taking stock of the implementation of Agenda 21 every year (*ibid.*, Vol. III. p.195).

The President also observed:

> "Secondly, it would be useful to determine more clearly the role, or the responsibility, of the countries of the North. I think that they have to preserve and restore their own domain (water, air, town, countryside), a task which their Governments are tackling unevenly. *That they have to refrain from any action harmful to the environment of the countries of the South.* Such is the purpose of France's very strict laws on the export of wastes." (*ibid.*, p. 194: emphasis added.)

It scarcely needs citation of authority to establish so self-evident a principle.

Dissenting opinion of Judge Palmer

58. ...It appears to me that what New Zealand has to show is that there is a prima facie case to examine the Judgment [of 1974]. It sought to do this by two arguments:

(a) the pertinent facts have changed increasing the risk of nuclear contamination;
(b) the state of international law had rapidly developed and progressed from the point it was at in 1974 so clarifying the standards to be applied to the dispute.

Either change, it was submitted, would be sufficient to trigger the process of examination by the Court under paragraph 63.

...

65. There is also analysis in the Request of what New Zealand considers to be inadequate assurances of safety by the French and details of documented accidents are given. France, it is said, has repeatedly claimed that the tests are safe but has limited or denied access to test sites. In my opinion the nature of the argument put forward by New Zealand suggests that if the legal issues permitted the case to proceed there would be significant evidence available to support the view that real environmental dangers flow from the testing done and planned by France in the South Pacific. In arriving at that conclusion I am not making any judgment about what the scientific evidence may ultimately show were it to be put before this Court and adjudicated upon.

66. France who is in the best position to know of the risks has provided some evidence to the Court. France says it has followed a policy of openness in making information available. There was little said by France about the potential risks long term being built up by cumulations of nuclear waste in the two atolls where testing is carried out. These wastes, France said, were trapped in vitrified rock. Furthermore the problems of shearing off of parts of the atoll and the development of fissures were attractive "Hollywood scenarios" but nothing more. The French presentation at the oral hearings went to some pains to make assurances about the safety of the tests. Large graphic presentations of the geomorphological structure of Mururoa were made. There was reference to a number of scientific studies that were before the Court. Counsel for France, Mr de Brichchambaut, said there was ample monitoring of the situation on a continuing basis. Precautions had been taken. France had observed its international legal obligations, he said.

The Calculus of Environmental Risk

67. The Court is not in a position to make definitive conclusions on the scientific evidence on the basis of the material put before it. Listening to the submissions at the oral hearings did, however, convince me that there were real issues at large here. The true question related to the assessment of the level of risk. The two nations appeared to have very different approaches to that subject. It is, however, an issue which could be determined were the Court to give it a full hearing.

...

69. It cannot be doubted that France has engaged in activities that have substantially altered the natural environment of the test sites in the Pacific. These actions have been intentional and they have been under scientific scrutiny, especially by French scientists. But the unintended repercussions of intentional human action are often the most important. The nature of the risks inherent in the activity itself would suggest caution to be appropriate. Some means of calculating those risks is necessary to arrive at a determination of whether New Zealand has satisfied the test [of a prima facie case]. This calculus I suggest should contain a number of elements:

- the magnitude of the recognizable risk of harm by nuclear contamination in the circumstances;
- the probability of the risk coming to pass;
- the utility and benefits of the conduct being assessed – viz. nuclear testing by France;
- the cost of the measures needed to avert the risk.

70. In my opinion what is required under the test the Court should apply is a risk-benefit analysis. There must be a balancing of the risks of the activity, the probability of harm, the utility of the activity and the measures needed to eliminate the risk. This is similar to a calculus of the risk analysis in the law of torts in some common law jurisdictions ... But it is submitted that it is an appropriate analytical construct with some modifications for measuring the issue here.

71. The gravity of the radiation harm if it occurs is likely to be serious for the marine environment. The magnitude of the risk that the harm will occur must be regarded as significant given the destructive force of nuclear explosions and the possibility of other disturbances of abnormal situations occurring in the course of the long life of the dangerous substances. The costs of averting the risk in this instance are low – they consist of France providing a fully scientifically verifiable environment impact assessment in accordance with modern environmental practice which demonstrates that the proposed tests will not result in nuclear contamination. No doubt France and New Zealand would differ greatly on the utility of nuclear testing but it can reasonably be said that the extra tests proposed cannot have great value given the number that have preceded them. They are of diminishing marginal value if they have any value at all. If the calculus of the risk analysis were applied in this way, then on these facts a prima facie case is made out by New Zealand in my opinion.

...

84. The obvious and overwhelming trend of these developments from Stockholm to Rio has been to establish a comprehensive set of norms to protect the global environment. There is a widespread recognition now that there are risks that threaten our common survival. We cannot permit the onward march of technology and development without giving attention to the environmental limits that must govern these issues. Otherwise the paradigm of sustainable development embraced by the world at the Rio Conference cannot be achieved.

...

93. In my view it would exert a salutary and needed influence on international environmental law for this Court to enter upon full hearings and a serious consideration of the issues of this case, whatever ultimate result was eventually reached. There is a pressing need to develop the law in the area. Given the possibility left open expressly in 1974 that in appropriate circumstances the Court could return to these issues, it would be possible to examine the 1974 decision in light of massive changes in the legal principles that have been developed in the period between the Court's two considerations of the issues. In the event, however, because a majority of the Court has taken another view New Zealand's effort to hold France accountable under the principles of international environmental law will fail.

CHAPTER 5

The development of environmental law in the European Community

1 INTRODUCTION

European Community environmental law has had a marked effect on the content and direction of environmental law in the United Kingdom. In some instances, this has led to the integration of European Community approaches, principles, values, and techniques of environmental regulation with typically British methods, such as those described in chapters 6 and 7. In this chapter we outline the development of legal methods and techniques used by the European Community in its environmental protection policy. We then categorise the main legislative approaches adopted. Finally, we consider the difficulties of implementing and enforcing European Community environmental law and the doctrines developed by the European Court of Justice in response.

The development of European Community law, and hence European Community environmental law, is most easily understood as a development of *international* law for a regional grouping of sovereign states that has broken new ground by developing institutions with power to legislate and to enforce law.

P Sands, 'European Community Environmental Law: The Evolution of a Regional Regime of International Environmental Protection', (1991) *Yale Law Journal* Vol 100, 2511-2523, at 2518-2519

The Community legal order, including its environmental law, remains a part of the old order of public international law from which it grew. Its approach is rooted in an international agreement, the Treaty of Rome, whose validity and effect continue to be governed by traditional rules of international law. In the case of *Van Gend en Loos*, the European Court called the Community "a new legal order *of international law*".[1] As such, the Community joins other specialised legal orders of international law, such as the European Court of Human Rights' regional human rights law and the international administrative law that international administrative tribunals apply.[2]

1 Case 26/62: *Algemene Transport-en Expeditie Ondermeming van Gend & Loos v Nederlandse Belastingadministratie* [1963] ECR 1, 2 (emphasis added).

2 See eg *de Merode v World Bank*, World Bank Admin, Trib Report Decision No 1, at 12-13 (1981) ('The Tribunal, which is an international tribunal, considers that its task is to decide internal disputes between the bank and its staff within the organised legal system of the World Bank and that it must apply the internal law of the Bank as the law governing the conditions of employment').

European Community law is, though, more distinctive than the classification of it as a form of international law or a hybrid of international and domestic law would suggest: it is a highly developed, *sui generis*, form of law. It is particularly astonishing that European Community law has developed not as 'soft' international law,[3] as envisaged by some of the parties to the Treaty of Rome 1957 which established the European Economic Community, but that it is distinctly 'hard' or enforceable law. However, although the doctrinal mechanisms are in place to ensure directly enforceable or directly effective environmental law, there are a number of practical limitations, for example a lack of information about the state of the environment. Doctrinal limitations also operate: for instance the requirement that to be enforceable in the national courts, environmental directives must be 'clear, precise and unconditional'. Such tests have been developed in the context of case law concerned primarily with 'individual' rights – financial and employment rights – and do not translate easily to the category of cases presented by environmental law which tend to deal with problems of *general* interest – the quality of air, conservation of flora and fauna, and the effect of development on the environment.

There remains considerable congruence between the objectives and content of international and Community environmental law. This is seen by the Community's wholesale adoption of the principle of sustainable development which, as discussed in the previous chapter, has developed in the context of international initiatives on environmental protection. As we explain in this chapter, sustainable development is the central tenet of the Community's Fifth Environmental Action Programme, *Towards Sustainability*[4] which provides a policy framework for future legislation and Community activity on the environment.

(a) The EEC to the European Union: a market in polluting substances

In 1951 France, Germany, Italy, Belgium, the Netherlands and Luxembourg signed the Treaty of Paris which brought into existence the European Coal and Steel Community (ECSC) at the start of 1952. The aim of this Treaty was to develop and supervise the production of steel and coal by building a single market in these within the structure of an international organisation. In 1957 the six participating Member States signed two Treaties of Rome, creating the European Atomic Energy Community (Euratom), and the European Economic Community (EEC). The effect of the creation of these three Communities was a single, unrestricted Western European market in potential pollutants – steel, coal, iron, and nuclear materials. However, the aims of the Communities were not solely economic. As stated in the preamble to the Treaty of Rome, its signatories were 'resolved by thus pooling their resources to preserve and strengthen peace and liberty'.

The core goal of the EEC was to achieve four fundamental 'freedoms': the free movement of goods, capital, services and people. These freedoms were

3 See ch 4, p131.
4 OJ C 138, 17.5.1993 (Brussels: Commission of the European Communities, 1993), see below pp 181-182.

expressed in Article 3 of the Treaty of Rome (the EEC Treaty), which consequently listed the EEC's activities as including the elimination of trade restrictions (customs duties and quotas) by establishing a common market, and abolishing obstacles to the free movement of persons, services and capital between Member States.[5] A system for ensuring that competition within the EEC was not distorted was to be instituted and common policy making in the spheres of agriculture, transport and fisheries was envisaged. More broadly, Article 3h of the Treaty referred to the 'approximation of the laws of the Member States to the extent required for the proper functioning of the common market'. A common customs tariff and a common commercial policy towards third countries was also to be established. The EEC Treaty created procedures whereby legislation could be adopted in pursuance of these activities by the Commission, the Assembly (the European Parliament after 1979) and the Council, the supervision and enforcement of which was entrusted to the European Court of Justice.

The character, development and operation of Community law was influenced by the dominant civil law tradition of the founding Member States. Since this legal tradition has legislation (the Code), or 'legislative positivism', at its core, the significant characteristic of the civil law tradition is purposive judicial interpretation of statutes, which tend to be marked by guiding principles and objectives. The role of the Treaty of Rome as the fundamental source of Community competence and the consequent teleological interpretation of the Treaty by the Court of Justice accord with this tradition. The purposive interpretation of the Treaty is particularly apparent in environmental cases.

The Treaty of Rome remained unamended for nearly 30 years until the Single European Act, signed in 1986, made a number of changes to the institutional structure and aims of the European Economic Community. This Act was intended to give strength to policy areas such as transport and financial services. Though contained in the Treaty of Rome, these areas had become immobilised due to unanimous voting in the Council and the informal resort to the 'Luxembourg Accords', by which the Council would endeavour to reach solutions that could be adopted unanimously should one Member State consider that a very important national interest was at stake. This amounted to a veto and often had the effect of delaying a decision indefinitely. Article 8a(1) of the Treaty, as amended by the Single European Act, set out the Act's objectives: to oblige the European Economic Community to adopt measures with the aim of establishing an internal area in which the free movement of goods, persons, services, and capital is ensured by the complete removal of physical, technical and fiscal barriers within the Community by 1992.[6] This commitment to the establishment of the internal market required national

5 Described more fully by S Weatherill and P Beaumont, *EC Law* (London: Penguin, 1993) pp 4-5; see also LN Lindberg, *The Political Dynamics of European Economic Integration* (Stanford: Stanford University Press, 1963).

6 European Commission, *White Paper on the Internal Market*, COM (85) 310 final, June 1985 on the meaning of the 'internal area'; see also CD Ehlermann, 'The Internal Market Following the Single European Act', (1987) CML Rev, Vol 24, 361-409, at 366.

rules at variance with it to be replaced with Community rules.[7] Importantly, this Article called for a qualified majority vote in the Council for measures based upon it.

In the years following the Single European Act, the Community came to recognise that the complete achievement of the internal area – 'an area without internal frontiers in which the free movement of goods, persons, services and capital is ensured'[8] – was dependent upon further European economic integration. As a result, plans were laid for fiscal and monetary harmonisation. The resulting Treaty on European Union ('Maastricht Treaty') was ratified in November 1993, amending the Treaty of Rome (now referred to as the Treaty Establishing the European Community – the EC Treaty) and creating a European Union. Although the central provisions of the Treaty on European Union are those establishing a timetable for progress towards economic and monetary union,[9] the Treaty also has political effects such as those arising from the declaration in Article 8a that nationals of a Member State shall also be citizens of the Union. The European Union is thus broader than the European Community, but is founded upon it.

So we see from this brief history of the European Union that its jurisdiction has expanded to encompass policy areas not originally included in the Treaty of Rome. Environmental protection is one such policy area and constitutes just one part of the wider European Union's activities. For this reason, when referring to the sum of its activities and competencies, the term 'European Union' is used; when describing activities falling specifically within the Treaty of Rome as amended, such as environmental protection, the European Community (EC) is used.

2 ORIGINS AND DEVELOPMENT OF EC ENVIRONMENTAL LAW AND POLICY

Before the establishment of the European Economic Community's environmental policy in 1972, there were few international measures relating to environmental protection. The most notable were the Convention for the Preservation of Wild Animals, Birds and Fish in Africa 1900 and the 1902 Convention for the Protection of Birds Useful to Agriculture. It was not until the 1972 United Nations Stockholm Conference on the Human Environment, convened following a General Assembly Resolution in 1968, that the impetus for international environmental measures gathered speed. The Conference produced a declaration of principles and an action plan for environmental protection which highlighted the problem of acid rain in Europe.[10]

7 Article 100a, allowing qualified majority voting in the Council for the approximation of national laws concerned with the regulation of products and services in derogation from Article 100 which requires unanimity, was inserted into the Treaty of Rome by Article 18 Single European Act 1986.

8 Article 8a EEC (now contained in Article 7a EC).

9 Articles 102a-109m EC.

10 See ch 4, pp 133-135.

After the Stockholm Declaration, the Heads of Member States of the Community declared the establishment of an environmental policy. The Declaration stated that 'economic expansion is not an end in itself...rather its aim is to reduce disparities in living conditions and to improve the quality and standard of living'. In response, the Commission drew up its First Environmental Action Programme in 1973[11] – a political declaration which provided the policy framework for EC action over the next four years. In the absence of a legislative foundation in the Treaty of Rome, the Commission relied upon a dynamic interpretation of the Treaty which gives 'the constant improvement of the living and working conditions of their peoples' as one of the Community's essential objectives. The Commission also relied upon Article 2 of the Treaty which declares the Community's tasks as promoting 'harmonious development', 'increased stability', 'raising the standard of living through the establishment of a common market and a programme of approx-imating Member States' economic policies'. In this respect, early environmental policy corresponded to the Community's social policy, an alliance justified on the basis of the affinity between environmental quality and social concerns such as public health and the condition of the working environment.

Competence to legislate on environmental matters was also assumed on economic grounds. A Council declaration on the adoption of the First Environmental Action Programme stated that the establishment of the common market could not be realised without an effective campaign against pollution and nuisance and an improvement in the quality of life and protection of the environment. In particular, the free movement of goods might be inhibited by Member States' differing product and process regulations set for 'environmental' reasons, and so be capable of hindering competition in the Community. The European Court of Justice confirmed in Case 91/79: *Commission v Italy*,[12] where it was stated that conditions relating to environmental protection 'may be a burden upon the undertakings to which they apply, and if there is no harmonisation of national provisions on the matter, competition may be appreciably distorted'.[13] The Court returned to these issues in Case 240/83: *Procureur de la République v Association de Défense Des Brûleurs D'huiles Usagées*.[14] In its strong support of environmental protection policy in this case, the Court of Justice took on the critics of this development, for example the House of Lords Select Committee on the European Communities, which had expressed the view that national pollution control does not directly affect the functioning of the common market: such control merely affects, and is one of the many factors which affect, the cost of production of a commodity.[15]

11 OJ C 112/1, 20.12.1973.

12 [1980] ECR 1099.

13 At 1106.

14 [1985] ECR 531.

15 House of Lords Select Committee on the Environment, *Approximation of Laws Under Article 100 of the Treaty of Rome: Environmental Problems of the Treaty of Rome*, Session 1978-79, Second Report HL (London: HMSO, 1978), 131, at 199. See, for a different view, G Close, 'Harmonisation of Laws: Use or Abuse of Powers under the EEC Treaty', [1978] ELRev, 461, at 468-472, who finds that anti-pollution costs are also an important feature in decisions concerning the location of new investment.

The Court of Justice's trump card was to present the Community's environmental policy as concerned with far more than the functioning of the common market. In a radical reading of the Treaty, the Court considered that the environment policy was necessary to protect an 'essential objective' of the Community – environmental protection.

The case grew out of a reference from a French court concerning Council Directive 75/439/EEC on the disposal of waste oils. Articles 2-4 of the Directive required Member States to take the measures necessary to ensure the safe collection and disposal of waste oils, preferably by recycling. Article 5 provided that if the aims of those Articles could not be met, then 'Member States shall take the necessary measures to ensure that one or more undertakings carry out the collection and/or disposal of the products offered to them by the holders, where appropriate in the zone assigned to them by the appropriate authorities'. Article 6 provided that 'any undertaking which disposes of waste oils must obtain a permit'. The French decree that implemented the Directive divided France into zones and authorised waste oil collectors and disposers to operate on a zone-by-zone basis. The French court asked the European Court of Justice whether Articles 5 and 6 were in conformity with the Treaty.

Case 240/83: *Procureur de la République v Association de Défense Des Brûleurs D'huiles Usagées* [1985] ECR 531

9. The national court asks whether the system of permits is compatible with the principles of free trade, free movement of goods and freedom of competition, but does not elaborate further. In that connection it should be borne in mind that the principles of free movement of goods and freedom of competition, together with freedom of trade as a fundamental right, are general principles of Community law of which the Court ensures observance. The above-mentioned principles of the directive should therefore be reviewed in the light of those principles.
10. As to whether the system of granting approvals by zones for the collection of waste oils is consistent with the principle of free movement of goods, the Commission and the Council, and also the Italian Government, emphasise in their observations that, in the first place, Article 5 of the directive permits the creation of zones only in exceptional circumstances, in particular in cases where no other, less restrictive, system seems to be feasible. They go on to argue that, in conformity with the Treaty, the directive as a whole does not obstruct the free movement of waste oils.
11. Whilst conceding that a system of approvals is bound to have a restrictive effect on freedom of trade, the Council and the Commission argue that the measure envisaged by Article 6 of the directive pursues an aim which is of general interest, by seeking to ensure that the disposal of waste oils is carried out in a way which avoids harm to the environment.
12. In the first place it should be observed that the principle of freedom of trade is not to be viewed in absolute terms but is subject to certain limits justified by the objectives of general interest pursued by the Community provided that the rights in question are not substantially impaired.
13. There is no reason to conclude that the directive has exceeded those limits.

> The directive must be seen in the perspective of environmental protection, which is one of the Community's essential objectives. It is evident, particularly from the third and seventh recitals in the preamble to the directive, that any legislation dealing with the disposal of waste oils must be designed to protect the environment from the harmful effects caused by the discharge, deposit or treatment of such products. It is also evident from the provisions of the directive as a whole that care has been taken to ensure that the principles of proportionality and non-discrimination will be served if certain restrictions should prove necessary. In particular, Article 5 of the directive permits the creation of a system of zoning "where the aims defined in Articles 2, 3 and 4 cannot otherwise be achieved".

...

An explicit legal base for the Community's environmental policy and law was provided by the insertion of Title VII on the Environment by Article 25 of the Single European Act 1986. This meant that in the majority of circumstances the EC could dispense with the need to find an economic rationale for environmental legislation. The inclusion of the Title confirmed the constitutional status of environmental policy in the Treaty, yet also reaffirmed the Community's de facto competence in environmental matters.

An economic nexus of sorts still remained. The Single European Act was concerned with environmental protection primarily because of the distorting effects differing national environmental laws had on competition and intra-Community trade. A further influence on the drafting of the Act was the likelihood of environmental harm caused by increased transport, industrial restructuring and enhanced economic growth accompanying fulfilment of the internal market. Environmental policy, alongside social policy, therefore came to be regarded by the Commission as a flanking policy to complement the internal market.

The Treaty on European Union confirms the legal base for environmental legislation. The Treaty amended Article 130s EEC, requiring unanimous voting in Council, to provide that, subject to some exceptions, environmental measures may be adopted under Article 189c EC by a qualified majority. The exceptions – provisions of a fiscal nature, certain measures concerning town and country planning, and measures significantly affecting a Member State's choice between different energy sources and supply – must be adopted by a unanimous vote. By inference therefore, these areas fall within the EC's jurisdiction. That town and country planning is mentioned in Article 130s EC is interesting given that a number of Member States have consistently argued that this has few international effects and is therefore a prime example of an area where competence should be reserved exclusively for Member States.

The economic implications of a Community-wide environmental policy are still significant, particularly in the post-Maastricht political climate of convergence criteria, competitiveness, and employment. The following extract from a Commission communication, or discussion document, gives a flavour of these concerns, particularly that environmental regulation and bureaucratic interference might impede the functioning of the market. 'Sustainable *growth*' is the desirable end, rather than sustainable development. This subtle turn of phrase sends a strong message to the 'economic agents' about what is expected of them by the Community in terms of compliance with environmental measures and economic and fiscal policies.

Commission of the European Communities, *Economic Growth and the Environment: Some Implications for Economic Policy Making,* Communication from the Commission to the European Parliament and Council COM(94) 465 final (Brussels: CEC), 3.11.1994

1. Introduction and Summary

The relation between Economic Growth and the Environment is a crucial one when studying the prosperity of the Member States of the European Community. Prosperity, or well-being in a broad sense, does not exclusively depend on economic welfare as conventionally measured, but also on the clean air we breathe and the health of the natural environment upon which we rely for many services. We used to take these for granted. Now, as our development becomes more intensive, pressures on the environment are becoming increasingly strong. Therefore, policies should aim at development patterns that respect the environment and can be sustained over time. In recognition of its key importance to the prosperity of the citizens of Europe, this principle of sustainable growth respecting the environment has been enshrined in the Treaty of the European Community as amended by the Treaty on European Union (Article 2) which entered into force in November, 1993. Similarly, Article 130r of the Treaty requires that environmental protection requirements must be integrated into the definition and implementation of other Community policies. This is fully in line with the commitments made by the Member States and the Community at the United Nations Conference on Environment and Development (UNCED, Rio de Janeiro, June 1992).

Consequently, the question arises which implications this new Community objective has for policy making in Europe.

The Commission has tentatively analysed the consequences of the principle of environmentally sustainable development for economic and fiscal policy making and wishes to present some first conclusions for discussion in this Communication. These points should be seen in the context of the Fifth Environmental Action Programme (COM(92) 23 and the White Paper on Growth, Competitiveness and Employment (COM (93) 700) which contain some building blocks for a strategy aimed at sustainable development in Europe. Obviously, sustainable development comprises a large number of facets which go well beyond the environmental aspects which are the focus of this Communication.

1. The stylised empirical facts of history show that there is no simple linear relationship between economic growth and pressure on the environment. While it is true that the emissions of some pollutants broadly grow in line with economic activity, there are many types of pressure on the environment that actually decrease as economies prosper. Clearly, this suggests that economic growth and environmentally sustainable development are not mutually exclusive. On the contrary, a case can even be made for arguing that, in the longer run, one is unlikely to be achievable without the other.

2. However, it is essential to point out that there is nothing automatic about such a move towards environmentally sustainable development. Although it is true that economic growth by itself generates additional resources that can be devoted to pollution abatement and environmental protection, much of this will only materialise if an appropriate policy framework is put into place.

3. Environmental policy making is presently changing course, aiming at sustainability by integrating environmental considerations in production and consumption processes in various sectors as of the early design stages of products. A stronger reliance on market based instruments is key to the success of this policy as both environmental effectiveness and cost-effectiveness require that economic agents are given the right signals.

4. Furthermore, an important advantage of this market-based approach is that it leaves it to individual economic agents to find the most promising solutions to environmental problems. Such a strategy could also contribute to deregulation and reducing bureaucratic interference that sometimes impedes the functioning of the market mechanism while preserving or even improving environmental quality.

...

8. It is of major importance to give economic agents time to adjust to the new sustainable growth. Hence, policy changes should be phased in gradually and predictably to limit adjustment costs.

...

10. Arriving at broad agreement between public authorities, employers and employees on policies for environmentally sustainable development would allow them to maximise the economic and environmental benefits of this strategy.

...

3 POLICY MAKING

The law of the European Union is the outcome of a distinctive and evolving policy process and reflects tensions which arise during that process between the interests of the Member States, scientific advisers, campaigning groups and policy-makers. The policy process has been the subject of much academic theorising. We outline the main theories below. Some of these theoretical strands are manifested in the detail of the Community's environmental laws.

The differing analytical and political theories used to explain the policy making process in the European Union may be grouped into three: neo-functionalist theory; intergovernmentalist theory and federalist accounts of European integration. Although the focus of these theories is on the roles of the various Community institutions and Member State officials, they also shed light on the Community and Member States' preference for differing environmental policy and legal directions.

Neo-functionalist theory, which has gained greatest currency in periods of deepening economic integration (in the 1950s and 1960s and from the late 1980s up to 1992), emphasises the central role played by the Commission and interest groups. The key concept of neo-functionalism is 'spillover', whereby initial steps towards integration trigger further economic and political cooperation. Neo-functionalism focuses less on the role of national civil servants in policy formation and more on their relationship with the Commission, explained through the concept of *engrenage* or co-option: national officials and representatives are gradually drawn into a new supranational decision making arena by an activist Commission. The theory predicts a shift to a new centre of gravity for decision making which is no longer at the national but the supranational European Union level.[16]

Neo-functionalism is now regarded by some as an unrealistically apolitical account of European integration. This is largely because the theory predicts a clear trajectory of progression towards greater integration in the EC: in reality, integration has proceeded in fits and starts and through a series of intergovernmental bargains. In addition, the political 'spillover' of economic integration and the increasing autonomy of supranational officials predicted by neo-functionalists seems to be lacking in the Community.

Intergovernmentalist theory, derived from analysis of international diplomacy, emphasises in contrast the role of the Council of Ministers, as representatives of the national governments. The picture is one of governments defending their national interests in the bargaining arena of Council meetings, and exercising a gatekeeper role by agreeing to cooperate only on those issues which they perceive as being within their national interest. This theory stresses the competencies of the European Council, the Council of Ministers and COREPER and the elaborate system of working groups and committees.

A Moravcsik, 'Preferences and Power in the EC: A Liberal, Intergovernmentalist Approach', (1993) ELRev Vol 31, No 4, 473-524

...

The liberal intergovernmentalist view seeks to account for major decisions in the history of the EC by positing a two-stage approach. In the first stage, national preferences are primarily determined by the constraints and opportunities imposed by economic interdependence. In the second stage, the outcomes of intergovernmental negotiations are determined by the relative bargaining power of governments and the functional incentives for institutionalization created by high transaction costs and the desire to control domestic agendas. This approach is grounded in fundamental concepts of international political economy, negotiation analysis, and regime theory.

The net economic interests of producers and popular preferences for public goods provide a solid foundation for explaining agricultural policy and industrial

16 See for example, E Haas, *The Unity of Europe: Political, Economic and Social Forces 1950-57* (Stanford: Stanford University Press, 1958).

trade liberalization, as well as socio-economic public goods provision, within the EC. These preferences tell us the goals of states, their alternatives, and – through the level of societal constraint on governments – the extent to which governments are willing to compromise. The distributional outcomes of intergovernmental negotiations are shaped by the unilateral and coalitional alternatives to agreement, as well as the opportunities for compromise and linkage.

...

By bringing together theories of preferences, bargaining and regimes, liberal intergovernmentalism provides plausible accounts for many aspects of the major decisions in the history of the EC in a way that is sharply distinct from neo-functionalism. Where neo-functionalism emphasizes domestic technocratic consensus, liberal intergovernmentalism stresses the role of relative power. Where neo-functionalism emphasizes the active role of supranational officials in shaping bargaining outcomes, liberal intergovernmentalism stresses instead passive institutions and the autonomy of national leaders.

...

A federalist account of policy making provides another perspective on integration in the European Union. This underlines the centrality of political ideas that foster integration towards a federal Europe, brokered by a strong European Parliament. From this perspective, the Council of Ministers is seen as acting as a brake on further integration. An adjustment to this account is provided by the concept of 'cooperative federalism' which has grown out of analysis of German and American political systems. This focuses on the effects of on-going bargaining within decision making structures shaped by codecision between European Union and national officers. It argues that in practice unanimity might prevail despite the formal relaxation of decisional rules, for example those which allow for a qualified majority vote in Council decision making. The 'Luxembourg Accords' (see 'The EEC to the European Union' above) therefore provide the antithesis to 'workable' federalism. An anti-federalist position on the part of the United Kingdom government may be seen in its vetoing the carbon tax proposal.[17]

The European Community's environmental law and policy has been generally understood as a functional spillover of its economic law and the general policy drive towards economic integration. The environmental policy making process is, however, more complicated than this. It is subject not only to the interests of Member States, but is also dependent on the advice of scientists, political advisers, and campaigning groups.

Rehbinder and Stewart identify a number of rationales for Community environmental law which provide an alternative to the neo-functionalist perspective, for example the belief that only Community action can arrest transboundary pollution. In their view, environmental priorities were set by action programmes which sought an improvement in environmental quality as an aim in its own right; the Community's environmental policy representing a

17 See ch 8, 'Economic instruments'.

new form of integration which cannot be fully explained by economic logic. They contend that the focus upon an economic rationale confuses the Community's motivation to enact environmental law with the constraints that it faced in doing so. Prior to the Single European Act 1986, environmental measures had to be based on Articles 100 and 235 EEC because of the absence of a specific legal base. This constrained Community environmental policy making to those activities which 'directly affect the establishment or functioning of the common market' (Article 100) or those which are 'necessary to attain...one of the objectives of the Community' (Article 235 EEC). To justify new policy proposals in the framework of the existing legal structure, the Community tended to address environmental problems that had some substantial economic impact as seen in the early emphasis on measures to regulate pollution from industrial activities and the relative neglect of land use and conservation of natural resources, flora and fauna.

E Rehbinder and R Stewart, 'Legal Integration in Federal Systems: European Community Environmental Law', (1985) *American Journal of Comparative Law* Vol 33, 371-447, at 428

...the development of a Community environmental policy could be interpreted as a product of the interrelation between already existing economic integration and the emergence of a new problem closely related to the economy. Since environmental problems arise to a large degree as a side effect of economic activities – if understood in the broad sense of including consumption activities – the existing economic integration required a concomitant integration of environmental policy in order to avoid the establishment of new barriers to trade or new distortions of competition. However, the fact that Community environmental policy through an incremental process of extending the scope and objectives of directives, has been largely emancipated from constraints of trade and competition policy and has developed as a separate policy in its own right indicates that environmental policies are not simply a function of pre-existing integrative steps.

The EC's environmental policy and law are not just the product of a functional 'spillover' or flanking policy of the EC's ultimate goal of economic integration. Environmental policy is highly politicised, both in terms of intergovernmental bargaining and power struggles between Member States (the intergovernmentalist position) and less prevalent, but still apparent, the drive towards centralisation of environmental polices (the federalist position).[18]

A further way of understanding the development of EC environmental policy and law is to look at policy making on the micro level by focusing on the psychology of decision making, including language, personnel, professional relationships and networks. A case study is provided by Kronsell's work on the making of the EC's Fifth Environmental Action Programme: *Towards*

18 See D Liefferink, *Environment and the Nation State* (Manchester: Manchester University Press, 1996), ch 2.

Sustainability,[19] the EC's plan of action for environmental measures and policy from 1992.[20] This describes more fluid arrangements and conditions for policy making than either the political intractability of inter-governmentalism or the naive economic incrementalism of neo-functionalism.

A Kronsell, 'A Sustainable Impact on the EC? An Analysis of the Making of the Fifth Environmental Action Programme', Paper given at the European Consortium for Political Research Workshop, 'Green Political Economy: Governmental Responses to Green Issues', Leyden, 1993

Networks

A network approach to inter-organizational relations becomes useful in order to understand the relations within issue-areas which 'transcend national boundaries and require participation by national as well as international organisations'.[21] The networks extend across the borders of political institutions and are composed of specialists in a given area. In the environmental area the specialists are often biologists, zoologists, limnologists, ecologists and some social scientists and legal experts.

...

In this paper I show that networks played an important role in forming the Fifth Environmental Action Programme. In broad terms this network involved policy makers and policy initiators in the Commission's Directorate General XI,[22] representatives from the national levels, the European Parliament Committee on the environment as well as the environmental organisations active at the European level.

...

Moving from one organisation to another is naturally important for network formation as it creates loyalties and friendships across institutional borders. Even though the EC institutions and the lobbying organizations are very different regarding organizational structure, aims, interests, representativity, responsibility and power, it is very common that individuals are recruited from one to the other. I spoke with one former non-governmental organisation (NGO) representative who went from local NGO activism to work in a national environment ministry, then to different NGOs at the European level and finally to the present position with the Commission as a consultant. Another individual came from a background with local government, to national representation in the Council to a position with the Commission, always within the environmental area.

This 'going in and out of different organisations' seems to be rather common. As a consequence, networks develop which transcend the institutional boundaries. The networks are built on personal relationships with colleagues

19 *Towards Sustainability – A European Community Programme of Policy and Action in Relation to the Environment and Sustainable Development* OJ C 138, 17.5.1993 (Brussels: CEC, 1993).

20 See below.

21 Jönsson, Christer (1986) 'Interorganization Theory and International Organization', *International Studies Association*, p 41.

22 The Directorate General of the European Commission for environment, public health and consumer protection.

at the former workplace. This is not consistent with the structure as it is envisaged by the Treaties where the Council is to represent the national interest, the Commission is to work in the European interest along with the European Parliament which is made up of political groups at the European level. Two policy processes develop: one being the formal process as laid down in the Treaties, and the other consisting of a network of individuals not limited by institutional boundaries.

...

It is clear that in the case of the Fifth Action Programme networks played a significant role: 'a well developed network is why the Fifth Action Programme has moved quickly and smoothly'.[23] What is it that makes policy making in networks run so smoothly?

Cohesion in networks

The frequency of interaction and the degree of cohesion varies between networks. Kingdon's case studies show that the more tightly knit a network is, the lower is the risk that the agenda shifts back and forth. What I would call a more cohesive network, Kingdon calls policy communities. He suggests that 'policy communities are a bit like academic disciplines, each with their own theories, ideas, preoccupations, and fads'.[24] He stresses that the issues which manage to reach the agenda fit the values that these specialists in the network have. The specialists in the network very often perceive the world in similar ways, as well as which problems and solutions should be considered. The interviews show that in the network connected to the Fifth Action Programme, the participants had similar views. In such tight networks the agendas are stable and not likely to shift very much. The problems and solutions focussed upon will be in line with the mainstream thinking within that network, thus it would be difficult for any issues running contrary to the world view of the policy network to reach that agenda. In other words, such a network has a bias towards certain problems and certain solutions...

My claim is that psychological aspects are also important to network cohesion. We know from everyday life that it is not enough to have the same background, nationality, education or knowledge to become close to a person. All the above variables do have an impact, but I suggest that what is also very important is the psychological aspect; do we like each other, and do we get along? Cognitive and affective factors become important. In connection with the development of the Fifth Action Programme, one Commission official said:

> 'A network is extremely important because a certain relationship develops and you can save enormously on time and energy. A goodwill develops with mutual respect and integrity; to a person who has been on both sides of the table this experience gives knowledge, but also a lot of respect and contacts.'

Affective factors are important for the relations between individuals in a network, and regarding the involvement with a particular issue or issue area. Policy makers put their efforts and energy into issues which concern, interest and/or

23 Commission official.

24 J Kingdom, *Agendas, Alternatives and Public Policies* (Boston: Little, Brown and Co, 1984) pp 140–145.

please them. One important and neglected cognitive aspect in the case of EC policy making and, perhaps, for international networks in general, is the role of language.[25] Language and communication across cultures is an important aspect considering network building, as it decides whether the policy makers can communicate and understand each other. In the EC there are nine official languages.

Summary

It is clear that there was a cohesive network involved in producing the Fifth Action Programme, but it was a network rather independent from DG XI. The network extended across the borders of the EC institutions and emerged from those responsible for the programme. It did include involvement with concerned people in DG XI: 'within DG XI we have already developed mutual respect and good relationships.' The consensus obtained for the Fifth Action Programme was reached because the network included different EC national representatives, especially from the countries which were perceived as obstinate in this case (Portugal, Spain, and Greece). There was at least one other network involved, a vertical one composed of people with similar views and values within the Dutch administrations and the Dutch scientific community. This national network could be used by the policy entrepreneurs to test the feasibility of the ideas expressed in the Fifth Action Programme.

4 POLICY AND LEGAL FRAMEWORK

A statement of the objectives of Community environmental law and a plan for future legislation is found in the five Environmental Programmes which create a framework for action by the Community.[26] Article 130s(3) EC confirms the central role of the Environmental Action Programmes in the legal and policy framework – 'The Council *shall* adopt the measures necessary for the implementation of these programmes'. The most recent, the Fifth Environmental Action Programme, departs from previous policy approaches by focusing on activities – industry, energy, transport, agriculture and tourism – rather than the protection of specific environmental media and in its concern with sources rather than receptors of pollution.[27] The determining characteristic, though, is the Programme's central theme of the desirability of achieving sustainability.

25 For a discussion on the role of language and communication in an international setting, see Jöhnsson, Christer (1990) *Communication in International Bargaining*, Pinter Publishers, London.

26 First Environmental Action Programme, (1973) OJ C 112/1, 20.12.1973; Second Environmental Action Programme, (1977) OJ C 139/1 17.5.1977; Third Environmental Action Programme, (1983) OJ C 46/1 7.2.1983; Fourth Environmental Action Programme, (1987) OJ C 328/1 19.10.1987; Fifth Environmental Action Programme, (1993) OJ C 138 17.5.1993.

27 See also Proposal for a European Parliament and Council Decision on the review of the European Community's programme of policy and action in relation to the environment and sustainable development, 'Towards Sustainability', COM(96) 648 final, 2.12.1996.

European Economic Community, *Fifth Environmental Action Programme: Towards Sustainability – A European Community Programme of Policy and Action in Relation to the Environment and Sustainable Development* OJ C 138, 17.5.1993 (Brussels: Commission of the European Communities, 1993)

CHAPTER 2
THE FIFTH PROGRAMME: A NEW STRATEGY FOR THE ENVIRONMENT AND SUSTAINABLE DEVELOPMENT

The overall objective of the Community is the improved and continued welfare of all its citizens. Together with political, economic and monetary union the Internal Market is designed to hold constituent Member States and their peoples together and to motivate and provide the framework for their social-economic growth. The long-term success of the Internal Market will be dependent upon the relative contributions of the industrial, energy, regional development and agricultural policies and the ability of the transport policy literally to deliver the goods. All of these policies are interdependent; the ultimate limiting factor for continued efficiency and growth as they interface with one another is the tolerance level of the natural environment.

Behind the strategy set out in this Programme is the ultimate aim of transforming the patterns of growth in the Community in such a way as to reach a sustainable development path. Among other things this implies that

- it be recognised that continued human activity and further economic and social development depend on the quality of the environment and its natural resources and on their satisfactory guardianship;
- since the reservoir of raw materials is finite, the flow of substances through the various stages of processing, consumption and use should be so managed as to facilitate or encourage optimum reuse and recycling, thereby avoiding wastage and preventing depletion of the natural resource stock;
- the behavioural trends of citizens within the Community should reflect an appreciation that natural resources are finite and that one individual's consumption or use of these resources must not be at the expense of another's; and that neither should one generation's consumption be at the expense of those following.

The development of such a strategy of sustainable development will require a considerable change in almost all main policy areas in which the Community is involved. It requires that environmental protection requirements be integrated into the definition and implementation of other Community policies, not just for the sake of the environment, but also for the sake of the continued efficiency of the other policy areas themselves.

...

In accordance with the European Council's Declaration 'The Environmental Imperative' the guiding principles for policy decisions under this Programme derive from the precautionary approach and the concept of shared responsibility, including effective implementation of the polluter pays principle.

This Programme continues to address major environmental issues such as climate change, acidification, water pollution, soil degradation and erosion, waste management, etc. However, rather than be directed solely at these issues, the strategy of the Programme is to create a new interplay between the main groups of Actors (government, enterprise, public) and the principal economic sectors (industry, energy, transport, agriculture and tourism) through the use of an extended, and integrated, range of instruments. This can best be done efficiently within the Community framework. Without an overall Community framework within which all these activities can be integrated and coordinated there is a danger that the actions carried out by individual Member States or regions, or by other actors will not have their full impact, or that the integrity of Community achievements or actions in other policy areas, notably the Internal Market could be called into question.

For each of the five main issues, *long-term* objectives are given as an indication of the sense of direction or thrust to be applied in the pursuit of sustainable development, certain *performance targets* are indicated for the period up to the year 2000 and a representative selection of *actions* is prescribed with a view to achieving the said targets. These objectives and targets do not constitute legal commitments but, rather, performance levels or achievements to be aimed at now in the interests of attaining a sustainable development path. Neither should all the actions indicated require legislation at Community or national level.

Sustainable development is a goal which will not be achieved over this Programme alone, but if effectively implemented, this Programme should mark a significant step on the way towards it.

This and other action programmes provide the policy framework for legislation. The legal framework of EC environmental policy is contained in primary legislation – Title XVI of the Treaty Establishing the European Communities (EC)(formerly Title VII). This provides a legal base for Community action in this area and for secondary legislation, most commonly directives and regulations. This Title was inserted into the Treaty by the Single European Act 1986. It was amended in a number of respects by the Treaty on European Union, shown here by italics.

The Treaty Establishing the European Communities (the EC Treaty), as amended by the Single European Act 1986 and the Treaty on European Union

TITLE XVI ENVIRONMENT
Article 130r
1. Community policy on the environment shall contribute to pursuit of the following objectives:

- *preserving, protecting and improving the quality of the environment;*
- *protecting human health;*
- *prudent and rational utilisation of natural resources;*
- *promoting measures at international level to deal with regional or worldwide environmental problems.*

2. Community policy on the environment shall aim at a high level of protection taking into account the diversity of situations in the various regions of the Community. It shall be based on the precautionary principle and on the principles that preventive action should be taken, that environmental damage should as a priority be rectified at source and that the polluter should pay. Environmental protection requirements must be integrated into the definition and implementation of other Community policies.

In this context, harmonisation measures answering these requirements shall include, where appropriate, a safeguard clause allowing Member States to take provisional measures, for non-economic environmental reasons, subject to a Community inspection procedure.

3. In preparing its policy on the environment, the Community shall take account of:
- *available scientific and technical data;*
- *environmental conditions in the various regions of the Community; the potential benefits and costs of action or lack of action;*
- *the economic and social development of the Community as a whole and the balanced development of its regions.*

4. Within their respective spheres of competence, the Community and the Member States shall cooperate with third countries and with the competent international organisations. The arrangements for Community cooperation may be the subject of agreements between the Community and the third parties concerned, which shall be negotiated and concluded in accordance with Article 228.

The previous subparagraph shall be without prejudice to Member States' competence to negotiate in international bodies and to conclude international agreements.

Article 130s

1. The Council, acting in accordance with the procedure referred to in Article 189c and after consulting the Economic and Social Committee, shall decide what action is to be taken by the Community in order to achieve the objectives referred to in Article 130r.

2. By way of derogation from the decision-making procedure provided for in paragraph 1 and without prejudice to Article 100a, the Council, acting unanimously on a proposal from the Commission and after consulting the European Parliament and the Economic and Social Committee, shall adopt:

- *provisions primarily of a fiscal nature;*
- *measures concerning town and country planning, land use with the exception of waste management and measures of a general nature, and management of water resources;*
- *measures significantly affecting a Member State's choice between different energy sources and the general structure of its energy supply.*

The Council may, under the conditions laid down in the preceding subparagraph, define those matters referred to in this paragraph on which decisions are to be taken by a qualified majority.

3. In other areas, general action programmes setting out priority objectives to be attained shall be adopted by the Council, acting in accordance with the procedure referred to in Article 189b and after consulting the Economic and Social Committee.

The Council, acting under the terms of paragraph 1 or paragraph 2 according to the case, shall adopt the measures necessary for the implementation of these programmes.

4. Without prejudice to certain measures of a Community nature, the Member States shall finance and implement the environment policy.

5. Without prejudice to the principle that the polluter should pay, if a measure based on the provisions of paragraph 1 involves costs deemed disproportionate for the public authorities of a Member State, the Council shall, in the act adopting that measure, lay down appropriate provisions in the form of:

- *temporary derogations; and/or*
- *financial support from the Cohesion fund to be set up no later than 31 December 1993 pursuant to Article 130d.*

Article 130t
The protective measures adopted pursuant to Article 130s shall not prevent any Member State from maintaining or introducing more stringent protective measures. *Such measures must be compatible with this Treaty. They shall be notified to the Commission.*

5 APPROACHES AND TECHNIQUES OF COMMUNITY ENVIRONMENTAL LAW

The Community's responsibilities and activities for environmental protection are wide ranging, as indicated by the objectives of environmental policy set out in Article 130r(1). An array of techniques has been developed by the Community in its environmental law in order to achieve these objectives. The environmental law of the EC can be arranged in three broad classes which represent the varying approaches adopted: protection of the environment by sectoral control of pollution; preventive and integrated law; and the regulation of land use for biodiversity and the protection of nature. The classes approximate to the chronological development of EC environmental law. There has been a gradual progression away from sectoral controls and towards the use of law based on principles of prevention of pollution and integrated pollution control. A number of different legal techniques are used in each class. Environmental standards, the imposition of procedural rules in development control, freedom of access to environmental information, and the designation of land for special protection are just a few of these.

(a) Sectoral controls

The Community's early response to environmental problems was to legislate to protect air and water: a sectoral approach. This forms the largest class of EC environmental law. The objectives of law in this category are diverse: to protect human health whilst also enhancing competitive conditions throughout the Community. The main legal techniques used are administratively enforced emission standards and environmental quality standards. A good example of an instrument in this class is Directive 778/80/EEC on the quality of water intended for human consumption, ('the Drinking Water Directive').[28] Not only does this Directive concern a single environmental medium – water – but also water for a specific use. The primary technique in this Directive is the establishment of environmental quality standards. These set an admissible level of a given pollutant in water, rather than setting emission limits for each source of pollution. The setting of specific standards compares sharply with the parallel pollution control techniques developed in the United Kingdom: achievement of the 'best practicable means'; and the setting of ambient standards which enhance discretion and rely upon local administration and enforcement.[29]

(b) Preventive and integrated law

This broadly defined class differs from the previous, more prevalent, class because the laws do not rely on the administration of substantive measures which control pollution in a particular environmental medium or from an industrial sector. This class contains environmental laws, described as integrated, or horizontal, which aim to regulate the sources of pollution. A common technique is the setting of certain *procedural* rules, for example Directive 85/337/EEC[30] requires that information about the effects of certain developments on the environment be considered in the planning process. Another example is the freedom of access to information on industrial activities, adopted in Directive 90/313/EEC on access to information on the environment,[31] Regulation 92/80/EEC on a Community eco-labelling scheme,[32] and Regulation 93/1836/EEC on the establishment of an eco-management and auditing scheme.[33] A common expectation of all these measures is that environmental groups and others will use this information to demand more effective application of environmental law from industry and enforcement agencies. The instruments in this class arguably form part of the EC's strategy to encourage compliance and enforcement by harnessing public participation and consumer choice (in the case of the Directive on an eco-labelling scheme) and bypassing national enforcement authorities. The recent use of integrated or horizontal measures relying upon freedom of access to environmental

28 OJ L 299, 30.8.1980. See further ch 9.
29 See ch 6.
30 See ch 10.
31 OJ L 158 23.6.1990.
32 OJ L 99 11.4.1992.
33 OJ L 168 10.7.1993. See further ch 8, pp 324-338.

information and the use of procedural mechanisms such as environmental assessment has been influenced by the practical problems of implementation and the political requirement that environmental legislation accords with the principle of subsidiarity.

(c) Regulation of land use

A third class of Community environmental law is directed towards encouraging biodiversity and protecting nature. The most common technique used in measures in this class is the *designation* of land for special protection. An early example is Directive 79/409/EEC on the conservation of wild birds,[34] which requires a sufficient diversity of habitats, particularly through the establishment of protected areas.[35] A similar technique is used in Directive 92/43/EEC on the conservation of natural habitats and of wild flora and fauna[36] to establish a European ecological network of special conservation areas.[37] This Directive makes linkages between the technique of designation of land for special protection and the development control systems (including environmental assessment) of the Member States[38] and consolidates existing administrative arrangements for designation of land for other purposes, for example the protection of wild birds. Directive 92/43/EEC represents a holistic approach to wildlife protection: birds and other species cannot be protected in isolation, and therefore their habitats must also be protected. The Directive underlines the way that EC environmental law transcends purely economic considerations; rather, it emphasises the necessity of protecting the environment for its own sake. However, as Article 6 of the Directive makes clear, the commitment to protect special areas of conservation is not absolute because the link with economic considerations is not altogether lost. A project likely to have a significant effect on the site may be granted development consent for 'imperative reasons of overriding public interest, including those of a social or economic nature'; although in the case of a 'priority' site the only considerations to have this effect are those relating to human or public safety.[39]

(d) Moving towards integration

We have outlined the different approaches to environmental protection adopted by the EC to give some idea of the wide range of techniques for environmental protection which have been used. Notwithstanding this variety, a trend can be seen of the EC increasingly favouring integrated and preventive measures based on freedom of access to information and procedural mechanisms such as environmental and risk assessment and placing less reliance on the setting and administration of substantive and prescriptive standards. This is particularly

34 OJ L 103, 27.4.1979.
35 See Case C-44/95: *Lappel Bank*, p 204.
36 OJ L 206, 22.7.1992.
37 See ch 11, pp 454 et seq for extracts from the Directive.
38 Article 6.
39 See Case C-44/95: *Lappel Bank*, p 204.

evident in the Community's commitment to integrated methods of pollution control in the Fourth Environmental Action Programme and by its adopting a Directive instituting a Community wide system of integrated pollution prevention and control.[40] This trend parallels the shift in British pollution control towards integrated methods epitomised by the system of Integrated Pollution Control in Part I of the Environmental Protection Act 1990.[41] The integrated nature of these instruments reinforces the element of preventive or anticipatory control which is undeniably present in much of Community environmental law. When pollution problems are approached predominantly as problems of air, water, or waste, the solution is usually to move the pollutant to where the environment is least protected. Integrated systems of pollution control allow alternative processes and products to be judged in the light of all possible paths or cycles of pollutants in the environment. Environmental harm might therefore be prevented by identifying possible changes to be made to the products or processes at an early stage in the authorisation process. Recognising the extent of damage caused by transfers of pollutants between media also provides an incentive to prevent pollution in the first place.

The commitment in the Fifth Environmental Action Programme to integrate not just pollution control but environmental protection *policies* into other areas of EC policy is a significant and related development. Integration in policy making may be seen as an attempt to avoid contradictions and inconsistencies between the different Directorates in the Commission. The provision on which this commitment was based, Article 130r(2) EEC,[42] is strengthened by its amendment by the Treaty on European Union so that it now reads: 'Environmental protection requirements must be integrated into the definition and implementation of other Community policies'. This requirement of policy integration is also the subject of the 'Declaration by the Member States on Assessment of Community Measures', annexed to the Treaty on European Union, which states: '...the Commission undertakes in its proposals, and the Member States undertake in implementing those proposals, to take full account of their environmental impact and the principle of sustainable growth'. To date, agriculture, energy, transport and Community procedures such as the distribution of structural funds have been subject to 'integrative' documents, but more significant steps remain tentative.

(e) The imperative of subsidiarity

A further significant development is the promulgation of environmental legislation and review of existing legislation to accord with the principle of subsidiarity. This principle first came to prominence in EC law in Article 130r(4) EEC. The principle was elevated to a general principle of Community constitutional

40 Directive 96/61/EEC on integrated pollution prevention and control, OJ L 257, 10.10.1996.

41 See ch 6.

42 Article 130r(2) EEC: 'environmental protection shall be a component of the Community's other policies'.

law by the Treaty on European Union and is now in Article 3b EC.

Article 3b

In the areas which do not fall within its exclusive competence, the Community shall take action only if, and in so far as, the objective of the proposed action cannot be sufficiently achieved by the Member States and can therefore by reason of the scale or effects of the proposed action be better achieved by the Community.

This principle regulates the exercise of competencies and powers attributed to the Community in relation to the Member States and, increasingly, local and regional authorities. The idea is that a central authority should have a subsidiary function, performing only those tasks which cannot be performed effectively at a more intermediate or local level. Subsidiarity favours non-centralisation; in the context of the European Union, the principle ensures political power cannot be taken from Member States' governments by the Union without common consent. The principle would therefore appear to give greater opportunity for Member States to insist that the Commission justify activity at Community level. Given its imprecise formulation and status as a legal principle, it is doubtful that in practice a Member State could rely on Article 3b to bring a challenge before the Court of Justice, although the principle has come close to being judicially interpreted (and approved) in *R v London Borough Transport Committee, ex p Freight Transport Association Ltd*[43] and was enthusiastically embraced by Smith LJ in *R v Secretary of State for Trade and Industry, ex p Duddridge.*[44] An inter-institutional agreement has been signed on procedures to check that the content and form of any proposed measure complies with subsidiarity.[45] The Commission has also embarked on a review to simplify, consolidate and update existing environmental legislation.[46] For example, the Commission plans to amend Directive 778/80/EEC on drinking water[47] and incorporate this and other Directives into framework instruments giving the Member States more room for manoeuvre in defining certain parameters.[48] In line with this principle, in the Fifth Environmental Action Programme[49] the Commission envisages shared responsibility between the Community, Member States, local authorities and industry, leading to a form of 'administrative subsidiarity' in which EC legislation establishes a regulatory

43 [1992] 1 CMLR 5.

44 [1995] Env LR 151 at 174. See further ch 1, p 18.

45 Inter-institutional Agreement on Procedures for Implementing the Principle of Subsidiarity, Bull EC 10-1993, 118-121.

46 Commission Report to the European Council on the Adaption of Existing Legislation to the Subsidiarity Principle, COM (93) 545 final, 24.11.1993 and Commission of the European Communities, ISEC Background Report B3/94 'Adapting Community Legislation to Subsidiarity'.

47 See further ch 9, pp 367-372.

48 See European Commission, Communication on a European Water Policy, COM(96) 59 final, 21.2.1996.

49 OJ C 138, 17.5.1993.

framework and Member States are given scope to interpret the Community's requirements. This calls for a review of present understandings of the policy and law making processes and their theoretical underpinnings. Some insights into the future possible workings of subsidiarity are gleaned from the Molitor Report (1995), the result of work by a group of independent experts charged with examining the impact of Community and national legislation on employment and competitiveness, and making proposals to alleviate and simplify legislation in line with the principle of subsidiarity.[50] The Report first stresses that streamlining and rationalising rules and regulations are an important part of Community policy to enhance global competitiveness and 'ensure that its positive effects on employment can be realised as rapidly as possible'.

The following extract is taken from the environment chapter of the report which closes with a succinct dissenting opinion.

Report of the Group of Independent Experts in Legislative and Administrative Simplification (the Molitor Report) COM(95) 288 final, 21.6.1995

5. Just as the reasons for Community action have evolved over time, as reflected in the changing legal bases in the Treaty, so has the approach to policy design. The bulk of existing legislation, dating from the 1970s and 1980s was a somewhat ad hoc response to specific political pressures and to growing interest in green issues. These mainly vertical directives were typically targeted at individual point of source emissions and set specific limit values or targets for each of a wide range of pollutants. Limits were changed, and legislation extended to cover new pollutants, as new scientific evidence became available.
6. This early regulatory approach tended to be too prescriptive and too rigid and hence not effective in achieving the Community's environmental objectives. It became increasingly apparent that such an approach did not adequately protect the environment, nor recognise the interdependence of environmental issues.
7. Recognition of these difficulties led to the development of a new approach which aims, as set out in the Fifth Environmental Action Programme of 1992, to set clear objectives whilst leaving Member States and/or business to decide how best to achieve them. It embodies three main principles:
   - reliance, when possible, on market based mechanisms rather than command and control regulation;
   - a move away from highly prescriptive rules towards greater flexibility for Member States and/or businesses to decide on implementation that would meet clearly defined objectives;
   - a move towards environmental quality standards and general permitting requirements.
8. The Commission has embarked on a major review of the main body of environmental legislation and, as confirmed in the 1992 Edinburgh

50 See also, Commission Report to the European Council on the Adaptation of Community Legislation to the Subsidiarity Principle COM(93) 545 final, 24.11.1993.

European Council conclusions, it intends "to simplify, consolidate and update existing texts, particularly those on air and water, to take new knowledge and technical progress into account".

...

WATER

30. The costs of water and of effluent disposal have increased significantly in recent years. The cumulative effect of Community legislation has not helped to reduce this cost and may have unnecessarily increased it. Companies either pay more for treatment or have to install and run their own effluent treatment plant. Adopting the flexibility principle, looking at the overall impact of various substances – allowing trade-offs – rather than setting limit values for individual substances, is likely to increase innovation and so increase the export capability – and hence job creation – to third country markets with specific local conditions and problems.

Proposal 19
All water quality legislation relating to the discharge of substances to them should be consolidated, taking full account of the trade-offs between them (and other pieces of legislation such as the proposed Integrated Pollution Prevention and Control Directive).

...

32. Guide levels in the Drinking Water Directive should be abandoned as they do not relate to scientific data, in general have no legal significance and also over-complicate the legislation. Further simplification would result from considerably reducing the number of standards set at Community level.

Proposal 21
The Drinking Water Directive (80/778/EEC) should be amended along the lines envisaged in the Commission proposal to drop all 40 guide levels, set values at EU level only for those parameters essential to protect public health whilst leaving Member States the flexibility to set additional parameters for regional or local supply, and leave Member States to set their own standards for aesthetic parameters (colour, taste, smell).

...

Dissenting opinion from Mr Pierre Carniti regarding the chapter on the environment

The chapter on the environment is unacceptable, because it treats environmental issues basically as obstacles to economic activity, whereas they should be seen from the point of view of improving people's quality of life.

6 A CASE OF SELECTIVE IMPLEMENTATION

Member States' institutions are bound to act in conformity with the binding rules laid down in Community law. This obligation is derived from the wording of Article 189 EC: that a regulation shall be 'binding in its entirety and directly applicable in all Member States; and a directive 'shall be binding, as to the result to be achieved, upon each Member State to which it is addressed'. 'Implementation' refers to the legal process of integrating Community principles into national law; by this process rights and duties contained in Community law are transferred to national legal systems and may be relied upon by individuals. The legal obligation upon Member States to give effect to Community law is then fulfilled. Implementation constitutes the meeting point between national law and legal traditions, and those of the Community; full and accurate transposition would make for uniform law throughout the Community.

In the context of environmental law, the obligation to implement directives includes a duty on the part of the Member States to bring about beneficial changes in the physical environment, in addition to the more basic obligation to transpose Community directives by enacting legislation. The extent of this obligation was decided by the European Court of Justice in Case C-337/89: *Commission v United Kingdom.*[51] Advocate General Lenz said there were two obligations: first, to transpose into national law the Drinking Water Directive's requirements; and, second, a further, absolute obligation to bring about physical changes in the environment.[52] The European Court of Justice has also developed general criteria for determining whether a directive has been fully implemented. For example, administrative measures such as circulars are inadequate as means to transpose directives.[53] A particularly strong stance on the obligation to implement was taken by the Court in Case C-361/88: *Commission v Germany*,[54] when it upheld a complaint that Germany had failed to secure legislative implementation of EC directives on air quality. Rejecting the defence that German legislation already conformed with the directives, the Court pointed out that implementation requires Member States to set in place a specific legal framework relevant to the Directive's subject matter to enable individuals to recognise clearly their rights and obligations under EC law.

In the environmental sector Community directives are seldom transposed in the national law of the Member States within the period prescribed.[55] When directives are implemented, the national laws are frequently defective in either form or content. The rate for practical implementation is decidedly lower, as borne out by Community and Member State official reports and the proportion of cases for practical infringement brought before the Court of Justice: at the end of 1990, 218 out of 371 proceedings brought by the Commission were for lack of 'effective application'. These issues are elaborated by the House of Lords Select Committee on the European Communities which attributes the problem of implementation of environmental directives to difficulties in drafting Community legislation in this area, the process of negotiation and adoption in the Council, and the differing styles and techniques of national legislation.[56]

51 Case C-337/89: *Commission v United Kingdom* [1992] ECR I-6103.

52 See further ch 9.

53 This was held to be the case in the environmental field in Case C-361/88: *Commission v Germany* [1991] ECR I-2567 and Case C-13/90: *Commission v France* [1991] ECR I-4327.

54 Case C-361/88: *Commission v Germany* [1991] ECR I-2567.

55 European Commission, Implementing Community Environmental Law, COM(96) 500 final, 28.11.996, p 2.

56 House of Lords Select Committee on the European Communities, Ninth Report, *Implementation and Enforcement of Environmental Legislation*, Session 1991-92 (London: HMSO, 1992), paras 15-25.

The relatively high rate of non-implementation or incorrect implementation may, to some extent, be attributed to the specific problems posed by environmental protection. First, since natural processes are not yet sufficiently understood the obligation to bring about physical changes is difficult to fulfil. Second, there is a lack of reliable information on the state of the environment and considerable variation in sampling techniques, between and within Member States. In addition, many directives confer discretionary powers to be exercised by Member States or competent bodies, raising the question of whether the exercise of such powers is capable of constituting a failure to implement a directive in *practice*. This is illustrated by Directive 85/337/EEC on environmental assessment which gives a discretion to Member States to determine appropriate criteria and thresholds to decide whether certain projects should be the subject of an environmental assessment. More specifically, a discretion lies with the local authority to determine whether a particular project is likely to have 'significant effects' on the environment and thus must be subject to an environmental assessment.

The poor implementation record for directives in general has been explained in terms of Member States resorting to 'selective application' of Community law in order to avoid the rigours of closer economic integration.[57] Environmental legislation has proved to be a suitably discrete area to be selectively discounted by Member States in this way. This practice may be encouraged by the extension of qualified majority voting for most environmental protection measures since Member States will be obliged to implement policies to which they may be opposed, a problem foreseen in a Declaration annexed to the Treaty on European Union stating that 'each Member State should fully and accurately transpose into national law the Community Directives addressed to it within the deadlines laid down therein'. Non-implementation or incorrect implementation of environmental law might be symptoms of continuing doubts about the Community's competence to legislate in this area. Even though the Member States formally transferred legislative powers to the Community when they signed the Single European Act 1986, this legal capacity has been compromised in practice by non-implementation and by increased recourse to the principle of subsidiarity.

7 ENFORCEMENT

(a) Procedure

Complaining to the European Commission under Articles 169 and 170 EC is the principal means of enforcing Community environmental law. The administrative and judicial procedure set out in these Articles enables any citizen or Member State to complain to the Commission on the grounds that Community provisions have not been applied, or have been incorrectly applied.

57 F Snyder, 'The Effectiveness of European Community Law: Institutions, Processes, Tools and Techniques', (1993) 56 MLR 19-54.

Following investigation, the Commission may refer the matter to the Court of Justice. Successful enforcement actions brought before the Court include that against the United Kingdom[58] for the failure to implement fully Directive 778/80/EEC on the quality of drinking water.[59] This Directive, adopted in 1980, was to be implemented in Member States' laws by 1982 and to have changed the physical environment in line with the standards set in the Directive by 1985. However, even by 1989, the maximum admissible concentration of nitrate was exceeded in 28 supply zones, each supplying approximately 10,000 people. A similar story of inadequate implementation may be told in the case of Directive 85/337/EEC on environmental assessment, the subject of chapter 10. This has been singled out by the Commission as problematic, especially as regards the public authority's evaluation of the developer's environmental statement; and because a large number of major construction projects, most frequently roads, have proceeded without an environmental assessment.[60]

This enforcement procedure is inherently reactive since it relies upon complaints being brought to the Commission's attention by pressure groups and members of the public. It is very slow, which creates significant problems in cases of irreversible environmental harm. The procedure is also premised upon Member States' cooperation since, until amendment by the Treaty on European Union, the only sanction available to the Court was political pressure in the form of an order that a Member State must fulfil its obligations under the Treaty. In the event of continued infringement, the Commission may now refer the matter back to the Court with a recommendation that the Member State pay a 'penalty payment'.[61]

The effectiveness of the enforcement procedure may still be questioned, as illustrated by the legal proceedings which followed the Court of Justice's finding in Case C-337/89: *Commission v United Kingdom*[62] that the United Kingdom had failed to comply with its obligations under EC law to implement fully the Drinking Water Directive. An action in judicial review was brought by Andrew Lees and Friends of the Earth, challenging the action that the Secretary of State for the Environment had taken to comply with the Court of Justice's declaration. The case goes some way, albeit negatively, to answering important questions about the enforcement procedure. What timetable should be set for full compliance with the Court's ruling? Precisely what action must be taken?

R v Secretary of State for the Environment, ex p Friends of the Earth [1994] 2 CMLR 760, Queen's Bench Division

Schiemann J: The United Kingdom has, since 1985, been in breach of an obligation ("the primary obligation"), contained in a directive ("the Directive")

58 Case C-337/89, *Commission v United Kingdom* [1992] ECR I-6103.
59 See ch 9, pp 370–372.
60 Ninth Annual Report to the European Parliament on Commission Monitoring and Application of Community Law (1993) OJ C 250/6, 28.9.1992, p 150.
61 Article 171(2) EC.
62 Case C-337/89: *Commission v United Kingdom* [1992] ECR I-6103; an extract from which is given in ch 9, pp 370–372.

adopted by the Council of the European Communities, to ensure that water intended for human consumption meets standards of wholesomeness set by the Community. In consequence, the United Kingdom is, and has been since 1985, under an obligation ("the secondary obligation") to rectify that breach of the primary obligation as soon as possible. A legislative mechanism exists in the United Kingdom which is adequate for securing that the breach is rectified. While the situation has improved since 1985, it is common ground that there are, and are likely to be for some years into the future continuing breaches of the primary obligation. The essential issue in the present case is whether the Secretary of State has used the United Kingdom's legislative mechanism for rectifying the breach of the primary obligation in a manner which is consonant with his obligation under English law bearing in mind that the law of the European Communities is part of our law.

...

Nature of the applications

These are two applications each by Andrew Lees and Friends of the Earth Limited ("FoE") (together "the applicants") for judicial review of decisions taken by the Secretary of State for the Environment ("the Secretary of State") under the Act on October 4, 1991, whereby he accepted undertakings from:

(a) Thames Water Utilities Limited ("Thames") to take steps which appeared to the Secretary of State appropriate for Thames to take for the purpose of securing or facilitating compliance with its duty under section 68(1)(a) to supply wholesome water as defined in the Water Supply (Water Quality) Regulations 1989 ("the Regulations"); and

(b) Anglian Water Services Limited ("Anglian") to take steps which appeared to the Secretary of State appropriate for Anglian to take for the purposes of securing or facilitating compliance with its duty under section 68(1)(a) to supply wholesome water as defined in the Regulations

and his concomitant decision not to make any enforcement orders pursuant to his duty under section 18 of the Act in respect of contraventions of the Regulations by Thames and Anglian.

...

The Position of the Secretary of State

The Secretary of State was, in 1991, faced with a situation in which the United Kingdom was in breach of its primary obligation. That was contested by the Secretary of State before the European Court of Justice. During that year he contended that the primary obligation imposed by the Directive on Member States was to use the best practicable means to secure compliance with the Directive. Since the judgment of the European Court of Justice he has accepted and accepts now that this country should never have arrived at this situation but the ineluctable fact is that is where we are. He submits, and I accept in the absence of evidence to the contrary, that the evidence makes clear that to arrive at a situation in which the undertakers were in a position to supply only wholesome water would take years rather than months. He accepts that the Act in section 18 provides that in that sort of situation the Secretary of State is, subject to section 19, to make an enforcement order. Such an order must "make such provision as is requisite for the purpose of securing compliance with the Regulations". He submits that such an order need not be made if "the company has given and is complying with an undertaking to take all such steps as it appears to him *for the time being* to be appropriate for the company to take for the purpose of securing or facilitating a compliance with the Regulations". Given that this country was in breach of its primary obligation, he accepts that he was and is under a duty by virtue of the country's secondary obligation to act speedily and effectively to arrive at a situation in which this country would no longer be in breach of its primary obligation. He submits that, for a variety of reasons set out in the affidavits filed on his behalf, this situation is more likely to be arrived at speedily if he uses the mechanism of an undertaking pursuant to section 19 rather than the mechanism of the enforcement order pursuant to section 18.

The Question for the Court

In my judgment the appropriate question for the court is whether the applicants have shown that the acceptance by the Secretary of State of the undertakings is an unlawful way of attempting to fulfil his duty to remedy the breach of the United Kingdom's primary obligation.

I now turn to consider each of the submissions advanced by Mr Beloff in support of the proposition that the Secretary of State erred in law in accepting these undertakings.

The applicants submit that the undertakings were not accepted for the purpose of actually securing compliance with the Directive's standards as laid down in the Regulations, but only for the purpose of securing or *facilitating* such compliance. They make that submission relying upon the following:

1. The undertakings were expressly given for the purposes *(sic) of securing or facilitating* compliance with the Regulations.
2. The notices of acceptance each expressly state that the Secretary of State is satisfied that the company is complying with an undertaking "to take all such steps as appear to him appropriate for the company to take for the purpose *(sic) of securing or facilitating* compliance with its duty to supply wholesome water."
3. At the time when he accepted the undertakings the Secretary of State was contending before the European Court that he was under no absolute duty to achieve a result and in that context an acceptance to facilitate would not have been a surprising course of action for the Secretary of State to have adopted.
4. The Act in section 19 uses the words "secure or facilitate" and so again an acceptance to facilitate would not have been a surprising course of action for the Secretary of State to have adopted.
5. Mr Lewis, authorised by the Secretary of State to make an affidavit on his behalf, nowhere therein states that the Secretary of State was at the relevant time alive to any distinction between facilitating and securing. This affidavit was sworn at a time when the Secretary of State had been alerted that one of the criticisms made by the applicants of the Secretary of State's acceptance of the undertakings was that acceptance of the undertakings was for the purpose of facilitating.

Mr Richards drew attention to repeated statements by Mr Lewis to the effect that the Secretary of State was conscious throughout this period of the need to secure compliance with the standards. The United Kingdom had submitted before the European Court of Justice that its obligation under the law of the Communities was only to take all practicable steps to secure compliance. True, that submission was not accepted and the United Kingdom was held to be in breach because it had failed to secure compliance, but what is significant in the present context is that the submission proceeded on the basis that the Secretary of State accepted that the aim in view was to secure compliance. There was no suggestion that all that was ultimately required was to facilitate compliance.

In my judgment when a challenge to action by the Secretary of State is based on an allegation of wrong motivation the court is entitled to look beyond the wording adopted in the document containing the decision under challenge, in this case the notices of acceptance, although that wording may in effect shift the onus of proof. Having looked at the affidavits sworn on behalf of the Secretary of State, the truthfulness of none of which is challenged, I am persuaded that the Secretary of State at the time when he accepted the undertakings did so intending to secure that ultimately the United Kingdom would comply with the standards. The question whether there was implicit in the Secretary of State's approach too great a degree of leisureliness is one to which I now turn.

The first error of approach: all practicable steps

The applicants submit that at the time of accepting the undertakings, the Secretary of State approached his duty to enforce on the basis that it was a duty only to use his best endeavours to achieve a compliance with the Directive's standards by taking all practicable steps, and not a duty to achieve the result required by the Directive as soon as possible. They submit that this was unlawful. They submit that there is a distinction between all practicable steps and all possible steps. What may not be practicable for the undertakers on their own may nonetheless be possible of achievement by the United Kingdom by taking appropriate Ministerial and Parliamentary action. Mr Beloff reminded the court that it has proved possible to get legislation through Parliament in a day or two. Extra funds can always be found if the political will is there. He submitted that, in circumstances where the United Kingdom is in breach of its primary obligation the secondary obligation is then to take all possible steps to remedy that breach as soon as possible.

I did not understand Mr Richards to be challenging this last proposition as such. In any event, I accept for present purposes that the secondary obligation is an obligation on the United Kingdom to rectify the breach as soon as possible and not merely as soon as practicable. Moreover, I accept that the wording frequently used on behalf of the Secretary of State in the evidence is to the effect that he is seeking to secure a result as soon as practicable.

However, in any particular case, it may be that it is not possible to achieve a result earlier than is practicable. In such a case, the use of the word practicable rather than possible does not necessarily betray a legally erroneous approach. In the present case there are considerable complexities in bringing *all* our water up to the standards. Many of these complexities are set out in the affidavits and are not disputed. To give an example, from Mr Lewis's affidavit, London is a city with millions of consumers. All those consumers need to have a water supply whilst a plant is constructed which will produce water which conforms to standard. The installation of the new processes required to remove pesticide residues will cause considerable disruptions at the treatment works and reduce the amount of water they can provide at present quality standards. The only way of coping with this temporary reduction in output is to take prior action to increase the output from other works and to use the London Ring Main to re-distribute water to meet the demand. The output from three of the eight major treatment works will need to be increased. The extent of disruptions caused by installation of additional treatment plant will vary from works to works but in some cases will be so considerable that it can not be undertaken until the London Ring Main is available and replacement supplies can readily be brought in. But it is impossible to combine the installation of additional treatment plant with the current hydraulic up-rating and the simultaneous construction of the London Ring Main.

The evidence does not show that the Secretary of State has, in accepting the undertakings, adopted a too leisurely approach. The applicants' evidence gives no possible alternative course of action on the ground which would have produced a situation in which the United Kingdom's water supply would now conform to standard or even would now be closer in time to conforming to standard. The only example of an unduly leisurely approach by the Secretary of State put forward by the applicants relies on the undoubted facts that:

1. the dates in several of the schedules are later than most of the non-binding dates in the Annexes to those schedules,
2. the undertakers have in some cases carried out the steps set out in the Annexes prior to the dates therein set out,
3. the Secretary of State has, since 1991, accepted further undertakings from the undertakers which are more stringent than the 1991 undertakings.

The first of these points is essentially a criticism of the grouping of the water supply zones in the schedules. I can illustrate the point by reference to the first Schedule to the Thames undertaking. The water supply zones set out in Part I are all the zones supplied by 14 treatment works. The end date for the construction of treatment plants which is given in Part 4 of the Schedule is March 31, 1995. The annexes to the Schedule indicate in relation to each of those treatment plants the date by which the new plant is to be commissioned. Only one of those dates is March 1995. All the others are earlier.

The secondary obligation of the United Kingdom is to bring all the plants up to standard as soon as possible. For reasons set out in Mr Lewis's affidavit this is more likely to be achieved if a certain degree of flexibility is left as to the order in which they are treated. The applicants have not shown that the incorporation into the schedules of enforceable dates in respect of each plant would be likely to lead to the sooner fulfilment of our secondary obligation.

The fact that it has proved possible for the undertakers to do or agree to do better than they undertook to do is not, in the absence of further evidence, proof that the Secretary of State at the time when he accepted the 1991 undertakings approached his duty in too leisurely a fashion.

The second error of approach: steps not results

The applicants submit that the undertakings were deficient because they required steps to be taken rather than results to be achieved and that, by accepting them, the Secretary of State was fettering *his own* ability to take further enforcement action so long as the applicants complied with the steps specified in the undertaking. [The effect on the ability of others to take enforcement action I return to later in this judgment. That was not the basis of this part of the applicants' submissions.]

I reject this submission for the following reasons:

1. the very wording of section 19 indicates that an undertaking should set out such steps as appear to the Secretary of State to be appropriate for the company to take for the purpose of securing a result. It must have been perfectly clear to both parties to each undertaking that the purpose of the exercise was to arrive at a situation in which there were no longer the contraventions specified in the Schedule. Undertaking or no undertaking, the undertakers remained in breach of section 68(1)(a) until the water was up to standard. There is no requirement to put into the undertaking itself an express requirement that the undertaker bring its water up to standard;
2. the Act does not provide that acceptance by the Secretary of State of an undertaking prevents the Secretary of State from taking further enforcement action. On the contrary, the words in section 19 "for the time being" envisage a continuing monitoring duty on the Secretary of State;
3. the undertakings expressly set out that they were given pursuant to section 19, refer to the phrase "for the time being" and contain no promise express or implied that the Secretary of State will not require more than is set out in the undertakings.

Lack of specificity

The applicants submit that "the undertakings accepted do not oblige the suppliers to take a sufficiently specific course of action to allow the Secretary of State to ascertain precisely whether effective action is being taken to secure compliance. Any detail is relegated to Annexes to the Schedules to the undertakings (which are specifically expressed not to form part of the undertakings)".

The ability of the Secretary of State to ascertain precisely whether effective action is being taken to secure compliance with the undertakings does not, in my judgment, depend on whether the timetable for the construction and commissioning of a plant is contained in the undertaking or in the Annexes to the Schedules. If there is any falling behind the programme set out in relation to any particular plant in the relevant annex, the Secretary of State will be able to ascertain it.

The arrangements which the Secretary of State makes to monitor the progress of the undertakers to the goal of conforming with the standards are not ones which require to be set out in the undertaking. Once one accepts that the Secretary of State is free to start enforcement action notwithstanding the existence of the undertakings then it follows that he has the whip hand should it be that the undertakers are not making what he would regard as sufficient progress. Whilst the point can be made, and indeed has been made by Mr

Beloff, that the Secretary of State never has enforced during the currency of an undertaking, the point would only be of conceivable use if it could be shown that the undertakers and the Secretary of State tended to wait until past the end date in the Schedules before looking to see whether or not there had been compliance. The evidence is all the other way. Target dates in the Annexes have regularly been beaten and tighter undertakings have been substituted for looser undertakings. All this indicates continued monitoring and a willingness and ability on the part of the Secretary of State to strive for conformity with standards prior to the dates specified in the Annexes.

Lack of precision and enforceability

Under this head, the applicants have developed their submissions that the Secretary of State, by accepting the undertakings in the form in which they are, has put it out of his power to secure compliance as soon as possible by the United Kingdom of its obligation to supply only wholesome water.

For reasons I have already developed, it is clear that the acceptance by the Secretary of State of the undertakings does not have the legal effect of inhibiting the Secretary of State's powers to serve an enforcement notice under the Act. It is true, as Mr Beloff submitted, that there is little in the undertakings which is of sufficient precision to allow of the taking of injunction proceedings for breach of the undertakings. In particular, the obligation to construct and commission treatment plants of unspecified design is, absent any further sanction, difficult to police.

However, the undertakers are manifestly in breach of section 68(1)(a) and there is no *legal* problem in asking for an injunction to restrain them from further supplying water which is not up to standard. The problem is purely practicable that meanwhile people must drink. The undertakings are designed to enable one to arrive at a situation in which all water conforms to standard. The Secretary of State, undertaking or no undertaking, can at any time, if he thinks it right, make use of the powers of making enforcement orders.

I do not doubt that there can be room for argument as to what steps on the ground are best designed to achieve the end which all agree must be achieved, namely the supply of water all of which is to conform to standard, but no such argument has been developed in the evidence or in front of me. In those circumstances the submissions as to whether the identification of those methods is as a matter of law for the court or for the Secretary of State can be left for the moment to academe. On any basis, their identification must initially be for the Secretary of State and his view can not be challenged until such time as someone puts forward an alternative view.

In his reply, Mr Beloff developed a different point which was concerned, not with the Secretary of State's powers of enforcement but with the powers of the individual Community citizen to secure by legal action a remedy for the continuing failure of the United Kingdom undertakers to supply only wholesome water of the standards prescribed by the Directive and the Regulations. His argument went as follows: the Community citizen has had since 1985 a right under Community law to wholesome water; such a right must be enforceable. Under the Act the only method of enforcement at the hands of an individual is that provided by section 22 and this only arises once an enforcement order has been made.

Therefore, by not making an enforcement order the Secretary of State deprives the individual of the possibility of enforcing his right under Community Law.

The essence of this submission is that by accepting an undertaking the Secretary of State is depriving the citizen of a right he enjoys under Community law and, therefore, the acceptance of the undertaking by the Secretary of State is illegal. The submission is not foreshadowed in the Form 86A and has not been the subject of detailed argument in front of me. However, in my judgment, it proceeds from at least one legally unsound premise, namely that it is possible for the Secretary of State, by his actions, to deprive a citizen of his rights under Community law. If the citizen has any rights under Community law then he can enforce them because they cannot be taken away from him by the Secretary of State. If he has no such rights then the point does not arise. In the circumstances, I do not need to decide whether he has such rights. None are expressly claimed in this action. That may be because there can be no suggestion that the limited company has suffered any damage and that there is no suggestion in the affidavits that the individual applicant has suffered any.

Conclusion

It has not been shown that by accepting these undertakings the Secretary of State breached any duty or acted illegally in any way. This application fails.

The most interesting aspects of the case are the extreme *pragmatism* of the court – in acknowledgment that Londoners must have water whilst the treatment plants are being built, and the imposition of the burden of proof on the *applicants* to show that the Secretary of State should have proceeded in some other way in order to secure compliance with the European Court of Justice's declaration. The case suggests that the absolute or primary obligation to comply with Directive 778/80/EEC by bringing about a change in the *physical* state of the environment is capable of being emasculated by the national courts' view of the nature and extent of the secondary obligation to comply with the Court of Justice's judgment because of the practicalities involved in securing higher standards of environmental protection. This is out of line with the strict approach taken by the Court of Justice to the breach of obligations in EC law. No reference to the Court of Justice was made for interpretation and clarification of the nature of the 'secondary obligation', as provided for under Article 177 EC, the Court of Appeal considering that the issues were sufficiently clear to be dealt with by the national courts. There is therefore a discrepancy between the absolute standard of compliance with Community law required by the Court of Justice and the liberal acceptance of practical difficulties in achieving this standard by the national courts. This represents the familiar 'implementation gap' of such modernist legal forms as Directive 778/80/EEC, which prescribe environmental quality standards. It is partly for this reason that there is increasing recourse to postmodern or 'post-regulatory' law in such self-regulatory techniques as environmental auditing.[63]

63 See further ch 8, pp 324–335.

(b) Individual protection

Even taking account of the likelihood of more effective enforcement by the imposition of fines by the European Court of Justice, and the possibility of greater congruence between the primary and secondary obligations to comply with EC law, the complaint and judicial procedure outlined above fails to take the place of the application of environmental law in *national* courts. The development of individual protection by the European Court of Justice, in particular via the doctrines of direct effect, indirect effect, and *Francovich* liability, confronts the limitations of the enforcement procedure.

Most Community environmental law is in the form of directives. Enforcement is often problematic because, although the result to be achieved by a directive is binding upon Member States, the manner in which that result is to be achieved is not. This is because Article 189(3) EC states: 'A directive shall be binding, as to the result to be achieved, upon each Member State to which it is addressed, but shall leave to the national authorities the choice of form and methods'. This is considered vital for the preservation of existing administrative systems and flexible implementation of EC law. However, this also means that directives are not directly applicable in the Member States' legal systems. Member States are therefore required to enact the necessary implementing measures to give effect to the directive. It was originally assumed that the corollary of not being directly applicable was that, unlike regulations and Treaty Articles, directives were not directly effective; that is, individuals were unable to rely upon their provisions before their national courts. As a result, the effectiveness of Community law relied heavily upon Member States discharging their obligations under the Treaty even though in many cases it was not in a Member State's interest to do so.

The European Court of Justice has now established that directives *are* capable of having direct effect in national courts where Member States have taken no, or insufficient, measures to transpose a directive's provisions into national law and where certain tests have been fulfilled.[64] This doctrine was expressed particularly clearly in *Marshall v Southampton and South West Hampshire Area Health Authority (No 1)*, a sex-discrimination case in which Mrs Marshall attempted (successfully) to rely upon rights contained in Directive 76/207/EEC on equal treatment:[65]

> Whereas the provisions of a directive appear as far as their subject matter is concerned to be unconditional and sufficiently precise, those provisions may be relied upon by an individual against the state where the state fails to implement the directive in national law by the end of the prescribed period or where it fails to implement the directive correctly.

64 Case 41/74: *Van Duyn v Home Office* [1974] ECR 1337; Case 148/78: *Pubblico Ministero v Ratti* [1979] ECR 1629; Case 8/81: *Becker v Finanzamt Münster-Innenstadt* [1982] ECR 53 and Case 152/84: *Marshall v Southampton and South West Hampshire Area Health Authority (No 1)* [1986] ECR 723.

65 Case 152/84: *Marshall v Southampton and South West Hampshire Area Health Authority (No 1)* [1986] ECR 723 at 748.

This doctrine lies at the core of the European Court of Justice's creation of a European 'common law', which permits the enforcement of Community law by protecting individuals' Community rights in a manner unprovided for by the Community's constitutional document – the Treaty of Rome. The doctrine of direct effect has developed largely in the context of law relating to free movement of persons and sex equality. Recognition of the significance of the direct effect doctrine in environmental law has taken far longer. This is partly because, until recently, an emphasis was placed on creating a corpus of Community environmental law, rather than its enforcement by individuals. In addition, the tests for direct effect pose a number of obstacles for plaintiffs seeking to rely on environmental directives. First, those directives which set out frameworks for action or confer discretion on Member States or competent authorities might well fail the tests of precision.[66] The judgment of the Divisional Court in *Wychavon District Council v Secretary of State for the Environment, ex p Velcourt*[67] suggests that this is the case with Directive 85/337/EEC on environmental assessment because it grants discretion to Member States to determine whether certain projects are likely to have a significant effect on the environment. Tucker J held that this discretion means the entire Directive should fail to have direct effect, suggesting also a misreading of the accepted principle of Community law that *individual* articles in a directive might have direct effect whilst others do not. Less difficulty is likely to be experienced on this point with those directives which set clear, quantifiable environmental standards.[68]

Second, there is a requirement that for direct effect of a directive to be possible, it should confer rights on individuals. This is problematic because many directives are designed primarily to protect the environment rather than confer some benefit on individuals. The test is however likely to be fulfilled in the case of directives which, whilst having as their primary purpose the protection and enhancement of the environment, are also intended to protect human health and safety. For example, the Court of Justice confirmed in Case C-58/89: *Commission v Germany*[69] that in terms of directives which are intended to protect public health, whenever non-compliance with the measures might endanger the health of persons, those concerned should be able to rely on mandatory rules in order to enforce their rights. In terms of national courts' interpretation of this test, the Divisional Court in *R v Secretary of State for the Environment*[70] sidestepped this issue of the Drinking Water Directive's direct effect, but the Court of Appeal was prepared to find it likely that Directive 778/80/EEC would have direct effect.

The direct effect of Directive 85/337/EEC on environmental assessment is more hazy. Article 6 gives members of the public certain rights of participation

66 This was the result in Case C-236/92: *Comitato di Coordinamento per la Difesa della Cava v Regione Lombardia* [1994] ECR I-483 concerning the direct effect of a framework directive on waste.

67 (1994) JEL Vol 6, No 2, 351.

68 Case C-58/89: *Commission v Germany* [1991] ECR I-4983, 5023 establishes that Directive 75/440/EEC, OJ L 194, 16.6.1975 on the quality of surface waters intended for abstraction is sufficiently clear and precise for this reason.

69 [1991] ECR I-4983, 5023.

70 [1995] Env LR 11.

in the assessment process. However, McCullogh J in *Twyford Parish Council v Secretary of State for the Environment*[71] was of the opinion that, notwithstanding his *obiter* comments that the Directive has direct effect, the applicants should not succeed because they had not suffered harm from the failure of the developers to produce an environmental assessment. The reasoning was that all the information which would have been derived from the compilation of a formal environmental assessment had come to light in some way or other. This novel reading of the direct effect doctrine suggests that whether a directive confers rights on individuals might be decided in future by reference to whether harm has been suffered. The possibility of a finding of direct effect is decidedly less likely still with Directive 92/423/EEC on the protection of habitats and fauna and flora. Since its purpose is the protection of certain species and their habitats, it might be argued that the Directive does not confer rights on individuals. This is a deeply anthropo-centric test which has the potential to prevent individuals relying on Community law which does not pertain directly to the protection of their health.[72]

Following *Marshall No 1*,[73] an individual will only be capable of relying upon a directive against a public body or 'emanation of the state', and not against a private body or another individual. The term 'public body' has since been couched in broad terms and, following *Griffin v South West Water Services Ltd*,[74] includes a private water company. Nevertheless, inequalities still exist between plaintiffs bringing an action to protect rights founded in Community law against public bodies and those against entirely private organisations. Where an individual does wish to bring an action against a private organisation, the doctrine of 'indirect effect', developed by the Court of Justice, might bring redress. According to this doctrine, methods of 'sympathetic interpretation' should be applied by national courts according to the duty on Member States under Article 5 EC to 'take all appropriate measures to ensure fulfilment of their Community obligations'.[75] This means that conflicting national law should be read in light of the wording and purpose of EC law. The scope of the doctrine has been extended.[76] This route relies upon the willingness and capacity of the national court to identify the relevance of 'sympathetic interpretation'.[77] Following the examples of judicial

71 [1992] 1 CMLR 276.

72 C Miller, 'Environmental Rights: English Fact or Fiction?' [1995] JLS, Vol 22, 374.

73 Case 152/84: *Marshall v Southampton and South West Hampshire Area Health Authority (No 1)* [1986] ECR 723; see also Case C-91/92: *Faccini Dori v Recreb Srl* [1994] ECR I-3325 which confirms the *obiter* statement in *Marshall No 1* denying the horizontal effect of directives.

74 [1995] IRLR 15.

75 The doctrine was first developed in Case 14/83: *Von Colson and Kamann v Land Nordrhein-Westfalen* [1984] ECR 1891.

76 A broader interpretation of the doctrine was advanced by the Court of Justice in Case C-106/89: *Marleasing SA v La Comercial Internacional de Alimentación SA* [1990] ECR I-4135: the obligation to interpret national provisions in the light of a Community measure was considered to apply whether 'the national provisions in question were enacted before or after the Directive'.

77 The scope for national courts to ignore an interpretation of national legislation in line with Community law has lessened in the light of Case C-32/93: *Webb v EMO Air Cargo (UK) Ltd* [1994] QB 718 in which the European Court of Justice set aside Lord Templeman's argument in *Duke v GEC Reliance Ltd* [1988] 1 All ER 626, HL, that methods of sympathetic interpretation may only be applied where a directive's provisions are directly effective.

resistance to the indirect effect doctrine in *R v Swale Borough Council and Medway Ports, ex p Royal Society for the Protection of Birds*[78] and *Wychavon District Council v Secretary of State for the Enviroment, ex p Velcourt*[79] it might be unduly optimistic to expect this approach to be widely adopted.

(c) *Francovich* liability

Following the Court of Justice's creative judgment in Joined Cases C-6/90: *Francovich v Italian State* and C-9/90: *Bonifaci v Belgian State*,[80] individuals who have suffered as a result of a Member State's failure to implement a directive may seek financial compensation from that state, even where the directive in question does not have direct effect. In principle, this judgment considerably strengthens the hand of private individuals seeking protection under Community rules before their national courts.

The use of *Francovich* liability as a mechanism of effective enforcement of EC environmental law is highly significant. At its most far-reaching, the legal effect of *Francovich*, when combined with the recognition of rights in environmental directives, is to create enforceable environmental rights which are not reliant upon the holding of private property.[81] This expression and enforcement of abstract, public rights in Community environmental law, contrasts with the specificity of private property rights which provided a conceptual framework for the development of environmental law in the United Kingdom.[82]

The judgment in Case C-337/89: *Commission v United Kingdom*[83] appears likely to trigger actions to establish *Francovich* liability since the Court stated explicitly that there was a legal interest in a full hearing, foreseeing liability for harm caused by poor water quality. However, *Francovich* liability might not be applied to the environmental field so easily as financial and employment cases. To establish state liability three conditions must be fulfilled:[84] the result required by a directive must include the conferring of rights for the benefit of individuals; the content of these rights may be determined by reference to the provisions of the directive; the existence of a causal link between the breach of the obligation of the state and the damage suffered by the person affected.[85] As discussed above, the first condition would be likely to be fulfilled. The second condition that the content of these rights must be determined by reference to the provisions of the directive is also likely to be fulfilled where specific limit values are given. The third condition, evidence of a causal link between the

78 (1991) JEL Vol 3, No 1, 135.
79 (1994) JEL Vol 6, No 2, 351.
80 Joined Cases C-6, 9/90: *Francovich and Bonifaci v Italy* [1991] ECR I-5357.
81 K Gray, 'Equitable Property', (1994) 47 CLP 157-214, at 206-7.
82 See ch 2.
83 Case C-337/89: *Commission v United Kingdom* [1992] ECR I-6103.
84 At para 40.
85 See joined Cases C-46/93: *Brasserie du Pêcheur SA v Germany* and Case C-48/93: *R v Secretary of State for Transport (Factortame III)* [1996] All ER (EC) 301 at paras 55-56 for the Court's definition of 'harm suffered'.

breach of the obligation of the state and the damage suffered by the individual, is likely to be extremely problematic in most environmental cases.[86]

8 LOSING THE ECONOMIC BASE: *LAPPEL BANK*

The European Community is now far more than an economic cooperation and trading group of Member States. The development of its environmental law confirms this. At least in formal terms, environmental law of the European Community was first based upon an economic concept of harmonisation in pursuance of economic efficiency; it is now concerned with ideas of the protection of human health and protection of the environment for its own sake. It remains the case, however, that European Community environmental law has developed within the confines of an aspirational policy framework of solid, but rapid, economic growth and it bears the marks of this influence, particularly the proposed dilution of provisions in line with the principle of subsidiarity.

A significant role for economic considerations in one important part of Community environmental law – habitat protection – is roundly dismissed by the European Court of Justice in Case C-44/95: *R v Secretary of State for the Environment, ex p Royal Society for the Protection of Birds (Lappel Bank)*. The Court's judgment on the interpretation of the directive on the conservation of wild birds is founded upon its assertion in Case 240/83: *Procureur de la République v Association de Défense Des Brûleurs D'huiles Usagées (ADBHU)*[87] that environmental protection is an 'essential objective' of the Community. The judgment in *Lappel Bank* is at variance with the policy of the Commission on competitiveness, and economic growth in the Community, and the measures it advances to simplify, or deregulate areas of environmental law. It also remains to be seen whether the Court's uncompromising stance on the role of economic considerations in certain decisions is matched in the future by its more practical recognition of environmental rights. History has shown that the Court's rhetoric, as well as its radical and creative interpretation of the EC treaty, has a tendency to have far-reaching effects.

Case C-44/95: *R v Secretary of State for the Environment ex p Royal Society for the Protection of Birds (Lappel Bank)* [1996] 3 CMLR 411

Judgment

1. By order of 9 February 1995, received at the Court on 24 February 1995, the House of Lords referred to the Court of Justice for a preliminary ruling under Article 177 of the EC Treaty two questions on the interpretation of Articles 2 and 4 of Council Directive 79/409/EEC of 2 April 1979 on the conservation of wild birds (OJ 1979 L 103 p. 1, hereinafter 'the Birds Directive').
2. Those questions were raised in proceedings between an association for the protection of birds (hereinafter 'the RSPB'), and the Secretary of State')

86 See ch 9, p 365 in the case of Directive 778/80/EEC.
87 [1985] ECR 531. See above.

concerning a decision designating a special protection area for the protection of wild birds.

3. The Birds Directive, which covers all species of birds naturally occurring in the wild in the European territory of the Member States to which the Treaty applies, provides, in Article 2, that the Member States are to take all necessary measures to maintain the population of all those species of birds at a level which corresponds in particular to ecological, scientific and cultural requirements, while taking account of economic and recreational requirements.
4. According to Article 3 of the Birds Directive, the Member States, having regard to the requirements mentioned in Article 2, are to take all the necessary measures to preserve, maintain or re-establish a sufficient diversity and area of habitats for all the protected species.
5. Pursuant to Article 4(1) of that Directive, the species mentioned in Annex I are to be the subject of special conservation measures concerning their habitat in order to ensure their survival and reproduction in their area of distribution. In particular, the Member States are to classify the most suitable territories in terms of number and size as special protection areas for the conservation of those species in the geographical sea and land area where the Directive applies.
6. According to Article 4(2), 'Member States shall take similar measures for regularly occurring migratory species not listed in Annex I, bearing in mind their need for protection in the geographical sea and land area where this Directive applies, as regards their breeding, moulting and wintering areas and staging posts along their migration routes. To this end, Member States shall pay particulat attention to the protection of wetlands and particularly to wetlands of international importance'.
7. Finally, according to Article 4(4), '[I]n respect of the areas referred to in paragraphs 1 and 2 above, Member States shall take appropriate steps to avoid pollution or deterioration of habitats or any disturbances affecting the birds, in so far as these would be significant having regard to the objectives of this Article. Outside these protection areas, Member States shall also strive to avoid pollution or deterioration of habitats'.
8. Council Directive 92/43/EEC of 21 May 1992 on the conservation of the natural habitats of wild fauna and flora (OJ 1992 L 206, p.7, hereinafter 'the Habitats Directive'), to be implemented in the United Kingdom by June 1994, provides in Article 7 that the obligations under Article 6(2), (3) and (4) are to replace any obligations arising under the first sentence of Article 4(4) of the Birds Directive in respect of areas classified pursuant to Article 4(1) or similarly recognized under Article 4(2) of that Directive. Article 6(2), (3) and (4) of the Habitats Directive is worded as follows:
    2. Member States shall take appropriate steps to avoid, in the special areas of conservation, the deterioration of natural habitats and the habitats of species as well as disturbance of the species for which the areas have been designated, in so far as such disturbance could be significant in relation to the objectives of this Directive.
    3. Any plan or project not directly connected with or necessary to the management of the site but likely to have a significant effect thereon,

either individually or in combination with other plans or projects, shall be subject to appropriate assessment of its implications for the site in view of the site's conservation objectives. In the light of the conclusions of the assessment of the implications for the site and subject to the provisions of paragraph 4, the competent national authorities shall agree to the plan or project only after having ascertained that it will not adversely affect the integrity of the site concerned and, if appropriate, after having obtained the opinion of the general public.

4. If, in spite of a negative assessment of the implications for the site and in the absence of alternative solutions, a plan or project must nevertheless be carried out for imperative reasons of overriding public interest, including those of a social or economic nature, the Member State shall take all compensatory measures necessary to ensure that the overall coherence of Natura 2000 is protected. It shall inform the Commission of the compensatory measures adopted.

   Where the site concerned hosts a priority natural habitat type and/or a priority species, the only considerations which may be raised are those relating to human health or public safety, to beneficial consequences of primary importance for the environment or, further to an opinion from the Commission, to other imperative reasons of overriding public interest.

9. The United Kingdom did not transpose the Habitats Directive until October 1994.
10. On 15 October 1993, the Secretary of State decided to designate the Medway Estuary and Marshes as a Special Protection Area (hereinafter 'SPA'). At the same time, he decided to exclude from it an area of about 22 hectares known as Lappel Bank.
11. According to the order for reference, the Medway Estuary and Marshes are an area of wetland of international importance covering 4,681 hectares on the north coast of Kent and listed under the Ramsar Convention. They are used by a number of wildfowl and wader species as a breeding and wintering area and as a staging post during spring and autumn migration. The site also supports breeding populations of the avocet and the little tern, which are listed in Annex I to the Birds Directive.
12. Lappel Bank is an area of inter-tidal mudflat immediately adjoining, at its northern end, the Port of Sheerness and falling geographically within the bounds of the Medway Estuary and Marshes. Lappel Bank shares several of the important ornithological qualities of the area as a whole. Although it does not support any of the species referred to in Article 4(1) of the Birds Directive, some of the bird species of the area are represented in significantly greater numbers than elsewhere in the Medway SPA. Lappel Bank is an important component of the overall estuarine ecosystem and the loss of that inter-tidal area would probably result in a reduction in the wader and wildfowl populations of the Medway Estuary and Marshes.
13. The Port of Sheerness is at present the fifth largest in the United Kingdom for cargo and freight handling. It is a flourishing commercial undertaking, well-located for sea traffic and access to its main domestic markets. The Port, which is also a significant employer in an area with a serious

unemployment problem, plans extended facilities for car storage and value added activities on vehicles and in the fruit and paper product market, in order better to compete with continental ports offering similar facilities. Lappel Bank is the only area into which the Port of Sheerness can realistically envisage expanding.

14. Accordingly, taking the view that the need not to inhibit the viability of the port and the significant contribution that expansion into the area of Lappel Bank would make to the local and national economy outweighed its nature conservation value, the Secretary of State decided to exclude that area from the Medway SPA.
15. The RSPB applied to the Divisional Court of the Queen's Bench Division to have the Secretary of State's decision quashed on the ground that he was not entitled, by virtue of the Birds Directive, to have regard to economic considerations when classifying an SPA. The Divisional Court found against the RSPB. On appeal by the RSPB, the Court of Appeal upheld that judgment. The RSPB therefore appealed to the House of Lords.
16. Uncertain as to how the Directive should be interpreted, the House of Lords stayed proceedings pending a preliminary ruling from the Court of Justice on the following questions:
    1. Is a Member State entitled to take account of the considerations mentioned in Article 2 of Directive 79/409/EEC of 2 April 1979 on the conservation of wildbirds in classification of an area as a Special Protection Area and/or in defining the boundaries of such an area pursuant to Article 4(1) and/or 4(2) of that Directive?
    2. If the answer to Question 1 is "no", may a Member State nevertheless take account of Article 2 considerations in the classification process in so far as:
       (a) they amount to a general interest which is superior to the general interest which is represented by the ecological objective of the Directive (i.e. the test which the European Court has laid down in, for example, *Commission* v *Germany* ("Leybucht Dykes") Case C-57/89, for derogation from the requirements of Article 4(4); or
       (b) they amount to imperative reasons of overriding public interest such as might be taken into account under Article 6(4) of Directive 92/43/EEC of 21 May 1992 on the conservation of natural habitats and of wild fauna and flora?'

The first question

17. The point of this question is whether Article 4(1) or (2) of the Birds Directive is to be interpreted as meaning that a Member State is authorized to take account of the economic requirements mentioned in Article 2 thereof when designating an SPA and defining its boundaries.
18. As a preliminary point, it must be borne in mind that, according to the ninth recital in the preamble to the Birds Directive, 'the preservation, maintenance or restoration of a sufficient diversity and area of habitats is essential to the conservation of all species of birds [covered by the Directive]', that 'certain species of birds should be the subject of special

conservation measures concerning their habitats in order to ensure their survival and reproduction in their area of distribution', and, finally, that 'such measures must also take account of migratory species'.

19. That recital is formally reflected in Articles 3 and 4 of the Directive. In paragraph 23 of its judgment in Case C-355/90 *Commission v Spain* [1993] ECR I-4221 (hereinafter *'Santoña Marshes'*) the Court pointed out that the first of those provisions imposes obligations of a general character, namely the obligation to ensure a sufficient diversity and area of habitats for all the birds referred to in the Directive, while the second contains specific obligations with regard to the species of birds listed in Annex I and the migratory species not listed in that Annex.
20. According to the United Kingdom Government and the Port of Sheerness Limited, Article 4 cannot be considered in isolation from Article 3. They state that Article 4 provides, in relation to certain species of particular interest, for the specific application of the general obligation imposed by Article 3. Since the latter provision allows account to be taken of economic requirements, the same should apply to Article 4(1) and (2).
21. The French Government reaches the same conclusion, observing that, when an SPA is created, the Member States take account of all the criteria mentioned in Article 2 of the Birds Directive, which is general in scope, and, therefore, *inter alia*, of economic requirements.
22. Those arguments cannot be upheld.
23. It must be noted first that Article 4 of the Birds Directive lays down a protection regime which is specifically targeted and reinforced both for the species listed in Annex I and for migratory species, an approach justified by the fact that they are, respectively, the most endangered species and the species constituting a common heritage of the Community (see Case C-169/89 *Van den Burg* [1990] ECR I-2143, paragraph 11).
24. Whilst Article 3 of the Birds Directive provides for account to be taken of the requirements mentioned in Article 2 for the implementation of general conservation measures, including the creation of protection areas, Article 4 makes no such reference for the implementation of special conservation measures, in particular the creation of SPAs.
25. Consequently, having regard to the aim of special protection pursued by Article 4 and the fact that, according to settled case-law (see in particular Case C-435/92 *APAS v Préfets de Maine-et-Loire and de la Loire Atlantique* [1994] ECR I-67, paragraph 20), Article 2 does not constitute an autonomous derogation from the general system of protection established by the Directive, it must be held (see paragraphs 17 and 18 of *Santoña Marshes*) – that the ecological requirements laid down by the former provision do not have to be balanced against the interests listed in the latter, in particular economic requirements.
26. It is the criteria laid down in paragraphs (1) and (2) of Article 4 which are to guide the Member States in designating and defining the boundaries of SPAs. It is clear from paragraphs 26 and 27 of *Santoña Marshes* that, notwithstanding the divergences between the various language versions of the last sub-paragraph of Article 4(1), the criteria in question are ornithological criteria.
27. In view of the foregoing, the answer to the first question must be that Article 4(1) or (2) of the Birds Directive is to be interpreted as meaning that a

Member State is not authorized to take account of the economic requirements mentioned in Article 2 thereof when designating an SPA and defining its boundaries.

The second question

The first part of the second question

28. By the first part of the second question, the national court seeks to ascertain whether Article 4(1) or (2) of the Birds Directive must be interpreted as allowing a Member State, when designating an SPA and defining its boundaries, to take account of economic requirements as constituting a general interest superior to that represented by the ecological objective of that Directive.
29. In its judgment in Case C-57/89 *Commission v Germany* [1991] ECR I-883, paragraphs 21 and 22 (hereinafter '*Leybucht Dykes*'), the Court held that the Member States may, in the context of Article 4(4) of the Birds Directive, reduce the extent of an SPA only on exceptional grounds, being grounds corresponding to a general interest superior to the general interest represented by the ecological objective of the Directive. It was held that economic requirements cannot be invoked in that context.
30. It is also clear from paragraph 19 of *Santoña Marshes* that, in the context of Article 4 of that Directive, considered as a whole, economic requirements cannot on any view correspond to a general interest superior to that represented by the ecological objective of the Directive.
31. Accordingly, without its being necessary to rule on the possible relevance of the grounds corresponding to a superior general interest for the purpose of classifying an SPA, the answer to the first part of the second question must be that Article 4(1) or (2) of the Birds Directive is to be interpreted as meaning that a Member State may not, when designating an SPA and defining its boundaries, take account of economic requirements as constructing a general interest superior to that represented by the ecological objective of that Directive.

The second part of the second question

32. By the second part of the second question, the House of Lords asks essentially whether Article 4(1) or (2) of the Birds Directive is to be interpreted as meaning that a Member State may, when designating an SPA and defining its boundaries, take account of economic requirements to the extent that they reflect imperative reasons of overriding public interest of the kind referred to in Article 6(4) of the Habitats Directive.
33. The United Kingdom Government considers that that question is relevant only to cases of classification decisions made after the expiry of the period for transposition of the Habitats Directive. Since that is not the case in the main proceedings, it considers that it is unnecessary to answer the question.
34. It is well settled that it is for the national courts alone, before which the proceedings are pending and which will be responsible for the eventual judgment, to determine, having regard to the particular features of each case, both the need for a preliminary ruling to enable them to give judgment and the relevance of the questions which they refer to the Court. A request

for a preliminary ruling from a national court may be rejected only if it is clear that the interpretation of Community law requested bears no relation to the true nature of the case of the subject-matter of the main action (see in particular Case C-129/94 *Ruiz Bernáldez* [1996] ECR I-1829, paragraph 7). That is, however, not the case in the main proceedings.

35. Consequently, it is necessary to examine the second part of the second question submitted by the national court.
36. It is important first to bear in mind that Article 7 of the Habitats Directive provides in particular that the obligations arising under Article 6(4) thereof are to apply, in place of any obligations arising under the first sentence of Article 4(4) of the Birds Directive, to the areas classified under Article 4(1) or similarly recognized under Article 4(2) of that Directive as from the date of implementation of the Habitats Directive or the date of classification or recognition by a Member State under the Birds Directive, whichever is the later.
37. As the Commission submits in its observations, Article 6(4) of the Habitats Directive, as inserted in the Birds Directive, has, following *Leybucht Dykes* where the point in issue was the reduction of an area already classified, widened the range of grounds justifying encroachment upon SPAs by expressly including therein reasons of a social or economic nature.
38. Thus, the imperative reasons of overriding public interest which may, pursuant to Article 6(4) of the Habitats Directive, justify a plan or project which would significantly affect an SPA in any event include grounds relating to a superior general interest of the kind identified in *Leybucht Dykes* and may where appropriate include grounds of a social or economic nature.
39. Next, although Article 6(3) and (4) of the Habitats Directive, in so far as it amended the first sentence of Article 4(4) of the Birds Directive, established a procedure enabling the Member States to adopt, for imperative reasons of overriding public interest and subject to certain conditions, a plan or a project adversely affecting an SPA and so made it possible to go back on a decision classifying such an area by reducing its extent, it nevertheless did not make any amendments regarding the initial stage of classification of an area as an SPA referred to in Article 4(1) and (2) of the Birds Directive.
40. It follows that, even under the Habitats Directive, the classification of sites as SPAs must in all circumstances be carried out in accordance with the criteria permitted under Article 4(1) and (2) of the Birds Directive.
41. Economic requirements, as an imperative reason of overriding public interest allowing a derogation from the obligation to classify a site according to its ecological value, cannot enter into consideration at that stage. But that does not, as the Commission has rightly pointed out, mean that they cannot be taken into account at a later stage under the procedure provided for by Article 6(3) and (4) of the Habitats Directive.
42. The answer to the second part of the second question must therefore be that Article 4(1) or (2) of the Birds Directive is to be interpreted as meaning that a Member State may not, when designating an SPA and defining its boundaries, take account of economic requirements which may constitute imperative reasons of overriding public interest of the kind referred to in Article 6(4) of the Habitats Directive.

...

In Part V we take up and elaborate many of the concerns of this chapter in the context of case studies concerning legal techniques for modifying farming so as to protect water from nitrate pollution (chapter 9), environmental assessment and the integration of planning and pollution controls (chapter 10), and the protection of habitats for geese, using international and Community law (chapter 11).

PART IV

Techniques for environmental protection

CHAPTER 6

Beyond Babylon: the development of pollution controls

1 INTRODUCTION

In this chapter we trace the development of some techniques for the control of pollution that are specific to environmental law. Meeting the challenges of pollution has given this area of law much of its distinctive flavour. As we will see, the recognition that it is necessary to take a holistic approach to the environment, rather than a sectoral one, has been slow. For this reason we will concentrate initially on air pollution. We will then show the ways in which the law has moved from regulation of specific substances emitted into a particular environmental medium to a more precautionary stance that seeks to minimise environmental damage as a whole, recognising that pollutants are not fixed in air, water or soil but move between these media.

This draws on the overarching theme of the book that the development of environmental law has been a process of moving from dealing with harm to the environment after it has occurred to attempting to prevent damage; or at least to set conditions that will ensure that the inevitable harm will be as small as possible. Britain, as the cradle of the industrial revolution, has a long history of industrial pollution and consequently a long track record of regulation of pollution from manufacturing industries. But it would be a mistake to think that pollution is a side effect of only industrial processes. No human settlement can avoid the problem of handling its wastes and every city since the dawn of civilisation has had problems with smoke and sewage disposal. Another reason for concentrating on air is because those who live with polluted air have no choice as to whether or not they breathe it, and it has always been the poor who live in the most polluted places.

The air of London was a problem before the industrial revolution. John Evelyn's treatise was written in 1661 and reprinted by the National Society for Clean Air in 1961. That it was still pertinent three hundred years later shows how intractable the problem is.

FUMIFUGIUM; or

The Inconvenience of the AER, AND
SMOAKE of LONDON DISSIPATED
TOGETHER With some REMEDIES humbly proposed
By John Evelyn Esq;
To His Sacred MAJESTIE AND To the PARLIAMENT now Assembled.

...I forbear to enlarge upon the rest of the conveniences which this August and Opulent City enjoies both by Sea and Land to accumulate her *Encomiums,* and render her the most considerable that the *Earth* has standing upon her ample bosome; because, it belongs to the *Orator* and the *Poet,* and is none of my Institution: But I will infer, that if this goodly City justly challenges what is her due, and merits all that can be said to reinforce her Praises, and give her *Title;* she is to be relieved from that which renders her less healthy, really offends her, and which darkens and eclipses all her other Attributes. And what is all this, but that Hellish and dismall Cloud of SEA-COALE? which is not onely perpetually imminent over her head; For as the Poet,

Conditur in tenebris altum caligine caelum:

but so universally mixed with the otherwise wholesome and excellent *Aer,* that her *Inhabitants* breathe nothing but an impure and thick Mist, accompanied with a fuliginous and filthy vapour, which renders them obnoxious to a thousand inconveniences, corrupting the *Lungs,* and disordering the entire habit of their Bodies; so that *Catharrs, Phthisicks, Coughs* and *Consumptions,* rage more in this one City, than in the whole Earth besides.

...since this is certain, that of all the common and familiar materials which emit it, the immoderate use of, and indulgence to *Sea-Coale* alone in the City of *London,* exposes it to one of the fowlest Inconveniences and reproaches, than possibly beffall so noble and other imcomparable City: And that, not from the *Culinary* fires, which for being weak, and lesse often fed below, is with such ease dispelled and scattered above, as it is hardly at all discernible, but from some few particular Tunnells and Issues, belonging only to *Brewers, Diers, Lime-burners, Salt* and *Sope-boylers,* and some other private Trades, *One* of whose *Spiracles* alone, does manifestly infect the *Aer,* more than all the Chimnies of *London* put together besides. And that this is not the least *Hyperbolic,* lest the best of Judges decide it, which I take to be our senses: Whilst these are belching it forth their sooty jaws, the City of *London* resembles the face rather of *Mount Aetna,* the *Court of Vulcan, Stromboli,* or the Suburbs of *Hell,* than an Assembly of Rational Creatures, and the Imperial seat of our incomparable *Monarch.* For when in all other places the *Aer* is most Serene and Pure, it is here Ecclipsed with such a Cloud of Sulphure, as the Sun itself, which gives day to all the World besides, is hardly able to penetrate and impart it here; and the weary *Traveller,* at many Miles distance, sooner smells, than sees the City to which he repairs. This is that pernicious Smoake which sullyes all her Glory, super-inducing a sooty Crust or Fur upon all that it lights, spoyling the moveables, tarnishing the Plate, Gildings and Furniture, and corroding the very Iron-bars and hardest Stones with these piercing and acrimonious Spirits which accompany its Sulphure; and executing more in one year, than exposed to the pure *Aer* of the Country it could effect in some hundreds;

___piceaque gravatum
Faedat nube diem;

It is this horrid Smoake which obscures our Churches, and makes our Palaces look old, which fouls our Clothes, and corrupts the Waters, so as the very Rain, and refreshing Dews which fall in the several Seasons, precipate this impure vapour, which, with its black and tenacious quality, spots and contaminates whatever is exposed to it.

The industrial revolution compounded this state of affairs described so graphically by John Evelyn and extended it to the new and enlarged manufacturing cities. The environmental problems in the nineteenth century were extensive and unprecedented.[1] It was clear something had to be done. The common law was unequal to the task and so legislation in the public interest became more and more important.

2 BEST PRACTICABLE MEANS

One of the most significant legal developments in pollution control was the transformation of the concept of 'best practicable means'. This shows how developments in law may take place as much through the dedication of individual enforcement officers as by interpretation by the courts or even legislative innovations. 'Best practicable means' had been a defence in the Smoke Nuisance Abatement (Metropolis) Act 1853 and continued as a defence in the Rivers Pollution Prevention Act 1876 where under section 12:

> the means used for rendering harmless any sewage matter or poisonous, noxious, or polluting solid or liquid matter falling or flowing or carried into any stream, are the best or only practicable and available means under the circumstances of the particular case.

In terms of air pollution from industrial works, in the Alkali Inspector's Ninth Annual Report of 1872, the Chief Inspector pointed out that the 1863 Alkali Act had outlived its usefulness because a uniform emission standard did not ensure clean air if many more factories came to the area and emitted according to the standard. Furthermore, emissions other than muriatic acid from alkali works were injurious. Parliament responded with an amendment Act, the Alkali Act 1874. Under section 5, in addition to the condensation of muriatic gas the owner of every alkali work should use the best practicable means of preventing the discharge of all other noxious gases from his works. In the hands of the Alkali Inspectors the concept of 'best practicable means' (bpm) became a sword with which to fight air pollution. But the real significance of the transformation from a defence to a weapon of attack is the way the Alkali Inspectors used it. The second Chief Inspector, Mr Fletcher, described 'best practicable means' as:

> ... more binding than a definite figure, even if that could be given, for it is an elastic band, and may be kept always tight as knowledge of the methods of suppressing the evils complained of increases.[2]

1 See further ch 2.
2 BPP (HC) 1878 quoted in L Guruswamy and S Tromans, 'Towards an Integrated Approach to Pollution Control: The Best Practicable Environmantal Option and its Antecedents', [1986] Journal of Planning Law, 643-655 at 645.

In the Alkali Etc Works Regulation Act 1906, section 5 of the Alkali Act 1874 was re-enacted under section 7 and explained under section 27:

> The expression 'best practicable means' where used with respect to the prevention of the escape of noxious and offensive gases, has reference not only to the provision and efficient maintenance of appliances adequate for preventing such escape, but also to the manner in which such appliances are used and to the proper supervision, by the owner, of any operation in which such gases are evolved.

The Inspectors adopted a conciliatory and co-operational approach to achieve compliance with bpm. The expertise of the Inspectors was welcomed by manufacturers because the Inspectors disseminated knowledge on ways to make use of the wastes, thereby giving the manufacturers good economic reasons to cooperate.

The 1906 Alkali Act also introduced the technique of 'scheduled processes' which functioned as a prior authorisation system. For alkali, hydrochloric acid and sulphuric acid works, specific statutory standards were set for emissions from registered works. But other registered works were required simply to use the 'best practicable means' to prevent the emission of noxious or offensive gases and to render those gases which were discharged harmless or inoffensive.

The combination under the 1906 Alkali Act of 'scheduled processes' and 'best practicable means' proved durable and able to adapt to advances in technology. More processes could easily be added to the schedule with the Alkali Inspectors bringing their technical expertise to the task of establishing the 'best practicable means' to render emissions harmless. In its report of 1976, the Royal Commission on Environmental Pollution praised the achievements of the Alkali Inspectorate in controlling industrial emissions (see extract from the report below). But operating the bpm system involved balancing interests and essentially conducting a cost/benefit analysis for a works and its neighbourhood. Critics have suggested that the balance of costs and benefits became too weighted towards the manufacturers under the 'practicable' part of the formula. Another criticism was that the Inspectorate operated a free consultancy service for manufacturers – in effect a subsidy for industry paid for by the public whom the Inspectors were supposed to be protecting from the emissions.

M Frankel *The Alkali Inspectorate: The Control of Industrial Air Pollution* (London: Social Audit, 1974) pp 45-46

Conclusion: Whose Interests Served? "These industrialists did not get up yesterday. That is why they become so successful. They know how to deal with officials. They need a different psychological approach. In my experience I have found that too much co-operation with them usually leads in the end to exploitation by them". J.C.Starkey, Chief Sanitary Inspector, Salford. November 1955.[3]

3 The Sanitarian, November 1955.

Who Pays? In a speech in February 1971, Secretary of State Peter Walker developed the principle that "he who causes pollution shall either be prevented from doing so, or if that is not possible, shall meet the cost of clearing up the pollution created".[4] The Alkali Inspectorate however, has never considered "making the polluter pay" to be one of its higher priorities. In June 1971, several months after Peter Walker's much publicised announcement, Mr Ireland was telling an audience in Sweden a tale with a different moral:

> "The design problems usually facing the industrialist and the inspectorate are concerned with how far we can go along the road to perfection in protecting the public, without financially embarrassing the industry, individual works or even the nation, for in the long run it is the public which pays, directly or indirectly".

As Mr Ireland suggests, the polluter is never ultimately made to pay. If pollution is uncontrolled, the burden is met by the community around the factory. If the polluter is forced to prevent emissions, the cost is passed on to the consumer in the form of higher prices. Yet the danger in removing pollution by this second course, as Mr Ireland sees it, is that the higher prices are felt abroad as well as at home. The result, he says, is that "no country can afford to risk its international trade by progressing at a much faster pace than its rivals (in controlling pollution) and thereby making its products uncompetitive.[5] The report commissioned by Peter Walker, *Pollution: Nuisance or Nemesis?*[6] addressed itself to just this point. It concluded that:

> "Such arguments should be resisted. International trade should reflect true comparative costs. These include the full social costs of production and hence must reflect pollution abatement costs. Some other country may prefer not to charge its producers for the pollution which they cause. That country is thereby reducing its economic welfare, not raising it, and Britain has no cause to follow suit".[7]

The Alkali Inspectorate's great attraction for industry lies in its loyalty to policies which reflect the values of the market - and it is by the market rather than by the needs of the public, that industry is governed.[8] Industry's sacrifices in the name of voluntary co-operation may, therefore, not be as burdensome as we are sometimes led to believe. As a previous Chief Inspector frankly explained in 1959:

> "'Best practicable means"...is in a large degree synonymous with running plant on sound economic and technical lines; so far as the chemical industry is concerned the more closely plant complies with statutory requirements the more profit it usually makes for the owner".[9]

4 Lecture, University of Cambridge, 24.2.71.
5 George E Davis Memorial Lecture, November 1970.
6 (1972), HMSO.
7 Page 64.
8 FE Ireland 'Control of Special Industrial Emissions in Britain', paper presented to the 2nd International Clean Air Conference in Washington, USA, December 1970.
9 JS Carter, 'The Alkali Act Etc Works Regulation Act 1906 and Alkali Etc Works Orders 1928 to 1958' in HW Cremer (ed) (1959) *Chemical Engineering Practice* Vol II.

Flexible standards - who benefits? The Inspectorate nevertheless claims that the "best practicable means" are in the interests of the public, largely because of their flexibility.

Mr Ireland has consistently argued against any system of statutory standards: "Statutory standards can only be altered by new Parliamentary legislation, but presumptive standards have the advantage that they can be altered at will by the chief inspector to take account of improving technology and the demands of the public for a better environment".

Yet the frequency with which presumptive standards change (perhaps once in 10 or 15 years) does not suggest that speed has been a vital consideration to the Inspectorate. In fact the most obvious examples of "inflexibility" are to be found in the Alkali Act itself, where four statutory standards have remained unchanged since 1906. Oddly enough, these standards do not seem to have inconvenienced the Inspectorate: in 1966 Deputy Chief Inspector Mahler explained that the standards "still represent a satisfactorily high standard of control over the operation of the processes concerned".[10]

Nor is it at all clear that the presumptive standards are as flexible as the Chief Inspector would have us believe. We asked a number of District Inspectors what they would do if a works, officially judged to be using the "best practicable means", was at the same time the cause of repeated justified complaints. Faced with this sudden dilemma one Inspector forgot all inhibitions over the interview transcript that was being prepared for his Chief Inspector. "Moan like hell" was his instant - and revealing - response. We pressed another Inspector further: would the situation not suggest that the "best practicable means" might need improving? This time we got the official answer: "Our standards are under review all the time. I would not press unilaterally for standards higher than the Inspectorate's policy".

Though the Alkali Inspectors are made "as autonomous as possible", the flexibility they allow works mainly in one direction: industry benefits from special consideration of its problems, but when the public needs greater protection the autonomy may run dry.

Industry, of course, is well able to safeguard its own interests since the trade associations are involved from the outset in setting standards. According to Mr Ireland:

"This participation by the trade associations is a good guarantee of their support in enforcing requirements amongst their members ... It is necessary to be able to negotiate with strong statutory powers in the background but that is where we keep our powers, only bringing them out when fair negotiation has failed to bring the proper response".[11] Paradoxically, if the Inspectorate were to use what Mr Ireland describes as its "strong" statutory powers, its present system of enforcement would disintegrate. The Inspectorate could force new works to accept its interpretation of the "best practicable means" by refusing to register dissenters under the Alkali Act. However the Inspectorate says it cannot refuse to renew the registration of an existing works, and that all it can do is prosecute.

10 EAJ Mahler (1966) 'Standards of Emission Under the Alkali Act', paper presented to the International Clean Air Congress, London, October 1966.

11 Ireland, Washington 1970, op cit.

This, in effect, would be to invite *the courts* to determine the "best practicable means" and, if prosecutions were frequent, would lead to the courts setting the standards leaving the Inspectorate only to administer their decisions.

The rarity of prosecutions in the past have left the Inspectorate as virtually the sole judge of "best practicable means". Industry has had little cause to engage in any serious conflict with the Inspectorate, for the system which has evolved serves it well. It can install pollution control equipment virtually at its convenience with "periods of grace" and "economic life" guarantees ensuring that outdated standards are never firmly revoked. It has the benefit of "uniformity of application of control measures", a policy which prevents a works whose emissions cause more nuisance than other works from spending more than its competitors to control emissions. And all this is backed up with the understanding that the Inspectorate will publicly support a works which meets its "best practicable means" requirement - even if there is justifiable public complaint.

Protecting the Polluted. What of the public? The Inspectorate's assurances that justified complaints will meet with immediate action have gathered dust in out-of-print annual reports. Allegations that registered works take advantage of the Inspectorate's poor surveillance are brushed aside, and requests for night-time inspections are received as if a slur on the name of registered works. Meanwhile standards are enforced by inspectors who may be 150 miles from works under their control and who make only a handful of inspections of each works in a year.

Emissions are tested infrequently and by the works themselves who are on their honour not to exploit the obvious opportunities for abuse. When an infraction is finally detected, the Inspectorate's response is most likely to be a private dressing-down for the management. Any form of public criticism, however useful this could be in bringing pressure for improvement, is scrupulously avoided - while prosecution is a fate reserved by the Inspectorate only for the most ungentlemanly of offenders.

Far from trying to give even the impression of independence from industry, the Inspectorate takes pride in the interdependence. The Inspectorate has rejected all calls for it to report in detail on the performance of individual works - although recommendations that it do so date back to the report of a Royal Commission in 1878.

3 CONTROL OF SMOKE

Air pollution from industrial processes may have been abated by the 1906 Alkali Act but the problems of smoke from furnaces and domestic fires continued. The London smog of December 1952 lasted for ten days and was responsible for 4,000 deaths more than usual. The smog was so severe that an opera performance at Sadlers Wells Theatre had to be cancelled because the audience could not see the stage.[12] A Committee on Air Pollution under the Chairmanship of Sir Hugh Beaver was set up with terms of reference 'to examine the nature, causes and effects of air pollution and the efficacy of present

12 National Society for Clean Air, *Pollution Handbook* (Brighton: NSCA, 1994) p 50.

preventive measures; to consider what further measures are practicable; and to make recommendations'. The Committee reported in 1953 with an interim report which was incorporated in the final report of 1954.

Committee on Air Pollution *Interim and Final Report 1953-54* Cmnd 9011, Cmnd 9322 (London: HMSO, 1954) (The Beaver Report) pp 6-7

6. In presenting this Report we wish to state our emphatic belief that air pollution on the scale with which we are familiar in this country today is a social and economic evil which should no longer be tolerated, and that it needs to be combated with the same conviction and energy as were applied one hundred years ago in securing pure water. We are convinced that given the will it can be prevented. To do this will require a national effort and will entail costs and sacrifices; the recommendations made in this Report will involve expenditure by the Government, local authorities, industry and householders alike. But we are confident that our proposals, if carried out, will secure happier and more healthy living conditions for millions of people, and that on all counts the cost of the cure will be far less than the national loss in allowing the evil to continue.

7. We are satisfied that the most serious immediate problem to be tackled is visible pollution by smoke, grit and dust, and we have been able to make definite recommendations in regard to these. We must emphasise that the problem is not one which can be solved overnight. Real improvement can be secured only by a continuous programme urgently and insistently carried out over a number of years. The objective of our recommendations is that by the end of ten to fifteen years the total smoke in all heavily populated areas would be reduced by something of the order of 80 per cent. This would mean a degree of freedom from air pollution which many parts of the country have not known for more than a century. With regard to gaseous pollution, there is not yet the knowledge to deal effectively with the whole problem; but we have made a number of recommendations for preventive action and have indicated the directions in which ultimate solutions may be found.

8. It is basic to all our recommendations that at the outset it should be made the declared national policy to secure clean air, and that a statement to this effect should find expression in the new legislation – the "Clean Air Act" – which we are recommending.

The recommendations of the Beaver Report were enacted in the Clean Air Acts of 1956 and 1968 to restrict smoke, grit and dust from commercial concerns not covered by the Alkali Acts. Of more significance was the control of smoke from domestic fires. Smoke control areas were designated with a prohibition on 'dark smoke' from chimneys. Smoke, dust and grit from furnaces were also controlled and these restrictions were enforced by local authority Environmental Health Officers. Leeson[13] writes that the 1956 Clean Air Act

13 J Leeson *Environmental Law* (London: Pitman, 1995) p 228.

'is entitled to be regarded as one of the most effective pieces of environmental legislation yet produced. Its implementation has replaced the dirty, smoke laden atmosphere of our cities and industrial areas, and the associated begrimed buildings and vestigial plant life, with the clear skies, clean building facades and regenerated parks and gardens enjoyed today'. This celebration of the Clean Air Acts rings true with those who can remember urban life in Britain before 1968, though it surprises those who are for good reason preoccupied with current pollution problems.

4 INTEGRATED POLLUTION CONTROL: THE EXPANSION OF BPM

Because laws for the control of pollution had so often been enacted in response to near disastrous situations, such as the London smog of 1952, the causes of the 'states of affairs', in the nuisance sense of the term, were treated as separate problems: industrial emissions to air; water pollution; smoke from domestic fires and furnaces; and so on. Not only were the laws fragmented but enforcement was entrusted to a bewildering array of agencies. This sectoral and fragmented perception failed to appreciate the integrated nature of environmental problems. With hindsight this seems astonishing given early evidence that, for instance, the 1863 Alkali Act's requirement that noxious gases be condensed led to pollution of freshwaters by sulphuric acid. But legislation was as reactive as judge made law, attempting to clear up messes as and where they seemed to be most severe.

The Royal Commission on Environmental Pollution's Fifth Report of 1976, *Air Pollution Control: An Integrated Approach*, went beyond its terms of reference and took a holistic view. The Royal Commission advocated that the environment should no longer be viewed as composed of the separate 'media' of air, water and soil but be seen as a whole. The fragmentation of the environment into environmental media was reflected in a separation of enforcement agencies: a situation that was, in the Commission's view, inefficient. So it recommended a single, unified body.

Royal Commission on Environmental Pollution, Fifth Report, *Air Pollution Control: An Integrated Approach* Cmnd 6371 (London: HMSO, 1976) pp 73-77

...

261. As our study progressed we found increasing difficulty in limiting our thinking to the control of air pollution alone. Because of the connections that exist between different forms of industrial pollution it makes little sense to look at one aspect of control in isolation. As the Royal Commission on Environmental Pollution our overriding concern is with the total effect of pollution on the environment; we could not be limited by the terms of reference for our present study to proposing arrangements for controlling air pollution which might increase the problems of water pollution and the disposal of industrial wastes or indeed, in some cases, of noise generation or derelict land.

...

263. The three principal forms of pollution - of air, water and land - are often very closely linked. In order to reduce atmospheric pollution, gases or dusts may be trapped in a spray of water or washed out of filters. This leaves polluted water, which if not discharged to a sewer or direct to a river or the sea can be piped into a lagoon to settle and dry out, leaving a solid waste disposal problem. The pollutant may even go full circle by blowing off the lagoon as a dust. Other examples of the possible transference of pollution include water seeping through refuse tips, smoke from the incineration of rubbish or sludge, and pollution of land where sewage sludge containing heavy metals is used as a fertiliser.

...

The approach to control

266. We have already discussed the method of working of the Alkali Inspectorate and the impressive improvements they have brought about in reducing industrial emission by their "best practicable means" policy and through their collaborative relations with industry. The essence of the matter is the Inspectorate's understanding of the technology of industrial processes. It is this knowledge which enables the Inspectorate to maintain effective pressure on industry for improved standards, for to be effective their requirements must be realistic in technological terms; it is this knowledge which qualifies the Inspectorate to become involved with industry in the design of new plant, thus ensuring that arrangements to control air pollution are considered as an integral part of design.

...

The role of the new inspectorate

271. We therefore propose a new unified inspectorate with widened responsibilities. The essential aim of creating this body (HMPI) would be to ensure an integrated approach to difficult industrial pollution problems at source, whether these affect air, water or land. HMPI would seek the optimum environmental improvement within the concept of "best practicable means", employing the knowledge of industrial processes and many of the present techniques of the Alkali Inspectorate to reduce or modify the wastes produced, whether solid, liquid or gaseous. In effect, we have in mind an expansion of the concept of "best practicable means" into an overall "best practicable environmental option". Where choices exist as to the sector of the environment to which wastes should be discharged, HMPI would be instrumental, in consultation with other bodies involved, in deciding how different sectors should be used to minimise environmental damage overall.

272. We envisage that HMPI would be centrally administered; they would form a small, technically highly qualified body which would focus on any industrial processes and plants creating difficult pollution problems. Despite this concentration on action "within the factory fence", because that is where the pollution arises, HMPI's fundamental concern would be with the wider environment outside the works, where the effects of pollution are primarily to be found.

(a) Best practicable environmental option

The legislative response to this seminal report was not exactly speedy. The Government did not reply until 1982 when Department of Environment *Pollution Paper 18* was published. The concept of 'best practicable environmental option' (BPEO) was acknowledged as being useful but the report's proposal for a new unified inspectorate was rejected. The Royal Commission on Environmental Pollution, however, persisted, discussed the subject in its Tenth and Eleventh Reports and then in 1988 devoted its Twelfth Report to the concept 'Best Practicable Environmental Option'. Note particularly the reference to the Brundtland Report of 1987[14] and how quickly its terminology, such as 'sustainable development', was adopted.

Royal Commission on Environmental Pollution, Twelfth Report, *Best Practicable Environmental Option* Cmnd 310 (London: HMSO, 1988) pp 38-39

CHAPTER 5
SYNOPSIS AND CONCLUSIONS
Introduction

5.1 Earlier reports from this Commission have been concerned with a specific subject, such as nuclear power or air pollution, or they have provided a review of the practice of pollution control in a range of given contexts. This report is different; it is concerned with the principles and practice of pollution in general. Accordingly, we have not considered it appropriate to make specific recommendations; instead we present here a synopsis of our approach and the main conclusions. These conclusions about BPEO are relevant to many of today's economic activities, not just environmental pollution. They are directed to anyone who is charged with taking decisions which must take account of the risks to the environment from pollution.

5.2 Natural resources have to be conserved if economic development is to take place in a sustainable manner. The health of this and future generations must be safeguarded. If fundamental necessities such as clean water are damaged by pollution, resources will have to be devoted either to the development of alternative sources or to remedial measures. The avoidance of pollution is therefore both a biological and economic necessity. During the course of our study, the report of the World Commission on Environment and Development was published and we commend it as an important statement on issues that concern us all.

5.3 Our primary objective in this study has been to develop a means of analysing pollution problems in the environment as a whole. In the past, each set of pollution control regulations has been concerned primarily with one or other of the environmental media, whether air, water or land. There is now increasing recognition of the need to consider interactions and transfers between different media. This multi-media approach was the rationale for the Commission's first

14 See further ch 4.

statement on BPEO in the Fifth Report, twelve years ago. BPEO was discussed again in the Commission's Tenth and Eleventh reports and since then it has been referred to in papers by industry, academics and government. However, we are concerned that the term BPEO has been used loosely and therefore we have sought to clarify the concept of BPEO...

> "A BPEO is the outcome of a systematic consultative and decision-making procedure which emphasises the protection and conservation of the environment across land, air and water. The BPEO procedure establishes, for a given set of objectives, the option that provides the most benefit or least damage to the environment as a whole, at acceptable cost, in the long term as well as in the short term."

5.4 The need to strike a balance between the degree of risk to the environment and the cost of the necessary measures introduces an element of subjective judgement into pollution control. In the absence of any statutory basis for implementing a multi-media BPEO approach, this report provides a code of good practice. Nevertheless, we envisage that experience will demonstrate that some aspects of BPEO should be incorporated within a legal framework.

Improving Current Practice: the BPEO Procedure

5.5 The task of selecting a BPEO in given circumstances should be carried out systematically, bearing in mind the requirements which we have identified...There we show how the environmental consequences of commercial, industrial and governmental decisions can be given proper and timely attention. This can be done by building on existing best practice in project planning and pollution control. Measures to deal with pollution and waste are often taken as an afterthought when the problems become pressing. However, we suggest that if attention is paid to the principles set out ...these decisions can be made with the benefit of foresight:

(i) Environmental considerations should be introduced into project planning at the earliest possible stage.
(ii) Alternative options should be sought diligently and imaginatively in order to identify as complete a set as possible.
(iii) The identification of potential damage to the environment should be done in such a way as to uncover the unusual and improbable as well as the familiar and likely.
(iv) The context within which items (i)-(iii) are considered should be sufficiently extensive to cover all the significant aspects of the project, whether local or remote, short or long term, and having regard to the people affected.
(v) The documentation associated with each project should be structured to make it possible to trace decisions back to the supporting evidence and arguments, so providing an "audit trail".
(vi) The documentation should include the origins of data used with any relevant information concerning their reliability. It should state the procedures used for evaluation of risks and the reasons for the decisions based on those evaluations.
(vii) In order to assist in taking decisions having social and political implications, the scientific evidence must be presented objectively.
(viii) The determination of acceptable cost should take full account of any

damage to the environment in addition to monetary costs. Financial considerations should not be overriding.
(ix) There must be appropriate and timely consultation with people and organisations directly affected. The circle of those involved in the taking of decisions should be appropriately wide.
(x) The procedure should be adaptable to incorporate innovations in methods of analysis and decision-making.

The Royal Commission's broad approach was, finally, put on a statutory footing in Part I of the Environmental Protection Act 1990. At the heart of the Integrated Pollution Control regime established by this Part of the Act is a requirement to achieve the Best Practicable Environmental Option.

As foreseen by the Royal Commission, implementation of the concept of BPEO needed an appropriate institutional framework, involving some body that could take an overall view. The government had originally rejected the Royal Commission's proposal for a new inspectorate but, finally, after an investigation into the efficiency of the Health and Safety Executive, the case for a unified body was made and Her Majesty's Inspectorate of Pollution was set up to cover England and Wales; Scotland and Northern Ireland having separate arrangements. It was an amalgamation of the Industrial Air Pollution Inspectorate (the Alkali Inspectorate had been renamed to reflect its wider remit), the Controlled Waste Inspectorate and the Radiochemical Inspectorate. The amalgamation was not smooth with serious internal conflict over, amongst other issues, the new Inspectorate's approach to inspection and enforcement. The Radiochemical Inspectorate fought for an 'arm's length' approach and eventually that emerged as successful over the old Alkali Inspectorate's flexible and conciliatory ways which aimed to educate industry to adopt better means to prevent pollution. HMIP initially also had difficulty in recruiting and keeping suitably qualified Inspectors. Under the Environment Act 1995 HMIP, the National Rivers Authority and waste regulatory authorities were combined into one Environment Agency – a logical extension of Integrated Pollution Control which treats the environment as a whole.

Under the Environmental Protection Act 1990, two regimes were established: Integrated Pollution Control and Local Authority Air Pollution Control. Both are licensing systems: operators must apply within appointed periods to the appropriate authority for an authorisation which may have conditions attached. The Secretary of State, exercising powers given in the Act, designates by Regulations those industrial processes that have the potential for significant releases of harmful substances. The Regulations have two parts: Part A deals with those processes which come under the regime of Integrated Pollution Control within the ambit of the Environment Agency and those in Part B (which are generally less harmful) come under the control of local authorities. In addition a number of particularly toxic substances are controlled.

The Integrated Pollution Control processes and substances are subject to centralised regulation of all discharges into the environment. The pollutants they emit are considered in their entirety before the Environment Agency decides what emissions and what levels of discharge are allowed and whether to air, water or land. This decision is structured by the objective that the Best Practical Environmental Option has been achieved.

(b) BATNEEC

Section 7 of the Environmental Protection Act 1990 provides that an implied condition of an authorisation for Integrated Pollution Control is that the Best Available Techniques Not Entailing Excessive Cost (BATNEEC) will be used '*having regard* to the best practicable environmental option'.

7(1) There shall be included in an authorisation-

(a) subject to paragraph (b) below, such specific conditions as the enforcing authority considers appropriate, when taken with the general condition implied by subsection (4) below, for achieving the objectives specified in subsection (2) below:
(b) such conditions as are specified in directions given by the Secretary of State under subsection (3) below; and
(c) such other conditions (if any) as appear to the enforcing authority to be appropriate;

...

(2) Those objectives are -

(a) ensuring that, in carrying on a prescribed process, the best available techniques not entailing excessive cost will be used -
    (i) for preventing the release of substances prescribed for any environmental medium into that medium or, where that is not practicable by such means, for reducing the release of such substances to a minimum and for rendering harmless any such substances which are so released; and
    (ii) for rendering harmless any other substances which might cause harm if released into any environmental medium;
(b) compliance with any directions by the Secretary of State given for the implementation of any obligations of the United Kingdom under the Community Treaties or international law relating to environmental protection;
(c) compliance with any limits or requirements and achievement of any quality standards or quality objectives prescribed by the Secretary of State under any of the relevant enactments;

...

(4) Subject to subsections (5) and (6) below, there is implied in every authorisation a general condition that, in carrying on the process to which the authorisation applies, the person carrying it on must use the best available techniques not entailing excessive cost -

(a) for preventing the release of substances prescribed for any environmental medium into that medium or, where that is not practicable by such means, for reducing the release of such substances to a minimum and for rendering harmless any such substances which are so released; and

(b) for rendering harmless any other substances which might cause harm if released into any environmental medium.

(5) In the application of subsections (1) to (4) above to authorisations granted by a local enforcing authority references to the release of substances into any environmental medium are to be read as references to the release of substances into the air.

(6) The obligation implied by virtue of subsection (4) above shall not apply in relation to any aspect of the process in question which is regulated by a condition imposed under subsection (1) above.

(7) The objectives referred to in subsection (2) above shall, where the process -

(a) is one designated for central control; and
(b) is likely to involve the release of substances into more than one environmental medium;

include the objective of ensuring that the best available techniques not entailing excessive cost will be used for minimising the pollution which may be caused to the environment taken as a whole by the releases having regard to the best practicable environmental option available as respects the substances which may be released.

In this extract from the Environmental Protection Act 1990 we can see that the BATNEEC technique is used in two ways in the licensing system. First it determines the objectives to be secured when setting conditions by the enforcing authority and, second – as an implied requirement of all authorisations – the 'residual' BATNEEC duty which applies to all aspects of the process other than those regulated by specific conditions. This covers the most detailed level of plant design and operation where only the operator can reasonably be expected to know and understand what the demands of pollution control require in practice. Note also that section 7(2)(b) provides the machinery by which obligations under Community or international law may be implemented into domestic law by this Act. There is a system of registers to which members of the public have access in order to achieve 'transparency' of decisions (see below).

The administration of IPC by the Environment Agency must now be read in conjunction with sections 4 and 39 of the Environment Act 1995.

Principal aim and objectives of the Agency

4. (1) It shall be the principal aim of the Agency (subject to and in accordance with the provisions of this Act or any other enactment and taking into account any likely costs) in discharging its functions so to protect or enhance the environment, taken as a whole, as to make the contribution towards attaining the objective of achieving sustainable development mentioned in subsection (3) below.

(2) The Ministers shall from time to time give guidance to the Agency with respect to objectives which they consider it appropriate for the Agency to pursue in the discharge of its functions.

(3) The guidance given under subsection (2) above must include guidance with respect to the contribution which, having regard to the Agency's responsibilities and resources, the Ministers consider it appropriate for the Agency to make, by the discharge of its functions, towards attaining the objectives of achieving sustainable development.

(4) In discharging its functions, the Agency shall have regard to guidance given under this section.

(5) The power to give guidance to the Agency under this section shall only be exercisable after consultation with the Agency and such other bodies or persons as the Ministers consider it appropriate to consult in relation to the guidance in question.

...

General duty of the new Agencies [the Environment Agency for England and Wales and the Scottish Environment Protection Agency] to have regard to costs and benefits in exercising powers

39. (1) Each new Agency -

(a) in considering whether or not to exercise any power conferred upon it by or under any enactment, or
(b) in deciding the manner in which to exercise any such power, shall, unless and to the extent that it is unreasonable for it to do so in view of the nature or purpose of the power or in the circumstances of the particular case, take into account the likely costs and benefits of the exercise or non-exercise of the power or its exercise in the manner in question.

(2) The duty imposed upon a new Agency by subsection (1) above does not affect its obligation, nevertheless, to discharge any duties, comply with any requirements, or pursue any objectives, imposed upon or given to it otherwise than in this section.

Section 4 of the Environment Act 1995 includes the first statutory reference to sustainable development in British domestic law.

This principal aim of achieving sustainable development also exists in relation to the national air strategy (see below). Section 4 makes clear that the Agency must take into account 'any likely costs' which the Act defines as including the likely costs to any person and to the environment. 'Costs' in this section relates to the Agency pursuing its principal aim of achieving sustainable development. Viscount Ullswater, Minister of State for the Environment, said during the passage of the Environment Bill that

> ...the inclusion of the reference to costs is therefore intended to ensure that the principal aim includes explicit recognition of both sides of the equation to reduce the risk of challenge in the courts from anyone who might seek to argue that sustainable development is to be interpreted exclusively in environmental terms.[14a]

Section 39 is explicitly telling the Agency to have regard to costs and benefits in exercising its powers in the same manner as the Inspectorate had always

14a Hansard, HL Vol 561, Col 1628

used best practicable means. Section 39(2) suggests that this duty does not affect the Agency's obligation to pursue the objective of sustainable development under section 4. In other words, section 39 relates to the Agency's more specific duties. It appears that a transmuted form of best practicable means lives on with 'practicable' explicitly defined as a cost/benefit analysis.

Part I of the Environmental Protection Act 1990 has the virtue of conceptual elegance and represents a clear departure from the traditional approach of controlling pollution sector by sector. It is however proving very difficult to implement in practice as the following extracts show:

***Ends Report No 227* (London: ENDS, 1993) pp 3-4**

IPC fails to deliver on BATNEEC and transparency

Integrated Pollution Control (IPC) is now well into its third year - but an in-depth study by ENDS has shown that the system is falling well short of expectations. (*Integrated Pollution Control: The First Three Years*, from ENDS) HM Inspectorate of Pollution (HMIP) has failed to force operators to address fundamental requirements of the Environmental Protection Act 1990, and vital information – including emission monitoring data – is not being entered on the public registers.

IPC came into force in April 1991, and was billed by the Government as "the most sophisticated system of pollution control in Europe". HMIP has now received well over 1,000 applications for IPC authorisations, and eventually the system will control around 5,000 of Britain's most polluting industrial processes.

To assess IPC's effectiveness and impact on industry, ENDS visited HMIP's public registers in Leeds, Bristol and Bedford between May and August 1993. We examined 666 applications received by 1 April 1993, when the regime was two years old, including 328 which had been authorised by that date. ENDS also scrutinised more recent applications and files relating to subsequent variations of authorisations. A questionnaire survey of operators who had been through the entire IPC process by April was also carried out, and backed up by telephone interviews with companies.

The study sheds light on how all the stages of the IPC process have been operating in practice, and also provides a wealth of new information on the costs of IPC to industry and on the diverse attitudes and approaches of companies to the new regime.

One of the major issues raised by the research is the transparency of the system. In our visits to the public registers, we were unable to find so much as a single item of monitoring data obtained by HMIP or its contractors in assessing companies' compliance with their authorisation conditions.

The IPÇ regulations oblige HMIP to place on the registers "all particulars of any monitoring information relating to the carrying on of a prescribed process under an authorisation ... obtained by the authority as a result of its own monitoring".

The absence of such information suggests either that no monitoring tests have been performed – which HMIP denies – or that it is failing in its duty to put the results into the public domain. Either way, the outcome is highly unsatisfactory - and lends a hollow ring to the promises that IPC would "maintain public confidence in the regulatory system through a clear and transparent system", and bring real data of companies' environmental performance into the open.

HMIP has roundly condemned complaints that the shift in emphasis towards greater "self-monitoring" by industry amounts to greater self-regulation. But in the absence of audit monitoring data, there can be no reassurance that operators are playing by the book in measuring and reporting their releases. Unless a strong and transparent monitoring policy is adopted quickly, the credibility of both HMIP and IPC will be severely damaged.

The study identifies several other key areas where transparency is lacking. Notably, the abandonment of HMIP's initial "arms' length" approach to industry means that many key decisions are now taken behind closed doors. Other problems include HMIP's failure to place all applications for variations on the registers.

The Inspectorate has also commonly responded to companies' failure to submit all the necessary information in their applications by issuing an authorisation, and only then insisting that the necessary information is supplied. But almost none of the reports submitted by companies have been placed on the registers because HMIP has taken the view that the regulations do not impose a clear duty on it to do so. The result has been that much information which should be in the public domain is being kept secret.

A second major finding of the report is that many companies have failed to fulfil their statutory duties at the first stage of the IPC process – and HMIP has not obliged them to do so.

Central requirements of the IPC regulations are that a company must demonstrate in its application that it will use the "best available techniques not entailing excessive cost" (BATNEEC) and the "best practicable environmental option" (BPEO). In both cases, it is difficult to see how such a justification could be made without a comparison of available processes or abatement options.

ENDS assessed the applications for all 328 processes that were authorised by 1 April 1993 to gauge the level of discussion of alternative processes or abatement techniques. The results are discouraging. More than half of applicants failed to discuss any alternatives, and only one-third did so to any great depth... And only a tiny fraction of firms supplied cost data to support claims that a process option had been rejected on the grounds of excessive cost...

Likewise, fewer than one-quarter of firms gave even slight consideration to the BPEO – though this is intended to be a cornerstone of IPC.

The picture is somewhat distorted by the extremely poor quality of the initial applications for combustion processes. But while there has been an improvement in the quality of BATNEEC and BPEO discussion over time, this has been slow and most applicants are still failing to address the issues fully. These shortcomings are particularly disappointing given the time now expended by HMIP in pre-application meetings with operators - an effort which appears to be detracting from its enforcement role...

A similar story applies to applicants' assessment of the environmental consequences of releases, also required under the IPC regulations. For the processes authorised by 1 April 1993, only 37% of applications offered some form of dispersion modelling and 23% offered some information on background pollution. And just 12% attempted to supply a meaningful assessment of the local environment and their impact upon it.

HMIP has often responded to these shortcomings by requesting further information via so-called Schedule 1 notices. These have sometimes had the desired effect, but in many cases the Inspectorate has given up and instead, as noted above, issued an authorisation containing conditions requiring submission of the missing information - generally some time after the authorisations have been issued.

...

Responses to ENDS' questionnaire survey showed that many companies expect IPC to bring them benefits... But overall, respondents viewed IPC as burdensome and unlikely to lead to significant environmental improvements. Probably industry's strongest objection to the system concerns the level of the cost-recovery charges payable to HMIP. Winning industry over to IPC may well have been easier had these not been imposed by the Government.

...

HMIP's efforts to preach the benefits of waste minimisation have evidently failed yet to convince many firms. However, the report also provides case studies of companies which, having taken their responsibilities under IPC seriously, expect to reap financial rewards from implementing waste reduction strategies.

...
and

***ENDS Report No 249* (London: ENDS, October 1995) pp 22-25**

In search of the best practicable BPEO

...
Haphazard application
...the Act left the ball in HMIP's court by offering no legal definition of BPEO. Furthermore, its requirement that operators use BATNEEC to prevent, minimise or render harmless releases presented HMIP with the thorny problem of deciding what, in practice, was meant by "harmless".

In practice, therefore, application of the BPEO ideal has been haphazard. ENDS' study of the implementation of IPC, published early in 1994, found that most operators had failed to even pay lip service to the concept in their applications for authorisation...And few had sought to justify their activities as BATNEEC by comparing the environmental impacts and costs of alternative process options.

HMIP has spent several years grappling with the problem. In April 1994, it published the "orange book" - a consultation document outlining a proposed methodology for assessing the overall environmental impact of process options, and weighing them against the costs. In effect, the approach is a merger of the BATNEEC and BPEO principles.

The proposals attracted widespread criticism. HMIP's plan for expressing the overall environmental impact of emissions as a single numerical value - the so-called Integrated Environmental Index (IEI) - came in for particularly strong criticism...

Overall, there must be some doubt that the BPEO assessment procedures currently on the table will provide the drive towards inherently clean technologies envisaged by the RCEP, and which was meant to be achieved by the 1990 Act. Indeed, the Act requires that, for prescribed substances, prevention and minimisation of releases at source are preferred to merely rendering them "harmless". HMIP's focus on "significant" releases in terms of environmental concentrations could, in principle, reward application of the traditional "dilute and disperse" approach.

5 PUBLIC PARTICIPATION

The question of the ease and effectiveness of public access to environmental information was the subject of a study in Scotland during 1994 and 1995. The law and administrative arrangements there are slightly different from those in England and Wales but these are possibly not so great that generalisations from the research cannot be extended to the whole of Britain. When reading this extract, bear in mind the exhortations and hopes expressed and implied in Agenda 21, the subject of chapter 4, for public participation.

J Rowan-Robinson, A Ross, W Walton and J Rothnie, 'Public Access to Environmental Information: A Means to What End?', (1996) *Journal of Environmental Law*, Vol 8 No 1, 19-42

The White Paper 'This Common Inheritance' states that the foundation of the Government's environmental policy is the ethical imperative of stewardship. ... The burden of stewardship, however, is not seen as resting on the Government alone. 'The responsibility for our environment is shared ... It is an obligation on us all' (para 1.38). The White Paper goes on to acknowledge the importance of public access to information about the environment if people are going to be able to assume their responsibility. 'If people are given the facts, they are best placed to make their own consumer decisions and to exert pressure for change as consumers, investors, lobbyists and electors' (para 1.20). The purpose of this Article is to make an assessment of the extent to which public access to certain sources of environmental information is likely to promote the notion of stewardship. ...

...However, stewardship is a very generalised concept and any assessment of the opportunities for the public to gain access to information requires a more precise measure of effectiveness. Such measure may be derived from an examination of the benefits which it is thought could arise from improved public access. These benefits or ends are not explicit but may be inferred from the discussion in the Tenth Report of the Royal Commission on Environmental Pollution[15] and from the White Paper.

The benefits of improved public access may be grouped under five general headings, all of which contribute to the stewardship objective:

* it will reassure the public and promote confidence on their part in the action being taken by the Government and by industry (the 'public reassurance' role). Secrecy, observed the RCEP (para 2.52), fuels fear – withdrawal of secrecy promotes public confidence;
* it will inform consumer choice, both in the demand for and in the consumption of goods (White Paper, para 1.20). For example, labelling may encourage consumers to opt for 'green' products; and information about the causes and consequences of pollution may encourage consumers to limit the use of cars and to reduce waste in the use of energy, water and so on (the 'personal responsibility' role);
* increased public scrutiny should encourage industry to take environmental protection seriously (the 'industry responsibility' role). The RCEP noted the CBI's conclusion that environmental pressures on industry should be recognised as 'helpful stimuli' rather than an obstruction (para 6.7);
* the knowledge that activities will come under public scrutiny should act as a 'vital discipline' for environmental protection agencies (RCEP, para 2.75) (the 'agency accountability' role);
* it will enable members of the public to play a role in policy formulation and decision-making on environmental matters (the 'public participation' role). People should be told the facts and what they mean, commented the White Paper (para 1.21) and given every opportunity to make their views known.

...

3. Public Registers

Although the Government believe that there is no single uniform way in which information relating to the environment can conveniently be made available to the public, public registers are considered to provide a key mechanism for the keeping and dissemination of information held by public authorities.[16] At a time when there was no general right for members of the public to have access to environmental information, public registers, maintained under particular codes of environmental legislation, offered a specific, if limited, right. ...

With one exception, our research confirms earlier work which shows that in absolute terms the level of use of public registers is low...

Table 1 shows that four of the local authority Radioactive Substances registers and four of the local authority IPC registers had received no visits at all. It should be noted, however, that a copy of both registers is also held at the HMIPI offices in Edinburgh and it is possible that enquiries were made there

15 Cmnd 9149, 'Tackling Pollution – Experience and Prospects', RCEP, Tenth Report, HMSO, 1984.

16 'Freedom of Access to Information on the Environment', Select Committee on the European Communities, (HL Paper 2), Session 1989-90, HMSO, 1989.

instead. More interest was shown in the planning register... The average number of people inspecting planning registers varied according to estimates from ten to sixty per week.

...

We think there are two explanations for the generally low level of use of registers. First of all, we share the conclusion of earlier research ... that there are shortcomings in the way in which registers operate and these shortcomings inhibit their use by the public. In reaching this conclusion, we acknowledge the difficulty faced by public authorities in providing an information service in a time of severe restrictions on public expenditure. The Government have increased the information burden on authorities...without providing additional resources for implementation. ...

The second explanation for the low level of use is the lack of what for want of a better term we refer to as a 'culture of participation'. Even if the shortcomings are remedied, in the absence of a culture of participation by the public in environmental regulation, no more than limited use by the public of registers should be expected. ...

5. Conclusions

The purpose of this Article has been to assess the extent to which public access to registers and reports as sources of environmental information is likely to promote the notion of stewardship. The contribution of these two sources has been measured by reference to the extent to which they promote public reassurance, industry responsibility, agency accountability and public participation. Our general conclusion is that registers play no more than a limited role. John[17] states that 'registration of data in publicly accessible registers presents perhaps the best possible means of making information public'. We do not agree. We think that registers offer an easy option for seeming to meet the pressure for greater public access to environmental information without actually achieving very much. They amount to little more than a gesture to promoting public access. Even the planning register, which shows a high level of use relative to other registers, is not very busy...

First of all, it was suggested to us by a number of environmental protection agencies and by industry that it is not worth putting more resources into developing public access because the public are apathetic. This view was also echoed by the local public interest groups, many of whom expressed frustration over their inability to mobilise public interest in the environment. National public interest groups agreed that it is difficult to mobilise the public but thought that the explanation lay not in apathy but in inhibition and hesitancy.

... On the other hand the study [on public participation in the formulation of a structure plan], concluded that 60% of those interviewed, when approached directly, were willing to express a view on the issues. In other words, they would not go out of their way to be involved but they were interested enough to volunteer a view if asked.

17 E John, 'Access to Environmental Information: Limitations of the UK Radioactive Substances Registers', *Journal of Environmental Law*, 1995, 7(1), 11-30.

This would suggest that what passes for apathy is, in many cases, a passive rather than an active interest in the environment. As John asserts 'silence or poorly articulated views by the general public should not be interpreted as public indifference or ignorance in the face of complex issues'. ... People with a passive interest in the environment are unlikely to have much direct use for public registers or reports. ...

...

Taking information to the public, or to a sector of the public, of course, raises questions of costs which cannot be ignored. It is cheaper to make information available for the public to come to than it is to take that same information to them. If environmental protection agencies and industry are to take a more proactive role, consideration will have to be given to the form in which the information is conveyed. For example, it would not be sensible to take the content of a public register around to a local community; but it might be practicable to require an applicant for a permit to notify neighbours, as happens now with planning applications; and it might also be practicable to supply community councils at regular intervals with a list of permit applications so that they can involve their community, a practice which also occurs with planning applications.

...

The second generalisation we draw from our research is that we do not think the movement towards increasing public access to information is carried through to active encouragement to the public to involve themselves in policy formulation and decision-making. Public participation is, of course, only one aspect of stewardship but together with the personal responsibility role that we referred to ... it is stewardship in its highest profile.

This lack of encouragement is evident at two levels. First of all, there has been no drive by central Government to involve the public in environmental issues in the same way as there was a drive to involve the public in the planning process during the 1970s. If people are to be encouraged to take on the stewardship role which the Government appears to envisage, it is not enough to set up a public register and to give public notice of proposed activities; people need to be educated and encouraged to involve themselves. Promoting awareness is not enough. It is necessary to identify and promote the opportunity, to promote a 'culture' of participation. If such a culture develops, then, as with planning control, public registers and public notices become useful vehicles for informing the public. If central Government is not prepared to encourage participation, there is unlikely to be much response at the local level...

...

An attempt to promote greater involvement by the public in local policy formulation and decision making on environmental matters could be channelled through local public interest groups. ...

If, however, public interest groups are to play a greater role with regard to participation, it will be important for environmental protection agencies to take positive steps to identify opportunities and to encourage their involvement. At the present, public interest groups are encountering barriers to participation, sixteen out of twenty-two public interest groups stated that the opportunities for participating in decisions by RPA [River Purification Authorities] were inadequate. The groups were largely unfamiliar with the decision-making processes of HMIPI; but nine which had attempted to involve themselves found HMIPI 'quite secretive and uncooperative'. Out of twenty-five groups, fourteen had felt that they were not given an adequate opportunity to get involved in decisions by SNH [Scottish Natural Heritage]. Local authorities fared better in the survey but even here quite a large minority of groups had experienced difficulty in the decision-making processes of environmental health and planning departments.

Even if encouragement is given at both central and local levels, the position will not change overnight. The culture of participation in planning is something that has evolved since the early 1970s. It will take some years for the results to begin showing through in the field of environmental regulation. The process may, however, be given impetus by the advent of a more environmentally aware generation.

6 ENVIRONMENTAL ASSESSMENT

The Environmental Protection Act 1990, in theory using BATNEEC to minimise pollution to the environment as a whole having regard to the BPEO, is still concerned with pollution from a particular site. The requirement for an environmental assessment, before planning permission is granted for development of a source of pollution on a specific site, widens the potential for pollution control very considerably since the assessment process can take into account effects beyond any particular parcel of land.[18] In chapter 10 we show, however, that developers are using environmental statements, as required under the environmental assessment regime, to justify their proposed developments.

7 MONITORING AIR QUALITY

The development of air pollution control has so far been directed to the sources of pollutants, assuming that these are static industrial plants or domestic buildings. Integrated Pollution Control and environmental assessment are potentially wide in scope but they still operate on the assumption that the atmosphere can absorb or disperse pollutants. Integrated Pollution Control seeks the BPEO for wastes but in most cases is not concerned with the best option of all: no wastes.

In towns and cities and near trunk roads the air is impaired by moving motor vehicles emitting fumes which come outside the ambit of the pollution controls we have discussed. In contrast, Part IV of the Environment Act 1995 is potentially all-embracing since it deals with the quality of the air.

Section 80 of the Environment Act 1995 requires the Secretary of State to prepare and publish a statement containing policies for a national air quality

18 Ch 10 deals with environmental assessment specifically; ch 7 considers the broader role of the planning system in controlling pollution.

strategy. Furthermore, the Secretary of State shall keep these policies for air quality under review and may modify the strategy (presumably to make it more stringent). The strategy must include standards relating to the quality of air, objectives for the restriction of the levels at which particular substances are present in the air and measures which are to be taken by local authorities and other persons for the purpose of achieving those objectives. Under section 82, every local authority shall conduct a review of the quality of the air in its area and, significantly, also assess the likely future air quality. If as a result of such a review it appears that air quality standards or objectives are not being achieved, nor are likely to be achieved, then the local authority shall designate air quality management areas and prepare an action plan in order to achieve the standards or objectives. There are reserve powers for the Secretary of State, or SEPA if the area is within Scotland, to give directions to a local authority if it appears that air quality standards or objectives are not being achieved.

This new strategy to control emissions from moving vehicles clearly has major implications for the motor manufacturing and oil industries. The following extract shows the scope of the strategy from the perspective of these industrial sectors.

'Air Quality – achieving the objectives', *Esso View* (London: ESSO, May 1996) pp 3-5

All of us share a desire to breathe good quality air. However, there remains a perception that air quality, particularly in cities, is getting worse largely because of the continuing increase in the number of motor vehicles.

In the face of these rising public concerns about vehicle emissions and their possible effects on air quality and health, the European Commission's Auto-Oil programme was set up in co-operation with the European motor and oil industries...

The programme was designed to provide policy-makers with an objective assessment of the most cost-effective package of measures, including vehicle technology improvements and possible fuel quality changes, necessary to reduce emissions from road transport to a level consistent with the attainment of new European Union (EU) air quality standards.

The motor and oil industries were asked to participate by the Commission; both agreed and fully support its principles, methodologies, data and results.

The foundation of the programme is the Commission's air quality studies, which took 1990 as a base year. With data collected from national governments and 140 municipal authorities, it built up a detailed pan-European picture of air quality at that date. Two fundamentals were studied – urban air pollution and ozone.

Next, the effects of agreed legislation, including that yet to be implemented, were considered so that air quality could be predicted through to the year 2010. Emissions from homes, factories and offices were included as well as those from road transport. Then the EU objectives, which are based on World Health Organisation guidelines or existing EU legislation and are the strictest in the world, were compared with the air quality predictions so that the size of the remaining gaps to be bridged by 2010 could be determined.

The conclusion of this piece of work has shown that air quality in Europe is improving and is set to improve even further. It is expected that some European objectives for air quality, including those for benzene and carbon monoxide, will be met earlier - by the year 2000 - even allowing for expected traffic growth. However, the studies have shown that for nitrogen oxides (NOx), ozone and particulates, additional measures, over and above those already agreed, will be required if Europe is to achieve these air quality objectives by 2010.

Urban pollutants were modelled in seven representative cities: Athens, Cologne, the Hague, London, Lyon, Madrid and Milan...

...

Another part of the Auto-Oil programme reviewed all known information on the relationships between emissions, fuel properties and engine technologies and [identified the further research needed] ... the European Programme on Emissions, Fuels and Engine Technologies (EPEFE) produced quantifiable results which provided an indispensable scientific basis for the Commission's cost-effective studies. These studies were aimed at finding the least costly package of measures needed to meet road transport's share of future air quality improvement.

...With NOx, for example, the studies show that a combination of better engine maintenance, tougher vehicle inspections, followed by the adoption of proven advanced technology for high-mileage trucks, buses and vans and improvements in passenger car technology, would produce a dramatic drop in NOx emissions. In addition, these measures would cause emissions of carbon monoxide and benzene to fall even further below their already achievable EU targets. Changes to petrol and diesel composition would do little to reduce NOx emissions and would be expensive and relatively ineffective compared to other measures.

...

Measures that focus on the control and maintenance of vehicles in use need to be introduced to ensure they continue to perform to the standard to which they were built. This would be the most cost-effective, least costly and quickest solution.

The RAC successfully demonstrated in tests on 60,000 cars that 12 per cent of vehicles caused 55 per cent of the pollution; just one poorly maintained car can emit as much pollution as up to 40 well-maintained modern vehicles. The UK Government is rightly starting to give greater emphasis to vehicle testing, and this solution would give everyone the opportunity to make a difference through their own actions...

8 CONCLUSION

Focusing on air pollution, we have traced the development over more than a century of some legal techniques which aim to achieve a cleaner environment. Pollution control will always be a matter of compromising and attempting to reconcile conflicting interests, but we have shown how the development of this area of environmental law has been a movement from a sectoral, reactive stance towards a proactive, integrated approach.

Now that the 1995 Environment Act sets in place a regime for a national air quality strategy we conclude with another extract from John Evelyn's treatise. For him, air purified of smoke and stenches could still be sweetened. It is always constructive to imagine positive improvements rather than merely the elimination of nuisances and a footnote to the 1825 edition of his treatise says it has been conjectured that the lime trees in St James's Park were planted in consequence. Other, more modern, positive contributions to air quality have been proposed by the Royal Commission on Environmental Pollution in their Eighteenth Report, *Transport and the Environment*, discussed further in chapter 8.

J Evelyn *Fumigium* (Brighton: NSCA, 1961)

PART III

An offer at the Improvement, and Melioation of the Aer of London, by Way of Plantation, etc.

...There is yet another expedient, which I here have to offer (were *This* of the poisonous and filthy *smoake* remov'd) by which the *City* and environs about it, might be rendred one of the most pleasant and agreeable places in the world. In order to this I propose,

That all low-grounds circumjacent to the City, especially *East* and *South-west*, be cast and contriv'd into square plots, or Fields of twenty, thirty, and forty *Akers*, or more, separated from each others by Fences of double *Palisads*, or *Contr'spaliers*, which should enclose a Plantation of an hundred and fifty, or more, feet deep, about each Field ... That these *Palisads* be elegantly planted, diligently kept and supply'd, with such *Shrubs*, as yield the most fragrant and odoriferous *Flowers*, and are aptest to tinge the Aer upon every gentle emission at a great distance: Such as are (for instance amongst many others) the *Sweet-brier*, all the *Periclymenas* and *Woodbinds*; the Common *white* and *yellow Jessamine*, both the *Syringas* or *Pipe trees*; the *Guelder-rose*, the *Musk*, and all other *Roses; Genista Hispanica*. To these may be added the *Rubus odoratus, Bayes, Junipier, Lignum-vitae, Lavender*: but above all, *Rosemary*, the *Flowers* whereof are credibly reported to give their scent above thirty Leagues off at Sea, upon the coasts of Spain; and at some distance towards the Meadow side, *Vines* yea *Hops*.

—Et Arbuta passim,
Et glaucus Salices, Casiamque Crocumque rubentem,
Et pinguem Tiliam & ferrugineos Hyacinthos, etc.

For there is a very sweet smelling *Sally*, and the blossoms of the *Tilia*, or *Lime-tree*, are incomparably fragrant, in brief, whatsoever is odoriferous and refreshing.

That the *Spaces*, or *Area* between these *Palisads*, and Fences, by employ'd in Beds and Bordures of *Pinks, Carnations, Cloves, Stock-gilly-flower, Primroses, Auriculas, Violets*, not forgetting the *White*, which are in flower twice a year, *April* and *August*; *Cowslips, Lillies, Narcissus, Strawberries*, whose very leaves as well as fruit, emit a *Cardiaque*, and most refreshing *Halitus*: also *Parietaria Lutea, Musk, Lemmon and Mastick Thyme; Spike, Cammomile, Balm, Mint, Marjoram, Pempernel, and Serpillum*, etc. which upon the least pressure and cutting, breathe out and betray their ravishing odours.

That the Fields, and Crofts within these Closures, or invironing Gardens, be, some of them, planted with *wild Thyme*, and others reserved for Plots of *Beans, Pease* (not *Cabbages*, whose rotten and perishing stalks have a very noisom and unhealthy smell, and therefore by *Hipocrates* utterly condemned near great Cities) but such blossom-bearing Grain as send forth their virtue at farthest distance, and are all of them *marketable* at *London*; by which means the *Aer* and *Winds* perpetually fann'd from so many circling and encompassing Hedges, fragrant Shrubs, Trees and Flowers may...not onely all that did approach the *Region*, which is properly design'd to be Flowery; but even the whole City, would be sensible of the sweet and ravishing varieties of the perfumes, as well as of the most delightful and pleasant objects, and places of Recreation for the Inhabitants...

CHAPTER 7

Land use controls: town planning and countryside designation

1 INTRODUCTION

Planning organises space and property, in a physical sense and in terms of allocating resources and legal rights of property development. It is of vital importance to environmental protection. In the previous chapter, we traced the development of pollution controls from the rudimentary controls in the nineteenth century to the onset of Integrated Pollution Control in the Environmental Protection Act 1990 and targets for purer air in the Environment Act 1995. In this chapter, we examine planning as a set of less direct but equally important controls for securing environmental protection – those relating to the use and development of land. We focus on town planning and countryside designation as two techniques for regulating environmentally harmful uses and development of land. Though not designed specifically as *environmental* measures, the planning and designation systems are actually very early examples of modern, precautionary environmental regulation which minimises harm before it occurs – the development of which is a recurrent theme of this book.

The modern planning system for granting development consent does not apply to most agricultural and forestry activities. For this reason, what amounts to a separate legal regime allowing land to be designated for special protection has evolved on an ad hoc basis. However, the role of planning in *preventing* environmental harm in the countryside is now better understood and this has led to some co-ordination between planning and the countryside designation regimes. In this chapter, we review and compare the respective functions of town planning and countryside designation in environmental protection and consider the prospects for the further integration of these legal regimes.

2 TOWN PLANNING

The town planning system offers a means by which development on land and the change of uses of land may be regulated on a day to day basis by local authorities, overseen by central government. A number of key features characterise the town planning system. The system is pragmatic, an important aspect of which is that it provides a means by which compromise may be reached between interests competing to develop or conserve land. The institutional arrangements and policy tools of the planning system regulate the use of land so as to encompass both interests to a greater or lesser degree. A further characteristic is the stability of the town planning system as a pervasive and significant social system. This stability is derived largely from the participation of interested groups and the public in the local planning authority's plan-making for land use, its decisions about whether to grant planning permission or not and, most visibly, at the local public planning inquiry. Such participation fosters legitimacy of the system and, in turn, acceptance of it. Another view, however, is that the planning system's various participation requirements contribute to an ideological bluff that planning decisions are consensual and publicly, rather than politically, determined. Notwithstanding its extreme stability as a social system, planning is flexible in the sense that it is capable of absorbing a number of often conflicting objectives and policy preoccupations. The 'weight' attributed to each or any of these objectives and policies varies according to current political priorities and economic expediency. Because they are expressed in policy guidance notes and circulars, they may be altered rapidly without undergoing formal examination in Parliament. Differing, and possibly conflicting, objectives and policy strands are therefore accommodated (often simultaneously) in the planning system. A collection of less formally articulated assumptions about the role of the planning system is held by planners, lawyers, and lay people. These assumptions and perspectives are identified by McAuslan as 'ideologies'.

P McAuslan, *Ideologies of Planning Law* (Oxford: Pergamon Press, 1980) pp 3-7

The three competing ideologies are as follows: firstly, that the law exists and should be used to protect private property and its institutions; this may be called the traditional common law approach to the role of the law. Secondly, the law exits and should be used to advance the public interest, if necessary against the interest of private property; this may be called the orthodox public administration and planning approach to the role of law. Thirdly, the law exists and should be used to advance the cause of public participation against both the orthodox public administration approach to the public interest and the common law approach of the overriding importance of private property; this may be called the radical or populist approach to the role of law. I shall say something about each legal ideology in general terms before going on to consider the role they and laws based on them play in three salient features of the planning system; public participation and debate, public development and initiatives and public regulation of private development and activities. Between them these salient features cover the main activities of the planning system into which there is a legal input...

Planning's historical origins lay in the need to do something about the horrendous living conditions of the new urban working classes in the mid-nineteenth century.[1] This involved taking powers to control and regulate the

1 W Ashworth, *The Genesis of Modern British Town Planning* (Routledge & Kegan Paul, London, 1954). P McAuslan, *Land, Law and Planning*, pp 37-48.

use of property, land and houses. To property-owners in urban areas, this was a new and unwelcome use of governmental power sanctioned by law, and their reaction was to seek the aid of courts and lawyers to protect them against these intrusions, as they saw them, of governmental power. Property-owners turned to the courts not just because they were the institutions provided for the resolution of conflicts but because lawyers and the common law that they had fashioned over the centuries were very much concerned with the protection and preservation of rights of property.

Two important reasons may be highlighted for this concern. Firstly, until well into the nineteenth century, the lawful exercise of political power and the possession and ownership of land were intimately related, so protection of private property was also a defence of the constitutional order. Nor was this a mere *ex post facto* rationalisation of what the judges were in fact doing; the relationship between property and constitution and the central importance of the law in upholding it had been at the forefront of John Locke's writings in the late seventeenth century[2] and he provided the main philosophical underpinnings for government for some considerable time thereafter. But in addition to this general reason there was, secondly, the practical matter that it was, almost by definition, the property-owners who used the courts and it was in the resolution of their disputes that the common law was formed. So the whole climate and ideology of the law stressed private property, its uses and transactions.

It was not surprising therefore that, presented with challenges by urban land-owners to government action, the courts developed principles, precedents and rules of statutory interpretation which were designed to protect those land-owners from that government action. For instance, where statutes were silent, as they often were, rules of procedure were imposed on public officials which gave land-owners an opportunity to put their case before action was taken against them.[3] No similar restriction had ever been imposed on land-owners in respect of their exercise of powers to, for example, evict tenants, because that would not have been a protection of but an interference with the rights of private property. Judgments were couched solely in terms of the need to protect land-owners against hasty government action with no regard being paid to the objective of the legislation or the living conditions of the working class, the property-less, for whose benefit the legislation was passed. That was an irrelevant consideration, and to the extent that it ever did impinge upon the judicial consciousness, it met the comfortable principle developed in the common law of nuisance that "what would be a nuisance in Belgrave Square would not necessarily be so in Bermondsey",[4] principles that the Public Health Act concepts of nuisance were trying to overturn.

The principles developed by the courts in the late nineteenth and early twentieth centuries to provide some protection for the urban land-owner against government action form the basis of the common law strand, the private property ideology, in the current planning law. Refined and more sophisticated, with

2 John Locke, *An Essay Concerning the True Original Extent and End of Civil Government*, Everyman's Library Edition London, 1953, ch ix, para 124.

3 *Cooper v Wandsworth Board of Works* (1863) 143 ER 414, started off this line of cases.

4 *Sturges v Bridgman* (1879) 11 Ch D 852 at p 865, CA.

more statute law to weave a way through, the principles of protection and defence of the rights of property-owners, the necessity to keep governmental powers within their proper limits (limits not defined by reference to the dictionary meaning of words but by reference to the judges' beliefs and assumptions, their ideology) are a, if not the, major concern of the courts in planning law. That law might be here to stay but for the traditionally educated lawyers (and as Lord Hailsham has reminded us, all our senior judges received their legal education thirty or more years ago),[5] it is none the less an intrusion, a statutory imposition on the common law of land use and land tenure which is the "natural" law on the subject. Nuisance law and the law of easements and restrictive covenants are not an intrusion, they have not been imposed *ab extra*, but have grown up naturally and in the law through the courts' response to changing social conditions. Development control under the planning acts, control of housing conditions under the housing acts, on the other hand, is imposed *ab extra*; they are not part of the normal or natural bundle of rights of the land-owner and as such are rightly subject to control in the interests of the land-owners.

The second competing ideology is what I have called the public interest ideology – the ideology of law as seen by the public administrator. The law is seen as providing the backing and legitimacy for a programme of action to advance the public interest, often and if necessary against the selfish interests of the private land-owner. This view of the role of the law is derived from the writing of Bentham, particularly his *Principles of Morals and Legislation*.[6] These principles inspired Chadwick, the earliest and most industrious of public health and housing reformers and the laws propounded and administered by him and his colleagues are the direct forebears of our current land use planning laws. The ideology of public interest is translated into laws which confer wide powers on administrators to do as they see fit and which either provide no redress or appeal (for how can there be redress against an administrator who is advancing the public interest) or redress within the administrative system only, i.e. an appeal from a lower to a higher administrator or from a local to a central government administrator. Special provisions may be made for the land-owner within this system but this is as much because experience has shown that to do so will lessen the chances of judicial interference or make more plausible provisions purporting to deny access to the courts, as because it is considered that the land-owner has any special claims to participate in the administrative process. These special provisions for the land-owner, however, need not deflect the administrator from doing what is considered necessary and right. Indeed for a long time, provided the formalities were observed, land-owners need be told little or nothing of the reasons for decisions in respect of property and their objection could be ignored.

This came about because the courts had been prepared to accept that there were limits on the extent to which they could protect the land-owner against governmental action taken in the public interest. Aided no doubt by the fact that as the nineteenth century gave way to the twentieth, judges and particularly

5 Lord Hailsham, Politics and the Law, BBC radio talk, 1 November 1977.

6 Ed W Harrison (Basil Blackwell & Co: Oxford, 1948). First published 1795.

Law Lords were appointed who had some familiarity with both Bentham's ideas and the senior officials in the reformed civil service, so the courts accepted that administration was different to adjudication; that the public interest was a legitimate concern for administrators to advance and have regard to; that public officials must be presumed to act in good faith and in the final analysis were accountable to Parliament for their actions and policies.

This acceptance of the public interest ideology was consolidated in two important cases decided by the House of Lords in 1911 and 1915,[7] significant dates when seen in the context of the existence since 1906 of the Liberal Government – one of the two great reforming administrations of this century. Since those dates there has, on the one hand, been a constant increase in the amount of legislation on land use planning motivated by and constructed in accordance with the public interest ideology and, on the other, a constant oscillation by the courts between their desire to reassert the right of private property against the all pervading bureaucracy and their sense of obligation to uphold the lawfully constituted authority of government. This oscillation has itself affected the structure and content of the legislation on land use planning. So the pursuit of the ideology of private property affected the pursuit of the ideology of public interest and vice versa in the enactment and operation of the law from its beginnings in the mid-nineteenth century. The discussion of the conflict as it affects the current system should not therefore lead us to conclude that it is a recent phenomenon brought on by particularly doctrinaire or oppressive legislation.

The third competing ideology (that law is a vehicle for the advancement of public participation) can claim as equally respectable a philosophical ancestry as the other two ideologies; that of J S Mill.[8] It is, however, the most recent and least developed of the ideologies both in practice, in terms that is of legislation, circulars and cases, and as a separate identifiable ideology backed by a separate and clearly identifiable constituency as the private property ideology is by the courts and the public interest ideology is by the administrators and planners. It is none the less an ideology of equal importance to the other two. It sees the law as the provider of rights of participation in the land use planning process not by virtue of the ownership of property but by virtue of the more abstract principles of democracy and justice.[9] These in turn come down to the argument that all who are likely to be affected by or who have, for whatever reason, an interest or concern in a proposed development of land or change in the environment should have the right of participation in the decision on that proposal just because they might be affected or are interested. This ideology, like the public interest ideology, denies the property-owner any special place in participation; such an interest is merely one of a great number to be considered in the democratic process of decision-making and by no means the most important, particularly when it is in conflict with the majority view; e.g. the

7 *Board of Education v Rice* [1911] AC 179; *Local Government Board v Arlidge* [1915] AC 120.

8 C Pateman, *Participation and Democratic Theory* (Cambridge University Press: Cambridge, 1970) ch 2.

9 J R Lucas, *Democracy and Participation*, Penguin Book 1976, for the best modern statement of this position.

tenants of a building have an equal if not a greater moral claim to participation than the landlord, public or private, present or absentee. This ideology differs, however, from that of public interest by denying that the public interest can be identified and acted upon by public servants on the basis of their own views and assumptions as to what is right and wrong. Public servants should act only after full public debate (and by public debate is meant a debate in which the general public can take a direct part) and subject always to continuous consultation with the public.

Respectable and old though its philosophical ancestry may be, in terms of law and practice, this ideology is not much more than twenty years old. If a single event or matter can be fixed on for a starting date, I would say that, with the advantage of hindsight, it was the Report of the Committee on Administrative Tribunals and Enquiries (the Franks Report)[10] of 1957 that set in motion the practice of participation, though it must be doubted whether any of the members of that august Committee would have subscribed then or would subscribe now to the ideology of public interest, which was considered to have become too dominant, and that of private property. But a call for openness, fairness and impartiality (the Committee's formulation of the attributes of good administration) cannot be confined to openness, fairness and impartiality for the land-owner but not for the rest of society so the changes in law and practice which came about as a result of the Franks Report have provided, unwittingly for this was not their purpose, some of the legal and administrative underpinnings for the growth of participation since then. Two further reports (the Planning Advisory Group's Report on the Future of Development Plans in 1965[11] and the Skeffington Report on People and Planning in 1969)[12] were specifically concerned with participation in the making of development plans but they too contributed to the general climate of feeling that participation was to be officially sanctioned and encouraged at least as regards local policy and plan-making. It is important to understand, however, that this ideology has now evolved beyond concern solely with procedural issues and its use in this book reflects that. As used here, the ideology of public participation embraces both procedural and substantive aspects. Procedural aspects take in the topics discussed above – more opportunities for ordinary people to be involved in decision-making in land use planning. Substantive aspects take in what may be called the alternative society; not just more lay input into the existing governmental system but new structures and processes of government which deliberately and significantly alter the balance between the governed and the governors; greater attention paid to social, community and ecological factors in decision-making and less attention paid to economic and technological factors which assume or are geared to reproducing the same kind of society that exists at present.[13] This

10 Cmnd 218.

11 HMSO 1965.

12 HMSO 1969.

13 There is no one volume statement of this position. Much of the discussion and evaluation of it has taken place through the medium of pamphlets, community newspapers and similar publications, but two important books are E F Schumacher, *Small is Beautiful*, Abacus 1974, and C B Macpherson, *The Life and Time of Liberal Democracy*, OUP 1977. See too Harford Thomas and James Robertson, An alternative agenda for party politics, the *Guardian*,

wider aspect of the ideology has the effect of putting it almost into the position of an ideology of opposition to existing governmental structures, processes and policies and this must be borne in mind throughout the ensuing discussion of the interplay of the three ideologies.

The three ideologies have been set out in a brief and stark form. In practice, they do not always come through so clearly nor must it be assumed that the courts *always* espouse the ideology of private property, or the planners and administrators the ideology of public interest. There are nuances in these ideologies as in that of public participation. But what is being argued here is that the law, administration and official interpretation in the area of land use planning are explicable in the terms of these ideologies and are based on these ideologies; and one of the causes of the general disarray in, and disillusion with, the planning system is the conflict between these ideologies, and in particular between the ideology of public participation on the one hand and the ideologies of private property and public interest on the other.

(a) Elements of the town planning system

Having suggested some general characteristics of the planning system and adopted McAuslan's triumvirate of ideologies as a prism through which to view planning law, we now outline its main elements. The Town and Country Planning Act 1990, as amended by the Planning and Compensation Act 1991, provides a system of controls for regulating development within a policy framework provided by development plans, and guidance notes issued by the Department of the Environment. The key ingredients of the modern town planning system are therefore the development plan, other 'material considerations', particularly policy guidance issued by central government, and

3 July 1978, the Town and Country Planning Association's evidence to the Windscale Inquiry, *Planning and Plutonium* 1977, and for the most up-to-date and succinct statement of this position, the following extract from a letter to *The Times* of 27 November 1978, from Professor S Cotgrove replying to Lord Rothschild's attack on 'econuts' is ideal:

> Secondly, and most important, the crux of the debate is about values, not facts. When environmentalists protest about reprocessing nuclear fuel or pollution they are protesting about a society which values economic and material goals more than quality of life and environmental protection. Nuclear power stations have for them come to have a deep symbolic significance. Their opposition stems from anxieties which go beyond technical questions of risk and safety. Above all, they are rooted in growing objections to large, remote, impersonal bureaucracies, increasing dependence on expert élites and reduced participation in the decisions which profoundly affect our lives.
>
> By contrast, the supporters of nuclear energy believe in a society dedicated above all to the production of wealth, in which efficiency, cost effectiveness and the needs of industry are the touchstones of policy. If the environment takes a knock or two, or if society takes some calculated risks, then this is the price we pay for the pursuit of the greater good.
>
> The acceptability of risk cannot be isolated from values. We take incalculable risks to save the life of a child. To cross the road, presumably even Lord Rothschild seeks zero risk. Where he and the environmentalists differ so passionately is for what goals, and to promote what kind of society, it is worth taking particular risks. Both are from this perspective rational.

various tools such as planning conditions and planning obligations for securing particular functions of the planning system (discussed below). 'Development' is defined broadly in section 55 of the 1990 Act as making a physical change or a 'material' change in the existing use of any buildings or land.

Meaning of 'development' and 'new development'

55.-(1) Subject to the following provisions of this section, in this Act, except where the context otherwise requires, "development" means the carrying out of building, engineering, mining or other operations in, on, over or under land, or the making of any material change in the use of any buildings or other land.

[(1A) For the purposes of this Act "building operations" includes –

(a) demolition of buildings;

(b) rebuilding;

(c) structural alterations of or additions to buildings; and

(d) other operations normally undertaken by a person carrying on business as a builder.]

(2) The following operations or uses of land shall not be taken for the purposes of this Act to involve development of the land-

(a) the carrying out for the maintenance, improvement or other alteration of any building of works which-

(i) affect only the interior of the building, or

(ii) do not materially affect the external appearance of the building and are not works for making good war damage or works begun after December 5, 1968 for the alteration of a building by providing additional space in it underground;

(b) the carrying out on land within the boundaries of a road by a local highway authority of any works required for the maintenance or improvement of the road;

(c) the carrying out by a local authority or statutory undertakers of any works for the purpose of inspecting, repairing or renewing any sewers, mains, pipes, cables or other apparatus, including the breaking open of any street or other land for that purpose;

(d) the use of any buildings or other land within the curtilage of a dwellinghouse for any purpose incidental to the enjoyment of the dwellinghouse as such;

(e) the use of any land for the purposes of agriculture or forestry (including afforestation) and the use for any of those purposes of any building occupied together with land so used;

(f) in the case of buildings or other land which are used for a purpose of any class specified in an order made by the Secretary of State under this section, the use of the buildings or other land or, subject to the provisions of the order, of any part of the buildings or the other land, for any purpose of the same class;

[(g) the demolition of any description of building specified in a direction given by the Secretary of State to local planning authorities generally or to a particular local planning authority.]

The inclusion of 'material change in the *use* of any building or any other land' as development for the purposes of the 1990 Act is unique to British planning law and makes for a category of development beyond *physical* changes to land to be controlled. There are also several exemptions from this definition of development set out in this section of the 1990 Act. See, in particular, the exemption in section 55(2)(e) for 'the use of any land for the purposes of agriculture or forestry (including afforestation) and the use for any purpose of any building occupied together with land so used'. In addition, two statutory instruments make a number of further exemptions. The Town and Country Planning (Use Class Order) 1987[14] excludes a variety of use changes from the definition of development. For example, a change of use of a building or other land from a crêche to a museum is deemed not to fall within the definition of a 'material change in the use of any buildings or other land' because they fall within the same 'class' in the statutory instrument. The second instrument, the Town and Country Planning (General Permitted Development Order) 1995,[15] automatically grants planning permission for a large number of activities. For example, in most instances, planning permission is not required for the installation of a satellite antenna, nor for the construction of an access road to a highway.

In dealing with an application for planning permission, the local planning authority must have regard to the provisions of the relevant development plans, and to 'any other material considerations' (section 70(2) of the 1990 Act). Such 'material considerations' include circulars, planning policy guidance notes, and representations made by third parties. Where the local planning authority has regard to the development plan (whether a structure, local, unitary or other plan) planning permission is to be determined in accordance with that plan unless 'material considerations' indicate otherwise (section 54A of the 1990 Act)(see below). This provision requires that particular 'weight' be given to development plan policies. Since 1988, information arising from the environmental assessment process is also a material consideration of the local planning authority.[16] The authority may grant planning permission either unconditionally or subject to such conditions as it thinks fit, or refuse planning permission (section 70(1) of the 1990 Act). In addition, the authority might enter into a contract with the developer. This may take the form of an agreement between the developer and authority, or a unilateral undertaking made by the developer, both of which are referred to in section 106 of the 1990 Act as a planning obligation. The applicant has a right of appeal to the Secretary of State against a refusal of planning permission, or if the authority has failed to determine the application within the prescribed period. Appeals are handled by a specialist Planning Inspectorate. 'Transferred' appeals may be recovered on request by the Secretary of State, in order to make a determination. The 1990 Act provides that a local planning authority may issue an enforcement notice where it appears both that there has been a breach of planning control and that it is expedient to do so. If at the end of the period for compliance the breach continues, the landowner is in breach of the notice and may be prosecuted in a Magistrates' Court.

14 SI 1987/764.
15 SI 1995/1418.
16 See further ch 10.

This is the basic legal framework of the planning system. The 1990 Act gives wide scope for the exercise of discretion by the local planning authority and by the Secretary of State on the basis of the prevailing planning policy, usually contained within circulars and planning policy guidance notes. Generally, very little is specified in law concerning the scope and content of planning policy, other than that its focus is the use and development of land. This creates the conditions for flexibility and accommodation in the planning system, in particular to take on board varying policies, including environmental protection.

(b) Policy change: the fall and rise of the development plan

The flexibility of the planning system to adopt and accommodate often conflicting objectives and policies is best illustrated by the changing legal status, and content, of the development plan. The significance of the development plan, like other material considerations (or ingredients) of the planning system, may be altered swiftly, most commonly by a change of planning policy set by the Department of the Environment.

Early planning legislation required borough and urban districts to prepare 'schemes' to regulate land use.[17] These schemes, setting out particular uses such as residential or industrial for stretches of land, were the precursors to the requirement in the 1947 Act that development plans be prepared for each area. These plans were to guide decisions about whether to grant or refuse applications for planning permission. However, development planning was criticised for being too detailed and subject to delays. The system was altered by the Town and Country Planning Act 1968 which introduced a two-tier system of structure (strategic) and local (more detailed) plans. In 1969 the Committee on Public Participation in Planning (the 'Skeffington Committee') published its report, *People and Planning*. The Committee was established to 'consider and report on the best methods, including publicity, of securing the participation of the public at the formative stage in the making of development plans for their area'. The Report told of their concerns about the scope of public participation in the democratic process of plan-making.

Committee on Public Participation in Planning (the 'Skeffington Committee'), *People and Planning* (London: HMSO, 1969).

10. The advantages that flow from involvement of the public have been recognised by several local planning authorities whose work has, to some extent, anticipated the requirements of the Town and Country Planning Act 1968. That being so, it may be asked why there has been so little to show from past efforts and why, generally, the public has made so little impact on the content of plans. The reasons vary from place to place; but two general points emerge. They are:

(i) First, most authorities have been far more successful in informing the public than in involving them. Publicity – the first step – is comparatively easy. To secure effective participation is more difficult.

17 See ch 3, 'Early planning law'.

(ii) Secondly, some of the authorities who have made intensive efforts to publicise their proposals have done so when those proposals were almost cut and dried. At that stage, those who have prepared the plan are deeply committed to it. There is a strong disinclination to alter proposals which have been taken so far; but from the public's point of view, the opportunity to comment has come so late that it can only be an opportunity to object. The authority are then regarded more as an antagonist than as the representative of the community and what was started in good will has ended in acrimony.

11. Where information comes too late and without preliminary public discussion there is the likelihood of frustration and hostility. It may be that the plan produced is the one best suited to the needs of the community but the reasons for decisions do not emerge, nor are people told why superficially attractive alternatives have been put aside. The failure to communicate has meant that the preparation of a plan, instead of being a bridge between the authority and the public, has become a barrier, reinforcing the separation that springs up so easily between the 'them' of the authority and the 'us' of the public.

Following the recommendations of the Skeffington Committee, the Town and Country Planning Act 1971 made opportunity for the local planning authority to increase rights of participation in plan-making, for example by holding a special, less formal variety of public inquiry. When preparing a structure or local plan the authority was to take steps to ensure that these plans are publicised and that people are given an opportunity to make representations.

Notwithstanding the enhanced place for public participation in plan-making, the status of the development plan was progressively weakened in a period of 'entrepreneurial planning' which held currency in the 1980s. This planning policy formed part of the Conservative Government's aim of 'releasing enterprise' or, as stated in a 1985 White Paper, 'Lifting the Burden' on business to bring about local economic regeneration. It included giving a greater priority to the right to develop land and, simultaneously, alleviating many of the legal and financial constraints imposed on development by the planning system. The Department of the Environment Circular 22/80, *Development Control: Policy and Practice* (1980) provides a very good example of this policy thrust.

> The planning system should play a helpful part in rebuilding the economy. Development control must avoid placing unjustified obstacles in the way of any development especially if it is for industry, commerce, housing or any other purpose relevant to the economic regeneration of the country...Local planning authorities are asked therefore to always grant planning permission, having regard to all material considerations, unless there are sound and clear-cut reasons for refusal.

This guidance was applied most clearly to housing projects: local authorities were required to undertake studies with the house building industry to ensure that sufficient land for private house building was allocated to meet the needs of the industry. Draft circulars mooted the withdrawal of green belt status from pockets of open land surrounded by existing housing development and the release of undeveloped land for house building. Similar policy was applied to road and airport projects.

In line with the policy aim of entrepreneurial planning, the Department of the Environment in 1988 stated that there should be a presumption in favour of development. This meant that planning consent for development projects was only to be refused by a local planning authority if the project was likely to 'cause demonstrable harm to interests of acknowledged importance'.

Department of the Environment, Planning Policy Guidance Note 1, *General Policy and Principles* (London: HMSO, 1988)

15....'the planning system fails in its function whenever it prevents, inhibits or delays development which can reasonably be permitted. There is always a presumption in favour of allowing applications for development, having regard to all material considerations, *unless that development would cause demonstrable harm to interests of acknowledged importance*' (emphasis added).

This presumption in favour of development, coupled with a host of deregulatory measures, changed the character of planning. The development plan was relegated in status to a material consideration on a par with any other. As a consequence of this policy, planning permission was often granted by the Secretary of State on appeal, even in cases in which the proposed project was in conflict with the relevant development plan at the local level. The planning system became 'appeal-led' rather than predominantly 'plan-led', with policy issues decided on a project-by-project basis rather than in relation to an overall planning framework.

A significant and surprising change to the status of the development plan was prompted by an Opposition amendment to the Planning and Compensation Bill which called for the local planning authority to have *primary* regard to the development plan. The resulting provision (section 26 of the Planning and Compensation Act 1991 which inserted section 54A into the Town and Country Planning Act 1990) was actually more far-reaching than the original Opposition amendment and amounts to a volte-face on policy on the status of the development plan.

> s 54A Status of development plans
>
> Where, in making any determination under the Planning Acts, regard is to be had to the development plan, the determination shall be made in accordance with the plan unless material considerations indicate otherwise.

This section is designed to be read in conjunction with section 70 of the 1990 Act:

> s 70 Determination of applications: general considerations
>
> (1) Where an application is made to a local planning authority for planning permission-
> (a) subject to sections 91 and 92, they may grant planning permission, either unconditionally or subject to such conditions as they think fit; or
> (b) they may refuse planning permission.
>
> (2) In dealing with such an application the authority shall have regard to the provisions of the development plan, so far as material to the application, and to any other material considerations.

The interplay of sections 54A and 70 is particularly significant when read in the light of sections 12(3A), 31(3), and 36(3) of the 1990 Act which require that certain environmental policies be included in unitary development, structure, and local plans, respectively. Section 31(3) is as follows (the wording is very similar in each case):

> s 31. (3) The policies shall...include policies in respect of -
> (a) the conservation of the natural beauty and amenity of the land;
> (b) the improvement of the physical environment; and
> (c) the management of traffic.

The change in policy, manifested in section 54A, arose because the Government was concerned about discontent in some quarters, particularly among planners, about the rise in successful appeals to the Secretary of State in which approved planning policy was ignored. This practice was seen to undermine the development plan process which, after all, provides the main democratic input into the planning system. The increase in the number of appeals also placed the Department of the Environment under strain. A possible further factor was that environmental considerations had now to be accommodated by the government, following pressure to fulfil obligations arising from European Community and international law. The planning system presented a suitable legal mechanism with which to achieve this accommodation. However, this could not be achieved without greater emphasis on plan making and the tempering of policies of deregulation and 'lifting the burden'. In 1987 the Planning Minister, William Waldegrave, had given a speech warning that government policy did not mean that development plan policies would be given little weight. In May 1991, during the final stages of the progress of the Planning and Compensation Bill through Parliament, the Minister reiterated this policy:

> We have always regarded the development plan as important although Circular 14/85 appeared to downgrade it by referring to it as only one of the material considerations. Those days are well behind us. Today's debate should leave no doubt as to the importance of the plan-led approach.

The effect of the amendment to the 1990 Act, the most important change in planning legislation since 1947, is that, where section 54A does apply, the decision maker must make a determination in accordance with the plan. Section 54A therefore sends a clear signal that the development plan has a greater legal status than previously.[18] However, the strength of this presumption in favour of the development plan is less clear. For example, in the first case in which the High Court interpreted the meaning of section 54A, *St Albans District Council v Secretary of State for the Environment and Allied Breweries Ltd* [1993] JPEL 374, the Deputy Judge, David Widdicombe QC, stated that 'undoubtedly section 54A does set up a presumption in favour of the development plan, but for its rebuttal it is sufficient if there are "material considerations which indicate otherwise" '. Such an interpretation rejects the argument that section 54A

18 See further I Gatenby and C Williams [1992] JPEL 110; and M Harrison 'A Presumption in Favour of Development?' [1992] JPEL 121-129.

creates a *strong* presumption in favour of the development plan. This case demonstrates also the general pragmatism of planning law: the result would have been the same if the planning inspector had applied section 54A because the local policy had been abandoned anyway.

St Albans District Council v Secretary of State for the Environment and Allied Breweries Ltd [1993] JPEL 374 (Queen's Bench Division, Mr D Widdicombe, QC sitting as a Deputy Judge, 23 November 1992)

The St Albans District Council refused planning permission for the redevelopment of the Abbey Tavern, a nineteenth century public house into a two storey office building. The Abbey Tavern is not a listed building but is in the St Albans Conservation Area, which includes the city centre.

On appeal, an inquiry was held and the Inspector gave his decision by letter dated April 6, 1992. By the time of the local inquiry, section 54A of the Town and Country Planning Act 1990 was in force.

The relevant development plan at the inquiry was the County Structure Plan 1988 and the District Local Plan of July 1985. The argument at the inquiry focused on two areas of policy involving office development and development in conservation areas. The Inspector allowed the appeal.

The Council applied to the High Court under s 288 of the 1990 Act to quash the Inspector's decision.

THE DEPUTY JUDGE said that the main issue was whether the Inspector had regard to and applied section 54A of the Town and Country Planning Act 1990, which stated:

> "Status of development plans:
> 54A. Where, in making any determination under the planning acts, regard is to be had to the development plan, the determination shall be made in accordance with the plan unless material considerations indicate otherwise."

That section was added by the Planning and Compensation Act 1991, and came into force on September 25, 1991. When the St Albans District Council had refused planning permission on November 6, 1990, the decision was governed by section 70(1) of the Act of 1990, which re-enacted the provision originally found in the Town and Country Planning Act 1947, namely: section 70(1):

> "70(1) Where an application is made to a local planning authority for planning permission-
> (2) In dealing with such an application the authority shall have regard to the provisions of the development plan, so far as material to the application, and to any other material considerations."

But by the time of the local inquiry into the appeals in December 1991, section 54A was in force. In cases to which it applied, of which this was one, it was apparent that section 54A had greatly increased the importance of the statutory development plan. However, it was common ground that section 54A did not apply to an application for demolition consent under section 74 of the Planning (Listed Buildings and Conservation Areas) Act 1990, but as the application for demolition consent in this case was dependent on the grant of planning permission for redevelopment, it was common ground that the consent to demolish stood or fell with the planning permission.

Mr Ground for the applicant council pointed to the difference between section 70(2) and section 54A. On section 70(2) he referred to *Simpson v Edinburgh Corpn* 1960 SC 313 where on p 318 Lord Guest said of its statutory predecessor: 'It requires the planning authority to consider the development plan, but does not oblige them to follow it.' He quoted Lord Donaldson MR in *Pehrsson v Secretary of State for the Environment* (1990) 61 P & CR 266 at 276 to the same effect.

As regards section 54A he drew attention to Planning Policy Guidance Note No. 1, paragraphs 25-27, which stated:

> 'The approach that decision-makers should take to the consideration of planning applications is set out in sections 70(2) and 54A of the 1990 Act (the latter inserted by section 26 of the 1991 Act). Section 70(2) requires the decision-maker to have regard to the development plan, so far as material to the application, and to any other material considerations. Where the development plan is material to the development proposal, and must therefore be taken into account, section 54A requires the application or appeal to be determined in accordance with the plan, unless material considerations indicate otherwise. In effect, this introduces a presumption in favour of development proposals which are in accordance with the development plan. An applicant who proposes a development which is clearly in conflict with the development plan would need to produce convincing reasons to demonstrate why the plan should not prevail. The plan to which sections 70(2) and 54A apply is the approved or adopted development plan for the area, and not any draft plan which may exist.
>
> ...
>
> Those deciding planning applications or appeals should therefore look to see whether the development plan contains policies or proposals which are relevant to the particular development proposal. Such material policies or proposals may either give support to a development proposal in a particular location or indicate that it is not appropriate. If the development plan does contain material policies or proposals and there are no other material considerations, the application or appeal should be determined in accordance with the development plan.
>
> Where there are other material considerations, the development plan should be taken as a starting point, and the other material considerations should be weighed in reaching a decision. One such consideration will be whether the development plan policies are up-to-date and apply to current circumstances, or whether they have been overtaken by events (the age of the plan is not in itself material). For example, policies and proposals in the plan may have been superseded by more recent planning guidance issued by the Government, or developments since the plan became operative may have rendered certain policies or proposals in the plan incapable of implementation or out of date.'

He (Mr Ground) emphasised the sentence: 'An applicant who proposes a development which is clearly in conflict with the development plan would need to produce convincing reasons to demonstrate why the plan should not prevail'.

...

Mr Ground submitted that in the decision letter the Inspector had failed to apply or had misapplied section 54A. He pointed out that the Inspector had made no reference to section 54A and, said Mr Ground, he treated the development plan on an equal footing with other material considerations such as the policies in the District Plan Review. Then the Inspector had stated his conclusion that the proposals would not result in demonstrable harm to the aims of employment and housing policies for the area. What the Inspector should have done, said Mr Ground, was to have identified the Development Plan policies, said whether the proposal conformed to them or not, and if they did not, he should have identified the material considerations which justified a departure. There was no recognition of the presumption in favour of the development plan. It was submitted that the decision had complied not with section 54A but with section 70(2) in which the development plan was just one, among others, of the material considerations to be taken into account.

Mr Aylesbury for the Secretary of State and Mr. Hicks for the second respondents, the developers, had supported the decision, and submitted that it was not necessary for the Inspector to have referred expressly to section 54A so long as the decision complied with it, which it did.

He (the Deputy Judge) agreed with Mr Aylesbury and Mr Hicks that the failure to refer expressly to section 54A was not fatal, so long as the requirements of the section were met. The Inspector had correctly identified the development plan and considered the relevant policies. He had mistakenly regarded the criteria for local firms in District Plan Policy 20 as still operative, but concluded that the proposals came some way to satisfying the criteria anyway.

Where he (the Deputy Judge) agreed with Mr Ground was that the Inspector appeared to make little or no distinction between the development plan policies and other policies and material considerations, so that at the end of the day it was by no means clear whether he had applied section 54A or section 70(2).

The bases for his conclusion were uncertain. Was the Inspector saying that the proposals were a departure from the development plan, but that there were material considerations which justified the departure, or was he saying, applying section 70(2) that he had taken all material considerations into account and had reached the stated conclusion? Because of the absence of any express reference to section 54A, and because of the phrase 'balancing the factors raised in the various local policies', he (the Deputy Judge) thought the latter was the more likely.

For those reasons, he (the Deputy Judge) would have been minded to quash that part of the decision for failure to comply with the approach laid down in section 54A. However, the court had a discretion and what had to be decided was whether there was any real possibility that the decision would be different if it were quashed. With some hesitation he had come to the conclusion that the decision would almost certainly have been the same if it were reconsidered by the Secretary of State with section 54A in mind. It appeared to him that any breach of Policy 20 had to be nominal in view of the abandonment of the criteria for local firms; and the fact, as found, that no demonstrable harm would result to the employment and housing policies for the area was a material consideration amply sufficient to justify a nominal departure from Policy 20, even allowing for the section 54A presumption in favour of the plan.

For those reasons therefore, although that part of the decision was defective for failure to comply with section 54A, in the exercise of discretion he (the Deputy Judge) declined to quash it.

A *strong* presumption apart, it would still seem to be the case that a *general* presumption in favour of the development plan exists. This is underlined by David Keene QC, Deputy Judge, in *R v Canterbury City Council, ex p Springimage Ltd* [1994] JPEL 427, in his acceptance that the Chief Planning Officer had misdirected the Planning Committee when he told them that section 54A meant that regard had to be had to the development plan and *then* to any material considerations. The Deputy Judge accepted that this failed to give development plans the additional weight to be attached to them under section 54A. The question remains whether there is a still a presumption in favour of granting planning permission? This issue arose in *Sainsbury plc v Secretary of State for the Environment* [1993] JPEL 651 in which a proposal to build an out of town supermarket which was not in accordance with the development plan was nevertheless granted planning permission. Development plan policy was to encourage town centre shopping development, such as that proposed by Waitrose, the economic viability of which was potentially jeopardised by Sainsbury's plans to build an out of town superstore. The case supports the view that where an application for planning permission is not in accordance with the relevant development plan this does not amount to deemed demonstrable harm, and the decision maker can still use the lack of demonstrable harm as a material consideration to overturn the presumption in favour of the plan. It would appear that the presumption in favour of development, which gave the planning system such a permissive air in the 1980s, remains, unless it can be shown that 'the development would cause demonstrable harm to interests of acknowledged importance'.[19]

Sainsbury plc v Secretary of State for the Environment [1993] JPEL 651, (Queen's Bench Division, Mr M Spence, QC sitting as a Deputy Judge, 22 December 1992)

Sainsbury's was refused permission to construct a food superstore near Sidcup. The town centre was about one mile away and planning permission had recently been granted for the development of a town centre site at Grassington Road as a supermarket and 21 shops.

On appeal, the Inspector identified the issues in paragraph 12 of his decision letter.

> 'With regard to impact upon Sidcup Town Centre, the Council did not seek to argue that the proposals would have an unduly harmful effect upon the existing centre. Their main concern was the importance of the Grassington Road proposals in enabling Sidcup to continue to perform its role as a major district centre.
>
> From the representations made and my inspection of the appeal site and its surroundings, it seems to me that the main issues remaining to be resolved are whether the use of the appeal site for a foodstore would cause demonstrable harm to the objective of promoting the Foots Cray area for industrial or business uses, and whether

19 Further on this issue, see M Purdue, 'The Impact of Section 54A', [1994] JPEL 399, on whether there is a battle of the presumptions; I Gatenby and C Williams, 'Section 54A: The Legal and Practical Implications', [1992] JPEL 110-120; and M Harrison, 'A Presumption in Favour of Planning Permission?', [1993] JPEL 121-129.

the appeal proposals would seriously affect prospects for the continuing vitality and viability of Sidcup Town Centre'.

The Inspector found in favour of Sainsbury's on the industry and business use aspects, but not on the issue of viability. The consequence was that attention focused on the proposed shopping re-development at Grassington Road.

In his overall conclusion the Inspector, after stating briefly the advantages of the proposal, said:

> 'However those advantages would to my mind be outweighed by the harmful effect that the proposals would have on the continuing vitality and viability of Sidcup Town Centre. The need for the proposed retail floorspace to be provided on the appeal site is not in my view such as to justify a decision being made in this case otherwise than in accordance with the provisions of the development plan'.

...The Inspector dismissed the appeal and the applicant appealed to the High Court under section 288 of the 1990 Act to quash the decision.

THE DEPUTY JUDGE said that Mr Read first submitted that the Inspector had failed to determine the appeal in terms of section 54A of the Town and Country Planning Act 1990. He said that plainly the Inspector had not determined the case on the basis of Policy S1 of the Adopted Local Plan which read: 'To resist shopping developments except within the confines of existing shopping centres...'.

It was common ground that the policy was outdated since more recent Government guidance. He said that section 54A of the Town and Country Planning Act 1990 requires the Inspector to determine the case in accordance with Policy S3, which read: 'To resist proposals likely to prejudice the strategic shopping role of Bexleyheath Town Centre or are likely to cause a serious decline in other centres.'

...

It had to be stressed that in this case a conclusion about the likely future of the Grassington Road scheme was crucial to the decision as to whether the Sainsbury proposal could seriously affect the vitality and viability of the centre as a whole. That was the main point in the case. The inquiry had lasted 13 days and much of the evidence was devoted to the point. The parties were entitled to expect a clear conclusion upon it.

...

In his (the Deputy Judge's) judgment the Inspector had not determined the main question in this case or at least had not done so properly. He had read the decision letter time and time again and listened attentively to the submissions, and he confessed that at the end of it he could not tell whether the Inspector had considered that the Waitrose scheme would be built or whether it would not if permission was granted for the Sainsbury superstore. The Inspector had said that he was not confident that it would be; this observation in itself was more consistent with an avoidance of the determination of the main question.

...

The Inspector was not inspired with confidence that the Waitrose scheme would proceed, but, that could not possibly be a reason for refusal. He (the Deputy Judge) rejected entirely the notion that a superstore proposal such as this could be refused permission just because the Inspector was not confident that another proposal would proceed. What was required was evidence and a conclusion that at least it was unlikely to do so. (That could be judged for example, by what had happened in other comparable cases.) Mere unsupported assertion by the other supermarket operator was scarcely the evidence which was required. The need for proper evidence and a proper conclusion applied particularly in cases such as this where the evidence, accepted by the Inspector, was that there was or would appear to be sufficient expenditure available for both schemes.

In his (the Deputy Judge's) judgment, at the very least it was unsafe to let the decision stand. That important point had to be resolved properly and clearly. The determination of it was not to be left to be inferred from other parts of the decision letter.

The fall and rise of the legal status of the development plan indicates that instruments of the planning system may be manipulated by planning policy to bring about certain results – in this case the demise of the development plan in the 1980s led to a less restrictive planning system. The excesses of the 'lifting the burden' policy and encouraging 'enabling' development have been curbed by the 1991 Act in line with an avowed policy of more balanced economic growth and achievement of the objectives of sustainable development. However, it is important to emphasise that the current status of the development plan remains subject to change vis-à-vis other imperatives by the introduction of new planning policy to which planners, developers, lawyers, and the public must quickly adjust. In addition, statutory provisions, such as section 54A of the 1990 Act, are open to varied interpretations by individuals in those groups as seen in the *St Albans* and *Sainsbury* cases. Nevertheless, as these show in the case of conservation of buildings and green field sites and the vitality of town centres, the priority given to the development plan by the local planning authority and, at appeal, the Secretary of State, has great significance for the level of environmental protection the planning system can deliver.

(c) Planning tools: conditions and obligations

The local planning authority has at its disposal a number of tools to enable it to achieve particular objectives. In terms of environmental protection, the most relevant of these are planning conditions and planning obligations.

The local planning authority has a power to impose 'such conditions as they see fit' under section 70(2) of the 1990 Act. The imposition of conditions can enable many development proposals to proceed where it would otherwise be necessary to refuse planning permission.[20] This power is, however, limited by public law principles of legality and rationality which have been developed by the courts in case law. We can see in these cases an example of McAuslan's ideology of private property at work. The House of Lords[21] has decided that

20 Planning Policy Guidance Note 1, *General Policy and Principles* (London: HMSO, 1992) para 46.

conditions must comply with three tests which elaborate these principles: the *Newbury* tests after the leading case on the legality of planning conditions. First, the condition must pursue a planning purpose and not an ulterior one. For example, imposing a condition that occupants of a proposed development should be on a council housing waiting list has been held as wrongly imposed for the non-planning purpose of assisting the authority to achieve its housing duties. Second, the condition must not be unreasonable. Conditions have been invalidated when they have imposed what the courts have interpreted as an unreasonable or unnecessary burden on the applicant. So, an unreasonable condition would require the developer to provide an access road, or a roundabout, at its own expense, even though this was only made necessary by the increased traffic generated by the development. The local planning authority cannot therefore impose a condition requiring the developer to provide infrastructure. Third, the condition must 'fairly and reasonably relate' to the development. This means that the condition must be related to planning needs arising from the actual purpose for which the permission is granted; in other words, there must be a reasonable connection with the development.

A second tool is the planning obligation, provided for under section 106 of the 1990 Act. Planning obligations include within their scope planning agreements, made between the developer and local planning authority and unilateral undertakings, declared by the developer alone. Planning obligations allow a developer either to enter into an agreement with the local planning authority or unilaterally to undertake to restrict the use or development of the land, to require specified operations on the land, or even to agree to pay money to the authority. The main purpose of the unilateral undertaking is to permit an applicant at the appeal stage to enter into an obligation that may remove an objection to planning permission being otherwise granted. The end result and objective of planning obligations has been pejoratively, but more accurately, referred to as planning 'gain'.

Planning obligations constitute a statutory contract between the developer and local planning authority. The obligation may be unconditional or subject to conditions. It may also impose restrictions or requirements for an indefinite or a specific period, so enabling an obligation to end when a planning permission expires. A planning obligation is a local land charge and so prospective buyers will become aware of it when making searches on the property. Section 106(5) of the 1990 Act provides specifically for enforcement of the terms of a planning obligation by injunction. In addition, section 106(6) of the 1990 Act provides that in the event of a breach of any requirement in a planning obligation to carry out any operations, the local planning authority may enter the land and carry them out itself, recovering the cost of doing so from the person against whom the obligation is enforceable.

Planning obligations hold a number of advantages for the local planning authority over the use of conditions. They enable the imposition of negative and positive covenants that will bind third parties who acquire the land in the future, as well as the original parties to the agreement. Unlike conditions,

21 *Newbury District Council v Secretary of State for the Environment* [1981] AC 578. See also Circular 11/95, *Conditions*, which imposes several further tests as a matter of policy.

monetary payments may also be made. It is also generally easier for an authority to enforce the terms of a planning agreement (by injunction), than a term of a planning condition (through the enforcement machinery outlined above). The negotiations and arrangements for a planning agreement are more consensual than those for a condition and are largely insulated from review by either the Secretary of State or the courts. The primary advantage of planning obligations, though, is that their scope is broader than that of planning conditions. Planning obligations enable an activity to be controlled or required which cannot be achieved by way of conditions. Where a proposed development would create a need for particular facilities or would have a damaging impact on the environment or local amenity and these difficulties cannot be satisfactorily resolved through the use of planning conditions, planning obligations can usually be sought or offered to overcome them. For example, the planning authority can make provision of physical or social infrastructure the subject of a planning obligation to overcome an objection to the proposal.[22]

The greater scope of planning obligations, when compared with planning conditions, is because, although a planning obligation must fulfil a planning purpose and must not be unreasonable (the first two *Newbury* tests), there is some question about whether it must also 'fairly and reasonably relate' to the development (the third *Newbury* test). The House of Lords decided in *Tesco Stores Ltd v Secretary of State for the Environment*[23] that the 'fairly and reasonably relate' formula is not appropriate to test the validity of planning obligations. Tesco had offered private funding for a £6.6m new road intended to relieve traffic congestion in return for a grant of planning permission for a superstore. The store was predicted to cause only 10% of the traffic congestion. The Secretary of State decided that the offer of funding was not a good ground for either granting or refusing permission. Tesco appealed on the basis that the offer of funding was a material consideration and that as the Secretary of State had failed to take it into account his decision was flawed. The House of Lords held that an obligation which had no connection whatsoever with the development, apart from the fact that it was offered by the developer, was not a material consideration. The test is whether the obligation has some connection with the development which is not *de minimis*. If that connection is established, then it must be taken into account but the weight to be attached to it is entirely within the discretion of the decision maker. That *Tesco* does not determine what is a *de minimis* connection suggests that there are few legal fetters on the local planning authority to seek planning gain, other than that the obligation fulfils a planning purpose, is not legally unreasonable, and the knowledge that if the authority attempts to extract too much in the way of benefits, the Secretary of State on appeal may grant planning permission without any planning obligation at all. So it is sometimes difficult to distinguish between the striking of agreements between the developer and the local planning authority and the extraction of planning gain from the developer, in return for a grant of planning permission. 'Moral panic' that planning permission has been bought in return for unrelated, but

22 See J Jowell and H Woolf, *de Smith: Administrative Law* (London: Sweet & Maxwell, 1995), para 22-032.
23 [1995] 2 All ER 636.

financially attractive, benefits, has ensued over this issue. This concern is addressed, but hardly laid to rest, in Lord Hoffmann's judgment in the House of Lords in *Tesco.*

***Tesco Stores Ltd v Secretary of State for the Environment* [1995] 2 All ER 636**

LORD HOFFMANN

...

(15) *Buying and selling planning permission*

This reluctance of the English courts to enter into questions of planning judgment means that they cannot intervene in cases in which there is sufficient connection between the development and a planning obligation to make it a material consideration but the obligation appears disproportionate to the external costs of the development. *Plymouth* [*R v Plymouth City Council, ex p Plymouth & South Devon Co-operative Society Ltd* (1993) 67 P & CR 78, CA] was such a case, leading to concern among academic writers and Steyn LJ in the present case that the court was condoning the sale of planning permission to the highest bidder. My Lords, to describe a planning decision as a bargain and sale is a vivid metaphor. But I venture to suggest that such a metaphor (and I could myself have used the more emotive term 'auction' rather than 'competition' to describe the process of decision-making in *Plymouth*) is an uncertain guide to the legality of a grant or refusal of planning permission. It is easy enough to apply in a clear case in which the planning authority has demanded or taken account of benefits which are quite unconnected with the proposed development. But in such a case the phrase merely adds colour to the statutory duty to have regard only to material considerations. In cases in which there is a sufficient connection, the application of the metaphor or its relevance to the legality of the planning decision may be highly debatable. I have already explained how in a case of competition such as *Plymouth*, in which it is contemplated that the grant of permission to one developer will be a reason for refusing it to another, it may be perfectly rational to choose the proposal which offers the greatest public benefit in terms of both the development itself and related external benefits. Or take the present case which is in some respects the converse of *Plymouth*. Tarmac says that Tesco's offer to pay £6.6m to build the WEL [West End Link] was a blatant attempt to buy the planning permission. Although it is true that Witney Bridge is a notorious bottleneck and the town very congested, the construction of a superstore would make the congestion only marginally worse than if the site had been developed under its existing permission for offices. Therefore an offer to pay for the whole road was wholly disproportionate and it would be quite unfair if Tarmac was disadvantaged because it was unable to match this offer. The Secretary of State in substance accepted this argument. His policy, even in cases of competition for a site, is obviously defensible on the ground that although it may not maximise the benefit for Witney, it does produce fairness between developers.

Tesco, on the other hand, says that nothing was further from its mind than to try to buy the planning permission. It made the offer because the local planning authority had said that in its view, no superstore should be allowed unless the WEL was built. Tesco says that this seemed a sensible attitude because although it was true that the development would add only marginally to the congestion which would have existed if offices had been built, this was an unrealistic comparison. In practice it was most unlikely that anyone would build offices in that part of Witney in the foreseeable future. The fact was that the development would make the existing traffic problems a good deal worse. In an ideal world it would have been fairer if the highway authority had paid for most of the road and Tesco only for a proportion which reflected the benefit to its development. But the highway authority had made it clear that it had no money for the WEL. So there was no point in Tesco offering anything less than the whole cost. Why should this be regarded as an improper attempt to buy the planning permission? The result of the Secretary of State's decision is that Witney will still get a superstore but no relief road. Why should that be in the public interest?

I think that Tesco's argument is also a perfectly respectable one. But the choice between a policy which emphasises the presumption in favour of development and fairness between developers, such as guided the Secretary of State in this case, and a policy of attempting to obtain the maximum legitimate public benefit which was pursued by the local planning authority in *Plymouth*, lies within the area of discretion which Parliament has entrusted to planning authorities. It is not a choice which should be imposed upon them by the courts.

I would therefore reject Mr Lockhart-Mummery's submission that Tesco's offer was not a material consideration. I think that it was open to the Secretary of State to have taken the same view as the Plymouth City did in *Plymouth* and given the planning permission to Tesco on the grounds that its proposals offered the greater public benefit. But the Secretary of State did not do so. Instead, he applied the policy of circular 16/91 and decided to attribute little or no weight to the offer. And so on the ground that its site was marginally more suitable, Tarmac got the permission.

...

We see in this judgment the familiar use of the 'public benefit' formulation to justify the striking of a bargain between the planning authority and a private developer, although the exact nature of the 'related external benefits' to be gained in this case might be questioned. *Tesco* suggests also a process of privatisation in the planning system in which developers contribute to the planning process, most directly financially, but also in terms of their influence as to what constitutes good planning, what is desirable development, and their definition of the '*public* interest', all in a context of private property development. The phraseology of the planning *obligation* suggests a sense of responsibility or duty to the public, and of stewardship towards the environment. This might enhance public acceptability of a project which might, after all, be little more than the consequence of a 'planning gain' in the old sense. For these reasons, planning obligations are legal techniques having considerable political, not to say cultural, significance. Another way of viewing the planning obligation is as an economic instrument since financial inducements are used to achieve certain goals. Planning obligations might therefore be grouped together with management agreements, although they work in the converse. Planning obligations require a developer to pay for certain public benefits connected in some way to a development. The management agreement requires that a developer refrain from developing land which constitutes a 'potentially damaging operation' in return for financial payments.[24] A final question is whether the conclusion of Lord Hoffmann's judgment, that it may be perfectly rational to choose the proposal which offers the greatest public benefit in terms of both the development itself and related external benefits, can be squared with the rhetoric and the demands of sustainable development in planning?

3 PLANNING FOR ENVIRONMENTAL PROTECTION

R Grove-White, 'Land Use Law and the Environment', (1991) *Journal of Law and Society*, Special issue on Law, Policy and the Environment, Vol 18, 32-47, at 32

The emergence of the environment as a mainstream political issue in Britain during the 1980s cannot be understood without an appreciation of the role of the land-use planning system. This system – best seen as an evolving web of law, policy and convention which regulates and orders a range of land uses in the United Kingdom – has been a powerful influence on the distinctive form in which environmental issues have emerged in a British context. This has been so not simply because of the regulatory constraints the system has provided, but also because of the 'cultural' framing created by the discourse and idioms of town and country planning law. These have helped to shape certain of the forms in which environmental tensions have been conceptualized and have found public expression.

On a more tangible level planning's concerns with the location of sources of pollution, the deposit of wastes and the allocation and use of natural resources such as minerals and aggregates mean that the planning system has central importance for environ-mental protection. Planning controls have particular relevance for air pollution, as explained by the Royal Commission on Environmental Pollution in its Fifth Report (1976). In the following, the Royal Commission identifies the general connections between planning and air pollution.

Royal Commission on Environmental Pollution, Fifth Report *Air Pollution Control: An Integrated Approach* Cmnd 6371 (London: HMSO, 1976) p 91

323. We have seen many examples during our study of the connection between pollution problems and planning. In most cases where pollution causes acute local problems, polluting industry is close to houses, shops or hospitals, or industry is so densely concentrated that the total pollution is unacceptable. Often these situations result from decisions taken many years ago when the development control was rudimentary and then, as now, many factors apart from pollution had to be taken into account. In a small industrialised country these situations are sometimes unavoidable. We have, however, seen cases where new housing development is still being allowed too close to polluting industry, or new polluting industry is allowed too close to houses. Here again, the decisions allowing these

24 See, on management agreements 'Control of land use in the countryside', below.

developments were not necessarily wrong, though they may lead to pollution problems in the future which will be difficult to resolve. Public expectations on environmental quality will no doubt continue to rise.

The specific roles which may be played by planning in controlling air pollution are listed by Wood in the following extract.

C Wood, *Planning Pollution Prevention: A Comparison of Siting Controls Over Air Pollution In Great Britain and the United States of America* (Manchester: Manchester University Press, 1989) pp 26-27

The role of land use controls

The land use planning agencies or authorities exert control at most stages in the pollution process but their most powerful potential contribution is in determining the nature of new development and redevelopment. Because pollution originates as waste from production and consumption activities, one of the key variables in pollution control – the geographical point at which additional waste is created – is determined once the location of these activities has been established. Therefore, because of their control over land use, planning agencies exercise an important influence on the spatial origin of wastes and consequently upon pollution levels and their distribution. These agencies are undoubtedly the principal controlling authorities in deciding the location of the pollution process, whether they recognise their position or not.

Control over the location of the pollution source is much more fundamental than other types of planning control over the pollution process. The new locations at which power is generated and at which goods are produced, and hence the location at which the associated wastes arise, are largely determined by grant or refusal of land use planning permits.

The locations at which products are used can be directly controlled by planning authorities. Apart from allocating land for the consumption of goods (e.g. residential areas) agencies have at least a voice in the determination of new road alignments (and also possess some indirect control over these ...[In sanctioning] types of seemingly relatively non-polluting development (such as sports stadia, commercial buildings and shopping centres) agencies are permitting so called *indirect* pollution sources to arise as the large numbers of motor vehicles travelling to and from them will emit significant quantities of air pollutants. Land use planning authorities can exert some direct control over the treatment of various wastes emitted from stationary sources by, for example, insisting upon particular air pollution emission levels (ie, requiring technical controls) or by specifying discharge height or by demanding certain building types for containment of pollutants.

The place at which the waste matter is disposed of is generally determined once a development is approved, although the precise location (and height) of, for example, a new chimney stack associated with the development may be subject to planning approval. Planning authorities have some control over waste diffusion, apart from the specification of stack heights or locations. They may, for example, insist on buffer zones and/or planting to remove pollutants from the atmosphere.

Land use planning agencies have a crucial role in controlling the damage arising from the resulting pollution, since they control the nature and location of receptors. In other words, apart from protecting the environment around a proposed new source of pollution, authorities can control damage from an existing source of pollution by determining the nature of new developments close to it. This may be achieved either through the granting or withholding of land use permits (eg, refusal of housing close to an oil refinery) or by the attachment of conditions (eg, that a school building be constructed so as to be separated from a major air pollution source by its playing fields).

It must be stressed that there are two stages in the planning process, the preparation of a plan and its implementation in the form of decisions on the use of specific areas of land. While all the controls mentioned above can be exercised in the absence of an overall land use plan, the potential role of the land use planner in ameliorating air pollution is not restricted either to attempting to ensure that the best anticipatory controls are imposed when development is permitted or to preventing such development. Rather, it extends to planning the future use of land to reduce air pollution by the preparation of implementable plans.

One final role must be mentioned. Apart from their controls at different stages in the pollution process, land use planning agencies are in a unique position – as a focus for consultation on both plan making and land use decision-taking – to play a central co-ordinating role in the control of pollution.

The town planning system embraces a more diverse range of objectives than solely environmental protection, including urban regeneration, affordable housing and industrial and commercial development. A crucial point is that environmental protection is therefore just one 'material consideration' amongst many others.

Royal Commission on Environmental Pollution, Fifth Report *Air Pollution Control: An Integrated Approach* Cmnd 6371 (London: HMSO, 1976) p 93

The need for cooperation

334. Pollution is only one of the factors which need to be taken into account in planning decisions and in many situations there will be other factors which have to be given equal or higher priority. There may be pressures on a local authority to improve housing or local employment opportunities, or an authority may wish, for example, to put derelict land into use. While this is not strictly a planning consideration, a local authority may also wish to secure the rate revenue from a major development. As always, there is the need to balance conflicting requirements.

335. Our concern is not that pollution is not always given top priority; it is that it is often dealt with inadequately, and sometimes forgotten altogether in the planning process. In part this stems from lack of guidance and advice. Planning officers and committees are not often pollution experts and they are necessarily dependent on advice on pollution matters. Such advice is not always available but even when it is, it is not always sought. We have seen evidence of lack of consultation between planning officers and those responsible for air pollution control, whether the latter are Environmental Health Officers of the local authorities concerned or of neighbouring authorities or the Alkali Inspectorate.

In this Report, the Royal Commission expressed a general concern that matters of pollution were not dealt with adequately in the planning process. The Commission considered that in most of those cases where pollution caused acute local problems, industry was located close by, and recommended that consultation to establish the pollution implications of proposals becomes common practice. There was some acceptance of the Royal Commission's recommendation by professional planning bodies. For example, in 1976, the Royal Town Planning Institute acknowledged the role of what was then known as the ecological movement in the general reassessment taking place of the objectives of planning. Over the following years, planning authorities and inquiry inspectors showed a greater readiness to cite particular forms of pollution such as noise, odour and air pollutants rather than rely on vague phrases such as 'prejudicial to amenity' in order to defend refusals of consent for environmentally unacceptable development. The planning system was recognised as offering an opportunity to anticipate and forestall environmental harm by refusing development consent or by separating incompatible land uses. In addition, green belt policies continued to perform a containment function and to protect land from development. However, the extent to which planning controls could be used to intervene further to prevent pollution was limited.

On the recommendation of the Royal Commission on Environmental Pollution's Report, Circular 71/77 *Local Government and Industrial Strategy* stated that planning conditions should not be used to deal with problems which are the subject of controls under separate environmental legislation and that planning conditions are considered unnecessary where they duplicate pollution controls. Planning has since trodden carefully in imposing controls in the form of conditions and obligations in areas in which other statutory controls exist. This separation in practice of planning from pollution controls is one effect of the creation of special laws, institutions and procedures for dealing with pollution, minerals extraction, industrial development and transport. It is another example of the sectoral approach to environmental protection which provided the context for the development of pollution controls, discussed in chapter 6. Some of the consequences of this approach are outlined in the following critique of the planning system's track record on protecting the environment.

D Hall, M Hebbert and H Lusser, 'The Planning Background', in A Blowers, (ed) *Planning for a Sustainable Environment* (London: Earthscan, 1993)

THE LIMITATIONS OF PLANNING

How has the postwar planning system performed from an environmental point of view? In practice, it has been an effective instrument for achieving the policy objectives of the 1940s, particularly the demarcation of built-up areas from the countryside and the designation and protection of national parks, landscape areas, and nature reserves.

But it has been far less successful in responding to new kinds of environmental concern. Once established as a regular branch of government at central and local levels, land-use planning became set in its ways. Its place in the scheme of government was assured but circumscribed. It was not allowed to trespass on the preserve of agricultural policy, which has an exceptionally tight political nexus with the farm supply, farming and food industries. So the town and country planning system has protected the rural land resource from building development but not from some of the uglier side-effects of agribusiness.

The same applies to the control of noise, noxious emissions and wastes from manufacturing and extractive industry. The planning system set up by the 1947 Act had the potential to place local authorities in a key role in the control of industrial pollution. It gave them powers to determine the nature, as well as the location of development; a statutory responsibility to consult and co-ordinate (with pollution control agencies) in plan-making and development control; and an ability, through positive planning, to coordinate environmental improvement on a broad scale.

But this 'comprehensive range of techniques...for pollution control', as Christopher Wood describes it,[25] was largely left unused. Wood analyses the reasons why: inadequate training, poor information, lack of central guidance, professional jealousies, and the fear – explored particularly in Blowers' study of pollution and planning in the brickfields[26] – that a tightening of local planning controls would lead to local job losses. There was also an important institutional factor. Industrial pollution control was the domain of the Alkali Inspectorate, now Her Majesty's Inspectorate of Pollution. In a later comparative study[27] of pollution control and planning in the UK and the USA, Wood documented the comparatively cosy relationship of Britain's national inspectorate with client industries and its tendency to discourage planning authorities from consideration of the environmental impacts on air and water of new industrial development.

...

Transport figures large in current environmentalism. Part of the original purpose of the postwar planning system was to reduce the wasteful transport of people and goods. The ideal was to reverse the trend towards big cities and enlarge the opportunity for small-town living. 'Decentralization means real homes for families within walking distance of pleasant work places and of playing fields and countryside', suggested an exhibition screen designed for the Town and Country Planners Association by Rose Gascoigne in the 1940s. The vision of balance and self-containment was partially realised in the postwar new towns. These great publicly financed projects were direct descendants of the garden city tradition. The original combination of the words 'garden' and 'city' implied something close to the heart of sustainability: modern manu-facturing industry purged of its grime, in balance with its natural setting. The new towns carried to an extreme the nineteenth-century hygienic desire for space, order (particularly the orderly segregation of land uses) and openness. However, they also sought to provide a good social and economic environment with a full range of the necessary social, community and welfare services and high levels of employment. As such, they were exemplary solutions to the nineteenth-century problems of pollution and overcrowding, although in the context of the late twentieth century they can

25 Wood, C (1976) *Town Planning and Pollution Control*, Manchester University Press.

26 Blowers, A (1984) *Something in the Air: Corporate Power and the Environment*, Harper and Row, New York.

27 Wood, C (1989) *Planning Pollution Prevention – A Comparison of Siting Controls Over Air Pollution in Great Britain and the USA*, Heinemann Newnes, London.

be criticised. New towns, like all other towns have no specific relationship with their surrounding countryside and draw much of the population, industry and financial resources from further afield. In their efforts to accommodate the car – and Milton Keynes, with its low density grid system designed to create areas free from traffic is a good example – they are no more sustainable than other towns. Inevitably, the new towns can be criticised when judged against criteria of sustainability that take a harsher view of car use; but in terms of open space and the design of residential areas they provide good examples of environmental quality that is accessible to a broad population.

Looking at much postwar development with the benefit of hindsight, we can see how town planning was forced astray in its response to rapidly rising car ownership and road transport. Effort was put into well-engineered new roads encompassing traffic-free precincts with concrete underpasses while neglecting the inequitable distribution of the car by class and age, as well as its heavy material demands and destructive environmental effects...

No doubt the potential was there in the postwar planning system to shape new developments in the interests of equity, personal safety and environmental quality. In too many areas, life has become less convenient, with services, schools and shops less accessible and with fewer facilities within walking distance of home. An increasing proportion of activities are structured for the benefit of the car-owning majority of households for whom, for example, the weekly trip to the supermarket has brought real benefits in terms of price, and the range of goods, as well as convenience. But there has been a price.[28] Mayer Hillman's research over several decades documents the erosion of local living environments by the motor car. Not all the blame lies at the door of retailers and service providers. It also reflects a failure of regulation and public policy. By comparison with neighbouring northern European countries, British planning has been remarkably slow to promote pedestrian and bicycle circulation.

As with pollution control, the potential for planning to direct transport policy into more environmentally sustainable directions remained dormant for a combination of political and administrative reasons, among them the low position of environmental generalists in the professional pecking order. As a result the most prominent shaping of public policy in new developments has been the wasteful and excessive standards imposed by engineers in the interests of vehicle flow and service maintenance. We have the worst of all worlds: undersized houses amidst oversized suburban roundabouts, car parks, mown verges and turning circles.

(a) The 'greening' of planning

In recent years the planning system has been the subject of a 'greening' process following greater recognition that, by granting planning permission for any new development, the planning authority is in effect sanctioning a new source of waste and pollution. This process has been motivated by debate about the

28 Hillman, M and Cleary, J (1992) 'A Prominent role for walking and cycling in future transport policy', in *A New Transport Policy for Britain* J Roberts et al (eds), Lawrence and Wishart, London.

principle of sustainable development which accompanied the Report of the World Commission on Environment and Development, *Our Common Future* (1987). The United Kingdom's commitment to sustainable development was set out in a White Paper on the environment, *This Common Inheritance.*[29] This identified the planning system as a particularly suitable forum for 'implementing' the principle, and triggered more detailed policy initiatives. For example, Planning Policy Guidance Note 1 *General Policy and Principles* (1992) which sets out the key elements of the government's philosophy on the planning system, charges planning with 'the objective of ensuring that development and growth are sustainable'. Planners were asked to address sustainable development on a local level: the Department of the Environment's *Regional Planning Guidance Note 7 for the Northern Region* (1993) makes this clear:

> The planning system, and the preparation of development plans in particular, can contribute to the objectives of ensuring that development and growth are sustainable. The sum total of decisions in the planning field, as elsewhere, should not deny future generations the best of today's environment. This should be expressed through policies adopted in development planning. (para 8-097)

The policy of achieving sustainable development in the planning system extends and combines the stewardship role and the public interest objective of planning which developed out of the public health movement during the nineteenth century.[30] The explicit recognition of the positive role of planning in environ-mental protection is strengthened by a swing back in favour of a plan-led planning system, directed by the insertion of section 54A into the Town and Country Planning Act 1990. As discussed above, this 'return to plans' provides an opportunity for environmental protection to be translated into planning policy. This is illustrated by the requirement to include environmental policies in unitary development plans or district-wide plans. The potential bite of this is shown by *Nawar v Secretary of State for the Environment.*[31] Here a policy in the local planning authority's draft unitary development plan, requiring that any loss of garden or open space would need to show compensatory benefit in environmental and landscape terms, was held to be a material consideration of the local planning authority. Section 54A also suggests that, if environmental considerations are contained in an applicable development plan, they may be capable of constituting legitimate reasons for the refusal of planning permission.

Debate on the role of planning in environmental protection has therefore broadened far beyond questions of preventing and controlling pollution to encompass issues relating to sustainable development. This may best be illustrated by the effect of transport policies on energy use, conservation and pollution as highlighted by the Royal Commission on Environmental Pollution's Eighteenth Report, *Transport and the Environment* (1994).[32] This emphasises the importance of combining *land use* policies with transport policies at local,

29 HM Government, *This Common Inheritance* Cmnd 1200 (London: HMSO, 1990).
30 See ch 2.
31 [1994] EGCS 132.
32 See ch 1 on 'The way we live'.

regional and national levels. Of particular relevance to this discussion are issues of the respective roles, interrelation and legal scope of planning and pollution control regimes.

(b) Interrelation of planning and pollution controls

There is growing acceptance of a role for planning in environmental protection. For example, the National Rivers Authority acknowledged the central part played by planning in protecting groundwaters from pollution. Groundwater forms part of the natural water cycle which is stored within underground strata (aquifers) and provides over a third of the public water supply. Groundwater is present in the many pores and fractures of the strata and is therefore more at risk from human activity than water contained in defined channels. As *Cambridge Water Co Ltd v Eastern Counties Leather plc*[33] shows, pollution of groundwater is almost impossible to 'clean up'; its *protection* is therefore of paramount concern. Planning contributes to this by operating as a precautionary measure.

National Rivers Authority, *Policy and Practice for the Protection of Groundwater* (Bristol: NRA, 1992)

RELATIONSHIP TO LAND USE PLANNING

Development and use of land is the one consistent element in the list of potential threats to the quality of groundwater; land use planning policies and procedures, therefore, play a significant role in effective groundwater protection.

The process begins at the development plan level. The Regional Planning Guidance procedures now in force provide an obvious route for appropriate policies to be incorporated which will have an impact on the whole of the development planning process. The Planning Policy Guidance Document PPG 12 (February 1992) draws particular attention to the protection of groundwater as a relevant and important environmental objective. Local plans, particularly the mineral and waste plans, are also very relevant to groundwater protection issues. The NRA will be incorporating groundwater protection objectives into its own model planning policies for Local Planning Authorities to consider as part of the development planning process.

...

Many developments may pose a direct or indirect threat to groundwater resources. Where planning permission is required (e.g. chemical stores, residential development, mineral extraction, industrial development) often the only control is by means of conditions on the permission document, an obligation (agreement or undertaking) under Section 106 of the 1990 Act, or by refusal of permission. It is, therefore, important to recognise developments that may be a potential risk to groundwater.

The latter Act introduces a "plan-led" system for Town and Country Planning for the first time. Regional guidance is issued by the Department of the

33 [1994] 2 AC 264, HL extracted as 'A modern postscript' to ch 2.

Environment. Structure Plans, Mineral Local Plans and Waste Local Plans are prepared by County Councils and other Local Plans produced by District Councils. The concepts detailed in this document are highly relevant for inclusion in these more strategic documents which can influence the locations of individual developments.

The NRA is a statutory consultee on development plans and many aspects of development control. In the case of plans, the NRA's views must be considered unless the Planning Authority can justify why its requirements are not to be included. The NRA is also a statutory consultee on Environmental Assessments where these are required.

Guidance to Planning Authorities is given by the Government in the form of Minerals Planning and Policy Guidance Notes. Recent issues (eg MPG 9 and PPG 12) emphasise the environmental importance of planning decisions and refer specifically to the need to ensure that groundwaters are adequately protected.

...

GROUNDWATER PROTECTION POLICY STATEMENTS

...

C.1 The NRA will liaise with Planning Authorities and others to encourage the location of new landfill sites in areas where groundwater is least vulnerable to pollution.

The NRA wishes to encourage developers and planning authorities to consider Non-Aquifers preferentially for new waste disposal activities. In some areas above ground landfills will need to be considered where sufficient below ground void space is not available. The NRA will make maps available and these should be taken into account in the drawing up of Structure and Waste Local Plans.

...

D.3 The NRA will recommend to the Local Planning Authority that it refuse Planning Permission for the redevelopment of contaminated sites where water resources could be adversely affected unless it is satisfied that the proposals include effective measures for the protection of groundwater and surface water quality. It will advise Local Planning Authorities where insufficient or technically weak information has been provided so that they can require the applicant to supplement the details provided.

On sites where contamination of the ground and groundwater pollution is highly likely, a thorough site investigation should take place prior to any application for Planning Permission. Investigation should include an assessment of the leaching characteristics of contaminants in the ground and of the geology/hydrogeology of the site, including existing groundwater quality. This information should support subsequent Planning Applications. These should include a strategy for dealing with contamination and minimising water pollution. Where the site investigation reveals significant groundwater pollution the development proposals should include details of the proposed remedial action.

D.4 The NRA will seek to ensure that Planning Permissions contain certain conditions designed to protect water resources. The NRA will strongly encourage the Local Planning Authorities to enter into planning obligations with developers under Section 106 of the Town and Country Act, 1990 (as substituted by Section 12 of the Planning and Compensation Act 1991) to control and monitor ground and groundwater contamination during and after redevelopment.

Planning obligations should require a remediation plan/method statement to be submitted for the approval of the local planning authority in consultation with the NRA. They should include details of further site investigation, chemical analysis, criteria and standards for removal or treatment of contaminated soil and final restoration. Details of foundations, covering material, drainage and groundwater quality monitoring programmes should also be included.

D.5 The NRA will, by liaison with Planning Authorities and industry, seek to influence the preferential location of new industrial development in areas which are not vulnerable to groundwater pollution.

The NRA will also, by liaison with HMIP and other regulatory bodies, seek to ensure that authorisations granted to industry prevent future contamination of land and groundwater.

It is important to recognise that land is continually being contaminated. The NRA wishes to ensure that these areas are minimised in the future, especially where new industries are located in green field sites. Through consultation on Draft Development Plans, the NRA will indicate areas vulnerable to groundwater pollution.

With this enhanced role for planning authorities in controlling pollution comes the possibility of overlapping with existing pollution controls. The opportunities for this are seen particularly clearly in *Gateshead Metropolitan Borough Council v Secretary of State for the Environment and Northumbrian Water Group*[34] which raises the issue of the extent to which the functions and efficiency of Her Majesty's Inspectorate of Pollution (now subsumed in the Environment Agency) may legitimately be taken into account by the Secretary of State for the Environment in the context of an appeal for planning permission. The Secretary of State for the Environment granted planning permission for a clinical waste incinerator near Gateshead. The Inspector appointed to hear the appeal had recommended that permission be refused. One of the issues which was taken into account by the Inspector was the local public's fear that dioxins emitted from the site would be harmful. The Secretary of State concluded that this issue could be satisfactorily addressed as part of the Integrated Pollution Control authorisation procedure. That decision was challenged by the local planning authority on the ground that the planning system and Integrated Pollution Control were so closely linked that it would be unreasonable to grant planning

34 [1995] Env LR 36.

permission without knowing if emissions could be adequately controlled under the Integrated Pollution Control authorisation. The High Court, confirmed by the Court of Appeal, decided that although the two statutory requirements overlapped, the extent of the overlap would vary on every occasion. Sullivan J held:

> ...just as the environmental impact of such emissions is a material planning consideration, so also is the existence of a stringent regime under the Environmental Protection Act 1990 for preventing or mitigating that impact and for rendering any emissions harmless.[35]

This reasoning makes clear that, in appropriate cases, misgivings by the local planning authority about a project's effect upon the environment may be resolved by imposing conditions in the Integrated Pollution Control authorisation process. The trust placed in the operation of the system of Integrated Pollution Control by Sullivan J, and endorsed by the Court of Appeal, circumscribes the means by which planning controls might *prevent* environmental pollution. Local planning authorities can still refuse planning permission on the grounds of harm to the environment, but they must adduce certain evidence of that harm. This is a countervailing approach to the precautionary principle, which guides policy making. The following passage is taken from the Court of Appeal judgment.

Gateshead Metropolitan Borough Council v Secretary of State for the Environment and Northumbrian Water Group [1995] Env LR 36, 40-50

GLIDEWELL LJ: This appeal relates to an activity which, in general terms, is subject to planning controls under the Town and Country Planning Act, and to control as a prescribed process under Part I of the Environmental Protection Act 1990. The main issue in the appeal is, what is the proper approach for the Secretary of State for the Environment to adopt where these two statutory regimes apply and, to an extent, overlap?

The Northumbrian Water Group Plc ("NWG") wish to construct and operate an incinerator for the disposal of clinical waste on a site some nine acres in extent, comprising about half of the area of the disused Felling Sewage Treatment Works at Wardley in the Metropolitan Borough of Gateshead. Under the Town and Country Planning Act planning permission is necessary for the construction of the incinerator and for the commencement of its use thereafter. The proposed incineration is a prescribed process within section 2 of the Environmental Protection (Prescribed Processes, etc.) Regulations 1991 as amended. An authorisation to carry on the process of incineration is therefore required by section 6 of the Environmental Protection Act 1990 and Schedule 1 of the Environmental Protection Act. In this case, the enforcing authority which is responsible for granting such an authorisation is HM Inspectorate of Pollution ("HMIP").

Two applications were made to Gateshead, the Local Planning Authority, for planning permission for the construction of the incinerator. The appeal is

35 At 44.

only concerned with the second, which was an outline application submitted on October 26, 1991. The application was refused by Gateshead by a notice dated February 4, 1991 for six reasons which I summarise as follows. The proposal is contrary to the provisions of the approved Development Plan, both the Local Plan and the County Structure Plan; the use of the land for waste disposal conflicts with the allocation of neighbouring land for industrial and/or warehousing purposes and could prejudice the development of that land; since there was no national or regional planning framework which identified the volume of clinical waste which was likely to arise, the proposal was premature, the applicants have failed to supply sufficient information that the plant could be operated without causing a nuisance to the locality; the applicants have failed to demonstrate that the overall effects on the environment, particularly in relation to health risk, have been fully investigated and taken account of. Then there was finally a ground relating to the reclamation and development of the site stating that no proposals have been submitted demonstrating how contamination arising from its previous use could be treated. That point does not arise in this appeal.

NWG appealed against the refusal to the Secretary of State. An inquiry into the appeal was heard by an Inspector of the Department of the Environment, Mr C. A. Jennings Bsc Ceng, with the assistance of Dr Waring, a Chemical Assessor, between April 9 and May 1, 1991. The Inspector and the assessor reported to the Secretary of State on August 3, 1992. The Inspector recommended that permission be refused. The Secretary of State by letter dated 24 May, 1993 allowed the appeal and granted outline permission subject to conditions. Gateshead applied to the High Court under section 288 of the Town and Country Planning Act 1990 for an order that the Secretary of State's decision be quashed. On September 29, 1993 Mr Jeremy Sullivan QC sitting as Deputy High Court Judge dismissed the application. Gateshead now appeal to this Court. The relevant provisions of the Town and Country Planning Act comprise sections 54A, 72(2) and 79(4). The effect of those sections is that, in determining the appeal the Secretary of State was required to decide in accordance with the provisions of the Development Plan unless material considerations indicated otherwise, and to decide in accordance with other material considerations.

In the Environmental Protection Act 1990, section 2(1) provides:

> "The Secretary of State may, by regulations, prescribe any description of process as a process for the carrying on of which after a prescribed date an authorisation is required under section 6 below."

It is agreed that the operation of the incinerator is such a process. By section 6(1)

> "No such person shall carry on a prescribed process after the date prescribed or determined for that description of process by..."

relevant regulations,

> "except under an authorisation granted by the enforcing authority and in accordance with the conditions to which it is subject."

The enforcing authority in this case means, strictly, the Chief Inspector, but in practice HMIP. Section 6(2) provides:

> "An application for any authorisation shall be made to the enforcing authority in accordance with Part I of Schedule 1 of the Act..."

Section 6 continues:

> (3)"Where an application is duly made to the enforcing authority, the authority shall grant the authorisation subject to the conditions required, authorisation to be imposed by section 7 below or refuse the application."
>
> (4)"An application shall not be granted unless the enforcing authority considers that the applicant will be able to carry on the process so as to comply with the conditions which would be included in the authorisation."

Section 7(1) deals with conditions which are required to be attached to any authorisation. By section 7(1)(a)

> "There shall be included in an authorisation – such specific conditions as the enforcing authority considers are appropriate...for achieving the objectives specified in subsection (2) below."

Those objectives are:

> "(a) ensuring that, in carrying on a prescribed process, the best available techniques not entailing excessive cost will be used-
> (i) for preventing the release of substances prescribed for any environmental medium into that medium or, where that is not practicable by such means, for reducing the release of such substances to a minimum and rendering harmless any such substances which are so released; and
> (ii) for rendering harmless any other substances which might cause harm if released into any environmental medium."

Finally by subsection (4)

> "Subject to subsections (5) and (6) below, there is implied in every authorisation a general condition that, in carrying on the process to which the authorisation applies, the person carrying it on use the best available techniques not entailing excessive cost for.."

precisely the same purposes as those set out in subsection (2). When the inquiry was held an application had been made to HM Inspectorate for an authorisation, but that had not yet been determined.

...

I comment first about the relationship between control under the Town and Country Planning Act and the Environmental Protection Act. In very broad terms the former is concerned with the control of the use of land, and the Environmental Protection Act with control (at least in the present respect) of the damaging effect on the environment of a process which causes pollution. Clearly these control regimes overlap.

Government policy overall is set out in a White Paper called "This Common Inheritance, Britain's Environmental Strategy", which is Cm 1200. The main part of this to which reference was made during the hearing of the appeal and before the Learned Deputy Judge is paragraph 6.39 which reads:

> "Planning control is primarily concerned with the type and location of new development and changes of use. Once broad land uses have been sanctioned by

> the planning process it is the job of the pollution control authorities to limit the adverse effects the operations may have on the environment. But in practice there is common ground. In considering whether to grant planning permission for a particular development a local authority must consider all the effects including potential pollution; permission should not be granted if that might expose people to danger."

There is also an earlier passage which is relevant in paragraph numbered 1.18 headed precautionary action. The latter part of that paragraph reads:

> "Where there are significant risks of damage to the environment, the Government will be prepared to take precautionary action to limit the use of potentially dangerous materials or the spread of potentially dangerous pollutants, even where scientific knowledge is not conclusive, if the balance of likely costs and benefits justifies it. This precautionary principle applies particularly where there are good grounds for judging either that action taken promptly at comparatively low cost may avoid more costly damage later, or that irreversible effects may follow if action is delayed".

More specific guidance relating to the application of Planning Control under the Planning Acts is to be given in a Planning Policy Guidance Note. This was in draft at the time of the inquiry. The Draft of Consultation was issued in June 1992 and, as I understand it, is still in this state. However, reference was made to it during the inquiry and Mr Mole, for Gateshead, has referred us to two paragraphs in particular. These are:

> "125. It is not the job of the planning system to duplicate controls which are the statutory responsibility of other bodies (including local authorities in their non-planning functions). Planning controls are not an appropriate means of regulating the detailed characteristics of industrial processes. Nor should planning authorities substitute their own judgment on pollution control issues for that of the bodies with the relevant expertise and the responsibility for statutory control over those matters.
>
> 126. While pollution controls seek to protect health in the environment, planning controls are concerned with the impact of the development on the use of land and the appropriate use of land. Where the potential for harm to man and the environment affects the use of land (eg by precluding the use of neighbouring land for a particular purpose or by making use of that land inappropriate because of, say, the risk to an underlying aquifer) then planning and pollution controls may overlap. It is important to provide safeguards against loss of amenity which may be caused by pollution. The dividing line between planning and pollution control considerations is therefore not always clear-cut. In such cases close consultation between planning and pollution control authorities will be important at all stages, in particular because it would not be sensible to grant planning permission for a development for which a necessary pollution control authorisation is unlikely to be forthcoming".

Neither the passages which I have read from the White Paper, nor those from the draft Planning Policy Guidance are statements of law. Nevertheless, it seems to me that they are sound statements of common sense. Mr Mole submits, and I agree, that the extent to which discharges from a proposed plan will necessarily or probably pollute the atmosphere and/or create an unacceptable risk of harm to human beings, animals or other organisms, is a material consideration to be taken into account when deciding whether to grant planning permission. The Deputy Judge accepted that submission also. But the Deputy Judge said at page 17 of his judgment, and in this respect I also agree with him,

> "Just as the environmental impact of such emissions is a material planning consideration, so also is the existence of a stringent regime under the Environmental Protection Act for preventing or mitigating that impact and for rendering any emissions harmless. It is too simplistic to say, 'The Secretary of State cannot leave the question of pollution to the Environmental Protection Act'."

...

The central issue is whether the Secretary of State is correct in saying that the controls under the Environmental Protection Act are adequate to deal with the concerns of the Inspector and the assessor. The decision which was to be made on the appeal to the Secretary of State lay in the area in which the regimes of control under the Planning Act and the Environmental Protection Act overlapped. If it had become clear at the inquiry that some of the discharges were bound to be unacceptable so that a refusal by HMIP to grant an authorisation would be the only proper course, the Secretary of State following his own express policy should have refused planning permission. But that was not the situation. At the conclusion of the inquiry, there was no clear evidence about the quality of the air in the vicinity of the site. Moreover, for the purposes of deciding what standards or recommendations as to emissions to apply, the Inspector described the site itself as "semi-rural", whilst the area of maximum impact to the east he described as "distinctly rural".

Once the information about air quality at both these locations was obtained, it was a matter for informed judgment (i) what, if any, increases in polluting discharges of various elements into the air were acceptable, and (ii) whether the best available techniques etc. would ensure that those discharges were kept within acceptable limits.

Those issues are clearly within the competence and jurisdiction of HMIP. If in the end the Inspectorate conclude that the best available techniques etc would not achieve the results required by section 7(2) and 7(4), it may well be that the proper course would be for them to refuse an authorisation. Certainly, in my view, since the issue has been expressly referred to them by the Secretary of State, they should not consider that the grant of planning permission inhibits them from refusing authorisation if they decide in their discretion that this is the proper course.

Thus, in my judgment, this was not a case in which it was apparent that a refusal of authorisation will, or will probably be, the only proper decision for HMIP to make. The Secretary of State was therefore justified in concluding that the areas of concern which led to the Inspector and the assessor recommending refusal were matters which could properly be decided by HMIP, and that their powers were adequate to deal with those concerns. ...

For these reasons, I conclude that the Secretary of State did not err in law, nor did he reach a decision which was irrational or in any other way outside his statutory powers...

The Secretary of State's argument for the 'separation' of planning from pollution issues, accepted by the Court of Appeal, derives from confidence that the pollution controls wielded by Her Majesty's Inspectorate of Pollution (HMIP) (now the Environment Agency) are achieving many of the aims of the Environmental Protection Act 1990. However, the most comprehensive study of the effectiveness of the Integrated Pollution Control regime, *Integrated Pollution Control: The First Three Years* (1994),[36] discussed in more detail in chapter 6, suggests that it has not ensured a real commitment to the key concepts of environmental protection underlying the 1990 Act. This report suggests that, in contrast to the Secretary of State's view held in *Gateshead*, the planning system can validly be concerned with the 'operational' element of facilities that are under the control of the Environment Agency. This case also suggests the possibility that more comprehensive planning control of damaging activities might be brought about by linking Integrated Pollution Control procedures with the planning system, for example by requiring a single assessment for the purpose of establishing the best practicable environmental option (BPEO),[37] which constitutes part of the authorisation procedure under Part I of the Environmental Protection Act 1990, and for planning authorisation requirements.

(c) Precautionary planning?

The planning system provides a forum for the application of precautionary measures (action which is taken in the face of uncertainty). Precaution has not generally been referred to as a distinct principle in planning policy but rather accords with the general preventive approach underpinning the system and its inherently preventive functions: screening development and controlling the location of polluting development. This state of affairs is changing, with more explicit reference to the principle being made in development plans,[38] planning literature,[39] and by pressure groups.[40] Furthermore, the amendment of the Environment Title of the EC Treaty to include an implicit reference to the European Union's competence in matters of town and country planning[41] suggests the possibility of a forceful combination of planning's preventive qualities with the European Union's specific commitment to the precautionary principle in Article 130r(2) EC. The precautionary principle has also been applied in the planning context in case law. In *Alfred McAlpine Homes (North) Ltd v Secretary of State for the Environment*,[42] the Secretary of State approved the Cheshire Replacement Development Plan, but modified it in a manner which severely restricted the release of green belt land for housing, as he is

36 Environmental Data Services Ltd, *Integrated Pollution Control: The First Three Years* (London: ENDS, 1994).

37 See ch 6.

38 For example Newbury District Council included such policies in its recently adopted local plan, *Planning Week*, 18 November 1993.

39 S Tromans, 'High Talk and Low Cunning: Putting Environmental Principles into Legal Practice', [1995] JPEL 779-796; and W Walton, A Ross-Robertson and J Rowan-Robertson, 'The Precautionary Principle and the UK Planning System', (1995) ELM 7(1) 35-40.

40 Campaign for the Protection of Rural England (CPRE), *General Policy and Principles: Response to the Department of the Environment's Draft Planning Policy Guidance Note 1* (London: CPRE, 1991) in which the CPRE suggest that the precautionary principle could be incorporated into planning policy informing planning authorities in the preparation of development plans and in the determination of planning applications.

41 Article 130s(2) EC.

42 [1994] NPC 138, CA.

entitled to do by section 35(1) of the Town and Country Planning Act 1990. The reason the Secretary of State gave for modifying the development plan was that he had applied the precautionary principle so as to reduce the risk of unacceptable consequences for the environment and character of Chester. The Secretary of State decided that future releases of green belt land should not go ahead until a more thorough examination has been carried out of the likely consequences of the loss of land on the character of the city and the long-standing protection of green belt areas. This decision rendered Alfred McAlpine Homes Ltd unable to build on their land. In the application for judicial review of this decision before the Queen's Bench Division, Moriarty J supported this cautious approach to the release of green belt land on the ground that a decision to maintain the green belt is capable of revocation, but a decision to relax the constraints is irrevocable. The judgment, followed by the Court of Appeal, is based on the irreversibility of environmental harm and acceptance of the need to take precautionary action in order to achieve sustainable development of land. Here, the planning system exercised its traditional function of controlling and preventing land use and development on land designated for special protection, in this case green belt land. This might be compared with planning's more complex function of controlling pollution examined in *Gateshead.* After all, the logic of the precautionary approach is to expand the scope of matters over which the planning authority has traditionally exercised controls to include, inter alia, the adequacy of pollution control authorities to limit and render harmless emissions. The former functions are legally acceptable. But the more far-reaching precautionary function of controlling pollution at its source (at the planning and design stages) was circumscribed in *Gateshead* because of the inevitable overlap and possible duplication with pollution controls exercised by HMIP. Both cases underline the distinction between the law and policy aspects of planning control. As a statement of policy, the precautionary principle may be disregarded at will. Inspectors will therefore use the term and give it such weight as they think appropriate in deciding whether or not the impacts of a particular development are such that planning permission should be refused. The application of the precautionary principle to planning decisions might also be lessened in practice because it remains broadly the case that it is for the local planning authority to demonstrate why an application should be refused rather than for the applicant to demonstrate why it should be permitted;[43] the latter representing the more precautionary approach.

(d) Legal scope of planning controls

Planning conditions which are designed to secure objectives of environmental protection must fulfil the *Newbury*[44] tests, as discussed above. It is clear that conditions may be imposed to regulate land use, for example to ensure decontamination of soil or the removal of chemicals, and to ensure proper

43 Walton et al, *supra*, at 35. A notable exception is that category of cases subject to environmental assessment.

44 *Newbury District Council v Secretary of State for the Environment* [1981] AC 578. See 'Planning Tools: Conditions and Obligations', above.

reinstatement of land after the use. Policy guidance suggests also that conditions may be imposed to protect amenity or limit the hours of operation of a facility.[45] As confirmed in *Gateshead*, less appropriate is the use of conditions to control the level of emissions from a proposed development where they are subject to pollution control.

The broader scope of planning obligations when compared with conditions is significant because it suggests that if a developer is prepared to agree to terms restricting the development or use of land in order to mitigate, or compensate for, the adverse effects of development on the environment, these terms may be far more extensive than mitigating measures which form the basis of planning conditions. It might then be possible for the *processes* and operations of a factory to be controlled with a view to minimising any possible nuisances by the terms of a planning obligation, whereas it has been considered undesirable to impose such restrictions on the working of a factory as part of a planning condition,[46] because conditions should 'fairly and reasonably' relate to the use and development of land.

It is unfortuante that financial restraints have been imposed on local authorities at the same time as greater responsibility for environmental protection. It is therefore perhaps understandable that planning obligations are used to mitigate the environmental effects of development or to compensate for them in some way. So, planning obligations might have as their objective that certain 'green gains' be achieved: that is, that some environmental (as opposed to the more usual infrastructure or financial) benefit be provided by the developer. 'Green gains' highlight particularly well the vexed question of related benefits: can compensatory 'gains' such as parkland ever fully compensate for, and be related to, the loss of wetlands? The courts have established that, if a developer proposes to mitigate the effects of his development by supplying some sort of public gain, the developer must identify it with precision and demonstrate that it was capable of implementation or achievement by a planning agreement or unilateral undertaking.[47] If there is a legally binding agreement or undertaking which would produce substantial environmental improvements to the existing site, this could appear to justify and offset the loss and adverse environmental effects and be seen as coming within the proper ambit of planning obligations. The courts have tended to follow a 'compensatory' approach rather than an 'alleviation' approach to planning gain in that the planning obligation does not *prevent* the loss but nevertheless makes it acceptable by the gain.[48]

45 Department of the Environment, Planning Policy Guidance Note 23, *Planning and Pollution Control* (London: HMSO, 1992), paras 3.24 and 3.25.

46 *Western Fish Products Ltd v Penwith District Council* [1981] 2 All ER 204.

47 *Collins v Secretary of State for the Environment and Langbaurgh on Tees Borough Council* [1996] JPEL 303; see also *Wimpey Homes Holdings Ltd v Secretary of State for the Environment* [1993] JPEL 919.

48 See P Healey, M Purdue, and J Ennis, *Negotiating Development: Rationales and Practice for Development Obligations and Planning Gain* (London: Spon, 1995); see also, S Boucher and S Whatmore, 'Green Gains? Planning by Agreement and Nature Conservation', (1993) JEPM Vol 36, No 1, 33.

There is a fine line between achieving greater congruence between the planning system and pollution control systems to achieve mitigation of adverse environmental effects, and guarding against unnecessary overlaps. In policy guidance, the line appears now to be drawn so as to dissuade planning authorities from imposing conditions and negotiating planning agreements to achieve mitigation which go beyond regulating the physical use of the land, as the following extract from the Department of the Environment's Planning Policy Guidance Note 23, *Planning and Pollution Control* (1992) shows. This demonstrates also the dynamic relationship between policy and law: the judgment of the court in *Gateshead* on the proper relationship between pollution control and planning authorities is incorporated wholesale into the policy guidance.

Department of the Environment, Planning Policy Guidance Note 23, *Planning and Pollution Control* (London: HMSO, 1992)

1.1 **The planning and pollution control systems are separate but complementary** in that both are designed to protect the environment from the potential harm caused by development and operations, but with different objectives. In recent years, increasing awareness of environmental priorities has led local planning authorities to take a greater interest in controlling polluting activities. Yet at the same time the effectiveness and scope of environmental protection legislation has expanded rapidly.

...

1.33 **The role of the planning system focuses on whether the development itself is an acceptable use of the land rather than the control of the processes or substances themselves.** It also assumes that the pollution control regime will operate effectively. In the case of developments with which this PPG is concerned, the material considerations are likely to include:

- location, taking into account such considerations as the reasons for selecting the chosen site itself;
- impact on amenity;
- the risk and impact of potential pollution from the development insofar as this might have an effect on the use of other land;
- prevention of nuisance;
- impact on the road and other transport networks and on the surrounding environment; and
- need, where relevant, and feasibility of restoring the land to standards for an appropriate after use.

Planning controls can therefore complement the pollution control regime, and thus help secure the proper operation and rehabilitation of potentially polluting development.

1.34 The dividing line between planning and pollution controls is not always clear cut. Both seek to protect the environment. Matters which will be relevant to a pollution control authorisation or licence may also be material considerations to be taken into account in planning decisions. The weight to be attached to such matters will depend on the scope of the pollution control system in each particular case.

...

3.24 Planning authorities should not therefore seek to control through planning measures matters that are the proper concern of the pollution control authority, except where planning matters can be clearly distinguished. For example, a planning condition would not normally be appropriate to control the level of emissions from a proposed development, where they are subject to pollution control; however, a planning condition may need to be imposed to protect amenity or limit the hours of operation of the plant.

3.25 Planning authorities may use conditions or planning obligations to meet planning goals to protect the environment, where these are relevant to the development proposed, for example, to:

- require the use of particular transport modes. Conditions and planning obligations may also be used to require the posting of notices requesting lorry drivers either to use or avoid particular routes, and operators may offer to restrict their lorries to particular routes. But a condition or planning obligation should not seek to control the right of passage over a public highway;
- ensure the decontamination of the soil or the removal of chemicals, and, where appropriate, the reinstatement of the land to the standards required for the agreed after use, if the use of the land ceases;
- ensure proper restoration and aftercare management of the land on landfill sites;
- require particular developments to make provision for recycling facilities, where appropriate.

The guidance states that planning legislation should not normally be used to secure objectives achievable under other legislation and that planning controls are not an appropriate means of regulating the detailed characteristics of industrial processes.

However, judicial sanctioning of expansive planning obligations in cases such as *Tesco Stores Ltd v Secretary of State for the Environment*[49] suggests that there might still be scope for planning obligations to deal with matters beyond the physical use of land and impose *standards* of performance or operation akin to those currently employed in pollution control authorisations.

4 CONTROL OF LAND USE IN THE COUNTRYSIDE

Another means of controlling the use and development of land is the designation of an area for special protection. On the whole, this has developed as a separate legal entity from town planning. This is because the use of land for agricultural and forestry purposes, the major determinants of the state of the environment in rural areas, is generally excluded from the scope of anticipatory land use

49 [1995] 2 All ER 636.

controls under the Town and Country Planning Act 1990, the title of the Act being something of a misnomer. Macrory and Sheate describe the exclusion of use of land for agricultural and forestry purposes as a *leitmotif* of the British planning system.[50] This state of affairs originates in the *Report of the Committee on Land Utilisation in Rural Areas*, the Scott Report (1943).[51] The Scott Report came out strongly with the view that prosperous farming was essential for aesthetic and social reasons as well as for food production. The dissenting opinion in the Report, given by Professor SR Dennison advocates rather that farmers be paid for conservation and that planning controls should be extended to the use and development of land in countryside areas. Professor Dennison's call for 'more comprehensive planning control' was not heeded; the Town and Country Planning Act 1947 excluded farming and forestry activities from the definition of 'development'. The conceptual, practical and legal split between the 'countryside' activities of agriculture and forestry and all other types of development, fostered by the majority opinion of the Scott Report, became settled in planning law and led to the evolution of different legal techniques for environmental protection in urban and rural areas. The focus here is on the legal technique of designating areas of land for special protection or treatment.

(a) Countryside designation

The National Parks and Access to the Countryside Act 1949[52] provides the basic machinery for the designation and administration of National Parks to be chosen for their landscape and recreational value, Areas of Outstanding Natural Beauty (AONBs) chosen on landscape grounds alone; and National Nature Reserves and Sites of Special Scientific Interest (SSSIs)[53] to safeguard places with special flora, fauna, physiography, or geology. Section 5 of the National Parks and Access to the Countryside Act 1949 included as the objectives of the Act: 'preserving and enhancing the natural beauty of the areas...and promoting their enjoyment by the public'. A new section 5 is inserted by section 61 of the Environment Act 1995 which reads:

> (1) The provisions of this Part of this Act shall have effect for the purpose-
> (a) of conserving and enhancing the natural beauty, wildlife and cultural heritage of the areas specified in the next following subsection; and
> (b) of promoting opportunities for the understanding and enjoyment of the special qualities of those areas by the public.

The modern United Kingdom conservation framework consists also of the Wildlife and Countryside Act 1981, amended in 1985 and 1991. Part II of the 1981 Act establishes a specific system of protection for SSSIs (the areas provided for in the 1949 Act because of their features of special interest). This is based on compensation payments being made to landowners or occupiers for profits

50 R Macrory and W Sheate, 'Agriculture and the European Community Environmental Assessment Directive: Lessons for Community Policy Making', (1989) *Journal of Common Market Studies* Vol 28, No 1, 68-81, at 78.

51 Cmnd 6378. The Report is discussed more fully in ch 3, 'Separation of land use controls – the town and the country'.

52 As amended by the Countryside Act 1968 and Part III of the Environment Act 1995.

53 Areas of Special Scientific Interest (ASSIs) in Northern Ireland.

foregone following notification of the site as a SSSI (section 28 of the 1981 Act) by one of the United Kingdom conservation bodies: English Nature, Scottish Natural Heritage and the Countryside Council for Wales. The notification sent by the conservation agency to an owner or occupier of a site contains a list of all operations which, in the agency's view, could damage the site. Notice must be given in writing by the occupier or owner of any such operations at least four months before they are carried out. During that period, the conservation agency will give consent to the operation, refuse it, or invite the owner or occupier to consider modifications which might avoid damaging the wildlife or site. Under section 15 of the 1981 Act, the conservation body may offer the owner or occupier a payment in return for a management agreement that protects the features of the site by restricting the operations that can be carried out. The following, taken from a 'menu' of potentially damaging operations, used by the nature conservancy agencies when drawing up management agreements, indicates the potential breadth of control.[54]

Nature Conservancy Council, *Site Management Plans for Conservation: A Working Guide* (Peterborough: NCC, 1991)

Operations likely to damage the features of special interest

1. Cultivation, including ploughing, rotovating, harrowing and re-seeding.
2. Changes in the grazing regime (including type of stock, intensity or seasonal pattern of grazing and cessation of grazing).
3. Changes in stock feeding practice.
4. Changes in the mowing or cutting regime (including hay-making to silage and cessation).
5. Application of manure, fertilisers and lime.
6. Application of pesticides, including herbicides (weedkillers).
7. Dumping, spreading or discharge of any materials.
8. Burning (and) changes in the pattern or frequency of burning.
9. The release into the site of any wild, feral or domestic animal*, plant or seed.

*'animal' includes any mammal, reptile, amphibian, bird, fish or invertebrate.

10. The killing or removal of any wild animal* including pest control.
11. The destruction, displacement, removal or cutting of any plant or plant remains, including tree, shrub, herb, hedge, dead or decaying wood, moss, lichen, fungus, leaf-mould, turf etc.
12. Changes in tree and/or wood management, including afforestation, planting, clear and selective felling, thinning, coppicing, modification of the stand or underwood, changes in species composition, cessation of management.

...

There are a number of problems with the system of designating SSSIs. Primarily, notification of a SSSI does not guarantee absolute protection: owners can

54 See also a judicial interpretation of what constitutes potentially damaging operations in *Sweet v Secretary of State for the Environment and Nature Conservancy Council* [1989] JPEL 927.

legally carry out damaging activities if they have given notice to a conservation agency and the four month period, available to the agencies to negotiate a management agreement, has expired. Damage may also be caused by third parties who are not covered by SSSI procedures, as seen in *Southern Water Authority v Nature Conservancy Council*,[55] in which the House of Lords decided that for the purposes of section 28 of the Wildlife and Countryside Act 1981, someone is an occupier if they have some form of stable relationship with the land. As a result, a water authority which carried out drainage works, described as an act of 'ecological vandalism' by the House of Lords, whilst temporarily working on a SSSI did not commit an offence under section 28 of the 1981 Act even though the company knew that its operations were 'potentially damaging'. Nor can SSSIs be isolated from the effects of development on adjacent or nearby land. A grant of planning permission constitutes a defence to the criminal offence of carrying out a potentially damaging operation;[56] local and private Acts of Parliament and Statutory Orders may also allow developments to proceed which damage the site.

Of particular significance is that even if the owners or occupiers agree to enter into a voluntary agreement, at present it is most likely that any agreement reached will be of a negative nature, that is not implementing a potentially damaging operation, rather than including more positive commitments to manage the land in some environmentally advantageous manner. This aspect of the designation system leaves the conservation agencies open to having to pay very large sums in compensation to landowners and occupiers. The practice subverts the principle of Community environmental policy that the 'polluter pays', and emphasises that, for purposes of controlling environmental damage, agriculture and forestry remain a special case. These aspects underline that notification of a SSSI might be disregarded.

Voluntariness is the main feature of the system of SSSI and other designations under the Wildlife and Countryside Act 1981. This reflects the assumption of the Scott Report that farmers are the 'nation's landscape gardeners' and 'guardians of the countryside'.[57] It is this feature, above all others, which has meant that the designation of a site as a SSSI has failed to safeguard wildlife sites. The National Audit Office recently reported that since 1987, there have been 869 cases of loss and damage to SSSIs in England alone. In 1993, 40 SSSIs suffered long term damage.[58] Several of the limitations of the SSSI system and its interplay with the planning system may be seen in *R v Poole Borough Council, ex p Beebee*.[59] The case underlines that planning permission may be granted although development is to take place on a SSSI. It shows also that the nature of the 'material considerations' formulation means that it is very difficult to challenge the weight given to the various considerations

55 [1992] 3 All ER 481.

56 Section 28(7) of the Wildlife and Countryside Act 1981, as amended; for example, in *R v Poole Borough Council, ex p Beebee* [1991] JPEL 643 the Council granted itself permission to build houses on a SSSI.

57 See ch 3.

58 National Audit Office, *Protecting and Managing SSSIs*, (see below)(London: HMSO, 1994).

59 [1991] JPEL 643.

including that the land is a SSSI, by the local planning authority. The strongly procedural rather than substantive nature of the environmental assessment process is also illustrated by this case.[60] Schiemann J considered that the information which would have come to light during the formal environmental assessment process, was already in the local planning authority's possession, thus effectively ignoring the contribution expert opinion and public participation (elements of a formal environmental assessment process) might make to gathering and evaluating information about the environmental effects of the development.

R v Poole Borough Council, ex p Beebee [1991] JPEL 643

In April 1989 Poole Borough Council granted itself planning permission for a housing development on land forming part of Canford Heath. The land was included in a site of special interest. The Nature Conservancy Council had objected to the development proposals and had requested the Secretary of State to call it in. This was refused. The applicants applied for judicial review.

SCHIEMANN J.,

...

The applicants' grounds of challenge were in substance threefold.

1. The Council had not taken into account a relevant consideration, namely the fact that the subject sites were part of an SSSI.
2. The Council had improperly failed to consider whether an environmental impact assessment should be carried out in relation to the subject sites prior to the grant of planning permission.
3. The Council had given excessive weight to the fact that in 1984 residential planning permission had been granted for the subject site and wrongly applied an alleged presumption in favour of the grant of planning permission.

The statute obliged local planning authorities to give reasons for *refusing* planning permission but did not oblige them to give reasons for *granting* planning permission. Statute gave those who have been refused planning permission a right of appeal on the merits but gave no right of appeal to those who disapproved of the grant of planning permission to another. Whereas in some countries there was a legal obligation on any public decision-making authority to set out in any decisions its motivation – that was the matters which it has taken into account – there was no such general rule in this country.

...

Nor was there in Town and Country Planning legislation, what could be found in some other statutes, a provision whereby any person affected by an unmotivated decision could write and ask for reasons...

...

Turning to examine the three grounds of challenge, first, the Council had not taken into account a relevant consideration, namely the fact that the subject

60 See further ch 10.

sites were part of an SSSI. That was the first submission. It was common ground that the subject sites were part of an SSSI and that this was a relevant consideration. Further, it was common ground that the Council knew that the NCC wished to extend the boundary of the existing SSSI so as to include the subject sites, and apparently took that factor into account.

The wording of the officer's report with its references to "intention to extend the boundaries of the SSSI" and "proposed SSSI boundary" was unfortunate and supported the applicants' contention that the Council might well have proceeded on the basis that the subject sites were not as yet within an SSSI. Hence Mr. Ryan's submission that the Council had failed to take into consideration a relevant consideration, namely that the subject sites were within an SSSI. That submission is justified.

However, although in general, once the submission had been accepted that the decision maker failed to take into account a relevant consideration, the decision would be quashed, he (Schiemann J.) did not think that the result should follow in the instant case. His reason for so holding was that the officer preparing the report, and the Council, had taken into account the substance of what they were required to take into account.

The procedure for establishing an SSSI under section 28 of the Wildlife and Countryside Act 1981 used to be that the NCC gave notice of a proposed notification to the owner, invited him to make representations, considered his representations and then decided whether or not to notify the owner that it considered the site to be one of special scientific interest and specifying operations which appeared to the Council likely to damage the flora or fauna on that site. If the owner, having been notified of the NCC's decision, thereafter carried out any notified operation without consent, he committed an offence. Further, the local planning authority was under an obligation to consult the NCC prior to granting any planning permission in relation to such a notified site. That regime proved to be defective because some owners who had been served with a notice of proposed notification thereupon set to and destroyed the site without waiting to see whether or not the notification was ever made.

By the Wildlife and Countryside (Amendment) Act of 1985 this loophole was closed and a different regime was established. Nowadays the site is protected whilst the NCC are considering representations. That protection is withdrawn if the NCC is persuaded by objections that the site should not be protected. ... The purpose of the old regime and the new regime, so far as presently relevant was to ensure that the planning authority, prior to granting any planning permission, was appraised of the fact that the NCC regard the site as one of special scientific interest. In the present case there was no doubt that the planning authority might not have been aware of the reasons for it. The fact that the planning authority might not have been aware that the site had been formally notified under the new regime did not deprive them of knowledge of any material underlying fact...

Turning to the second submission, this was that the Council had improperly failed to consider whether an environmental impact assessment should be carried out in relation to the subject sites prior to the grant of planning permission. It was common ground that this was not considered by the Council, and it was common ground that they were not obliged as a matter of law to carry out such an environmental impact assessment. However, Mr Ryan submitted that they should have considered whether or not to carry out such an environmental impact assessment and that their failure so to consider should lead to the permissions being quashed.

...

This point could be disposed of when one remembered that the purpose, in circumstances such as the present, of any environmental assessment was to draw to the attention of the authority material relevant to the coming of a decision. In the present case it seemed that the appropriate bodies, the NCC and the BHS [British Herpetological Society], had drawn the significant factors to the attention of the authority, and so the authority had in their possession the substance of what they would have had if they had applied their minds to the 1988 Regulations and had prepared such an environmental statement. The substance of all the environmental information which was likely to emerge from going through the formal process envisaged by the regulations had already emerged and was apparently present in the Council's mind. In those circumstances it would be wrong to quash either of their resolutions on the basis of this submission.

Turning to the third one, this was that the Council had given excessive weight to the fact that in 1984 residential planning permission had been granted for the subject sites and wrongly applied an alleged presumption in favour of the grant of planning permission. Mr Ryan submitted that this case raised a point of general concern as to the proper approach to a planning application in an area which had the highest status in conservation terms. He pointed out that the site here was (a) an SSSI under the Wildlife and Countryside Act 1981; (b) part of a candidate special protection area under section 3 of the 1981 Act and Article 4 of the EEC Birds Directive; and (c) the home of several species protected under Part I of the 1981 Act, the Birds Directive and the Berne Convention.

He submitted that, given those statutory and policy considerations, it was an error for the Council to treat this as a site where any presumption in favour of planning permission applied.

In substance, he submitted that this application should have been considered on its merits and he submitted that instead it laboured under a substantial disadvantage in having a presumption erected from the previous planning history. He did not, and could not, have contended that the previous planning history was irrelevant. The background to his submission was that on April 25, 1984, permission had been granted to develop a large part of Canford Heath including the subject sites for residential purposes.

That permission was granted subject to two conditions of present relevance:

> "2. Application for approval of any 'Reserved Matter' must be made not later than the expiration of three years beginning with the date of this permission.
>
> 3. The development to which this passage relates must be begun not later than whichever is the later of the following dates:
> (i) the expiration of five years from the date of grant of outline planning permission or,
> (ii) the expiration of two years from the final approval of the Reserved Matters..."

Mr Ryan made the point that at the time of the consideration of this matter by the Development Control Sub-Committee on April 6, 1989, the outline permission could not be implemented without further ado because the three year limit for the application approval of the reserved matter had elapsed. He conceded that, by virtue of section 31A of the Town and Country Planning Act 1971, application could have been made for the development of the land without complying with this condition but pointed out that it never was made, still less granted. In those circumstances he submitted that the officer advising the committee had erred in asserting that the subject sites enjoyed the benefit of the 1984 permission. The point was of importance, he submitted because the officer's report, after referring to the 1984 outline permission granted for the whole of the central Canford Heath, including this site, continued:

> "There is then a full presumption in favour of renewing an outline (permissions) unless there are overriding reasons for not so doing. Here the only change is that of the NCC proposing to extend the SSSI into the known development area in the interests of nature conservancy".

Later in the report he referred to the subject sites as enjoying the benefit of the 1984 permission and also referred to the long-held presumption in favour of development. Mr Ryan submitted that the committee were misled as to the status in law of the 1984 permission.

It was worth reminding oneself that the committee were not concerned with any attempt to implement the 1984 permission but rather with an application for a new permission. The 1984 permission was relevant as part of the planning background, as was the fact that in the planning of the area it had long been assumed that these sites would go for residential development. The essence of Mr Ryan's complaint did not turn on the technicality as to whether or not the 1984 permission was at the date of the report still capable of being implemented but rather on what he said was a misleading approach to be found in the report and its references to presumption.

Having looked at all the evidence he [Schiemann J] was not persuaded that the committee here were misled at all. Planning circulars and structure plans were full of broad statements with many presumptions, many of which were mutually irreconcilable so that in a particular case one had to give way to another. Neither the instant report nor the planning circulars were to be read as though they were taxation statutes to be carefully construed. The local authority officers who drafted these reports were not by training or inclination in general endowed with the skill of Parliamentary draftsmen. It seemed that Mr Garrard was absolutely right when he said that there was a balance to be struck. There were strong policy/historical arguments in favour of a grant and strong conservation reasons against the grant. That was the matter with which the committee grappled at some length and came down in the favour of adhering to their earlier policy, notwithstanding the fact that they knew that the NCC were anxious that this site should be preserved for perfectly good ecological reasons.

When one looked at the evidence as a whole rather than the odd isolated phrase in one or another of the documents before the Council, there was no reason to suppose that the Council took into account any significant matter which they should not have taken into account, or that they had failed to take into account any significant matter which they ought to have taken into account; or that they had committed some other error which should lead to this permission being quashed. Some of the criticisms made by Mr Ryan of this phrase or that did have force. But at the end of the day the court had to sit back, as it were, and ask itself whether there was anything which vitiated the decision-making processes and which would make it desirable for the Council to look at this matter again.

(b) European designations

The system of countryside designation outlined above has been developed further to comply with European Community law. This process began with the adoption by the European Community of Directive 79/409/EEC on the conservation of wild birds.[61] The Birds Directive arose from public concern over the customary annual hunting of migratory birds in Southern Europe and Northern Africa, and from scientific research conducted by the European Commission which indicated that the number of species of European birds was falling. In terms of control of land use, the Birds Directive requires that Member States must preserve, maintain or re-establish a sufficient diversity and area of habitats so that bird populations are maintained. The most suitable land and sea territories for these birds are classified as special protection areas (SPAs).[62] Within these areas, Member States are obliged in Article 4(4) of the Directive to 'take appropriate steps to avoid pollution or deterioration of the habitats or any disturbances affecting the birds'. Outside these areas, there is a residual duty on Member States to 'strive to avoid pollution or deterioration of habitats'.

In the United Kingdom, before land can be designated as an SPA by an order made by the Secretary of State for the Environment, it must be notified as a SSSI to secure legal protection of it under the Wildlife and Countryside Act 1981. The conservation agencies advise the Secretary of State which areas should be considered for designation and consult with any landowners and the local authorities. The purpose of such orders is normally to provide sanctuary to particularly vulnerable groups of birds. The protection given by the orders can vary to meet particular circumstances. To date 86 SPAs have been designated, 54 of which are coastal. A further 151 potential SPAs have been identified.[63] In line with the precautionary principle, potential SPAs also attract legal protection under the Directive.

61 OJ L 103, 25.4.1979, p 1. See ch 11, 'Designation as a Special Protection Area'.

62 See Case C-57/89: *Commission v Germany* (*Leybucht Dykes*) [1991] ECR I-883 and Case C-355/90: *Commission v Spain* (*Santoña Marshes*) and Case C-44/95: *R v Secretary of State for the Environment, ex p RSPB (Lappel Bank)* ([1996] 3 CMLR 411, UK proceedings reported at [1995] JEL Vol 7, No 2, 245), on which, see ch 5, 'Losing the economic base: *Lappel Bank*'.

63 HC Deb 16 May 1994 cc 375-376; see P Hughes, 'The Habitats Directive and the UK Conservation Framework', Research paper 94/90, 15 July 1994, House of Commons Library.

Most recently EC Directive 92/43/EEC on the conservation of natural habitats and of wild fauna and flora (the 'Habitats Directive')[64] has led to significant changes in the system of land designation. The Habitats Directive aims to contribute towards ensuring biodiversity through the conservation of natural habitats and of wild flora and fauna. It will do this by establishing a coherent network of conservation sites throughout Europe. The sites will contain specific natural habitat types (listed in Annex I to the Directive) and species (listed in Annex II). The Habitats Directive sites will be known as special areas of conservation (SACs), but the network will also include the special protection areas (SPAs) already designated under the Birds Directive: the whole network to be called Natura 2000. Member States must select sites on the basis of the habitats and species present, using criteria set out in Stage I of Annex III of the Habitats Directive. These include the degree of representivity of the site, the area of the site compared to its total area in a Member State, the density of a species population at a site, and the isolation of that population. SACs must finally be designated by the year 2004. However, as soon as a site is placed on the Community's draft list, it will be subject to article 6 of the Directive, which provides protection for SACs. Article 6 requires Member States to establish the necessary conservation measures for SACs. Furthermore, under Article 6(3):

> Any plan or project not directly connected with or necessary to the management of the site but likely to have a significant effect thereon, either individually or in combination with other plans or projects, shall be subject to appropriate assessment of its implications for the site in view of the site's conservation objectives...the competent national authorities shall agree to the plan or project only after having ascertained that it will not adversely affect the integrity of the site concerned, and, if appropriate, after having obtained the opinion of the general public.

If a plan or project must be carried out for reasons of overriding public interest (including those of a social or economic nature) the Member State must take all compensatory measures to ensure that the overall coherence of the network is protected, and shall inform the European Commission of compensatory measures taken. If a site includes a priority species and/or priority habitat type (these are identified by an asterisk in the Directive's Annexes), then the only considerations that may be raised are human health or public safety, or those of primary importance to the environment. The Directive therefore provides a two-tier system of protection: ordinary SACs may be overridden on social or economic grounds, but 'priority' SACs may only be overridden on grounds of public health or safety.

The Directive is transposed into United Kingdom law by statutory instrument – The Conservation (Natural Habitats, &c) Regulations 1994 (the 'Habitats Regulations'),[65] not through new primary legislation. As with other areas of environmental law, such as environmental assessment[66] the United Kingdom government chose to implement Community law through

64 OJ L206 22.2.1992.
65 SI 1994/2716.
66 See ch 10, 'Implementation of Directive 85/337/EEC'.

existing legal machinery and administrative structures. The existing SSSI system therefore forms the bedrock for the European site network, as it was similarly used to implement the Birds Directive. The SAC system in the United Kingdom will also echo the SSSI system in favouring compensation and voluntary agreement rather than compulsion. The legal and social impacts of this are seen in relation to habitat protection for geese, discussed in chapter 11.

The Habitats Regulations 1994 do depart from the voluntary approach to nature conservation in one important respect: the Secretary of State for the Environment may make a special nature conservation order over a European site which produces a *ban* on potentially damaging operations for an indefinite period and confers absolute protection.[67] It is likely that such an order will be made in cases in which a management agreement could not be negotiated and the site is in danger. This system of protection depends, however, upon how willing the Secretary of State is to make a special conservation order in the first place; the Secretary of State may also direct a conservation agency to give consent to an operation if he or she is satisfied that there is no alternative solution and that the operation must be carried out for certain imperative reasons of overriding public interest (which may be of a social or economic nature). In all other cases of European sites (SPAs under the Birds Directive and SACs under the Habitats Directive), only the normal protection offered to SSSIs applies.

(c) Planning for conservation

In recent years, planning has become closely associated with the aims of conservation and the means by which designated land is protected.[68] This is particularly apparent in Regulation 54 of the Conservation (Natural Habitats, &c) Regulations 1994, which implements the requirement contained in Article 6 of the Habitats Directive that competent national authorities consider the effect of development on a European site when deciding whether or not to grant planning permission. This amounts to a duty to conduct an assessment of whether the development is likely to have a significant effect on the site in terms of the ecological objectives for which the site was classified or designated. The local planning authority may only grant planning permission having ascertained that it will not affect the integrity of any European site – the coherence of its ecological structure and function – across its whole area, that enables it to sustain the habitat and the levels of populations for which it was classified.

However, a hierarchy of protection exists which reflects the Habitats Directive's two-tier structure. For a 'standard' European site, if the authority is satisfied that there are reasons of overriding public interest (including social

67 Regulation 22 of the Habitat Regulations 1994, SI 1994/2716.

68 See Department of the Environment, Planning Policy Guidance Note 9, *Nature Conservation* (London: HMSO, 1994), which sets out the government's policies on the role of planning in nature conservation.

and economic reasons) the authority may agree to the development notwithstanding that it will have adverse effects. In the case of a 'priority' site (as marked in Annex I of the Directive), the authority can only grant planning permission for reasons relating to human health. This hierarchy, derived from European Community law, acknowledges and permits the fulfilment of objectives other than environmental protection in the planning system. Following from this, there is some emphasis in planning guidance that 'conservation and development can be compatible'[69] and that care should be taken by the local planning authority 'to avoid unnecessary constraints on development'.[70] Imaginative use of planning conditions and obligations is also encouraged, particularly when these enable a development to proceed, perhaps by providing a 'compensatory' benefit.

Department of the Environment, Planning Policy Guidance Note 9, *Nature Conservation* (London: HMSO, 1994)

NATURE CONSERVATION AND DEVELOPMENT CONTROL

27. Nature conservation can be a significant material consideration in determining many planning applications, especially in or near SSSIs, where there are statutory requirements to consult English Nature. But local planning authorities should not refuse permission if development can be subject to conditions that will prevent damaging impacts on wildlife habitats or important physical features, or if other material factors are sufficient to override nature conservation considerations.

...

28. Where there is a risk of damage to a designated site' the planning authority should consider the use of conditions or planning obligations in the interests of nature conservation. Conditions can be used, for example, to require areas to be fenced or bunded off to protect them, or to restrict operations or uses to specific times of year. Planning obligations can accompany permissions in order to secure long-term management, to provide nature conservation features to compensate for any such features lost when development takes place...

5 CONCLUSION

The systems of town planning and countryside protection have traditionally operated in relief: the planning system aims at blanket coverage – all 'development' requires planning permission unless specifically exempted, whereas the system of countryside designation demarcates only particular areas for special protection. A more holistic approach to the control of land use and development may now be seen in the *general* requirement that nature conservation objectives be taken into account in all planning activities affecting rural and coastal land

69 Department of the Environment, Planning Policy Guidance Note 9, *Nature Conservation*, (London: HMSO, 1994), para 3.

70 Ibid, para 18.

use and in urban areas where there is wildlife of local importance. For example, structure plans should now identify key conservation sites such as SSSIs, so that the wildlife characteristics of the area can be placed in a national and international setting, and local plans should identify nature conservation interests and ensure that provisions are made for their protection, with an emphasis also on international designations. The regimes employ similar legal tools: the planning agreement and management agreement both rely upon contract for their legal form, financial inducements.[71] The integration of planning controls and countryside protection regimes arises from a recognition that planning performs an important role in *preventing* environ-mental harm and that this function may have a far wider application than town planning. This trend of integrating previously separate land use controls has been directed by European Community law and parallels the gradual integration of pollution controls discussed in the previous chapter.

The function and scope of planning controls have broadened considerably from their original remit of securing public health by removing nuisances and regulating the building of dwellings[72] to achieving sustainable development. This suggests that environmental protection might well constitute a further ideological strand to those McAuslan identifies in the planning system, quoted at the beginning of this chapter. This broadening has been possible because planning legislation has always had, as at least one of its goals, the provision of a healthier environment. The environmental agenda in some respects merely draws upon planning's latent stewardship role and public interest objectives. The difference is that planning's concern with environmental protection in planning is now emphasised in planning law. The existence and adequacy of pollution control regimes is a legitimate material consideration of the local planning authority when considering an application for planning permission,[73] as is an environmental assessment of a project.[74] Perhaps the clearest sign of the greater priority given to environmental protection in planning is the acceptance in policy guidance that planning offers a practical means by which the nebulous concept of sustainable development may be implemented, and therefore that obligations in international law be fulfilled.[75] So far, the rhetoric of sustainable development remains advanced only in policy; the exact legal scope of planning controls – planning conditions and obligations – to control industrial processes as well as the physical shape of the land is not settled. The doubt arises because, in forging legitimate roles for itself in pollution control and nature conservation, planning has inevitably pulled away from its solid foundation of controlling land use and development; the extent to which legally enforceable conditions and obligations can give practical expression to planning's new and broader roles – beyond land use and development control – is therefore still uncertain. But it is important to remember that planning's

71 On this type of legal instrument, see further, ch 8, 'Economic instruments'.

72 See ch 3, 'Early planning law'.

73 *Gateshead Metropolitan Borough Council v Secretary of State for the Environment* [1995] Env LR 37.

74 See further 'Implementation of Directive 85/337/EEC', ch 10.

75 See ch 4.

current preoccupation with environmental protection is a reflection of the contemporary ascendancy of concerns for environmental protection in the wider society: the malleability of the planning system ensures that this priority might be subject to further policy changes.

CHAPTER 8

Alternative environmental protection

1 INTRODUCTION

Most of this book has told of the development and growth of regulation to deal with environmental problems. Most commonly a traditional model of regulation by administratively determined and enforced standards, often referred to as 'command and control', has been followed. We have seen in a number of cases how the effects of this regulation whether at international, Community or national level have been different from those aimed for. Another way to describe this is 'implementation failure', or even 'regulatory failure'. This gap between aspiration and reality in law is a continuing theme. This can arise from a failure of political will, from the material or institutional limitations of organisations, and even from the psychology and professional background of those charged with bringing a law into effect.[1] We have also seen the specific problems which environmental protection poses law: problems of causation, scientific uncertainty, and cumulation of adverse effects on the environment.

Recognition of the failures and inherent limitations of the traditional regulatory model to achieve environmental protection has arisen from criticism on two counts. The first critique has been levelled by economists who consider that 'command and control' type regulation is neither efficient in economic terms, nor effective in changing people's behaviour. The second allegation is that such methods take insufficient account of public perceptions of pollution and allow too little public participation, the development of pollution controls having traditionally been settled within closed policy communities made up of specialist public officials and industrial representatives. More sophisticated, but also more democratic methods, are required. The range of methods and techniques of environmental protection which offer an alternative to 'command and control' regulation is very broad. In this chapter we consider only some, albeit diverse, alternatives. We divide these into two categories: alternatives *within* society and alternatives *for* society. Those within society include the use of economic instruments, fostering self-regulation and supporting green consumerism by providing the conditions for effective consumer choice. The second category, alternatives *for* society, includes 'voluntary simplicity' and direct action for social change.

1 A Weale, *The New Politics of Pollution* (Manchester: Manchester University Press, 1992) pp 154-155.

The first category of alternatives is by far the more prevalent. The development of these has been described as part of a process of ecological modernisation or reformism. The institutional context of ecological modernisation is discussed in the following. We shall see that a major influence along the way to ecological modernisation is the idea of sustainable development which integrates environmental issues and economic concerns.

MA Hajer *The Politics of Environmental Discourse: Ecological Modernisation and the Policy Process* (Oxford: Oxford University Press, 1995) p 74-101

To be able to understand the present dynamics of ecological modernization we will have to go back to at least the early 1970s when the environment quite suddenly became a political topic in modern societies. Since that day environmental discourse has taken many twists and turns, from the collective concern about the prophecies of doom of a coming resource crisis that would bring the whole world to a grinding halt, to the localized concern over the pollution of water, soil, and air; from the concerns about the possibility that the modern world will come to an end with the bang of a nuclear catastrophe to the idea that Western civilization is slowly ruining its heritage now cathedrals and sculptures crumble away as the consequence of acid rains. The historical sequence of emblematic issues is often retold in the literature. Yet there is a parallel story that is not often told. While the alleged catastrophes made the headlines and have always dominated both the academic and popular literature, there was another process that laid the foundations of the present age of ecological modernization. Here I want to reconstruct the specific argumentative interplay between the state, the environmental movement, and key expert organizations that made ecological modernization into such a powerful force.

...

During the 1970s radical factions of the environmental movement increasingly broke with the discursive order of lobbying and interest group politics. Initially the environmental movement had mimicked the institutional structures of established interest-groups that had always oriented themselves towards the state. The radical factions, however, neither wanted nor were able to negotiate demands with the state. They related to other political actors and opponents no longer in terms of negotiations, compromise, reform, or improvement. Politics was not a matter of gradual progress to be brought about by organised pressure-group activity and a strategy of inclusion. The new social movements thought in terms of sharp anomalies such as yes-no, them-us, the desirable and the intolerable, etc. Especially in continental Europe, the environmental movement in fact constituted an independent discourse coalition, complete with alternative life-styles and new structures of organization embracing alternative communicative practices such as mass demonstrations, and separate newspapers and radio stations...

Its actions were typically supported by slogans starting with 'stop', 'ban', or 'freeze' and its concern was formulated in exclusionary terms: 'no part of it [could] be meaningfully sacrificed...without negating the concern itself.'[2] After

2 Offe 1985: 831.

all, what was at stake was not so much the specific way in which energy was generated or bottles were handled after their economic lives, what was at stake was their very identity or survival.[3] This did not allow for any kind of exchange or trade-off. Given this perception of the environmental problem it is hardly surprising that nuclear power plants became the focus of the environmental protest in the course of the 1970s. Cotgrove and Duff have pointed out the deep symbolic significance of nuclear power stations in this respect: 'centralized, technologically complex and hazardous, and reinforcing all those trends in society which environmentalists most fear and dislike – the increasing domination of experts, threatening the freedom of the individual, and reinforcing totalitarian tendencies'.[4]...The *Total Kritik* of the anti-nuclear movement, as it became known in Germany, and the metaphorical meaning of nuclear power therein, meant that pragmatic alternatives were not sought. That would imply a denial of the fact that nuclear power stood for a much bigger problem.

...Yet, as society changes so the environmental movement changes. In the early 1980s the environmental movement found new incentives and changed its political strategies and organizational structures. The environmentalists of the 1980s were less radical, more practical, and were much more policy- oriented. The movement's emphases were no longer on alternatives for society, it started to focus on presenting practical alternatives within society instead. Technology was no longer the focus of critique but increasingly came to be seen as the discourse of solutions. A new type of knowledge became relevant. Activists should no longer be qualified to discuss the crisis-ridden nature of the capitalist system on a reasonably well-informed level, they were now valued for various sorts of expertise (such as scientific or engineering know-how, or media, management, or marketing skills). Nor did the environmental movement any longer rely solely on mass meetings for its political support. Instead it aimed to maximise its campaign funds by extending both its formal membership ('giro-activism') and its wider political support – something that was completely disregarded in the 1970s. To the extent that it continued to stage mass demonstrations the meanings of these gatherings changed radically. From exercises in grassroots democracy and alternative lifestyles, mass-mobilisation became an instrumental means to back up the activities by pressure-groups and lobbyists. The environmental movement now also emphasised the importance of media presence and behind-the-scenes political lobbying, again something that was inconceivable under the old identity-oriented movement. In short, in the 1980s the environmental movement took up the role of counter-expert, illuminating alternative solutions to what were increasingly seen again as environmental problems (thus bracketing deeper institutional causes). The problem-makers of the 1970s had become the problem-solvers of the 1980s.

The Emergence of Ecological Modernization Explained

How should this change within the movement be explained? At least four reasons can be given. First of all, radical environmentalism was caught up by the

3 See Cohen 1985; Melucci 1985.

4 Cotgrove and Duff 1980: 338. Hence it would be quite wrong to suggest that environmentalism was largely a politics of 'single issue negativism' as Paehlke (1989) suggests.

economic recession of the late 1970s. In the face of the economic slowdown environmental issues suddenly lost out against the concern over inflation and mass unemployment. The basic insecurity over the economic future of national societies frustrated the validity of the discourse of selected growth. In order to maintain its social credibility environmental discourse had to find ways to reconcile economic restructuring with environmental care, or so it seemed. Of course, within the radical political discourse the argument could have been to blame the same practices for both the environmental and economic problems. This in fact obviously happened, but somehow that claim became marginalized in environmental discourse. Secondly, important changes occurred within the environmental movement itself. Even with the rather reluctant professionalization of the environmental movement at the time, the activity of professionals eroded identity orientation and favoured a strategic model. Inside the NGO-elites there was a growing awareness that the radical confrontational style unnecessarily constrained the advancement of the environmental movement as a social power. 'Soft technologists' like Amory Lovins surfaced, arguing that the resolution of many environmental problems was well within the reach of a reformist environmental strategy. The practice of mass demonstrations was recognised as a dead-end and NGOs started to think about alternatives.

The third factor was the emergence of other issues such as acid rain or the diminishing ozone layer, that were not necessarily as politically illuminating as nuclear power, but that none the less seemed to be a promising basis for a further extension of the social influence of the environmental movement. The practice of strategic campaigning that had been pioneered by NGOs like Friends of the Earth and the Sierra Club, suggested the tactic of exploiting the importance of the emblematic issues for the general public understanding of environmental problems. Again there was a play on the symbolic, metaphorical meaning of key issues, yet this time they had to qualify on different criteria. Rather than illustrating the perverted nature of the system at large to the radical core of the counter-culture, they now had to illustrate the vast threats that various industrial practices formed to society as a whole.

The fourth factor consisted in the political fact that an alternative discourse was available. Ideas of ecological modernization had, by then, already overcome their growing pains. Work in academic circles and expert organizations now provided an alternative conceptual language and delivered concrete solutions that suggested pragmatic ways of overcoming environmental problems. It strongly suggested that for many issues solutions could indeed be found, e.g. experiments had been conducted that hinted that energy savings of up to 40 per cent were feasible at reasonable costs. Hence what came out in the 1980s was that during the 1970s environmental politics had not only been made on the streets: a far less visible, but undoubtedly essential development of environmental discourse had taken place in the domain of policy-making institutions and think-tanks. This activity originated for the first phase of political upheaval over *Limits to Growth.* Since then policy-makers and environmental experts had staged a host of conferences and produced a stream of reports in their effort to find effective ways of regulating environmental problems. Here they could take up much work that had been done before. An important example is the Pigouvian analysis in economics, which drew attention to the social costs of private enterprise.[5] The original idea stemmed from the 1920s; it had been taken up again in the 1950s and was now channelled into the policy-making arena thanks to the activities of easily identifiable mediating institutions. A key role was played by secondary policy institutes such as the OECD, the UNEP, and the UN-ECE, which had started their own environmental directorates or committees in the early 1970s. They became actively involved in the study of environmental problems and the design of policy instruments. From the late 1970s onwards these institutes started to produce evidence that the initial legalistic governmental response to the environmental challenge produced highly unsatisfactory results.[6] ...

With hindsight we can identify at least three different tracks along which the repositioning in environmental discourse in the late 1970s and early 1980s took place. Together they facilitated the formation of national discourse-coalitions around the ideas of ecological modernization in the decade to come.[7]

The first track is related to the publication and subsequent take up of the *World Conservation Strategy* (WCS) in 1980.[8] This report marked the emergence of a coalition in environmental politics oriented towards policy-making and explicitly arguing for a strategy of sustainable development. The report was the joint product of the moderate NGOs, the International Union for the Conservation of Nature and the World Wildlife Fund together with the UNEP, and was written in collaboration with the FAO and the UNESCO. These organizations had been working hard on a world-wide survey of endangered habitats and eco-systems. They argued strongly for a strategy of sustainable development based on efficient resource utilization and considerate environmental planning. Their agenda was to promote the conservation of nature and to this purpose the WCS came up with many suggestions for environmental policy making.

...

A second track along which this repositioning in environmental discourse took place was linked to the activities of the OECD. The OECD Environment Committee, launched in 1970, functioned as a think-tank and mediator for ideas that sprang up in academia. The main thrust of the OECD story-line was that pollution problems mostly indicated a gross inefficiency and that the costs of pollution should be borne by the polluters (the 'polluter pays principle').[9] As a primarily economic organization the OECD put special emphasis on the relationship of economy and environment. A key moment here was the meeting of Environment Ministers of the OECD member states in May 1979. The official Declaration on Anticipatory Policies did not go much further than the suggestion of incorporating the environmental considerations at an early stage of decision-making and a plea for the use of economic and fiscal instruments instead of

5 See Weale 1992: 158 ff; Kapp 1950.

6 Especially significant in this respect were the *State of the Environment* reports that the OECD started to issue from 1979 onwards.

7 Reports by the OECD Directorate, the UNEP, and similar organizations put a heavy emphasis on the serious health effects of a continuation of basic features of the industrial society such as high sulphur emissions.

8 Anon, 1980.

9 Of special relevance in this context is *The Costs and Benefits of Sulphur Oxide Control* (OECD 1981b).

concentrating on legal regulatory instruments. Yet the papers give a better idea of the underlying arguments that were important in the OECD attempt to push ecological modernization to the fore. There it was typically argued that 'In the changed economic conditions greater emphasis will have to be placed on the complementarity and compatibility of environmental and economic policies'.[10] The positive-sum game format that became characteristic of ecological modernization was simply born out of necessity: for environmental policies to survive they needed to work with the grain of time. What is more, environmental policy was not only positioned as non-contradictory to economic policy, it was also suggested as a potential instrument for economic recovery...

The third track that helped to bring about this redefinition of the environmental conflict were the debates within the United Nations commissions on issues of development, safety, and environment. It is undisputed that the Brundtland Report, *Our Common Future* (1987), is to be seen as a sequel to the Brandt Report, *North-South: A Programme for Survival* (1980) and *Common Crisis* (1983) and the report *Common Security* (1982) of the Palme Commission.[11] This sequence of UN reports signifies a continued concern with the need for increased multilateral co-operation which was strongly inspired by Western European social-democratic ideas.[12] So as in the OECD story-line we see an emphasis on the need to look at economics and environmental issues as essentially intertwined. Yet this time the background of the connection between environmental issues and economic issues of development was not rooted in efficiency but stemmed from the social-democratic background of this particular brand of UN work. The UN commissions problematized the dark side of the post-war boom in production and Western welfare and in fact tried to elaborate (or keep alive) a discourse of shared global problems stemming from a perspective of solidarity. This elaborated on the state-oriented social-democratic tradition that had been outlined by the social-democratic Keynesian economists such as Galbraith and Tinbergen.[13] As such the WCED most definitely had a critical edge. It explicitly aimed to get environmental issues out of the periphery of politics (as conservation issues) and sought to link them to core – i.e. economic – concerns. Likewise it aimed to resist the dichotomy between environment and development which had been the obstacle that split North and South at the 1972 Stockholm Conference...

... ecological modernization is essentially an efficiency-oriented approach to the environment. This is what made it possible for ecological modernization to become the dominant discourse within the environmental domain...

10 OECD 1980, 60-1.

11 Independent Commission on International Development Issues (Brandt Commission) 1980, 1983, Independent Commission on Disarmament and Security Issues (Palme Commission) 1982. See also Redclift 1987. For a discussion of these reports see Ekins 1992, ch 2.

12 Note that the chairpersons of the subsequent commission were all leaders of Western European social-democratic parties.

13 See Galbraith 1967; Tinbergen 1977. Interestingly the latter author's work on the New Internationalist Order had generated interest from the Club of Rome which even led to the commissioning of the 1977 report.

It is important to note also that ecological modernisation is sympathetic to ideas of deregulation, and that, in advocating the use of certain alternatives to command and control, a political ideology may also be being pursued. Indeed, it is in the environmental field that the effects of the 'climate of euphoric deregulation'[14] may be seen most clearly. There is also a significant European Community dimension to the process of ecological modernisation. This arises from recognition of the difficulties of implementing administratively set and controlled standards at Community level, particularly given resistance to such standards. Aside from these practical difficulties of implementation and enforcement, the European Community follows the zeitgeist of deregulation.[15] However, the avowed reason for developing alternatives to traditional methods of regulation, set out in the Fifth Environmental Action Programme, below, is the need to influence different types of behaviour and respond to different environmental problems.

Fifth Environmental Action Programme, *Towards Sustainability: A European Community Programme of Policy and Action in Relation to the Environment and Sustainable Development* OJ C 138, 17.5.1993 (Brussels: Commission of the European Communities, 1993) pp 67-68

CHAPTER 7

BROADENING THE RANGE OF INSTRUMENTS

One of the principal strengths of the European Community, as distinct from other international institutions such as the United Nations agencies and OECD, is that it is a legislative body; when it acts in a legislative capacity its measures are binding on its constituent Member States. Under the first four action programmes, Community activity has predominantly been in the form of Council Directives and Regulations. A great majority of the measures adopted have been designed to respond to clearly identified problems or to apply controls to certain processes or activities, though there are notable exceptions, such as the measures on environmental impact assessments, protection of wild fauna and flora and access to environmental information. Many of the Directives serve the dual process of protecting the environment and eliminating distortions of competition within the Internal Market.

As a consequence of this legislative activity, the Community and its constituent Member States have achieved a significant degree of success in containing threats to public health and the environment, which cannot be ignored and should not be understated, and now have a body of law which, though relatively young and far from complete, provides a very solid foundation for the further steps which require to be undertaken in the years ahead.

There will be a continuing need to legislate measures at Community level, particularly in respect of

- the establishment of fundamental levels of environmental care and protection;

14 F Ost, 'A Game Without Rules? The Ecological Self-Organisation of Firms', in G Teubner, L Farmer and D Murphy, *Environmental Law and Ecological Responsibility* (Chichester: Wiley, 1995) p 354.

15 See Molitor Report, pp 188-189.

- Community commitments to wider international agreements; and
- common standards and/or controls which may be deemed necessary or expedient to preserve the integrity of the Internal Market.

But it is not feasible to adopt a Directive or Regulation which says: 'Thou shalt act in a sustainable manner'. Also because of the broad scope of many of the present-day environment issues and the threats to our biosphere posed by current trends in political, economic and social life, it is imperative to focus on the causes of environment-based problems in a different manner. It is essential to go to the roots of these problems – human activity, human values in relation to the environment and natural resources and human behaviour and consumption patterns.

In order to bring about substantial changes in current trends and practices and to involve all sectors of society, in a spirit of shared responsibility, a broader mix of 'instruments' needs to be developed and applied. Environmental policy will rest on four main sets of instruments: regulatory instruments, market-based instruments (including economic and fiscal instruments and voluntary agreements), horizontal supporting instruments (research, information, education etc.) and financial support mechanisms...

2 ECONOMIC INSTRUMENTS

It has been said that the development and use of economic instruments is central to the process of ecological modernisation. But economic instruments have broader functions than environmental protection and their use is significant in administrative, political, and constitutional terms as well as for environmental reasons. This is explored by Daintith, who uses 'dominium' to describe strategies such as economic instruments, in contrast to the more regular command and control type administrative methods of governance – 'imperium'. Although writing in the late 1980s about 'Thatcher's Britain', his analysis of the changing methods and styles of regulation applies equally well to the form of governance exercised by the European Community. As mentioned above, the European Community's activity in promulgating laws on a carbon tax, on environmental auditing and management styles and on eco-labelling suggests that it has come to rely on a broader range of methods of regulation than command and control because of difficulties in achieving harmonised environmental quality and emission standards, and because of the difficulties it has experienced in enforcing such laws.[16] In other words, the European Community's most recent legislation on environmental protection shows more signs of dominium than imperium.

T Daintith, 'The Executive Power Today: Bargaining and Economic Control', in J Jowell and D Oliver (eds), *The Changing Constitution* (Oxford: Oxford University Press, 1989), pp 193-218

...

The main resources available to government for persuading people to change their behaviour are two: first, the command of law, backed in the last

16 See ch 5.

resort by force, carrying with it the threat of harm to those who do not comply; and second, the possession of wealth, carrying with it the promise of benefit for those who do. The first is simply exemplified by the use of the criminal law to compel car-drivers and their passengers to wear seat belts; the second by the offering of grants to people to improve the insulation in their houses. The usual association of the first resources with sanctions, and the second with benefits, can be reversed: a relaxation of legal commands (for example, a tax reduction or exemption) can be used to reward compliance, and a withdrawal of benefits, such as government contracts or grants, can be used to 'punish' non-compliance. For the sake of consistency I use the term *imperium* to describe the government's use of the command of law in aid of its policy objectives, and the term *dominium* to describe the employment of the wealth of government for this purpose.

...

A practical example may help to clarify the meaning of these terms, and will show incidentally the wide range of potential policy choices which government may need to consider in relation to a given problem. When oil and gas began to be discovered under the British sector of the North Sea from the early 1960s onward, government assumed that the massive investment in rigs, platforms, barges, and other equipment would bring major opportunities for British industry. A report published in 1972 showed, however, that British industry was winning a disappointingly low share of orders, and was likely to go on doing so in the absence of government intervention: one of the reasons was that many of the major companies searching for and finding oil and gas under petroleum production licences were American and had a strong propensity to stick to their United States suppliers for all items of equipment, even down to such mundane necessities as chicken wire. What forms might government intervention take? Using *imperium*, it could promulgate legislation (or use existing legal powers, if available) to prohibit or tax the importation or use of foreign equipment; or, more subtly, to set compulsory standards with which only British manufacturers (warned well in advance) would find it easy to conform; or to require licensees to buy British in preference to foreign goods where supplied on competitive terms. Using *dominium*, it could offer subsidies to British manufacturers of relevant equipment, or to licensees who purchased British, rather than foreign, equipment. Alternatively, *dominium* could be employed through the licence, which is in the nature of a grant to the licensee of the right to obtain for himself, against payment of a royalty, petroleum over which the State has proprietary rights. A preference in favour of British equipment could be made a term of the licence; or an undertaking to exercise such a preference, or evidence of having purchased such equipment in the past, could be made a criterion for the award of a licence. Forms of intervention other than through *imperium* or *dominium* might also be considered: government could content itself with a campaign of exhortation to licensees to buy British, or with the dissemination of information to licensees and manufacturers alike (though such measures will almost certainly involve government expenditure, and can therefore be seen as a form of *dominium*).

In the event, the government employed a variety of measures. It offered a subsidy to purchasers of British-made equipment; set up a specialized unit within the appropriate department to encourage and monitor British orders;

made an informal agreement with the organization representing the main North Sea licensees, the United Kingdom Offshore Operators' Association, on tendering rules that would give British manufacturers 'full and fair opportunity' to compete for orders; and made acceptance and (where appropriate) past observance of this agreement one of the informal criteria considered by the minister in allocating petroleum licences among competing applicants. In all these measures, the government eschewed the use of its *imperium*, but relied on *dominium*, both directly and as a support for arrangements concluded through a process of negotiation with interested parties. This kind of complex, many-pronged approach to problems is today commonplace: the straightforward deployment of *imperium* is the exception, not the rule.

Economic instruments have not only been associated with a certain style of governance. Since the World Commission on Environment and Development reported in *Our Common Future* (1987), economic instruments have been viewed as one means of 'operationalising' or achieving sustainable development. This is for many of the reasons given by Hajer above, but particularly that the elites of the most important intergovernmental and non-governmental organisations began to see that an accommodation between environmental and economic goals was the way forward for environmental protection. After all, the hard line intransigence of the environmental movement in the 1960s and 1970s had not achieved the aims of easing economic pressures on the environment and reversing environmental deterioration. The vocabulary of sustainable development in the WCED report is economic in nature. There is, for example, a concern that economic growth might be arrested should the logic of environmentalism be pursued in a strict sense. Ostensibly to allow developing countries to embark, or to continue, upon economic growth paths enjoyed by the developed world, the WCED advocated a five- to ten-fold increase in manufacturing output.

World Commission on Environment and Development, *Our Common Future* (Oxford: Oxford University Press, 1987), p 1

This Commission believes that people can build a future that is more prosperous, more just, and more secure. Our report, *Our Common Future*, is not a prediction of ever increasing environmental decay, poverty, and hardship in an ever more polluted world among ever decreasing resources. We see instead the possibility for a new era of economic growth, one that must be based on policies that sustain and expand the environmental resource base. And we believe such growth to be absolutely essential to relieve the great poverty that is deepening in much of the developing world.

The prescriptions of the WCED to achieve sustainable economic growth were taken up by Pearce, amongst others, who expanded them into a 'blueprint' for a green economy. Central terms in this blueprint are 'valuation', 'cost-benefit analysis', 'balancing', and 'trade-offs'. An underlying assumption is that the use of economic instruments fosters public participation. It is claimed also that monetisation extends beyond the simple, democratic, 'one man one vote' model of registering public opinion since the *intensity* of feeling that people attach to environmental protection may be measured through their monetary valuation of a river, a view, or a clean beach. Individual choice therefore replaces common and politically determined policies for environmental protection. An extract from Pearce et al's 'Blueprint' on the use of contingent valuation to determine how much people are willing to pay for a particular environmental resource is given below.

D Pearce, A Markandya and E Barbier, *Blueprint for a Green Economy* (London: Earthscan, 1989), pp 51-57

...

Economics and environmental values

Care and concern for the environment can be thought of as positive preferences for cleaner air and water, less noise, protection of wildlife, and so on. Economics is about choice, and choice relates to situations in which we have preferences for certain things but in which we cannot choose everything we like because of income limitation. Very simply, given limited resources, the rational thing to do is to choose between our preferences in an effort to get the most satisfaction – or "welfare", to use the economist's term – we can. If we apply economics to environmental issues, then, we should expect to obtain some insights into the desirability of improving the environment further, taking the social objective of increasing people's overall satisfaction (or welfare) as given.

...

The uses of monetary measures

...

At its simplest, what we seek is some expression of how much people are willing to pay to preserve or improve the environment. Such measures automatically express not just the fact of a preference for the environment, but also the intensity of that preference. Instead of "one man one vote", then, monetization quite explicitly reflects the depth of feeling contained in each vote.

If, of course, the issue is one of losing an environmental benefit, we may wish to rephrase the problem in terms of individuals' willingness to accept monetary compensation for the loss, rather than their willingness to prevent the loss. This can result in very large implied values of environmental quality. Our first reason for seeking a monetary measure, then, is that it will, to some considerable extent, reflect the strength of feeling for the environmental asset in question.

The second reason arises out of the first: provided the monetary measures that are revealed are sufficiently large, they offer a supportive argument for environmental quality. The usefulness of such arguments in turn arises from the fact that voters, politicians, and civil servants are readily used to the meaning of gains and losses that are expressed in pounds or dollars.

To say that a particular species in danger from some development is valued very highly because of the vocal expression of concern is one thing. To support that argument with a monetary expression of that concern makes the case for preservation stronger than if any one argument is used alone.

The third reason for wanting to make the effort at monetization is that it may permit comparison with other monetary benefits arising from alternative uses of funds.

The point here is that preserving and improving the environment is never a free option: it costs money and uses up real resources. This is true whether actual expenditures are incurred to preserve a habitat or insulate houses against noise or introduce sulphur emission reductions, or whether the cost of preservation is in terms of some benefit foregone. Preserving a wetlands area, for example, may well be at the cost of the agricultural output had the land been drained. If a monetary measure of environmental benefits can be secured, it can be compared to the monetary benefits of the agricultural output. This will help in any analysis of the extent to which it is socially worthwhile to preserve the land. The option with the biggest net benefits – i.e. the excess of benefits over costs – will be the one that is preferred, subject to any other considerations relating, say, to the interests of future generations.

The reasoning above may be formalized. The exercise of comparing the costs and benefits of two or more options of the use of land in the manner discussed is known as cost-benefit analysis.

Cost-benefit analysis (or CBA for short) makes operational the very simple, and rational, idea that decisions should be based on some weighing up of the advantages and disadvantages of an action.

At the moment, it is important to stress that CBA is not the only way to assist in decisions of the kind under consideration. There are other approaches which may be preferred. But CBA is the only one which explicitly makes the effort to compare like with like using a single measuring rod of benefits and costs, money.

This approach has been criticised widely. The following extract takes issue, fundamentally, but still from an economics perspective, with Pearce et al.

M Jacobs, *The Green Economy: Environment, Sustainable Development and the Politics of the Future* (London: Pluto Press,1989) pp 207-215

The problems of monetary valuation

Criticisms of monetary valuation in fact fall into two categories. In some cases the problems are merely technical. It can be accepted that there *is* a monetary value to be found, but for one reason or another the techniques available are unable to discover it with much accuracy. But in other cases the problems lie deeper. It is not 'accuracy' which is at issue, but the whole idea that meaningful monetary values exist at all.

...

Prices, incomes and monetary values

The indeterminacy of monetary values may not simply be an empirical matter, a question of observed behaviour. Important philosophical issues are raised by the hypothetical preference approach to valuation. This approach is based on the idea that a thing's value is discovered when it is placed in a market. That is, it equates value with *price*, generated by the interaction of supply and demand.

Given this concept of value, the hypothetical exercises are an explicit attempt to replicate the conditions in a market, facing the respondents with an environmental good and asking them to say how much they would be willing to pay for it, just as if it were a commodity in a shop. The more like a real market the exercise conditions are made, the more 'accurate' the results are claimed to be. This is the basis of the notion of 'hypothetical market bias', which is said to occur when the conditions are not much like a real market. 'True' values are obtained, the theory goes, when the invented market is as lifelike as possible.

There is no doubt that price is one way of valuing things. For most ordinary commodities which are traded in markets and consumed individually (that is, whose value is appreciated solely by the purchaser), price indeed seems a reasonable means of valuation. It is in turn, and more importantly, a practical method of deciding what should be produced and by whom it should be consumed. But it is not the only way in which things can be valued; and it is not obvious that what is appropriate for toothbrushes and ice cream must necessarily be right for such things as beautiful landscapes and rare species. Public environmental goods such as these are not 'commodities', since they are not traded in markets and are not consumed individually – their value is appreciated collectively. It is therefore not enough to argue that simply because other types of goods are valued in markets, so these goods should be also. However like real markets the hypothetical ones are designed to be, they may not be the appropriate means of valuation.

There are two strong objections to valuation in markets. The first is that the values obtained depend upon the incomes of the consumers. This is true of all prices; it is particularly obvious in hypothetical exercises where respondents are specifically asked about their 'willingness to pay'. Clearly one's willingness to pay for a good is constrained by one's ability to do so. Yet it does not seem fair to say that because one is unable to pay therefore one doesn't actually desire the good. On the contrary, the welfare gain that one might make by a particular environmental change – say, a reduction in air pollution – might be greater the lower one's income. Poorer people tend to live in more polluted neighbourhoods and have less access to the countryside. So they might value a reduction in pollution levels more highly than richer people: their gain in welfare (which is ultimately what economists seek to measure) might be greater.[17] But of course in a hypothetical market it is likely to show up as less, since they are less able to pay for it. This is indeed what evidence from such exercises indicates.[18]

...

17 ND Hanley, 'Using Contingent Valuation to Value Environmental Improvements', *Applied Economics*, 20(4), 1988, pp 541-50. Another study, D Brookshire, B Ives, and W Schulze, 'The Valuation of Aesthetic Preferences', *Journal of Environmental Economics and Management* 3 (4), 1976, pp 325-46, found a smaller difference in valuations between different income groups.

18 It is true that the rainforest can be shown to have a higher value when the potential for renewable crops and northern citizens' existence values are taken into account. This is argued, for example, by D Pearce, *An Economic Approach to Saving the Rainforest*, London Environmental Economics Centre, August 1990. But it does not alter the basic case. There are other parts of the natural environment where these special conditions of the rainforest do not apply.

The second objection to valuing the environment by inventing markets for it is that this is inappropriate for public goods which are consumed collectively by society as a whole (or parts of it) rather than individually. In a market consumers behave as individuals; they are motivated by self-interest. Consumption in markets is something each individual or household does by itself, for itself. This is not to denigrate consumers or their behaviour; it is almost impossible to act in any other way for most of the many hundreds of different purchase decisions which we all have to make. We cannot hope to make these decisions with other people, or even to know how they are behaving, let alone to know what the overall outcome of everyone's purchases might be.

It has long been recognised, however, that market behaviour with respect to public goods is problematic. This is because once such goods (for example, a lighthouse or the police) are provided, people cannot be excluded from consuming them. If asked to pay for them in a market, people will therefore tend to 'free ride': the price obtained will be less than the real value of the good to them...

...

There is ample evidence to show that people's valuations in the political arena are different from their market ones – that is, that their behaviour as *citizens* is different from their behaviour as *consumers*. For example, in opinion polls (which are proxies for democratic choice) substantial majorities of people say that they wish to protect the environment, and are willing to pay higher taxes and prices to do so. But as consumers they continue to buy goods and services which cause serious environmental degradation. This may be partly to do with ignorance, or lack of choice. But it is equally explicable in terms of the prisoner's dilemma of market consumption. To put it succinctly: since no one knows whether, if they use less electricity, everyone else will also, and since if everyone doesn't there is no point in their not doing so, they don't. If, however, everyone were forced to cut their electricity consumption by higher prices or taxes, the same people might accept this as the price of doing something about global warming. In the one case, as consumers, people's behaviour is individualistic and self-interested; in the other, as citizens, it has at least the opportunity to acknowledge wider interests and values, including in this case those of future generations.

The arguments for the use of economic instruments have been rehearsed at the international and European Community level, as well as at the national level by writers such as Pearce and Jacobs. The Royal Commission on Environmental Pollution has examined the arguments in theory, and in practice by commissioning studies on the use of charging schemes in the Tees and Forth Estuaries. The Royal Commission's conclusion is that rather than being straightforward deregulation the use of economic instruments requires a tight regulatory structure, at least in the setting-up period. The Commission also challenges the economists' concept of 'optimal pollution', by analysing the use of economic instruments from an equity as well as an efficiency standpoint.

Royal Commission on Environmental Pollution, Sixteenth Report, *Freshwater Quality*, Cmnd 1966 (London: HMSO, 1992) pp 140-144

CHAPTER 8

ECONOMIC INSTRUMENTS

Economic analysis of pollution

8.1 The pollution of freshwater can cause harm to human health, to ecological systems and to public amenity. The prevention of pollution therefore provides benefits to society. However, the implementation of policies to improve water quality imposes costs. Water companies in England and Wales, for example, will have to spend more than £7 billion over the years 1989 to 1991 to improve discharges from sewage treatment works and storm overflows. It is essential, therefore, to analyse the costs of policies to reduce pollution in relation to their benefits. Policies which are efficient – in the sense that they lead to larger improvements in environmental quality, for a given expenditure of public and private resources, than alternative policies – make further environmental improvements possible. Economic analysis helps to illuminate the principles of environmental policy.

8.2 Practical decisions about pollution are influenced, explicitly or implicitly, by evaluations of costs and benefits. Policies which require public expenditure are usually subject to budgetary scrutiny. Policies which require private expenditure – such as the implementation of regulations which restrict permitted effluents – are evaluated (and sometimes opposed) by those who must incur the costs. Other costs are not reflected in actual expenditure: for example, the cost of there being no birds to see as one walks beside a lake. But individuals take account of these costs in deciding whether to oppose specific pollution policies. The economic analysis of costs and benefits provides 'a consistent procedure for evaluating decisions in terms of their consequences', and thereby for choosing efficient environmental policies.

8.3 Cost-benefit analysis might consider, for example, a decision to reduce the level of a pollutant in a body of water. The pollution control authority would evaluate different water quality objectives, and different policies for achieving these objectives. In a simple exercise, it could estimate costs in three different ways. The first (Cost 1) would be the cost of the pollution itself – equivalent to the benefits foregone because of it. Thus if pollution is not reduced, people's walks might be less enjoyable, recreational enterprises might not be established around the waterbody, or there might be irreversible changes in local flora and fauna. The second (Cost 2) would be the cost of reducing pollution by the technique of prevention: the cost to enterprises (and households) of reducing those activities which result in discharge of the pollutants to the waterbody. The third (Cost 3) would be the cost of reducing the pollution by the alternative technique of treatment: the cost to the pollution control authority of achieving the same reduction by treating the water to remove or neutralise the pollutant. There is no reason, in general, to suppose that Costs 1, 2 and 3 will be the same. They will almost certainly be borne by different groups of people. Each of the estimates, in a thorough analysis, would include indirect as well as direct costs; for example, the costs of water treatment incurred by public authorities, the costs to households of having new water treatment facilities built in the vicinity, and the costs to enterprises of shortages of appropriate skills. The costs should also include increased pollution of other sorts if effluent were disposed of to land or air rather than water, and even the costs of preparing cost/benefit analyses. The implications of borrowing or raising taxes should be ignored in a full appraisal.

8.4 The pollution control authority, in an ideal system, would adopt those policies whose implementation involved costs which, when fully evaluated, were smaller than their benefits. If Cost 2 or Cost 3 were less than Cost 1, in the example above, then it would decide to reduce pollution by the cheaper of the two techniques (or by the cheapest combination). The result, under certain special circumstances, and if the policy were pursued fully, is that society would end up with what the Royal Commission Minority Report in 1972 called the 'optimum amount of pollution': for each pollutant, that level at which the marginal cost of reducing pollution becomes just greater, for society as a whole, than the marginal benefit of the reduction. We will see later that the practical problems in arriving at such a result are dauntingly difficult. The concept of an 'optimum amount' of pollution (which has been central to the economic analysis of social costs for more than 30 years) can itself be criticised, as will be seen in paragraph 8.11. Yet the objective of evaluating the costs and benefits of different policies remains of essential importance.

8.5 Environmental policies pose many problems for cost/benefit analysis. There are few accepted standards for studies. Analysts often neglect distributional effects, that is, the impact of policies on different individuals and groups in society. In addition, they have great difficulty in assigning values to benefits such as nature preservation, which in Robert Dorfman's words 'have no natural monetary values'; they pay little attention to uncertainty; they treat the costs of achieving standards superficially and consider too few alternative policies; they assume that policies will be executed with full efficiency. But similar problems would arise in any systematic effort to evaluate the costs of environmental policies. Some such effort is, however, an essential component of environmental improvement.

8.6 The use of market mechanisms to control pollution is a particular case of the application of economic analysis to environmental policy. The principal mechanisms – which include charges on pollution discharged, and permits to discharge pollutants – are discussed in reports prepared for the Commission. Charges establish the price to be paid for pollution, and allow the market to determine the total quantity of pollution; permits ration the total quantity, and allow the market to determine the price. A thorough economic analysis of alternative pollution control policies, it is suggested in these reports, would show that such mechanisms constitute the most efficient (or least costly) instruments for achieving desired environmental standards. They permit flexibility in compliance, so that firms with low costs of controlling pollution make relatively greater reductions in pollution than firms with high costs. Because the level of charges (or the quantity of permits) is established on the basis of benefits to be achieved, pollution can also be reduced most in those places where it does most damage. If a unit of effluent has no known effect on wildlife when discharged into a fast-flowing river but does significant damage when discharged into a sluggish river, then reductions in effluent at the latter are more 'cost-effective', all other things being equal, than reductions at the former.

8.7 Market mechanisms such as charges and auctioned permits have the further advantage that they make harmful activities more expensive. This gives 'producers and consumers clear signals about the costs of using environmental resources'. Some policies to control pollution by using economic instruments may also provide extra revenue to public authorities: they may yield more in new revenue than they cost to administer. These revenues could in turn be used to finance further investments in environmental improvement, as will be discussed later. But they could also be seen as a generally efficient form of taxation, in the sense that the activities which are subject to tax – and thus to discouragement – are themselves harmful. The overall additional benefit of the policy (to all members of society) should however be equal to its overall additional costs.

8.8 The use of market mechanisms in environmental policy has been discussed fairly intensively since the early 1970s, at least during successive cyclical upturns in political interest in environmental pollution. There is considerable experience of charging schemes in France, Germany and the Netherlands, which we discuss in paragraphs 8.24-8.39, and of tradeable permit schemes in the United States. Even in the former Soviet Union, the 'ecological reformation of the economy' of 1987 included 'the introduction of financial incentives for natural resource conservation and on levels of pollution emissions'. Starting in 1991, enterprises were to pay pollution fees, charged 'for standardized air or water pollutant emissions, and for waste storage as well as fines levied for exceeding the established standards'.

8.9 There has been rather little international interest, nonetheless, in adopting a comprehensive economic approach to pollution, in which market mechanisms provide some sort of alternative to environmental regulation. This may in part reflect a reasonable scepticism about the larger claims made for deregulation. The use of market mechanisms in environmental policy should indeed be seen as a form of regulation, and not as an alternative to it. Charges and permit schemes require new regulations – for example, to restrict discharge of pollutants without paying a charge or obtaining a permit, or to create new property rights – and new administrative activities. An essential element of the economic approach must be to include a systematic analysis of the costs and benefits associated with alternative regulation policies. In different circumstances, such analysis might favour regulation by permits, or by charges, or by uniform discharge standards.

8.10 Even the more limited claims for market mechanisms have, however, received surprisingly little support in the United Kingdom and elsewhere. The economic arguments have remained strong but contrary political arguments have prevailed. The point made by the Royal Commission majority in 1972 – that, in the absence of regulatory limits, pollution charges allow people to 'pay the charge and discharge without limitation'– has been central to these political arguments. Pollution control authorities have been reluctant to relinquish physical limits on discharges of pollutants, even when alternative policies seem likely to lead to significant reductions in the costs of preventing pollution – a point that we discuss further in paragraph 8.22.

8.11 Such concerns reflect serious conceptual difficulties for environmental policy. The Royal Commission's definition of pollution refers to 'hazards, harm, damage, and interference'. But if to pollute is to cause harm, then the concept of an optimum amount of pollution is unavoidably troublesome. It is coherent only in the context of the analysis of a whole range of public decisions, in which the harm caused by a certain amount of pollution needs to be compared with the harm which would be caused if resources were diverted from other important purposes, not connected with pollution (and seldom within the control of the pollution control authorities). Public policy might thus compare the harm caused by a small reduction in oxygen levels in a river – for example, reducing the number and diversity of fish – with the harm which would be caused if fewer resources were available for other desirable objectives, such as providing infant and nursery care. To attempt to impose very strict limits on pollution risks diverting scarce resources from activities which might be valued much more highly by society than the elimination of a marginal unit of pollution.

8.12 The measurement of environmental benefits has been the subject of intense recent study. Evaluation surveys now attempt to elicit how much people would be willing to pay for beautiful views (and even for the knowledge that other people have beautiful views). But the measurement problems remain considerable. It is relatively easy to think about how much one would pay for the sorts of services – like visits to a lake with good quality water for swimming – which have close market substitutes. It is much less easy when the 'services' are indivisible, such as distant views of a lake. One does not usually think about how much one would pay for Windermere to be unspoilt, any more than one thinks about how much one would pay for the conservation of the Royal Navy. In the example of swimming, people are more like consumers; in the example of an unspoilt lake, they are more like citizens. But the respondents in environmental benefit surveys are citizens as well as consumers. A citizen might influence water policy by voting for a party which promises to preserve Windermere, for example, or by joining a conservation organisation, or by stating a willingness to pay heavily for walks around lakes, or by expressing an opinion about the use of environmental benefit surveys. It is important to note too that policy decisions, such as to establish uniform permitted levels of pollution, themselves influence subjective valuations of environmental benefits. People do not have time, for example, to study the scientific basis of all environmental directives, and must devise some sort of algorithm or shortcut for their own decision-making. They might thus be willing to pay large amounts of money to prevent the level of nitrate in water from exceeding European Community limits. They might pay much less, perhaps, to prevent certain specific risks associated with nitrate in water.

8.13 The problems of evaluating benefits and therefore of balancing costs and benefits at the margin are so great that the relevant authorities usually specify the desirable environmental standards that they wish to be attained. The costs of achieving these standards are often not directly considered by them, although they may not normally attempt to set standards for which the costs of compliance are clearly very high, especially if immediate compliance is required. It is interesting in this connection that the pollution inspectorate in England and Wales normally takes into account the costs involved in arriving at BATNEEC solutions,[19] in that it is prepared on occasions to allow firms several years' grace in order to achieve full compliance.

8.14 The continuing integration of European environmental regulations makes the need to estimate the costs and benefits of implementing these regulations particularly urgent. Community-wide water directives, for example, are dauntingly difficult subjects for full-scale cost-benefit analysis, given the enormous variations in physical conditions and valuations of benefits. But the systematic incorporation of economic considerations into Community environmental decision taking is correspondingly important. The higher the standards that the Community attempts to set, the higher the costs of compliance are likely to be, and the greater the potential for conflict between environmental objectives and other desirable objectives of society.

8.15 The use of economic analysis, including the appropriate use of economic instruments, is in our view an essential component of effective policies to reduce pollution. Although we are a Royal Commission on Environmental Pollution, we cannot consider pollution as though it were the only problem confronting our society. The cost of reducing pollution must be weighed against the costs of attempting to remedy other social problems. This effort is greatly facilitated by systematic economic analysis. The economists' conception of an 'optimum amount of pollution' can, however, be seen as unattractive and even inconsistent, as was noted earlier. This reflects a tension between two different ways of looking at the economics of pollution, corresponding to the perspectives of efficiency and of equity.

8.16 If it is assumed that the 'economic problem', in relation to environmental harm, 'is to maximise the value of production' then it is not unreasonable to speak of 'optimum pollution'. But for anyone concerned with policy, this is not, of course, the only objective. To judge the effects of pollution exclusively in terms of, for example, 'the value of the fish lost' versus 'the value of the product which the contamination of the stream makes possible' is to ignore essential aspects of policy concerned with equity. The person who contaminates a stream (person A) harms another person (person B) who hoped to use the stream; he harms the fish; he may harm future people, unknown or even unborn, who might have used the stream in the distant future. Under certain circumstances, the most efficient solution may be attained if person B pays person A to stop polluting the stream. But the solution is most unlikely to be equitable, and equity, too, is a component of policy choice.

19 See ch 6.

8.17 Pollution charging schemes should be efficient, and they also have the advantage from the perspective of equity, noted by the Royal Commission minority in 1972, that they are a 'means of making the polluter pay for the damage done by his pollution'. They thus reinforce the widely accepted objective of implementing the 'polluter pays' principle. This principle is not always easy to interpret. There are many kinds of harm, including but not confined to environmental pollution, which people impose on others, without being expected to pay. Sometimes the harm is so minor that it is not worth requiring (or requesting) payment; sometimes the harm is not recognised as such under current legislation; sometimes the person imposing the harm cannot reasonably be expected to have foreseen the effects of his actions; sometimes the harm results from the cumulative actions of a large number of persons. We cannot therefore, as a Commission concerned with environmental pollution, recommend that all polluters should always pay for all the harm they do. But we do consider that charging schemes represent a practical way of making producers and consumers more aware of the cost imposed by water pollution; we look in chapter 9 at other, complementary measures, including proposals for public reporting of the 'output' of certain pollutants. Charging schemes should, however, help to make possible progressive reductions in pollution over a long period and an eventual transition to conditions in which acceptable levels of pollution are both low and declining.

Some case studies

8.18 There is an extensive literature on the theory of market mechanisms in the environmental context. We asked London Economics to provide a paper giving a general overview of the scope for applying market mechanisms for the control of water pollution. It compared charges and tradeable permits as substitutes for traditional regulatory approaches to controlling water pollution. In order to look more closely at how market mechanisms might work in practice, we commissioned Stirling University and Mr J. Pezzey to report on "how a range of market mechanisms might operate in order to control a single measure of pollution, BOD [Biological Oxygen Demand], in the Forth Estuary". This work built on research carried out by the University with support from the Economic and Social Research Council (ESRC). We also considered the study by Newcastle University into the feasibility of a charging scheme designed to control pollution in the Tees Estuary. This work was commissioned by the Government in 1974 as part of its response to the Royal Commission's Third Report. Rivers and estuaries differ in a number of ways, in particular in their ability to disperse pollutants; we felt that nonetheless these reports provided valuable insights into how market mechanisms might operate in freshwater systems.

8.19 The Tees study...investigated how a charging scheme might be used instead of the statutory system of discharge consents to achieve target water quality standards in an estuary which was, at the time of the study, grossly polluted with industrial effluents and raw sewage. The study indicated that such a scheme would be very complex with charges varying substantially along the estuary for each pollutant. In addition, the calculations depended on the validity of several assumptions. It was assumed that dischargers were not able to take advantage of economies of scale when investing in pollution abatement; that no discharger dominated discharges to the estuary; and that dischargers acted to minimise their costs. Since these assumptions did not hold good for sewerage undertakers, who had considerable scope for economies of scale, sewage treatment works were not covered by the proposed charging scheme. Moreover, the charging scheme required the authorities to have access to substantial quantities of information about the costs of investment options available to dischargers – information that, in practice, is not likely to be generally available. The study also considered the effect of certain simplified charging schemes, requiring only limited information from dischargers. Making the same assumptions as described above, it was concluded that, in economic terms, such schemes could be more efficient at improving river quality than an inflexible application of regulatory controls. They would not, however, ensure that target water quality standards were achieved.

The Royal Commission was examining the use of economic instruments in the context of water pollution, in a measured way. In contrast, the European Community's position has been one of wholehearted acceptance of the narrow arguments underpinning the use of economic instruments.

European Community, *Fifth Environmental Action Programme: Towards Sustainability – A European Community Programme of Policy and Action in Relation to the Environment and Sustainable Development* OJ C 138, 17.5.1993, pp 70-72

7.4. The Economic Approach: Getting the Prices Right
Although the value of many environmental assets is difficult to measure in monetary terms and, in the case of particularly important or rare elements should not be priced in any event, valuations, pricing and accounting mechanisms have a pivotal role to play in the achievement of sustaintable development. Economic valuations can help economic agents to take environmental impacts into account when they take investment or consumption decisions. Where market forces are relevant, prices should reflect the full cost to society of production and consumption, including the environmental costs.

...

Use of economic and fiscal incentives
In order to get the prices right and to create market based incentives for environmentally friendly economic behaviour, the use of economic and fiscal instruments will have to constitute an increasingly important part of the overall approach. The fundamental aim of these instruments will be to internalize all external environmental costs incurred during the whole life-cycle of products from source through production, distribution, use and final disposal, so that environmentally-friendly products will not be at a competitive disadvantage in the market place vis-à-vis products which cause pollution and waste. In this respect, two options are possible: a pricing approach and one related to quantity.

While the Community and the Member States are currently engaged in the former, it will be important to study also the extent to which possible options such as tradeable permits could be utilized to control or reduce quantities. It will be of increasing importance to ensure that the range of instruments will be applied in a cost effective way so as to avoid unnecessary adjustment costs to the economy of the Community to minimise adverse distributional consequences and to achieve optimum environmental benefit. In developing such instruments, it will also be important to consider not only the potential impact on the local and wider environment but also their economic efficiency and regional impact.

A first important category of economic instruments consists of charges and levies. They are well understood and used, for instance in the field of water pollution. They have been developed in the past primarily to create the necessary funds for clean-up operations and infrastructures such as water treatment installations, and will remain important for these and other similar purposes such as waste disposal. However, in line with the polluter-pays principle, such charges should be progressively reorientated towards discouraging pollution at source and encouraging clean production processes, through market signals.

...

As a second category, fiscal incentives can exert considerable influence on patterns of consumption and behaviour. Environmental considerations are already being taken into account in the fiscal area within the Community: ready examples include the differentiated duties being applied by the Member States in the case of unleaded and leaded petrol, the proposal for a Council Directive on excise duties on motor fuels from agricultural sources[20] and the energy/ carbon tax envisaged in the Commission Communication 'A Community Strategy to limit carbon dioxide emissions and to improve energy efficiency'.[21]

This policy was followed by a proposal for a Council Directive introducing a carbon tax, from which the following is taken.

Amended proposal for a Council Directive introducing a tax on carbon dioxide emissions and energy COM(95) 172 final, 10.5.1995

...

Whereas, the Community's action programmes for the environment adopted in 1973, 1977, 1983, 1987 and 1992 stress the importance of reducing and preventing air pollution, whereas the 1987-92 environmental action programme stresses the importance of concentrating Community action on the priority area of reducing air pollution at source;

Whereas, at its meeting in Dublin in June 1990, the European Council pressed for the adoption, at the earliest possible opportunity, of targets and strategies for limiting emissions of greenhouse gases; whereas carbon dioxide emissions are the major component of such gases;

20 COM(92) 36 final, 28.2.1992
21 SEC(91) 1744 final, 14.10.1991

Whereas, at its meeting on 29 October 1990, the Council concluded that aggregate carbon dioxide emissions should be stabilised at 1990 levels by the year 2000;

Whereas the global dimension of the greenhouse effect has been recognised; whereas this phenomenon should be tackled at that level;

Whereas the introduction of a carbon dioxide/energy tax is an essential element of an overall strategy for improving the efficient use of energy and bringing about changes in the use of forms of energy in favour of less-polluting sources;

...

Whereas the tax must be levied on fossil energy sources as regards its objective of limiting carbon dioxide emissions and on all forms of energy as regards its objective of promoting efficient use of energy; whereas use of energy sources as feed stocks should be excluded; whereas, however, as regards the taxation of energy as such, steps should be taken to avoid distortions between various energy sources arising in connection with the extraction process; whereas the arrangements should provide for appropriate treatment of electricity;

Whereas, in order to promote the use of alternative sources of energy, renewable sources should be excluded from the scope of the tax;

Whereas, in order to achieve these two objectives, the tax should be based on the energy content and on the level of carbon dioxide emissions from the products used;

...

HAS ADOPTED THIS DIRECTIVE

Article 1

1. The Member States shall apply a harmonised tax on the products specified in Article 3 and to be levied on carbon dioxide emissions and energy content, in accordance with the provisions of this Directive.

...

Article 3

1. The tax referred to in Article 1(1) shall be levied on the products specified below and intended for use as heating fuels or as motor fuels:

a. coal, lignite, peat and their derivatives (coke, gas, etc.), with the exception of blast-furnace gas, falling within CN codes 2701 to 2705;
b. natural gas falling within CN codes 2711 21 00 to 2711 29 00;
c. mineral oils as defined in Article 2(1) of Directive 92/81/EEC on the harmonisation of the structures of excise duties on mineral oils;[22]
d. ethyl and methyl alcohol falling within CN codes 2207 and 2905 where obtained by distillation from products specified at (a) to (c).

2. The tax referred to in Article 1(1) shall also be levied on;

a. any other product intended for use as motor fuel or as an additive or extended in motor fuels, with the exception of those specified in paragraph 3;

22 OJ No L316, 31.10.1992, Directive last amended by Directive 94/74/EEC (OJ L365, 31.12.1994).

b. electricity falling within CN code 2716, and heat, generated;
   - in hydroelectric installations with a capacity of over 10 MW;
   - or using products falling within CN codes 2612, 2844 10 to 2844 50 and 2845 10;

3. The tax referred to in Article 1(1) shall not be levied on:

- fuel wood and wood charcoal falling within CN codes 4401 and 4402, and products resulting from the distillation or processing of wood;
- any product of agricultural or vegetable origin obtained directly or after chemical modification, and in particular alcohols falling within CN codes 2207 and 2905 and crude or esterified vegetable oils falling within CN codes 1507 to 1518.
- forms of energy of solar, wind, tidal and geothermal origin, or from biomass transformation.

4. Products specified in paragraphs 1 and 2 and used in metallurgical or electrolytic processes shall be regarded as being intended for use as heating fuels.

TITLE II – CHARGEABLE EVENT AND CHARGEABILITY

Article 4
1. The chargeable event for the tax shall be the extraction or manufacture of the products specified in Article 3 on the territory of the Community, ..., or their importation into that territory;

...

TITLE IV – DETERMINATION OF THE TAX BASE

Article 7
The tax base shall be:

- for the energy component of the tax: the energy content of the products specified in Article 3(1) and (2). However, electricity as specified in Article 3(2)(b) and that generated using the products referred to above shall be taxed on the basis of the electricity generated, the said products used being exempt from the tax;
- for the carbon dioxide component of the tax: the volume of carbon dioxide emitted on combustion in the presence of excess oxygen of the products specified in Article 3(1) and (2)(a).

Notwithstanding the optimism of the Fifth Environmental Action Programme about the use of economic instruments, the adoption of the proposed carbon tax Directive has proved problematic. This is not only because of the complexity of its provisions but also for political reasons. The United Kingdom government in particular is opposed to this proposal and has vetoed its adoption.

3 OBLIQUE REGULATION

There is a raft of laws which are intended primarily to protect workers' health or citizens' comfort which have the beneficial side effect of protecting the wider environment. We call this 'oblique regulation'. Under this heading is included the control of noise,[23] much health and safety regulation, particularly the Control of Substances Hazardous to Health (COSHH) Regulations 1988, now regulated by COSHH Regulations 1994,[23a] and the statutory nuisance regime operated by local authorities' Environmental Health Officers.

Health and Safety Executive, *What You Should Know About COSHH*, (London: HSE, 1990)

What are hazardous substances?
A hazardous substance is any solid, liquid, dust, fume, vapour, gas, or micro-organism that may be harmful to *your* health. Common substances like chemicals, cleaning solvents, and pesticides can be hazardous.

The types of health hazards could include:

- poisoning
- skin burns and irritation
- asphyxiation
- long-term health effects such as cancer.

COSHH covers *all* hazardous substances used, handled, processed, stored, transported, or disposed of at work. The only exceptions are asbestos, lead, materials that are harmful due solely to any radiation hazard, and substances in mines – and these are covered by their own regulations.

...

Your employer may be required by COSHH to:

- Assess workers' health risks and determine ways to remove or reduce them.
- Implement measures to control risks. For example, your employer might find substitutes for hazardous substances, change or enclose work processes, add ventilation, or where other controls are not practical, provide personal protective equipment.
- Monitor workers' exposure to risks and perform health surveillance where necessary.
- Inform, instruct, and train workers in the nature and degree of the hazard, and the precautions to take to protect themselves and others.

...

COSHH requires you to:

- Cooperate with your employer in meeting COSHH obligations
- Make full and proper use of control measures such as ventilation and storage facilities
- Select, wear, and store personal protective equipment properly
- Practice good hygiene and follow company rules
- Learn and follow proper means of using, handling, storing, and disposing of hazardous substances

23 See J Leeson, *Environmental Law* (London: Pitman, 1995) ch 12, for a comprehensive treatment of noise regulation.
23a SI 1994/3246.

- Know what to do in case of an emergency
- Report promptly any inadequacies or defects in control measures or protective equipment.

There is also a European dimension to 'oblique regulation'. EC Directive 82/501/EEC on the major accident hazards of certain industrial activities (the 'Seveso' Directive) requires the assessment of risks from hazardous works.[24] The Directive requires that Member States must take all measures to require that manufacturers engaged in listed activities prove to the competent authorities that they have identified existing major accident hazards and adopted appropriate safety measures and provided persons working with sufficient information and training in order to ensure their safety. The emphasis is on procedural rules of participation, consultation, assessment and freedom of access to information.

4 SELF-REGULATION: ENVIRONMENTAL MANAGEMENT AND AUDITING SYSTEMS

On the whole, business has been successful in convincing governments that it knows best how to change itself to contribute to sustainable development and should be left free to determine how this should be done. The development of 'environmental management' techniques has been an effective part of this lobbying strategy and from which a 'green corporate culture' has apparently been created. In the following, the authors discuss the background to the development of environmental management strategy in the United Kingdom.

J Moxen and P Strachan, 'The Formulation of Standards for Environmental Management Systems: Structural and Cultural Issues', (1995) *Greener Management International*, Issue 12, 33-48

...During the last three decades, when firms have responded to environmental pressures they have tended to do so in a way that suggests one of two stances. This is not to imply that firms have not changed stances or that their responses to pressures have always been planned, complementary or consistent. It is plain that firms have at one time or another done any number of these things. However, certain stances towards environmental pressure can be inferred from the behaviour of firms, and mostly these fall into one of two camps. Admittedly, these camps are broad and heterogeneous, but significant differences do distinguish one from the other, and for the purposes of the analysis, this is what matters. These differences are primarily concerned with the vision of the future and the strategy for getting there implicit within the stances. In some firms, the vision and the strategy implied by their stance are explicitly recognised and expressed in policy statements and plans. Of course, in many firms, the strategic implications of the stance towards pressures is not formally recognised... The

24 OJ L230, 5.8.1982, as amended by Directive 87/216/EEC, OJ L85, 19.3.1985.

fact is that the two principal stances of the last thirty years are each associated with a distinctive environmental strategy and goal. The characteristics of the strategies are discussed below.

The Scientific and Technical Strategy

This strategy emerged in the early 1970s when UK firms started to think seriously about the impact on the environment of waste and emissions. This was largely a response to increasing statutory pressures to resolve pollution concerns. Not surprisingly, this strategy was rooted firmly in the explanations that successful environmental organisations provided of their own endeavours. In these explanations, the standard of environmental performance was treated as a function of the technical abilities of staff. The technical or scientific skills of a firm's staff were held largely responsible for reducing the amount of waste and emissions generated when processing raw materials into goods. In line with this explanation, the strategy consisted of the application of scientific and technical skills to resolve waste and emission problems, and this strategy is one that many organisations still favour.

The UK Government has encouraged this view by setting environmental protection in the context of legislative limits for pollutants in effluent, emissions and waste, along with the technologies required to control them. For example, two recent initiatives of this type taken by the UK Government include the Environmental Protection Act (1990) and the Environmental Technology Best Practice Programme launched in 1994. Thus, this remains an important strategy, and, according to Eden, 'An overwhelmingly technical orientation to change is displayed by business ... Technological innovation is construed as the means to improve environmental performance and reach environmental standards'.

This strategy has much value and the technical fixes generated by it have, without question, improved the environmental performance of industry (see WCED, *Our Common Future*). However, this strategy reflects the now-dated view that the scope of environmental issues that the firm must face is small, requiring only technical adjustments to production processes and reductions in waste and emissions. The environmental concerns of the general public and those of customers have increased immeasurably in the last decade or so. The relationship between business and the environment has been radically re-appraised and firms are now required to set standards for facets of their operations that were not previously considered environmentally sensitive. Reflecting these changes in the values and perceptions of the public, the UK Government has made it clear that it expects industry to pursue a policy of continuously improving the design and operation of administrative and production processes, and the environmental standards of goods and services. In the context of these social changes, 'the problem of environmental damage by business is a complex and multi-faceted issue which requires more than a technological fix to solve the problem'.

As a consequence of these pressures, environmental issues have been forced onto the strategic and operational agendas of business managers. This recognition has led to the development and spread of a second strategy for environmental improvement, this time one which is not merely technical but, rather, explicitly managerial. Although this second strategy is stronger than the first because of its focus on management, it too is unlikely to achieve the goal of continuous improvement. The central thrust of this strategy is to establish within the firm the management systems prescribed by the standards; however, continuous improvement will only be won by laying aside conventional management philosophies and innovating in the design and operation of formal structures and in the field of human resource policies.

The Managerial Strategy

The development of this strategy has passed through two stages: first, the formulation of environmental guidelines and principles by national and international bodies and an attempt by the business community to adhere to these codes by developing its own ad hoc initiatives; second, the formulation of 'generic' environmental management systems to consolidate these earlier initiatives and provide a uniform approach to environmental management in industry.

The Formulation of Guidelines and Principles and other Measures

A precursor to the development of generic standards for environmental management systems was the proliferation of environmental guidelines and principles by leading national and international bodies. The purpose of these guidelines is to articulate a business and environmental ethic, map the key environmental issues and problems raised by contemporary business and urge managers to develop the organisational and technical means to revoke these practices and to develop more sustainable alternatives. By endorsing these guidelines, the business community has sought to highlight its commitment to continuously upgrading its environmental record.

A number of environmental guidelines and principles exist, and some of the better-known ones include: the Chemical Industries Responsible Care Programme; the CBI Environment Business Forum Agenda for Voluntary Action; the International Chamber of Commerce Business Charter for Sustainable Development; and the Coalition of Environmentally Responsible Economics (CERES) Principles (formerly the Valdez Principles).

...

[The CERES Principles are:]

1. Protect the biosphere
2. Use natural resources in a sustainable way
3. Reduce and dispose of waste safely
4. Improve energy efficiency and conservation
5. Reduce environmental risks
6. Market safe products and services
7. Compensate for damage caused by operations
8. Fully disclose environmental risks
9. Appoint environmental directors and managers
10. Assess and audit environmental performance

Across industry, the business community has responded to the CERES Principles and similar pronouncements by developing, in an incremental manner, their own ad hoc environmental management initiatives. This has included, among others, the appointment of environmental directors and managers, the development of mission statements, programmes and audits, and the utilisation of Total Quality Management (TQM) philosophies and principles and the associated human resource policies...British Telecommunications (BT), for example, has taken the latter route and has had some success in integrating environmental considerations into the organisation via business planning functions and the company's quality management systems.

Overall, however, developments in this area have been patchy, success limited, and there is some confusion about the way forward. This confusion is reflected in the frustration of the business community and the lack of a consensus on how to deliver environmental excellence. Charters, mission statements and other policy initiatives are now a common feature of the business world, but the management systems needed to change organisations and deliver these objectives are frequently absent.

...

A Regulation has been adopted at Community level for environmental management by business. It is the linchpin of a framework in which business may regulate itself. Self-regulation models such as this eco-audit and management scheme represent a departure from modernist forms of regulation which tend to rely on compliance with centrally set standards, by recourse to sanctions if necessary, the self-regulation model is both more fluid and complex. Networks of responsibility are set up which are activated by the exchange of information, training of key personnel, and external verification of the audit and management systems. Responsibility for environmental protection extends even to the public, since the publicity requirements of this model draw in the vigilant citizen or environmental group as an external check.

COUNCIL REGULATION (EEC) No 1836/93 of 29 June 1993, OJ L168, 10.7.1993, allowing voluntary participation by companies in the industrial sector in a Community eco-management and audit scheme

...

Whereas the programme "Towards Sustainability", presented by the Commission and approved as to its general approach by the Council resolution of 1 February 1993, underlines the role and responsibilities of companies, both to reinforce the economy and to protect the environment throughout the Community;

Whereas industry has its own responsibility to manage the environmental impact of its activities and should therefore adopt a pro-active approach in this field;

Whereas this responsibility calls for companies to establish and implement environmental policies, objectives and programmes and effective environmental management systems; whereas companies should adopt an environmental policy which, in addition to providing for compliance with all relevant regulatory requirements aims at the reasonable continuous improvement of environmental performance;

Whereas the application of environmental management systems by companies shall take account of the need to ensure awareness and training of workers in the establishment and implementation of such systems;

Whereas environmental management systems should include environmental auditing procedures to help management assess compliance with the system and the effectiveness of the system in fulfilling the company's environmental policy;

Whereas the provision of information to the public, by companies, on the environmental aspects of their activities is an essential element of good environmental management and a response to the growing interest of the public in information on this subject;

Whereas companies should therefore be encouraged to produce and disseminate periodic environmental statements containing information for the public on the factual environmental situation in their industrial sites and on their environmental policies, programmes, objectives and management systems;

Whereas the transparency and credibility of companies' activities in this field are enhanced when the companies' environmental policies, programmes, management systems, audit procedures and environmental statements are examined to verify that they meet the relevant requirements of this Regulation and when the environmental statements are validated by accredited environmental verifiers;

Whereas it is necessary to provide for an independent and neutral accreditation and supervision of environmental verifiers in order to ensure the credibility of the scheme;

Whereas companies should be encouraged to participate in such a scheme on a voluntary basis; whereas, in order to ensure an equal implementation of the scheme throughout the Community, the rules, procedures and essential requirements have to be the same in each Member State;

...

Whereas, in order to avoid unjustified burdens on companies and to ensure consistency between the Community scheme and national, European and international standards for environmental management systems and audits, those standards recognized by the Commission according to an appropriate procedure shall be considered as meeting the corresponding requirements of this Regulation and companies should not be required to duplicate the relevant procedures;

...

HAS ADOPTED THIS REGULATION:

Article 1

The eco-management and audit scheme and its objectives

1. A Community scheme allowing voluntary participation by companies performing industrial activities, hereinafter referred to as the 'Community eco-management and audit scheme' or 'the scheme', is hereby established for the evaluation and improvement of the environmental performance of industrial activities and the provision of the relevant information to the public.

2. The objective of the scheme shall be to promote continuous improvements in the environmental performance of industrial activities by:

(a) the establishment and implementation of environmental policies, programmes and management systems by companies, in relation to their sites;

(b) the systematic, objective and periodic evaluation of the performance of such elements;
(c) the provision of information of environmental performance to the public.

3. The scheme shall be without prejudice to existing Community or national laws or technical standards regarding environmental controls and without prejudice to the duties of companies under those laws and standards.

Article 2

Definitions

For the purposes of this Regulation:

(a) *environmental policy* shall mean the company's overall aims and principles of action with respect to the environment including compliance with all relevant regulatory requirements regarding the environment;
(b) *environmental review* shall mean an initial comprehensive analysis of the environmental issues, impact and performance related to activities at a site;
(c) *environmental programme* shall mean a description of the company's specific objectives and activities to ensure greater protection of the environment at a given site, including a description of the measures taken or envisaged to achieve such objectives and where appropriate the deadlines set for implementation of such measures;
(d) *environmental objectives* shall mean the detailed goals, in terms of environmental performance, which a company sets itself;
(e) *environmental management system* shall mean that part of the overall management system which includes the organizational structure, responsibilities, practices, procedures, processes and resources for determining and implementing the environmental policy;
(f) *environmental audit* shall mean a management tool comprising a systematic, documented, periodic and objective evaluation of the performance of the organization, management system and processes designed to protect the environment with the aim of:
    (i) facilitating management control of practices which may have impact on the environment;
    (ii) assessing compliance with company environmental policies;
(g) *audit cycle* shall mean the period of time in which all the activities in a given site are audited, according to the requirements of Article 4 and Annex II, on all the relevant environmental aspects mentioned in Annex 1.C;
(h) *environmental statement* shall mean a statement prepared by the company in line with the requirements of this Regulation and, in particular, of Article 5;

...

Article 3

Participation in the scheme

The scheme is open to companies operating a site or sites where an industrial activity is performed. In order for a site to be registered in the scheme the company must:

(a) adopt a company environmental policy, in accordance with the relevant requirements in Annex 1, which, in addition to providing for compliance with all relevant regulatory requirements regarding the environment, must include commitments aimed at the reasonable continuous improvement of environmental performance, with a view to reducing environmental impacts to levels not exceeding those corresponding to economically viable application of best available technology;
(b) conduct an environmental review of the site on the aspects referred to in Annex 1, part C;
(c) introduce, in the light of the results of that review, an environmental programme for the site and an environmental management system applicable to all activities at the site. The environmental programme will be aimed at achieving the commitments contained in the company environmental policy towards continuous improvement of environmental performance. The environmental management system must comply with the requirements of Annex 1;
(d) carry out, or cause to be carried out, in accordance with Article 4, environmental audits at the sites concerned;
(e) set objectives at the highest appropriate management level, aimed at the continuous improvement of environmental performance in the light of the findings of the audit, and appropriately revise the environmental programme to enable the set objectives to be achieved at the site;
(f) prepare, in accordance with Article 5, an environmental statement specific to each site audited. The first statement must also include the information referred to in Annex V;
(g) have the environmental policy, programme, management system, review or audit procedure and environmental statement or statements examined to verify that they meet the relevant requirements of this Regulation and the environmental statements validated in accordance with Article 4 and Annex III;
(h) forward the validated environmental statement to the competent body of the Member State where the site is located and disseminate it as appropriate to the public in the State after registration of the site in question in accordance with Article 8.

Article 4

Auditing and validation
1. The internal environmental audit of a site may be conducted by either auditors belonging to the company or external persons or organizations acting on its behalf. In both cases the audit shall be performed in line with the criteria set out in part C of Annex I and in Annex II.

...

Article 9

Publication of the list of registered sites
The competent bodies directly, or via the national authorities as decided by the Member State concerned, shall communicate to the Commission before the end of each year the lists referred to in Article 8 and updates thereof.

Each year the Commission shall publish in the *Official Journal of the European Communities* a list of all the registered sites in the Community.

...

ANNEX I

REQUIREMENTS CONCERNING ENVIRONMENTAL POLICIES, PROGRAMMES AND MANAGEMENT SYSTEMS

A. Environmental policies, objectives and programmes

1. The company environmental policy, and the programme for the site, shall be established in writing. Associated documents will explain how the environmental programme and the management system at the site relate to the policy and systems of the company as a whole.

2. The company environmental policy shall be adopted and periodically reviewed, in particular in the light of environmental audits, and revised as appropriate, at the highest management level. It shall be communicated to the company's personnel and be publicly available.

...

B. Environmental management systems

The environmental management system shall be designed, implemented and maintained in such a way as to ensure the fulfilment of the requirements defined below.

1. *Environmental policy, objectives and programmes*

The establishment and periodical review, and revision as appropriate, of the company's environmental policy, objectives and programmes for the site, at the highest appropriate management level.

2. *Organization and personnel*

Responsibility and authority

Definition and documentation of responsibility, authority and interrelations of key personnel who manage, perform and monitor work affecting the environment.

Management representative

Appointment of a management representative having authority and responsibility for ensuring that the management system is implemented and maintained.

Personnel, communications and training

Ensuring among personnel at all levels, awareness of:

(a) the importance of compliance with the environmental policy and objectives, and with the requirements applicable under the management system established;
(b) the potential environmental effects of their work activities and the environmental benefits of improved performance;
(c) their roles and responsibilities in achieving compliance with the environmental policy and objectives, and with the requirements of the management system;

(d) The potential consequences of departure from the agreed operating procedures.

Identifying training needs, and providing appropriate training for all personnel whose work may have a significant effect upon the environment.

The company shall establish and maintain procedures for receiving, documenting and responding to communications (internal and external) from relevant interested parties concerning its environmental effects and management.

...

C. Issues to be covered

The following issues shall be addressed, within the framework of the environmental policy and programmes and of environmental audits.

1. Assessment, control, and reduction of the impact of the activity concerned on the various sectors of the environment.
2. Energy management, savings and choice.
3. Raw materials management, savings, choice and transportation; water management and savings.
4. Waste avoidance, recycling, reuse, transportation and disposal.
5. Evaluation, control and reduction of noise within and outside the site.
6. Selection of new production processes and changes to production processes.
7. Product planning (design, packaging, transportation, use and disposal).
8. Environmental performance and practices of contractors, subcontractors and suppliers.
9. Prevention and limitation of environmental accidents.
10. Contingency procedures in cases of environmental issues.
11. Staff information and training on environmental issues.
12. External information on environmental issues.

Regulation 1863/93/EEC uses the terminology of responsibility, stewardship and sustainability and stresses freedom of access to information on the environment. It is the freedom of access to information and the publicity requirements of the regulation which, surprisingly, have drawn the sharpest criticism. This is not because of the likely ineffectiveness of such provisions but because of the opportunities for self-promotion they offer. This aspect of self-regulation is assessed in the following passage, which asks provocatively whether audit and management systems (and eco-labelling) have the power to seduce.

F Ost, 'A Game Without Rules? The Ecological Self-Organisation of Firms', in G Teubner, L Farmer and D Murphy, *Environmental Law and Ecological Responsibility* (Chichester: Wiley, 1994) pp 352-355

...

Eco-audit and eco-label: right to know or power to seduce?

Two regulations of the Council of the European Communities...one for a "Community Environmental Audit Scheme" (eco-audit), the other for a "Community System of Ecological Labelling" (eco-labelling), further illustrate the political will to increase firms' self-responsibility in the area of environmental protection. These two texts are, moreover, part of a line of preventive action aimed at reducing nuisances at source, by rational planning of production and the promotion of clean technologies and products. In both cases, the point is to make the policy pursued by the firm in these areas more transparent, make the public aware of the efforts being made and to award the most efficient firms with a sort of good conduct certificate that they would be authorised to use in their publicity campaigns. The public's supposed preference for products and firms with that distinction would then, through the flexible play of the law of supply and demand on the market, lead to the repayment of investments made and to the launching of a general campaign in favour of the most environment-friendly technologies.

Positive as these prospects are, we propose, however, to put a few critical questions in connection with them, inspired by the same concerns as have guided us up to now. Should one, for instance, favour a system of deliberate self-commitment by certain firms in sectors they have chosen, or instead one of respect by *all* firms for *legal* obligations? Are the procedures for awarding the eco-label and doing the eco-audit of a sufficiently adversary nature? Do they give guarantees of independence and impartiality? Is the publicity that seems to be the real objective of both schemes inspired by a genuine concern for public information, or does it derive more from a media message? In other words, is the game one where the cards are on the table, or is it instead related to a game like poker where all moves, including bluffs and cheating, are permitted?

To answer these questions, let us consider each of the regulatory texts. First the eco-audit. This is a tool for the firm's environmental administration, consisting in the systematic, periodic, objective evaluation of its policy, programme and equipment in the sphere. In addition to better information for the public and authorities, it is expected to bring a steady improvement in the performance of firms. Among these aims there is also that of respect for the various legal regulations...

This system will not, however, be of general application. It is planned to reserve it to firms that deliberately commit themselves to it. Article 3 provides that enterprises "may" ask for entry to the audit scheme, for one or several of their industrial sites...They will in this case conform to the rules of the audit, including in particular the obligation to "establish, in accordance with their own needs and choices, an internal system for environment protection", and, of course, the obligation to have the audit done regularly, have it evaluated, and keep it available to the public and the authorities (Art. 3).

The text further provides for a system of certification by outside auditors of the reliability of the audit reports. This system requires that a variety of national and supra-national authorities be set up. It is further provided that "Member States may engage in action to promote the eco-audit scheme, in particular by introducing appropriate incentives to encourage participation in the eco-audit scheme (reduction in charges for pollution emitted, loans, priorities in public contracts etc.)".

What is one to think of this system? It will first of all be noted that, following the logic of self-responsibility, it has a purely voluntary foundation. Firms conform to it if they want to, and for the sites...where they feel that it might be advantageous. They are to develop an internal system of environment protection "in accordance with their own needs and choices". It will be agreed that this is to push the logic of "self" very far. One would, however, have no objections if it were established that this sort of scheme is, as the Preamble says, a complement to and not a substitute for the general legal obligations. If it means doing more than the law and better, then so much the better; if on the contrary the point is the *ad hoc* negotiation of the application of obligatory texts, with the state sometimes "buying" conformity in the form of reductions in charges or of loans, it is clear that this sort of scheme would be unacceptable... Is our criticism misplaced because the text explicitly rules out this hypothesis? Certainly the most flagrant abuses are unlikely; it is not unrealistic, by contrast, to fear that this scheme of self-responsibilization will gradually, in a climate of euphoric deregulation, replace the normative framework that is both binding and general. In that case, would we not see a growing differentiation between a few very efficient enterprises, at the cutting edge of research in terms of clean technology, and the bulk of the industrial sector whose polluting activities would scarcely be censured any longer? Moreover, how is one to guarantee that the bound measures by "clean" firms would be maintained once they had acquired a dominant market share or ecology has gone out of fashion – especially since in the meantime the present binding mechanism would have been weakened? Here too, then, it is important for progress in the direction of self-responsibility to be accompanied by corresponding progress in the direction of defining general, binding normative objectives. Here again, the game model is instructive: the players' inventiveness has meaning only against the background of the rules of the game.

Our second question relates to the nature of the publicity attached to the audit. In connection with this, the text studied contains a number of very informative passages. The Preamble (old version) says that there is a "clear need to *improve public acceptance* of certain activities (of firms) through greater transparency"; further on there is talk of developing a "*partnership*" with the public (here again we almost explicitly come up against the model of the positive sum co-operative game). Several provisions echo this concern for information/ seduction of the public: ... Article 5 provides for an "environment statement" to be drawn up to inform the "wider public". Written in "summary, non-technical form", it should however "fully and objectively" reflect the results of the audit and likewise be certified by outside verification...Article 11 provides that firms entered in the eco-audit scheme should have the right to use the eco-audit *logo* for sites and/or production activities covered. Finally, Article 12 provides that states may also join this great promotion campaign by "publicizing the eco-audit scheme and informing the public about it".

Many precautions have certainly been taken to guarantee the objectivity of the information contained in the audit report and the outside auditors have the specific mission of ensuring the reliability of these documents. One cannot, however, avoid the impression that the real *raison d'etre* of the text is the concern to reinforce the firm's image. In these circumstances, this "licence to seduce" ought not to be a substitute for a much more fundamental legal institution, namely the citizen's "right to know", since every attack on the environment can be analyzed as a detriment to the "common goods" that the Belgian and French Civil Codes (Art. 714) claim belong to no-one and are for the benefit of all. Another EC Directive, dated 7 June 1990, on "the freedom of access to environment-related information" might serve as a reference here. It makes access to information (through the authorities, it is true) a genuine right enjoyed by "every physical or legal person asking for it, without any need to show an interest" (Art. 3). Refusal to communicate the information requested would have to be for stated reasons, and the person turned down would have a remedy (Art. 4). The scope of this principle is further extended by Art. 6, which makes it a duty on states to ensure that "information relating to the environment held by agencies with public responsibilities related to the environment and controlled by the public authorities should be made available on the same terms". One can see the potential field of application of this principle, even if at present it remains encumbered by numerous exceptions (Art. 3). Starting from the idea that the environmental game is at least as much conflictual as co-operative, we admit our preference for this logic of "cards on the table" information over the publicity system of the audit. The regulation on ecological labelling leads us to a similar conclusion.

Schemes such as the eco-audit and management system rest on large assumptions: first, the existence of an identifiable 'corporate culture'; and second, that a corporate culture can be adapted to become environmentally aware and environmentally responsible. The following extract questions whether such assumptions are well-founded or even desirable.

A Crane, 'Rhetoric and Reality in the Greening of Organisational Culture', (1995) *Greener Management International*, Issue 12, 49-62

...

The Cultural Fix

The arguments depicting the development of a strong and highly-integrative corporate culture in order to provide social cohesion and a common guiding force for the organisation are by now well known (see, for example, Peters and Waterman, *In Search of Excellence*). Of most significance perhaps is the causal relationship that is either explicitly or implicitly established between culture and performance in such models. This cultural fix prescription has evidently proved popular too in the green business literature where it is commonly seen as a means to promote greener corporate management, strategy and marketing. Primarily, the major objective is to develop a 'strong' culture – one that permeates and binds corporate members and fosters a sense of identity and commitment to common environmental goals and aspirations within the organisation. Culture is therefore regarded in this sense as that which is shared...Conceived thus, a strong green corporate culture would require an overriding consensus of environmental beliefs and values between individuals and their organisation. Bernstein states the case succinctly and unambiguously:

> Green is a catalyst, forcing the most reticent of companies to communicate, raise its profile, state what it stands for. Every company will need to examine, possibly change, almost certainly articulate, its corporate culture.

Most commonly, the central element in this process of developing a strong green culture is the cascade of core values from top management downwards. The 'greenness' of the corporation's culture is thus determined in the executive suite, usually by the founder – 'caring capitalists' such as Anita Roddick of The Body Shop or Ben Cohen of Ben & Jerry's for example – and subsequently disseminated among employees throughout the lower levels of the corporation. This corporate vision or mission can be articulated in a number of ways, either directly through cultural artefacts such as corporate environmental statements and policies, or indirectly through symbolic acts of managerial greenness (such as Anita Roddick's well-publicised trips to indigenous people of Mexico and South America). Since these cultural manipulations need to be correctly interpreted and understood by employees, effective corporate communication can be regarded as the principal conduit for 'cultural greenewal'.

The argument that corporate cultures will have to be defined and changed in order to respond to green pressures is almost uniformly advocated by green business writers. That much of the work in this area is characterised by little more than 'technicist kitsch' should not be ignored. It appears further that even well-established researchers in the field proselytise a virtually identical creed. For example, Welford...states:

> Corporate culture...constitutes a distinctive character of the organisation. The challenge facing the modern business is therefore how it can redefine and change its corporate culture in such a way as to be consistent with the concept of sustainable development. Senior management will have to take the lead.

Several factors can be said to account for the popularity of the cultural fix model, but primarily these stem from two main elements of the culture discourse: in terms of its theoretical applicability, there is the moral dimension of organisational culture; and in practical terms, there is the wide-scale marketing of the corporate culture concept itself in the management field.

The popular view of culture as the essential ingredient in the greening of business can be attributed to some extent to the need to locate organisational greening within some kind of conceptual framework. The position of environmentalism within organisation studies and within management theory generally is as yet unclear and open to interpretation.

Perhaps the greatest advantage offered by the concept of organisational culture is that it allows us to explore the rather less conspicuous *moral* dimension of economic institutions. Any community that can be distinguished in terms of its unique culture must in some way be held together by reciprocal relationships of obligation and responsibility – that is, by moral relationships. It is through this moral dimension that we are able to conceive of environmental issues as being a social responsibility of corporations, an ethical dilemma for managers to deal with, or a means by which employees and other stakeholders can express their own personal values. In essence, the concept of organisational culture provides a conceptual bridge between, on one side the abstract normative prescriptions which underlie the principles of corporate social responsibility and business ethics, and on the other the social realities of everyday organisational life.

Alvesson and Berg argue that the dramatic growth and popularity of the concept of organisational culture is also attributable to the way in which it has been effectively formulated and sold as a 'product' to managers. The seductive promise of corporate culture has been that it can be managed in such a way as to achieve social integration and commitment in order to provide a vehicle for long-term competitive advantage, innovation and productivity. It is the propagation of this (relatively unproven) link between culture and performance that has been instrumental in the increasing importance being attached to cultural considerations in the field of corporate environmentalism. Effective environmental management, it is frequently argued, depends on the successful integration of greener values throughout the organisation. Essentially, the message from environmental literature is clear: improved environmental performance requires greener corporate cultures.

Is There Such a Thing as a Green Corporate Culture?

In order for the concept of corporate culture to be a useful term analytically, then it must be possible to observe evidence of qualitative differences between organisations both in terms of their common behaviours and their shared underlying assumptions and values. Although it appears intuitively plausible that we can begin to differentiate between corporate environmental behaviour (or performance) in this way, we must also consider the extent to which it is true that corporations can embody greener values and assumptions than others. Two major caveats are apparent in the assumption that we can identify and recognise specifically 'green' cultures: first that an overarching and unifying corporate culture might not actually exist in practice, except at the most superficial of levels; and second that attempts to conform to such prescriptions might drive out the very moral reflection that is necessary to maintain a moral or socially responsible agenda for environmental issues in business.

...

Growing Greener Cultures

Clearly then there are doubts that should be raised concerning the popular proposition that the organisation can exhibit a culture that integrates the environmental values of its constituent members, and that this will subsequently lead to better environmental performance. Perhaps even more importantly however, we must also question the extent to which such a 'greener' culture can be grown and developed through deliberate management action. The assertion that corporate culture can in some way be controlled and managed is probably the most controversial and contested notion within the organisational culture discourse. It is evident, however, that the same level of questioning and debate has not been forthcoming in the environmental field. There is a common, but evidently myopic and even potentially damaging assumption that because culture *must* change in order to bring about environmental improvements in the business sector then of course it *can* change and that top management *will* indeed change it. There is very little evidence advanced in support of this claim outside of accounts that are either brief and anecdotal or self-reported. There is little reason to expect that the majority of managers will attempt to green their organisational culture; there is even less reason to expect that even those that do will achieve the sort of success that is promised to them from the managerialist pulpit.

...

5 BUYING THE GREEN LIFESTYLE

Consumers consume more than the products and services they buy. They also purchase a company's image, its social, economic and environmental record. The thrust of green consumerism is to change the course of rampant consumerism rather than to curb its excesses. Its emphasis remains freedom of action of the individual – to buy a particular product, choose a particular mode of transport, all in all to buy a particular lifestyle, with constraints only at the edges. Green consumerism even offers a further layer of satisfaction than that usually derived from the material reward of consumption – the taking part in a broader movement (the environmental movement), and the easing of a green conscience. To use Jacob's argument, green consumerism permits the fusion of individuals' behaviour as citizens and as consumers.[25]

In the 1980s the influence of the green movement on public values and consumer awareness left manufacturers and retailers reeling, so unprepared were they for the demand for apparently environmentally benign products and services. The *Green Consumer Guide* responded to, but also fuelled, this demand.

J Elkington & J Hailes, *The Green Consumer Guide* (London: Victor Gollancz, 1989) pp 1-3

The Green Consumer

Every day of the week, whether we are shopping for simple necessities or for luxury items, for fish fingers or for fur coats, we are making choices that affect the environmental quality of the world we live in.

Take a bite out of a hamburger, we are told, and we may be taking a bite out of the world's rainforests. Buy the wrong car and we may end up not only with a large fuel bill, but also with fewer trees and, quite possibly, less intelligent children. Spray a handful of hair gel or a mist of furniture polish from certain aerosols, and you help destroy the planet's atmosphere – increasing everybody's chances of contracting skin cancer.

Few of us can spot the links between what we do day-to-day and the environmental destruction which is happening around the world. How many fast-fooders know about what is happening to the world's tropical forests, for example? Yet cattle ranching has been one of the causes of deforestation in countries like Brazil and Costa Rica, particularly from the mid-1970s to the mid-1980s. A good deal of the meat produced went into fast-food products of one kind or another...

And how many of us, even if we have seen TV programmes on the newly-discovered Antarctic 'ozone hole', could say exactly what chlorofluorocarbons (CFCs) are? However, the dramatic success of the anti-CFC campaign means that millions of us *do* now know about the Earth's protective ozone layer. And we are also beginning to be aware of the damage that the CFC propellants used to squirt many products through the nozzle of an aerosol, that pinnacle of convenience in twentieth-century packaging, can do to the ozone layer.

25 See above, pp 310-312.

But more and more of us want to do the right thing – we simply don't know how. Clearly, if the relevant information is presented in the right way, then more and more of us will become sufficiently interested to take action, through our day-to-day decisions.

Part of the solution, in fact, is in your hands. Whether you are in the supermarket, the garage; the garden centre or the travel agent's, this first edition of *The Green Consumer Guide* tells you which products to avoid and which to buy.

The *Guide* does not promote a 'hair-shirt' lifestyle. It is designed to appeal to a 'sandals-to-Saabs' spectrum of consumers. The information provided is intended to ensure that, whatever your lifestyle, you will know where to find attractive, cost-competitive products and services which are environmentally acceptable and – as far as possible – a pleasure to use.

...

The real message of the *Guide* is that the Green Consumer is here and is already having a tremendous impact. Remember the changes that have already taken place: the replacement of 'hard' detergents with 'soft', more biodegradable products; the gradual shift from leaded to unleaded petrol; and the growth in demand for health foods and organically grown produce.

...

It is the consumer's ability to change from Brand X to Brand Y – or even more worrying for manufacturers and retailers, to stop buying a particular product altogether – that makes producers sit up and take notice.

The European Community has adopted a two pronged approach to achieve more environmentally friendly business and consumption patterns: the environmental management and auditing system (EMAS) set up by Regulation 93/1863/EEC, discussed above, and an eco-labelling regime for providing information. Significantly, both are voluntary. The aim of Regulation 92/880/EEC on a Community eco-label[26] is that information is provided so that consumers may differentiate between products and services on environmental grounds. The system follows the 'cradle to grave' principle taking into account every stage of a product's life from manufacture, through transport and use, to disposal, and every stage of service provision. The manufacturer, importer or service provider applies for a label and, if one is awarded by the competent authorities, the firm enters into a contract with the authorities and may use the label. We see here a good example of Daintith's 'dominium' technique of governance discussed above. The eco-labelling scheme has been subjected to the same criticisms as for EMAS.[27]

Most of the information about the qualities and environmental impacts of products and services is derived, not from eco-labelling but from advertisements issued by the manufacturers and providers of those products and services. But, as with other categories of advertisements, many 'green' advertisements do not function as a source of information for consumer wants that originate within the individual but, rather, force a shift in the locus of decision in the purchase of 'green' goods to the producer where it is subject to control. The

26 OJ L 99, 11.4.1992.

27 See critique of EMAS by Ost, p 332 above.

advertising industry very capably appropriates the spirit, language, and images of the environmental movement, but falls short of taking on its message of resistance, political and direct action, and profound change in consumption patterns and living conditions. The following extract outlines the method and problem of green advertising and evaluates one response – regulation of the advertising industry *by* the advertising industry. The limits of law can be seen in controlling 'unfair' advertisements, which rely on the juxtaposition of images and language to carry across the message that a particular product is environmentally benign.

J Holder, 'Regulating Green Advertising in the Motor Car Industry', (1991) *Journal of Law and Society*, Vol 18, No 3, 323-343

The 'ultimate green machine' is a phrase used to describe a motor car from the 'new generation'[28] of vehicles. In such advertisements, the advertising industry stands between mass production and mass 'green' consumption.[29] Similar advertising techniques have recently been employed in large numbers to sell products which appear to conform to the demands of 'green consumerism', that is the use of individual consumer preference to promote less environmentally damaging products and services. This advertising practice has been popularly regarded as a response to consumer demands for information upon environ-mentally benign products fuelled by a sense of responsibility towards the environment. Such a liberal view of advertising is adhered to by the Advertising Standards Authority (hereafter, the ASA) which states that 'it is to the credit of the advertising industry that they have responded to this green movement'.[30] However the use of the language of the environmental protection movement and green imagery by the advertising industry has been criticized. Green advertisements have been perceived as a means to create and foster new consumer desires and to inject competition into the market in a way that does not rely upon price and even denies it as a factor. Green advertisements have been described as misleading, 'downright false', and also unfair as words such as 'natural', 'real' and 'green' have become thoroughly polluted with misuse.

Within green consumerism, the regulation of advertising is emerging as a key issue alongside that of the need for a comprehensive labelling system. The concern about green advertising may be seen on two levels. The first is that of misleading or deceptive advertising involving the accuracy of facts. The second level is 'unfair' advertising or the more subtle means by which value may be seen to be added to the product during exchange.

...

The particular problems raised by green advertising and the effectiveness of private and public regulation will be illustrated by current advertisements for motor cars. This example has been chosen because cars, perhaps the 'archetypal commodity',[31] are commonly not regarded as 'green' even by the

28 SAAB advertisement, *The Guardian*, 31 January 1990.
29 S Irvine, *Beyond Green Advertising*, Friends of the Earth Discussion Paper No 1 (1989) 12.
30 ASA Case Report No 171, Editorial, 'A Shade too Green?'.
31 S Ewen, *Captains of Consciousness*, (1976), p 202.

motoring industry. Car advertisements in this area therefore tend to be potent sources of persuasion. Further, motor car advertisements offer an example of the two levels on which advertisements may be seen to 'work'. The problem of inaccurate facts has been addressed by legislation and the ASA. Car advertisements also offer opportunity for regulation or acting upon the 'signifier' or meaning level. On this level, much use has been made in advertisements of the idea that the car is:

> not merely an idiosyncratic mode of transport but an artifact of multi-dimensional significance within the culture.[32]

...

THE PROBLEM OF 'GREEN' ADVERTISING

The rhetoric and visual language of 'green' advertising tends to reconcile the contradictions between mass consumption and an environmental conscience. In this process inaccurate information and latent messages or signifiers have been used. As stated, the concern about green advertising may be seen on two levels: misleading or deceptive advertising and the second level of unfair advertising. The provision of accurate information has been seen as one condition for the optimal operation of a competitive market. Failure in the area by way of fraud or barriers to the consumers' search for information may lead to an inefficient allocation of consumer resources.[33] The accuracy of facts and claims is particularly important with regard to green advertising since the consumer is generally unable to test the claims made in areas where scientists do not agree. Further, inaccurate information may mean that a consumer becomes disillusioned with all green products.

Unfair advertising works on a less overt level to that of misleading advertising. Unfair advertising has been broadly classified as that which involves psychological exploitation.[34] A more useful distinction may be drawn between 'legitimate exploitation' and 'illegitimate' exploitation. This distinction raises the question of how far advertisers may excite, distress or alarm the consumer by some form of 'green' advertising such as that which documents environmental decay if a message of prudent or sensible behaviour underlies the advertisement. Unfair advertisements have been described as those which abuse or unjustifiably arouse sentiments of fear or are likely to influence a consumer or the public in any other improper manner.[35]

...

1. *Misleading Factual Claims*

Misleading factual claims and inaccurate information in green advertisements are a special category monitoring project by the ASA (report no. 178). From July to December 1989, the ASA looked at sixty-nine press advertisements of

32 Ibid, p 203.

33 I Ramsay, *Consumer Protection* (1989) p 573.

34 E Ackroyd, 'Proper Functions of Advertising', in *Advertising and the Community* A Wilson (ed) (1968).

35 Definition in draft EC Directive, see D Glass, 'Misleading Advertisements - the Law Responds' (1989) NLJ 1643.

which ten needed further enquiries. For example, a factual inaccuracy was made recently in an advertisement for the Austin Metro Surf. It was claimed that the car was designed to run on unleaded petrol and was thus 'as ozone friendly as it was economical'. The advertisers acknowledged that they had no evidence to support the claim's implication that there was a connection between the use of unleaded petrol and damage to the ozone layer. The statement was found to be incorrect because lead is too heavy to reach the stratosphere and cannot interfere with the composition of the earth's ozone layer (ASA Report no. 178).

Similarly objection was taken to a national press advertisement for the Citroen BX Diesel Turbo which included the claim that 'while you're looking after the pennies, you're also looking after the planet; diesel is lead free'. The ASA upheld the complaint that the advertisement was misleading in that it suggested that diesel-powered cars would not pollute the environment despite evidence that the fumes produced by a diesel engine using lead-free fuel remained noxious (ASA report no. 178).

...

2. *Appealing to Nature and the Natural*

Appeals to nature as a major referent system appear to be the basis of many 'green' advertisements. In such a way an individual's knowledge of nature is appropriated by advertisers.[36] The use of natural imagery – or a 'bundle of positive connotations' – in advertisements is a particularly strong selling point. According to Williamson, such imagery encompasses knowledge and values from the outside referent system, or anterior knowledge which enables the consumer to internalize and make sense of the advertisement.[37] As a referent system, nature may be 'implied' and used as a signifier in relation to a product. Thus a product is placed within a hollowed-out knowledge of 'nature' and draws its significance from that.

...

In the current 'green generation' of car advertisements, the 'rawness' and 'danger' of nature[38] is exchanged for a celebration of nature and denial of technology. However some advertisements still show the car placed quite literally in 'nature', not in order that technology be channelled through nature and come to overcome it...but rather to connect the product with nature. In some recent advertisements, cars have been placed in natural settings. The juxtaposition of a car speeding through a forest ('Put your foot down, cut pollution', SAAB, *The Observer,* 12 November 1989) is such as to give the car an aura of the natural. Similarly a car's catalytic converter was 'tested' in America 14,000 feet up a mountain, 'because the air is very clear up there' (Rover 800 series, *The Independent,* 4 May 1990). Applying Williamson's analysis to 'green' advertisements, such advertisements may be seen to shake the meaning out of the natural referent system and insert their own meaning. Thus the natural system comes to be filled with products that summarize nature. Consumers are

36 J Williamson, *Decoding Advertisements* (1978) 135.
37 Ibid, p 123.
38 Ibid, p 123.

urged to buy and attain 'the natural'. In 'green advertising' the attaining of the natural is portrayed as imperative and as part of a collective movement.

3. *Fostering a Sense of Participating in Collective Action*
In *Critique of Commodity Aesthetics*, Haug suggests that collective action which moves beyond the private sphere and is not self-interested is an alien exception to the capitalist system.[39] Collective action, or the high degree of satisfaction derived from such communal action is appropriated by the advertising industry which generally relies upon individual interests and action in consumption. Haug states that 'there is a whole illusion industry hard at work constructing just such illusory satisfaction',[40] which displaces the very purpose of collective action. The importance of the collective praxis is apparent in 'green' advertising. Faced with the prospect of environmental decay and disasters, normally isolated consumers form an ad hoc community. The community has been artificially reflected in some advertisements.

Campaign magazine's ten rules for green advertisers includes the tip to 'induce a sense of pride inspired by being part of the movement'.[41] The Saab advertisement campaign seems to follow this rule carefully. The opening of one advert urges 'sign a petition, lobby your local MP, form a demonstration, buy a Saab' (*The Observer,* 12 November 1989). The essence of green consumerism is that of individual action forming part of a larger movement. However the manipulation of satisfaction derived from collective action tends to divert attention away from the main issue and makes consumption the goal of collective movements rather than social change. Williamson concludes that the need for '...relationships and human meaning appropriated by advertisements is one that if only it was not diverted could radically change the society we live in'.[42]

Therefore the power of collective action may be seen to become marginalized and minimalized. The fostering of a sense of belonging to the green movement by consumption may be regarded as exploiting the need to participate in collective action. This manipulation of human weaknesses and vulnerability is a further form of psychological exploitation and may be categorised as 'unfair' advertising.

4. *Exploitation of Concern for the Environment*
...the following extract from a recent Audi advertisement is in the form of a direct appeal to the consumer and may be seen to be 'unfair' in the sense defined:

> Isn't lead already affecting our children's brains? Isn't carbon monoxide poisoning the air we breathe even as we speak? And frankly, hasn't the car done the environment enough damage over the years? (*The Observer,* 19 November 1989).

'Green' advertisements such as the above have tended to make frequent references to children and to the 'next generation'. This technique was employed

39 W Haug, *Critique of Commodity Aesthetics* (1971) 119.
40 Ibid, p 120.
41 Quoted in *Socialist Worker*, 7 October 1989.
42 Williamson, op cit, p 14.

in a recent Volvo advertisement which depicted eighteen young children and babies sitting on or near a Volvo. The advertisement read 'Volvo announce free catalytic converters for all those people who don't own Volvos'. The use of such references may be criticised as exploiting consumers' fears for the environment and the effect that environmental decay may have upon 'our children' hence falling within the ambit of the 'unfair' advertisement.

...

REGULATION OF 'GREEN' ADVERTISEMENTS

...

3. *Self-regulation*

The present system of advertising control is predominantly self-regulatory. At the apex of the disciplinary system is the Code of Advertising Practice Committee and the ASA. The Committee draws up the British Code of Advertising Practice ('the code') which is based on the principle that advertisements should be 'legal, decent, honest, and truthful'.[43] The Government view is that self-regulation is a better way of controlling advertising than relying on statute (Committee on European Communities, HL, 5.4.1978). This view has been attributed to the fact that self-regulation reduces rule-making and enforcement costs and may be seen to be a more flexible means of control than legislation. In particular the ASA's sanctions of publicity and denial of access to the media have been praised as cheaper and quicker than legal action.[44] However the ASA has been criticised as a 'safety valve' for consumer dissatisfaction with advertising, thus questioning its independence and effectiveness.

...

Misleading 'green' advertisements are brought to the ASA's attention by complaints from the public. The ASA works on a case-by-case basis with reference to its code. The examples of misleading factual statements made in motor car advertisements described above indicate that the ASA's main concern is with urging the manufacturers and producers to make more vigorous checks on scientific-based claims in the future. In each case, enforcement of the code was by informal pressure and adverse publicity in the form of case reports rather than the ultimate sanction of denial of access to the media. The handling of potentially 'unfair' advertisements by the ASA may be seen as more controversial.

The Molony Committee concluded that psychological claims were to be controlled by the ASA and subsequently the ASA has formally come to control claims in this area. Although the concept of 'unfair' advertising is not recognised in United Kingdom law a form of 'unfairness' appears to be recognised in the code. Under the heading that advertisements should be honest, the code states that:

> No advertiser should seek to take improper advantage of any characteristic or circumstance which may make consumers vulnerable; as, for example, by exploiting their credibility or their lack of experience or knowledge (para. 4.1.).

43 38th Report HL Committee on European Communities (1978), iv-v, para 7, extract in Ramsay, op cit, pp 389-90.

44 Ibid.

Further, para. 15.1. states that 'without good reason, no advertisement should play on fear or distress'. The psychological exploitation form of 'unfair' advertising would therefore appear to be included in the code. However the ASA has made a number of statements concerning the limits of its powers in this area which has affected its handling of unfair green advertising.

It has recently been suggested that green claims which were implied through images rather than baldly stated were unlikely to be criticised.[45] For instance the ASA did not object to an advertisement for unleaded fuel which featured an illustration of rolling countryside. While 'appreciating the complainant's point that pollution from cars can damage the countryside', the ASA felt that 'the message of the advertisement was clear: a car which runs on unleaded fuel does less damage to the environment than one which does not'. In case report no. 171, the ASA editorial states that with regard to green advertisements, '...in such cases we are concerned solely with maintaining the factual accuracy of advertisements and insisting on objective standards', and that complaints which go beyond factual claims lie outside the limits of its powers. This approach to the green issue has as its base the association's policy on freedom of opinion. The ASA believes that to consider matters other than factual statements would entail an entitlement to correct the opinion of advertisers. The ASA see the central question as:

> when does the advertiser's selection, presentation and arrangement of facts to boost his argument require to be tested against an objective yardstick and when must it simply be accepted as uncheckable because of the absence of agreement as to what yardstick for assessment would be appropriate or just? (case report no. 168).

ALTERNATIVES TO THE REGULATORY FRAMEWORK

Deficiencies in the control of unfair advertising have led to the employment of a number of methods which work outside the regulatory framework. Such alternatives to the existing regulatory provisions include corrective advertising by advertisers to neutralise the damage of their misleading statements. The United Kingdom rejected this technique because of practical difficulties in its use in the United States. A further alternative legal measure used in the United States is that of counter-advertising which obliges the media to carry advertising prepared by consumer interest groups. However it is unclear whether such a measure could apply to the controversial area of unfair advertising.

Cranston maintains that the independence of the enforcement procedure may be ensured by empowering private individuals or public interest groups to take legal action.[46] For example, consumer groups in Germany have the right to seek injunctive relief against deceptive claims. However these approaches tend to require the development of an unfairness doctrine and a shift in the underlying theoretical perspective of advertising from that of a liberal approach to a more critical view.

Green advertising throws up the double-edged problem of claims that are difficult to test and the fact that advertising may work by psychological

45 Environmental Data Services Ltd (1990) Report No 191, 16-24.

46 R Cranston, *Consumers and the Law* (2nd edn, 1984) p 56.

exploitation. A non-legal approach to increase consumer education may not be appropriate in areas of technical complexity. An information-based response has been regarded as a 'weak response to the problem'[47] by consumer groups and environmentalists by identifying the problem of green advertising as that of inadequate consumer information. Legal regulation is therefore required which acknowledges the exploitation potential of advertising. These aims may be reconcilable if effective consumer interest participation was assured in the policy-making process. The participation of such groups may be encouraged by measures such as subsidies as proposed by Trebilcock. A regulatory process which more faithfully represents the consumer interest may lead to regulation that adopts a wider definition of deceitful advertising to encompass exaggeration, half-truths and ambiguities, thus acknowledging the potential of advertising such as 'green' advertisements to work by psychological abuse as well as by misleading statements.

6 VOLUNTARY SIMPLICITY AND ALTERNATIVE LIFESTYLES: POST- MATERIALISM

Not all are buying the green consumer puff.

P Marshall, *Nature's Web: An Exploration of Ecological Thinking* (London: Simon & Schuster, 1992), pp 416-417

Simple in means, rich in ends

In their lifestyle, deep ecologists advocate voluntary simplicity, a way of life which is 'inwardly rich but outwardly poor'. Modesty and humility are considered central virtues. Their guiding principle is to be 'simple in means, rich in ends'. It means living at one with the Earth; as Devall puts it, 'nothing forced, nothing violent, just settling into our place'. They go in search of the primitive and ancient ways. They value ritual and ceremony. Cultivating ecological consciousness means for them cultivating what the American academic Theodore Roszak has called the 'rhapsodic intellect'.

On a practical level, deep ecologists are in defence of the Earth. This involves principally protecting wilderness areas, living in bioregions based on natural and not political boundaries, and decreasing the human population.

Wilderness areas, deep ecologists insist, are essential for the well-being of the human spirit as well as the vitality of the ecosphere. To escape from cities and parks and to experience the wild, they argue, is to develop a sense of place and to realize how nature follows its own processes. Like Thoreau, they believe that 'in wilderness is the preservation of the world'.

This extract suggests that to change one's way of life rather than merely one's patterns of consumption is on the fringes of the social spectrum of

47 H Beale, R Craswell, and S Salop, 'The Efficient Regulation of Consumer Information (1981) 24 Journal of Law and Economics 491, extract in Ramsay, op cit, p 67.

environmentalism. But below we find the Royal Commission on Environmental Pollution advocating more simple ways of living. The difference is that the Royal Commission feels that governments have a role to play in inducing people to make these changes. The Royal Commission deals with the fact that most of us live and work in towns, not wilderness.

Royal Commission on Environmental Pollution, Eighteenth Report *Transport and the Environment*, Cmnd 2674 (London: HMSO, 1994) pp 88-89

Greening the way we live

6.36 The [...] perspective discussed here highlights the importance of the way people choose to live. It diagnoses the environmental damage caused by transport as an inherent consequence of present lifestyles in developed countries, and makes the assumption that the situation can be radically changed as a result of the initiatives by local communities. In part this would involve reversing the changes in lifestyles which were identified earlier in this report (2.17-2.27)[48] as being closely associated with the recent growth of transport, but many people envisage a process going much further than that.

6.37 The central aim would be to make the inhabitants of each town or neighbourhood as far as possible self-sufficient by redesigning the urban fabric and also the urban metabolism. A major reduction in energy use for transport would be one contribution to that; and greater self-sufficiency in other respects would greatly reduce demand for the transport of goods and people. Although urban areas are where most people live, the same aim could also be pursued by similar methods in rural areas.

6.38 Advocates of self-sufficiency nevertheless differ in the way they view transport. One writer has envisaged a society emerging towards the end of the next century based on local self-sufficiency, but in which people will travel a great deal and almost the only remaining requirement for government on a large scale will be 'a world agency...to provide traffic control'. More usually, a new approach to transport has been seen as one of the crucial steps towards a self-sufficient community. As another writer puts it, 'turning too much living space into road space destroys the inner form and balance of the city'. The city is viewed as 'an organism, an eco-system, with its own internal life, creative energy and interdependence', and the criterion used in planning and transport decisions should be 'how well the city encourages or discourages creative relationships between people'. Reassessments of transport policies from this perspective have often been associated with opposition to proposals for large-scale road construction or, in one case (the German city of Freiburg-im-Breisgau), opposition to construction of an underground light-rail line.

6.39 A central feature of the self-sufficient lifestyle is the possibility for an able-bodied person to make all everyday journeys within the neighbourhood on foot or by cycle. These modes of travel use no fossil fuel, and very little energy: someone weighing 70 kg has been estimated to use 0.14 megajoule/

48 See ch 1, 'How we live'.

kilometre when walking and 0.035 megajoule/kilometre when riding a 20 kg bicycle, whereas cars on commuting journeys in built-up areas have been estimated to use 2.8 megajoules/passenger-kilometre on average and cars on other urban journeys 1.8 megajoules/passenger-kilometre. Ideally there would also be a communal same-day delivery service (as in Freiburg and in Zurich) so that, even when shopping for bulky goods, people can travel on foot, by cycle or by public transport rather than by car.

6.40 A number of cities claim to be pioneers of greener transport policies as well as Freiburg..., they include York (which the Commission visited), and Delft (which the Commission also visited), Groningen and Munster on the continent. In all of them, between a half and a third of journeys not made on foot are made by cycle, compared with less than 3% in the UK as a whole. Large areas of these cities exclude motor traffic, and the rest of the city has safe and attractive cycle routes. Safe storage for cycles has been established at key points. Other policies include better provision for pedestrians and linkages between other transport modes, for example through park and ride schemes.

6.41 The cities which have been most successful in encouraging journeys on foot or by cycle tend to be of a particular type: medium-sized, free-standing, with a population in the range 150,000 to 450,000, and usually flat. In economic terms they are relatively self-contained, and not in serious competition with other urban centres nearby. They are compactly built, with their central area on a medieval street-plan. Cities like this provide a pleasant lifestyle for many people, with a rich social and cultural life. They are often university cities, and the non-student part of their populations is to a degree self-selected people who like such a lifestyle and gravitate to them, and those for whom it would not be attractive to choose to live somewhere else.

6.42 One view of experience so far would be that radical policies aimed at reducing car use are inherently more suitable for cities of the kind just described. In that case it would be unwise to assume that the same policies could be equally successful elsewhere. Another view would be that, while (for historical and cultural reasons connected with civic identity) cities of this kind have been able to reach a consensus about such policies more quickly and more easily, they represent the leading edge of a general trend. Certainly there seems to be a much wider movement in local communities towards systematic policies for reducing reliance on cars, even if the eventual limits of such policies remain unclear.

6.43 Changes in lifestyles have an important role to play in creating a sustainable transport system for the UK. They need to embrace, not only greater resort to walking and cycling, but far-reaching changes in the way people perceive and use other modes of transport. New lifestyles cannot be imposed by governments. It is not likely they could be brought about solely by education or persuasion, or by other promotional measures, on a sufficient scale to resolve the basic dilemmas of present transport policies. Greener lifestyles will have to spread over a period of time. They will have more appeal to people at certain periods of their lives, and may be taken up more readily in some areas of the country than in others. Their eventual success will depend on the action taken by central and local government to provide frameworks within which individual choices can be exercised in an environmentally responsible way.

The literature on voluntary simplicity is extensive[49] and, generally, romantic in contrast to the Royal Commission's practical and pragmatic approach. But when environmentalists from across the social spectrum all pull in the same direction it is possible to achieve change. Government policy on transport has changed, moving away from its obsession with road building and appearing more receptive to some environmental concerns.[50] The Royal Commission's Report appeared coincidentally with a widespread campaign by a variety of 'road protests' all over the country. The combination of the weighty and worthy Royal Commission, middle class protestors, and 'alternative' cultural events ('carnivals for change') shifted the juggernaut of the road lobby. For once, policy change occurred without significant inputs from the European Community.

7 DIRECT ACTION AND DESTABILISATION: THE NEW *TOTAL KRITIK*

Parts of the modern environmental movement claim to be the direct descendants of radical groups which have constituted a dissident tradition in Britain since the seventeenth century: The Diggers, The Levellers, The Chartists, and the socialists of the arts and crafts movement.[51] This is a counterpoise to the ecological modernisation and reformism of those who joined the ranks of non-governmental organisations and institutionalised environmental pressure groups. The radicalism of some environmental action groups is an expression of a new *Total Kritik* (the term used originally to describe the German anti-nuclear movement of the 1970s and 1980s) in which alternatives are advocated *for* society, not *within* society. In the United Kingdom, the road building programme has overtaken the nuclear question as a galvanising issue for many. The anti-road protesters combine romanticism (of notions of community and alternative, ecological ways of life) with a critique of the rationality of mainstream notions of social progress.

The individualism of green consumerism, and even of voluntary simplicity, compares with the communitarianism of many direct action groups. The centrality of 'community' to these groups perhaps explains why the car culture which relies on notions of freedom of the individual for its legitimacy is targeted for action. In addition, the paraphernalia of road transport – heavy traffic, bypasses,

49 See D Elgin *Voluntary Simplicity* (New York: William Morrow, 1981); A Sharma 'The Voluntary Simplicity Consumer: A Comparative Study', *Psychological Reports* 63(3) 859-869; J Dominguez and V Robin, *Your Money or Your Life* (New York: Viking/Penguin); D Shi *The Simple Life: Plain Living and High Thinking in American Culture* (New York: Oxford University Press, 1985).

50 For example, see Policy Planning Guidance Note 13, *Transport* (London: HMSO, 1994).

51 See ch 3, 'Utopianism and the garden city movement'.

and dual carriageways – dissects, and disrupts communities. Road transport also supports commuter lifestyles which fragment communities and localities.

A further characteristic of these campaigning and direct action groups is their broad platform, so that many of their concerns go beyond what is conventionally called 'environmental'. Roadalert describe this, below, as one aspect of the death of single issue politics. This reveals also the integration of environmental protection concerns in a wider agenda of social and distributive justice, criminal justice, and protection of public rights of demonstration and action. These environmental protection campaigns are kept alive by such dissident groups; social diversity is as important to sustainable development as biodiversity. The following offers a quite different message from those given out by mainstream environmental groups and green consumerist organisations, and uses a different medium. However, the persuasiveness of the images, cultural signifiers and appeals to collective action are similar, though on the 'other side', to those in the motor car advertisements discussed above. Roadalert makes appeals for the use of traditional methods of campaign, for example writing to the local council, alongside advocating direct action, of the type exercised by Reclaim the Streets.

To: roadalert@gn.apc.org

From: wildwood

1:52 pm 24 SEP 1996
The RUSSLAND BEECHES
Lake District National Park
Cars or trees?

ACTION ALERT.
THE LAKE DISTRICT NATIONAL PARK AUTHORITY (LDNPA) ARE ABOUT TO FELL 54 MAGNIFICENT 150 YEAR OLD BEECH TREES NEAR LAKE WINDERMERE as they pose a minuscule hazard to motorists driving along a narrow and hardly used lane.
THE FINAL DECISION TO FELL (OR SPARE) THE TREES WILL BE TAKEN AT A MEETING OF THE PARK AUTHORITY ON OCTOBER 1.
The Lake District is where Wordsworth wrote "Daffodils".

ACTION NEEDED;
Letter, fax and e-mail objections to the felling are needed to show public opposition to this vandalism, which is more about a bureaucratic concern with insurance than any real threat to the passing public. The earlier decision to fell was only by a 8-6 vote by the committee so quick action will help.

THE FACTS:
The beeches were given to the Park in 1984 for safekeeping. The trees are much loved by local people, who are those who would be most "at risk" from the trees. A 3,500 name petition to save the trees has been gathered, but virtually ignored by the Park Authority. Last weekend there was a well attended party for the trees to reinforce and show local opposition.

Both the Authority and the protestors have taken expert advice, and there is agreement that some trees should be felled. The Park's expert is recommending all 54 beeches be felled, as a precaution, while the protesters' own more experienced advisor says that only up to nine trees are potentially dangerous.

Geoff Dellow, a protester, has said "If this decision goes ahead it will send shock waves over Britain to all of those who have mature trees overhanging roads and footpaths".

Marianne Bennett, who overlooks the trees has said: "The trees were given to the park to protect them. Instead they are to destroy them".

John Toothill, a National Park officer has said: "We have looked after the trees for 12 years but now they are like sick old people who need drastic surgery." (?!)

Theo Hopkins of Native Forest Network, England, has said: "Britain is particularly short of biologically rich old and fungi infested trees. That the trees are full of fungi is a reason for a National Park to keep them, not to fell the trees".

Among proposed options to save the trees is the simple one of closing the road in high winds or heavy snow.

COMMENT:
Readers of this alert may consider that the trees were there before the metalled road, so it is the road that is the problem and not the trees, thus the Park Authority should not be protecting drivers who are going too fast to stop for a fallen bough, but protecting the environment, and no trees should be felled.

This is a typical case of the environment taking second place to the bureaucratic wish never to be in a position to be blamed by anyone, however minute the risk.

CONTACT:
For more information, phone local campaigner [...]

TO OBJECT:
Write, fax or email to:
The Lake District National Park at [...]

KILL YOUR CAR AND NOT THE TREES
(for a fungi, the trees are merely lunch.)

Date: 26 Sep 1996
To: roadalert@gn.apc.org

From: rts@gn.apc.org (Reclaim the Streets!)

Subject: September mailout
September 1996
Well, it's been a while since the last newsletter so for all those who don't know, here's a round up of what's been going on and what RTS are planning next!

STREET PARTY 96
The summer kicked off with the M41 job on 23rd July. 10,000 people dancing on the motorway, chilling out on the central reservation, planting trees in the fast lane, and twenty foot skirted ladies grooving to the sound of happiness from the hard shoulder! It was great to see the Met and "pals" powerless yet again to put a stop to the spontaneous coincidence of people reclaiming their space. The post-party response was excellent – the answerphone/postbox was jammed with exuberant "nice one!"s and "when's the next party?" for weeks after.
...

RAID
On the morning of Friday 2nd August, the RTS office and one person's private home were raided by police who seized computers as well as various personal effects. At the moment it seems as though at least one person is to be charged with conspiracy to cause criminal damage to the M41. Don't worry about the computer – the database was PGPd so there's no chance of them having got hold of your details! Pretty Good Privacy (PGP) is a special means of encrypting any information on your computer that you don't want certain people to get hold of. For details of how you can use this yourselves, call the RTS office.

STOP THE CLAMPDOWN – RECLAIM THE FUTURE!
A 3 Day Event including a massive parade, party and action against the CJA, JSA, Scotland Yard and life as we know it happening at the end of September! Reclaim The Streets, Advance Party, Freedom Network and other grassroots groups are working in solidarity with the Liverpool Dockers who have been fighting for a year against "casualisation", after Merseyside Docks and Harbour Company sacked 500 workers. Not only is that a bit crap but there's the environmental issue i.e. legit dockers are choosy about what cargo they handle – no toxics, no nuclear waste – while the scabs will handle anything for £32 quid an hour!

Anyway, we're fighting back and forging links with STOP THE CLAMPDOWN, RECLAIM THE FUTURE on 28, 29, 30 September in Liverpool so come up and play! The plan for the weekend is a massive march/party through Liverpool on Saturday 28th meeting at Myrtle Parade, Liverpool at 12 noon. The day after there will be relaxation, workshops, direct action training and entertainment and on Monday 30th there will be a mass action, meeting 10am at Seaforth Docks, Liverpool. For transport/accommodation details, ring us here at the office on [...] nearer the time.

AROUND THE STREETS IN 80 DAYS
Birmingham Street Party happened on 17th August as well as another one the same day in Bath. The Brighton Street Party turned into a march after police stormed in and arrested about 90 party-goers on a random we-don't-like-your-face-and-what's-that-poem-you're-reading-basis!
Cambridge then held a very successful Street Party on 14th September, with over 1,000 people attending.

October 19 Manchester RTS – meet 1 pm Albert Square (ends 6pm)???? Party and info help line [...]

In London, we got active in support of the Tube Workers. There was a special Critical Mass on 7th August followed by an occupation of the London Underground Headquarters where an opportunity was taken to have a chat with Chairman Peter Ford, as to his involvement in the exploitation of his tube workers. There were 11 arrests but no charges as yet. The FIT (Forward Intelligence – special branch) team were there – true to form – to take snapshots.

People have been getting active all over London with a West London, North London and South London Critical Mass adding to the Hackney and Central London Masses. On Friday 30th August there was a critical mass in Oxford, followed by, you guessed it, another Street Party. There was also a road block in West London on 25th July.

Anti-JSA (Job Seekers Allowance) demos are kicking off nationwide – the changes in benefit rules that will come into operation on October 7th are going to affect a great number of people involved in campaigning. There are actions planned nationwide for the 7th.

The second phase of work on the Newbury Bypass has begun. There were six days of protest at the Flim-Flam Festival 25th to 30th August and, as ever, they need support down there. For info ring Third Battle of Newbury [...]

The A30 camps down in Fairmile, Devon, also need support a.s.a.p. They know for certain that they are due to start building the road on 1st October and it is very likely that the evictions will be in late September. Their no is [...]

ANARCHIST INFILTRATORS!
The press have been having a blue fit recently about the infiltration of RTS by a "lunatic anarchist fringe".

The summer's activities have successfully destroyed the myth of single issue politics. No issue exists in isolation from other issues, as they all have a common cause: the state and the fatcats. Whenever issues are brought together and similarities identified the media always insinuates some "outside agitators" as the cause behind any action that lies outside their rigidly defined stereotypes.

8 LEGAL RADICALISM

In the nineteenth century, public law to control pollution developed as a response to the limitations of the common law to prevent nuisances. After a century and a half of legislative action, the limitations of this have now also become clear. There is a sense that legal devices need to be developed which are more responsive to the nature of environmental problems. It is also recognised that environmental problems are not single issue. They form part of wider social problems – of inequality, disenfranchisement, and poverty.

A theme of this book is that the common law has hitherto dealt with environmental problems in the same manner as it has traditionally dealt with other problems – on an individualised basis and by favouring private property. For example, we saw in *St Helen's Smelting Co v Tipping*[52] the upholding of ideas of protection of private property by the House of Lords' interpretation of the scope of private nuisance to deal with harmful acidic emissions from the smelting company.[53] It is notable in this case that people's health was hardly an overriding concern. To some extent, this favouring of private property rights has prevailed, at least on the part of the courts. The environmental movement has pushed more for a growth in regulation than in changes to the structure and norms of private law, although it is fair to say that creative use of contract has been made in statutes.[54] The environmental agenda has challenged leading concepts of private law, for example causation and the burden of proof.[55] And some prophesy that there might be more widespread restructuring of the tools of private law, such as the trust, to accommodate the need to protect *common* property. This development of more 'equitable property' and its protection is considered in the following passage in which Gray radicalises the trust, an ancient legal tool.

K Gray, 'Equitable Property' (1994) *Current Legal Problems* Vol 47, 157-214

In more recent years a number of related factors have conduced in the United States to a gathering recognition of the general social stake in property. It has even become possible to suggest that all rights of land ownership should be commuted forthwith to 'socially derived privileges' of use. Indeed, with the proliferation of zoning law and the remorseless intrusion of regulation following the National Environmental Policy Act 1969, the fee simple estate in land may already have been stripped back to a mere usufructuary title heavily conditioned by the public interest. Such developments are readily understood as exemplifying a 'principle of stewardship, under which ownership or possession of land is viewed as a trust, with attendant obligations to future generations as well as to the present'. The steady infiltration of this notion of stewardship inevitably impresses on land tenure a range of social obligations which effectively create a public beneficial entitlement in respect of ecologically critical assets. Meanwhile the advent of this new civic property in strategic environmental resources merges quite harmoniously with other contemporary American social and intellectual themes. The community-oriented aspect of the new environmental property confirms and complements the insights of the ecofeminist movement and also blends easily with the communitarian vision of property advanced in much recent economic and philosophic theory. Additional intellectual sustenance for the current socialisation of property relationships can be derived from the modern rediscovery of the 'land ethic' first proposed

52 (1865) 11 ER 1483.
53 See ch 2, 'The role of the common law of nuisance'.
54 Examples of statutory contracts include the planning obligation (see ch 7, pp 262-266) and voluntary agreements in water protection law (see ch 9, pp 377-380) and in conservation law (see ch 7, pp 287-288).
55 See ch 1, 'Precaution: soft science/ hard values'.

by Aldo Leopold over four decades ago.[56] Leopold's call for the adoption of a cooperative 'land ethic' was aimed at enlarging 'the boundaries of the community to include soils, waters, plants, and animals, or collectively: the land'. For Leopold it had become imperative to bring about 'the extension of the social conscience from people to land'.

Civic claims in respect of the environment have received further significant afforcement in the continuing evolution of the American version of historic doctrines of 'public trust'. In its original formulation the American public trust doctrine confirmed merely the state ownership of navigable waters and tidelands on behalf of all citizens. More recently courts and state agencies have seemed willing to oversee important extensions of both the character and the coverage of the doctrine. It is now clear that the purposes of the public trust doctrine extend no less to the protection of environmental and recreational values than to the preservation of commercial navigation and fishery. It is increasingly apparent that the ultimate role of the public trust doctrine may lie, not in its traditional function as justifying state taking, but rather in promoting a public beneficial ownership which is opposable against government itself. Even more radically there is now strong reason to believe that the doctrine of public trust can relate to objects far beyond its initial scope, thereby extending to such resources as wild country and parkland, wildlife, and perhaps even areas of general recreational utility or historic interest.

The reinvigorated notion of public trust has clearly become a vital weapon in the battle for environmental protection currently being waged in the United States courts. As Alison Rieser has indicated, the theory of public trust now provides an immensely significant doctrinal vehicle for subordinating both private and government ownership to a 'property interest held by the "unorganised public" in the ecological integrity of natural resources'.[57] Similarly Richard Lazarus has predicted that the likely outcome of modern environmental legislation will be the creation of 'modified property rights' for the citizen in many forms of natural resource not hitherto regarded as susceptible to communal proprietary claims.[58] Even in the vexed area of American 'takings' jurisprudence some commentators have begun to discern the 'hidden influence' of the idea that 'land and natural resources are common property'.[59] It has suddenly become realistic to envisage the creation of a 'new property' which consists, not of individual private property rights, but of 'new collective private property rights' in respect of the common pool resources of the natural land base.[60]

...

The advantages conferred by this trust model may be substantial indeed. For the first time it becomes meaningful to claim on behalf of the citizenry a 'property' interest comprising enforceable access to such inherent public goods

56 See 'The Land Ethic', in A Leopold, *A Sand County Almanac* (New York and Oxford, 1987 (first published 1949)).

57 'Ecological Preservation as a Public Property Right: An Emerging Doctrine in Search of a Theory', 15 Harv Envtl L Rev 393, 426 (1991).

58 RJ Lazarus, 77 Iowa L Rev 1739, 1759 (1992).

59 See TN Tideman, 'Takings, Moral Evolution, and Justice', 88 Col L Rev 1714, 1728 (1988).

60 See RH Nelson, 'Private Rights to Government Actions: How Modern Property Rights Evolve', (1986) U Ill L Rev 361, 373.

as clean air, unpolluted rivers and seaways, ozone regeneration, recreational enjoyment of wild country, and the sustainable development of land and marine areas. The moral parameters which have come to delimit the exclusory dimension of 'property' thus go some way towards converting green politics into relatively good communitarian law.[61] The environmental trust also generates rather less tangible – though perhaps ultimately more important – public benefits. The equitable property conferred by the new trust includes shared rights of access to the regenerative socialising dimensions of public environmental goods.[62]

...

There is increasing evidence on all sides that we are slowly recognising some concept of social trust in relation to the natural environment. This gathering perception of stewardship emulates something of the greater humility expressed in the Australian Aboriginal's orientation towards land resources. We may be starting to have a more cogent sense of obligation than of ownership, and this realisation is, of course, the necessary precursor of a new equilibrium with our environment. But a law of ecological responsibility which confirms civic property rights in natural resources would certainly impart a new environmental twist to the Lockean notion of a person's 'property' in his 'life, liberty and estate'. Are we really beginning to acknowledge some form of trust relationship which confers public rights of reasonable access and due administration in respect of environmental assets? Inevitably there will remain some who cannot, even in their wildest dreams, envisage such 'equitable property' vested in the community.[63]

Yet there is today one set of institutions which, in this and many other contexts, may convert even your wildest thoughts into present reality. These institutions are, of course, the institutions of the European Community or European Union. It is salutary to remember that the European Court's decision in 1991 in *Francovich v Italian State*[64] now imposes on member states a civil liability to compensate individuals for damage suffered by reason of a member state's failure to implement a Community directive. This liability will arise where the result laid down by the relevant directive involves the conferment of rights on the individual, and in many instances the *Francovich* ruling – if it remains good law – offers the individual citizen of Europe a broad and effective means of enforcing Community law.

In this context it is instructive to cast another glance at the litigation in *Commission of the European Communities v Federal Republic of Germany*[65] which also came before the European Court in 1991. Here the Court eventually

61 'Property in Thin Air', (1991) Cambridge LJ 252,297. See also JP Byrne, 'Green Property', 7 Const Comm 239 (1990).

62 K Carol Rose has confirmed that we should expect 'socialising activities' to 'give rise to inherently public property insofar as those activities require certain specific locations' (53 U Chi L Rev 711, 777 (1986)).

63 See, however, Sir Harry Woolf, 'Are the Judiciary Environmentally Myopic?' (1992) Vol 4, No 1 JEL 1.

64 Cases C-6/90, 9/90 [1993] 2 CMLR 66.

65 Joint Cases C-361/88 [1991] ECR I-2567 and C-59/89 [1991] ECR I-2607.

upheld a complaint that Germany had failed to secure legislative implementation of Community directives aimed at curbing air pollution caused by lead and sulphur dioxide emissions. The German defence had been in part that German practice was already in substantial conformity with the thrust of the relevant directives: there was in fact no air pollution in Germany in excess of the limit values prescribed in these directives. The European Court rejected this defence, pointing out that true implementation of a directive requires not merely de facto compliance but also that each member state must actually set in place a specific legal framework relevant to the directive's subject, containing provisions sufficiently precise, clear and transparent to enable individuals to ascertain their rights and obligations. The Advocate General emphasised that the relevant directives were intended to give 'individuals, ordinary citizens...the right that the air which they breathe should comply with the quality standards which have been laid down'. Individuals, he said, have the right under Community law 'to rely on those quality standards when they are infringed, either in fact or by the measures adopted by the public authorities'.[66] The Court agreed that without the actual transposition of the directives into specific provisions of the national legal system individuals would not be 'in a position to know with certainty the full extent of their rights in order to rely on them where appropriate'.[67] Only the enactment of 'mandatory rules' by the member state would enable citizens to assert their rights.

Viewed from the objective distance of this side of the Channel, such an approach begins to resemble, as perhaps nothing else, the recognition of a beneficiary's right to insist that trust assets are not merely conserved by chance or fortunate practice but are instead fully subjected to governance in accordance with the terms of the relevant trust instrument. The European Court has come close to conceding the existence of an individual right to the effective and structured management of the ecosystem on behalf of all citizens. Taken in conjunction with the *Francovich* ruling, the stance of the Court in *Commission of the European Communities v Federal Republic of Germany* seems to recognise something which looks awfully like a right in the citizen to demand the proper and conscientious administration of a public trust in which he is regarded as having enforceable rights of a beneficial character.

66 [1991] ECR I-2567, 2591.
67 [1991] ECR I-2607, 2632.

PART V

Applications of modern environmental law

CHAPTER 9

The case of nitrate: farming for environmental protection

1 INTRODUCTION

In this chapter we deal with the legal responses to a particular environmental problem: nitrate in water from farming. As the first of our case studies, it demonstrates an early legal initiative for environmental protection by the European Community. In contrast to the broad brush and integrated approach of environmental assessment, discussed in chapter 10, the focus here is on a single substance in one medium and one sector of the economy. The response to the nitrate problem also illustrates the dynamic relationship between European Community laws framed to protect the environment and United Kingdom environmental law. However, the EC's legislation was itself a reaction to work done by the World Health Organisation (WHO) which is an agency of the United Nations, so again we see an initiative from an international institution having very real effects on the law and, here, literally on the ground.

In this chapter we consider the nature of nitrate pollution of water from farming, European Community law aimed to control this problem, and the British responses. These responses have been to provide information to farmers, to designate water protection zones and nitrate sensitive areas and to formulate a code of good agricultural practice.

2 NITRATE POLLUTION OF WATER

Nitrate is naturally present in the soil and is essential for plant growth. When crops are harvested the nitrate that was used during their growth is taken away; to maintain the fertility of the soil it must be replaced, either by applying it to the soil as an inorganic fertiliser or in the form of farmyard manure. At the level of mere replacement, fertilising with either artificial nitrate or manure is essential to good farming. Also, crucially, poor land may be made more fertile with high concentrations of nitrate. This fertilisation of poor land to improve and make it productive has changed the face of large tracts of rural Britain since the 1940s and enabled farmers to grow grain on an unprecedented scale.

If there is more nitrate in the soil than growing plants can take up, rainwater may wash the nitrate away, either down through the soil to the groundwater or as 'runoff' to the nearest stream or river. The nitrate from any given farm may end up anywhere in the water of a whole catchment area. In some soils the particles are very small so the water seeps slowly down to the aquifer underground; a process that in chalk soils may take decades. Since there is a high nitrogen content in manure, rain falling on farmyards may carry nitrate to streams or onto ploughed land where it then seeps down or runs off. Cultivation of soil releases nitrate that was formerly fixed, so if grassland is ploughed up there is very often more residual nitrate in the soil than is needed for growing the crop.

So the application of some nitrate is essential, but if too much is put on there is a potential water pollution problem. Excessive loading of nitrate in drinking water may, possibly, be associated with risks to human health in the forms of 'blue baby' syndrome (methaemglobinaemia) and stomach cancer. The WHO guidelines aim to safeguard health on the assumption of life-long consumption and are intended for use by countries as a basis for the development of standards which, if properly implemented, will ensure the safety of drinking water supplies. When a guideline value is exceeded this should be a signal to countries to investigate the cause with a view to remedial action. There are two figures: the higher of which should only be exceeded on exceptional occasions; and the lower which is a target for countries to aim for.

Quite apart from the possibility of nitrate harming human health, too much nitrate in surface waters can cause these waters to become 'eutrophic,' or over-enriched, so that plant growth becomes excessive. This may mean that the plants in the water take up most of the available oxygen, leaving insufficient oxygen for fish, or blanket weed may cover mud flats so that birds cannot feed on the worms and shrimps that live in the mud.

The problem of nitrate pollution of water from farming has proved to have a complexity unforeseen when legislation to control nitrate inputs to protect human health was first proposed by the European Commission. This was an early legal expression of the precautionary principle: the Commission has not waited for conclusive scientific evidence as to whether nitrate is harmful to human health but instead acted on the assumption that it may be and has tried to reduce the amounts of the substance to which people are exposed. This is justified by the fact that people must drink water and that they will be taking in a good deal of nitrate anyway by eating green vegetables, which are good for their health. The complexity of the problem comes from scientific uncertainties as to the behaviour of nitrate in soils and water; doubts as to whether nitrate is harmful to humans; and from the social organisation of the farming industry.

Compared with manufacturing industry where the polluters will generally be in large cities, and a specific industry such as chemical manu-facturing which may be concentrated in only a few places, there are a great many individual farms widely dispersed throughout the European Union, on land that is in private ownership. This dispersal of farms, though, is only part of the explanation of why controlling the activities of farmers is so difficult. In the extract below, Lowe et al discuss the relationship between farmers and the state. This may go some way to explaining why pollution caused by farmers is such an intractable problem in Britain.

P Lowe, G Cox, M MacEwan, T O'Riordan and M Winter, *Countryside Conflicts* (Aldershot: Gower, 1986), pp 87-90

It is not difficult to demonstrate, then, that in terms of both its remarkable achievements and its equally remarkable autonomy agriculture is an exceptional industry. Just as the emergence and persistence of this 'exceptionalism' presents a complex story, so there is no simple explanation for the ways in which it has been sustained, though analysis of the power of the farming and landowning lobby has to be central to any explanation.

A Unique Partnership

Given a statutory role in the annual round of decision-making on farm prices by the Agriculture Act 1947, agricultural interests developed and consolidated their governmental links, particularly with the Ministry of Agriculture. Already by the early 1960s, the relationship between the National Farmers Union and government was, according to Self and Storing, 'unique in its range and intensity'. Later commentators have tended only to confirm and amplify that judgement. Indeed, in recent analyses of British politics, agriculture has been cited as perhaps the one unequivocal example of an economic sector where an interest group has been officially recognised by the state and incorporated into the process of decision-making, not merely to represent its members but to play a joint role in the political management of the sector.

The NFU has derived considerable political advantage from its symbiotic relationship with the Ministry of Agriculture, Fisheries and Food – through the ministry's single-minded commitment to the farmers' cause, through the NFU's entrenched role in policy-making and through its privileged access on a routine basis to centres of decision-making, including the highest levels of government. This is the key to the NFU's influence and it is significant that, in the inter-war years, before it achieved this intimate relationship with the ministry – indeed, before the ministry became so closely involved in the management of the agricultural sector – the NFU was a relatively weak and marginal interest group. Nowadays, the ministry and the union are in constant contact at all levels over the myriad of issues, large and small, that arise in the development and implementation of agricultural policy.

The NFU's working partnership with the state has enabled it to exert an influence which has been disproportionate, given that its membership is too small directly to determine the outcome of elections and that it does not have at its disposal the direct economic sanctions available to some other key business organisations or trade unions. But the partnership has also placed constraints on the NFU. As Self and Storing noted, 'the tendency of the close concordat has been as much to debilitate the union as to hamper the government'. The constraints on MAFF from other government departments concerned at the financial and other implications of developments in agricultural policy have also been significant. The NFU does not have such a close relationship with these other departments and, far from being in a position to dictate terms, it has in fact been highly dependent upon the goodwill of successive governments. It has been the sheer reluctance of governments to change farm policy in any fundamental way which has most obviously benefited agricultural interests, particularly the large farmers who dominate the NFU, and has been the most significant of the factors conferring power on the NFU. Throughout the post-war period, the farming and landowning lobby and the state have been moving in tandem with a powerful momentum in pursuit of the same broad priorities.

Although their most important channel of access to decision-makers is through MAFF, the NFU and the Country Landowner's Association have not neglected other political channels, including other government departments, the European Commission, local government, Parliament and the mass media. The agricultural interest enjoys an in-built bias in most representative assemblies, which they have been able to exploit. Through their traditional social and political leadership of rural areas, farmers and landowners tend to be disproportionately represented on parish, district and county councils and in the British and European Parliaments. They are a sizeable minority in the Commons, particularly on the Conservative side; and a majority of the Lords. Most members of Tory Cabinets are landowners or have agricultural connections, and even Labour Cabinets usually have a few. At the very least, this ensures an informed hearing for the farming lobby. The NFU has developed particularly effective links with Parliament – so much so that when the CBI, of which it is an influential member, decided to improve its lobbying arrangements in the late 1970s, it modelled its new system on the NFU's, adopting in particular that organisation's practice of central coordination and encouragement of contacts between its members and MPs in the constituencies.

An important corollary of the partnership between the farming lobby and the state has been a reluctance to resort to legislative control of the activities of farmers. In any case, the relatively modest legislative base – much of it very dated – on which MAFF operates has meant that much policy-making has been accompanied by considerable latitude and discretion for producers. Understandably, therefore, a 'what we have we hold' mentality has prevailed in relation to many of the issues of public concern discussed above, and much of the apparent power of the lobby has derived from its ability to resist fundamental changes on matters such as planning controls and de-rating by working to bolster and sustain an already engineered consensus with government.

During the past decade, however various factors have ensured greater prominence and contention for questions of agricultural policy. These include the excesses of the Common Agricultural Policy; the shift of the burden for agricultural support from the taxpayer to the consumer which followed EEC entry; rising unease over animal welfare; and political interest in the welfare of rural communities. But the most serious challenge to the privileges of farmers arises from conservationists. As the Society for the Responsible Use of Resources in Agriculture and on the Land (RURAL) notes in the report of its inaugural meeting held in April 1983, 'farmers are becoming increasingly aware that they are under threat of their freedom of action because of the strength of public opinion about the way land is being managed'.

Indeed, so concerned have the NFU and the CLA become with the drift of public opinion that they have recently sought funds for an unprecedented £27,000 study to be conducted by the Centre for Agricultural Strategy, Reading University, and designed to counter criticism of the farming community and improve agriculture's public image. This was also the specific objective of 'The

Backbone of Britain' campaign. The ministry meanwhile has acknowledged concern: in May 1984 it appointed as special adviser a farmer prominent in both the NFU and the CLA; and in July it established an Environment Coordination Unit with a staff of six, to be headed by a food scientist with the rank of Assistant Secretary, the fourth highest in Whitehall.

The struggle to counter the increasingly articulate voices of the industry's critics presents the farming and landowning lobby with perhaps its sternest task to date. The lobby's unique partnership with the state depends upon its ability to discipline its own members such that they voluntarily comply with agreements reached with government and cooperate with the implementation of policy. Thus the struggle is at the same time a critical internal process of education and inducement in which the NFU and the CLA cannot afford to be unsuccessful, though the authority of their leadership is much less strong than it once was. This broader struggle is especially challenging because it takes them beyond the somewhat circumscribed channels of political influence in which they have been so effective during the post-war period.

3 THE LEGAL PROBLEM

Despite more than a century of legislation designed to protect the quality of drinking water, the legal standard in Britain remained that of 'wholesome' until the Water Supply (Water Quality) Regulations 1989, passed under section 52 of the Water Act 1989 (reformulated in the Water Resources Act 1991), to comply with Directive 80/778/EEC on drinking water (see below), for the first time defined quality scientifically. The Act set limits which must not be exceeded for a list of substances, including nitrate.

The general criminal offence of causing or knowingly permitting water pollution is contained in section 85(1) of the Water Resources Act 1991:

> A person contravenes this section if he causes or knowingly permits any poisonous, noxious or polluting matter to enter any controlled waters.

Such law is by its very nature limited because it is inherently reactive: both common law and criminal law operate after the pollution has taken place.[1] Another crucial limitation is that the law is narrowly focused on causation: a discrete incident must be found to have caused the pollution and an identifiable person must have been responsible for the incident. Nitrate pollution of water simply does not fit with this sort of law since the harm may be an accumulation over many years from different sources and many of the individuals involved may be impossible to trace by the time the harm becomes measurable. The problem is deteriorating water quality: pervasive pollution from *diffuse* sources, over a long period of time, will be the cause of waters failing to meet the drinking water standards and eutrophic stretches of water. Farming is a major contributor to this insidious kind of pollution.

1 W Howarth, 'Agricultural Pollution and the Aquatic Environment', in W Howarth and C Rodgers, *Agriculture, Conservation and Land Use* (Cardiff: University of Wales Press, 1992), p 59.

To tackle the problem of nitrate pollution, a wholly different form of proactive and preventive law was needed. In the following section we focus on the way that innovative Community law has been transposed to Britain. We first deal with the European Community directives concerned with the quality of drinking water and discuss the differences between the European and British approaches to water pollution.

4 EUROPEAN COMMUNITY LAW

The problem of the level of nitrate in water abstracted for drinking only exists, in a strictly legal sense, as a result of European Community directives. In 1970 the WHO European Standards for Drinking Water first suggested that 100mg/l was a safe limit, with 50mg/l as the target, so the British government circulated the water authorities to this effect. The authorities were able to comply with the safe limit but had problems reaching the target level.

(a) Emission standards or water quality objectives?

As part of the First Environmental Action Programme, the European Community directed its attention to water pollution and legislated to lessen it. There is no overall framework directive, such as there is for waste, but rather the approach is selective and not all pollutants in all waters are covered. The directives tend to either adopt emission standards to reduce dangerous substances or impose quality objectives on waters, according to the use that is to be made of those waters. As we saw in chapter 5, the European Community's approach is to compile and enforce common standards of emissions so as not to distort competition between Member States: more stringent standards in one state would impose higher costs on industry there than would be imposed in a state with lax standards. Disadvantages of this approach are that it does not work well for pollution from diffuse sources, or where there are many polluters in an area.

In contrast, Britain has long favoured a different approach of setting water quality objectives, whereby the purpose for which the receiving waters are to be used determines what emissions are permitted. The reason for the British approach originates in the nineteenth century. The problem of alkali deposits associated with the chemical industry in this period highlighted the difficulty of relying on a uniform emission standard.[2] The Alkali Act 1863 set a uniform standard of a 95% reduction of noxious vapours; but this did not ensure clean air as many more factories were being built. The result was that even though they all conformed to the 95% reduction within ten years the Alkali Inspector was reporting that the pollution was as bad as it had ever been. Parliament responded with the 1874 Alkali Act introducing 'best practicable means'.[3] The conflict between the European

2 See ch 2, 'Legislation and control of industrial activities'.

3 S Elworthy, 'Environmental Law in the Nineteenth and Early Twentieth Centuries', in G Weick (ed), *National and European Law on the Threshold to the Single Market* (Frankfurt am Main: Lang, 1993) p 43.

and British approaches to water pollution – emission standards or water quality objectives – has proved unresolvable. A compromise was reached by which either system would be permissible. Britain, alone among the other Member States, follows the water quality objectives approach.

Directive 75/440/EEC, OJ L194, 25.7.1975 on surface water for drinking was the first directive concerned with water of the First Environmental Action Programme. It specifies that surface water must be classified into three categories, A1, A2 and A3 corresponding to the three standard methods of treatment required to transform surface water into drinking water. A1 water requires only simple physical treatment such as filtration; A2 water requires normal physical treatment, chemical treatment and disinfection; while A3 water requires intensive physical and chemical treatment and disinfection. Any water failing to meet the worst category may not be abstracted for drinking unless the circumstances are exceptional.

Directive 76/464/EEC, OJ L129, 18.5.1976 on dangerous substances in water deals with the elimination or reduction of pollution of inland, coastal and territorial waters by particular dangerous substances. It was intended to be a framework directive with daughter directives to follow in due course. The Directive has two lists: an A list and a B list. The A list includes exceptionally toxic or persistent substances and the intention is to eliminate pollution from them. Any discharge must have been consented to by a 'competent national authority'. This consent may either set emission standards on the discharges that do not exceed limit standards, or emission standards are set for quality objectives for the receiving waters. The quality objectives are set by the Member State. The standards and objectives are to be set in daughter directives. Until a daughter directive has been agreed, A list substances are treated as B list ones, in which case pollution should be reduced. All discharges require a consent which sets emission standards with the aim of achieving environmental quality objectives. These are set at Member State level but states must introduce a reduction programme for these substances.

The following EC directives are designed to tackle the problem of nitrate pollution of water.

(b) EC Directive 80/778/EEC on the quality of drinking water

In 1980 the European Community issued Council Directive 80/778/EEC[4] on the quality of water intended for human consumption which set standards for drinking water expressed as permitted levels of specified substances. Acting on the World Health Organisation (WHO) guidelines for nitrate levels in drinking water, the European Community set a limit of 50mg/l (the WHO target level rather than the safe limit of 100mg/l), with a guide level of 25 mg/l. It has been argued, particularly by the National Farmers Union, that the European Community level is entirely arbitrary and there was no justification for halving the WHO limit. This does not seem to be the case, however, because the WHO revised its levels in 1984 to 45mg/l and 15mg/l to take account of the importance of green vegetables in the European diet.

4 OJ L229 30.8.1980.

When Directive 80/778/EEC came into force in 1985, Britain at first attempted to derogate under Article 9(1), which allows for exemptions of supplies of water exceeding maximum admissible concentrations (MACs) in order to take account of 'situations arising from the nature and structure of the ground in the area from which the supply in question emanates'. The non-governmental organisation, Friends of the Earth, complained to the Commission that the United Kingdom had failed to implement the Directive. The extract below is taken from their complaint to the Commission.

House of Commons Environment Committee, *Pollution of Rivers and Estuaries, Third Report (1986-7) Friends of the Earth evidence: Complaint to the Commission of the European Communities* (London: HMSO, 1987) Annex 5, pp 194-196

1. Formal Infringement

The United Kingdom has not integrated the Community measure into national law by the most appropriate forms and measures to ensure that the Directive is effective. In particular, section 11 of the Water Act 1973, which *inter alia* obliges local authorities "... to take such steps from time to time as may be necessary for ascertaining the sufficiency and wholesomeness of water supplies within their area...", to notify the relevant water undertaker of "... any insufficient or unwholesomeness in those supplies..." and requires water undertakers "... to provide a supply of wholesome water...".

There is no statutory definition of "wholesome" drinking water in UK law and there is no statutory reference to the parameters in the Directive. The only guidance upon the matter is in Department of the Environment Circular 20/82 which states that "The Secretaries of State will regard compliance with the terms of the Directive as a necessary characteristic but not a complete definition of any water that is to be considered wholesome". This is confirmed by the Nitrate Coordination Group (NCG): "In implementing the Directive, the Government have advised water undertakers that they would regard compliance with the terms of the Directive as a necessary characteristic but not a complete definition of any water that is to be considered wholesome". (Nitrate Coordination Group (1986) Nitrate in Water, para 1.7, Pollution Paper No.26).

Thus there is a formal infringement of the Community measure.

2. Actual Infringement

The Nitrate Coordination Group (NCG) report that "DOE (Department of the Environment) received 52 applications from the nitrate parameter before July 1985. These supplies affected a population of 921,000. The Department has granted derogations under Article 9(1)(a) of the Directive provided the nitrate concentration in any supply does not exceed a three monthly average of 80 mg per litre and a maximum of 100 mg per litre" (NCG, para 1.116). The areas concerned are covered by the Anglian, Severn Trent and Yorkshire Water Authorities.

...

Nitrate is Toxic

The World Health Organisation's (WHO) Guidelines for Drinking Water state that there is conflicting evidence about the level of nitrates in water which cause methaemglobinaemia ("blue-baby" syndrome). The WHO notes that "Infants, in contrast to adults, are also deficient in two specific enzymes that can convert methaemoglobin back to haemoglobin". The WHO also reports that although the clinical manifestations of infantile methaemoglobinaemia may not be apparent at up to 89 mg of nitrate per litre, "undesirable increases in methaemoglobin in the blood do occur". This is one reason why the WHO recommends a guideline value of 44.5 mg of nitrate per litre (World Health Organisation (1984) Guidelines for Drinking Water Quality, Vol.1, p.57, Geneva).

The WHO Guidelines indicate that it is nonsense to describe nitrate as non-toxic. Furthermore, Annex 1 to the Directive states that "Certain of these substances (which include nitrate) may even be toxic when present in excessive amounts". It is certainly arguable that excessive amounts of nitrate in water are toxic and thus ineligible for derogation under Article 9.

The Nature and Structure of the Ground

Article 9.1 of the Directive provides for derogations in order to take account of "situations arising from the nature and structure of the ground in the area from which the supply in question emanates".

The Government applies Article 9.1 "... when the nature and structure of the ground is a material factor causing the particular MAC to be exceeded..." (DOE letter of 10 November 1983 to Water Authorities and Water Companies).

The British Geological Survey recently concluded that: "... the principal source of the nitrate problem in groundwater is leaching from arable land".

The Nitrate Coordination Group (NCG) report that "The research undertaken during 1975-82 in the outcrop of major aquifers showed high concentrations of nitrate, generally in excess of 100 mg NO3/1, invariably present in the unsaturated zone pore-water beneath long-standing arable land, suggesting leaching losses in excess of 50 kg N/ha. By comparison the concentrations beneath unfertilised and lightly fertilised permanent grassland were much lower (normally less than 10 mg NO3/1) (Para 3.15).

The NCG continue: "A relationship between intensive arable cropping sustained by increasing large nitrogen fertiliser applications and high rates of nitrate leaching to groundwater was inferred. High nitrate concentrations were accompanied by elevated levels of other solutes, notably sulphate, chloride and some trace elements, derived either directly from fertilisers or mobilised from soils by farming practices".

As arable land is the principal source of nitrate in groundwater, it must also be a significant source of nitrate in surface waters (due to ground water "capture" by rivers).

Additional nitrate in rivers is derived from surface water runoff (including top soil which has been eroded from arable land), farm wastes (silage liquor and slurry) and effluents from sewage treatment works. According to the NCG: "For 10 sampling points (on 25 rivers in England, Scotland and Wales), mean nitrate concentrations for 1981-84 were greater than in any previous periods. These are primarily in arable farming areas such as East Anglia".

There is thus strong evidence showing that nitrate in both ground and surface water sources is largely derived from agricultural inputs. The MAC is not exceeded because of "situations arising from the nature and structure of the ground in the area from which the supply in question emanates".

. . .

The Government uses Article 9(1) as a device to evade compliance with the MAC for nitrate.

In 1987 the European Commission began formal proceedings under Article 169 of the EC Treaty against the United Kingdom for failing to implement the drinking water directive in its domestic legislation and failing correctly to apply the Directive. The United Kingdom government had argued that there was nothing else it could possibly do to secure the required water quality and it should not be held liable for the actions of third parties, for example the privatised water companies.

In 1988, on advice from the Department of Environment's lawyers that Britain would lose the case, the government announced that existing dispensations allowing water undertakers to continue supplying water above the 50mg/l limit were being withdrawn.

In January 1992 the European Court of Justice, following Advocate General Lenz's Opinion, gave judgment that Britain had failed to fulfil its obligations under the EC Treaty by not complying with the nitrate limit in the drinking water Directive. The European Court of Justice stated that the United Kingdom had failed to ensure that the quality of water supplied in 28 areas in England conforms to the requirements of the Directive concerning nitrate. In finding against the United Kingdom, the Court gave a clear signal that the quality standards in the Directive must be satisfied. An extract from the Judgment follows.

Case C-337/89: *Commission v United Kingdom* [1992] ECR I-6103

Nitrates Levels

17. The Commission claim that water supplied in 28 supply zones in England does not conform to the maximum admissible concentration (hereinafter referred to as "MAC") of 50 mg/l for nitrates and that the excessive levels are not justified by the derogations provided for in Article 9 of the directive.

18. The United Kingdom Government argues, first, that the directive does not impose an obligation to achieve a result but merely requires Member States to take all practicable steps to comply with the standards laid down. The United Kingdom claims to have done so in this case. It adds that the failure to achieve the objective is due to extraneous factors relating in particular to techniques used in agriculture.

19. It argues further that the Commission's view that a State is in breach of the directive where the MAC is not observed, even if the State has taken all practicable steps to secure compliance, would mean that the directive would be infringed wherever a MAC was exceeded after 18 July 1985 even though the excessive level went unnoticed when the inspections required by the

directive were carried out. The State would therefore be in breach of the directive even before it was afforded the opportunity of verifying whether there was a breach and of remedying the situation.

20. That argument cannot be upheld.

21. It follows from Article 7(6) of the directive that the Member States must take the steps necessary to ensure that water intended for human consumption at least meets the requirements specified in Annex I.

22. That result had to be achieved within a period of five years from notification of the directive (Article 19), that period being longer than that allowed for implementation of the directive, namely two years from notification (Article 18), in order to enable Member States to satisfy the above-mentioned requirements.

23. As the Court stated in its judgment in Case 228/87: *Pretura Unifacata di Torino* v *Persons Unknown* [1988] ECR 5099 (paragraph 10), the only derogations from the obligation on Member States to ensure that water intended for human consumption conforms to the requirements of the directive are those provided for in Articles 9, 10 and 20. The first of those provisions permits derogations to take account of situations arising from the nature and structure of the ground in the area from which the supply in question comes, as well as situations arising from exceptional meteorological conditions; the second authorizes derogations in the event of emergencies; and, finally, the third provision permits Member States, in exceptional cases and for geographically defined population groups, to submit a special request to the Commission in order to obtain a longer period for compliance with Annex I.

24. The directive therefore requires Member States to ensure that certain results are achieved and, except within the limits of the derogations laid down, they may not rely on special circumstances in order to justify a failure to discharge that obligation.

25. It follows that the defendant's claim that it took all practicable steps to secure compliance cannot justify, except within the limits of the derogations expressly laid down, its failure to comply with the requirement to ensure that water intended for human consumption at least meets the requirements of Annex I of the directive.

26. Finally, the United Kingdom Government claims that it granted derogations under Article 9 of the directive for the zones in which the MAC specified for nitrates was exceeded and that it notified those derogations to the Commission on 9 October 1985. The Commission did not express any view concerning those derogations until it issued the letter of formal notice on 11 August 1987, in which it stated that, where the MAC for nitrates had been exceeded, Article 9 could not be used as a basis for the derogations so notified. The United Kingdom Government considers that in those circumstances the Commission, instead of proceeding with its complaint, should have automatically granted the United Kingdom an extension of the time-limit notwithstanding the expiry of the period within which a request under Article 20 must be submitted.

27. As the Court held in its judgment in Case C-42/89: *Commission v Belgium* [1990] ECR I-2821, mentioned above (paragraph 23), a request under Article 20 of the directive for a longer period for complying with Annex I must be made within the period laid down in Article 19 for implementation of the directive. Notification of the derogations in accordance with Article 9 of the directive occurred after 18 July 1985, that is to say after that period had expired. Consequently, it is unnecessary to rule on the request made by the United Kingdom Government.

28. The second complaint is therefore also well founded.

...

38. In the light of all the foregoing considerations, it must be held that, by failing, first, to implement Council Directive 80/778/EEC of 15 July 1980 in the regulations applicable in Scotland and Northern Ireland and, as regards water used in the food industry, also in England and Wales and, secondly, to ensure that the quality of water supplied in 28 supply zones in England conforms to the requirements of the directive concerning nitrates, the United Kingdom has failed to fulfil its obligations under the EEC Treaty.

Costs

39. Under Article 69(2) of the Rules of Procedure the unsuccessful party is to pay the costs if they have been asked for in the successful party's pleading. Since the United Kingdom has for the most part failed in its submissions, it must be ordered to pay the costs.

(c) Directive 91/676/EEC on the protection of water against pollution caused by nitrates from agricultural sources

Directive 91/676/EEC on the protection of water against pollution caused by nitrates from agricultural sources[5] was adopted by the Member States. This is an an important directive for several reasons. First, it is an example of the integration of environmental policy with other policies of the European Community. This aim is clearly expressed in the preamble to the Directive:

> Whereas the reform of the common agriculture policy set out in the Commission's green paper 'Perspectives for the Common Agricultural Policy' indicated that, while the use of nitrogen-containing fertilizers and manures is necessary for Community agriculture, excessive use of fertilizers constitutes an environmental risk, that common action is needed to control the problem arising from intensive livestock production and that agricultural policy must take greater account of environmental policy.

Under the Directive, Member States are required to designate 'vulnerable zones' within two years (Nitrate Vulnerable Zones – NVZs). These are defined in the Directive as areas where inland or groundwaters intended for drinking are

5 OJ L135, 30.5.1991.

likely to contain more than 50 mg/l nitrate if protective action is not taken. The Directive lays down detailed regulatory requirements to have effect in these zones. With the aim of protecting all waters, Member States must establish codes of good agricultural practice, again within two years.

The precautionary principle is satisfied by the Directives discussed above. Directive 91/676/EEC on nitrate from agricultural sources goes even further. It is a proactive piece of legislation which aims to reduce the *sources* of nitrate pollution, and is wide in scope, extending beyond concerns with human health to the stability of aquatic ecosystems, particularly the North Sea where there are extensive areas of weed as a result of the nitrogen enrichment of the water in several rivers which flow into it.

5 THE BRITISH RESPONSE: PROACTIVE LAW

Directive 76/464/EEC on dangerous substances in water, discussed above, had a fundamental impact in Britain because the government had to formalise its system of quality objectives for receiving waters. As mentioned, at first this was done with a guidance circular but the European Commission was not satisfied with this as an implementing measure. Britain was not the only Member State to use circulars to implement directives. The issue was finally resolved by the European Court of Justice in Case C-361/88: *Commission v Germany*,[6] which makes it clear that a change in domestic law is required to implement European Community law, since mere administrative measures may be altered at any time. Statutory water quality objectives were therefore introduced in sections 104 and 105 of the Water Act 1989 and are now contained in sections 82 and 83 of the Water Resources Act 1991, as seen below:

> 82(1) The Secretary of State may, in relation to any description of controlled waters (being a description applying to some or all of the waters of a particular class or of two or more different classes), by regulations prescribe a system of classifying the quality of those waters according to criteria specified in the regulations.
>
> (2) The criteria specified in regulations under this section in relation to any classification shall consist of one or more of the following, that is to say-
>
> (a) general requirements as to the purpose for which the waters to which the classification is applied are to be suitable;
> (b) specific requirements as to the substances that are to be present in or absent from the water and as to the concentrations of substances which are or are to be required to be present in the water;
> (c) specific requirements as to other characteristics of those waters and for the purposes of any such classification regulations under this section may provide that the question whether prescribed requirements are satisfied may be determined by reference to such samples as may be prescribed.
>
> 83(1) For the purposes of maintaining and improving the quality of controlled waters the Secretary of State may, by serving a notice on the Authority specifying-

6 [1991] ECR I-2567.

(a) one or more of the classifications for the time being prescribed under section 82 above; and
(b) in relation to each specified classification, a date to establish the water quality objectives for any waters which are, or are included in, waters of a description prescribed for the purposes of that section.

(2) The water quality objectives for any waters to which a notice under this section relates shall be the satisfaction by those waters, on and at all times after each date specified in the notice, of the requirements which at the time of the notice were the requirements for the classification in relation to which the date is so specified.

Section 84 of the Water Resources Act 1991 requires that when the Environment Agency is granting discharge consents it must ensure compliance with these statutory water quality objectives.

Several proactive measures to prevent pollution occurring at source were enacted in the Water Act 1989 and are now re-enacted in the Water Resources Act 1991. These include the provision of information, measures to encourage good storage practices, the designation of nitrate vulnerable zones and nitrate sensitive areas, and the formulation of a code of good agricultural practice.

It was at first thought that the nitrate problem was caused by over enthusiastic applications of inorganic fertilisers onto arable land. Whilst this has, indeed, been a part of the problem, it became clear that manure spreading was the source of a great deal of the pollution. This has added greatly to the complexity of the problem of controlling nitrate applications because it is difficult to establish exactly how much nitrate there will be in a load of manure. And, if spreading the manure must be limited, then it must be stored adequately. Many dairy and pig farms did not have adequate manure storage facilities. The realisation that too much manure was the real problem of course challenged the view held by many outside farming that the 'artificiality' of inorganic fertilisers was to blame; nothing can be more 'natural' than manure.

(a) Information

Section 202 of the Water Resources Act 1991 is a general power that allows the Environment Agency to ask for information which will assist it to prevent water pollution. The section authorises the Agency to operate in an advisory role, which hopefully also enables Agency officers to establish a cooperative relationship with farmers so that potential problems can be discussed at an early stage and measures taken to avoid pollution. Such measures may be very simple such as avoiding spreading manure near to a watercourse or may entail installing large and expensive storage facilities.[7]

(b) Storage

Section 86 of the Water Resources Act 1991 gives power to the Environment Agency to prohibit discharges. This power however only extends to discharges from 'a building or from any fixed plant' which, though potentially useful in

7 However, there is also evidence that some farmers are responding to these attentions from the Environment Agency by going out of dairy farming and into arable instead.

other cases, would not catch many farm waste disposal systems such as mobile slurry spreaders.

Before the 1989 Act, agriculture accounted for about 12% of reported pollution incidents, but these were considered to be only a small proportion of those that actually occurred.[8] 87% of all reported farm pollution incidents were due to organic wastes. This figure breaks down as cow slurry 55%, silage 20%, pig slurry 10% and poultry manure 2%. Oil accounted for a further 3%. Section 92 of the Water Resources Act 1991 provides for the setting of minimum standards for keeping and handling silage, slurry and agricultural fuel on new or altered facilities. Most existing facilities are exempt but the Environment Agency may serve a notice requiring improvements to be made if, in the Agency's opinion, there is a significant risk of pollution. Failure to abide by the terms of a notice is a criminal offence. The central offence is not for causing pollution but rather for failing to take precautions to prevent it.

Schedule 22 to the Environment Act 1995 gives the Environment Agency new powers to serve a works notice on a polluter or potential polluter to carry out works. The new secton 161(D) of the Water Resources Act makes it an offence not to comply with a notice. In the event of non-compliance, section 161 of the Water Resources Act allows the Environment Agency to carry out operations itself to prevent or clean up pollution and to recover the cost of doing so from the offender. This again is a very powerful measure which could be used if a farm does not comply with the Regulations for safe storage of polluting material. However it would only be useful for point sources such as slurry tanks and, crucially, it assumes a financially solvent farmer.

The law's concentration on the adequacy of storage facilities for farmyard wastes has resulted in great expense, arguably without solving the problem. A discussion paper by the Sustainable Agriculture, Food and Environment (SAFE) Alliance offers a critique of this focus.

P Lowe, J Clark, S Seymour and N Ward *Pollution Control on Dairy Farms: An evaluation of current policy and procedure* (London: Sustainable Agriculture, Food and Environment (SAFE), 1992) p 17

Conclusion

The primary aim of the regulation of pollution by farm wastes ought to be the protection of the environment, yet our analysis reveals serious flaws in the present set of policies which compromise that objective. Principally this is because they are geared to the needs of agriculture. Government policies tackle farm waste pollution problems within the confines of existing farming systems and focus primarily on containment rather than on the generation of waste and its safe management and disposal. At the same time, policies target pollution incidents but fail to address diffuse pollution issues and the role of everyday farming practices. This approach has enabled most farmers to accommodate new demands without altering course, but is likely to be much less successful in protecting the environment. What is needed is a new approach to policy,

8 National Rivers Authority, *The Influence of Agriculture on the Quality of Natural Waters in England and Wales*, Water Quality Series No 6 (Bristol: NRA, 1992).

which seeks to minimise the generation of waste and to reintegrate its use within the production cycle.

While the technical standards of waste facilities do need to be improved, this single minded policy commitment to a 'technical fix' has several significant implications. Even judged within its own logic, it is uncertain how successful technological solutions will be in reducing pollution. None of the present controls can guarantee the quality of waste installations, and in any case farmers may avoid the procedures altogether.

Moreover, to the extent that sizeable investment in facilities engenders complacency, a sense of technical security on the part of the farmer could have the effect of downgrading the importance of careful management, on which the effectiveness of any technology depends. At the same time, while an upgrading, albeit slow, of waste containment facilities may well in time lead to fewer incidents, the extent to which storage capacity is increased may well influence the seriousness of those events which do occur: the larger the facility; the greater the potential for concentrated environmental damage. A policy of 'contain and dispose' for farm wastes may actually increase the risk of serious water pollution incidents.

The financial and technical decisions encouraged by current policies also have implications for future policy choices. Regulation could well become more stringent in the future; for example, restrictions on slurry spreading, a requirement for treatment (in part because this would reduce odour), or controls on stocking rates. This could force more fundamental consideration of the generation and disposal of such large quantities of highly polluting livestock wastes. But the fact of substantial existing investment in technical infrastructures would make such a reorientation that much more difficult. In the first three years of the current grant scheme over £120 million has been invested. The wisdom of committing such considerable sums of public and private money to the containment of the problem rather than to tackling it at its source must be questioned.

The focus on point sources and technical solutions reflects, in part, the traditional approach to pollution control, oriented towards gross pollution from factory and sewerage outfalls. But agriculture is unamenable to such a 'pipeline' approach. On the one hand, treatment processes that would yield an acceptable discharge from farm wastes are not available (as they are for many sewerage and trade effluents). On the other hand, as an extensive user of land, agriculture is inherently less circumscribed. Pollution control, by focusing on point source incidents, reinforces the assumption that pollution is the consequence of inappropriate or careless waste disposal, not the outcome of a production process that is unsound. But farming is not simply another industrial activity generating flows of waste; it is the primary force in the management of the rural environment.

(c) Water protection zones

Section 93 of the Water Resources Act 1991 gives powers to the Secretary of State to designate water protection zones after consulting the Minister of Agriculture, Fisheries and Food. In effect a local water pollution law operates within each zone, with the Environment Agency prohibiting or restricting activities which are likely to pollute water, with criminal sanctions for breaches. This provision existed under the Control of Pollution Act 1974 but was never used. It appeared in the Water Act 1989 and has been rewritten into the Water Resources Act 1991. This measure would be particularly useful for protecting especially sensitive areas, for protecting groundwaters and for dealing with diffuse problems such as pesticide and fertiliser run-off. A limitation is that the powers are restrictive or prohibitive only and do not include the power to require positive works to be carried out.

(d) Nitrate Sensitive Areas

Whilst still in the European Community's legislative pipeline, Directive 91/676/EEC on nitrate from agricultural sources prompted an inclusion in the Water Act 1989 of a provision to prevent the pollution of water by nitrate: the designation of land as Nitrate Sensitive Areas (NSAs) in which farming would be modified to prevent nitrate leaching to groundwater. An area is generally chosen if it forms the catchment for a water supply. Section 112 of the Water Act 1989, now sections 94 and 95 of the Water Resources Act 1991, gave powers to the Minister of Agriculture, Fisheries and Food and the Secretary of State for the Environment to designate Nitrate Sensitive Areas. Following an application by the Environment Agency, these bodies may jointly designate areas of land to prevent or control the entry of nitrate into controlled waters as a result of anything done in connection with, or the use of, any land for agricultural purposes.

Within the area, the aim is to change or prohibit activities in order to protect the water. Here different legal tools can be deployed as appropriate to the problem. In the Nitrate Sensitive Areas this has involved a voluntary contract in the form of a management agreement between the Minister of Agriculture and the farmer. Should this fail to achieve its objectives, powers exist to make the arrangement compulsory and to resort to additional criminal sanctions.

A farmer may apply to the Minister to join the scheme and a voluntary management agreement is then entered into.

> Where any land has been designated as a nitrate sensitive area by an order under this section and the relevant Minister considers it appropriate to do so... he may... enter into an agreement under which, in consideration of payments to be made by the relevant Minister (a) the owner... or (b) (the tenant)... accepts such obligations with respect to the management.

Then 'in consideration of payments' from the Ministry, the farmer agrees to abide by the terms of agreement. The terms are set out in the Nitrate Sensitive Areas Designation Order.[9] An agreement must allow the Ministry to monitor compliance with the terms or to assess its effectiveness by going onto the land, installing equipment, taking samples and examining records. If a farmer fails, without reasonable excuse, to comply with any of the provisions of an agreement the Minster may terminate it and recover the whole or any part of any payment already made. The payments vary both from area to area and between options, according to how onerous the obligations of the agreement are.

9 SI 1990/1013.

The designation of an area is an important measure which contains within it and deploys a number of different forms of law which co-exist and interact. Proactive or preventive law is superimposed on, and interferes with, ancient English land law in which the social relationship between landlord and tenant is expressed as greater or lesser interests in the land. The detailed treatment of the landlord and tenant relationship in the Nitrate Sensitive Areas arises because the terms of the management agreements are designed to change the long term character of the land which could substantially affect the profitability of the farm. An agreement binds successors in title of the offeree but not, if the offeree is a tenant, the landlord who takes the land in hand later, nor a subsequent tenant. The Water Act 1989 amended the Agricultural Holdings Act 1986 to give protection to tenants who joined a Nitrate Sensitive Area scheme, providing that if the landlord gave his consent, nothing done for the management agreement would amount to a breach of tenancy. The Minister may impose mandatory requirements, prohibitions or restrictions with or without payments.

A variety of forms of law appear in the provisions for Nitrate Sensitive Areas. As well as land law, contract has been incorporated and used for the management agreements between the Minister and the farmers which have been entered into voluntarily and whose terms are enforced as contractual obligations. In the classical form a contract cannot bind third parties. In the Nitrate Sensitive Areas this form has been modified:

> s 94 (3) An agreement such as is mentioned in section (2) above between the relevant Minister and a person having an interest in any land shall bind all persons deriving title from or under that person to the extent that the agreement is expressed to bind that land in relation to those persons.

As a legal form, contract has other advantages that go beyond the convenience of enforceability and have more to do with wider obligations that may be mobilised to reinforce the law. Atiyah[10] writes that contract is that part of the law that deals with obligations that are self-imposed. As such it is said that a contract implies freedom of individual choice as to whether or not to be bound by its terms. It has become elevated above other obligations and operates on a moral plane that gives it primacy even if, in practical commercial contexts, contracts are often broken.

Criminal law also plays a role in the legal regime of Nitrate Sensitive Areas. Section 94(4)(d) of the Water Resources Act 1991 says:

> ... an order under this section... may
>
> (d) provide that a contravention of a requirement, prohibition or restriction contained in the order or in a condition of a consent given in relation to or for the purposes of any such prohibition or restriction shall be an offence...

The offence of breaching a mandatory requirement carries the penalties of a fine or imprisonment or both. This power to use the sanction of the criminal law has not been implemented in the Designation Order but is significant as a symbol: for many farmers in the Nitrate Sensitive Areas it is possible the stigma

10 PS Atiyah, *An Introduction to the Law of Contract*, 3rd edn (Oxford: Clarendon Press, 1981) p 20.

of being labelled a criminal offender could be worse than the bare punishment since they are often leaders in the rural community.

The government placed great emphasis on the voluntary participation of farmers in the Nitrate Sensitive Areas but also reminded them of the more coercive measures that were available, in reserve as it were. For example the Minister at the time, John Gummer, in a MAFF News Release announcing the candidate areas for designation finished with:

> Finally I must emphasise that, in accordance with the Government's policy on nitrate, all agricultural practices or restrictions introduced under this pilot scheme will be on a voluntary basis. Should these measures not prove effective, the 1989 Water Act provides for compulsory powers as a fallback.

The proactive element of the Nitrate Sensitive Areas legal regime is first of all the designation of the land that forms the catchment areas of boreholes. The procedure for designating land as a Nitrate Sensitive Area is specified in Schedule 12 of the Water Resources Act 1991. The Environment Agency makes an application to the Minister for a designation order if, following section 5(2) of the Water Resources Act 1991, it appears to the Agency:

> s 5(2)
>
> (a) that pollution is or is likely to be caused by the entry of nitrate into controlled waters as a result of, or of anything done in connection with, the use of particular land in England and Wales for agricultural purposes; and
>
> (b) that the provisions for the time being in force in relation to those waters and that land are not sufficient, in the opinion of the Authority, for preventing or controlling such entry of nitrate into those waters.

Pollution is taken to be at, or above the 50mg/l level for nitrate set by Directive 80/778/EEC on drinking water. The Environment Agency must identify both the controlled waters that appear to the Agency to be, or likely to be, entered by nitrate and the area in which farming needs to be modified to prevent this. The Authority then serves a notice on the Minister and the Secretary of State, who may not make an order without the consent of the Treasury.

Once the land has been designated, the next step is to specify in what ways land use must change. The powers to require, restrict or prohibit activities are as wide as the Minister considers appropriate, only circumscribed by their relevance to preventing the entry of nitrate to waters. The obligations need not all be specified in the original designation order but may be detailed in subsequent orders relating to the area. Should there be any doubt as to the scope of the powers available this is spelt out in the Water Resources Act 1991 at section 94:

> (5) An order under this section may
>
> (a) make different provision for different cases, including different provision in relation to different persons, circumstances or localities; and
>
> (b) contain such supplemental, consequential and transitional provisions as the relevant Minister considers appropriate.

An innovation, in legal terms, is the power to require positive acts to be done by farmers such as planting a cover crop in the autumn. This is a feature of

Nitrate Sensitive Areas that goes beyond the provision for water protection or 'vulnerable zones', where only restrictions or prohibitions are possible.

The majority of the obligations are to reduce applications of inorganic nitrogen fertiliser. As we have said nitrate reaches the water from many sources and along many pathways but the application of inorganic nitrogen fertiliser is one source that can be controlled relatively easily. Differing amounts of fertiliser for wheat and barley, oilseed rape and forage crops are specified together with planting dates. Applications of inorganic nitrogen fertiliser to grassland and cultivation of grassland are also restricted. Other obligations concern the storage and application of slurry, poultry manure and liquid sewage sludge. As well as the basic scheme, there is a further option to join a premium scheme with higher payments under which arable land is converted to unfertilised grassland or trees are planted under the Farm Woodland Scheme. This option is designed to fundamentally change the character of the land.

The real significance of the Nitrate Sensitive Areas scheme is that it goes to the root of the problem by coupling land use with water protection and restricting intensive farming for the sake of drinking water and the amenity quality of surface waters. It also interacts with other preventive legal measures, such as the codes for good agricultural practice to prevent pollution and the Regulations for the storage of slurry, silage and fuel oil; all of which are designed to mitigate pollution of water from farming.

(e) Code of good agricultural practice for the protection of water

The code of practice as a legal form is a relatively new development but already there are several variations. The legal status of codes may differ but a common feature is that there is a good deal of negotiation with those who will eventually have to follow it before a code is officially issued – with the expectation that they will be more willing to comply than if it had been imposed without discussion. The early Nitrate Sensitive Areas had a legal significance and an importance beyond the control of nitrate levels in the areas: they provided a way to discuss and try out the practical implications for farming before the publication of the new code of good agricultural practice for the protection of water which applies to all farmers throughout the country. The consultation process was wide and thorough and discussions with the farmers in the Nitrate Sensitive Areas were influential. The significance of this can be appreciated from estimates in 1991 that nearly half of the dairy farmers of Britain were in danger of polluting water, if they were not already doing so, unless they made major changes to their farming. As well as this, levels of nitrate in groundwater where arable farming seemed to be the cause were in danger of exceeding the European Community limit in most of the Midlands and East Anglia. The code of good agricultural practice for the protection of water, provided for by section 97 of the Water Resources Act 1991, is now central to the Environment Agency's strategy for mitigating agricultural water pollution.

The House of Commons Select Committee on the Environment which reported on the pollution of rivers and estuaries in 1987 realised that much of this pollution came from farming. The Committee directed many of its questions to the effectiveness of the code of good agricultural practice for the prevention of pollution that had been set up under the Control of Pollution Act 1974.

House of Commons Select Committee on the Environment, Third Report (1986-87), *Pollution of Rivers and Estuaries* (London: HMSO, 1987) ch 6, Evidence, pp xxv-xxviii

Pollution by Agriculture

Hayricks and duckponds are rare sights on today's farm. Silage stores and slurry pits seem to be their successors. This is a big industry, where intensive livestock and arable farming cause major unwanted by-products which can lead to water pollution. South West Water told us that modern agriculture was the main cause of deterioration of river quality in their area. They saw this as:

> "a direct, unwelcome consequence of national agricultural policy which has concentrated on increasing production without adequate consideration of wider implications."

We heard similar comments in Switzerland, West Germany and the Netherlands. Mr Waldergrave recognised that

> "clearly there is a relationship between increase in some of the output and the increase in problems that go along with output"

and Lord Belstead said that his Ministry had...

> "tried to respond to this serious concern that if you keep on increasing production there is going to be an increased danger of pollution."

The Council for the Protection of Rural England (CPRE) took this further by saying that the patterns of financial incentives to farmers – capital grants and price support offered to farmers under CAP – have encouraged the pursuit of crop production objectives "sometimes to the exclusion of other objectives". The CPRE suggest that a review of financial incentives to farmers might, in the end, lead to less pollution of our rivers.

Agricultural pollution is a wide topic and we received much evidence covering many different matters. We therefore limit ourselves here to those aspects which seem to us to be most pressing. These are:

(i) pollution incidents related to slurry and silage
(ii) dispersed pollution by nitrates
(iii) future changes in land use
(iv) fish farming.

A common thread was the operation of MAFF's Code of Good Agricultural Practice and the current preference for exhortation over regulation. We therefore start with a brief look at the role of MAFF.

Ministry of Agriculture, Fisheries and Food (MAFF)

Our major concern about agricultural pollution is the complacent attitude of MAFF. Their evidence to us barely conceded that agricultural pollution has been heavily implicated as one of two major threats to water quality. Despite a major Royal Commission Report and our own report on the Wildlife and Countryside Act, we sense that MAFF neglects to provide the strong lead needed to induce more farmers to adopt pro-conservation and anti-pollution farming practices. MAFF's failure to take farm pollution seriously is encapsulated in its ineffective approach of "positive encouragement". Our concern is exemplified by the fact that there is still no one single division within MAFF with overall responsibility for policy on conservation and pollution. Lord Belstead described to us the relatively recent organisational arrangements in MAFF which include an Environmental Steering Committee chaired by a Deputy Secretary and a Lands and Environmental Affairs Group headed by an Under-Secretary. Despite these changes, we consider that a single division should be created as a matter of urgency, and the new division should be headed by a senior official of at least Under-Secretary rank.

Farmers and COPA

Under the Control of Pollution Act farmers enjoy a defence from prosecution if they pollute a stream or river where:

> the entry in question [into the water course] is attributable to an act or omission which is in accordance with good agricultural practice.

Good agricultural practice is defined by MAFF's Code of Good Agricultural Practice. We received almost no criticism of the substance of this Code. Nevertheless, we heard innumerable complaints that the Code is simply not observed. We were also frequently told that if farmers would only adhere to the Code there could be no agricultural pollution problem at all.

The special defence which farmers enjoy under COPA seems to us quite unwarranted. MAFF told us that they know of no case where a farmer had successfully used this defence, and of only one case where a farmer had even attempted it. We cannot think of circumstances where pollution of a stream or a river by a farmer could be justifiably excused on the grounds that "it accorded with good agricultural practice". The two are mutually exclusive. The special defence leads unjustified weight to a feeling that farmers warrant separate consideration when it comes to water pollution. This is not appropriate. We therefore think that s.31(2)(c) of COPA should be repealed at the first opportunity.

...

Code of Good Agricultural Practice

The Code of Good Agricultural Practice may be a good concept, but the reality does not withstand very close scrutiny. The actual Code (price £2) is primarily a reference list to some twenty other documents published by MAFF. A farmer would need to spend up to £20 to acquire all these documents which together constitute the Code and which "stand some six inches tall". They are not widely available. MAFF stressed that farmers would not need to acquire every document which makes up the Code. They reported that they had circulated an introductory leaflet about the Code to each of the 225,000 farms in England and Wales and had distributed a total of 67,000 leaflets in 1985-86 covering constituent parts of the Code. However, it is clear from MAFF's leaflet distribution figures that these leaflets still reach only a small proportion of farmers. Our overall impression is that the Code of Good

Agricultural Practice is little known, and in reality often ignored. In its current form the Code is purely advisory and could not become a basis for statutory control without very substantial revision.

Despite this very strongly worded recommendation by a Parliamentary Select Committee, the government's response in the Water Act 1989 was a change in the status of the code, but only so that a contravention can be taken into account by the Environment Agency when determining, under section 85 of the Water Resources Act 1991, whether to prosecute for causing or knowingly permitting a discharge of poisonous, noxious or polluting or solid waste matter to any controlled water without proper authority. It is no longer a defence but failure to abide by it can be seen as evidence for prosecution.

The status of the new code of good agricultural practice, first introduced under the Water Act 1989, can be interpreted as a small retreat for the farmers from a favoured position but nonetheless remains indicative of a 'special relationship' between the state and the farming lobby which is far from fading.

Section 116 of the Water Act 1989, re-enacted as section 97 of the Water Resources Act 1991, gave powers to the Secretary of State and the Minister to issue a new code of good agricultural practice for the prevention of pollution. This includes a code for the prevention of pollution of water, one for the safe use of pesticides on farms and holdings, one for the agricultural use of sewage sludge and another for the protection of air. The code for the protection of water, published in July 1991, instructs farmers on how to dispose of their animal wastes to minimise water pollution and devotes a whole section to nitrate.

Ministry of Agriculture, Fisheries and Food, *Code of Good Agricultural Practice for the Protection of Water* (London: MAFF Pubs, 1991) pp 60-62

Nitrate

258. This section of the Code covers the nitrogen lost as nitrate from farmland and the way you can cut down this loss at little or no extra cost. In some cases, better farming methods will reduce both the cost and the amount of nitrate lost by leaching (that is the nitrate washed away by water draining from the soil).

259. Nitrate leaching causes nitrogen to be lost from soils. Nitrate is lost to surface waters by run-off or through land drains and to groundwater. The amount of nitrogen lost depends on weather, soil and farming system.

260. There is concern over the increasing amount of nitrate in many of our drinking water sources, particularly groundwaters. There is also concern over the amount of nitrogen reaching our rivers, estuaries and seas. The Pilot Nitrate Scheme was set up during 1989/90 to look at ways of cutting down the amount of nitrate lost from a range of mainly agricultural water catchments.

261. In some catchments, action beyond the Good Agricultural Practice described in this Code will be needed to keep water below 50 mg/l nitrate which is the most nitrate allowed in drinking water.

Section 112 and Schedule 11 of the Water Act 1989 consider the designation of Nitrate Sensitive Areas where the Government considers it appropriate to control the amount of nitrate going into water from agricultural land. The National Rivers Authority (NRA) are responsible for suggesting areas for designation by the Government.

262. A lot of nitrate is released if permanent grassland is ploughed up and changed to arable. Nitrate will be lost by leaching for several years. This practice should be avoided if possible.

If permanent grassland needs reseeding do it with as little cultivation as possible and make sure that grass covers the field by early October.

263. If grass leys are grown in rotation with arable crops, sow the first crop as soon as possible after the grass has been ploughed up. Following winter cereal crops should be drilled early.

When you are reseeding leys, do it with as little cultivation as possible and try to get the crop to cover the land by early October.

Organic Manures

264. Animal manure and other organic wastes such as sewage sludge contain different amounts and forms of nitrogen. When you apply them to the soil, the soluble nitrogen is turned into nitrate in a few weeks. The rest of the nitrogen takes longer to break down and be converted to nitrate.

265. Because of the different form of nitrogen and the different rates at which they can be used by the crop, the risk of losing nitrate by leaching is higher than from inorganic fertilisers. To avoid losing too much from leaching do not apply more than 250 kg/ha of total nitrogen in organic manure in any 12 months. You should not apply more available nitrogen than the crop needs.

266. Apply organic manures which have a lot of available nitrogen when they can be used by the crop. This type of manure includes cow slurry, pig slurry, poultry manures and liquid sewage sludges. To cut down the risk of nitrate leaching, application to arable land in the autumn or early winter should be avoided whenever practicable.

267. You can apply organic manures that do not contain much nitrogen that can easily be converted to nitrate, at any time. These include farmyard manure and sewage sludge cake.

Inorganic Nitrogen Fertiliser

268. To keep the amount of nitrate lost from the soil as low as possible, carefully work out the amount of inorganic nitrogen fertiliser you need. Do not use more than the economic optimum in each field. Work out how much nitrogen is in the soil and how much the crop needs. Take into account the type of soil, previous cropping and the use of animal manure and other organic wastes when you are working out how much nitrogen a crop can get from the soil itself.

Do not apply extra fertiliser to be on the safe side. Applying above the economic optimum will increase the amount of nitrate lost by leaching.

6 CONCLUSION

The European Community's series of Environment Action Programmes has resulted in several directives concerned with the quality of water. These have been of progressively wider scope and are now designed to extend beyond the quality of drinking water for human consumption to the protection of aquatic ecosystems of both fresh and sea water. The precautionary principle finds legal expression in preventive directives which, it is hoped, will give more effective protection to waters by regulating the sources of pollution than laws which only come into operation once the harm has been done.

Britain has had to adapt both institutions and law in response to these developments. This response may have initially been reluctant but there is now a tranche of strong laws which, in theory, give the Environment Agency powers to prevent much pollution from farming. The regulations for storing polluting substances on farms are, arguably, not truly preventive since they do not address the fundamental problem of an over-abundance of manure.

The Environment Agency may now also play an educational role as well as an enforcement one within the farming community. The code of good agricultural practice for the protection of water shows that the educational function goes both ways. Farmers had the opportunity to contribute to its drafting and so it now reflects the realities of farming. However, its status remains ambiguous: no longer is it a defence against a prosecution for polluting water but neither is contravention of it an offence per se. It is possible that this ambiguous status is sometimes useful to the Environment Agency because the officers' educational and advisory role on preventing water pollution need not be jeopardised. It would be interesting to know if the majority of farmers have a copy of the new code. It has been discussed extensively in the farming press, so they may perhaps have some knowledge of its provisions.

The powers to prevent pollution now available to the Environment Agency have had considerable effect in some parts of the country, though not at all the intended effect. In Suffolk, several farmers have been so alarmed by the threat of prosecution if they have inadequate storage for the manure from their dairy cows that they have sold the cows and changed to arable farming, which pays very well now.[11] In the South West Water area the same thing has happened but there steep hillsides have been changed from pasture to plantations of maize, with attendant problems of soil erosion.[12] These examples show the limitations of concentrating on preventing a single substance going into a single medium. In other parts of the country, however, it appears that the recommendations for optimal applications of inorganic fertiliser are resulting in farmers using much less.[13] A change to farming in a more environmentally friendly way is taking a long time.

11 S Elworthy (1996), 'Legal Obstacles to Integrating Environmental Concerns in the CAP' in K Van Dael (ed) Recente Ontwikke-Lingen in het Europees Milieurect (Antwerp: Kluwer Rechtswetenschappen Belgie, 1997) pp 1-35.

12 Pers comm from an official of the Environment Agency, July 1996.

13 Pers comm. Scottish Agricultural College, Aberdeen, July 1996.

Over-enthusiastic application of nitrate was initially seen by the WHO, the European Community and the United Kingdom as solely a problem of water pollution. The following extract shows that now, a quarter of a century since the WHO first issued its nitrate guideline for drinking water, our environmental thinking has advanced so soil and water are no longer viewed as though they are quite separate.

Royal Commission on Environmental Pollution, Nineteenth Report, Sustainable Use of Soil, Cm 3165 (London: HMSO, 1996) pp 59-63

Nutrient leaching from agricultural land

Nitrogen

5.42 In the UK, nitrate levels in upland waters are generally correlated with atmospheric inputs; in lowland waters, soils are the main source (but industrial waste water, sewage effluents and run-off from farm wastes and silage are also important).

...

5.46 There is a long-term link between the use of inorganic nitrogen fertiliser and nitrate losses. The more fertiliser used, the greater the yield and the more nitrogen there is in plant residues (straw, stubble, roots). This can lead to an increase in soil organic nitrogen and in the potential for nitrate leaching after mineralisation of organic matter. Practices which increase soil organic matter therefore increase the long-term potential for nitrate leaching.

5.47 In the short term, leaching can be minimised if soil nitrogen remains in an organic form. Cover crops (including unfertilised grass) and minimum tillage can help directly to reduce mineralisation, which takes place at the surface of the soil. Incorporation of residues results in an initial increase in mineralisation, followed by a population explosion of soil micro-organisms which exhausts the supply of available nitrogen. Subsequent cultivation will increase mineralisation, with release of nitrate.

5.48 Nitrate leaching can also be reduced by using commercial nitrification inhibitors, such as dicyandiamide, applied to the soil either directly before slurries or granular fertilisers, or with ammonium-based liquid fertilisers. These chemicals inhibit (or, in some cases, kill) the bacteria which convert ammonium to nitrate. By slowing down the rate at which this conversion occurs, improvements in yield, as well as reduction in nitrogen loss (through leaching or as nitrous oxide emissions), can be achieved. Their use in a strategy to control nitrate losses was considered in the Netherlands but was not favoured because of concern about possible persistence in groundwater of these inhibitors.

Schemes to reduce nitrate leaching

5.49 The pilot Nitrate Sensitive Areas (NSAs) Scheme was introduced in ten areas in England in 1990 to investigate ways of reducing nitrate losses from agriculture to groundwater. Farmers entering this voluntary scheme are compensated for costs incurred and production losses. After the first three years,

MAFF reported that conversion of arable land to extensive grassland, the establishment of cover crops and restrictions on the use of animal manure were particularly effective in reducing nitrate losses. While the NSA scheme has the potential to reduce nitrate leaching, it is difficult to draw meaningful conclusions about its efficacy over such a limited period, given the large annual variations in nitrate production, cycling and loss and the fact that movement of nitrate to groundwater takes many years. A further 22 NSAs were designated in England in 1994 and the scheme is now part of the UK agri-environment programme... There are no NSAs in Wales, Scotland or Northern Ireland.

5.50 The 1991 EC Nitrate Directive aims to reduce 'water pollution caused or induced by nitrate from agricultural sources' through the designation of Nitrate Vulnerable Zones... It is proposed to designate 70 sites in England. There are two NVZ proposals in each of Scotland and Wales, where a smaller proportion of land is cultivated and less use made of groundwater for public water supply. The Ythan catchment in north-east Scotland was proposed because of severe eutrophication of the river estuary. The relative contributions of nitrate and phosphate to this eutrophication are being studied.

5.51 We welcome the expansion of the NSA scheme and its continuation under the UK agri-environment programme. Although it is too early to assess the effects, we believe that the NSA scheme and the appropriate management of farmland in the NVZs will bring long-term environmental benefits.

CHAPTER 10

The road ahead: environmental assessment

1 INTRODUCTION

In this chapter we consider a different technique of environmental protection from those discussed so far: environmental assessment. As a *procedural* requirement that the likely effects of development be taken into account before planning permission is granted for certain projects, environmental assessment is strikingly different from substantive and prescriptive measures, such as Directive 80/778/EEC on the quality of drinking water (see previous chapter), which have so far made up the bulk of modern environmental law. We choose environmental assessment as the subject of this chapter because it represents a number of significant developments in environmental law, discussed throughout this book – the development of integrated and preventive methods of control, the fostering of responsibility for, or stewardship of, the environment, and the growing acceptance of the validity of precautionary measures. Environmental assessment also provides a conceptual and practical bridge between pollution controls, such as those discussed in chapter 6, and the controls over the use and development of land in chapter 7. Whilst it is possible that planning's role in protecting the environment might be realised through the use of environmental assessment, as we shall see in this chapter the technique is open to abuse.

Environmental assessment has been developed most fully by the European Community in the form of Council Directive 85/337/EEC.[1] This is the product of the first attempt of the European Community to influence Member States' planning systems. In formal terms, the Community had no competence in this area. By definition, a sovereign state controls its own land. This was also a recognition of the cultural significance of land use. The implementation of Directive 85/337/EEC in the United Kingdom illuminates an important theme of the book – the integration of different layers of law. Environmental assessment is a European Community legal technique which is integrated with existing national or 'indigenous' methods of scrutinising the environmental effects of a development.

Once again, we use a case study to explain what environmental assessment is and its practical effects, in particular how it is used to identify and mitigate the adverse effects of development on the environment. The case study is the

1 OJ L175, 5.7.1985, p 40.

Thanet Way bypass in the north east corner of Kent. The bypass was proposed by Kent County Council Highways and Transport department and was determined by the Planning Department of the same council. A planning inquiry was held following the calling in of the project by the Secretary of State for Transport. Permission to construct the bypass was granted by the Secretary of State in 1994. The road is now being built. At a local level, controversy over the project was intense. On a national level, it remains a lower profile than the causes célèbres – the M3 extension through Twyford Down and the Newbury bypass – but nevertheless raises many similar issues of the role of public participation in road projects, the conservation of the countryside versus enhanced amenity in urban areas, and the effectiveness and environmental effects of the road building programme. In choosing this case study we return to our brief discussion in chapter 1 of the environmental and health effects of transport and the dilemmas of road use and building. The desirability of a holistic approach is again raised. The case study highlights other important points: that environmental harm arises from more diverse sources than the typical factory outlet, and that public bodies (in this case a county council) may be responsible for officially sanctioning environmentally harmful development. It addresses in a practical way philo-sophical questions about the meaning of 'the environment' and its protection: whose environment is to be protected, and for what reasons? Does the environment have intrinsic value? Can loss of natural resources or a habitat be compensated for?

Before turning to the case study, we discuss the concept, origins and characteristics of environmental assessment, its development by the European Community, and the legal framework and political machinations which constitute the implementation of Directive 85/337/EEC in the United Kingdom.

2 THE CONCEPT OF ENVIRONMENTAL ASSESSMENT – THE ACCEPTED VERSION

Environmental assessment was first introduced in the United States in 1969[2] as a requirement for assessing the environmental impact of major actions, physical land use projects as well as policies, which might significantly affect the quality of the environment. Environmental assessment is a means of drawing together expert and public opinion of a project or policy's environmental effects and ensuring that this information is taken into account by decision makers before a decision is made. The conceptual premise of environmental assessment is that introducing information about the effects of development into a decision making process encourages an informed choice to be made between environmental and other objectives, possibly resulting in less environmentally harmful decisions. Changing the rules governing the generation and use of knowledge

2 A system of environmental assessment was established by s 102(2)(c) of the National Environmental Policy Act (NEPA) 1969, 42 USC 4321-4361.

is thought also to change the intellectual and political culture of decision making so that decision makers become generally more aware of the environmental consequences of their decisions. Environmental assessment is the archetypal interdisciplinary technique: as a legal process it is reliant upon scientific methods and contributes to essentially political planning procedures.

This conceptual basis of environmental assessment relies upon a set of presumptions that the causes and effects of harm can be predicted and that the significance of these effects can be measured, both of which may, at times, prove unsupportable. This is because, as we have emphasised throughout the book, the effects of change on ecological systems are not well enough understood yet to be accurately predicted and pollutants might accumulate and react in ways which are not easily foreseeable.

(a) Characteristics of environmental assessment

Environmental assessment sets procedural requirements for decision making, rather than containing specific standards. Environmental assessment rules relate to the style and structure of decision making. The element of legal control is indirect: environmental assessment provides a conduit by which information may enter decision making procedures, but, in theory at least, will not determine the outcomes of these procedures. This means that should an environmental assessment establish that significant environmental harm will ensue from a particular development or project, this will be taken into account, but will not necessarily lead to the project or policy being refused.

The procedure is anticipatory, providing information about potential impacts *before* a final decision is taken (most commonly at the authorisation stage of planning procedures). This offers the possibility of imposing conditions about the siting of development and the mitigation of harmful environmental effects before harm occurs. If the environmental assessment procedure is not followed, enforcement action may be taken even though harm may not have arisen. The anticipatory control exercised by environmental assessment relies upon its imposing a 'burden of proof' on the developer to demonstrate that a proposed project is acceptable in environmental terms at the planning stage and that adverse effects may be mitigated. This duty on the developer to take account of the environmental effects of a proposal interferes with the right to develop expressed in the prevailing policy presumption in favour of development,[3] and, most significantly, encourages a general perception of development as potentially environmentally harmful. This type of control contrasts markedly with controls which specify a form or quantity of pollution, state of environ-mental harm, or nuisance which must not be allowed to arise. Such controls are retrospective in the sense that they may only be enforced after the standard has been exceeded and, commonly, after a harmful incident has occurred.

A further important characteristic of environmental assessment is that it encourages an awareness of pollutants moving between environmental

3 See ch 7.

media. This was novel to the United Kingdom's regulatory approach until the establishment of the Integrated Pollution Control system under Part I of the Environmental Protection Act 1990. The general approach had been to control pollution by industrial sector, as with the Alkali Acts, or by environmental medium, as in the Rivers Pollution Prevention Act 1876 and the subsequent Rivers (Prevention of Pollution) Act 1951.[4] As discussed in chapter 6, little attention was given to devising integrated and co-ordinated institutions which would allow environmental considerations to affect a wide range of policy concerns. Environmental assessment works against this sectoral trend by establishing procedures for *integrated* policy and rule making. When pollution problems are approached predominantly as problems of air, water, or waste, the solution is usually to move the pollutant to the least protected parts of the environment. Integrated systems of pollution control allow alternative processes and products to be judged in the light of all the possible paths or cycles of pollutants in the environment. Environmental harm might therefore be prevented by identifying possible changes to be made to the products or processes at an early stage in the authorisation process. This reinforces the element of anticipatory control. Environmental assessment is a response to some of the inadequacies of sectoral controls, but nevertheless, as we will see, retains the pragmatism which informed the concept of 'best practicable means' and, latterly, 'best practicable environmental option'.

(b) 'Implementing' sustainable development via environmental assessment

In recent years, environmental assessment has been acknowledged as having a role in 'implementing' the principle of sustainable development by assisting decision makers to take account of the quality of development – its effects upon the conservation of natural resources – as well as its location and quantity.[5] Environmental assessment permits decision makers to balance (and possibly trade-off) detrimental environmental effects against economic benefits – one of the less avowed aspects of sustainable development. The Brundtland Report identifies environmental assessment of projects and policies as offering a strategy for sustainable industrial development, alongside the use of economic instruments.[6] This role is formally acknowledged by the international community in the Rio Declaration (1992):

> Principle 17: Environmental Impact Assessment as a national instrument shall be undertaken for proposed activities that are likely to have a significant adverse impact on the environment and are subject to a decision of a competent national authority.

4 See ch 2, 'Legislation and contol of industrial activities'.

5 See Experts Group on Environmental Law of the World Commission of Environment and Development, *Environmental Protection and Sustainable Development* (London, Dordrecht: Graham and Trotman/Martinus Nijhoff, 1986).

6 World Commission on Environment and Development, *Our Common Future* (Oxford: Oxford University Press, 1987) pp 221-224.

The prospects for environmental assessment giving effect to sustainable development relies on a broad definition of 'activities', so that for example the environmental effects of policies and programmes, as well as development projects, might be assessed and taken into account by decision makers. This is explored below. Some mention is made of environmental assessment's participatory elements as contributing to sustainable development.

B Dalal-Clayton, 'Environmental Assessment and Sustainable Development', (1994) *EIA Newsletter* No 9, 3-4

Much effort is now being made to consider how environmental assessment (including strategic environmental assessment) can play a more effective role in support of sustainable development. ...At the International Institute for Environment and Development (IIED), we take sustainable development to mean achieving a quality of life that can be maintained for many generations because it is:

- socially desirable, fulfilling people's cultural, material and spiritual needs in equitable ways;
- economically viable, paying for itself, with costs not exceeding income, and
- ecologically sustainable, maintaining the long-term viability of supporting ecosystems.

As Carley[7] has pointed out, 'good decisions come about from a steady improvement of the process of decision-making and participation, and enhanced human resource and institutional capabilities at national, regional and local levels'.

Many methods of analysis can contribute to these processes: by building up a picture of the tasks necessary to promote sustainable development (e.g. political change, good governance, institutional co-ordination, equitable resource distribution, etc); by offering resources which can be applied to those tasks; and by contributing to the development of a national consensus leading to purposive action. The relevant techniques, taken together, form a suite or framework which has been called 'sustainability analysis' (SA).[8] The latter has been defined as:[9]

'A generic term which embraces the aim of assessing the extent to which projects, programmes and policies are able to satisfy the goals and imperatives of sustainable development, particularly the integration of environment and development in decision-making.

A framework for SA will, *inter alia*, need to comprise a suite or 'tool kit' of methodologies and approaches which:

7 Carley, M (1994) *Policy Management Systems and Methods of Analysis for Sustainable Agriculture and Rural Development*, FAO, Rome, and IIED, London.

8 Dalal-Clayton, DB (1993) *Modified EIA and Indicators of Sustainability: First Steps Towards Sustainability Analysis*, Environmental Planning Issues, No 1, IIED, London.

9 Dalal-Clayton, DB and Sadler, B (in preparation) *More Effective Environmental Assessment: A Key Tool in Sustainability Analysis*, Environmental Planning Issues, IIED, London.

- explicitly focus on the trade-offs between the biophysical, social and economic aspects of the projects, programmes and policies, recognising that these take place within a framework of political decision-making;
- are undertaken in a systematic, integrative and transparent way;
- are participative (not just consultative), to the extent possible and practicable in the context of prevailing socio-cultural-political circumstances;
- need to operate within a set of defined criteria and guidelines for sustainable development, recognising that these may often only be best practice approximations; and
- recognise that EA is a major point of departure because it is a process which is well institutionalised in policy and law.

For environmental assessment to play a more effective role in sustainable development, ways need to be found that enable it to make a full contribution to policy – and decision-making. A major opportunity lies in the momentum now gathering weight, in the follow-up to UNCED, to develop national sustainable development strategies (NSDSs) and to promote the concept of sustainable development. The experiences of past strategies have been reviewed recently by IIED and IUCN, identifying approaches which have worked well and those which have been less successful.[10] This work has defined a strategy for sustainable development as a 'participatory and cyclical process to achieve economic, ecological and social objectives in a balanced and integrated manner. The process encompasses the definition of policies and action plans, their implementation, monitoring and regular review'. The process should not, therefore, be a one-shot event but one which is on-going, enabling lessons learnt from defining and implementing previous strategies, and the current one, to feed into refining, amending and improving it as circumstances and situations change. Some of the elements of the strategy cycle will follow on from the other; others (e.g. information analysis, monitoring and evaluation, and some implementation) will proceed throughout the cycle. However, there are many dilemmas for those charged with developing an NSDS or similar plan. For example: the political context in which a strategy is developed; identifying the key objective; building strategy capacity – through a single spine discipline or via a 'tool kit' approach; and setting the limits of consultation and participation...

A key challenge, therefore, is to ensure that those responsible for defining the process for the development of such strategies and for making consequential policy and action decisions, provide mechanisms (including legal and institutional) that enable sustainability analysis – and particularly environmental assessment to play a full part at all stages in the process.

We see here the assumption that social change to deal with environmental problems will come from consensus about the aim of sustainable development, and the instruments by which it might be 'implemented'. This can be

10 Carew-Reid, J, Prescott-Allen, R, Bass, S and Dalal-Clayton, DB (1994) *Strategies for National Sustainable Development: A Handbook for their Planning and Implementation*, IIED and IUCN, in association with Earthscan, London.

questioned. Perhaps change might also arise from contradictions and conflict? It also suggests a heavy reliance on scientism to provide a 'tool-kit' for change. Some of the effects of these unquestioned assumptions can be seen in the case study.

In this and similar literature, achieving sustainable development has been most closely tied to strategic environmental assessment – the assessment of plans and programmes of action as well as projects. This is because strategic environmental assessment is thought to be more able to take account of the broader picture of environmental effects and the interrelation of environmental and economic factors than project-based assessment can ever hope to do. The prospects for a statutory requirement for strategic environmental assessment are slim. Early drafts of a European Community instrument on strategic environmental assessment were under discussion in the early 1990s, but were abandoned at the end of 1996 due to a veto by the United Kingdom government.

3 ENVIRONMENTAL ASSESSMENT IN LAW AND PRACTICE

(a) Development of environmental assessment by the EC

As noted above, environmental assessment originated in the United States in 1969. It has since been developed by a number of international organisations, most fully by the European Community. In 1985, Directive 85/337/EEC on the assessment of the effects of certain public and private projects on the environment was adopted by the Council of the European Community. The Directive's adoption was delayed because of long standing political intransigence by some Member States in the Council which accords with intergovernmental accounts of the Community policy making process.[11] This explains the diluted tenor of some of its provisions. For example, the Directive applies only to development projects and not to policies as well, as provided for by early drafts.

The aims of Directive 85/337/EEC are set out in its preamble, the key parts of which are below. Note particularly the references to the creating of competitive conditions as justification for adopting environmental law in this period (no explicit legal base for such measures yet exists in the EEC Treaty), and the desirability of preventive action, which was to become a guiding principle of European Community environmental law. Articles 2 and 4 are the central provisions to determine the application of the Directive to certain development projects which are listed in Annex I and Annex II to the Directive (not given). Major projects listed in Annex I, including power stations, refineries, motorways and major roads, *must* always be subject to prior environmental assessment (Article 4(1)). For those projects listed under Annex II (including pig or poultry farming units, mineral extraction, food manufacture, tanneries and paper manufacturing), there must be an environmental assessment only

11 See ch 5, 'Policy making'.

'where Member States consider that their characteristics so require' (Article 4(2)). This means that a project listed under Annex II does not automatically have to have an environmental assessment. The question of whether an assessment is required or not depends on whether a project is judged by the Member States to have 'significant environmental effects' by virtue of its size, location, and characteristics (Article 2). Member States may prescribe more explicit thresholds and criteria to determine 'significance' and therefore which of the projects falling under Annex II are to be subject to an assessment (Article 4(2)). This grants considerable discretion to Member States to determine whether an environmental assessment is necessary for a particular project.

Note the essentially procedural nature of the Directive. What does it have to say if an adverse environmental assessment is the result of the procedures? Must development consent be refused in such circumstances? Compare Directive 85/337/EEC with Directive 92/43/EEC on the conservation of natural habitats and wild fauna and flora[12] on this point. Does the requirement in Article 3 amount to an integrated approach? Finally, what does '*significant* effects on the environment' mean?

Council Directive 85/337/EEC on the assessment of the effects of certain public and private projects on the environment OJ L 175, 5.7.1985, p 40.

Preamble

...

Whereas the 1973[13] and 1977[14] action programmes of the European Communities, as well as the 1983[15] action programme, the main outlines of which have been approved by the Council of the European Communities and the representatives of the Governments of the Member States, stress that the best environmental policy consists in preventing the creation of pollution or nuisances at source, rather than subsequently trying to counteract their effects; whereas they affirm the need to take effects on the environment into account at the earliest possible stage in all the technical planning and decision-making processes; whereas to that end, they provide for the implementation of procedures to evaluate such effects;

...

Whereas the disparities between the laws in force in the various Member States with regard to the assessment of the environmental effects of public and private projects may create unfavourable competitive conditions and thereby directly affect the functioning of the common market; whereas, therefore it is necessary to approximate national laws in this field pursuant to Article 100 of the Treaty;

...

12 OJ L 206, 22.7.1992. See below p 454
13 OJ No 169, 9.7.1980, p 14.
14 OJ No 66, 15.3.1982, p 89.
15 OJ No C 185, 27.7.1981, p 8.

Whereas development consent for public and private projects which are likely to have significant effects on the environment should be granted only after prior assessment of the likely significant environmental effects of these projects has been carried out; whereas this assessment must be conducted on the basis of the appropriate information supplied by the developer, which may be supplemented by the authorities and by the people who may be concerned by the project in question;

...

Whereas the effects of a project on the environment must be assessed in order to take account of concerns to protect human health, to contribute by means of a better environment to the quality of life, to ensure maintenance of the diversity of species and to maintain the reproductive capacity of the ecosystem as a basic source for life;

...

Article 1

1. This Directive shall apply to the assessment of the environmental effects of those public and private projects which are likely to have significant effects on the environment.

2. For the purposes of this Directive:
'project' means:

- the execution of construction works or of other installations or schemes,
- other interventions in the natural surroundings and landscape including those involving the extraction of mineral resources;

'developer' means:

the applicant for authorization for a private project or the public authority which initiates a project;

'development consent' means:

the decision of the competent authority or authorities which entitles the developer to proceed with the project.

3. The competent authority or authorities shall be that or those which the Member States designate as responsible for performing the duties arising from this Directive.

...

Article 2

1. Member States shall adopt all measures necessary to ensure that, before consent is given, projects likely to have significant effects on the environment by virtue, *inter alia*, of their nature, size or location are made subject to an assessment with regard to their effects.

These projects are defined in Article 4.

2. The environmental impact assessment may be integrated into the existing procedures for consent to projects in the Member States, or, failing this, into

other procedures or into procedures to be established to comply with the aims of this Directive.

...

Article 3
The environmental impact assessment will identify, describe and assess in an appropriate manner, in the light of each individual case and in accordance with Articles 4 to 11, the direct and indirect effects of a project on the following factors:

- human beings, fauna and flora,
- soil, water, air, climate and the landscape,
- the inter-action between the factors mentioned in the first and second indents,
- material assets and the cultural heritage.

Article 4
1. Subject to Article 2(3), projects of the classes listed in Annex I shall be made subject to an assessment in accordance with Articles 5 to 10.

2. Projects of the classes listed in Annex II shall be made subject to an assessment in accordance with Articles 5 to 10, where Member States consider that their characteristics so require.

To this end Member States may *inter alia* specify certain types of projects as being subject to an assessment or may establish the criteria and/or thresholds necessary to determine which of the projects of the classes listed in Annex II are to be subject to an assessment in accordance with Articles 5 to 10.

Article 5
1. In the case of projects which, pursuant to Article 4, must be subjected to an environmental impact assessment in accordance with Articles 5 to 10, Member States shall adopt the necessary measures to ensure that the developer supplies in an appropriate form the information specified in Annex III inasmuch as:

(a) the Member States consider that the information is relevant to a given stage of the consent procedure and to the specific characteristics of a particular project or type of project and of the environmental features likely to be affected;
(b) the Member States consider that a developer may reasonably be required to compile this information having regard *inter alia* to current knowledge and methods of assessment.

2. The information to be provided by the developer in accordance with paragraph 1 shall include at least:

- a description of the project comprising information on the site, design and size of the project,
- a description of the measures envisaged in order to avoid, reduce and, if possible, remedy significant adverse effects,
- the data required to identify and assess the main effects which the project is likely to have on the environment,
- a non-technical summary of the information mentioned in indents 1 to 3.

3. Where they consider it necessary, Member States shall ensure that any authorities with relevant information in their possession make this information available to the developer.

Article 6
1. Member States shall take the measures necessary to ensure that the authorities likely to be concerned by the project by reason of their specific environmental responsibilities are given an opportunity to express their opinion on the request for development consent. Member States shall designate the authorities to be consulted for this purpose in general terms or in each case when the request for consent is made. The information gathered pursuant to Article 5 shall be forwarded to those authorities. Detailed arrangements for consultation shall be laid down by the Member States.

2. Member States shall ensure that:

- any request for development consent and any information gathered pursuant to Article 5 are made available to the public,
- the public concerned is given the opportunity to express an opinion before the project is initiated.

...

[Article 7 concerns the arrangements for cross-border assessment]

Article 8
Information gathered pursuant to Articles 5, 6 and 7 must be taken into consideration in the development consent procedure.

...

(b) Refining environmental assessment

Since the Directive has been in force, a number of concerns about the environmental assessment procedure and problems with enforcement has been expressed by the European Commission,[16] in particular that it has been applied unevenly across the Community. The number of environmental assessments has certainly varied between Member States: a dozen or fewer in Denmark and Portugal, 1,000 in Germany, to 5,500 in France. This concern formed the basis of proposals to amend the Directive,[17] expected to come into force in 1997.

In terms of departing from usual administrative practice in the United Kingdom, the most significant proposed amendments to the Directive are that 'competent authorities' would be *obliged* to take account of the information on environmental impacts obtained in the course of the procedures and to publish

16 Commission of the European Communities, *Report from the Commission on the Implementation of Directive 85/337* COM(93) 28, 2.4.1993 Vol 12 Annex for United Kingdom, Vol 13 Annex for all Member States (Brussels: Commission of the European Communities, 1993).

17 Common Position (EC) No 40/96, adopted by the Council on 25 June 1996 with a view to amending Directive 85/337 (1996) C 248, Vol 39/75, 26.8.1996.

not only their decisions on development consent, but also to give the 'main reasons and considerations' on which they based a decision to refuse consent or, alternatively, to grant consent despite receiving unfavourable opinions from statutory consultees or the public.[18] This is significant because currently planners exercise considerable discretion to take account of a large number of often conflicting considerations; this amendment would implicitly require planners to give weight to information arising from the environmental assessment process.

There is also a proposal to clarify the circumstances under which Annex II projects (which require environmental assessment only where the project would be likely to have significant effects on the environment) should be subject to an assessment by introducing a 'screening' procedure. A new Annex III would give details of the selection criteria of projects which might require environmental assessment: these criteria include the characteristics of the project itself, for example, its size, the use of natural resources, waste and nuisance generation, and impact on landscapes of cultural or archeological and historical significance. Authorities would also take account of the sensitivity of the environment liable to be affected by the project; for instance if it is an area where any European Community environmental quality standards are already being exceeded or if it is liable to have a significant effect on special areas designated by Member States according to Community law,[19] including those designated under Directive 79/409/EEC on the protection of wild birds[20] and Directive 92/43/EEC on the conservation of habitats and of wild fauna and flora,[21] (on which, see the following chapter). For all other Annex II projects, the competent authority would have to determine the applicability of environmental assessment rules and therefore whether the environmental impact is likely to be 'significant' on the basis of thresholds set by the Member States and selection criteria laid down in the new Annex III discussed above. The rationale of these proposed reforms is to bring greater awareness to the planning authority of the need for an environmental assessment and to provide a more systematic approach to environmental assessment throughout the Community.

Deficiencies in consultation have led to the proposal to impose a duty on the competent authority to define in advance which of the information in Annex III (now Annex IV) of Directive 85/337/EEC should be provided by the developer.[22] This introduces a 'scoping' requirement to permit interested parties, the local planning authority and statutory consultees to ascertain the scope and intensity of investigation. A new duty of consultation seeks also to ensure that both the public and statutory bodies are asked about the project. This extends to proposals for better consultation between Member States over projects that give rise to 'significant adverse effects' in the environment in

18 Art 1(11) of the Common Position Amending Directive 85/337, op cit.
19 Annex III of the Common Position, op cit.
20 Directive 79/409/EEC on the conservation of wild birds, OJ L 103, 27.4.1979.
21 Directive 92/43/EEC on the conservation of natural habitats and of wild fauna and flora, OJ L206, 22.7. 1992.
22 Art 1(7) of the Common Position, op cit.

another Member State.[23] This latter proposal is part of the international Treaty signed at Espoo, Finland, on transboundary environmental assessment.[24] This provides a further example of the process of integrating different layers of law, in this case international and Community law.

4 ENVIRONMENTAL ASSESSMENT IN THE UK

(a) Informal environmental assessment

Even before Directive 85/337/EEC was implemented in the United Kingdom, the assessment of the effects of development on the environment was clearly a feature of the land use planning system. For example, information about the likely environmental impact of a project could be obtained under the procedure set out in the General Development Order 1977.[25] Guidance issued by the Department of the Environment made clear the need to assess the environmental effects of specific categories of development such as the storage of hazardous materials.[26] Environmental assessments were also conducted outside the town and country development consent system when the proposed project fell outside the statutory definition of 'development',[27] or became the subject of a public planning inquiry. For example, prior to statutory environmental assessment, projects such as the Thanet Way bypass would have been subject to informal guidance on the evaluation of road projects.[28] One aspect of this guidance was a requirement that a feasibility study be conducted to consider a number of alternative corridors or routes. There was also provision for participation in the planning procedures and the publication of a statement on traffic needs, and any other material factors. Interestingly, there was a requirement that where the evidence appears to favour one alternative both on economic and environmental grounds, the feasibility study was to draw attention to this and it was to be taken into account by those authorising the development in deciding the route. These procedures operated by courtesy of the Secretary of State, and not by law, so that certain schemes were excluded from the procedures which were not enforceable. Planning legislation and official guidance imposed few constraints upon the decision maker for judging

23 Art 1(9) of the Common Position, op cit.

24 United Nations Economic Commission for Europe, *Convention on Environmental Impact Assessment in a Transboundary Context*, Espoo, Finland, 30 ILM 800, 25.2.1991, which requires notification of any party affected by any transboundary activity to be informed as early as possible and to participate in the environmental assessment.

25 Reg 5 of the Town and Country Planning General Development Order 1977, (SI 1977/289) (enacted under s 25 of the Town and Country Planning Act 1971, as amended).

26 Circular 1/72, *Development Involving the Use of Storage in Bulk of Hazardous Material* (London: HMSO, 1972).

27 For example, a de facto environmental assessment arose from the statutory requirement that official notices about a road building project 'shall state the general effect of the proposed scheme', Highways Act 1959, Sch 1, para 7.

28 Such as that contained in Department of the Environment Circular 30/73, *Participation in Road Planning* (London: HMSO, 1973).

the weight to be given to environmental information obtained by these various means. The evidential value of the information could therefore be judged by the local planning authority so long as it constituted a 'material consideration' as defined by the courts. This discretion gave planners and the Secretary of State ample opportunity to examine, but also to dismiss, the significance of environmental effects of individual projects. And, while not denying that the informal assessment procedures generally permitted assessment of the impact of a proposed development on the surrounding area, this was carried out in relation to a specific site. In contrast, Directive 85/337/EEC is designed to require an assessment with respect to the wider environment and in terms of the cumulation and interaction of the effects of development on the environment.

Furthermore these informal procedures did not entitle a decision maker to insist on the submission and analysis of environmental information.

(b) Implementation of Directive 85/337/EEC

The aims of Directive 85/337/EEC are incorporated into the existing planning procedures. This enables information about the effects of development on the environment to be considered as part of the planning process. In projects where environmental assessment is required, planning permission may not be granted unless the assessment has been taken into consideration. Unlike the law on the control of pollution, which is subject specific, environmental assessment takes account of a wide range of issues associated with the environment. In terms of priority, the assessment is not the most influential consideration in the final decision whether to grant planning permission; it is one factor that must be taken into account among many others.

Faced with a requirement to implement Directive 85/337/EEC, the government's view was that environmental assessment was 'implicit in the United Kingdom's town and country planning system'.[29] For this reason mainly, the government intended to achieve the Directive's results by absorbing its requirements into the existing legislative and administrative arrangements for applying for development consent. This was also thought to reduce the risk of imposing significant new burdens on either developers or planning authorities; approximating the Directive's requirements to the then discretionary assessment procedures was in line with the government's policy of 'lifting the burden' on enterprise.[30] The possibilities for conflict in incorporating a Community instrument which imposed a burden of proof on developers and restricted developers' freedom of action with regard to their property within a permissive, development-oriented planning system were thereby minimised.

Directive 85/337/EEC was first implemented by the Town and Country Planning (Assessment of Environmental Effects) Regulations ('the 1988

29 House of Lords Select Committee on the European Communities, Eleventh Report, *Environmental Assessment of Projects*, Session 1980-81 (London, HMSO, 1981) para 31 and pp 131-136; see also *Hansard* Parliamentary Debates (1981b) 30 April 1981 cols 1311-1347.

30 See further ch 7, p 253.

Environmental Effects Regulations')[31] on 15 July 1988 under powers contained in section 2(2) of the European Communities Act 1972. To implement fully the Directive forty further sets of regulations have been enacted so far. Which regulations cover a particular project is determined by its nature(for example an afforestation project is covered by different regulations from a harbour project) and its geographical location (different regulations apply in Scotland from those in Northern Ireland or England and Wales). Nevertheless, the regulations are broadly similar. In cases where there is a dispute as to whether an assessment should be carried out there is an appeal procedure to the Secretary of State for the Environment. The courts appear reluctant to intervene in the actual merits of the decision reached by the planning authority on this point.[32] Approximately 2,300 statutory environmental assessments have been conducted in the United Kingdom since 1988. When combined with the number of environmental statements submitted voluntarily to planning authorities, this increases to approximately 16,500.

Although environmental assessment has formalised procedures for eliciting information about the effects of development on the environment, no statutory guidance is given in the implementing regulations as to what weight should be given to information arising from these procedures. There is no provision to parallel section 54A of the Town and Country Planning Act 1990 which gives clear guidance that priority should be given to the relevant development plan in determining a planning application over other 'material considerations'.[33] This aspect of the practical impact of Directive 85/337/EEC is seen in the Thanet Way case study.

5 THE THANET WAY BYPASS

This project is a highway being constructed by Kent County Council from Whitstable to Herne Bay (the Thanet Way) in the north east corner of Kent. The highway constitutes a 'bypass' of the two towns. The project was proposed by a public developer, the Highways and Transportation Department of Kent County Council, and fell to be decided by the local planning authority of the same council. The project was the subject of a public local planning inquiry which ran for seven months from September 1992. In September 1994 the Secretary of State for Transport accepted the Planning Inspector's recommendation to grant consent for the project under the Highways Act 1980 and Acquisition of Land Act 1981 and various orders relating to side roads and compulsory purchase of property.

The original Thanet Way was built in the 1930s to improve access to Kent's coastal towns – Whitstable, Herne Bay, and the Isle of Thanet. By the late

31 SI 1988/1199.
32 See *R v Swale Borough Council, ex p Royal Society for the Protection of Birds* [1991] JPEL 39.
33 See ch 7, 'Policy change: the fall and rise of the development plan'.

1980s, traffic on the Way was at or above the limits of its capacity. The dualling, or upgrading, of the Thanet Way, including the bypass skirting Whitstable and Herne Bay, was expected to help cope with the predicted increase in traffic brought by the Channel tunnel development and also to balance economic growth in the county, away from the main centre of Ashford and to the less economically strong areas in the north east of the county such as Whitstable. The project, designed to serve the expansion of trans-European transport, was considered by the County Council to be vital to the economic regeneration of the area. The project has also enjoyed high level support. In 1986 the Secretary of State for Transport confirmed the inclusion of the dualling of the Way in the Council's Highway Programme on the basis that it was a project of regional importance. The Way was identified in the County's 1989 Structure Plan as a primary route. This development plan states that it is imperative that such routes have sufficient capacity in order to bring about economic growth and prosperity in the area.[34]

The Thanet area has been given Assisted Area Status, making it eligible for funding from the European Community for infrastructure projects, creating the potential for conflict between the two aims of the European Community of economic regeneration and environmental protection.[35] Regional Planning Guidance Note 9, issued by the Department of the Environment, states that 'local planning authorities should ensure that their land-use allocations reflect the potential offered by both Assisted Area Status and European Community funding'. However, unusually, the Thanet Way bypass project was funded primarily by a Department of Transport grant.

As is the case with many road building projects, the bypass triggered confrontation between those objecting to the project and the public authorities proposing it. As part of a county-wide road plan, the project was regarded as being the result of little local input. Opposition came particularly from those arguing that the road would be intrusive to the area's landscape and would destroy valuable agricultural and woodland areas. Those supporting the project tended to live in Whitstable and Herne Bay and thought they would be relieved of traffic congestion and air pollutants should the bypass be built.

The bypass was proposed as a new dual carriageway on a green field site to the south of the existing road and Whitstable and Herne Bay towns. The route is 6.9 miles long. The planned road runs close to a village and conservation area, through a golf course, along the edge of a Special Landscape Area and through a Site of Nature Conservation Interest. A public consultation exercise carried out by the County Surveyor in 1988 led to this 'off-line' bypass route first being proposed by the Council, as opposed to various 'on-line' routes previously suggested by the Council which would have been built on the existing road structure. Consultation with the affected golf club and parish council led to a proposal to create a tunnel, built at existing ground level with the ground of the golf course extended to cover the structure. It was expected that, in

34 Kent County Council, Structure Plan (1989) policy T1.

35 See ch 11 on the European Community's regional development schemes, pp 453–454.

addition to removing the dual carriageway from view, this would also reduce noise pollution, provide opportunities for landscaping, and permit access over the tunnel, allowing golf to continue to be played. A planning application was submitted in 1989 under regulation 4 of the Town and Country Planning General Development Regulations 1976. In January 1991, the Secretary of State for the Environment directed the County Council not to deem to grant itself permission for the bypass without his authorisation.

An environmental assessment was required of the proposed bypass by the 1988 Environmental Effects Regulations. Other sections of the Thanet Way (A299) which runs between Faversham and Monkton were already being built at the time that this bypass was proposed, and so the environmental assessment process here related to the single outstanding section of road that was planned to link the existing sections – between Whitstable and Herne Bay. The Highways and Transportation Department of Kent County Council compiled the Environmental Statement with considerable help from the Council's planning department. The Statement evaluated several alternative routes to the published route. However, representations were made to the planning department by local groups that this evaluation was unsatisfactory, particularly because a 'do-nothing' alternative had not been evaluated fully. Planners responsible for the project informally sought the European Commission's advice on the adequacy of the Environmental Statement they had helped to compile. The Commission, which was currently investigating a number of other complaints about the application of the Directive's requirements in the United Kingdom, advised the Council to amend its existing evaluation of alternative routes by compiling an addendum of supplementary information to the Environmental Statement which outlined a 'do-nothing' alternative. It did this several weeks before the planning inquiry.

The project raises a number of important issues about the environmental assessment process. The first issue is the extent of the requirement to review alternative projects. The Thanet Way project is a test case for the scope of the evaluation of alternatives in environmental assessment, as reflected in the Planning Inspector's report which focuses almost exclusively on this question of alternative routes to the published (or favoured) route. The second issue is the legal status of undertakings made by the developer to alleviate environmental harm in the environmental statement. Another issue is the manner in which the cumulative effects of development are dealt with in the planning process, since the bypass constituted just one section of a larger road building programme in the county. This in turn, raises the question of the adequacy of a project-based environmental impact assessment system as opposed to a more strategic approach.

The generic problem of bypass development is discussed by the Royal Commission on Environmental Pollution, in their Eighteenth Report, *Transport and the Environment* which seeks to set out the conditions for sustainable transport. The Royal Commission begins this part of the report by reviewing the environmental and social impact of heavy road traffic on communities and the prospects that these impacts might be lessened by bypass development.

Royal Commission on Environmental Pollution, Eighteenth Report, *Transport and the Environment* Cmnd 2674 (London: HMSO, 1994) pp 50-51

Impact on communities

4.27 Heavy road traffic disrupts the life of communities. A US study showed that, as traffic volumes increased, social contacts within streets declined. There were also other differences in behaviour. Where traffic was heavier, people no longer lingered on the pavement, they did not use their front gardens, and those living in the busiest of the three streets studied spent less time in the front rooms of their house. Families who could afford to do so moved away from the area.[36]

4.28 The most obvious obstacle to social contacts is a motorway or other fenced road (or a railway line) which pedestrians are not allowed to cross. A road which pedestrians can cross may also be a formidable obstacle, especially for the old, young children and their mothers. These groups are less likely to have access to a car and are therefore more dependent on contacts within walking distance. Even if a pedestrian crossing or subway is provided, the detour involved may well discourage these less mobile groups. In the case of subways, anxiety about the risk of criminal attacks may be an important additional psychological obstacle.

4.29 Noise was discussed above primarily in the context of annoyance caused to people in their homes but has an even more marked effect on people in the streets. Traffic noise may well prevent conversation or at least make it difficult and uncivilised. Where traffic is heavy, people on the pavements will be exposed to relatively high concentrations of pollutants. Quite apart from the implications for health many people notice the unpleasant smell and taste of exhaust fumes. Last but not least, there is the risk of accidents...

4.30 The combined effect of these factors is to make the streets unpleasant places in which to spend time. The use made of the street declines. Space which was an important possession of local people has been taken from them over the years, and made the preserve of people in cars who happen to be passing through. Children no longer play on the pavement or make unaccompanied journeys along the street to school. A reduction in the numbers of people walking through the streets creates the conditions for an increase in the crime rate, and a vicious circle may develop which drives down still further the number of journeys made on foot.

4.31 Local authorities are now trying to make considerable efforts to reverse this process. In particular they are applying traffic calming measures with the aim of reducing speeds and discouraging traffic from using residential streets when there are other routes available. Often this is an essential element in revitalising town centres and inner city areas. Another approach to reducing

36 Appleyard, D and Lintell, M (1972) The environmental quality of city streets: The residents' viewpoint, *American Institution of Planners Journal*, March 1972, 84-101.

the effects of road traffic, emphasised by DOT, is to build bypasses for villages and small towns.

4.32 While quality of life can be a subjective concept, there seems to be very widespread agreement that heavy car and lorry traffic is causing serious damage and conflict. We consider it should be a basic objective of a sustainable transport policy:

> **TO IMPROVE THE QUALITY OF LIFE, PARTICULARLY IN TOWNS AND CITIES, BY REDUCING THE DOMINANCE OF CARS AND LORRIES AND PROVIDING ALTERNATIVE MEANS OF ACCESS**

In the next section, and in chapter 11, we propose some specific targets for moving towards this objective.

4.33 The construction of bypasses often improves conditions in the towns and villages bypassed and leads to a freer flow of traffic, which reduces emissions from vehicles. On the other hand some evidence suggested that the problems may reappear somewhere else (in effect being pushed along the road) and the bypassed centre may wither because of the loss of trade. It was also suggested that the extent to which traffic is transferred to bypasses is overestimated; and that in some circumstances it would be environmentally preferable, and more cost-effective, to achieve the benefit to the local community through traffic restraint and traffic calming, rather than by building a new road. At a minimum, traffic management could be adopted much more quickly as an interim solution.

4.34 Bypasses form an increasingly important component of the trunk road programme.[37] It is disturbing that there is a lack of consensus about their overall effect. DOT's Bypass Demonstration Project is intended to establish best practice in this field by maximising the benefits which six towns obtain from bypasses. However, there is also a need for research to throw light on the overall effectiveness of bypass schemes. This should take the form of studying a representative selection of towns and villages three or four years after a bypass has been completed to ascertain whether the environmental, traffic and safety objectives have been achieved in practice.[38] **We recommend that DOT:**

- i. **make comparative studies of representative towns and villages before and after the completion of bypasses in order to improve understanding of their environmental and other effects;**
- ii. **investigate whether some towns and villages could obtain most of the benefits of a bypass more effectively and with less environmental damage, through traffic management measures.**

The case for bypass development is not clear-cut. The 'alternatives' to building a bypass – traffic calming measures and traffic management measures – were not clearly discussed in the Environmental Statement compiled by the Highways and Transportation Department of Kent County Council. The category of

37 Department of Transport (1994), *Trunk Roads in England 1994 Review*, HMSO.
38 Evidence from Transportation Planning Associates.

'alternatives' presented in the Environmental Statement was of more limited scope and focused on the different routes which the road might take.

(a) Alternative routes: the 'need' for the project

Environmental assessment law requires that the main alternatives to a particular design or site of project are to be studied by the developer and may be provided as supplementary information in the environmental statement.[39] In Kent County Council's Environmental Statement for the Thanet Way bypass the various alternative routes were assessed in a section headed 'The Need for the Scheme'. This part of the Statement, and a brief introduction to the scheme, are given below.

Kent County Council Highways and Transportation, A299 Route Improvement, *Whitstable to Herne Bay, Environmental Statement,* March 1991

1. INTRODUCTION

1.1 The A299 Thanet Way runs between the end of the M2 at Faversham and the A253 at Monkton a distance of 28km (18 miles). It was decided in 1986 by the Secretar[ies] of State for the Environment and Transport that the dualling of the A299 was a project of regional importance.

1.2 The dualling of the sections of the Thanet Way between the M2 and Whitstable and between Herne Bay and Monkton are already under construction or about to commence on site this year. These sections received planning consent where necessary and the Side Roads and Compulsory Purchase Orders for this work were confirmed. This Environmental Statement refers to the single outstanding section that will link the works already under way.

1.3 It is proposed to construct a new dual carriageway to the south of the existing route and the settlements of Chesterfield and Greenhill. The scheme would remove through traffic from the existing route and allow it to carry just local traffic.

1.4 This document summarises the environmental effects of the published scheme in accordance with the Town and Country Planning (Assessment of Environmental Effects) Regulations 1988. It includes as an Appendix, a non-technical summary which is also available separately, free of charge.

2. THE SCHEME

2.1 The Need for the Scheme

The dualling of the A299 Thanet Way as a whole is a desirable project for a number of reasons. The perception of the Thanet Way as an unsafe and busy road, as it is now, has potential effects throughout the area. The County Council's initial submission for central government funding stated:

> 'Improved access to the area, the north east corner of Kent, is essential for the retention of existing industry and for attracting new industry to this area of high unemployment.

39 Sch 3 to the Environmental Effects Regulations 1988.

> An increase in holiday makers is also likely, many being put off at present by the Thanet Way's notoriety as a dangerous and congested road.'

The need to bolster the economy and accessibility of Thanet, Whitstable and Herne Bay has been heightened by the construction of the Channel Tunnel and the concern about the future of the port of Ramsgate. The dualling of the Thanet Way will also increase the accessibility of Manston airport.

The dualling of the Thanet Way will reduce transport costs to companies and individuals. The scheme will reduce congestion and delays, reducing journey times significantly. If the Thanet Way were not improved, accidents would increase as traffic grows.

The section of Thanet Way between Whitstable and Herne Bay is the most congested. On the most heavily used part – between Chesterfield and Greenhill roundabouts – current traffic flows average 25,000 vehicles per day, increasing considerably during the holiday periods. This is well above the normal design limit for a single carriageway road. By the year 2010, traffic flows on the part of the Thanet Way between Chesterfield and Greenhill are expected to rise to between 35,000 and 43,000 vehicles per day on average. Without the proposed improvements there would be a significant increase in safety and congestion problems. Six roundabouts and a number of lesser junctions on the existing Thanet Way will be bypassed by the proposed scheme.

It is proposed to improve the whole length of the A299 Thanet Way. Schemes have already been successfully through the statutory procedures for improving the rural section to dual carriageway standard, and those sections are either about to be constructed, already under construction, or completed. This central section of the A299 Thanet Way passes through several built up areas and following extensive public consultation, an off line route has been adopted, passing to the south of the residential areas.

...

2.4 Alternative Routes Considered

Public Consultation

The findings of the first public consultation carried out on this section of the Thanet Way in 1988 was that there was no one scheme option that was clearly better than the others. The schemes presented to the public were all derivatives of an 'on-line' solution.

A further consultation was carried out in 1989 when an 'off-line' solution was promoted as well as two on line solutions. This 'off-line' solution was included following severe pressure from the public at the 1988 consultation.

The three schemes were identified by colours and are detailed in the following text.

Common to all schemes was the western end of the routes which basically followed an approved scheme dating from 1964 but updated to current design standards.

Red Route

This scheme was originally exhibited in 1988 and proved to be the most popular at that consultation. Following the line of the existing road, the scheme used flyover junctions at all except one location with local roads passing beneath the dual carriageway.

This high level route would have created severe noise pollution and substantial visual intrusion. Through and local traffic would not have been segregated. During construction there would have been severe disruption to traffic. Ten buildings would have been required for demolition with an effect on two listed buildings.

Of the public who responded to the consultation in 1989, only 3% supported this scheme.

Green Route

This scheme was developed following the first public consultation to provide an 'on-line' solution using underpass solutions at junctions allowing local roads to pass over the dual carriageway at existing ground level.

The Green Route proved more favourable than the Red Route, reducing noise and visual intrusion. Twenty buildings would have been required for demolition with an effect on two listed buildings. The underpass junctions with the substantial retaining walls required to construct them, would have created a 'canyon effect' in the built environment introducing community severance. Through and local traffic would not have been segregated.

Of the public who responded to the consultation in 1989, 33% supported this scheme.

Blue Route

This scheme formed the 'off-line' route at the public consultation in 1989. Leaving the existing road west of Long Reach at Whitstable, the route passed to the south of the residential areas at Chesterfield and Greenhill before returning to join the existing road at Eddington.

Bypassing the existing road, the Blue Route would segregate through traffic from local traffic movements. The removal of through traffic would give the opportunity to provide traffic and safety measures to the existing road. Local traffic movements would also remain unaffected.

The route would provide an improvement in reducing traffic noise and air pollution in the built environment it bypasses. There would be a noise reduction at all properties adjacent to the existing route. However, the Blue Route would affect a number of properties in areas that are currently quiet and rural. Detailed information can be found in the Framework at Appendix 1 [not included].

Community severance in the existing built environment would be reduced by the Blue Route. There would also be no requirement for land take from the school playing fields at Church Street, Whitstable.

The Blue Route would allow far greater scope for providing mitigating measures by earth mounding and landscape planting than would be possible in the urban area.

The Blue Route would provide the cheapest engineering solution to the traffic problems representing the best value for money. It would also give a far greater capacity for future traffic growth.

Of the public who responded to the consultation in 1989, 61% supported this scheme.

Preferred Route
Following the public consultation in 1989, the County Council assessed all public responses and using these together with all information gathered from other consultees and internal investigations approved the Blue Route as the Preferred Route for this section of the Thanet Way.

[The Environmental Statement continues to discuss the Preferred Route (the 'Blue Route') as the Published Scheme.]

The County Council's preference for the 'Blue Route'is reinforced in the Non-Technical Summary of the Environmental Statement (required for public participation purposes by the Environmental Effects Regulations 1988). This is also headed 'The Need for the Scheme', and offers a precis of the above. The Non-Technical Summary contains no information relating to the effects of the project on the environment.

Whilst the identification and presentation of alternative routes using scientific models (in the Framework, referred to in the passage from the Environmental Statement above) gave an appearance of objectivity in the Environmental Statement, the main alternatives were treated in such a way as to substantiate the *proposed* route and design. In lieu of a proper examination of alternaitve routes, the Highways and Transportation Department concluded in the Statement that there is a need for the bypass. A parish group, opposing the road, thought that 'the environmental statement has started from the premise that the proposal is both necessary and desirable and is disturbingly biased...the statement does not properly compare the published route with other viable alternatives which would clearly expose the published route's shortcomings'. The Council for the Protection of Rural England was similarly of the view that the Environmental Statement was flawed because it did not properly evaluate alternative routes.

(b) Mitigating measures and environmental gains

Environmental assessment law requires that the measures envisaged to 'avoid, reduce, or remedy' significant adverse environmental effects must be specified in the developer's environmental statement.[40] These might include reducing noise by planting trees and building screening devices, damping down areas during construction to limit dust, and restricting operations to particular times or weather conditions. Such measures are a key feature of the Council's Environmental Statement of the Thanet Way project: a 300m long twin bore tunnel to minimise the final impact of the road on a golf course, extensive earth works to create a hill upon which golf could continue to be played, shrub and tree planting, and screening to reduce visual impact and noise. The considerable scope of these measures reflects the economic importance of the project. The road was believed to be essential to the economy of the north east of Kent which had hitherto failed to attract industry and business centred on the Channel Tunnel.

40 Sch 3 to the Environmental Effects Regulations 1988.

The Statement indicates not only the local planning authority's intention to minimise impacts, but its proposal to enhance the landscape, to 'integrate the road into its landscape setting and to provide a valuable wildlife habitat' by planting an avenue of willow and creating a number of settling ponds:

> The intention here is to turn the unavoidable intrusion of the road to an advantage by introducing a strong new landscape element which will reflect and enhance the history and character of the existing landscape...two balancing ponds in the bypass section of the road will be treated as an opportunity to introduce an attractive landscape feature.

The identification and description of such mitigating measures alleviates some of the concerns about the environmental impact of the proposed project. The effect is to balance environmental harms against measures which are positive in nature, in some instances to create 'environmental gains'.[41] The positive connotations of terms such as 'environment', 'nature', 'landscape', and 'amenity' are combined with the proposed development in the Environmental Statement. The project's contribution to the local community is emphasised, encouraging an accommodation of diverse interests concerned with it. In identifying the environmental gains to be made from the development, natural resources are aligned with exchangeable 'goods', and environmental harms are presented as separate, remediable, and compensatable problems.

Kent County Council Transportation and Highways Department conclude in the Environmental Statement that they favour the 'off-line' route because it offers a greater opportunity for successful mitigation than the dualling of an 'on-line' route through Whitstable. The Secretary of State for Transport agreed with this in his decision letter and commented that 'there is no doubt that the Council are conscious of the need for sensitive measures to lessen the impact of the (proposed) route'. English Nature made representations at the public local planning inquiry that the full impact of the development, including substantial loss of verges, hedges, and wayside trees was not evaluated. In English Nature's view, such losses could not be compensated for by transplanting or replanting. They also claimed that the conservation value of the site had been underestimated because only flora had been assessed; no account was taken of the size of the site, its 'naturalness', fragility, and the spatial and ecological relationship to adjacent habitats.

The expressions of intent in the Environmental Statement to mitigate impacts and to create environmental gains play a part in making the project acceptable to the public and the planners. The legal status of such information is less clear. How, for example, does the planner use the information contained in an environmental statement? Can such expressions of intent be legally enforced? In the Thanet Way case, the expressions of intent formed the basis of planning conditions and planning obligations. The County Planning Officer granted planning permission subject to a number of conditions – planting

41 For a discussion of this term, see S Boucher and S Whatmore, 'Green Gains? Planning by Agreement and Nature Conservation', (1993) *Journal of Environmental Planning and Management* Vol 36, No 1, 33-51.

trees, ground mounding, and provision of new hedges, all of which were described as mitigating measures in the developer's Environmental Statement. The role of such measures in determining a planning application and forming part of a 'legal agreement' (most likely a planning obligation) is described below:

> The assessment shows how it would work and we can then say well you must do this...that is why the mitigating factors identified in the statement must be capable of working. They (developers) might have put in vague information... then we find that they don't work and that's where we get problems and we may have to get involved with legal agreements with them.
>
> (Planning officer, Kent County Council)

More generally, the extent to which planning conditions and planning obligations are based on information contained in an environmental statement, particularly mitigating measures, is more difficult to determine. This is because proposals are often modified as a result of suggestions made during the consultation process, rendering it unnecessary to attach conditions to a grant of planning permission. Mitigating measures described in environmental statements might also allow developers to pre-empt conditions that planners are likely to impose. It is likely to be the case that where conditions are imposed which originate in information provided by the developer in an environmental statement, these tend to relate more to the construction of the development (the control of dust and noise) than to any on-going activities on the site such as controlling processes, the latter falling more squarely within the ambit of pollution control agencies' responsibilities.

(c) Cumulative effects of development

The bypass of Whitstable to Herne Bay, a route of 6.9 miles, formed part of a wider highway project: the dualling, or 'upgrading' of the whole 18 mile length of the Thanet Way (A299) from Faversham to Monkton on the Isle of Thanet. The Thanet Way was therefore divided into sections for the purposes of planning authorisation and construction. At the time that the bypass application was made for the section of the Way between Whitstable and Herne Bay, three out of four sections of the road had been the subject of planning inquiries and one of these had already been completed. Dividing one project into a number of separate sections for planning and construction purposes is common practice, but this raises questions about the adequacy of an environmental assessment of one section of a wider scheme, particularly when this is viewed in isolation from the whole development. In the case of the Thanet Way, no account was taken in the Environmental Statement of the likely cumulative effects of all the sections of the route. Instead, one part of the wider scheme – a 6.9 mile section of road forming the bypass – was dealt with in the environmental assessment process. In considering the limited scope of the Environmental Statement in this case, the following comments by the Royal Commission on Environmental Pollution are apt.

Royal Commission on Environmental Pollution, Eighteenth Report, *Transport and the Environment*, Cmnd 2674 (London: HMSO, 1994)

9.61 The fact that environmental assessments have been carried out does not mean that satisfactory standards have necessarily been achieved. There has been widespread criticism, endorsed by the Standing Advisory Committee on Trunk Road Assessment, of the nature and quality of environmental assessments of trunk road proposals. SACTRA found, for instance, that 'where a series of individual schemes has been generated by a Route Identification Study or ... when a series of schemes taken altogether amount *de facto* to an improved route, detailed environmental assessments are always made but only of the individual component schemes. Corresponding assessments are not made at the aggregate level in relation to the overall route and its regional impact.'[42] Others argued in evidence to the Royal Commission that environmental assessment has been made at too late a stage, when fundamental alternatives cannot be evaluated, and with inadequate opportunities for public involvement in decisions and that the issues are effectively marginalised by excessive reliance on cost-benefit analysis...

9.62 Following SACTRA's recommendations, the government has published revised guidance on environmental assessment.[43] This takes a broader view than the previous guidance and goes some way towards the three stage assessment procedure recommended by SACTRA. It also acknowledges that 'in some cases assessment may need to cover the combined and cumulative impacts of several schemes'[44] because this may result in a better choice of alignment and design in both environmental and traffic terms...

(d) Role of the developer's environmental statement

There is a perception amongst developers and some planners that the environmental assessment process speeds a project through the various development consent procedures. The developer's environmental statement may be used to justify a particular proposal, as borne out by a Kent County Council Transportation and Highways Officer, describing the Thanet Way project:

> They [the planning department] are very keen that we can justify exactly what we are doing....although the final decision is really Kent judging Kent, judging itself, they are still very conscious of the need and they press us on the environmental statement very hard to make sure that we justify exactly what we are doing.

The Thanet Way case suggests that the compilation of an environmental statement was informed not only by the need to establish the 'likely significant

42 Department of Transport, The Standing Advisory Committee on Trunk Road Assessment (1992), Assessing the environmental impact of road schemes, HMSO (cited as DOT/SACTRA, 1992).

43 Department of Transport, Scottish Office Industry Department, Welsh Office, Department of the Environment for Northern Ireland (1993), *Design Manual for Roads and Bridges* Vol 11, Environmental Assessment, HMSO.

44 Para 1.6 in *Design Manual* 1993.

effects' of the development on the environment as required by the 1988 Environmental Effects Regulations, but also by judgments about the public profile of the project, the local authority's support of it, and the need to justify the development by the developer. The vagueness of the 'significant effects' test, particularly when unrestrained by concise, quantitative criteria means that there is considerable scope for criteria other than a project's likely environmental effects to inform planners' judgments about the applicability of environmental assessment rules. This underlines that environmental assessment has acquired functions beyond predicting harm to the environment. The environmental statement in particular is capable of being used in a non-neutral manner by developers and planning authorities alike to advance, support, or justify a project – for example by publicising the 'need' for the particular development.

We have seen also how the developer's environmental statement can be used to assuage concerns about the proposed development by presenting plans to mitigate its effects and enhance the local environment in some way. Perhaps this is why developers tend to describe mitigating measures comprehensively in the environmental statement, particularly those that are positive in nature. In contrast, few developers identify alternative sites and processes in their environmental statements or examine pollution control measures at the planning stage.

The primary responsibility for conducting the environmental assessment rests with the developer, either public or private, in the form of compiling an environmental statement. The environmental statement presents the *developer's* perception of the proposed project, the type and extent of environmental harm likely to arise, and the main alternatives to it. This has several important consequences. It contributes to a view of environmental assessment as a single document (the environmental statement) which supplements the planning application, rather than an entire and complex information gathering, evaluation and decision making process. Considerable discretion is given to the developer to determine the scope of the assessment, select, and present information about the main alternatives to the proposal, the interaction and cumulation of any adverse effects, and their mitigation. This discretionary leverage can mean that information about the predicted environmental effects of the proposed development is not documented objectively. By contributing directly to the fulfilment of legal environmental assessment requirements, the developer acquires partial responsibility for environmental protection but, in so doing, is capable also of controlling the assessment procedure by interpreting and presenting scientific information in the most favourable light.

(e) Environmental assessment and the planning inquiry

The Secretary of State for the Environment made the Thanet Way project the subject of a local public planning inquiry – the traditional forum in the British planning system for resolving conflict over a development and determining its environmental effects. Conflict at the inquiry was heightened because the issues gave rise to clear divisions of opinion and participators made explicit use of the inquiry to promote alternative routes. The Transportation and Highways Department's Environmental Statement became one part of the adversarial apparatus of the inquiry. Information about the environmental effects of the development, contained in the Statement, was selected and highlighted by witnesses in their oral presentations in a disjointed manner and to support their arguments.

There were other problems with the inclusion of information from the environmental assessment process in the planning inquiry. The Statement was not referred to as a coherent document, nor was it given a particular status in the inquiry. The legal relevance of it as a document representative of a process of inquiry in itself was not explained. The use of the developer's Environmental Statement by various expert witnesses led to information contained in the Statement being duplicated in their proofs of evidence, for example on the environmental implications of traffic related pollutant releases and the effects of development on conservation areas.

The use of the developer's Environmental Statement by opponents and supporters of the Thanet Way bypass had major effects. Attention was diverted away from the Environmental Statement as an integrated document because proofs of evidence became the focus of attention. In addition, the practice of dealing with issues arising from the Environmental Statement, but elaborated in individual proofs of evidence, meant that the cumulation and interaction of environmental impacts were not fully addressed.

Several more general concerns with planning inquiries on road projects are raised by the Royal Commission on Environmental Pollution in their Eighteenth Report. Some of these have considerable relevance for the Thanet Way project, particularly those relating to public participation, the limited scope of inquiries dealing with one section of a larger route, and the overall problem that inquiries take place within boundaries set by the prevailing government policy. The Royal Commission makes several radical recommendations which, if taken up, might alter the conduct, and possibly the result, of future planning inquiries on road projects such as the Thanet Way.

Royal Commission on Environmental Pollution, Eighteenth Report, *Transport and the Environment*, Cmnd 2674 (London: HMSO, 1994) pp 226-227

Inquiry procedure

13.85 Pending the integration of national road schemes into the planning system, there is scope to improve existing practices...

13.86 The lack of public discussion of the policies which are expressed in White Papers and individual road proposals has often been criticised. The Joint Nature Conservation Committee's evidence referred to the 'lack of opportunities for debating or challenging transport policy prior to the announcement of proposals for individual schemes; and the limited input made by environmental appraisals in initial stages of consultation'. Others criticised the lack of opportunity to consider whole routes at inquiries. Instead individual schemes were promoted piecemeal, their combined effects never opened for consideration and choices effectively truncated by decisions on earlier schemes in the same route.

13.87 The government's announcement in August 1993 of measures to speed up the road programme acknowledged the force of some of these objections, stating that 'time is wasted because possible objections to a scheme are not resolved at the outset'. It is now experimenting with conferences of interested parties to discuss scheme options before public consultation takes place. This is an improvement so far as it goes and we await the results with interest. The new approach must be implemented very positively if it is to answer the criticisms cited above. We consider that the conferences must be sufficiently representative to command public confidence; must systematically explore alternatives other than road building (including the promotion of other modes of transport); work carefully through the likely interactions with land use patterns; and have available adequate environmental appraisals. At this early stage in a proposed scheme, these should be widely based (as SACTRA recommended) covering broad national and environmental issues and corridor and regional effects as appropriate. They should contain sufficient information to enable the relative merits of options (including the use of other modes, as well as 'do-nothing', and comprehensive demand management) to be compared. Even were all these conditions to be fulfilled, we doubt whether the existing institutional system would enable links to be made between road planning and wider development issues in a wholly satisfactory manner.

...

13.89 Although trunk road schemes are now promoted by the Highways Agency, the Secretary of State remains responsible for the scale and content of the road programme and, following an Inspector's report, jointly with the Secretary of State for the Environment, for decisions on individual schemes. The difficulty is that, although decisions may be wholly dispassionate, such deep involvement of a single department makes it difficult to demonstrate convincingly that this is so. One of the principal objections to the procedure adopted in inquiries concerns the status of the National Road Traffic Forecasts. These are not challengeable at inquiries, as was confirmed by the House of Lords in the case of *Bushell v Secretary of State for Transport and the Environment* [1981] AC 75, [1980] 2 All ER 608. The government has stated that they are not a target and that it is not desirable that they should be achieved but they are still used as evidence of the need for a road scheme. The key point is that, although road schemes can be dropped at any stage in their development, and this has happened to some high profile schemes while our report has been in progress, the impression created is that public inquiries have been largely restricted to considering the scope of a proposed road and have not probed alternative strategies which would remove the need for it. The administration would defend this as a proper restriction since the role of the inquiry, in its view, is to consider public objections but not evaluate or determine policy. The proper place for the latter would be Parliament. This argument would be more convincing if there were sufficient evidence that Parliament regularly offered the opportunity of scrutinising the road programme and if many trunk road schemes were not designed to meet regional (or even local) needs rather than national ones. In our view, there is a need both for Parliamentary scrutiny of the broad thrust of policies and for opportunities for local people to question the policies as applied to their locality. The failure to allow the latter is symptomatic of a flawed policy; it certainly creates a deep sense of frustration amongst those affected. We therefore recommend that the rules of procedure governing inquiries into trunk road proposals and compulsory purchase orders be amended so as to permit government witnesses to answer questions about the merits of government policy and allow the inspector to take account of the interaction of the proposal with other government policies.

(f) Perceptions of the environment in environmental assessment

Planners' views and assumptions about the environment commonly reflect a fundamental distinction between the environment as a 'public good' and a view of the intrinsic qualities of the environment. The former, encompassing primarily issues of public health and the public use of the environment for recreation, has the attainment and preservation of amenity as its focus and may be labelled a 'public environmental interest'. The latter represents a departure from human centred understandings of the environment – an 'ecological interest'. Directive 85/337/EEC caters for both. It is directed towards the prediction and mitigation of impacts on both human health and population (public environmental interests) and on fauna, flora, soil, and landscape (ecological interests).

These differing perceptions of the environment came to the fore in the course of the environmental assessment process for the Thanet Way bypass. Planners dealt with environmental assessment in such a way as to emphasise the environment as a public good. Their working perspective was a concern with amenity and public health considerations. The bypass which was proposed to skirt Whitstable and Herne Bay was expected to confer benefits to the towns' residents of less traffic related air and noise pollution. The Environmental Statement justified the bypass in these terms; the public health benefits of the proposed project were stated to be greater than if the Thanet Way dualling took place along the length of the existing route which cuts through the two towns. In slicing through a Site of Special Scientific Interest, the development would also be detrimental to surrounding open countryside and the landscape. The public environmental interests of the development were, however, prioritised by those supporting the project: the selfishness of the conservationist and agricultural lobby, compared with the amenity and public health value of the project for the towns' residents was a key theme in the public inquiry. This emphasis is evocative of the guiding preoccupations and principles of public health, amenity and the salubrious suburb of early planning law.[45] An important consequence of this perspective is a receptiveness towards projects in which concerns about public health are addressed, notwithstanding damage to the ecological quality of a habitat. The identification and negotiation of 'trade-offs' in the form of compensatory and mitigating measures as environmental gains, was encouraged by the planners in addressing the effects of the development on the countryside and landscape. This gives an appearance of balance in the planning process.

45 See ch 3, 'Early planning law'.

6 SO WHAT IS GOING ON HERE?

Environmental assessment has been hailed by some environmentalists as a procedure by which more 'environmentally friendly' decisions are made in the light of an objective assessment of the effects of a project by scientists, various experts, and public opinion – all in all a panacea for planning. Environmental assessment certainly puts environmental protection on the agenda for developers, planners, councillors, and campaigning groups. And yet, projects which have been the subject of an environmental assessment process and which are likely to have detrimental effects might still be granted planning permission. No absolute protection is accorded by environmental assessment. This raises the question of whether an adverse environmental statement would have had much effect on the planning procedures and eventual decision in the Thanet Way case. Perhaps a more worrying trend indicated by the case study is that in reality environmental assessment may operate as a developers' charter, the assessment process being used by developers to advance their projects in environmental terms. This is because at the basis of environmental assessment, as with the planning inquiry, is an idea of due process which confers legitimacy on a project. That a project has been subject to environmental assessment suggests that environmental concerns have been adequately addressed, notwithstanding that many assessments are partial, and even operate as a means by which a proposed project might be publicised and gain public approval. This suggests considerable discordance between the aims of Directive 85/337/EEC and its practical implementation in the United Kingdom. It means also that planning is capable of giving expression to environmental concerns through environmental assessment but, ultimately, might also constrain the power and radicalism of the environmental movement. We trace the potential for this in planning's containment of radical and popular movements in the post second world war period.[46]

Environmental assessment supports a view that the planning system is sufficiently flexible to take account of a whole manner of concerns, including those relating to the environment, and contributes to an idea of balance between economic and environmental interests in the context of individual planning applications. This aspect of environmental assessment draws upon the prevalence of more fundamental ideas of balance between developmental and environmental interests in society, the clearest expression of which is the principle of sustainable development. The appeal of this idea of balance suggests that the planning system might yet prove resistant to reforms giving greater priority to environmental protection. That is to say that perhaps the primary function of environmental assessment is to fulfil the social and political need for information on the effects of development on the environment to be assessed and weighed in balance with other, particularly economic, considerations.

46 See ch 3.

7 IS STRATEGIC ENVIRONMENTAL ASSESSMENT THE WAY FORWARD?

At this stage it is worth asking whether strategic environmental assessment, the assessment of plans and policies, might make amends for the failure of the present environmental assessment process to take account of the wider picture of road strategy and effects of this on the environment. As we have mentioned, it is strategic environmental assessment which has been most closely associated with the implementation and achievement of sustainable development. The Royal Commission on Environmental Pollution advocates this extension of environmental assessment to encompass policy decisions giving greater emphasis to environmental issues. This is viewed also as a means by which the best practicable environmental option, a principle of pollution control (BPEO),[47] might be applied to strengthen the planning system. A thorough assessment of alternatives might then be made, on environmental grounds. On reading the following from the Royal Commission's Eighteenth Report, it is interesting to question what might have been the practical effects of conducting a strategic environmental assessment of road transport policy relating to the Thanet Way and other projects. Might applying BPEO have delivered a more reasoned, imaginative, and fully integrated assessment of environmental effects in this case? The government's response to these aspects of the Report then follows. This takes a more limited view of BPEO.

Royal Commission on Environmental Pollution, Eighteenth Report, *Transport and the Environment*, Cmnd 2674 (London: HMSO, 1994) pp 155-228

Strengthening the planning system

9.55 In many cases policy decisions rather than 'immutable trends' have shaped land use and transport patterns. Policy makers and service providers appear to have been too ready to seek road-based solutions to transport demands without sufficient systematic explorations of alternatives. Strategic environmental assessment provides an alternative for such exploration, and a means to identify the Best Practicable Environmental Option (BPEO) in transport policy. Extending the latter concept, explored by the Royal Commission in its Twelfth Report, means that when transport policies are developed or transport decisions taken, attention must be paid to assessing how best the environment (land, air and water) can be protected from damage, at an acceptable cost. It will include assessment of demand management options, using the land use planning or other instruments. A key element in the BPEO approach is the imaginative search for alternative options. In this context, these should include non-transport options, and options which do not involve the construction of new infrastructure, or which make use of alternative modes, possibly in conjunction with demand management methods. That the government has stressed the link between land use plans and transport policies and programmes is a helpful development in

47 See ch 6, pp 225-227.

this respect although we wish to see similar links established at regional, national and international levels. Clear, quantified targets must be established to provide a framework for environmental appraisals.

9.56 **We recommend that decision-making at all levels of transport policy be based on the identification and pursuit of the best practicable environmental option.** It should be an integral part of planning procedures and should inform regional, structure and local planning as well as decisions on applications for planning permission. The long-term aim of this approach would be to provide people with access to the goods, services and activities they desire, without unsustainable environmental degradation. In this sense, the planning system is an instrument for designing flexibility and personal choice into developments.

...

13.94 ...The European Commission has for some time been considering a directive requiring the environmental assessment of policies, plans and programmes. Progress towards a formal proposal is at present blocked largely because of opposition by countries including the UK which see great practical difficulties in drafting a legislative requirement which would be equally applicable to the systems of government in all Member States. The UK has taken this view in the light of its experience in producing, in 1981, a guide for its own officials to use in assessing policies and programmes – 'Policy Appraisal and the Environment: A Guide for Government Departments'. The government should work more positively with the European Commission and other Member States to develop a means of ensuring that policies receive thorough environmental appraisal.

HM Government, *Transport The Way Forward: The Government's Response to the Transport Debate* Cm 3234 (London: HMSO, 1996) p 71

Environmental assessment

11.56 The appraisal of trunk road schemes for their environmental effects has been a major issue in the transport debate. For many years the Government has promoted standards of environmental impact assessment for transport policies that have set the standard internationally. The DOT [Department of Transport] published its *Manual of Environmental Appraisal* in 1983 (expanded in 1993 as volume 11 of the Design Manual for Roads and Bridges) and it has complied with European Directive 85/337/EEC since it came into force in 1988.

...

Best Practicable Environmental Option

The RCEP report on transport advocates the concept of "best practicable environmental option" (BPEO)...

This...recognises the need to accommodate non-environmental considerations. These may include safety, engineering feasibility, economic benefits and affordability. For Government investment, a very important non-environmental consideration that must be taken into account is the benefit that the new infrastructure will provide for users and for others indirectly affected by the proposal.

At the level of individual trunk road schemes, the Department of Transport, having identified the benefits that a proposed scheme would bring, already searches for the best practicable environmental way of achieving them, taking account of the other factors mentioned. This is ensured through a combination of the environmental objectives set for the Highways Agency by the Secretary of State, and the well-established process of environmental assessment.

The likely environmental effects of individual schemes (both positive and negative) are taken into account when the roads programme is reviewed. With a view to ensuring that environmental factors are given due weight in strategic decision-making, the Department is examining the scope for assessing environmental factors above scheme level and for achieving closer integration of trunk roads with land use planning...

Strategic Traffic and Environmental Appraisal

11.60 As part of its follow-up to both the 1992 and 1994 SACTRA reports (on "Assessing the Environmental Impact of Road Schemes" and "Trunk Roads and the Generation of Traffic" respectively) the Department of Transport is reviewing its advice to consultants on strategic traffic appraisal. The traffic levels carried by a new road scheme will be affected by whether, and when, neighbouring schemes are implemented. For a robust assessment of both the traffic and environmental effects of any particular scheme, it is important to take a strategic view of the traffic effects taking account of the neighbouring schemes and their timing, but in a way that remains focused on the "core" scheme.

...

11.62 As another part of the follow-up to the 1992 SACTRA report, the Department of Transport is considering the scope for assessing the total and cumulative environmental effects of the trunk road programme as a whole. This reflects a popular perception that, while individual road schemes may seem to be justified when viewed separately, the cumulative effect of all the schemes that are liable to be built over a period of a decade or more might make unacceptable inroads on the total national "capital" of certain sensitive categories of land, or on the proportion of the population subjected to unacceptable levels of noise and other emissions. If practicable, this approach would provide greater insight into the overall impact of the road programme, and enable a better judgement to be made of the best practicable options for the road programme and for transport infrastructure more generally.

CHAPTER 11

Room for the geese: nature conservation and designation

1 INTRODUCTION

In this chapter we again use a case study to explore the themes of the book: the layering of United Kingdom, European Community and international law; the importance of a holistic and integrated approach to the environment; and the usefulness of deploying a variety of legal techniques to achieve environmental protection. We draw out that environmental law is not static but has developed in specific historical contexts and, above all, that it attempts to reflect developing scientific knowledge as well as increased social awareness of the importance of environmental protection. By grounding the law, literally, on a four mile square parcel of land and water – the area of our study – we demonstrate and discuss many of the issues that arise when law and administration grapple with the complexities of ecosystems.

We describe and discuss a real place which has been selected for protection in order to conserve particular species and natural features. This site shows the way the law for nature conservation has developed over the last four decades. The case study emphasises that legislation may be the outcome of a policy process but it is only the beginning of the story. The dedication of the administrators is what makes the difference between successful and unsuccessful practical implementation of the law. We have already highlighted this point in chapter 6 when we saw how the nineteenth century Alkali Inspectors used 'best practicable means' as a sword with which to fight air pollution.

We explore in some detail the implications of the legal technique of designation of an area of land for special treatment, outlined in chapter 7. Our site for study was chosen initially because it promised a diversity of competing land uses in a small area and so, clearly, successful management would entail minimising conflict between these interests in order to conserve the ecosystems that have provided a wealth of habitats for many different species. Part of our site is a National Nature Reserve. We deliberately chose a site in Scotland because the agency responsible for the conservation project is Scottish Natural Heritage, which combines the equivalent functions of English Nature and the Countryside Commission in England; a fusion which achieves a more holistic approach,[1] a recurring theme of this book.

1 *Chairman's Preface to Sustainable Development and the Natural Heritage: the SNH Approach*, (Perth: SNH, 1993).

Law and administration for nature conservation, in effect, consists largely of regulating what people may and may not do on land, so it follows that nature conservation managers need to be aware of the range of attitudes that people have towards the land. The following is intended as a background against which the developments in the case study take place. It is also worth emphasising here that there is considerable scope for conflicts of interest between groups of people who use the site: the estate, the crofters, the SNH personnel, research scientists, the Ministry of Defence and the tourists who come to the area for fishing, shooting, birdwatching, amateur botany, vigorous hill walking and using the beaches. That a cooperative modus vivendi exists is one of the major successes of the National Nature Reserve.

C Smout, Raleigh Lecture, November 1990, *The Highlands and the Roots of Green Consciousness, 1750–1990* (Perth: SNH, 1990) pp 24-28

...It is possible to classify attitudes towards land use in many different ways. Perhaps six main types of attitude have dominated Scottish experience in the last 250 years, and they fall into two broad categories. There are three types that I would group together as traditional, and three I would group together as post-romantic. Of the traditional types, the first is to regard the land as a resource from which to make a living by farming, forestry and commercial fishing; and the second to regard the land as a resource for the private, aristocratic pursuits of hunting, shooting and sport fishing. These two attitudes have existed since time immemorial: they were the only attitudes known before the eighteenth century, and completely dominated land use, law and public policy in the Highlands throughout the eighteenth and nineteenth centuries, though in varying proportions and with very varying consequences for those who lived there, depending precisely on what was involved. Small-scale crofting, associated with potato husbandry and kelping on the islands, which dominated 1750-1820, was also associated with a population explosion and had very different social effects from the sheep farming and deer forests that dominated the next century and were associated with clearance and the maintenance of land as empty space. This contrast bred a bitter antipathy of crofter and small farmer towards large farmer and landowner without in the least rocking the secure foundations of landed power. Crofter, farmer, forester, laird, who farm by land and sea, plant trees and shoot, survive today as the social, economic and political backbone of Highland life, perhaps more reconciled towards one another in the second half of the twentieth century than for two hundred years, and this by the pressure of mutual dependence on various forms of agricultural subsidy and mutual antipathy towards non-traditional forms of land use.

The third attitude is to regard land as a resource for industry, which I also classify as traditional as it has fascinated entrepreneurs and planners, mainly outsiders, since Sir George Hay's iron works in Wester Ross in the seventeenth century. By and large it has been a sad disappointment; the eighteenth century was littered with failed ironworks, mines and textile undertakings, and the twentieth century with pulp mills, aluminium smelters and rig yards. Even hydro power and the nuclear industry never realised the immense hopes vested in them by Tom Johnston and the post-war Secretaries of State, as agencies for reviving the Highlands by providing power for light industry. The main importance of those hopes for the Hydro Board historically lie in explaining why Scotland, almost alone of advanced industrial countries has no land designated as national parks.

All three of these traditional attitudes to land usage, (and the first two, related to agriculture and private sport, are much the most important) leave out of account any interest the outsider might have in using the Highlands, or any scenic or scientific value the land might have. They are fundamentally informed by an ancient way of seeing nature as resilient and there to be exploited and the land as providing a way of making a living or pursuing a private pleasure.

The next three attitudes I have classed as post-romantic, as none of them would have been thinkable before the age of Ossian.[2] Number four in my list is an attitude that regards the land as an invigorating obstacle course...

The fifth attitude is a century older, and follows Thomas Gray and Wordsworth in seeing unspoiled landscape as refreshment to the spirit, so something to be maintained in its entirety and contemplated in its tranquility. There was much emphasis on this throughout the nineteenth century, but only on the part of intellectual romantics with no influence on public policy: in the first half of the twentieth century they allied very effectively with those who held the fourth view (of land as an arena for public recreation) to put pressure on government to declare national parks...

The sixth and last attitude is to regard land not only as a recreational and scenic resource for man, but also as a refuge for plants, birds and animals seen as interesting and worth preserving for their own sake. This attitude had, as we have seen, very little public emphasis in Britain, and particularly little in the Scottish Highlands, until after the Second World War. Then it grew dramatically...

The three attitudes towards the Highlands that I have called post-romantic were all held predominantly by outsiders to the Highlands, and thus became the main reason for the tourist trade servicing sport, scenery admirers and nature lovers, which flourished exceedingly in the age of mass leisure and car ownership, 1960-1990...

...Highland society, in fact, has come to accord a differential scale of respect to the three post-romantic attitudes. Mass sport and recreation may be unacceptable to some landowners and farmers because of what they regard as trespass, but it is seen to provide jobs and does not interfere with traditional land use in other ways. Scenic appreciation is less welcome if it gives rise to criticism of forestry policies and fish farming, or limits development in National Scenic Areas. Nature appreciation seems to have been least welcome of all, at least since the 1981 Wildlife and Countryside Act gave teeth to the Nature Conservancy Council to interfere substantially with the rights of landowners, forestry companies and farmers to do what they liked with their property, by

2 A legendary Gaelic bard. James Macpherson (1736-96) drew on Gaelic oral traditions to write, in English, epic poems ascribed to 'Ossian'. These were translated into all the chief European languages and became a potent influence in the Romantic revival (London: Chambers Encyclopaedia, Int Learning Systems, 1973).

declaring SSSIs. It is of course quite likely that a single person will combine many attitudes in one; a visitor who climbs a mountain, admires the view and identifies with pleasure a peregrine falcon on the crags has all three of the post-romantic attitudes.

...So where does this leave us? This lecture has, I hope, demonstrated how all our attitudes towards the land and nature have a history, indeed, how they have come to be twisted and directed by history. But a last and more important point might be made. The situation at the moment is a potential disaster because too many on the development side cannot see either that the Highlands belong to a wider British society than seems to be visible from Inverness, or that man is an animal along with other animals on this fragile planet; and on the other side, too many see economic change only in simple and emotional terms of man's encroachment on nature's kingdom. One might well consider that the only possible way forward is to bring to our aid a holistic ecology concerned with developing overall land use strategies according to the strains the land can bear, treating man as an animal who fits in with the natural world instead of trying to smash through it...

2 THE CASE STUDY – LOCH DRUIDIBEG

The area of our case study is Loch Druidibeg National Nature Reserve on South Uist, an island in the Outer Hebrides. We have chosen this site partly because it provides a tangible illustration of the development of nature conservation law in the United Kingdom since the Second World War, but mainly because designation of Loch Druidibeg as a Nature Reserve has been effective. The loch was declared a National Nature Reserve because one of the few remaining native populations of greylag geese in the British Isles lives throughout the year in the Uists with Loch Druidibeg as an important breeding site.[3]

The management of the Nature Reserve over a period of nearly forty years has succeeded in rescuing a species that was endangered – the greylag goose – to the point where it is viable again, exporting breeding pairs to other islands and to mainland Scotland, where once it was common. The site is an important one for other birds, animals and plants and now, with the develop-ment of nature conservation law more generally, enjoys protection under both international agreements and European Community law, as well as United Kingdom law. We will outline the way these developments in conservation law have resulted in superimposed designations on the site so that now there is a layering of laws. International, Community, national and local laws make up this complex pattern, with a degree of interaction between the layers. Interestingly, legal protection from the European Community came late, for reasons already discussed in chapter 5.

The following extract from a leaflet for walkers, produced by the Western Isles Tourism Development Programme, introduces the area of our case study:

3 G Churchill, SNH Area Officer, Uists and Barra, *Loch Druidibeg Management Plan* (1995), para 2.1.1.

Western Isles Walks

Machair

The flat, sandy coastal plain, which stretches down the western fringe of the Uists is known as machair. It is considered to be unique in terms of the rich plant and bird life it sustains.

The machair developed as the fine white sand, which consists of the crushed and pulverised remnants of innumerable sea shells, was steadily blown onto the land. This sand eventually became intermixed with the darker, acidic peat and has a liming effect which produces a fertile natural grassland.

The machair has been worked by generations of crofters with a variety of crops which they change round from year to year. This keeps the soil fertile and helps stop the soil being blown away. The ploughed patches are generally fertilised using seaweed collected from the beach.

The main crops grown are hay, silage and corn, all of which are used as winter feed for livestock. Sheep and cattle graze various parts of the machair during the winter months, before going out onto the improved land and the moorland areas for the summer.

Traditional crofting and farming practices serve to maintain and enhance the wildlife interest of the machair. During the summer months the machair plays host to a stunning display of wild flowers which creates a wonderful, colourful mosaic.

...

Wildlife

The full range of habitats from the sea eastwards to the hills is reflected in the variety of birds seen within the Reserve. Offshore, seabirds such as gannets, skuas and auks may be seen passing through. Eiders ride the waves joined by long-tailed ducks in the winter when small flocks of waders such as sanderling or turnstone may be feeding along the tide line. Other waders live here throughout the year and breed on the machair.

The Reserve supports about 100 pairs each of oystercatcher and lapwing. About 50 pairs of ringed plover hide their nests and eggs on shingle or the bare soil of fallow areas of the machair. Breeding dunlin are normally associated with the uplands, but in the Uists they nest at sea level in rough hummocky pasture. Redshank and snipe prefer damper areas and ditches. In early summer a corncrake or two may be heard calling in the hayfields or iris beds.

The machair lochs provide good feeding for a variety of wildfowl in winter, including goldeneye, wigeon and whooper swans. Some of them – notably mute swan, mallard, teal and tufted duck remain to breed in the summer, with an occasional shoveler and little grebe. Arctic terns nest on some of the islands along with a few pairs of herons.

The coastal lochs, such as Groigearraidh, tend to be salty, but benefit from the lime which leaches through the surrounding machair soils into the lochs. Loch Druidibeg itself is shallow and peaty so it has a more limited range of freshwater plants and animals. Sticklebacks (two species) and both brown and sea trout are found here.

The greylag geese live here all the year round, one of the few remaining native populations in Britain. ... Red-throated diver breed on some of the smaller hill lochs, with golden plover on the hill slopes. Golden eagle, hen harrier, merlin and short-eared owl breed in the hills around the Reserve, but may hunt over both moor and machair. The plantation along the Loch Sgioport road is a refuge for a variety of small woodland birds.

Red deer were re-introduced to South Uist by the Estate in 1975. Although they are not often seen in this area, you may hear stags roaring in the autumn.

Rabbit, hedgehog and ferret (domesticated polecat) have also been introduced deliberately. None of these introductions were beneficial. Rabbits now exist in large numbers on the machair, where they reduce the grazing available for domestic stock and their burrows contribute to erosion of the sandy ground. Ferrets have been lost or released during rabbit trapping. They also kill other small mammals and birds, including domestic fowl, so they do considerable damage. Feral cats living on the machair have a similar diet. Hedgehogs have spread widely since they were first introduced in 1974: they have been found robbing henhouses, so they probably take eggs from ground nesting birds too.

The mammal population which lives on the Reserve consists of brown rats, short-tailed voles, field mice, house mice and pygmy shrews. Some of these, and the rabbits, provide food for the birds of prey which hunt over the area. There are also otters, which live around the loch.

Plantation

The plantation forms part of Loch Druidibeg National Nature Reserve ... It is not a natural woodland, but was originally planted by the owners of South Uist Estate...The plantation now has a variety of native and exotic trees, including birch, hazel, alder, Norway maple, together with the only group of mature Scots pine to be found in the Uists and three monkey puzzle trees. The area provides an interesting contrast to the native scrub woodland found on the islands in Loch Druidibeg.

The plantation provides food and shelter for a variety of small birds such as robin, greenfinch, some thrush and blackbird. Cuckoos are also often seen around the plantation where they fool meadow pipits into rearing their fledgelings. The plantation also plays host to a number of butterflies, moths and dragonflies.

3 NATURE CONSERVATION

NW Moore *The Bird of Time* (Cambridge: CUP, 1987), p xvi

...A glance at political manifestos and at the editorial and business columns of newspapers shows clearly that most do not perceive the extent of human dependence on nature. If it is mentioned at all, nature is usually relegated to 'Nature Notes' and whimsical articles about Natterjack Toads. Conservation is made to look frivolous, sentimental and backward looking, opposing development and more concerned with the past than the future.

...Conservation is both a subject and an aim. It involves fundamental and applied science, technology, economics, administration and politics and requires the understanding of people and society. It is motivated by strong feelings as well as by objective reasoning.

This points to the nature of the fundamental challenge that conservation of natural systems presents to law in that conservation is both a subject and an aim. There are two dynamic thrusts embedded in this: first, that the subject – nature – is constantly changing and second, that as our knowledge of natural systems increases, so must management of conservation sites develop.

As will be shown below, there have been changes in the ecological character of Loch Druidibeg as a wetland site. The changes arise from natural trends and 'man' induced trends. It also illustrates an important issue as to the meaning of nature conservation: to what extent does this include preservation? Arguably, it is not possible to have 'preservation' of an ecosystem since that implies a static state, whereas living systems constantly change. 'Conservation' rather is dynamic: good conservation enhances biodiversity. Much of the biodiversity of the machairs of the Western Isles is the result of people living and working on the land for thousands of years. This is strikingly apparent in our case study: the ecological health of the Loch Druidibeg National Nature Reserve is intimately connected with active crofting.

G Churchill *Loch Druidibeg National Nature Reserve Management Plan*, 1995

2.3 FACTORS INFLUENCING MANAGEMENT

2.3.1. Natural Trends

Two of the major natural trends likely to influence management are erosion and deposition. At present the coast is in a phase of erosion which is mainly the result of marine erosion during winter storms, most recently in January 1993, and this looks likely to continue for the foreseeable future. The natural cycle of this coast suggests that it will eventually start to grow seawards again. Until this point it is important that human activity does not exacerbate the coastal erosion.

Erosional problems created by overgrazing (rabbits) pose a serious threat to the landforms on the machair. The rabbit populations of the machair are so high that several large erosional scarps and a multitude of small pits and hollows have been created. Wind erosion then enlarges these scarps and many parts of the machair are eroding as a result. The escarpment area at Drimsdale is particularly badly affected. The rabbits also cause problems for the crofters and it is recommended that action is taken to reduce the damage caused by rabbits. This is highlighted in the Site Documentation Report for the Ardivachar to Stoneybridge GCR [Geological Conservation Review] Site.

The greylag goose breeding population on the Reserve has decreased over recent years. In the 1970s 65-70 pairs of geese were thought to be breeding on Loch Druidibeg (Sharrock 1976) but by 1982 the number had fallen to 38 pairs (Pickup 1982). A survey by SNH staff in 1994 found 13 pairs of geese breeding on Loch Druidibeg. However, during this same period the overall population of greylag geese in the Uists has increased to an estimated 2165 birds in August

1994 (GGMC 1994). The cause for the decline of Loch Druidibeg as a major breeding area in the Uists is as yet unknown.

Fluctuating water levels could adversely alter the salinity of brackish waters and affect associated invertebrate populations. The changing water levels of Loch Druidibeg which occur during the breeding season could seriously disrupt ground nesting birds along its shoreline.

Although useful cover for birds, the continued spread of *Rhododendron ponticum* on the reserve will affect the plantation, the surrounding area and the islands on Loch Druidibeg, with subsequent loss of valuable natural habitats.

2.3.2 Man Induced Trends

The continuation of cattle and sheep grazing along with the associated cultivation regimes on the machair are fundamental to the long term conservation of the floristic features of interest. Changes to excessive numbers of stock, grazing routines and cultivation methods (use of artificial fertilisers and pesticides) would have a considerable effect on plant species diversity and bird breeding success. However, currently cultivation of the Stilligarry machair is very limited which may be having an adverse effect on its features of interest and therefore this situation needs to be addressed.

Changes to the profile of the land such as levelling hummocks on the escarpment effectively remove the features of geomorphological importance of the machair. Therefore, any activities of this kind should avoid areas where key features occur.

Vehicles straying away from existing machair tracks could cause erosion leading to blowouts and increase disturbance to breeding birds. The condition of existing tracks needs to be monitored to avoid further erosion.

Removal of sand and gravel from sensitive areas of the shore is likely to increase erosion and coastal retreat. There is small scale removal of sand and gravel from borrow pits in the machair and in some cases there are several pits in close proximity. These are further being enlarged by rabbits and wind erosion. The number of pits requires rationalising and restoration of those no longer in use.

Increased recreational use of the beach and machair areas could cause an increase in noise pollution, disturbance during breeding season and localised coastal erosion. Any new tourism initiatives should be given careful consideration and subsequently monitored.

Oil pollution on the shore would endanger marine animals and local wader populations.

Uncontrolled muirburn on the reserve could have devastating effects on the plantation and wildlife.

Sheep along with the re-introduced Red Deer (c.1975) are causing some damage to the vegetation on some of the islands, primarily browsing of trees. Scaring techniques have been used but this problem needs to be monitored. Perhaps the most worrying introductions are the increasing numbers of ferrets and hedgehogs to be seen on the reserve. These animals and their effect on the populations of breeding birds need to be closely monitored. Fishing on the loch is very small scale at present but if it is increased could affect fish stocks and disturb birds.

4 DESIGNATION

The body of laws for nature conservation has expanded dramatically over the last half century since the enactment of the National Parks and Access to the Countryside Act 1949 (see below) which put in place the British system of designated areas of land considered to need special protection because of their nature conservation interest. As well as these laws which are obviously concerned specifically with nature conservation, in recent years many other Acts have included conservation indirectly. For example, under three of the 1991 Water Acts which apply in England and Wales, the whole range of regulatory bodies – the ministers, the Environment Agency, drainage boards, and water and sewerage undertakers – must exercise their powers so as to enhance conservation.[4] This might be considered rather weak law which can only be enforced by judicial review, but in practice it has proved quite effective in creating an administrative culture which does pay some attention to conservation of nature. Nonetheless, the laws for nature conservation are too often site or species specific which makes them unable to tackle deep seated problems in the wider environment.

More specifically we explore the legal technique of designating an area of land for special treatment. Designation of a parcel of land for a particular purpose means that within the boundaries of the area a local law can operate overriding some normal property rights. Designation offers a means by which law can regulate space. It can be a very powerful legal tool having significant effects on the human social world both within and outwith the designated area. However designation may also be problematic, as is any boundary drawing exercise. In *Sweet v Secretary of State for the Environment and Nature Conservancy Council*,[5] concerning the designation of a Site of Special Scientific Interest, it was held that it is possible to designate a penumbra of land that does not have the same scientific interest as the core area provided it belongs to the same environmental unit. What is not clear is whether surr-ounding 'buffer zone' land may be designated.

Designation may be counterproductive: the manager of land nearby may rationalise destroying similar features of interest on the undesignated land, on the ground that it could have been designated but was not.[6] Even so, pragmatically, designation is useful in a variety of contexts. When drawing up structure or local plans, planners may be made aware that the designated area is unsuitable for industrial development, for example. As we saw in chapter 7, the designation of land for special protection is a 'material consideration'; an individual planning application may fail, or have conditions attached, in order to maintain the scenic integrity of an area. The close relationship that designation has with the planning system in the United Kingdom is therefore the source of many of its strengths but also the fatal weakness at the heart of nature conservation law in Britain. The planning system does not provide absolute protection for natural conservation sites.

4 Water Industry Act 1991, s 3(2); Water Resources Act 1991, s 16(1); Land Drainage Act 1991, s 12(1).

5 [1989] JPEL 927.

6 See: P Lowe, G Cox, E MacEwen, T O'Riordan and M Winter *Countryside Conflicts* (Aldershot: Gower, 1986); and S Elworthy *Farming for Drinking Water* (Aldershot: Avebury, 1994).

Designation is used for a variety of purposes: Conservation Areas in towns and cities to protect the built environment; Nitrate Vulnerable Zones and Nitrate Sensitive Areas in which farming is modified to protect drinking water (see chapter 9); Environmentally Sensitive Areas in which traditional farming is encouraged by the offer of management agreements; and sites for nature conservation or for landscape protection. Our case study area is the site of several 'environmental' des-ignations; some embedded in one another and some intersecting these; some designations are for protection of species and some for protection of habitats or geological features. There are also 'agricultural' designations: the site is in a Less Favoured Area and there is an Environmentally Sensitive Area intersecting the Reserve. Whilst not a designation as such, there is a large zone owned by the Ministry of Defence for rocket shooting. Most significantly, the site is in a part of Scotland that now enjoys European Union designation for Objective 1 development funding and support. As will be shown, these designations interact with one another and though they are generally mutually reinforcing, they may conflict. The Environmentally Sensitive Area designation has particular relevance for our study because it stresses the relationship between nature conservation and agriculture.

Since nature conservation relies so much on the legal technique of designation and there are so many possible designation types, to illustrate simply how the technique works in practice, we have adopted a chronological schema. Our starting point is the post Second World War project which redefined the use and development of land in Britain.[7]

5 THE POST-WAR CONSERVATION PROJECT

The designation of sites for nature conservation grew out of a strategy evolved by voluntary organisations for the protection of common lands for recreational purposes.[8] The government of reconstruction after the war included a Ministry of Town and Country Planning which took a broad brush approach. The Ministry set up the Wildlife Conservation Special Committee, chaired by the biologist Sir Julian Huxley, to consider setting up National Parks. The following extract from the Report of the Huxley Committee remains the best articulation of the reasons for having nature reserves. To modern readers it may have a rather anthropocentric tone, but that in itself illustrates cultural change since the 1940s.

Conservation of Nature in England and Wales **(Report of the Wild Life Conservation Special Committee)(The Huxley Report), Cmd 7122 (London: HMSO, 1947), pp 12-13**

37. The need to save for posterity the most valuable and interesting of the sites which remain can hardly be denied. In the national museums the State has

7 See also ch 3, 'The post-war planning project: 1944 and onwards'.
8 S Ball and S Bell *Environmental Law* (London: Blackstone, 1991), p 342.

long recognised its responsibility for the collection and preservation of objects of artistic, scientific and cultural value. It has more recently recognised (and interpreted broadly) its responsiblity for the protection, acquisition and custody of ancient monuments of historic and pre-historic importance. There is but a narrow gap between these and the reserves, which are both ancient monuments and living museums – a living embodiment of the past history of the land. The parallel with geological monuments is even closer...

The need for a constructive scientific policy

38. We wish to stress the view, however, that undue emphasis has usually been placed on the merely passive idea implied in the word conservation. The outlook hitherto has been rather to protect something *against* something else. This is perhaps to be expected when there is pressure by many interests upon a limited amount of land, and there is no central directive. We do not base our conclusions on this negative attitude. There is a positive need for reserves of varying types because they are required in pursuit of an active policy – a policy which will make the best use of the nation's heritage not only for the advancement of pure knowledge, though that in itself can be considered a sufficient aim, but for the application of that knowledge for the greater benefit of man. The acceptance by the Government of the widened responsibilities proposed...would certainly entail the need for reserves where the scientific studies, research and experiment, which alone can provide the data upon which a practical and active policy can be based, could be carried out with an assurance of continuity and support. The only criterion applied therefore in selecting the areas and sites recommended...has been whether their scientific value was such as to earn them a place in a carefully balanced scheme considered as a whole...

The need for educational facilities

39. In addition to the aesthetic, recreational and scientific aspects of conservation that have been discussed above, there is the educational aspect. This, although it merits a place of its own, is also in many ways complementary to each and all of the others. The true appreciation of scenery rests in part upon, and is certainly enhanced by, some understanding of what may be likened to its bony structure – the forms and dispositions of the rocks and the variety of landscape which these induce, the shapes of the valleys and summits, the flow of the streams, the cliffs and dunes and flats of the past, and all the rich verdure with which they are clothed. These are things which can invigorate and refresh the mind and upon which a deep culture can be based. The more widely this appreciation can be diffused, the sounder will be the mental and physical health of the nation and the safer will become the places where these pleasures are to be enjoyed. The spread of education in these matters is a *sine qua non* to the effective maintainance both of National Parks and nature reserves. Penalties for destruction or defacement should be imposed, but as deterrents they are less effective than a powerful public opinion.

40. And there are other considerations. Students have to be trained, and teachers must learn how to train them. It has for long been the practice of many universities to take students of field subjects – biologists, geologists,

physiographers, foresters and the like – to visit selected parts of the country where they can study and have demonstrated to them in the field the actual working of the principles that they have been, or will be, taught in the lecture room. A similar practice has more recently begun to develop in the higher forms at schools. This development we regard as of the highest importance in the teaching of the three main branches of science with which we are concerned; its successful continuation depends upon the conservation of appropriate areas of country. We go further. We consider...that small educational reserves or experimental plots should be made available if possible to all schools for courses in biology, geography and nature study, or at least to all the larger towns. Without such facilities the teaching of these subjects tends to become warped or lifeless.

41. The educational benefits to be had from a constructive wild life policy extend beyond the cultivation of a healthy public opinion and the technical training of science students to the wider sphere of general and adult education. In this context we may quote a sentence from the third report of the Nature Reserves Investigation Committee who in commending their proposals say -

> 'A serious student, whatever his calling, who could visit and have intelligently demonstrated to him even a good sample of the sites here proposed, would have received a liberal education in one of the most stimulating and formative fields of thought'.

HOW THESE NEEDS CAN BE SATISFIED

The material requirements

42. Reduced to its simplest terms, the satisfaction of the needs outlined in the preceding section requires-

land
scientific man-power
money.

All three are commodities that have to be acquired in a competitive market. Fortunately, there are facts that mitigate the severity of this competition. The land most suitable for reservation on biological grounds and still available is mainly land which has suffered the least disturbance by man; that is, where land which has up to the present been for one reason or another beyond the margin of economic development, or woodland which is not being exploited commercially to any appreciable extent. The scientific man-power would in any event need specialised training – for the higher grades a post-graduate course analogous to the specialised training given to foresters, and for the lower grades a somewhat simpler course in the scientific principles of nature conservation. We do not anticipate that, given reasonable terms of employment such as those set out in the White Paper on the Scientific Civil Service (Cmnd. 6679), there would be any lack of good candidates, nor that there would be any insuperable difficulties in arranging for the appropriate courses to be given. There are now suitable biologists who could be transferred to this service without making a serious competitive drain on other equally important biological requirements, and who would be sufficient, if working as a single team, to form a nucleus round which in time a permanent cadre could be built up. Furthermore, the value of having a section of the nation's biologists devoted to this service, cooperating with allied services and applied sciences (such as agriculture, forestry and veterinary science), should not be overlooked. Biology can hardly be applied effectively to the many problems that arise from the fact that wild life impinges on man's domestic stocks or economic crops unless there is adequate land and staff dedicated first and foremost to observing, and gaining experience in the management of, that wild life and natural conditions under which it flourishes or fails. The provision of money from public funds must obviously depend upon the size of the sums estimated as sufficient to meet immediate and recurrent charges and the relevant value of the return to the State on the expenditure incurred. On this last we are prepared to assert that our proposals, if accepted and vigorously carried through, would prove a most profitable business transaction, quite apart from the gains in those higher values that cannot be quantified in terms of money.

6 NATIONAL NATURE RESERVES IN SCOTLAND

The Scottish Wild Life Conservation Committee was appointed in 1946, under the chairmanship of Professor James Ritchie, to consider and advise the Scottish National Parks Committee as to the steps which should be taken to conserve wildlife in Scotland. In 1947 the Committee submitted its first Report on the Conservation of Nature in Scotland, which was mainly concerned with the necessary arrangements for administration.

The Nature Reserves Investigation Committee had confined itself to England and Wales, so without an equivalent information base for Scotland the Ritchie Committee set about gathering data. Regional Committees based on the university centres were set up, suggestions were invited from individuals and from scientific bodies, and an appeal was made to the general public through the press so that a preliminary survey could be made.[9] By 1949 the Committee submitted its Final Report.

***Nature Reserves in Scotland: Final Report by the Scottish National Parks Committee and the Scottish Wild Life Conservation Committee,* Dept of Health for Scotland Cmd 7814 (Edinburgh: HMSO, 1949), p 6**

II. NATURE RESERVES

5. In our first Report we expressed the opinion that the establishment of nature reserves for the conservation of habitats representative of Scottish conditions and their particular assemblages of plants and animals, for the preservation of rare species, and for scientific research and for educational purposes, is an essential requirement for the safeguarding of wild life in Scotland. We wish to repeat here our view that the reserves which we recommend, while adding to the amenity of the countryside, will in no way conflict with the good management of neighbouring properties. These reserves will be used as areas

9 *Nature Reserves in Scotland: Final Report by the Scottish National Parks Committee and the Scottish Wild Life Conservation Committee,* Cmnd 7814, (Edinburgh: HMSO, 1949) p 5.

for research, where, amongst other things, information may be obtained about plant and animal fluctuations under natural conditions.

...

(b) National Nature Reserves

For the conservation and study of plant and animal communities as well as of geological monuments, there will be required National Nature Reserves to include (1) particular conditions of habitat and terrain, such as primitive forest, peat, moss, sand dunes, etc; (2) individual species of plants and animals in need of conservation; and (3) outstanding geological features. Such National Reserves would be under constant and close scientific scrutiny, for little is known about the factors producing changes in plant and animal communities, and such knowledge would be of economic value to agriculture, forestry, and fisheries, and would afford invaluable guidance in controlling the natural amenities in the proposed National Parks. These National Nature Reserves would in general be owned by the State, and would be controlled by the Scottish Committee of the Nature Conservation Board. While, however, a proprietor was anxious to collaborate in the conservation of wild life, and willing to covenant to that end, the property might remain in his ownership.

Access by the public to National Nature Reserves would be subject to control by the Biological Service.

The Report contains a list of recommended Nature Reserves and Conservation Areas. The entry for Loch Druidibeg follows.

NNR23 Loch Druidibeg, South Uist (land: 2,048 acres (8.28 sq kms.)(water: 883 acres (3.57 sq kms.)

One-inch Sheets: Ordnance Survey, 68,69; Popular Edition, 23

This large freshwater loch with many islets is situated in the interior of South Uist, between Loch Skiport and Grogarry. It is of importance as a wild-fowl breeding ground, particularly for the greylag goose whose status in Great Britain has become precarious.

Many of the islets, bearing native scrub or introduced shrubs, possess a shade flora. A plantation along the north shore of the loch provides in this treeless district attractive cover for resident and migratory birds. Included in this reserve is a stretch of *machair* with good examples of *machair* lochs...These lochs, characteristic of the Uist west coast, are shallow, lying on shell sand with low 'grassy' or swampy verges in contrast with the steeper rocky shores of the acid lochs of the interior. They contain a rich aquatic vegetation besides possessing a good 'swamp' flora; the hydrobiology of a few has been investigated.

As well as recommending the designation of National Nature Reserves, Conservation Areas, National Parks, Geological Monuments, Local Nature Reserves and Local Educational Reserves, and proposing that there should be a Biological Service, the Huxley Report recommended drawing up a schedule of sites.

***Conservation of Nature in England and Wales (Report of the Wild Life Conservation Special Committee)*, Cmd 7122 (London: HMSO, 1947), p 26**

Schedule of Sites of Special Scientific Importance and production of handbooks

71. If the methods suggested for dealing with these areas are to be effectively applied, it will be necessary for each area to be inspected by qualified scientists at the earliest possible date in order that a schedule may be drawn up setting out the precise features and sites which are considered to be of the greatest scientific value, together with any other relevant information which may be required by the local planning authorities and the Advisory Committees...and that these schedules should be made available to the appropriate authorities and should be open to consultation by any member of the public. We recommend that this should be among the first duties laid upon the proposed Biological Service. This Service should also be required to produce for each area, in consultation or collaboration with the appropriate officers of the National Parks Commission handbooks similar in kind to those recommended...for National Nature Reserves.

7 THE NATIONAL PARKS AND ACCESS TO THE COUNTRYSIDE ACT 1949

The Huxley and the Ritchie Committees liaised closely: as the Huxley Committee remarked 'Plants and animals do not recognise political borders, and although there are features peculiar to Scotland, there are many sites which take an essential place in any balanced scheme for the conservation of wild life on the continuous land mass of Great Britain, and which are necessary complements to sites recommended on the English side of the Border'.[10] The recommendations of the two Reports were largely enacted in the National Parks and Access to the Countryside Act 1949. The recommended Biological Service became the Nature Conservancy.

It is worth noting that under section 23 of the National Parks and Access to the Countryside Act 1949 (see below), SSSIs were merely important sites that were on a list for the benefit of the scientific community. Though the local planning authority was informed of sites in its area, quite often the landowner or occupier of a site would not know that it was on the list, nor indeed of the existence of the list. It follows that landowners and occupiers were, at this date, under no legal obligation to protect the sites. Local planning departments would consult the Nature Conservancy before determining an application for planning permission for development, but as we have seen in chapter 3, agriculture and forestry were outwith the remit of the Town and Country Planning Act 1947 so the legal regime for protecting these sites was extremely weak.

10 Huxley Report, op cit, para 91.

National Parks and Access to the Countryside Act 1949

PART III
NATURE CONSERVATION
15. In this Part of this Act the expression 'nature reserve' means land managed for the purpose-

(a) of providing, under suitable conditions and control, special opportunities for the study of, and research into, matters relating to the fauna and flora of Great Britain and the physical conditions in which they live, and for the study of geological and physiographical features of special interest in the area, or

(b) of preserving flora, fauna or geological or physiographical features of special interest in the area, or for both of these purposes.

16. (1) The Nature Conservancy may enter into an agreement with every owner, lessee and occupier of any land, being land as to which it appears to the Conservancy expedient in the national interest that it should be managed as a nature reserve, for securing that it shall be so managed.

(2) Any such agreement may impose such restrictions as may be expedient for the purposes of the agreement on the exercise of rights over the land by the persons who can be bound by the agreement.

(3) Any such agreement-

(a) may provide for the management of the land in such manner, the carrying out thereon of such work and the doing thereon of such other things as may be expedient for the purposes of the agreement;

(b) may provide for any of the matters mentioned in the last foregoing paragraph being carried out, or for the cost thereof being defrayed, either by the said owner or other persons, or by the Conservancy, or partly in one way and partly in another;

(c) may contain such other provisions as to the making of payments by the Conservancy, and in particular for the payment by them of compensation for the effect of the restrictions mentioned in the last foregoing subsection, as may be specified in the agreement.

...

17. (1) Subject to the provisions of the next following subsection, where the Nature Conservancy are satisfied as respects any land that it is expedient in the national interest that it should be managed as a nature reserve, they may acquire the land compulsorily.

(2) The Nature Conservancy shall not acquire any interest in land under the last foregoing subsection unless they are satisfied that they are unable, as respects that interest, to conclude on terms appearing to them reasonable an agreement under the last foregoing section containing such provisions as in their opinion are required for securing that the land will be satisfactorily managed as a nature reserve.

[s. 18 powers to enter into management agreements with owners]

[s. 19 requirement to make Declarations that areas are nature reserves]

20. (1) The Nature Conservancy may, as respects land which is being managed as a nature reserve under an agreement entered into with them [under powers given in s. 18] or land held by them which is being managed as a nature reserve, make byelaws for the protection of the reserve:

> Provided that byelaws under this section shall not have effect as respects any land in a reserve unless a declaration under the last foregoing section is in force declaring that the land is being managed as a nature reserve and notice of the declaration has been published in pursuance of that section.

(2) Without prejudice to the generality of the last foregoing subsection, byelaws under this section-

> (a) may provide for prohibiting or restricting the entry into, or movement within, nature reserves of persons, vehicles, boats or animals;
>
> (b) may prohibit or restrict the killing, taking, molesting or disturbance of living creatures of any description in a nature reserve, the taking, destruction or disturbance of eggs of any such creature, the taking of, or interference with, vegetation of any description in a nature reserve, or the doing of anything therein which will interfere with the soil or damage any object in the reserve;
>
> (c) may prohibit or restrict the shooting of birds or of birds of any description within such area surrounding or adjoining a nature reserve (whether the area be of land or of sea) as appears to the Nature Conservancy requisite for the protection of the reserve;
>
> (d) may contain provisions prohibiting the depositing of rubbish and the leaving of litter in a nature reserve;
>
> (e) may prohibit or restrict, or provide for prohibiting or restricting, the lighting of fires in a nature reserve, or the doing of anything likely to cause a fire in a nature reserve;
>
> (f) may provide for the issue, on such terms and subject to such conditions as may be specified in the byelaws, of permits authorising entry into a nature reserve or the doing of anything therein which would otherwise be unlawful, whether under the byelaws or otherwise;
>
> (g) may be made so as to relate either to the whole or to any part of the reserve or, in the case of byelaws made under paragraph (c) of this subsection, of any such surrounding or adjoining area as is mentioned in that paragraph, and may make different provisions for different parts thereof:

...

23. Where the Nature Conservancy are of opinion that any area of land, not being land for the time being managed as a nature reserve, is of special interest

by reasons of its flora, fauna or geological or physiographical features, it shall be the duty of the Conservancy to notify that fact to the [local planning authority, originally] in whose area the land is situated.

8 ESTABLISHMENT OF THE RESERVE

Loch Druidibeg was designated as a National Nature Reserve in 1958 using the power for purchase given in section 17(1) of the National Parks and Access to the Countryside Act 1949. The original area covered was the loch and the surrounding moorland. The first Management Plan was prepared in March 1960. The principal objectives followed directly from the reasons for establishment and the evaluation of features of conservation interest:[11]

1. To conserve the stocks of greylag geese breeding within the Reserve.
2. To measure the size of the breeding population of greylag geese and other wildfowl and study their habits.
3. To initiate systematic recording of the fauna and flora, climate, hydrology and geology.

In 1962 the National Nature Reserve was extended to the western shore. This addition was by a Nature Reserve Agreement between the Nature Conservancy Council and South Uist Estates under section 17(2) of the National Parks and Access to the Countryside Act 1949, to complete the area recommended in the Ritchie Report. The extension was declared a National Nature Reserve, as required by section 19 of the 1949 Act. This extension includes three smaller lochs which, in contrast to Loch Druidibeg, are nutrient rich and support large populations of trout. The 'machair' or coastal grassland plain also lies between Loch Druidibeg and the western shore and is home to a rich variety of birds, wild animals and plants.

> There must be few places in the British Isles to compare with the Southern Isles, where one may traverse from the sandy beaches of the west, over machair, wetland, rough pasture and moorland to reach the seacliff and sealoch panoramas of the east coast within four miles of the start point.[12]

The Reserve, along with all National Nature Reserves, was re-notified as an SSSI under section 28 of the Wildlife and Countryside Act 1981 in 1987. It is through the system of SSSIs that the United Kingdom system gives legal protection to important nature conservation sites.[13]

11 *Loch Druidibeg Management Plan*, 1995, op cit, p 10.
12 P Cunningham, T Dix and P Snow *Birdwatching in the Outer Hebrides* (Argyll: Saker Press, 1995), p 26.
13 See ch 7, 'Countryside designation'.

9 INTERNATIONAL LAW

(a) Designation as a Ramsar site

S Lyster *International Wildlife Law* (Cambridge: Grotius Pubs, 1985), p 183

THE CONVENTION ON WETLANDS OF INTERNATIONAL IMPORTANCE ESPECIALLY AS WATERFOWL HABITAT ('RAMSAR')

1. Background

Wetlands are amongst the most productive life-support systems on earth, and their conservation is important for biological, hydrological and economic reasons. They provide essential habitat for hundreds of species of waterfowl, fish, amphibians, reptiles, mammals and plants. They act as natural sponges which control floods and droughts. A sub-tropical saltmarsh may produce organic material at more than twice the rate of the most fertile hayfield ... In spite of their valuable functions, wetlands in many parts of the world have been destroyed at an alarming rate in recent decades by drainage, land reclamation and pollution.

A series of international conferences and technical meetings was held in the 1960s, mainly under the auspices of the International Waterfowl Research Bureau ('IWRB'), in an effort to stem this tide of destruction. As a result of these discussions, the Convention on Wetlands of International Importance Especially as Waterfowl Habitat[14] was drawn up and was eventually signed on 2 February 1971 in the Iranian town of Ramsar...Ramsar came into force on 21 December 1975.

The UK signed the Ramsar Convention in 1973. There are now 88 Contracting Parties which may rise to 95 if all the Eastern European newly independent countries sign. Since three-quarters of the world's land is covered by the signatory states, Ramsar is a convention more important than the number of participating states suggests.[15]

Convention on Wetlands of International Importance especially as Waterfowl Habitat, Ramsar, 2.2.1971 as amended by the Protocol of 3.12.1982

The Contracting Parties,

Recognizing the interdependence of Man and his environment;

Considering the fundamental ecological functions of wetlands as regulators of water regimes and as habitats supporting a characteristic flora and fauna, especially waterfowl;

Being convinced that wetlands constitute a resource of great economic, cultural, scientific and recreational value, the loss of which would be irreparable;

14 11 ILM 963; UKTS no 34 (1976), Cmd 6465.

15 GVT Matthews *The Ramsar Convention on Wetlands: Its History and Development* (Gland: International Waterfowl and Wetlands Research Bureau, 1993).

Desiring to stem the progressive encroachment on and loss of wetlands now and in the future;

Recognizing that waterfowl in their seasonal migrations may transcend frontiers and so should be regarded as an international resource;

Being confident that the conservation of wetlands and their flora and fauna can be ensured by combining far-sighted national policies with co-ordinated international action;

Have agreed as follows:

Article 1
1. For the purpose of this Convention wetlands are areas of marsh, fen, peatland or water, whether natural or artificial, permanent or temporary, with water that is static or flowing, fresh, brackish or salt, including areas of marine water the depth of which at low tide does not exceed six metres.
2. For the purpose of this Convention waterfowl are birds ecologically dependent on wetlands.

Article 2
1. Each Contracting Party shall designate suitable wetlands within its territory for inclusion in a List of Wetlands of International Importance, hereinafter referred to as 'the list' which is maintained by the bureau established under Article 8. The boundaries of each wetland shall be precisely described and also delimited on a map and they may incorporate riparian and coastal zones adjacent to the wetlands, and islands or bodies of marine water deeper than six metres at low tide lying within the wetlands, especially where these have importance as waterfowl habitat.
2. Wetlands should be selected for the List on account of their international significance in terms of ecology, botany, zoology, limnology or hydrology. In the first instance wetlands of international importance to waterfowl at any season should be included.
...
6. Each Contracting Party shall consider its international responsibilities for the conservation, management and wise use of migratory stocks of waterfowl, both when designating entries for the List and when exercising its right to change entries in the List relating to wetlands within its territory.

Article 3
1. The Contracting Parties shall formulate and implement their planning so as to promote the conservation of the wetlands included in the List, and as far as possible the wise use of wetlands in their territory.
2. Each Contracting Party shall arrange to be informed at the earliest possible time if the ecological character of any wetland in its territory and included in the List has changed, is changing or is likely to change as the result of technological developments, pollution or other human interference. Information on such changes shall be passed without delay to the organization or government responsible for the continuing bureau duties specified in Article 8.

Article 4
1. Each Contracting Party shall promote the conservation of wetlands and waterfowl by establishing nature reserves on wetlands, whether they are included in the List or not, and provide adequately for their wardening.
2. Where a Contracting Party in its urgent national interest, deletes or restricts the boundaries of a wetland included in the List, it should as far as possible compensate for any loss of wetland resources, and in particular it should create additional nature reserves for waterfowl and for the protection, either in the same area or elsewhere, of an adequate portion of the original habitat.
3. The Contracting Parties shall encourage research and the exchange of data and publications regarding wetlands and their flora and fauna.
4. The Contracting Parties shall endeavour through management to increase waterfowl populations on appropriate wetlands.
5. The Contracting Parties shall promote the training of personnel competent in the fields of wetland research, management and wardening.

Articles 6 and 7 of the Convention of International Importance especially as Waterfowl Habitat as amended by the Conference of the Parties on 28.5.1987
Article 6
1. There shall be established a Conference of the Contracting Parties to review and promote the implementation of this Convention...
2. The Conference of the Contracting Parties shall be competent:

(a) to discuss the implementation of this Convention;
(b) to discuss additions to and changes in the List;
(c) to consider information regarding changes in the ecological character of wetlands included in the List provided in accordance with paragraph 2 of Article 3;
(d) to make general or specific recommendations to the Contracting Parties regarding the conservation, management and wise use of wetlands and their flora and fauna;
(e) to request relevant international bodies to prepare reports and statistics on matters which are essentially international in character affecting wetlands;
(f) to adopt other recommendations, or resolutions, to promote the functioning of this Convention.

3. The Contracting Parties shall ensure that those responsible at all levels for wetlands management shall be informed of, and take into consideration, recommendations of such Conferences concerning the conservation, management and wise use of wetlands and their flora and fauna.
...
Article 7
1. The representatives of the Contracting Parties at such conferences shall include persons who are experts on wetlands or waterfowl by reason of knowledge and experience gained in scientific, administrative or other appropriate capacity.
...

The recommendations under Article 6.1(d) do not have the same legal force as the Convention itself but are soft law. The language of the Convention may be the mandatory 'shall' but its nature overall is permissive.[16] The body of recommendations of the meetings under the Ramsar Convention is an example of soft international law proving dynamic and successful with the discretion given to signatory states, freeing them to be creative and cooperative. The result has been large areas of protected sites and the series of meetings has extended the scope of the original Convention considerably.

On signing, states must designate at least one national wetland site. These sites may be designated unilaterally but guidelines have been developed at formal meetings since the Convention. These guidelines are now known as the Montreux Criteria for identifying sites and the Cagliari Conference in 1980 decided that they should be used for assessing wetlands of international importance. The following table shows the criteria for identifying these wetlands.

Source: Mathews (1993) and Navid (1989) – from C Neild and R Rice *A Review of UK Compliance with the Ramsar Convention on Wetlands of International Importance Especially as Waterfowl Habitat* (London: Friends of the Earth, 1996), p 6

The Montreux criteria identified are subdivided into three categories:
The wetlands must meet at least one of the criteria below:

1. Criteria for representative or unique wetlands:

(a) it is a particularly good representative example of a natural or near-natural wetland characteristic of the appropriate biogeographical region; or

(b) it is a particularly good representative example of a natural or near-natural wetland, common to more than one biogeographical region; or

(c) it is a particularly good representative example of a wetland, which plays a substantial hydrogeological, biological or ecological role in the natural functioning of a major river basin or coastal system, especially when it is located in the trans-border position; or

(d) it is an example of a specific type of wetland, rare or unusual in the appropriate biogeographical region.

2. General criteria based on plants or animals:
A wetland should be considered internationally important if:

(a)it supports an appreciable assemblage of rare, vulnerable, or endangered species or subspecies of any plant or animal, or an appreciable number of any one or more of these species; or

(b)it is of special value for maintaining the genetic and ecological diversity of a region because of the quality and peculiarities of its flora and fauna; or

(c)it is of special value as a habitat of plants or animals at a critical stage of their biological cycles; or

(d)it is of special value for its endemic plant or animal species or communities.

3. Specific criteria for using waterfowl to identify wetlands of importance:
A wetland should be considered internationally important if:

(a) it regularly supports 20,000 waterfowl; or

16 See ch 4.

(b) it regularly supports substantial numbers of individuals from particular groups of waterfowl, indicative of wetland values, productivity or diversity; or
(c) where data on populations are available, it regularly supports 1% of individuals in a population of one species or subspecies of waterfowl.

Loch Druidibeg is one of the 80 Ramsar Sites which have been designated in the United Kingdom.

The Sixth Meeting of the Contracting Parties to the Ramsar Convention met in Brisbane, Australia during March 1996. The United Kingdom's National Report to this meeting described the state of the Nature Reserve in 1995.

Extract from UK's National Report to the 6th Meeting of the Contracting Parties to the Ramsar Convention

6. Lochs Druidibeg, A'Machair and Stilligary

Change in Legal Status
Parts of the listed Ramsar site have been identified as part of a possible SAC[17] (South Uist Machair).

Change in Ecological Character
A marked decline in the area of arable land now under cultivation on the machair within the site has taken place over the last 50 years. This is associated with a decrease in cattle farming, and increase in sheep numbers and a decline in cultivation since the second world war. Traditional low-intensity agricultural practices play an important role in sustaining the high floral diversity and large populations of breeding waders characteristic of the machair on Uist. The introduction of management agreements is being explored as a means of getting disused arable land back into traditional rotational cultivation, and maintaining or re-establishing beneficial grazing regimes and fodder production practices.

Large numbers of Rabbits *Oryctolagus cuniculus* are exacerbating erosion of the machair through burrowing and heavily grazing the vegetation. Several large scrapes and many small pits and hollows have developed. Wind erosion enlarges these pits and many areas of the machair are eroding as a result. A project is currently being developed to eradicate and exclude rabbits from the reserve. The accidental introduction of feral Ferrets and Hedgehogs *Erinaceus europaeus* to this area pose a serious threat to the large numbers of nesting birds. A research project aiming to quantify the impact of these introduced species will begin in summer 1995. Sheep *Ovis amon* and Red Deer *Cervus elaphus* are causing browsing damage to relict woodland vegetation on some of the islands of Loch Druidibeg. Scaring techniques have been used and the scale of damage monitored.

17 Special Area of Conservation under Directive 92/43/EEC on the conservation of natural habitats and of wild fauna and flora. See below 'European Community law', p 454.

Management Plan
The Management Plan for the NNR was revised in 1994 and came into force in 1995.

A confidential draft of this report prepared by the Joint Nature Conservation Committee for the Department of the Environment was leaked to Friends of the Earth. This showed that more than half of the United Kingdom Ramsar sites had been damaged or seriously threatened during the previous three years. Friends of the Earth wrote to the secretariat of the Ramsar Convention urging that the 15 most threatened United Kingdom sites, amongst them Loch Druidibeg, be added to the Montreux Record. This would trigger an assessment by an international panel of experts.

C Heild and T Rice *A Review of UK Compliance with the Ramsar Convention on Wetlands of International Importance Especially as Waterfowl Habitat* (London: Friends of the Earth, 1996), p 42

APPENDIX 1: Damage and potential threats to Ramsar sites.

Definitions
Damage to a Ramsar site is defined as: a permanent or temporary change in the ecological character of a wetland as a result of direct or indirect human activity.
Threat to a Ramsar site is defined as: a possible change in ecological character as a result of direct or indirect human activity, (e.g. if there is public pressure on the site or nutrient enrichment from sewage and agricultural sources).

Designated Sites
...Lochs Druidibeg, A'Machair and Stilligarry

Damage 1992-96
...Insufficient management, erosion (rabbits/wind), Woodland damage (sheep/deer browsing).

Threats
...Accidental introduction of species (hedgehogs and ferrets) causing threat to ground nesting birds.

Enforcement of the obligation to conserve wetlands generally and listed sites in particular under the Ramsar Convention is a problem. Regional economic co-ordination organisations (such as the European Union) are not allowed to be signatories to the Convention so the listed sites do not automatically enjoy protection under Community law. This lacuna has been filled by Directive 92/43/EEC on the conservation of natural habitats and of wild fauna and flora which is discussed below. The following, from the resolutions of the Brisbane meeting show why the Ramsar Convention has proved durable and dynamic. Note the attention to devising scientific definitions that will be of practical use and also the emphasis on cooperation between states and the panel of experts.

Ramsar Convention, Brisbane, Australia, 19-27 March 1996

Resolutions and Recommendations

Resolution VI.1

WORKING DEFINITIONS OF ECOLOGICAL CHARACTER, GUIDELINES FOR DESCRIBING AND MAINTAINING THE ECOLOGICAL CHARACTER OF LISTED SITES, AND GUIDELINES FOR OPERATION OF THE MONTREUX RECORD

1. **CONSIDERING** that Article 3.2 of the Convention states that each Contracting Party 'shall arrange to be informed at the earliest possible time if the ecological character of any wetland in its territory and included in the List [...] has changed, is changing, or is likely to change as the result of technological developments, pollution or other human interference';

2. **RECALLING** that Recommendation 4.8 instructed the Bureau to maintain a record of listed sites where change in ecological character had occurred, was occurring, or was likely to occur, and that Resolution 5.4 established guidelines for operating the record, to be known as the Montreux Record;

3. **FURTHER RECALLING** that Recommendation 5.2 emphasized the need for further studies of the concepts of 'ecological character' and 'change in ecological character', and instructed the Bureau, with the support of the Scientific and Technical Review Panel (STRP) and partner organizations, to report to the present meeting on the results of such studies;

4. **NOTING** the results of the work carried out by the STRP and during Technical Session B of the present meeting;

5. **RECOGNIZING** the need for definitions and guidelines to assist Contracting Parties with implementation of Article 3.2 and, in particular, with maintaining the ecological character of listed sites;

6. **FURTHER RECOGNIZING** the need for revised guidelines to ensure effective operation of the Montreux Record;

7. **NOTING** that Resolution VI.13 of the present meeting seeks to address the deficiencies in essential baseline data provided by the Contracting Parties in the form of Information Sheets on Ramsar Wetlands; and

8. **AWARE** of the existence of many successful environmental monitoring programmes world-wide (including those which rely on the involvement and enthusiasm of local communities) and of the value of Early Warning Systems to allow Contracting Parties to take sufficiently prompt actions to prevent changes in the ecological character of listed sites;

9. **ACCEPTS** working definitions, to be assessed further during the 1997-1999 triennium, of 'ecological character' and 'change in ecological character', together with the guidelines for describing and maintaining ecological character of listed sites, as contained in the Annex to the present resolution, recognizing that these working definitions are relevant to the management of wetlands in general;

10. **REQUESTS** the Contracting Parties and the Bureau, with the advice of the STRP, to implement the revised procedure for operation of the Montreux Record, as contained in the Annex to the present resolution;

11. **CALLS ON** Contracting Parties to support the development, by the relevant authorities within their territories, of Early Warning Systems for detecting, and initiating action in response to, change in ecological character; and

12. **INSTRUCTS** the STRP, in cooperation with the Bureau and partner organizations, and the wider scientific community, to liaise with the Standing Committee, in order to identify the effects of application of the present resolution, especially at specific sites, and to report accordingly to the 7th Meeting of the Conference of the Parties.

Annex to Resolution VI.1
WORKING DEFINITIONS OF ECOLOGICAL CHARACTER, GUIDELINES FOR DESCRIBING AND MAINTAINING THE ECOLOGICAL CHARACTER OF LISTED SITES, AND GUIDELINES FOR OPERATION OF THE MONTREUX RECORD

1. Working Definitions
1.1 Ecological character
The 'ecological character' is the structure and inter-relationships between the biological, chemical, and physical components of the wetland. These derive from the interactions of individual processes, functions, attributes and values of the ecosystem(s);

1.2 Change[18] in ecological character
'Change in ecological character' of a wetland is the impairment or imbalance in any of those processes and functions which maintain the wetland and its products, attributes and values.
The following notes on wetland processes, functions, values, products and attributes, are derived from the *Ramsar Convention Manual* (Davis, 1994), and *Wetland Conservation: A Review of Current Issues and Required Action* (Dugan, 1990); 'Building a new approach to the investigation and assessment of wetland ecosystem functioning' in Mitsch, *Global Wetlands: Old World and New* (Maltby, 1994); and 'Defining new procedures of functional assessment for European river marginal wetlands ecosystems' (Maltby, in press).

Processes are changes or reactions which occur naturally within wetland ecosystems. They may be physical, chemical or biological.

Functions are activities or actions which occur naturally in wetlands as a product of the interactions between the ecosystem structure and processes. Functions include flood water control; nutrient, sediment and contaminant retention; food web support; shoreline stabilization and erosion controls; storm protection; and stabilization of local climatic conditions; particularly rainfall and temperature.

18 Change in the ecological character of a site is interpreted as meaning adverse change, in line with the context of Article 3.2 of the Convention and Recommendation 4.8 (1990), which established the Montreux Record. The definition refers explicitly to adverse change caused by human activities. It excludes the process of natural evolutionary change occurring in wetlands. It is also recognised that wetland restoration and/or rehabilitation programmes may lead to favourable human-induced changes in ecological character.

Values are the perceived benefits to society, either direct or indirect, that result from wetland functions. These values include human welfare, environmental quality and wildlife support.

Products generated by wetlands include: wildlife resources, fisheries, forest resources; forage resources; agricultural resources; and water supply. These products are generated by the interactions between the biological, chemical and physical components of a wetland.

Attributes of a wetland include biological diversity and unique cultural and heritage features. These attributes may lead to certain uses or the derivation of particular products, but they may also have intrinsic, unquantifiable importance.

...

3. Guidelines for operation of the Montreux Record

3.1 The Montreux Record is the principal tool of the Convention for highlighting those sites where an adverse change in ecological character has occurred, is occurring, or is likely to occur, and which are therefore in need of priority conservation attention. It shall be maintained as part of the Ramsar Database and shall be subject to continuous review.

3.2 The following procedure should be observed when considering the possible inclusion of a listed site in the Montreux Record:

3.2.1. A Contracting Party may request inclusion of a site in the Montreux Record, because of potential or actual adverse change in its ecological character, in order to draw attention to the need for action or support. Alternatively, the Bureau, on receipt of information on actual or possible adverse change from partner organizations, other international or national NGOs, or other interested bodies, may draw the attention of the Contracting Party concerned to this information and enquire whether a Ramsar site should be included in the Montreux Record. A site can only be included in the Record with the approval of the Contracting Party concerned.

3.2.2 The Bureau will pass the information received from partner organizations, other international or national NGOs, or other interested bodies, to the Contracting Party, together with a concise, voluntary questionnaire...normally to be returned to the Bureau within three months. However, this deadline should be flexible to take into account the circumstances of developing countries and Contracting Parties whose economies are in transition.

3.2.3 The completed questionnaire will, with the agreement of the Contracting Party, be forwarded by the Bureau to the Scientific and Technical Review Panel (STRP) for advice in line with the 'Working Definitions and Guidelines for Describing and Maintaining the Ecological Character of Listed Sites'. The Bureau will, with the agreement of the Contracting Party, relay the completed questionnaire to the original source of the information. If the Contracting Party is not able to agree to this, the Bureau will relay the Contracting Party's decision.

3.2.4 Any technical comment or advice provided by the STRP will be forwarded by the Bureau to the Contracting Party and to the source of the information first received by the Bureau (if different from the Contracting Party).

3.2.5 The Bureau will discuss the STRP's comments and advice with the Contracting Party concerned, with the aim of determining what steps might be taken, including a decision as to whether the site should be included in the Montreux Record. The STRP and other interested bodies will, where appropriate, be informed of the decision made by the Contracting Party, in consultation with the Bureau.

3.2.6 Within the framework of their National Reports, Contracting Parties shall provide a report to the Convention Bureau on the conservation status of any sites included in the Montreux Record. If necessary further information will be provided to the Bureau on request.

Resolution VI.9 is concerned with cooperation with the Convention on Biological Diversity.[19] VI.9.14 invites the Third Meeting of the Conference of the Contracting Parties to the Biodiversity Convention, held in November 1996, to include in its agenda a report on progress achieved and problems encountered in implementing the Ramsar Convention because of the complementarity of the two Conventions. Resolution VI.10 calls for coordination between Ramsar and the Global Environment Facility and its implementing agencies, the World Bank, UNDP and UNEP.

(b) Designation as a biosphere reserve

Loch Druidibeg National Nature Reserve was given Biosphere Reserve status by the United Nations Education, Scientific and Cultural Organisation (UNESCO) in June 1976. This is an international designation which has no specific legal base and to which no specific legal protection attaches. It is primarily for educational and research purposes: UNESCO's Man and the Biosphere Network of significant examples of the biosphere throughout the world establishes a benchmark against which long-term changes to the biosphere can be studied. In the following, note how the features of interest include some, such as seaweeds and seals, that are in the sea rather than on the land. This is significant because United Kingdom nature conservation designations have traditionally focused on land. The powers which existed to designate marine areas were largely ignored until clearer provision for Marine Nature Reserves was made in the Conservation (Natural Habitats &c) Regulations 1994.[20]

UNESCO Man and the Biosphere (MAB) Information System, Biosphere Reserves, Compilation 4, October 1986

Physical Features

The underlying rock is the remains of an ancient eroded platform of Lewisian gneiss. The eastern section of the reserve is a gently sloping basin of peat

19 See ch 4, p 126.

20 SI 1994/ 2716, Reg 33. See LM Warren 'Law and Policy for Marine Protected Areas' in CP Rodgers (ed) *Nature Conservation and Countryside Law* (Cardiff: University of Wales Press, 1996), pp 65-88.

moorland, including Loch Druidibeg, which is shallow with many islands. The western part is 'machair', formed from shell sand, blown inland by the prevailing westerlies, making the peat more fertile. There are dunes along the coast and several small lochs which are eutrophic in the west grading to ologotrophic in the east. The climate is temperate moist oceanic.

Vegetation

The eastern section is least affected by man and has moorland vegetation with raised and low bog, dwarf shrub and deciduous bog shrub. The western section is predominantly machair, with freshwater marsh, reed swamp, dune grasslands and dune slack mires to permanent pasture inland. There are few trees but some scrub occurs on the islands in Loch Druidibeg and a small experimental plantation of the once native hardwoods of the Outer Islands has been established. The machair grasslands are rich in species, both cultivated and uncultivated, including the largest British fern, the royal fern *Osmunda regalis* is among them. Machair lochs contain species not commonly found in northern Scotland. The fucoid seaweeds *(Phaeophycacea)* are well represented in the marine plant associations.

Fauna

The reserve was established as a sanctuary for the biggest surviving population of greylag geese *Anser anser* in Britain. Mammals include short-tailed vole *Microtus agrestis* and otter *Lutra lutra* by Loch Druidibeg. The grey seal *Halichoerus grypus* is common offshore. Typical moorland birds occur in the east while duck and several species of waders breed and overwinter in the lochs and marshy areas of the west. The lochs and running waters contain salmon *Salmo salar* and both sea and brown trout *lmo trutta subspp.* The common eel *Anguilla vulgaris* occurs and two species of stickleback, three-spined *Gasterosteus aculeatus* and nine-spined *Pungitius pungitius.* Some of the freshwater aquatic species are uncommon or not found in mainland freshwaters. Over 900 species of invertebrate have been identified.

(c) Designation as a Geological Conservation Review Site

The area is also a Geological Conservation Review Site of importance as the following extracts from the National Nature Reserve Management Plan show. The Geological Conservation Review designation is the result of the attempt by the National Conservancy Council (now SNH) to redress the imbalance between the biological importance of sites (which has been the main impulse for designating a site as a SSSI) and its geological importance which has hitherto received less attention. In time, inclusion of a site on SNH's Geological Conservation Review Site will mean that it will automatically be notified as a SSSI and thus attract legal protection.

GCR Block: Lewisian
Name of Site: Loch Skipport
Grid Ref: NF 812384

Present Status:The GCR site largely overlaps in part with the existing NNR Loch Druidibeg.

Statement of Interest:
The gneisses of this site record some of the best evidence for late Scourian and Laxfordian structural and metamorphic history. Many of the gneisses are in orthopyroxene-clinopyroxene granulite facies, though the metadolerites of the Scourie dyke suite show only amphibolite or garnet-clinopyroxene bearing assemblages. The gneisses contain metasedimentary horizons, the outcrop of which traces out late Scourian and Laxfordian folds. Early (Scourian) basic rocks are extensively and spectacularly agmatised; intruded and broken up by various ages of granitic veins, and this area is probably one of the best areas of Lewisian rock for any study of migmatisation. The Laxfordian deformation was locally intense, the Scourie dykes are now almost concordant with the gneissic banding and have been deformed by several phases of folding; this is the type area for the development of the late Laxfordian (F4) fold set. The site shows a wide range of Lewisian rock types and affords an important record of regional structural and metamorphic history.

and

GCR

Part of the Reserve is covered by the Ardivachar – Stoneybridge Geological Conservation Review Site.

Citation
GCR Block: Beach Complexes
Name of Site: Ardivachar – Stoneybridge, South Uist
Grid Ref: NF 758472 – NF 727334

Present Status:
a. The GCR site overlaps in part with the existing SSSI named Howmore Estuary etc. and the Loch Druidibeg NNR
b. The GCR site is a new earth science site.

Further GCR Interest:
The site also contains an area believed to be of GCR standard for the following interest:

Precambrian

Statement of Interest:
A single beach complex extending for more than 20kms from Ardivachar to Stoneybridge. To the north, Gualann Island represents the remains of the much larger submerged and fragmented dune and machair system, dissected portions of which are seen scattered throughout the site. The coastal dunes display a wide variety of erosional forms whilst inland, on the low flat machair plain, are extensive areas of redepositional dune hummocks and an especially well developed and prominent escarpment edge. Here, the landform assemblage conforms with the classic beach-dune-machair sequence in its type location, the Uists. From beach to 'blackland' the sequence includes coastal dune ridge, low, flat, seasonally

flooded machair plain, retreating escarpment, hilly machair backslope and machair loch. The low machair plain represents the ultimate stage in machair development formed as a result of deflation by scarp retreat. This site includes the area in the Hebrides where most research into machair development has been undertaken. The extensive, continuously developed system and the range and variety of erosional and depositional forms found makes this site of outstanding geomorphological importance as a beach complex.

10 EUROPEAN COMMUNITY LAW

(a) Designation as a Special Protection Area

In August 1982 Loch Druidibeg National Nature Reserve was declared a Special Protection Area under Directive 79/409/EEC[21] on the conservation of wild birds. It fulfils the criteria for designation since it is important for breeding greylag geese, waders, hen harriers and corncrakes. It will shortly be incorporated into the larger South Uist Machair Special Protection Area now being designated.

Council Directive of 2 April 1979 on the Conservation of Wild Birds (79/409/ EEC), OJ L 103, 27.4.1979

...

Whereas a large number of species of wild birds naturally occurring in the European territory of the Member States are declining in number, very rapidly in some cases; whereas this decline represents a serious threat to the conservation of the natural environment, particularly because of the biological balances threatened thereby;

Whereas the species of wild birds naturally occurring in the European territory of the Member States are mainly migratory species; whereas such species constitute a common heritage and whereas effective bird protection is typically a trans-frontier environment problem entailing common responsibilities;

...

Article 1

1. This Directive relates to the conservation of all species of naturally occurring birds in the wild state in the European territory of the Member States to which the Treaty applies. It covers the protection, management and control of these species and lays down rules for their exploitation.
2. It shall apply to birds, their eggs, nests and habitats.

...

Article 4

1. The species mentioned in Annex I shall be the subject of special conservation measures concerning their habitat in order to ensure their survival and reproduction in their area of distribution.

21 OJ L 103, 25.4.1979.

In this connection, account shall be taken of:
(a) species in danger of extinction;
(b) species vulnerable to specific changes in their habitat;
(c) species considered rare because of small populations or restricted local distribution;
(d) other species requiring particular attention for reasons of the specific nature of their habitat.

Trends and variations in population levels shall be taken into account as a background for evaluations.

Member States shall classify in particular the most suitable territories in number and size as special protection areas for the conservation of these species, taking into account their protection requirements in the geographical sea and land area where this Directive applies.

2. Member States shall take similar measures for regularly occurring migratory species not listed in Annex I, bearing in mind their need for protection in the geographical sea and land area where this Directive applies, as regards their breeding, moulting and wintering areas and staging posts along their migration routes. To this end, Member States shall pay particular attention to the protection of wetlands and particularly to wetlands of international importance.

3. Member States shall send the Commission all relevant information so that it may take appropriate initiatives with a view to the coordination necessary to ensure that the areas provided for in paragraphs 1 and 2 above form a coherent whole which meets the protection requirements of these species in the geographical sea and land area where this Directive applies.

4. In respect of the protection areas referred to in paragraphs 1 and 2 above, Member States shall take appropriate steps to avoid pollution or deterioration of habitats or any disturbances affecting the birds, in so far as these would be significant having regard to the objectives of this Article. Outside these protection areas, Member States shall also strive to avoid pollution or deterioration of the habitats.

...

Note that Article 4(2) obliges Member States to pay particular attention to wetlands of international importance, thereby effectively implementing the Ramsar Convention in Community law.

In Loch Druidibeg we have three layers of designation for the protection of birds: a United Kingdom National Nature Reserve, an international Ramsar Site and a European Community Special Protection Area. In theory this further designation as a Special Protection Area (SPA) gives additional legal protection. SPAs are crucial to the European Union's Natura 2000 ecological network of nature conservation sites under Article 3 of Directive 92/43/EEC on the conservation of natural habitats and of wild fauna and flora (see below), which contributes to fulfilling obligations under the Biodiversity Convention signed in 1992 at Rio.[22] The larger South Uist Machair SPA designation is to provide

22 See ch 4, p 126 for the text of this.

a larger site in the Natura 2000 network. It is interesting to see that this network builds on the thinking of the Huxley Committee of the 1940s, that plants and animals do not recognise political borders.

The protection accorded to SPAs could be overridden if it can be shown that a development project is of major public interest, be it social or economic.[23] This means that in the very unlikely event of the United Kingdom government deciding to, say, drain Loch Druidibeg for a development purpose, then this might be permitted under the terms of the Directive. This hypothetical development scheme throws into relief one of the potential conflicts of interest between designations: in this case the conflict would be between the two European Community aims of economic development for North West Scotland under Objective 1 regional development and the nature conservation objective of both the Birds Directive and the Habitats Directive.[23a] The underlying problem, however, is that in Britain the whole legal structure for conservation still rests on the shaky foundation of the SSSI system.[24]

The designation of Loch Druidibeg as an SPA seems to have no immediate practical effect since the obligations of the Birds Directive were being complied with, in line with the management plan for the National Nature Reserve, before the Directive was adopted.

(b) Designation as a Special Area of Conservation

Directive 92/43/EEC on the conservation of natural habitats and of wild fauna and flora (see below) has been implemented in the United Kingdom by the Conservation (Natural Habitats etc) Regulations 1994 (SI 1994/2716). The Directive has as its main focus the creation of an ecological network called Natura 2000 made up of special areas of conservation designated under the Habitats Directive and Special Protection Areas under the Birds Directive. The whole National Nature Reserve is a potential Special Area of Conservation (SAC) for the machair, the lochs and the species 'Najas flexilis'. Another possible SAC has been proposed for the whole of South Uist Machair which would extend the machair addition to the original Reserve by an orthogonal limb running north to south, coinciding with the coastal part of

23 In Case C-355/90: *Commission v Spain (Marismas de Santoña)* [1993] ECR I-883 the European Court of Justice decided that Spain was in breach of the Birds Directive for failing to designate the Santoña Marshes which fulfilled the objective ornithological criteria of the Directive. In Case C-57/89: *Commission v Germany (Leybucht Dykes)* [1991] ECR I-883 the ECJ decided that the only exceptions to Art 4(4) obligations were where the works were necessary for reasons of public health or public safety, not for economic or recreational reasons. This decision was reversed by Art 6 of the Habitats Directive. In Case C-44/95: *R v Secretary of State for the Environment, ex p RSPB (Lappel Bank)*, see ch 5, 'Losing the economic base: *Lappel Bank*', the ECJ again confirmed that economic considerations could not override ornithological criteria when designating a site. However, Art 6(4) of the Habitats Directive allows a Member State to allow development of an existing SPA for imperative reasons of overriding public interest.

23a See further J Scott *Development Dilemmas in the European Community* (Buckingham: Open University Press, 1995).

24 See further ch 7, 'Countryside designation'.

the Geological Conservation Review site. This possible SAC has now been submitted to the Commission for consideration as part of the Natura 2000 network.

Council Directive 92/43/EEC of 21 May 1992 on the Conservation of Natural Habitats and of Wild Fauna and Flora, OJ L 206, 21.5.1992.

...

Whereas, the main aim of this Directive being to promote the maintenance of biodiversity, taking account of economic, social, cultural and regional requirements, this Directive makes a contribution to the general objective of sustainable development; whereas the maintenance of such diversity may in certain cases require the maintenance, or indeed the encouragement, of human activities;

Whereas, in the European territory of the Member States, natural habitats are continuing to deteriorate and an increasing number of wild species are seriously threatened; whereas given that the threatened habitats and species form part of the Community's natural heritage and the threats to them are often of a transboundary nature, it is necessary to take measures at Community level in order to conserve them;

Whereas, in view of the threats to certain types of natural habitat and certain species, it is necessary to define them as having priority in order to favour the early implementation of measures to conserve them;

Whereas, in order to ensure the restoration or maintenance of natural habitats and species of Community interest at a favourable conservation status, it is necessary to designate special areas of conservation in order to create a coherent European ecological network according to a specified timetable;

Whereas all the areas designated, including those classified now or in the future as special protection areas pursuant to Council Directive 79/409/EEC of 2 April 1979 on the conservation of wild birds,[25] will have to be incorporated into the coherent European ecological network;

...

Conservation of natural habitats and habitats of species

Article 3

1. A coherent European ecological network of special areas of conservation shall be set up under the title Natura 2000. This network, composed of sites hosting the natural habitat types listed in Annex I and habitats of the species listed in Annex II, shall enable the natural habitat types and the species' habitats concerned to be maintained or, where appropriate, restored at a favourable conservation status in their natural range.

25 OJ L103, 25.4.1979, p 1. Directive as last amended by Directive 91/244/EEC (OJ L 115, 8.5.1991, p 41).

The Natura 2000 network shall include the special protection areas classified by the Member States pursuant to Directive 79/409/EEC.
2. Each Member State shall contribute to the creation of Natura 2000 in proportion to the representation within its territory of the natural habitat types and the habitats of species referred to in paragraph 1. To that effect each Member State shall designate, in accordance with Article 4, sites as special areas of conservation taking account of the objectives set out in paragraph 1.
3. Where they consider it necessary, Member States shall endeavour to improve the ecological coherence of Natura 2000 by maintaining, and where appropriate developing, features of the landscape which are of importance for wild fauna and flora.

Article 4
1. On the basis of criteria set out in Annex III (Stage 1) and relevant scientific information, each Member State shall propose a list of sites indicating which natural habitat types in Annex I and which species in Annex II that are native to its territory the sites host. For animal species ranging over wide areas these sites shall correspond to the places within the natural range of such species which present the physical or biological factors essential to their life and reproduction. For aquatic species which range over wide areas, such sites will be proposed only where there is a clearly identifiable area representing the physical and biological factors essential to their life and reproduction. Where appropriate, Member States shall propose adaptation of the lists in the light of the results of the surveillance referred to in Article 11.
The list shall be transmitted to the Commission within three years of the notification of this Directive, together with information on each site. That information shall include a map of the site, its name, location, extent and the data resulting from application of the criteria specified in Annex III (Stage 1) provided in a format established by the Commission in accordance with the procedure laid down in Article 21.
...

Article 6
1. For special areas of conservation, Member States shall establish the necessary measures invoking, if need be, appropriate management plans specifically designed for the site or integrated into other development plans, and appropriate statutory, administrative or contractual measures which correspond to the ecological requirements of the natural habitat types in Annex I and the species in Annex II present on the sites.
2. Member States shall take appropriate steps to avoid, in the special areas of conservation, the deterioration of natural habitats and habitats of species as well as disturbance of the species for which the areas have been designated, in so far as such disturbance could be significant in relation to the objectives of this Directive.
3. Any plan or project not directly connected with or necessary to the management of the site but likely to have a significant effect thereon, either individually or in combination with other plans or projects, shall be subject to appropriate assessment of its implications for the site in view of the

site's conservation objectives. In the light of the conclusions of the assessment of the implications of the site and subject to the provisions of paragraph 4, the competent national authorities shall agree to the plan or project only after having ascertained that it will not adversely affect the integrity of the site and, if appropriate, after having obtained the opinion of the general public.

4. If, in spite of a negative assessment of the implications for the site and in the absence of alternative solutions, a plan or project must nevertheless be carried out for imperative reasons of overriding public interest, including those of a social or economic nature, the Member State shall take all compensatory measures necessary to ensure that the overall coherence of Natura 2000 is protected. It shall inform the Commission of the compensatory measures adopted.

Whereas the site concerned hosts a priority natural habitat type and/or a priority species, the only considerations which may be raised are those relating to human health or public safety, to beneficial consequences of primary importance for the environment or, further to an opinion from the Commission, to other imperative reasons of overriding public interest.

...

11 AGRICULTURAL DESIGNATIONS

Loch Druidibeg National Nature Reserve lies within the Less Favoured Area which covers all of north west Scotland.

As the United Kingdom's report to the Ramsar Convention Conference points out, changes in farming and crofting in the Loch Druidibeg Nature Reserve have been going on for the last fifty years. South Uist crofters have responded to the Common Agricultural Policy of the European Community along with farmers all over the European Union. The increased numbers of sheep mentioned in the Ramsar report are such a response but less fertile, sparsely populated and remote areas are disadvantaged in a common policy. However, it was conflicts over land use in England that spurred the United Kingdom government to find a way to resolve the incompatibility of modern, intensive farming with conservation of the countryside.

P Wathern, 'Less Favoured and Environmentally Sensitive Areas: a European dimension to the rural environment' in W Howarth and CP Rodgers (eds), *Agriculture, Conservation and Land Use* (Cardiff: University of Wales Press, 1992), pp 187-189

Thus, it can be seen that environmental regulation and policy style in the UK are influenced significantly by EC membership. However, this is also a forum in which the UK is able to exert an influence. This interplay is equally evident in relation to the rural environment, especially in sparsely populated areas. By far the greatest influence of the EC upon the rural environment is through the Common Agricultural Policy (CAP). Most of the massive CAP budget goes into support for large intensive farms (the guarantee section), with relatively little to aid the small farmer.

In 1989 a mere 4.9 per cent was allotted to the guidance section which mainly benefits small farmers, even though they comprised about thirty per cent of the total within the EC. In part this maldistribution can be explained in terms of the emphasis on price support in the CAP which constitutes, in effect, a subsidy on production. It is also a reflection of the free-trade provisions of the Treaty of Rome which, in essence, demand that all producers must be treated alike with none given favoured treatment over other comparable producers. Special support can only be channelled to particular groups of farmers if they are rendered in some way 'not comparable' with the remainder. Two designations have been adopted at an EC level in order to achieve this objective with respect to special groups of farmers. These are provided for in the Less Favoured Areas (LFA) and Environmentally Sensitive Areas (ESA) programmes...

These programmes can be regarded, in part, as an acknowledgement of the need to balance the various demands currently placed upon the rural environment in the UK. No longer simply used for producing agricultural commodities, rural areas are also needed to provide land for growing timber, for water supply and as recreational space for an increasingly urban population. In addition, rural areas, especially the wild uplands, provide an increasingly valuable resource for wildlife and landscape conservation. The fate of human populations within these areas is also an integral consideration in securing their long-term future, for the character of even the upland areas is dependent upon the continuation of low intensity management. However, the rural areas have their own special social and economic problems. They have a long history of depopulation coupled with a decline in the importance of agriculture to the rural economy...

Both the LFA and ESA policies seek to sustain the rural economy through payments of cash subsidies. There are, however, important differences between the schemes related not only to the basis for legal support, but also to the targeting of the payments. The LFA is a relatively old policy dating from 1975.[26] It provides for payments which are largely subsidies on production. As such, the policy can be regarded as merely a continuation of the basic CAP philosophy with respect to subsidies [the increase in the numbers of sheep grazing around Loch Druidibeg is a response to this policy]...The ESA policy, however, represents somewhat of a revolution in the way that payments are made to farmers *pro rata* on their land holding for a variety of services and activities.

The European Community Regulation on improving the efficiency of agricultural structures[27] was the result of the United Kingdom's initiative. Article 19(1) provides for Member States to establish national schemes for 'the introduction or continued use of agricultural production practices compatible with the requirements of conserving the natural habitat ensuring an adequate income for farmers' within specially designated environmentally sensitive areas defined in Article 19(2) as being 'of recognised importance from an ecological or landscape

26 Directive 75/268/EEC on mountain and hill farming in certain less favoured areas, OJ 18, L128 19.5.1975.
27 OJ L93, p 1, 30.3.1985.

point of view'. Even though the United Kingdom government had proposed the ESA provisions at European Community level, it had no domestic legal base on which to implement the scheme until the Agriculture Act 1986. Section 17 put in place what came to be known in United Kingdom agricultural policy circles as the 'twin track' policy, coupling conservation and agriculture.

Agriculture Act 1986

s. 17 Duty to balance interests in exercise of agricultural functions:

(1) In discharging any functions connected with agriculture in relation to any land the Minister shall, so far as is consistent with the proper and efficient discharge of those functions, have regard to and endeavour to achieve a reasonable balance between the following considerations -

(a) the promotion and maintenance of a stable and efficient agricultural industry;
(b) the economic and social interests of rural areas;
(c) the conservation and enhancement of the natural beauty and amenity of the countryside (including its flora and fauna and geological and physiographical features) and of any features of archaeological interest there; and
(d) the promotion of the enjoyment of the countryside by the public.

In Scotland twenty areas were investigated with a view to designation and short listed to two priority areas and three of lower priority.[28] The machair lands of the Uists and Benbecula was one of the two Scottish priority areas but it was not designated initially, possibly because of conflict with the European Community Integrated Development Programme which was providing assistance for crofters to improve their holdings.[29] This is a historic example of conflict between designations and lends credence to our conjecture that there could be conflict between the European Union Objective 1 regional development programme and the nature conservation designations. Whilst it is most unlikely that there would be a development project which would damage Loch Druidibeg directly, such as the drainage we suggested above as a hypothetical project, a significant increase in tourism might create a conflict.

The Machair of the Uists and Benbecula, Barra and Vatersay was finally designated as an ESA in 1988. Wathern assesses the ESA programme as having 'produced a system for subsidizing farmers which does not encourage them to increase production, but rather to continue to manage their farms in an environmentally benign way. Indeed in the South Downs ESA and in the Scottish ESAs a more positive approach has been adopted which goes beyond merely maintaining the status quo by seeking to improve environmental quality'.[30] In 1993 the ESA of our case study was revised and extended. Participation is again entirely voluntary but this time those who join the scheme are being offered more money in exchange for more management expectations.

28 Wathern, op cit, p 203.
29 See Wathern, op cit, p 204.
30 Wathern, op cit, p 206.

The Scottish Office Agriculture and Fisheries Department *M/ESA 1* 1994 p 5

Explanatory Leaflet for Crofters and Farmers

Part III How to Join the ESA Scheme

Who is eligible to join the Scheme?
9. To be eligible, you must be an individual crofter or farmer with an interest in agricultural land wholly or partly within the designated Area and be in a position to undertake the required management of this land. Applicants will normally be individual crofting or farming tenants or owner occupiers; however, applications from others with an interest in agricultural land, for example, partnerships, trusts and possibly joint applications from tenants and landlords may be acceptable. The critical point is that the applicant must be in a position to undertake his/her side of the agreement. Common grazings committees are also eligible to join the Scheme in their own right and guidance is given in a separate leaflet.

Do I have to inform anyone else if I apply?
10. If you are a tenant the answer is 'YES'. It is an important requirement that you notify your landlord when you enter an agreement by sending him or her the notification form which accompanies this leaflet. This informs your landlord of your intention to apply and lists the main conditions of the agreement. The Department will ask you to confirm on the application form that you have notified your landlord, but will not require any written approval from him/her before accepting your application unless the land belongs to the Crown and is managed by the Crown Estates Commissioners, in which case consent of the Crown Commissioners will be required. You should, however, ensure that your tenancy agreement will not be adversely affected by joining the Scheme, or that the tenancy does not contain any conditions which will affect your ability to undertake the Scheme requirements.

What about joint applications between landlord and tenant?
11. As mentioned above, these will be considered, but the persons concerned will need to agree amongst themselves the division of ESA responsibilities and payments.

Can I apply to bring part of my croft or farm into the Scheme even if all of the land is in the designated area?
12. No. Applications must relate to all land farmed as a single business within the ESA. Individual crofters or farmers must bring into the Scheme their traditional share of the common machair and parts of the common grazings which have been apportioned for their own exclusive use together with any inbye land.

...

Will it be possible to bring land into the Scheme if it is already designated as a Site of Special Scientific Interest (SSSI), National Nature Reserve (NNR), National Scenic Area (NSA) or Scheduled Ancient Monument?
15. Yes; these designations do not affect eligibility to join the Scheme. However, if you already have a management agreement with Scottish Natural Heritage (SNH), Historic Scotland (HS) or Local Authority, which provides payments in relation to particular areas of land, then the land in question may be ineligible

for ESA payments. Rules have been drawn up to prevent double-funding by public agencies and we will discuss cases of this sort with applicants either before or after an application has been submitted.

Explanatory Leaflet for Common Grazings Committees M/ESA 1A – 1994, p 3

What are the aims of this ESA?

5. In order to conserve and enhance the characteristic landscape and habitats and to protect features of historic interest, the main aims of the ESA are:

- to protect, enhance and extend the existing natural and semi-natural habitats of wetlands and water margins, unimproved and herb rich grassland, dunes, coastal grassland and maritime heath;
- to protect features or areas of historic or archaeological interest and allow for their management;
- to encourage the introduction or continuation of rotational cropping or fodder production in a way which conserves and enhances the natural heritage value of both the machair and non-machair land.

The Environmentally Sensitive Area designation is important as a buffer zone for the Reserve but the encouragement given to crofters by it for positive conservation runs up against the Common Agricultural Policy subsidy regime that favours sheep. The European Commission's ban on exporting beef and cattle from Britain[31] is now the major obstacle to keeping cattle and therefore threatens the conservation value of the site. Scottish Natural Heritage is exploring ways to address this.

12 CROFTING AND RARE SPECIES

The original (1958) National Nature Reserve was designated amongst other things for the benefit of the birds, particularly the greylag geese, but on the machair extension (of 1962, see above) to the Reserve the crofters fill an essential role in a complex ecosystem. On the moorland their activities are less beneficial since they tend to burn it too much and too often. Reseeding the grass on the blackland together with the encouragement of machair fencing as part of the Integrated Development Programme during the 1980s improved the grazing for stock but this was not necessarily good for the habitat, which can now be overgrazed. The stock are taken off the machair in summer and ideally should be out on the hill allowing some of the blackland to be used for growing hay, as was done traditionally. Paradoxically though, it is quite possible that the Integrated Development Programme made a contribution to the recovery of goose numbers: better grazing for the crofters' cattle and sheep on the reseeded areas was also better grazing for the geese.

The greylag goose population in the Uists as a whole has increased to around 2,500. The key to this success has been the work of the Goose

31 OJ L 78/47, 27.3.1996.

Management Committee on which sit representatives from Scottish Natural Heritage, the estates which own most of the land in the Uists, the Crofters' Union, the Crofters' Commission and the Scottish Office Agriculture and Fisheries Department. This Goose Management Committee meets at intervals and operates as a forum for discussion and co-operation. For instance, the Goose Committee holds a stock of goose scarers which it can lend to crofters, as well as giving advice and recording complaints. Twice a year there is a goose count involving crofters, the estates and agencies so the success or failure of a strategy may be monitored regularly.

13 CONCLUSION

This case study has shown that the conceptual basis of nature conservation has developed since the National Nature Reserve was first designated in the 1950s, from metaphorically fencing off an area for anthropocentric nature study to positive conservation that seeks to enhance the habitats. The legal developments have been that British law operated first, then there were international designations which, whilst still resting on the imperfect British system with the fatal flaw of inadequate protection for SSSIs, do enable submissions by NGOs such as Friends of the Earth to bring pressure to bear on the government in international forums. Then European Community nature conservation law, implementing international conventions, is putting in place the ambitious Natura 2000 programme. In theory, this allows for some enforcement by the European Court of Justice should the United Kingdom fail to implement the Birds and Habitats Directives properly.

Loch Druidibeg National Nature Reserve exemplifies an interesting assemblage of designations but the wildlife cannot survive by the law alone. It needs good advice to the crofters, management schemes for them, and good will and co-operation from them.

Epilogue

EPILOGUE

Environmental justice

The last few years have seen an explosion of legislation aimed at protecting the environment. Environmental law is now a mainstream legal discipline. We should be aware though that environmental law, as it has been conventionally defined, practised and taught, has contributed to the social justice requirements of sustainable development being marginalised. This is because environmental law has generally defined 'the environment' narrowly as environmental media – air, water and land – and 'nature conservation', and part of the sustainable development agenda has been absorbed into the existing legal framework, rendering its effects more rhetorical than practical. Many are doing the sustainable development dance. We see this buzzword in a whole range of legal documents – international treaties, planning policy guidance notes, and also in corporate plans and advertisements; a process of dispersing, and very possibly diluting, environmental responsibilities.

The Nairobi Declaration 1982, adopted by the United Nations, spelt out the social justice dimension of sustainable development. Progress, even in acknowledging this dimension, has been grindingly slow. Worldwide, environmental harms still bear most heavily on the poor, the young, the old, and the vulnerable and it has always been the poor who live in the most polluted places. And the landscape of environmental law in the United Kingdom is littered with the failed challenges of those who wish not necessarily to create a better world but to be able to live and breathe in this one.

There has been a deliberate misreading of the political and economic implications of sustainable development, with a consistent emphasis on *inter*-generational equity, rather than on the equally significant imperative of *intra*-generational equity – the redistribution of resources for those alive now. The danger is that this emptying of content of sustainable development will lead to little more than bequeathing our status quo to future generations, instead of a radical realignment of social relations now. The objective of sustainable development is, after all, to make a better world not just a 'cleaner environment'. We need to relearn that social, as well as pollution externalities, to use the economists' jargon, derive from unsustainable ways of life and production. The next stage must be to make clearer linkages between environmental harms and social injustice. In the meantime, the silence in environmental law on *social* justice remains significant and potentially harmful.

There has been much discussion, outside law, about the nature of 'nature' and what is and is not 'the environment', let alone what should be done. This should not be ignored by those who wish to transform the way things are at present. Harvey highlights the centrality of this:

> The present battles being waged over the concepts of 'nature' and the 'environment' are of immense importance. All critical examinations of the relation to nature are simultaneously critical examinations of society. The incredible vigour with which ruling interests have sought to contain, shape, mystify and muddy the contemporary debate over nature and environment (for the most part within discourses of 'ecological modernisation', 'sustainability', 'green consumerism' or the commodification and sale of 'nature' as a cultural spectacle) testifies to the seriousness.[1]

Law is, however, fundamental to this attempt to 'contain, shape, mystify and muddy' the debate. The weakness of much of the law in practice contrasts with its rhetoric of environmental concern, sustainability and stewardship: this contrast is the product of compromise. The generality of the law is shaped by, and serves best, the interests of large capital but there are opportunities - opportunities that can be seized and opportunities that must be seized. What is at stake is using the law to empower people to redefine their relationships with nature and with each other.

1 D Harvey, *Justice, Nature and the Geography of Difference* (Oxford: Blackwell, 1996) p 174.

Bibliography and further reading

Adams, J. *Risk* (London: University College London Press, 1995).

Atiyah, P. S. *An Introduction to the Law of Contract* (London: Weidenfeld and Nicholson, 1981).

– 'Railway Nuisances in the English Common Law: A Historical Footnote' (1980) 23 *Journal of Law and Economics*, 191.

Ball, S. and Bell, S. *Environmental Law: The Law and Policy Relating to the Environment*, 3rd ed. (London: Blackstone Press, 1994).

Banuri, T. and Marglin, F. A. *Who Will Save the Forests? Knowledge, Power and Environmental Destruction* (London: Zed Books, 1993).

Barry, J. 'Deep Ecology and the Undermining of Green Politics' in Holder, J. et al (eds), *Perspectives on the Environment* (Aldershot: Avebury, 1993).

Beevers, R. *The Garden City Utopia* (Hampshire: Macmillan, 1988).

Birnie, P. and Boyle, A. *International Law and The Environment* (Oxford: Clarendon Press, 1993).

Birtles, W. and Stein, R. *Planning and Environmental Law* (London: Longman, 1994).

Blowers, A. (ed) *Planning for a Sustainable Environment: A Report by the Town and Country Planning Association* (London: Earthscan, 1993).

Boucher, S. and Whatmore, S. 'Green Gains? Planning by Agreement and Nature Conservation' (1993) *Journal of Environmental Planning and Management*, Vol. 36, No. 1, 33.

Brenner, J. F. 'Nuisance Law and the Industrial Revolution' (1974) 3 *Journal of Legal Studies*, 403.

Caldwell, L. K. *Between Two Worlds: Science, the Environmental Movement and Policy Choice* (Cambridge: Cambridge University Press, 1992).

Cameron, J. and Werksman, J. 'The Precautionary Principle: A Policy for Action in the Face of Uncertainty', CIEL Background Paper (London: FIELD, 1991).

Campaign for the Protection of Rural England (CPRE), *General Policy and Principles: Response to the Department of the Environment's Draft Planning Policy Guidance Note 1* (London: CPRE, 1991).

Carley, M. and Christie, I. *Managing Sustainable Development* (London: Earthscan, 1992).

Carson, R. *The Silent Spring* (London: Penguin, 1963).

Checkland, S. G. *The Rise of Industrial Society in England 1815-1855* (London: Longmans, 1969).

Chief Inspector of the Alkali Inspectorate, *Ninth Annual Report* (London: HMSO, 1873).

Close, G. 'Harmonisation of Laws: Use or Abuse of Powers under the EEC Treaty' (1978) *European Law Review*, Vol. 3, 461.

Coates, I. 'Environmental Concern in Britain 1919-1949: Diversity and Continuity', in Elworthy, S. et al (eds) *Perspectives on the Environment* 2 (Aldershot: Avebury, 1995).

Commission of the European Communities (CEC), *Implementing Community Environmental Law* COM(96) 500 final, 28.11.1996 (Brussels: CEC, 1996).

– *Report of the Group of Independent Experts in Legislative and Administrative Simplification* COM(95) 288 final, 21.6.1995 (Brussels: CEC, 1995).

– *Economic Growth and the Environment: Some Implications for Economic Policy Making* COM(94) 465 final, 3.11.1994 (Brussels: CEC, 1994).

– *Green Paper on Remedying Environmental Damage* COM(93) 47 final (Brussels: CEC, 1993).

– *Tenth Annual Report to the European Parliament on Commission Monitoring of the Application of Community Law*, OJ C 233/6, 30.8.1993 (Brussels: CEC, 1993).

– *Commission Report to the European Council on the Adaptation of Community Legislation to the Subsidiarity Principle* COM(93) 545 final, 24.11.1993 (Brussels: CEC, 1993).

Committee on Public Participation in Planning (Skeffington Committee), *People and Planning* (London: HMSO, 1969).

Committee on Air Pollution (Beaver Committee), *Air Pollution*, 1953-54 Interim and Final Report, Cmd 9011, Cmd 9322 (London: HMSO).

Committee on Land Utilisation in Rural Areas (Scott Committee) *Land Utilisation in Rural Areas* Cmnd. 6378 (London: HMSO, 1943).

Conway, R. and Barbier, E. *After the Green Revolution: Sustainable Agriculture and Development* (London: Earthscan, 1990).

Crane, A. 'Rhetoric and Reality in the Greening of Organisational Culture' (1995) 12 *Greener Management International*, 49.

Crook, S., Pakulski J. and Waters, M. *Postmodernization: Change in Advanced Society* (London: Sage, 1992).

Cullingworth, J. B. and Nadin, V. *Town and Country Planning in Britain*, 11th ed. (London: Routledge, 1994).

Cunningham, P., Dix, T. and Snow, P. *Birdwatching in the Outer Hebrides* (Argyll: Saker Press, 1995).

Daintith, T. 'The Executive Power Today: Bargaining and Economic Control', in Jowell, J. and Oliver, D. (eds) *The Changing Constitution* (Oxford: Oxford University Press, 1989).

Dalal-Clayton, B. *Getting to Grips with Green Plans* (London: Earthscan, 1996).

Department of the Environment, Circular 11/95 *Conditions* (London: HMSO, 1995).

– *Planning Controls over Agricultural and Forestry Development and Rural Building Conversions* (London: HMSO, 1995).

– Planning Policy Guidance Note 9 *Nature Conservation* (London: HMSO, 1994).

– Planning Policy Guidance Note 13 *Transport* (London: HMSO, 1994).

– *Regional Planning Guidance for the Northern Region* (London: HMSO, 1993).

– Planning Policy Guidance Note 23 *Planning and Pollution Control* (London: HMSO, 1992).

– Planning Policy Guidance Note 1 *General Policy and Principles* (London: HMSO, 1992).
– Planning Policy Guidance Note 1 *General Policy and Principles* (London: HMSO, 1988).
– Circular 22/80 *Development Control: Policy and Practice* (London: HMSO, 1980).
– Circular 71/77 *Local Government and Industrial Strategy* (London: HMSO, 1977).
Dobson, A. *The Green Reader* (London: Andre Deutsch, 1991).
– *Green Political Thought* (London: Unwin Hyman, 1990).
Ehlermann, C. D. 'The Internal Market Following the Single European Act' (1987) *Common Market Law Review*, 361.
Elkington, J. and Hailes, J. *The Green Consumer Guide* (London: Victor Gollancz, 1989).
Elgin, D. *Voluntary Simplicity: Towards a Life that is Outwardly Simple and Inwardly Rich* (New York: William Morrow, 1981).
Elworthy, S. *Farming for Drinking Water: Nitrate Pollution of Water - An Assessment of a Regulatory Regime* (Aldershot: Avebury, 1994).
– 'Environmental Law in the Nineteenth Century and Early Twentieth Centuries', in Weick, G. (ed) *National and European Law on the Threshold to the Single Market* (Frankfurt am Main: Peter Lang, 1993).
Elworthy, S. et al (eds.) *Perspectives on the Environment 2* (Aldershot: Avebury, 1995).
Environmental Data Services Ltd (ENDS Ltd), *Integrated Pollution Control: The First Three Years* (London: ENDS Ltd, 1994).
European Economic Community, *Fifth Environmental Action Programme: Towards Sustainability - A European Community Programme of Policy and Action in Relation to the Environment and Sustainable Development* OJ C 138, 17.5.1993 (Brussels: Commission of the European Communities, 1993).
Evans, D. *A History of Nature Conservation in Britain* (London: Routledge, 1992).
Evelyn, J. *Fumifugium* (Brighton: National Society for Clean Air, 1961).
Evernden, N. *The Social Creation of Nature* (Baltimore: John Hopkins University Press, 1993).
Experts Group on Environmental Law of the World Commission of Environment and Development, *Environmental Protection and Sustainable Development* (Dordrecht: Graham and Trotman/Martinus Nijhoff, 1986).
Faure, M., Vervaele, J. and Weale, A. *Environmental Standards in the European Union in an Interdisciplinary Framework* (London: Blackstone Press, 1994).
Frankel, M. *The Alkali Inspectorate: The Control of Industrial Air Pollution* (London: Social Audit, 1974).
Füredi, F. 'The Dangers of Safety' (1996) *Living Marxism*, 17.
Gatenby, I. and Williams, C. 'Section 54A: The Legal and Practical Implications' [1992] *Journal of Planning and Environmental Law*, 110.
Gillot, J. and Kumar, M. *Science and the Retreat From Reason* (London: Merlin Press, 1995).
Girouard, M. *Cities and People: A Social and Architectural History* (New Haven/ London: Yale University Press: 1985).

Gore, A. *Earth in the Balance: Ecology and the Human Spirit* (New York: Penguin, 1993).

Grant, M. *Urban Planning Law* (London: Sweet and Maxwell, 1982).

Gray, K. 'Equitable Property', (1994) *Current Legal Problems* Vol. 47 (II), 157.

Gray, T. S. (ed) *UK Environmental Policy in the 1990s* (London: Macmillan, 1995).

Grove-White, R. 'Land Use Law and the Environment', (1991) *Journal of Law and Society*, Vol. 18, Special Issue: 'Environment, Law and Policy', 32.

Guruswamy L. D. and Tromans, S. 'Towards an Integrated Approach to Pollution Control: The Best Practicable Environmental Option and its Antecedents' [1986] *Journal of Planning and Environmental Law*, 643.

Haas, E. *The Unity of Europe: Political, Economic and Social Forces 1950-57* (Stanford: Stanford University Press, 1958).

Hajer, M. A. *The Politics of Environmental Discourse: Ecological Modernisation and the Policy Process* (Oxford: Oxford University Press, 1995).

Hall, D., Hebbert, M. and Lusser, H. 'The Planning Background', in Blowers, A. (ed), *Planning for a Sustainable Environment* (London: Earthscan, 1993).

Handler, T. (ed) *Regulating the European Environment*, 2nd ed (London: Baker and McKenzie, 1993).

Hardy, D. *From Garden Cities to New Towns: Campaigning for Town and Country Planning 1889-1946* (London: Spon, 1991)

– *From New Towns to Green Politics: Campaigning for Town and Country Planning 1946-1990* (London: Spon, 1991).

Hardy D. and Ward C. *Arcadia for All: The Legacy of a Makeshift Landscape* (London: Mansell, 1984).

Harrison, M. 'A Presumption in Favour of Development?' [1992] *Journal of Planning and Environmental Law,* 121.

Harvey, D. *Justice, Nature and the Geography of Difference* (Oxford: Blackwell, 1996).

Healey, P., Purdue, M. and Ennis, F. *Negotiating Development: Rationales and Practice for Development Obligations and Planning Gain* (London: Spon, 1995).

Health and Safety Executive, *What You Should Know About COSHH*, (London: HSE, 1990).

Helm, D. (ed) *Economic Policy Towards the Environment* (Oxford: Blackstone Press, 1991).

HM Government, *Transport The Way Forward: The Government's Response to the Transport Debate,* Cm 3234 (London: HMSO, 1996).

– *This Common Inheritance* (London: HMSO, 1990).

Holder, J. 'Regulating Green Advertising in the Motor Car Industry' (1991) *Journal of Law and Society*, Vol. 18, No. 3, 323.

Holder, J. et al (eds) *Perspectives on the Environment*, (Aldershot: Avebury, 1993).

House of Commons Select Committee on the Environment, Third Report Session 1986-7, *Pollution of Rivers and Estuaries* (London: HMSO, 1987).

House of Lords Select Committee on the European Communities, Ninth Report, *Implementation and Enforcement of Environmental Legislation*, Session 1991-92 HL Paper 53 (London: HMSO, 1992).

– Eleventh Report, *Environmental Assessment of Projects*, Session 1980-81 (London, HMSO, 1981).

– *Approximation of Laws Under Article 100 of the Treaty of Rome: Environmental Problems of the Treaty of Rome*, Session 1978-9, Second Report HL 131 (London: HMSO, 1978).

House of Lords Select Committee on Noxious Vapours, *Report on Injury from Noxious Vapours*, BPP 14 (London: HMSO, 1862).

Howard, E. *Garden Cities of Tomorrow* (London: Faber and Faber, 1946).

Howarth, W. 'Agricultural Pollution and the Aquatic Environment', in Howarth, W. and Rodgers, C. *Agriculture, Conservation and Land Use* (Cardiff: University of Wales Press, 1992).

Howarth, W. *Wisdom's Law of Watercourses*, 5th ed. (London: Shaw and Sons, 1992).

IUCN (The World Conservation Union) et al *Caring for the Earth: A Strategy for Sustainable Living* (Gland: IUCN, 1991).

Jacobs, M. *The Green Economy: Environment, Sustainable Development and the Politics of the Future* (London: Pluto Press, 1989).

Jowell, J. and Woolf, H. *de Smith: Administrative Law* (London: Sweet and Maxwell, 1995).

Kiss, A. and Shelton, D. *International Environmental Law* (London: Transnational Publishers Inc./Graham & Trotman, 1991).

Krämer, L. *European Environmental Law Casebook* (London: Sweet and Maxwell, 1993).

Kropotkin, P. *Address to the Young* (London: Lighthouse Publications, 1885).

Lane, P. and Peto, M. *Blackstone's Guide to the Environment Act 1995* (London: Blackstone Press, 1995).

Ledgerwood, G., Street, E. and Therivel, R. *The Environmental Audit and Business Strategy* (London: Pitman, 1992).

Leeson, J. *Environmental Law* (London: Pitman, 1995).

Liefferink, D. *Environment and the Nation State* (Manchester: Manchester University Press, 1996).

Lindberg, L. N. *The Political Dynamics of European Economic Integration* (Oxford/Stanford: Oxford University Press/Stanford University Press, 1963).

Lomas, O. and McEldowney, J. (eds) *Frontiers of Environmental Law* (London: Chancery, 1991).

Lowe, P., Cox, G., McEwen, E., O'Riordan, T. and Winter, M. *Countryside Conflicts* (Aldershot: Gower, 1986).

Lyster, S. *International Wildlife Law* (Cambridge: Grotius, 1985).

Matthews, G. V. *The Ramsar Convention on Wetlands: Its History and Development* (Gland: International Waterfowl and Wetlands Research Bureau, 1993).

MacFadyen, D. *Sir Ebenezer Howard and the Town Planning Movement* (Manchester: Manchester University Press, 1970).

MacLaren, J. P. S. 'Nuisance law and the Industrial Revolution - Some Lessons from History' (1983) *Oxford Journal of Legal Studies*, Vol. 3, No. 2, 155.

Macrory, R. and Sheate, W. 'Agriculture and the European Community Environmental Assessment Directive: Lessons for Community Policy Making' (1989) *Journal of Common Market Studies*, Vol. 28, No. 1, 68.

Macrory, R. 'British Environmental Law: Major Strands and Characteristics' (1989) *Connecticut Journal of International Law* Vol. 4, No. 2, 287.

Malcolm, R. *A Guidebook to Environmental Law* (London: Sweet and Maxwell, 1994).
Markandya, A. and Richardson, J. *Environmental Economics* (London: Earthscan, 1992).
Marshall, P. *Nature's Web: An Exploration of Ecological Thinking* (London: Simon and Schuster, 1992).
McAuslan, P. *Ideologies of Planning Law* (Oxford: Pergamon Press, 1980).
– *Land, Law and Planning* (London: Weidenfeld and Nicholson, 1975).
McEldowney, J. and McEldowney, S. *Environmental Law and Science* (London: Longman, 1996).
Miller, C. 'Environmental Rights: English Fact or Fiction?' (1995) *Journal of Law and Society*, 374.
Miller C. and Wood C. *Planning and Pollution: An Examination of the Role of Land Use Planning in the Protection of Environmental Quality* (Oxford: Oxford University Press, 1983).
Millichap, D. 'Law, Myth and Community: A Reinterpretation of Planning's Justification and Rationale' (1995) *Planning Perspectives*, Vol. 10, 279.
– 'Sustainability - A Long Established Concern of Planning [1993] *Journal of Planning and Environmental Law*, 1111.
Ministry of Agriculture, Fisheries and Food, *Code of Good Agricultural Practice for the Protection of Water* (London: HMSO, 1991).
Moore, N.W. *The Bird of Time* (Cambridge: Cambridge University Press, 1987).
Moravcsik, A. 'Preferences and Power in the EC: A Liberal, Intergovernmentalist Approach' (1993) *European Law Review*, Vol. 31, No. 4, 473.
Morris W. *'Hopes and Fears for Art as the Lesser Arts of Life'* (1877), in *Collected Works* Vol. XXII (London: Longman, 1914).
– *'The Earthly Paradise'*, Prologue (1898), in *Collected Works* (London: Longman, 1914).
Moxen, J. and Strachan, P. 'The Formulation of Standards for Environmental Management Systems: Structural and Cultural Issues' (1995) 12 *Greener Management International*, 33.
Murdie, A. *Environmental Law and Citizen Action* (London: Earthscan, 1993).
Myerson, G. and Rydin, Y. 'Environment and Planning: A Tale of the Mundane and Sublime' (1994) *Space and Society*, Vol. 12, 437.
National Society for Clean Air, *Pollution Handbook* (Brighton: NSCA, 1994).
National Audit Office, *Protecting and Managing Sites of Special Scientific Interest* (London: HMSO, 1994).
National Rivers Authority, *Policy and Practice for the Protection of Groundwater* (Bristol: NRA, 1992).
– The Influence of Agriculture on the Quality of Natural Waters in England and Wales, Water Quality Series No. 2 (Bristol: NRA, 1992).
Nature Conservancy Council (NCC), *Site Management Plans for Conservation: A Working Guide* (Peterborough: NCC, 1991).
Neild, C. and Rice, R. *A Review of UK Compliance with the Ramsar Convention on Wetlands of International Importance Especially as Waterfowl Habitat* (London: Friends of the Earth, 1996).

Ogus, A. 'Water Rights Diluted: *Cambridge Water Co.* v. *Eastern Counties Leather*' (1994) *Journal of Environmental Law,* Vol. 6, No. 1, 151.
Ogus A. and Richardson, G. 'Economics and the Environment: A Study of Private Nuisance' (1977) *Cambridge Law Review,* Vol. 36, 284.
O'Riordan, T. and Cameron, J. *Interpreting the Precautionary Principle* (London: Cameron May, 1994).
Ost, F. 'A Game Without Rules? The Ecological Self-Organisation of Firms', in Teubner, G., Farmer, L. and Murphy, D. (eds) *Environmental Law and Ecological Responsibility* (Chichester: Wiley, 1994).
Passmore, J. *Man's Responsibility for Nature* (London: Duckworth, 1974).
Pearce, B. J. 'Property Rights and Development Control' (1981) *Town Planning Review,* Vol. 52, 45.
Pearce, D., Markandya, A. and Barbier, E. *Blueprint for a Green Economy* (London: Earthscan, 1989).
Pepper, D. *The Roots of Modern Environmentalism* (London: Routledge, 1986).
Porrit, J. and Winner, D. *The Coming of the Greens* (London: Fontana, 1988).
Purdue, M. 'The Impact of Section 54A' [1994] *Journal of Planning and Environmental Law,* 399.
Redclift, M. *Sustainable Development: Exploring the Contradictions* (London: Routledge, 1992).
Rehbinder, E. and Stewart, R. 'Legal Integration in Federal Systems: European Community Environmental Law' (1985) *American Journal of Comparative Law,* Vol. 33, 371.
Reid, C. (ed) *Environmental Law in Scotland* (Edinburgh: W. Green/Sweet and Maxwell, 1992).
Robinson, N. A. *Agenda 21: Earth's Action Plan* (New York: Oceana Publications Inc., 1993).
Rodgers, C. P (ed) *Nature Conservation and Countryside Law* (Cardiff: University of Wales Press, 1996).
Rowan-Robinson, J., Ross, A., Walton, W. and Rothnie, J. 'Public Access to Environmental Information: A Means to What End?', (1996) *Journal of Environmental Law,* Vol. 8, No. 1. 19.
Royal Commission on the Pollution of Rivers (of 1865), Third Report, *The Rivers Aire and Calder,* Cmnd. 3850 (London: HMSO, 1867).
Royal Commission on Pollution of Rivers (of 1868) Fifth Report, *Pollution Arising from Mining Operations and Metal Manufacturing,* Cmnd. 951 (London: HMSO, 1874).
– *Fourth Report on the Pollution of Rivers in Scotland,* Cmnd. 603 (London: HMSO, 1872).
– *Report on the Process of Treating Sewage,* Cmnd. 181 (London: HMSO, 1870).
Royal Commission on Environmental Pollution, Nineteenth Report, *Sustainable Use of Soil,* Cm 3165 (London: HMSO, 1996).
– Eighteenth Report *Transport and the Environment,* Cmnd. 2674 (London, HMSO, 1994).
– Sixteenth Report, *Freshwater Quality,* Cmnd. 1966 (London: HMSO, 1992).
– Twelfth Report, *Best Practicable Environmental Option,* Cm. 310 (London, HMSO, 1988).

– *Fifth Report: Air Pollution Control: An Integrated Approach,* Cmnd. 6371 (London: HMSO, 1976).
Royal Commission on Salmon Fisheries, *Report on Fisheries in England and Wales*, BPP 2768 (London: HMSO, 1861).
Royal Commission on Sewage Disposal, Final Report, *General Summary of Conclusions and Recommendations* (1914-16) Cmnd. 7821 (London: HMSO).
– Ninth Report, *Disposal of Wastes from Manufacturing Processes* (1914-16) Cmnd. 7819 (London: HMSO).
– Eighth Report, *Standards and Tests for Sewage and Sewage Effluents Discharging into Rivers and Streams* (1912-13) Cmnd. 6464 (London: HMSO).
Royal Sanitary Commission (Royal Commission on Sanitary Laws) *First Report* (1968-1869) BPP 4218 (London: HMSO, 1969).
Sands, P. 'European Community Environmental Law: The Evolution of a Regional Regime of International Environmental Protection', (1991) *Yale Law Journal*, Vol. 100, 2511.
Scott, J. *Development Dilemmas in the European Community* (Buckingham: Open University Press, 1995).
Scottish National Parks Committee and the Scottish Wild Life Conservation Committee (Department of Health for Scotland), Final Report, *Nature Reserves in Scotland*, Cmd 7814 (Edinburgh: HMSO, 1949).
Scottish Natural Heritage, *Sustainable Development and the Natural Heritage: The SNH Approach* (Perth: SNH, 1993).
Shackley, S. 'Mission to Model Earth', in Elworthy, S. et al (eds) *Perspectives on the Environment 2* (Aldershot: Avebury, 1995).
Shove, E. 'Threats and Defences in the Built Environment', in Elworthy, S. et al (eds.) *Perspectives on the Environment 2* (Aldershot: Avebury, 1995).
Smith, S. C. 'How Law Hides Risk', in Teubner, G., Farmer, L. and Murphy, D. (eds.) *Environmental Law and Ecological Responsibility* (Chichester: Wiley, 1994).
Smout, C. *The Highlands and the Roots of Green Consciousness, 1750 - 1990* (Perth: SNH, 1990).
Snyder, F. 'The Effectiveness of European Community Law: Institutions, Processes, Tools and Techniques' (1993) 56 *Modern Law Review*, 19.
– *New Directions in European Community Law* (London: Weidenfeld and Nicholson, 1990).
Steele, J. 'Private Law and the Environment: Nuisance in Context' (1995) *Legal Studies*, Vol. 15, No. 2, 236.
Sustainable Agriculture, Food and Environment (SAFE) Alliance, *Pollution Control on Dairy Farms* (London: SAFE, 1992).
Sweeney, J. M., Oliver, C. T. and Leech, N. E. *The International Legal System*, 3rd ed. (Westbury/New York: Foundation Press, 1988).
Tarlock, A. D. 'The Futile Search for Environment Laws Based on "Good Science"' (1996) *International Journal of Biosciences and the Law*, Vol. 1, No. 1, 9.
Teubner, G., Farmer, L. and Murphy, D. (eds) *Environmental Law and Ecological Responsibility* (Chichester: Wiley, 1994).
Therivel, R. *Strategic Environmental Assessment* (London: Earthscan, 1992).

Tromans, S. 'High Talk and Low Cunning: Putting Environmental Principles into Legal Practice' [1995] *Journal of Planning and Environmental Law,* 779.

– *The Environmental Protection Act 1990* 2nd ed (London: Sweet and Maxwell, 1993).

Velikovsky, I. *Earth in Upheaval* (London: Abacus, 1973).

Walton, W., Ross-Robertson, A. and Rowan-Robertson, J. 'The Precautionary Principle and the UK Planning System' (1995) *Environmental Law and Management,* Vol. 7, No. 1, 35.

Warren, L. M., 'Law and Policy for Marine Protected Areas', in Rodgers, C. P. (ed) *Nature Conservation and Countryside Law* (Cardiff: University of Wales Press, 1996).

Warrens, K. *Chemical Foundations: The Alkali Industry in Britain Until 1926* (Oxford: Clarendon, 1980).

Wathern, P. 'Less Favoured and Environmentally Sensitive Areas: a European Dimension to the Rural Environment', in Howarth, W. and Rodgers, C. P (eds) *Agriculture, Conservation and Land Use* (Cardiff: University of Wales Press, 1992).

Weale, A. *The New Politics of Pollution* (Manchester: Manchester University Press, 1992).

Weatherill, S. and Beaumont, P. *EC Law* (London: Penguin, 1993).

Wild Life Conservation Special Committee, *Conservation of Nature in England and Wales,* Cmnd 7122 (London: HMSO, 1947).

Wilson, G. 'The Development of Environmental Law in Nineteenth Century Britain', in Weick, G. (ed.), *National and European Law on the Threshold to the Single Market* (Frankfurt am Main: Peter Lang, 1993).

Wood, C. *Environmental Impact Assessment: A Comparative Review* (London: Longman, 1995).

– *Planning Pollution Prevention: A Comparison of Siting Controls Over Air Pollution In Great Britain and the United States of America* (Manchester: Manchester University Press, 1989).

World Commission on Environment and Development, *Our Common Future: Report of the Brundtland Commission* (Oxford: Oxford University Press, 1987).

Index

Access to information, 234-8, 332
Advertisements, 339-46
  British Code, 344-5
  'green',
    problems with, 341-4
    rules (*Campaign*), 343
    self-regulation, 344-6
  misleading, 340-2, 344-5, 346
    corrective to, 345
    counter-, 345
  motor car industry, 340-4
  unfair, 340, 341-2, 343-5
Agenda 21, 37, 123, 144-53
  consumption patterns, 145-51
  customary international law, as, 151, 153
  global instrument, as, 144
  implementation of, 123-4, 150
  labelling, 149
  Local, 37-40, 151-2
  monitoring of, 145, 151
  nature of, 150-1
  participation requirements, effect of, 151-3
  pricing, environmental, 150
  'soft law', as, 124, 145, 151, 154
  sustainable development, 124
    agenda for, 145
    precautionary principle, and, 154-64
  waste, 149
Agrarianism, 101-3
Agriculture. *See also* FARM; FARMER
  Codes,
    good agricultural practice (COPA), 382-3
    protection of water, for, 380, 383-4
  criticism of modern, 108
  designations, 457-61
  Environmentally Sensitive Areas, 457-61
  exclusion from 'development', 106
  industry, as, 363-5, 376, 381
  Less Favoured Areas, 457
  maintenance and needs of (Scott Report), 104-6
  planning, and, 243, 269-70, 285-6
  pollution, nitrate etc, from, 361 *et seq.* *See also* NITRATE POLLUTION
Agriculture-*contd*
  pollution, nitrate etc, from-*contd*
    House of Commons Select Committee Report, 381-3
  post-War expansion of, 106-7
Air pollution, 15-16, 40, 43-4
  Beaver Report, 221-2
    Clean Air Act, in response to, 222-3
  chemical works, 48-9, 61-2, 65, 217-21
  control measures, 215 *et seq*
    'best practicable means' concept, 217-21
    EC, 184
    exhaust emissions. *See* TRAFFIC POLLUTION
    local authority air pollution control, 227
    nineteenth century legislation, 61-2, 65
    planning controls, 266-9
    smoke, for, 221-3
    See also INTEGRATED POLLUTION CONTROL
  Derby Committee, 49-50, 61
  Evelyn (John), treatise on, 215-17, 241-2
  industrialisation, and, 48-9, 217
  monitoring, 238-40
  reducing levels of (Royal Commission Reports), 43-4, 224
Air quality
  national policies, 238-9
    industry's views on, 239-40
Alkali works
  Alkali Inspectorate, renaming and amalgamation of, 227
  'best practicable means' concept, and, 217-21, 366
Alternative lifestyles, 346-9
Alternative protection methods, 299 *et seq*. *See also* ECOLOGICAL MODERNISATION; ENVIRONMENTAL MOVEMENT
Amenity/ies
  first Planning Act, concept in, 94-6
  preservation of (Dennison Report), 105-6
Arcadia. *See* UTOPIANISM

Area of outstanding natural beauty, 286
Assessment. *See also* ENVIRONMENTAL ASSESSMENT
  risk (hazardous works), 324
Asthma, 23. *See also* AIR POLLUTION
Auditing, 324-37. *See also* ENVIRONMENTAL MANAGEMENT
  EC Regulation, 327-32

Beach
  GCR site, 450-1
Beaver Report, 221-2
Best available techniques not entailing excessive cost, 228-9, 231, 232
'Best practicable environmental option', 225-8, 232
  ENDS Report, 233-4
  meaning, 226
  single assessment for planning and pollution control, 281
  statutory footing for, 227
  strategic environmental assessment identifying, 419-21
  Transport the Way Forward, 420-1
'Best practicable means', 217-21, 224
Bicycle
  use of, 347-9
Biosphere Reserve, 449-50
Birds, 110, 185, 204-11, 293
  EC Directive on, 204, 293, 452-4
  greylag geese, reserve for, 425-7, 450, 461. *See also* CONSERVATION:Loch Druidibeg
  special protection areas, 293, 451-2. *See also* CONSERVATION
  waterfowl, protection of habitat, 439-43
Bourneville, 84, 87
Brown, Lancelot (Capability), 90
Brundtland Commission/Report, 139-40, 225, 304, 391
Building operations, 250. *See also* TOWN AND COUNTRY PLANNING

CBI, 326
CERES principles, 326-7
Cancer
  exhaust emissions, and, 43-4
Car. *See* ADVERTISING; TRAFFIC POLLUTION; TRANSPORT
Carbon dioxide emissions. *See also* TRAFFIC POLLUTION
  tax on, proposal for, 320-4
***Caring for the Earth* (1991)**, 140-4
  global instrument, need for, 144. *See also* AGENDA 21
  nine principles, 141
Chadwick, Edwin, 83
Chamber of Commerce, 326
Charges and levies, 314-16, 318, 320
Chemical industry, 48-51, 61-2, 217-21
  guidelines for management, 326
Christianity
  stewardship tradition, 29-31
Civil liability
  entitlement to, 54
  European Community system, 78-81
    product liability, 79-80
  restricted role for (*Cambridge Water*), 47, 67-79
    importance of case, 76-7
Coal industry, 50-1
Codes of practice. *See* AGRICULTURE
Common law, 54-60, 65-6, 76-7
Company. *See* INDUSTRY
Conceptual basis, 3-4
Conservation. *See also* NATURE
  area designation, 286-95, 430-1, 449-56, 461-2
    AONB, 286
    agricultural, 457-61
    background to (Huxley Committee), 431-4, 435-6
    EC, 185, 293-5, 451-6
    planning, and, 289-93, 430
    purposes, 431
    Scotland. *See* NATIONAL NATURE RESERVE
    towns, in, 431
    voluntary nature of, 288
    See also 'SAC', 'SPA', 'SSSI' *below*
  biodiversity enhanced by, 428
  case study (Loch Druidibeg), 425 *et seq*
    agricultural designations, 457-61
    background to, 430-8
    Biosphere Reserve, 449-50
    birds on, summary of protection for, 453
    changes to site, 428
    crofting, effect of, 461
    EC law, and, 452-6
    Environmentally Sensitive Area, as, 457-61
    factors influencing management, 428-9
    Friends of the Earth review, 445
    Geological Conservation Review Site, 450-1
    Less Favoured Area, as, 457
    management plan, 444
    Montreux Criteria/Record, 443, 445-9
    Ramsar Convention, and, 439-43, 444, 445-9
    Reserve, designation as, 438-9, 443, 449, 461-2
    Ritchie Committee entry, 435
    Special Area of Conservation, as, 454-6
    Special Protection Area, as, 451-2, 453-4

Conservation–*contd*
European law, 185, 293-5, 451-6
groups,
start of, 110. *See also* ENVIRONMENTAL MOVEMENT
UK, 287
SAC, 294-5, 454-6
SPA, 293, 451-4
notification as SSSI, 293
number of, 293
SSSI, 286-9, 430
compensation to landowners, 287
damage to, statistics, 288
Huxley Committee proposal for, 435-6
original status, 436
planning permission for development on, 288-93
scope of protection, 287-8
subject and aim, as, 427-8
Consumer
advertising ethics, and, 340-6. *See also* ADVERTISEMENTS
behaviour as, 312
green, 338-45
Guide, extract, 338-9
lifestyle, 346-9. *See also* ENVIRONMENTAL MOVEMENT
Consumption patterns
changes to make sustainable, 145-51
research into, need for, 147
Control. *See* LAW; POLLUTION
Controlled Waste Inspectorate, 227
Convention on Biological Diversity. *See* RIO CONFERENCE
Cost-benefit analysis, 310, 313-14, 317
Council for the Preservation of Rural England, 107, 110-11, 117-19
Countryside. *See also* NATIONAL PARKS; NATURE
access to, 109, 111-13
Ramblers' Federations, and, 108-9
designation of. *See* CONSERVATION
development in, 117-119, 295-6
planning permission for, 288-93, 295-6
Planning Policy Guidance, 296
pollution by farmers. *See* NITRATE POLLUTION
protection of, 107-11, 114, 243, 285-96
assessment of effects of development, 295-6
European site, ban possible, 295
See also CONSERVATION

Damage control, 8-9
Demolition, 250. *See also* TOWN AND COUNTRY PLANNING
Dennison, Professor S R, 104, 105-6, 286
Derby Committee
report, 49, 61, 66
extract, 49-50
Designation. *See* CONSERVATION
Direct action, 349-53
Dower Committee, 111
Drains
legislation for installation of, 59, 83
sewage. *See* SEWAGE

Earth's Action Plan. *See* AGENDA 21
Ecological change
importance of understanding, 4-7
irreversible, 6
Ecological modernisation, 300-5
European dimension, 305
'instruments' required for, 306 *et seq*
Ecology, 27-8
deep, 33-4, 346
function of, 28
Economics
economic instruments, 306-22
categories of, 306, 320
development and use of, 306-8, 312-19, 322
Royal Commission Report extract, 313-19
environmental harm, and, 317-18
fiscal incentives, 319-20
monetization, 309-12
sustainable development, and, 319-20
tax, use of, 320-4
Electricity transmission/supply
risk to health from, 18-22
Emission. *See also* AIR POLLUTION; TRAFFIC POLLUTION; WATER
standards, 366-7
English Nature, 287
Environment. *See also* NATURE
concept of, 25-34, 35, 37, 465-6
legal, 465
consciousness-raising relationships with nature, 33-4
different views of, relevance of, 28-9
environmental norm, 27
garden, nature as, 34
indoor, 36-7
man's relationship to, 29-33
utopia, as, 85
'wilderness experience' of nature, 33-4
Environment Agency
aims and objectives, 229-31
creation of, 227
discharge consents, 374
exercise of powers, cost exercise, 230
IPC administered by, 229
sustainable development, and, 230-1
Environmental assessment, 388 *et seq*
alternatives to project, requirement for, 407

Environmental assessment–*contd*
anticipatory nature of, 390, 391
appeal, 402
avoidance, etc, measures to be specified in, 410
criticism of, 413-14, 418
EC law, 389, 391, 394-400
consultation duty, 399-400
extract from Directive, 395-8
implementation of Directive, 192, 401-2
projects affected, 394, 399
proposals to amend, 398-9
effect of, on planning decision, 418
General Development Order, under, 400-1
informal assessment, 400-1
integrated pollution control, as part of, 391
introduction of, 389, 394-5
justification of project by, danger of, 413-14
'material consideration' for planning authority, 251, 401
mitigating measures, 410-12, 414, 417
nature of, 390-1
perceptions on the environment in, 417
'ecological interest', 417
'public environmental interest', 417
planning conditions/obligations, extent based on, 412
precautionary principle, and, 157, 159-62
purpose of, 389-90, 418
requirement for, 238, 400-402
responsibility for, 414
Royal Commission extracts, 405-6, 413, 415-17, 419-21
statistics, 398, 402
strategic, advantages of, 419-21
sustainable development, role in, 391-4
extract on, 392-3
Rio Declaration acknowledges, 391-2
Thanet Way bypass case, 402-17
alternative routes, 407-10
assessment adequacy questioned, 404, 410
background to, 402-4
economic importance of road, 410
'environmental gains' proposed, 411-12
issues raised by, 404
limited scope of assessment, 412-13
planning inquiry on, 414-15
public good, emphasis on, 417
UNEP guidelines on goals of, 160-2
weight of, 390
Environmental management, 324 *et seq*
advertising techniques, 340-6. *See also* ADVERTISEMENTS
assumptions behind schemes, 335-7
Environmental management–*contd*
EC Regulation on, 327-32, 339
criticism of, 332-5
green corporate culture, 324, 335-7
UK strategy, 324-7
guidelines, 326-7
management strategy, 326
scientific and technical strategy, 325-6
Environmental movement, 114-19, 299 *et seq*
direct action, 349-53
characteristics of groups, 349-50
Reclaim the Streets (RTS), 350, 351-3
Roadalert appeal, 350-1
Friends of the Earth. *See* FRIENDS OF THE EARTH
green consumerism, 338-6, 349. *See also* ADVERTISEMENTS
green corporate culture. *See* ENVIRONMENTAL MANAGEMENT
Greenpeace, 124-5
instruments, mix required in future, 306. *See also* ECONOMICS
law, radicalism in, 353-7
origins, 300-5
voluntary simplicity, 346-9
Environmentally Sensitive Area, 431, 457-61
joining, advice on, 459-61
European Atomic Energy Community, 166
European Coal and Steel Community, 166
European Commission
complaint to, 191-2
FoE, by (water quality), 368-70
European Community, 165 *et seq*
air protection, 184, 189, 192-9
background to, 165-8
carbon tax proposed, 320-4
civil liability for damage, 78-81
insurance, 79, 81
polluter pays principle, 79, 80
prevention principle, 79
Court of Justice, reference to, 192
fines, imposition of, 200
strict approach of, 199
designation (countryside), 293-5, 451-6
agricultural, 457-9
SACs, 294-5, 454-6
SPAs, 293, 451-4
Directives,
binding nature, 189-90, 200
circulars used to implement, 373
direct effect doctrine, 201-3
drinking water, on, 184, 187, 189, 192-9, 367-3
environmental assessment, 395-8

European Community-*contd*
Directives-*contd*
equal treatment, 200
failure to implement, 192-9, 200, 203, 368-70
flora and fauna habitats, 205-6, 209-10, 294-5, 454-6
hazardous waste shipments, 80
nitrate pollution from agriculture, 377
product liability, 79
'Seveso', 324
waste/landfill waste, proposals for liability for, 81
wild birds, on, 204, 293, 452-4
EEC Treaty/EC Treaty. *See* 'Treaty of Rome' *below*
eco-labelling regime, 332-5, 339
eco-management and audit system (EMAS), 327-32, 339
criticism of, 332-5
ecological modernisation, and, 305
economic instruments, approach to, 319-20
Environmental Action Programmes, 166, 169, 176-9, 186
Fifth. *See 'Towards Sustainability' below*
environmental assessments, 388, 389, 394-400
Directive extract, 395-8
implementation in UK, 401-2
projects affected, 394-5, 399
Environmentally Sensitive Areas, 457-61
hazards works, risk assessment, 324
internal market, commitment to, 167-8
land protection, 185
law (environmental), in, 183 *et seq*
enforcement, 191-204
infringement, 192-9, 200, 203, 368-70
land use regulation, 183, 185
preventive and integrated law, 183, 184-6
primary legislation, basis in, 181-3
sectoral control of pollution, 183, 184
subsidiarity. *See* 'subsidiarity principle' *below*
techniques used, 183
Less Favoured Areas, 457-61
Luxembourg Accords, 167, 175
Maastricht Treaty (Treaty of EU), 168, 171
Member States,
complaint to Commission, 191-2
difficulties in complying, 190-1
extent of, cases on, 190
failure to implement law, case on, 192-9, 200, 203
Francovich liability of, 203-4
'implementation', meaning, 190

European Community-*contd*
Member States-*contd*
national courts of, direct effect in, 200-3
obligations of, 189-91
Natura 2000, 294, 453, 454, 455
planning competence of EU, 281
policy for environment, outline,
constitutional status, 171
economic requirements, and, 172-3, 176, 204-11
'essential objective', protection as, 170
integration in, move to, 186
legal basis for, 181-3
process of, 173-9
statement of, 179
precautionary principle, EU commitment to, 281
regulations, binding nature of, 189-90
subsidiarity principle, 185, 186-9
Article setting out, 187
Molitor Report extract, 188-9
review by Commission, 187
sustainable development concept in, 166, 172-3, 179-81
sustainable growth preferred, 171-2
Towards Sustainability, 166, 177-81, 186, 187
extracts from, 180-1, 305-6, 319-20
network cohesion, 177-9
Treaty of Paris, 166
Treaty of Rome, 166-8, 181-3
extract, as amended, 181-3
water pollution. *See* NITRATE POLLUTION; WATER
European Court of Justice, 192, 199, 200
European Economic Community, 166-7. *See also* EUROPEAN COMMUNITY
European Union. *See also* EUROPEAN COMMUNITY
creation of, 168
distinguished from European Community, 168
policy making process in, 173-9
federalist account of, 175-7
intergovernmentalism, 174-5
neo-functionalism, 173-4
Evelyn, John
treatise on air pollution (1661), 215-17, 241-2
Exhaust emissions. *See* TRAFFIC POLLUTION
Expert evidence, 14

Farm
Dairy, Pollution Control, 375-6
fuel oil pollution, 375, 380
manure and slurry on, 380-4. *See also* NITRATE POLLUTION

Farm–*contd*
organic/alternative, 114-19
temporary structures on, 114-15
wastes, 375-6. *See also* NITRATE POLLUTION
Farmer, 104-5
compensation for, 103-4
National Farmers' Union, 363-5
nation's landscape gardeners, as, 288
nitrate sensitive areas scheme, joining, 377-80
pollution caused by. *See* NITRATE POLLUTION
Farming. *See* AGRICULTURE; NITRATE POLLUTION
Fiscal incentives, 320. *See also* ECONOMICS
Fish, 50-1. *See also* RIVER; WATER
farming, 381
Flora and fauna. *See* EUROPEAN COMMUNITY; NATURE
Forestry, 243, 285
France
nuclear tests by, judgments on, 155-64
***Francovich* liability**, 203-4
Franks Report, 248
Friends of the Earth
complaint to Commission, UK failure on water standards, 368-70
complaint to secretariat of Ramsar Convention, 445
Fumes. 48-51, 56, 61-2. *See also* AIR POLLUTION

Gaia, 35
Garden
formal, 90
Garden cities, 84-9, 102, 113
Geese. *See* BIRDS
Geological Conservation Review Site, 450-1
Germany
Total Kritik, 349
vorsorgeprinzip, 16-17
Global concerns, 8, 10, 13
Gaian philosophy, 35
Green Belt, 111, 253, 269
release for housing, 281-2
Green consumer, 338-46
Green corporate culture. *See* ENVIRONMENTAL MANAGEMENT
Green economy, 308-12
Blueprint, extract, 309-10
Green field sites, 100-1
Greenpeace
Rainbow Warrior, sinking of, 124-5
Groundwater
nitrate pollution, 361-2, 372-3, 380
protection, 67-9, 273-6
Guidelines
management systems, for, 326-7
Guidelines–*contd*
Policy Planning Guidance, 284-5, 296
UNEP, 160-2

Hazardous waste/substances
EC Directive, 80
HSE document on Regulations, 323-4
storage effects, 400
Health and safety at work
controls, 322-4
Hebrides, Outer
Loch Druidibeg Nature Reserve, 425 *et seq*
Her Majesty's Inspectorate of Pollution, 224, 227, 231. *See also* INTEGRATED POLLUTION CONTROL
failings, 232-4
Historical background, 47 *et seq*
nineteenth century, changes in, 47, 48 *et seq*
Holism, 4, 107, 215, 422, 425
Housing. *See* GARDEN CITIES; PUBLIC HEALTH; TEMPORARY STRUCTURES; TOWN AND COUNTRY PLANNING
Howard, Ebenezer, 87-9
Huxley Committee
Report extracts, 431-4, 435-6

IUCN, 138-9
Industrial Air Pollution Inspectorate, 227
Industrialisation
effect of, 47, 48-54. *See also* AIR POLLUTION; ALKALI WORKS; CHEMICAL INDUSTRY; COAL INDUSTRY
Industry. *See also* AIR POLLUTION; WATER
agriculture as, 363-5, 376, 381
alkali. *See* ALKALI WORKS
chemical. *See* CHEMICAL INDUSTRY
coal, 50-1
effect of. *See* AIR POLLUTION
hazardous works, 323-4
'lifting the burden' on, 253, 401
self-regulation by, 324 *et seq*. *See also* ENVIRONMENTAL MANAGEMENT
Information
Environment Agency power to obtain, 374
planning permission, prior to, *See* ENVIRONMENTAL ASSESSMENT
public access to, 234-8, 332
Inquiry, local public planning, 414-17
Integrated pollution control (IPC)
administration. *See* ENVIRONMENT AGENCY
best available techniques not entailing excessive cost, 228-9, 231, 232
ENDS Report on, 233-4
best practicable environmental option, 225-8, 232, 234
one assessment for planning and pollution control, 281

Integrated pollution control–*contd*
EC/international law compliance, 229
establishment of regime for, 227
implementation difficulties, 231-4, 281
inspectorate for enforcement (HMIP), 224, 227, 231
licensing, 227
local authority air pollution control, 227
monitoring, 231-2
move to, from sectoral control, 215, 223, 240-1
planning controls, relation with, 275-81
registers, 229, 231-2, 235-7
Royal Commission Report, 223-5, 268-9
International Court of Justice, 124, 154-5
nuclear tests in South Pacific, judgments on, 155-64
International law, 123 *et seq*
Agenda 21. *See* AGENDA 21
background, 123-4
Caring for the Earth (1991), 140-4
sustainable development, meaning, 141, *see also* SUSTAINABLE DEVELOPMENT
custom, 130-2
Agenda 21, and, 151, 153
evidence of, 130
example, 131
European law. *See* EUROPEAN COMMUNITY
Nairobi Declaration (1982), 135-8, 139, 465
need for, 143-4
precautionary principle, 16-17, 154, 157, 159-60
Ramsar site, designation as, 439-42
'soft law', 124, 131-2, 138, 145
sources, 124-32
Stockholm Declaration (1972), 133-5
Principle 21, 134-5
treaties, 124, 125-30
example, 126-30
process, 125
Vienna Convention on, 125
United Nations Environment Programme (UNEP), 135
World Charter for Nature, 138-9
World Commission on Environment and Development, 139-40, 304
Brundtland Report, 140, 304
World Conservation Union (IUCN), 138-9

Kropotkin, Prince Peter, 86, 89, 102, 107

Labelling, 149, 184
eco-, 184, 332-5, 339
Land pollution, 224. *See also* INTEGRATED POLLUTION CONTROL; LAND USE; WASTE
Land use. *See also* COUNTRYSIDE
agriculture. *See* AGRICULTURE
air pollution, and, 267-8
controls, 82 *et seq*, 243 *et seq*. *See also* CONSERVATION; TOWN AND COUNTRY PLANNING
origins of, summary, 113-14
designation. *See* CONSERVATION
EC regulation, 185
groundwater pollution, and, 273-6, 380
industrial. *See* INDUSTRY
Land Utilisation in Rural Areas, Committee on, 103-5
'non-natural' use, 56, 67
owner's control over, 54-60
plotlanders, by, 102-3
pressure groups, 107
private property rights, 59-60, 353-4
public health challenge to, 83
Scottish attitude to, 423-5
tortious actions, 54-9
urban and countryside, separation of, 106-7, 114, 286
water pollution from, 385-7. *See also* AGRICULTURE; NITRATE POLLUTION
Lappel Bank
ECJ case on, 204-11
Law
causal chain, 14, 15
historical context, 47-8, 61-5
'implementation failure', 299
international. *See* EUROPEAN COMMUNITY; INTERNATIONAL LAW
jurisdiction, 34
mainstream discipline, environmental law as, 465
nineteenth century developments, 47, 53-4, 61-6
piecemeal protection of, 54, 66
planning. *See* TOWN AND COUNTRY PLANNING
radicalism in, 353-7
role of, 3-4, 37
scientists' contribution to, 7-9
trusts, environmental use of, 354-7
use of science in, 7-9, 13-15
expert evidence, 14
Legal principles, 4. *See also* LAW
Legislation. *See* LAW
Letchworth, 89, 113
Leukaemia, 19, 21
Licensing, 227
Local Authority Air Pollution Control
establishment of, 227
Local concerns, 34-5. *See also* LOCAL GOVERNMENT; TOWN AND COUNTRY PLANNING

Local government, 37-40. *See also* PUBLIC HEALTH
  Agenda 21, effect on, 151-3
  restricted scope of, 39
Local planning authority. *See* TOWN AND COUNTRY PLANNING
Loch Druidibeg. *See* CONSERVATION
London smog, 221
Less Favoured Areas, 457

Management. *See* ENVIRONMENTAL MANAGEMENT
Marine life, 449
Market mechanisms. *See also* ECONOMICS
  use of, 314-16
Mining
  efflux from, 50-1
Mobile homes, 114-19
Molitor Report, 188-9
Monetary valuation, 310-12
Montreux Criteria/Record, 443, 445-9
Morris, William, 85-6, 102, 107
Motor car. *See* ADVERTISING; TRAFFIC POLLUTION; TRANSPORT
Motor fuels. *See* AGRICULTURE; TRAFFIC POLLUTION

Nairobi Declaration (1982), 135-8, 139, 465
National Farmers' Union, 363-5
National Nature Reserves, 286, 423, 434-6
  case study (Scotland), 425-7, 438-9
  crofting, and, 461
  establishment of, 434-6
National parks
  Act establishing, 112-13, 286, 436-8
  origins, 111-12, 431
  pre-War support for, 97
National Rivers Authority, 227, 273
  Policy and Practice for Protection of Groundwater, 273-6
National Trust, 110
Natura 2000, 294, 453, 454, 455
Nature. *See also* COUNTRYSIDE; ENVIRONMENT
  appeal to, in advert, 342-3
  Conservancy, 436, 437-8
  conservation. *See* CONSERVATION
  designation of areas. *See* CONSERVATION
  English Nature, 287
  Flora and Fauna Directive. *See* EUROPEAN COMMUNITY
  idealisation of, 102
  man's stewardship of. *See* STEWARDSHIP
  meaning, 465-6
  World Charter for, 138-9
Nature Conservancy, 436, 437-8
Negligence, 67
New towns, 270-1. *See also* GARDEN CITIES
New Zealand, 154-164
Nitrate pollution, 361 *et seq*
  agricultural policy, background, 363-5
  Code of Good Practice for the Protection of Water, 383-4
  Dangerous Substances in Water Directive, 367, 373
    implementation by UK, 373-4
  Drinking Water Directive, 367-72
    case on failure by UK to implement, 370-2
    FoE complaint on UK failure, 368-70
    standards for drinking water, 367
    UK attempt to derogate, 368
  drinking water pollution offence, 365
  EC law, general approach of, 366-7
  effects,
    eutrophic effect, 362
    human health, on, 362
  Environment Agency's powers, 374-5
  fertiliser use, 386
    reductions required, 380
  information to prevent, 374-5
  level for, 366, 379
  manure and slurry,
    Code for, 384
    manure spreading, 374
    storage, 374-5
  Nitrate from Agricultural Sources Directive, 377
  'nitrate sensitive area (NSA)' designation, 377-80, 386
    offence, provision for, 378
  nitrate vulnerable zones, 387, 431
  Protection of Water from, Directive, 372-3
    sources of pollution, reduction in, 373
  Sustainable Use of Soil (Royal Commission Report), 386-7
  use of nitrates by farmers, 361-2, 374
  WHO guidelines, 362, 366
  water protection zones, 376-7
Noise, 56, 58
Non-governmental organisations, 302. *See also* ENVIRONMENTAL MOVEMENT
Nuclear energy
  anti-nuclear protest (*Total Kritik*), 349
  non-ionising radiation, 18-20
  nuclear tests by France, International Court judgments, 154-64
Nuisance, 56-9
  doctrine of, case on, 57-8
  foreseeability of damage, 72-3
  limitations of tort of, 58-9, 67, 70-2
  sewers, from, 64-5
  strict liability, 58

OECD, 303-5
Owen, Robert, 86-7

Park. *See* NATIONAL PARKS
Participation
Agenda 21, and, 151-3
public, 237-8, 247-8, 252-3
Pastoralism, 101-2
Paths (walkers'), 111-12. *See also* RAMBLERS' FEDERATIONS
Perchloroethene
case on leakage of, 67-79
European Community standard for, 78
Philosophy
nature and man, traditions of, 29-30, 35
Physical exercise
government promotion of, 42
Planning. *See* TOWN AND COUNTRY PLANNING
Planning obligation
conditions contrasted, 263, 283
local land charge, as, 262
nature of, 262-3
significance of, 265
uses, 283
groundwater protection, 275
validity, case on, 263, 264-5
Politics, 37-40
fear, of, 12
local government, 37-40
democracy in, 39-40
science, relation to, 11
single issue, end of, 350, 353
Polluter pays principle, 318, 320. *See also* ECONOMICS
Pollution. *See also* AIR POLLUTION; INDUSTRY; NITRATE POLLUTION; WASTE; WATER
concentrations and consequences, as, 26
control techniques, 215 *et seq*
'best practicable environmental option', 225-8
'best practicable means', 217-21, 224
EC, 184-6. *See also* EUROPEAN COMMUNITY
integrated, 223-34, 391. *See also* ENVIRONMENTAL ASSESSMENT; INTEGRATED POLLUTION CONTROL
planning controls, and, 273-81, 282-5
cultural construction of, 24-5
definition (Royal Commission's), 316
economic analysis (Royal Commission Report), 312-19
HMIP, 224, 227, 231
HMIPI (Scotland), 235, 238
'historic', 67
meaning, 26-7
moral element, 26, 27
traffic. *See* TRAFFIC POLLUTION
Pollution of Rivers and Estuaries, 381-3
Port Sunlight, 87
Poverty, 144, 154
Precautionary principle, 17-18, 22, 154-64, 281-2. *See also* ENVIRONMENTAL ASSESSMENT
Product liability
civil liability, EC Directive, 79
Property. *See* LAND USE
Public
access to information, 234-8
behaviour patterns, changing, 306-8
valuations made by, 312
Public health, 48 *et seq*, 64-5, 82-4. *See also* DRAINS
environmental assessment, emphasis in, 417
planning, and, 246-7, 297
proprietorial rights, challenge to, 83-4
sanitation policy in first Planning Act, 92, 94
town planning, and, 100

Radiation. *See* NUCLEAR ENERGY
Radiochemical Inspectorate, 227
Ramblers' Federations, 107, 108-9
Ramsar Convention, 439-43
Brisbane (6th) meeting, 444
recommendations, 445-9
enforcement under, 445
FoE complaint to secretariat of, 445
UK Report to, 444, 457
Reclaim the Streets (RTS), 350, 351-3
Regional (environment), 35
Registers, public
IPC, 229, 231-2, 235-6
planning, 236
use made of, 236-7
Regulatory methods
range of, 306
Resilience
concept of, 4-7
Rio Conference, 124, 125
Agenda 21, negotiation at, 144. *See also* AGENDA 21
Convention on Biological Diversity, 126-30, 449
conservation measures, 128, 129
identification and monitoring, 128
objectives, 127-8
precautionary principle, 154
principle, 128
United States' objections, 130
sustainable development as theme, 124, 125, 391-2
Riparian rights, 54-5
Risk
apprehension of, 26
Risk assessment
cultural construction of, 22-4
Ritchie Committee, 434,436

River
industrialisation on, effect of, 50-1
National Rivers Authority, 227, 273-6
nuisance, scope of, 60, 64-5
pollution in,
'best practicable means' concept, 217-21
nitrate. *See* NITRATE POLLUTION
Pollution of Rivers and Estuaries, 381-3
Royal Commission on, 52, 60, 61, 63, 318-19
sewage, 52, 63-6
riparian rights, 54-5
trespass, 55-6
Roadalert, 350-3
Roads. *See* TRANSPORT
Royal Commission Reports
air pollution,
best practicable option, 225-7
cooperation, need for, 268-9
integrated approach, 223-5
freshwater quality, 312-19
river pollution, 52, 60, 61
recommendations, 63
sustainable use of soil, 386-7
transport and the environment, 40-4, 272-3, 347-9
bypass development, 404-6
environmental assessment procedure, 413
inquiry procedure, 415-17
strategic environmental assessment, 419-20
***Rylands v Fletcher*, rule in**, 56, 67, 70-2
foreseeability of damage, 73-6

SPAs, 293, 451-4
SSSIs. *See* CONSERVATION
Safety issues, 17-18
Salmon fisheries, report on, 50-1
Sanitation. *See* DRAINS; PUBLIC HEALTH
Science, 7-25
changes to, and new forms of, 12, 13
law, scientists' contribution to, 7
politics, relation to, 11
scepticism about, 11-12, 13
scientism, 9-11, 13
Scotland
agricultural designation of NW, 457
Highlands, 423-5
land use, attitudes to, 423-4
Loch Druidibeg case study. *See* CONSERVATION
National Nature Reserve. *See* NATIONAL NATURE RESERVES
Report on public access to information in, 234-8
Ritchie Committee (wild life conservation), 434-5
Scotland–*contd*
Scottish Environmental Protection Agency, 230
Scottish Natural Heritage, 287, 422
Scott Report (1943), 103-5, 111, 286, 288
Scottish Environmental Protection Agency, 230
Scottish Wild Life Conservation Committee (Ritchie Committee), 434-5
Sea
designation for nature in, 449
Self-regulation, 324-37. *See also* ENVIRONMENTAL MANAGEMENT
Self-sufficiency, 347-9
Sewage, 52, 63-4, 65-6, 92, 94
Shopping
superstores, effect of, 41-2
Sites of Special Scientific Interest. *See* CONSERVATION
Skeffington Report (1969), 248, 252-3
Smallholders, 114-19
Smoke, 221-3. *See also* AIR POLLUTION
Social justice, 465
Socialism
utopian ideas, and, 84-9, 107, 349
Soil Association, 107-8
Spatial scales, 34-7
controversy, and, 40
Special Area of Conservation (SAC), 294-5, 454-6
Special Protection Area, 293, 451-4
Spence, Thomas, 85, 89
Squatter
rural, 103
State
transition to, 54
Statutory controls. *See* LAW
Stewardship
Christian tradition of, 29-31
public participation as aspect of, 237, 272
trust law, and, 354
western tradition of, 90-1
White Paper, in, 234
Stockholm Declaration (1972), 133-5
tenth anniversary of, 135
Strategic environmental assessment, 419-21
Sustainability, 4-7, 37-40. *See also* SUSTAINABLE DEVELOPMENT
consumption, and, 145-51
principles for, 141
'sustainability analysis (SA)', 392-3
Towards Sustainability. *See* EUROPEAN COMMUNITY
Sustainable development
Agenda 21, theme of, 124, 145, 154-64
British law, in, 230

Sustainable development–*contd*
Brundtland Report on, 140, 391
Caring for the Earth, and, 141-4
concept of,
contradictions in, 142-4
evolution, 132
misreading of, 465
environmental assessment, role of, 391-4
environmental management strategy for, 324-7
European Community, in, 166 *et seq*. *See also* EUROPEAN COMMUNITY
global instrument for. *See* AGENDA 21
international response to need for, 133-41. *See also* INTERNATIONAL LAW
local, 151-3
meaning, 141, 142
planning, and, 271-3, 297
precautionary principle, and, 154-64
strategies for, 393
UN Commission on, 145

Tax. *See also* ECONOMICS
carbon dioxide emissions, on, 320-4
Temporal scales, 34-7
Temporary structures, 114-19
Textiles, 51
Thanet Way bypass. *See* ENVIRONMENTAL ASSESSMENT
Tort, 54-9. *See also* NUISANCE
limitations of liability, 67 *et seq*
Total Kritik, 349
Town and country planning, 91-100, 243 *et seq*
agricultural land, 106-7, 243
air pollution, relevance for, 266-9
control over source, 267-8
appeals, 251, 255
application for planning permission, 251-616
cases, 256-61
considerations for determination. *See* 'material considerations' *below*
discretion of planning authority, 252, 265
refusal, 251, 254, 272, 282
breach of control, 251
'building operations', 250
'buying and selling' planning permission, case on, 264-5
conditions, imposition of,
contrasted with obligation, 263
power to impose, 261-2
scope of, 282-3
use to protect environment, 269, 284-5
countryside, separate treatment of. *See* COUNTRYSIDE

Town and country planning–*contd*
development,
meaning, 250-1, 286
presumption in favour of, 253-4
development plan, 249, 252
introduction of, 98-100
participation of public in area plan, 252-4
presumption in favour of, 255-6, 259-61
rebuttal of presumption in favour, cases on, 255-9
status of, 254-6, 261
two tier system, 252
early goals of, 92
enforcement notice, 251
entrepreneurial planning, 253-5, 261
deregulatory measures, 253-4
environmental assessments. *See* ENVIRONMENTAL ASSESSMENT
environmental issues, and, 266-85, 296-8
criticisms of separatist approach, 269-71
Planning Policy Guidance Note, 284-5
pollution control, planning's role in, 273-81, 282-5, 297
precautionary measures, 281-2
sustainability, and, 271-3
European Union, and, 281
features and ideologies of, 243-9
first Planning Act, 92-3
amenity, centrality to, and meaning of, 94-6
criticism of, 94
Green Belt. *See* GREEN BELT
integrated pollution control, relation with, 275-81
Land Utilisation in Rural Areas, Committee on (Scott Report), 103-5, 111, 286, 288
legislation, 92-100
local planning authority,
planning agreement with developer, 262, 263, 264-5
powers, 261-6
See also 'application for planning permission' *above*
local public planning inquiry, 414-15
Royal Commission Report on, 415-17
material considerations, 251, 254-5, 259
environmental assessment evidence, 251, 401
environmental protection one of, 268
pollution controls, 279-80
obligations, imposition of. *See* PLANNING OBLIGATION
origins of, 113-14, 244-5

Town and country planning–*contd*
post-War developments in, 98-100, 248-9, 269-71
car ownership, and, 271
precautionary principle, and, 281-2
private landowners, effect on, 99-100, 244-6
public interest, 265, 272
SSSIs. *See* CONSERVATION
schemes, first requirement for, 96-7
temporary and mobile structures, controls on, 114-19
Traffic pollution, 22-5. *See also* AIR POLLUTION
car use, increase in, and, 40-3, 405
carbon tax, Council Directive for, 320-4
control strategies, 238-9
cultural construction of, 24-5
fuel duties, 320
Transport. *See also* TRAFFIC POLLUTION
anti-road protests, 349-53
bicycle or foot, energy use compared with car, 347-8
impact of traffic on communities, 405-6
planning, and, 270-1
reducing car use, policies for, 347-9
road building policy, 349
Royal Commission Report, 40-4, 272-3, 347-9
bypasses, 405-6
environmental assessment procedure, 413
inquiry procedure, 415-17
strategic environmental assessment, 419-20
traffic calming measures, 405
Transport The Way Forward, 420-1
Treaties (international), 125-30
Trespass, 55-6
Trust
public, US notion of, 355
social, for environment, concept of, 356-7

United Kingdom
Member State of EC. *See also* EUROPEAN COMMUNITY
failure to implement Drinking Water Directive, 192-9
pollution control, contrasted with EC techniques, 184
United Nations
Agenda 21 monitoring, 145
Environment Programme (UNEP), 135, 137-8, 140, 303
General Assembly Resolutions, 133, 138
International Court of Justice. *See* INTERNATIONAL COURT OF JUSTICE
United Nations–*contd*
Nairobi Declaration, 135-8, 139, 465
sustainable development, Commission on, 145
World Health Organisation, 361, 362, 366
United States of America
air pollution siting controls, 267
counter-advertising, 345
declaration on Convention on Biological Diversity, 130
environmental assessment in, 389
land ownership rights, 354
public trusts in, 355
Utopianism, 84-9, 113
environment as, origins, 85
modern variant, 114

Value, environmental, 308-12, 319-20. *See also* ECONOMICS
Vehicle testing, 240. *See also* TRAFFIC POLLUTION
Voluntary simplicity, 346-9

Wales
Countryside Council, 287
War (World, II), 98-100, 106-7
effect of, and access to land, 111, 113-14
Waste, 149
disposal, planning controls, 267-8
farm, 375-6. *See also* NITRATE POLLUTION
landfill, 81
nuclear, 155-64
oils, 170-1
Water
dangerous substances in, 367, 373
Drinking Water Directive (Quality), 184, 187, 189, 365
extract, 367-73
implementation in UK, case on, 192-9
emission standards, 366-7
escape of, 56
groundwater, 273-6, 361-2, 372-3, 380
legislative control, nineteenth century, 61-2
pollution, 63-4. *See also* RIVER
clean-up operations, 320
criminal offence, 365
EC measures to prevent, 184, 189, 365-73, 384-5
nitrates and farm waste. *See* AGRICULTURE; NITRATE POLLUTION
UK approach, 366-7, 373-4
protection zones, 376-7
quality, 366-7
supply, 83
surface, 367

Water closets, 83
Welwyn Garden City, 89, 113
Western Isles
leaflet for walkers in, 425-7
Wetlands
Lappel Bank, case on, 204-11
Loch Druidibeg case study, 425 *et seq*. *See also* CONSERVATION
Montreux Criteria/Record, 443, 445-9
Ramsar Convention. *See* RAMSAR CONVENTION
White Paper
Lifting the Burden, 253, 401
This Common Inheritance, 234, 272, 278
Wild life. *See also* BIRDS; CONSERVATION; COUNTRYSIDE; NATURE
Flora and Fauna Directive, 205-6, 209-10, 294-5, 454-6
Wool, 51
World Charter for Nature, 138-9
World Commission on Environment and Development, 139-40, 141, 272
Our Common Future, 139-40, 141, 272, 308-9
World Conservation Strategy, 138, 303
World Conservation Union, 138-9, 140
World Health Organisation, 361, 362, 366
World Wide Fund for Nature, 138, 140

www.ingramcontent.com/pod-product-compliance
Lightning Source LLC
LaVergne TN
LVHW052212200926
848481LV00001B/90
9780521613538